ACCA

Strategic Professional – Options

Advanced Financial Management (AFM)

EXAM KIT

PUBLISHING

British Library Cataloguing-in-Publication Data

A catalogue record for this book is available from the British Library.

Published by:

Kaplan Publishing UK
Unit 2 The Business Centre
Molly Millar's Lane
Wokingham
Berkshire
RG41 2QZ

ISBN: 978-1-83996-152-6

Printed and bound in Great Britain

Acknowledgements

These materials are reviewed by the ACCA examining team. The objective of the review is to ensure that the material properly covers the syllabus and study guide outcomes, used by the examining team in setting the exams, in the appropriate breadth and depth. The review does not ensure that every eventuality, combination or application of examinable topics is addressed by the ACCA Approved Content. Nor does the review comprise a detailed technical check of the content as the Approved Content Provider has its own quality assurance processes in place in this respect.

The past ACCA examination questions are the copyright of the Association of Chartered Certified Accountants. The original answers to the questions from June 1994 onwards were produced by the examiners themselves and have been adapted by Kaplan Publishing.

We are grateful to the Chartered Institute of Management Accountants and the Institute of Chartered Accountants in England and Wales for permission to reproduce past examination questions. The answers have been prepared by Kaplan Publishing.

Kaplan Publishing are constantly finding new ways to make a difference to your studies and our exciting online resources really do offer something different to students looking for exam success.

This book comes with free MyKaplan online resources so that you can study anytime, anywhere. **This free online resource is not sold separately and is included in the price of the book.**

Having purchased this book, you have access to the following online study materials:

CONTENT	ACCA (including FBT, FMA, FFA)		FIA (excluding FBT, FMA, FFA)	
	Text	Kit	Text	Kit
Electronic version of the book	✓	✓	✓	✓
Knowledge checks with instant answers	✓		✓	
Material updates	✓	✓	✓	✓
Latest official ACCA exam questions*		✓		
Timed questions with an online tutor debrief using video icon***		✓		
Consolidation Test including questions and answers	✓		✓	

* Excludes BT, MA, FA, FBT, FMA, FFA; for all other papers includes a selection of questions, as released by ACCA

*** Excludes BT, MA, FA, LW, FBT, FMA and FFA

How to access your online resources

Kaplan Financial students will already have a MyKaplan account and these extra resources will be available to you online. You do not need to register again, as this process was completed when you enrolled. If you are having problems accessing online materials, please ask your course administrator.

If you are not studying with Kaplan and did not purchase your book via a Kaplan website, to unlock your extra online resources please go to www.mykaplan.co.uk/addabook (even if you have set up an account and registered books previously). You will then need to enter the ISBN number (on the title page and back cover) and the unique pass key number contained in the scratch panel below to gain access. You will also be required to enter additional information during this process to set up or confirm your account details.

If you purchased through the Kaplan Publishing website you will automatically receive an e-mail invitation to MyKaplan. Please register your details using this email to gain access to your content. If you do not receive the e-mail or book content, please contact Kaplan Publishing.

Your Code and Information

This code can only be used once for the registration of one book online. This registration and your online content will expire when the final sittings for the examinations covered by this book have taken place. Please allow one hour from the time you submit your book details for us to process your request.

Please scratch the film to access your unique code.

Please be aware that this code is case-sensitive and you will need to include the dashes within the passcode, but not when entering the ISBN.

CONTENTS

Section

Versions of some questions in this Exam Kit may also be available on the ACCA Practice Platform on the ACCA website. They are a very useful reference, in particular to attempt using ACCA's exam software. However, you should be aware that ACCA will decide when those questions will be amended for syllabus changes or replaced, so they may differ slightly from the versions in this Exam Kit

---

Key features in this edition

In addition to providing a wide ranging bank of real past exam questions, we have also included in this edition:

- An analysis of all of the recent examinations.

- AFM specific information and advice on exam technique.

- Our recommended approach to make your revision for this particular subject as effective as possible.

  This includes step by step guidance on how best to use our Kaplan material (Study Text, Pocket Notes and Exam Kit) at this stage in your studies.

- Enhanced tutorial answers packed with specific key answer tips, technical tutorial notes and exam technique tips from our experienced tutors.

- Complementary online resources including full tutor debriefs and question assistance to point you in the right direction when you get stuck.

Versions of some questions in this Exam Kit may also be available on the ACCA Practice Platform on the ACCA website. They are a very useful reference, in particular to attempt using ACCA's exam software. However, you should be aware that ACCA will decide when those questions will be amended for syllabus changes or replaced, so they may differ slightly from the versions in this Exam Kit.

You will find a wealth of other resources to help you with your studies on the following sites:

www.mykaplan.co.uk

https://www.accaglobal.com/gb/en/student/exam-support-resources/professional-exams-study-resources/p4.html

Quality and accuracy are of the utmost importance to us so if you spot an error in any of our products, please send an email to mykaplanreporting@kaplan.com with full details.

Our Quality Co-ordinator will work with our technical team to verify the error and take action to ensure it is corrected in future editions.

INDEX TO QUESTIONS AND ANSWERS

INTRODUCTION

The majority of the questions within this kit are past ACCA exam questions. The index identifies which sitting the questions were from. An 'A' next to the question in the index means that the past exam question has been adapted in some way. For example, past exam questions have been modified to reflect the current format of the exam where Professional Skills Marks make up 10 of the 50 marks in each Section A question and 5 of the 25 marks in each Section B question.

KEY TO THE INDEX

ENHANCEMENTS

We have added the following enhancements to the answers in this exam kit:

Key answer tips

All answers include key answer tips to help your understanding of each question.

Tutorial note

Many answers include more tutorial notes to explain some of the technical points in more detail.

ONLINE ENHANCEMENTS

 *Answer debrief*

For selected questions, we recommend that they are to be completed in full exam conditions (i.e. properly timed in a closed book environment).

In addition to the examining team's technical answer, enhanced with key answer tips and tutorial notes in this exam kit, online you can find an answer debrief by a top tutor that:

- works through the question in full

- explains key elements of the answer

- ensures that the easy marks are obtained as quickly as possible.

These questions are indicated with the 'video' icon in the index.

Answer debriefs will be available on MyKaplan at:

www.mykaplan.co.uk

SECTION A-TYPE QUESTIONS

SECTION B-TYPE QUESTIONS

ANALYSIS OF PAST EXAMS

The table below summarises the key topics that have been tested in the published questions from recent Advanced Financial Management examinations. The list of topics matches the chapter titles in the Kaplan Study Text.

Note that the references are to the number of the question in this edition of the Exam Kit.

Topic	Mar/Jun 19	Sep/Dec 19	March 20	Sep/Dec 20	Mar/Jun 21	Sep/Dec 21
The role and responsibility of the financial manager	4, 59, 74	29	13, Q3 in Ch 5	Q1 in Ch 5	18, 76	77
Investment appraisal	4	21	40			5
International operations and international investment appraisal		21		Q2 in Ch 5		
The financing decision		21	13		18, 41	5
The dividend decision		29				
WACC	59		13	Q1 in Ch 5		
Risk adjusted WACC and APV		21			41	5
Option pricing	4					
An introduction to risk management		21	40	Q2 in Ch 5		
Hedging foreign exchange risk		21	Q3 in Ch 5		76	
Hedging interest rate risk	74			75		77
Strategic aspects of acquisitions		51	13	Q1 in Ch 5	18	
Business valuation	59	51	13		18	60
Corporate failure/ reconstruction	59			Q1 in Ch 5	18	60

SPECIFIC AFM EXAM INFORMATION

THE EXAM

FORMAT OF THE EXAM

		Number of marks
Section A:	One compulsory question worth 50 marks	50
Section B:	Two compulsory questions worth 25 marks each	50
		100

Total time allowed: 3 hours and 15 minutes

AIM

To apply relevant knowledge, skills and exercise professional judgement as expected of a senior financial executive or advisor, in taking or recommending decisions relating to the financial management of an organisation.

OBJECTIVES

On successful completion of this exam, candidates should be able to:

- Explain and evaluate the role and responsibility of the senior financial executive or advisor in meeting conflicting needs of stakeholders and recognise the role of international financial institutions in the financial management of multinationals

- Evaluate potential investment decisions and assessing their financial and strategic consequences, both domestically and internationally

- Assess and plan acquisitions and mergers as an alternative growth strategy

- Evaluate and advise on alternative corporate re-organisation strategies

- Apply and evaluate alternative advanced treasury and risk management techniques

- Apply a range of professional skills in addressing requirements within the Advanced Financial Management exam, and in preparation for, or to support, current work experience

- Apply employability and technology skills

PASS MARK

The pass mark is 50%.

DETAILED SYLLABUS

The detailed syllabus and study guide written by the ACCA can be found at:

https://www.accaglobal.com/gb/en/student/exam-support-resources/professional-exams-study-resources/p4/syllabus-study-guide.html

---

EXAM TECHNIQUE

EXAMINATION TIPS – COMPUTER BASED EXAM (CBE)

In addition to reading the tips contained here, we recommend that you review the resources available on the ACCA Global Website before sitting the CBE. Here you will find guidance documents, videos and a link to the CBE question practice platform.

Before the exam starts – You will be given 10 minutes to read the introductory page and the four pages of instructions. These will be the same for each AFM exam and therefore it is important that you familiarise yourself with these (using the ACCA practice exams) during your revision. The exam time (3 hours and 15 minutes) will start automatically at the end of the 10 minutes or earlier if requested by you.

Plan your strategy before you go in; allocating 90 minutes to Section A, 45 minutes to each question in Section B (1.8 minutes per mark) and 15 minutes to skim through the questions at the start and as a buffer to review your answers at the end.

Planning your answers - When the exam starts spend a few minutes skimming through the whole exam to get a feel for what is included. Once you have done this carry out an initial review of Section A. This will include a number of **exhibits** breaking down the scenario into relevant sections and including the detailed requirement. It will also include a list of the summarised **requirements** and an option to complete your answer in a **word processing** document and/or a **spreadsheet** document.

You can move around and resize the windows that you open to lay the screen out in a format that suits you.

Now **copy and paste** the specifics of the requirement into your answer document, perhaps highlighting in bold the different parts of the requirement and the verb used, to make sure that you **answer all parts of all requirements**. Once complete review the exhibits in detail, highlighting and making notes as you do so and copy and pasting any relevant information to your answer document. These steps will help with your planning and structure but will also enable you to minimise the number of windows you have open.

The procedure will be similar for Section B.

Completing your answers – Start by revisiting the relevant exhibits for each requirement. Decide on the use of a word processing format, a spreadsheet format or both. For calculations, use a logical and well laid out structure. Calculations should be labelled and referenced in to any relevant discussion. For discursive answers use bold headings and sub-headings and professional language. Ensure all aspects of the requirement are covered in a sensible and balanced way. It is vital that you relate your answer to the specific circumstances given. In Section A you will usually be required to produce a report. Head up your answer as a report and use the requirements as a basis for your introduction.

If you get completely stuck with a question, return to it later.

If you do not understand what a question is asking, state your assumptions. Even if you do not answer in precisely the way the examiner hoped, you should be given some credit, if your assumptions are reasonable.

Finally, use your buffer time to read through the answers, ensuring they are clear and organised, and to make any necessary changes.

KAPLAN'S RECOMMENDED REVISION APPROACH

QUESTION PRACTICE IS THE KEY TO SUCCESS

Success in professional examinations relies upon you acquiring a firm grasp of the required knowledge at the tuition phase. In order to be able to do the questions, knowledge is essential.

However, the difference between success and failure often hinges on your exam technique on the day and making the most of the revision phase of your studies.

The **Kaplan Study Text** is the starting point, designed to provide the underpinning knowledge to tackle all questions. However, in the revision phase, poring over textbooks is not the answer.

Kaplan Online tests help you consolidate your knowledge and understanding and are a useful tool to check whether you can remember key topic areas.

Kaplan Pocket Notes are designed to help you quickly revise a topic area; however you then need to practise questions. There is a need to progress to full exam standard questions as soon as possible, and to tie your exam technique and technical knowledge together.

The importance of question practice cannot be over-emphasised.

The recommended approach below is designed by expert tutors in the field, in conjunction with their knowledge of the examiner and their recent real exams.

The approach taken for the Applied Knowledge and Applied Skills exams is to revise by topic area. However, with the Strategic Professional exams, a multi topic approach is required to answer the scenario-based questions.

You need to practise as many questions as possible in the time you have left.

OUR AIM

Our aim is to get you to the stage where you can attempt exam standard questions confidently, to time, in a closed book environment, with no supplementary help (i.e. to simulate the real examination experience).

Practising your exam technique on real past examination questions, in timed conditions, is also vitally important for you to assess your progress and identify areas of weakness that may need more attention in the final run up to the examination.

In order to achieve this we recognise that initially you may feel the need to practise some questions with open book help and exceed the required time.

The approach below shows you which questions you should use to build up to coping with exam standard question practice, and references to the sources of information available should you need to revisit a topic area in more detail.

Remember that in the real examination, all you have to do is:

- attempt all questions required by the exam

- only spend the allotted time on each question, and

- get them at least 50% right!

Try to practise this approach on every question you attempt from now to the real exam.

EXAMINER'S COMMENTS

We have included many of the examiner's comments to the examination questions in this kit for you to see the main pitfalls that students fall into with regard to technical content.

However, too many times in the general section of the report, the examiner comments that students had failed due to:

- 'misallocation of time'

- 'running out of time' and

- showing signs of 'spending too much time on an earlier question and clearly rushing the answer to a subsequent question'.

Good exam technique is vital.

STRATEGIC PROFESSIONAL COMPUTER BASED EXAMINATIONS

We advise consulting the ACCA Global website for additional CBE revision resources. On the ACCA website there is a CBE demonstration. It is **ESSENTIAL** that you attempt this before your real CBE. You will become familiar with how to move around the CBE screens and the way that questions are formatted, increasing your confidence and speed in the actual exam.

Be sure you understand how to use the **software** before you start the exam. If in doubt, ask the assessment centre staff to explain it to you.

Questions are **displayed on the screen** and answers are entered using keyboard and mouse.

For additional support with your studies please also refer to the ACCA Global website.

THE KAPLAN AFM REVISION PLAN

Stage 1: Assess areas of strengths and weaknesses

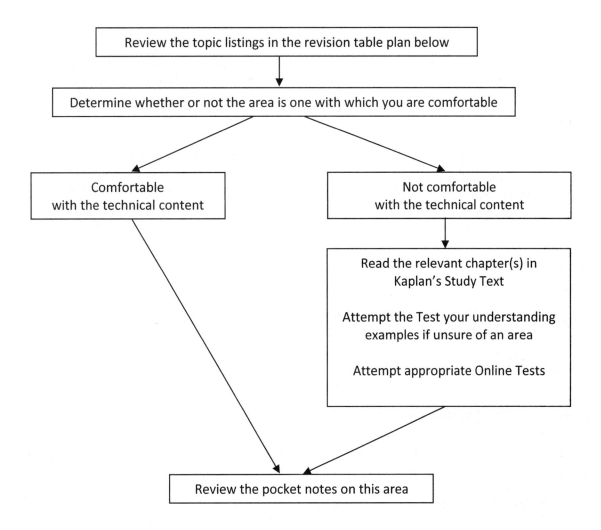

Stage 2: Practise questions

Follow the order of revision of topics as recommended in the revision table plan below and attempt the questions in the order suggested.

Try to avoid referring to textbooks and notes and the model answer until you have completed your attempt.

Try to answer the question in the allotted time.

Review your attempt with the model answer and assess how much of the answer you achieved in the allocated exam time.

Fill in the self-assessment box below and decide on your best course of action.

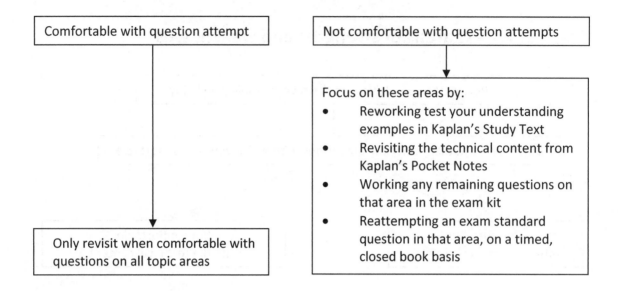

Note that:

 The 'answer debrief' questions have an online debrief where a tutor talks you through the exam technique and approach to that question and works the question in full.

Stage 3: Final pre-exam revision

We recommend that you **attempt at least one three hour and fifteen minutes mock examination** containing a set of previously unseen exam standard questions.

It is important that you get a feel for the breadth of coverage of a real exam without advanced knowledge of the topic areas covered – just as you will expect to see on the real exam day.

Ideally this mock should be sat in timed, closed book, real exam conditions and could be a mock examination offered by your tuition provider.

KAPLAN'S DETAILED REVISION PLAN

Module 1: Investment appraisal and WACC

Topic	Study Text Chapter	Pocket notes Chapter	Questions to attempt	Tutor guidance	Date attempted	Self-assessment
WACC	6	6	–	Before you can start appraising projects, it is vital to understand how the WACC can be calculated. Notice that several formulae used to derive WACC appear on the formula sheet. Make sure you identify which need to be learned and which are given.		
Investment appraisal	2	2	37	Investment appraisal is very commonly tested. Make sure you understand NPV and MIRR in particular.		
Foreign investment appraisal	3	3	3	Foreign NPV is very similar to 'normal' NPV. The parity theories are frequently tested, so learn how to apply the formulae.		
Risk adjusted WACC	7	7	33	Degearing and regearing betas is one of the examiner's favourite topics. The formula is given in the exam, but learn how to apply it.		
APV	7	7	5, 38	APV questions are very common. The key is to remember to discount the investment cash flows at an ungeared cost of equity and the financing cash flows using the risk free rate.		
Module 1 Revision Test			*1, 30, 32, 35, 39*	*Attempt these questions to check your understanding of Module 1 topics.*		

Module 2: Acquisitions and business valuation

Topic	Study Text Chapter	Pocket notes Chapter	Questions to attempt	Tutor guidance	Date attempted	Self-assessment
Strategic aspects of acquisitions	12	12	–	Valuation questions tend to contain calculations and discussion. This chapter covers the key discursive aspects.		
Free cash flow analysis	13	13	7, 11	The examiner's favourite method of business valuation is the discounted free cash flow approach, so revise the method from Chapter 13.		
Business valuation	13	13	6, 51	Now cover the other valuation methods. Questions will tend to mix discursive and computational elements, so focus on both aspects.		
Module 2 Revision Test			*12, 13, 46, 49, 50*	*Attempt these questions to check your understanding of Module 1 and 2 topics.*		

Module 3: Option pricing, corporate failure and roles/responsibilities of the financial manager

Topic	Study Text Chapter	Pocket notes Chapter	Questions to attempt	Tutor guidance	Date attempted	Self-assessment
Option pricing	8	8	2, 4, 52	The Black Scholes formulae are given on the formula sheet, but make sure you can apply them in various circumstances.		
Corporate failure/ reconstruction	14	14	15, 28, 53	This is a very topical area, so highly examinable. Learn the indicators of financial distress and the calculation of ratios.		
Roles/responsibilities of the financial manager	1	1	29			
Module 3 Revision Test			*14, 16, 24, 25, 31*	*Attempt these questions to check your understanding of Module 1, 2 and 3 topics.*		

Module 4: Risk management and hedging

Topic	Study Text Chapter	Pocket notes Chapter	Questions to attempt	Tutor guidance	Date attempted	Self-assessment
Risk management	9	9	35, 40	Chapter 9 gives a good introduction to risk management topics.		
Hedging – currency risk	10	10	20, 74, 76	Learn the different methods of hedging. The key here is to adapt a systematic approach, laying out your workings carefully so that you don't get muddled.		
Hedging – interest rate risk	11	11	65, 67	As with currency hedging, learn all the methods, and the advantages and disadvantages of using each of them.		
Swaps	10, 11	10, 11	68, 72	Swaps are often overlooked by some students who focus mainly on futures and options. However, they are quite frequently tested.		
Module 4 Revision Test			**21, 71, 73, 75**	**Attempt these questions to check your understanding of Module 1, 2, 3 and 4 topics.**		

Note that not all of the questions are referred to in the programme above. The remaining questions are available in the kit for extra practice for those who require more questions on some areas.

MATHEMATICAL TABLES AND FORMULAE SHEET

Modigliani and Miller Proposition 2 (with tax)

$$k_e = k_e^i + (1 - T)(k_e^i - k_d) \frac{V_d}{V_e}$$

The Capital Asset Pricing Model

$$E(r_i) = R_f + \beta_i(E(r_m) - R_f)$$

The asset beta formula

$$\beta_a = \left[\frac{V_e}{(V_e + V_d(1-T))} \beta_e \right] + \left[\frac{V_d(1-T)}{(V_e + V_d(1-T))} \beta_d \right]$$

The Growth Model

$$P_0 = \frac{D_0(1+g)}{(r_e - g)}$$

Gordon's growth approximation

$$g = br_e$$

The weighted average cost of capital

$$WACC = \left[\frac{V_e}{V_e + V_d} \right] k_e + \left[\frac{V_d}{V_e + V_d} \right] k_d(1-T)$$

The Fisher formula

$$(1+i) = (1+r)(1+h)$$

Purchasing power parity and interest rate parity

$$S_1 = S_0 \times \frac{(1+h_c)}{(1+h_b)} \qquad F_0 = S_0 \times \frac{(1+i_c)}{(1+i_b)}$$

AFM: ADVANCED FINANCIAL MANAGEMENT

Modified Internal Rate of Return

$$MIRR = \left[\frac{PV_R}{PV_I}\right]^{\frac{1}{n}}(1+r_e)-1$$

The Black-Scholes option pricing model

$$c = P_aN(d_1) - P_eN(d_2)e^{-rt}$$

Where:

$$d_1 = \frac{\ln(P_a/P_e)+(r+0.5s^2)t}{s\sqrt{t}}$$

$$d_2 = d_1 - s\sqrt{t}$$

The Put Call Parity relationship

$$p = c - P_a + P_ee^{-rt}$$

MATHEMATICAL TABLES

Standard normal distribution table

	0.00	0.01	0.02	0.03	0.04	0.05	0.06	0.07	0.08	0.09
0.0	.0000	.0040	.0080	.0120	.0159	.0199	.0239	.0279	.0319	.0359
0.1	.0398	.0438	.0478	.0517	.0557	.0596	.0636	.0675	.0714	.0753
0.2	.0793	.0832	.0871	.0910	.0948	.0987	.1026	.1064	.1103	.1141
0.3	.1179	.1217	.1255	.1293	.1331	.1368	.1406	.1443	.1480	.1517
0.4	.1554	.1591	.1628	.1664	.1700	.1736	.1772	.1808	.1844	.1879
0.5	.1915	.1950	.1985	.2019	.2054	.2088	.2123	.2157	.2190	.2224
0.6	.2257	.2291	.2324	.2357	.2389	.2422	.2454	.2486	.2518	.2549
0.7	.2580	.2611	.2642	.2673	.2704	.2734	.2764	.2794	.2823	.2852
0.8	.2881	.2910	.2939	.2967	.2995	.3023	.3051	.3078	.3106	.3133
0.9	.3159	.3186	.3212	.3238	.3264	.3289	.3315	.3340	.3365	.3389
1.0	.3413	.3438	.3461	.3485	.3508	.3531	.3554	.3577	.3599	.3621
1.1	.3643	.3665	.3686	.3708	.3729	.3749	.3770	.3790	.3810	.3830
1.2	.3849	.3869	.3888	.3907	.3925	.3944	.3962	.3980	.3997	.4015
1.3	.4032	.4049	.4066	.4082	.4099	.4115	.4131	.4147	.4162	.4177
1.4	.4192	.4207	.4222	.4236	.4251	.4265	.4279	.4292	.4306	.4319
1.5	.4332	.4345	.4357	.4370	.4382	.4394	.4406	.4418	.4430	.4441
1.6	.4452	.4463	.4474	.4485	.4495	.4505	.4515	.4525	.4535	.4545
1.7	.4554	.4564	.4573	.4582	.4591	.4599	.4608	.4616	.4625	.4633
1.8	.4641	.4649	.4656	.4664	.4671	.4678	.4686	.4693	.4699	.4706
1.9	.4713	.4719	.4726	.4732	.4738	.4744	.4750	.4756	.4762	.4767
2.0	.4772	.4778	.4783	.4788	.4793	.4798	.4803	.4808	.4812	.4817
2.1	.4821	.4826	.4830	.4834	.4838	.4842	.4846	.4850	.4854	.4857
2.2	.4861	.4865	.4868	.4871	.4875	.4878	.4881	.4884	.4887	.4890
2.3	.4893	.4896	.4898	.4901	.4904	.4906	.4909	.4911	.4913	.4916
2.4	.4918	.4920	.4922	.4925	.4927	.4929	.4931	.4932	.4934	.4936
2.5	.4938	.4940	.4941	.4943	.4945	.4946	.4948	.4949	.4951	.4952
2.6	.4953	.4955	.4956	.4957	.4959	.4960	.4961	.4962	.4963	.4964
2.7	.4965	.4966	.4967	.4968	.4969	.4970	.4971	.4972	.4973	.4974
2.8	.4974	.4975	.4976	.4977	.4977	.4978	.4979	.4980	.4980	.4981
2.9	.4981	.4982	.4983	.4983	.4984	.4984	.4985	.4985	.4986	.4986
3.0	.4987	.4987	.4987	.4988	.4988	.4989	.4989	.4989	.4990	.4990

This table can be used to calculate $N(d_1)$, the cumulative normal distribution function needed for the Black-Scholes model of option pricing. If $d_1 > 0$, add 0.5 to the relevant number above. If $d_1 < 0$, subtract the relevant number above from 0.5.

Present value table

Present value of 1, i.e. $(1 + r)^{-n}$

where   r = discount rate

n = number of periods until payment

Periods (n)	1%	2%	3%	4%	5%	6%	7%	8%	9%	10%
1	0.990	0.980	0.971	0.962	0.952	0.943	0.935	0.926	0.917	0.909
2	0.980	0.961	0.943	0.925	0.907	0.890	0.873	0.857	0.842	0.826
3	0.971	0.942	0.915	0.889	0.864	0.840	0.816	0.794	0.772	0.751
4	0.961	0.924	0.888	0.855	0.823	0.792	0.763	0.735	0.708	0.683
5	0.951	0.906	0.863	0.822	0.784	0.747	0.713	0.681	0.650	0.621
6	0.942	0.888	0.837	0.790	0.746	0.705	0.666	0.630	0.596	0.564
7	0.933	0.871	0.813	0.760	0.711	0.665	0.623	0.583	0.547	0.513
8	0.923	0.853	0.789	0.731	0.677	0.627	0.582	0.540	0.502	0.467
9	0.914	0.837	0.766	0.703	0.645	0.592	0.544	0.500	0.460	0.424
10	0.905	0.820	0.744	0.676	0.614	0.558	0.508	0.463	0.422	0.386
11	0.896	0.804	0.722	0.650	0.585	0.527	0.475	0.429	0.388	0.350
12	0.887	0.788	0.701	0.625	0.557	0.497	0.444	0.397	0.356	0.319
13	0.879	0.773	0.681	0.601	0.530	0.469	0.415	0.368	0.326	0.290
14	0.870	0.758	0.661	0.577	0.505	0.442	0.388	0.340	0.299	0.263
15	0.861	0.743	0.642	0.555	0.481	0.417	0.362	0.315	0.275	0.239

Periods (n)	11%	12%	13%	14%	15%	16%	17%	18%	19%	20%
1	0.901	0.893	0.885	0.877	0.870	0.862	0.855	0.847	0.840	0.833
2	0.812	0.797	0.783	0.769	0.756	0.743	0.731	0.718	0.706	0.694
3	0.731	0.712	0.693	0.675	0.658	0.641	0.624	0.609	0.593	0.579
4	0.659	0.636	0.613	0.592	0.572	0.552	0.534	0.516	0.499	0.482
5	0.593	0.567	0.543	0.519	0.497	0.476	0.456	0.437	0.419	0.402
6	0.535	0.507	0.480	0.456	0.432	0.410	0.390	0.370	0.352	0.335
7	0.482	0.452	0.425	0.400	0.376	0.354	0.333	0.314	0.296	0.279
8	0.434	0.404	0.376	0.351	0.327	0.305	0.285	0.266	0.249	0.233
9	0.391	0.361	0.333	0.308	0.284	0.263	0.243	0.225	0.206	0.194
10	0.352	0.322	0.295	0.270	0.247	0.227	0.208	0.191	0.176	0.162
11	0.317	0.287	0.261	0.237	0.215	0.195	0.178	0.162	0.148	0.135
12	0.286	0.257	0.231	0.208	0.187	0.168	0.152	0.137	0.124	0.112
13	0.258	0.229	0.204	0.182	0.163	0.145	0.130	0.116	0.104	0.933
14	0.232	0.205	0.181	0.160	0.141	0.125	0.111	0.099	0.088	0.078
15	0.209	0.183	0.160	0.140	0.123	0.108	0.095	0.084	0.074	0.065

Annuity table

Present value of an annuity of 1, i.e. $\dfrac{1-(1+r)^{-n}}{r}$

where   r = interest rate

         n = number of periods

Periods (n)	1%	2%	3%	4%	5%	6%	7%	8%	9%	10%
1	0.990	0.980	0.971	0.962	0.952	0.943	0.935	0.926	0.917	0.909
2	1.970	1.942	1.913	1.886	1.859	1.833	1.808	.1783	1.759	1.736
3	2.941	2.884	2.829	2.775	2.723	2.673	2.624	2.577	2.531	2.487
4	3.902	3.808	3.717	3.630	3.546	3.465	3.387	3.312	3.240	3.170
5	4.853	4.713	4.580	4.452	4.329	4.212	4.100	3.993	3.890	3.791
6	5.795	5.601	5.417	5.242	5.076	4.917	4.767	4.623	4.486	4.355
7	6.728	6.472	6.230	6.002	5.786	5.582	5.389	5.206	5.033	4.868
8	7.652	7.325	7.020	6.733	6.463	6.210	5.971	5.747	5.535	5.335
9	8.566	8.162	7.786	7.435	7.108	6.802	6.515	6.247	5.995	5.759
10	9.471	8.893	8.530	8.111	7.722	7.360	7.024	6.710	6.418	6.145
11	10.37	9.787	9.253	8.760	8.306	7.887	7.499	7.139	6.805	6.495
12	11.26	10.58	9.954	9.385	8.863	8.384	7.943	7.536	7.161	6.814
13	12.13	11.35	10.63	9.986	9.394	8.853	8.358	7.904	7.487	7.103
14	13.00	12.11	11.30	10.56	9.899	9.295	8.745	8.244	7.786	7.367
15	13.87	12.85	11.94	11.12	10.38	9.712	9.108	8.559	8.061	7.606

Periods (n)	11%	12%	13%	14%	15%	16%	17%	18%	19%	20%
1	0.901	0.893	0.885	0.877	0.870	0.862	0.855	0.847	0.840	0.833
2	1.713	1.690	1.668	1.647	1.626	1.605	1.585	1.566	1.547	1.528
3	2.444	2.402	2.361	2.322	2.283	2.246	2.210	2.174	2.140	2.106
4	3.102	3.037	2.974	2.914	2.855	2.798	2.743	2.690	2.639	2.589
5	3.696	3.605	3.517	3.433	3.352	3.274	3.199	3.127	3.058	2.991
6	4.231	4.111	3.998	3.889	3.784	3.685	3.589	3.496	3.410	3.326
7	4.712	4.564	4.423	4.288	4.160	4.039	3.922	3.812	3.706	3.605
8	5.146	4.968	4.799	4.639	4.487	4.344	4.207	4.078	3.954	3.837
9	5.537	5.328	5.132	4.946	4.772	4.607	4.451	4.303	4.163	4.031
10	5.889	5.650	5.426	5.216	5.019	4.833	4.659	4.494	4.339	4.192
11	6.207	5.938	5.687	5.453	5.234	5.029	4.836	4.656	4.586	4.327
12	6.492	6.194	5.918	5.660	5.421	5.197	4.988	4.793	4.611	4.439
13	6.750	6.424	6.122	5.842	5.583	5.342	5.118	4.910	4.715	4.533
14	6.982	6.628	6.302	6.002	5.724	5.468	5.229	5.008	4.802	4.611
15	7.191	6.811	6.462	6.142	5.847	5.575	5.324	5.092	4.876	4.675

Section 1

PRACTICE QUESTIONS – SECTION A

ADVANCED INVESTMENT APPRAISAL

1   TRAMONT CO (DEC 11)

Tramont Co is a listed company that is based in the USA and manufactures electronic devices. One of its devices, the X-IT, is produced exclusively for the American market. Tramont Co is considering ceasing the production of the X-IT gradually over a period of four years because it needs the manufacturing facilities used to make the X-IT for other products.

The government of Gamala, a country based in south-east Asia, is keen to develop its manufacturing industry and has offered Tramont Co first rights to produce the X-IT in Gamala and sell it to the USA market for a period of four years. At the end of the four-year period, the full production rights will be sold to a government backed company for Gamalan Rupiahs (GR) 450 million after tax (this amount is not subject to inflationary increases). Tramont Co has to decide whether to continue production of the X-IT in the USA for the next four years or to move the production to Gamala immediately.

Currently each X-IT unit sold makes a unit contribution of $20. This unit contribution is not expected to be subject to any inflationary increase in the next four years. Next year's production and sales estimated at 40,000 units will fall by 20% each year for the following three years. It is anticipated that after four years the production of X-IT will stop. It is expected that the financial impact of the gradual closure over the four years will be cost neutral (the revenue from sale of assets will equal the closure costs). If production is stopped immediately, the excess assets would be sold for $2.3 million and the costs of closure, including redundancy costs of excess labour, would be $1.7 million.

The following information relates to the production of the X-IT moving to Gamala. The Gamalan project will require an initial investment of GR 230 million, to pay for the cost of land and buildings (GR 150 million) and machinery (GR 80 million). The cost of machinery is tax allowable and will be depreciated on a straight line basis over the next four years, at the end of which it will have a negligible value.

Tramont Co will also need GR 40 million for working capital immediately. It is expected that the working capital requirement will increase in line with the annual inflation rate in Gamala. When the project is sold, the working capital will not form part of the sale price and will be released back to Tramont Co.

Production and sales of the device are expected to be 12,000 units in the first year, rising to 22,000 units, 47,000 units and 60,000 units in the next three years respectively.

The following revenues and costs apply to the first year of operation:

- Each unit will be sold for $70
- The variable cost per unit comprising of locally sourced materials and labour will be GR 1,350, and

- In addition to the variable cost above, each unit will require a component bought from Tramont Co for $7, on which Tramont Co makes $4 contribution per unit
- Total fixed costs for the first year will be GR 30 million.

The costs are expected to increase by their countries' respective rates of inflation, but the selling price will remain fixed at $70 per unit for the four-year period.

The annual corporation tax rate in Gamala is 20% and Tramont Co currently pays corporation tax at a rate of 30% per year. Both countries' corporation taxes are payable in the year that the tax liability arises. A bi-lateral tax treaty exists between the USA and Gamala, which permits offset of overseas tax against any US tax liability on overseas earnings. The USA and Gamalan tax authorities allow losses to be carried forward and written off against future profits for taxation purposes.

Tramont Co has decided to finance the project by borrowing the funds required in Gamala. The commercial borrowing rate is 13% but the Gamalan government has offered Tramont Co a 6% subsidised loan for the entire amount of the initial funds required. The Gamalan government has agreed that it will not ask for the loan to be repaid as long as Tramont Co fulfils its contract to undertake the project for the four years. Tramont Co can borrow dollar funds at an interest rate of 5%.

Tramont Co's financing consists of 25 million shares currently trading at $2.40 each and $40 million 7% bonds trading at $1,428 per $1,000. Tramont Co's quoted beta is 1.17. The current risk free rate of return is estimated at 3% and the market risk premium is 6%. Due to the nature of the project, it is estimated that the beta applicable to the project if it is all-equity financed will be 0.4 more than the current all-equity financed beta of Tramont Co. If the Gamalan project is undertaken, the cost of capital applicable to the cash flows in the USA is expected to be 7%.

The spot exchange rate between the dollar and the Gamalan Rupiah is GR 55 per $1. The annual inflation rates are currently 3% in the USA and 9% in Gamala. It can be assumed that these inflation rates will not change for the foreseeable future. All net cash flows arising from the project will be remitted back to Tramont Co at the end of each year.

There are two main political parties in Gamala: the Gamala Liberal (GL) Party and the Gamala Republican (GR) Party. Gamala is currently governed by the GL Party but general elections are due to be held soon. If the GR Party wins the election, it promises to increase taxes of international companies operating in Gamala and review any commercial benefits given to these businesses by the previous government.

Required:

(a) **Prepare a report for the Board of Directors (BoD) of Tramont Co that**

    (i) **Evaluates whether or not Tramont Co should undertake the project to produce the X-IT in Gamala and cease its production in the USA immediately. In the evaluation, include all relevant calculations in the form of a financial assessment and explain any assumptions made.**

        It is suggested that the financial assessment should be based on present value of the operating cash flows from the Gamalan project, discounted by an appropriate all-equity rate, and adjusted by the present value of all other relevant cash flows. **(27 marks)**

    (ii) **Discusses the potential change in government and other business factors that Tramont Co should consider before making a final decision.** **(8 marks)**

(b) Although not mandatory for external reporting purposes, one of the members of the BoD suggested that adopting a triple bottom line approach when monitoring the X-IT investment after its implementation, would provide a better assessment of how successful it has been.

Discuss how adopting aspects of triple bottom line reporting may provide a better assessment of the success of the X-IT. **(5 marks)**

Professional marks will be awarded for the demonstration of skill in communication, analysis and evaluation, scepticism and commercial acumen in your answer. **(10 marks)**

(Total: 50 marks)

2 CHMURA CO (DEC 13)

Since becoming independent just over 20 years ago, the country of Mehgam has adopted protectionist measures which have made it difficult for multinational companies to trade there. However, recently, after discussions with the World Trade Organisation (WTO), it seems likely that Mehgam will reduce its protectionist measures significantly.

Encouraged by these discussions, Chmura Co, a company producing packaged foods, is considering a project to set up a manufacturing base in Mehgam to sell its goods there and in other regional countries nearby. An initial investigation costing $500,000 established that Mehgam had appropriate manufacturing facilities, adequate transport links and a reasonably skilled but cheap work force. The investigation concluded that, if the protectionist measures were reduced, then the demand potential for Chmura Co's products looked promising. It is also felt that an early entry into Mehgam would give Chmura Co an advantage over its competitors for a period of five years, after which the current project will cease, due to the development of new advanced manufacturing processes.

Mehgam's currency, the Peso (MP), is currently trading at MP72 per $1. Setting up the manufacturing base in Mehgam will require an initial investment of MP2,500 million immediately, to cover the cost of land and buildings (MP1,250 million) and machinery (MP1,250 million). Tax allowable depreciation is available on the machinery at an annual rate of 10% on cost on a straight-line basis. A balancing adjustment will be required at the end of year five, when it is expected that the machinery will be sold for MP500 million (after inflation). The market value of the land and buildings in five years' time is estimated to be 80% of the current value. These amounts are inclusive of any tax impact.

Chmura Co will require MP200 million for working capital immediately. It is not expected that any further injections of working capital will be required for the five years. When the project ceases at the end of the fifth year, the working capital will be released back to Chmura Co.

Production of the packaged foods will take place in batches of product mixes. These batches will then be sold to supermarket chains, wholesalers and distributors in Mehgam and its neighbouring countries, who will repackage them to their individual requirements. All sales will be in MP. The estimated average number of batches produced and sold each year is given below:

Year	1	2	3	4	5
Batches produced and sold	10,000	15,000	30,000	26,000	15,000

The current selling price for each batch is estimated to be MP115,200. The costs related to producing and selling each batch are currently estimated to be MP46,500. In addition to these costs, a number of products will need a special packaging material which Chmura Co will send to Mehgam. Currently the cost of the special packaging material is $200 per batch. Training and development costs, related to the production of the batches, are estimated to be 80% of the production and selling costs (excluding the cost of the special packaging) in the first year, before falling to 20% of these costs (excluding the cost of the special packaging) in the second year, and then nil for the remaining years. It is expected that the costs relating to the production and sale of each batch will increase annually by 10% but the selling price and the special packaging costs will only increase by 5% every year.

The current annual corporation tax rate in Mehgam is 25% and Chmura Co pays annual corporation tax at a rate of 20% in the country where it is based. Both countries' taxes are payable in the year that the tax liability arises. A bi-lateral tax treaty exists between the two countries which permits offset of overseas tax against any tax liabilities Chmura Co incurs on overseas earnings.

The risk-adjusted cost of capital applicable to the project on $-based cash flows is 12%, which is considerably higher than the return on short-dated $ treasury bills of 4%. The current rate of inflation in Mehgam is 8%, and in the country where Chmura Co is based, it is 2%. It can be assumed that these inflation rates will not change for the foreseeable future. All net cash flows from the project will be remitted back to Chmura Co at the end of each year.

Chmura Co's finance director is of the opinion that there are many uncertainties surrounding the project and has assessed that the cash flows can vary by a standard deviation of as much as 35% because of these uncertainties.

Recently Bulud Co offered Chmura Co the option to sell the entire project to Bulud Co for $28 million at the start of year three. Chmura Co will make the decision of whether or not to sell the project at the end of year two.

Required:

(a) **Discuss the role of the World Trade Organisation (WTO) and the possible benefits and drawbacks to Mehgam of reducing protectionist measures.** **(7 marks)**

(b) **Prepare an evaluative report for the Board of Directors of Chmura Co which addresses the following parts and recommends an appropriate course of action:**

    (i) **An estimate of the value of the project before considering Bulud Co's offer. Show all relevant calculations** **(14 marks)**

    (ii) **An estimate of the value of the project taking into account Bulud Co's offer. Show all relevant calculations** **(5 marks)**

    Note: in the Computer Based Exam (CBE), the "BSOP calculator" spreadsheet option will be provided to help you to answer this question.

    (iii) **A discussion of the assumptions made in parts (i) and (ii) above and the additional business risks which Chmura Co should consider before it makes the final decision whether or not to undertake the project.** **(14 marks)**

Professional marks will be awarded for the demonstration of skill in communication, analysis and evaluation, scepticism and commercial acumen in your answer. **(10 marks)**

(Total: 50 marks)

3   YILANDWE (JUN 15)

Yilandwe, whose currency is the Yilandwe Rand (YR), has faced extremely difficult economic challenges in the past 25 years because of some questionable economic policies and political decisions made by its previous governments. Although Yilandwe's population is generally poor, its people are nevertheless well-educated and ambitious. Just over three years ago, a new government took office and since then it has imposed a number of strict monetary and fiscal controls, including an annual corporation tax rate of 40%, in an attempt to bring Yilandwe out of its difficulties. As a result, the annual rate of inflation has fallen rapidly from a high of 65% to its current level of 33%. These strict monetary and fiscal controls have made Yilandwe's government popular in the larger cities and towns, but less popular in the rural areas which seem to have suffered disproportionately from the strict monetary and fiscal controls.

It is expected that Yilandwe's annual inflation rate will continue to fall in the coming few years as follows:

Year	Inflation rate
1	22.0%
2	14.7%
3 onwards	9.8%

Yilandwe's government has decided to continue the progress made so far, by encouraging foreign direct investment into the country. Recently, government representatives held trade shows internationally and offered businesses a number of concessions, including:

(i)   zero corporation tax payable in the first two years of operation; and

(ii)   an opportunity to carry forward tax losses and write them off against future profits made after the first two years.

The government representatives also promised international companies investing in Yilandwe prime locations in towns and cities with good transport links.

Imoni Co

Imoni Co, a large listed company based in the USA with the US dollar ($) as its currency, manufactures high tech diagnostic components for machinery, which it exports worldwide. After attending one of the trade shows, Imoni Co is considering setting up an assembly plant in Yilandwe where parts would be sent and assembled into a specific type of component, which is currently being assembled in the USA. Once assembled, the component will be exported directly to companies based in the European Union (EU). These exports will be invoiced in Euro (€).

Assembly plant in Yilandwe: financial and other data projections

It is initially assumed that the project will last for four years. The four-year project will require investments of YR21,000 million for land and buildings, YR18,000 million for machinery and YR9,600 million for working capital to be made immediately. The working capital will need to be increased annually at the start of each of the next three years by Yilandwe's inflation rate and it is assumed that this will be released at the end of the project's life.

It can be assumed that the assembly plant can be built very quickly and production started almost immediately. This is because the basic facilities and infrastructure are already in place as the plant will be built on the premises and grounds of a school. The school is ideally located, near the main highway and railway lines. As a result, the school will close and the children currently studying there will be relocated to other schools in the city. The government has kindly agreed to provide free buses to take the children to these schools for a period of six months to give parents time to arrange appropriate transport in the future for their children.

The current selling price of each component is €700 and this price is likely to increase by the average EU rate of inflation from year 1 onwards.

The number of components expected to be sold every year are as follows:

Year	1	2	3	4
Sales component units (000s)	150	480	730	360

The parts needed to assemble into the components in Yilandwe will be sent from the USA by Imoni Co at a cost of $200 per component unit, from which Imoni Co would currently earn a pre-tax contribution of $40 for each component unit. However, Imoni Co feels that it can negotiate with Yilandwe's government and increase the transfer price to $280 per component unit. The variable costs related to assembling the components in Yilandwe are currently

YR15,960 per component unit. The current annual fixed costs of the assembly plant are YR4,600 million. All these costs, wherever incurred, are expected to increase by that country's annual inflation every year from year 1 onwards.

Imoni Co pays corporation tax on profits at an annual rate of 20% in the USA. The tax in both the USA and Yilandwe is payable in the year that the tax liability arises. A bilateral tax treaty exists between Yilandwe and the USA. Tax allowable depreciation is available at 25% per year on the machinery on a straight-line basis.

Imoni Co will expect annual royalties from the assembly plant to be made every year. The normal annual royalty fee is currently $20 million, but Imoni Co feels that it can negotiate this with Yilandwe's government and increase the royalty fee by 80%. Once agreed, this fee will not be subject to any inflationary increase in the project's four-year period.

If Imoni Co does decide to invest in an assembly plant in Yilandwe, its exports from the USA to the EU will fall and it will incur redundancy costs. As a result, Imoni Co's after-tax cash flows will reduce by the following amounts:

Year	1	2	3	4
Redundancy and lost contribution	20,000	55,697	57,368	59,089

Imoni Co normally uses its cost of capital of 9% to assess new projects. However, the finance director suggests that Imoni Co should use a project specific discount rate of 12% instead.

Other financial information

Current spot rates

Euro per Dollar	€0.714/$1
YR per Euro	YR142/€1
YR per Dollar	YR101.4/$1

Forecast future rates based on expected inflation rate differentials

Year	1	2	3	4
YR/$1	120.1	133.7	142.5	151.9
Year	1	2	3	4
YR/€1	165.0	180.2	190.2	200.8

Expected inflation rates

EU expected inflation rate: Next two years	5%
EU expected inflation rate: Year 3 onwards	4%
USA expected inflation rate: Year 1 onwards	3%

Required:

(a)   Discuss the possible benefits and drawbacks to Imoni Co of setting up its own assembly plant in Yilandwe, compared to licensing a company based in Yilandwe to undertake the assembly on its behalf.   **(4 marks)**

(b)   Prepare a report which:

(i)   Evaluates the financial acceptability of the investment in the assembly plant in Yilandwe   **(20 marks)**

(ii)   Discusses the assumptions made in producing the estimates, and the other risks and issues which Imoni Co should consider before making the final decision;   **(14 marks)**

(iii) Provides a reasoned recommendation on whether or not Imoni Co should invest in the assembly plant in Yilandwe.   **(2 marks)**

Professional marks will be awarded for the demonstration of skill in communication, analysis and evaluation, scepticism and commercial acumen in your answer.   **(10 marks)**

(Total: 50 marks)

4   TALAM CO (MAR/JUN 19)

    Answer debrief

The following exhibits, available on the left-hand side of the screen (in the CBE exam), provide information relevant to the question.

1   **Talam Co**

2   **Uwa Project**

3   **Jigu Project as a real option**

4   **Biodegradable drones and related issues**

This information should be used to answer the question requirements within your chosen response option(s).

Talam Co

Talam Co, a listed company, aims to manufacture innovative engineering products which are environmentally friendly and sustainable. These products have been highly marketable because of their affordability. Talam Co's mission statement also states its desire to operate to the highest ethical standards. These commitments have meant that Talam Co has a very high reputation and a high share price compared to its competitors.

Talam Co is considering a new project, the Uwa Project, to manufacture drones for use in the agricultural industry, which are at least 50% biodegradable, at competitive prices. The drones will enable farmers to increase crop yields and reduce crop damage. Manufacture of drones is a new business area for Talam Co. The project is expected to last for four years.

Talam Co will also work on the Jigu Project (a follow-on project to the Uwa Project) to make 95%+ biodegradable drones. It is expected that the Jigu Project will last for a further five years after the Uwa Project has finished. If the Uwa Project is discontinued or sold sooner than four years, the Jigu Project could still be undertaken after four years.

Uwa Project

The following number of drones are expected to be produced and sold:

Year	1	2	3	4
Number of drones sold	4,300	19,200	35,600	25,400

In the first year, for each drone, it is expected that the selling price will be $1,200 and the variable costs will be $480. The total annual direct fixed costs will be $2.7m. After the first year, the selling price is expected to increase by 8% annually, the variable costs by 4% annually and the fixed costs by 10% annually, for the next three years. Training costs are expected to be 200% of the variable costs in year 1, 60% in year 2, and 10% in each of years 3 and 4. There is substantial uncertainty about the drones produced and sold, and Talam Co estimates the project to have a standard deviation of 30%.

At the start of every year, the Uwa Project will need working capital. In the first year, this will be 20% of sales revenue. In subsequent years, the project will require additional or a reduction in working capital of 10% for every $1 increase or decrease in sales revenue respectively. The working capital is expected to be fully recovered when the Uwa Project ceases.

The Uwa Project will need $35m of machinery to produce the drones at the start of the project. Tax allowable depreciation is available on the machinery at 15% per year on a straight-line basis. The machinery is expected to be sold for $7m (post-inflation) at the end of the project. Talam Co makes sufficient profits from its other activities to take advantage of any tax loss relief. Tax is paid in the year it falls due.

Honua Co's offer

Honua Co, whose main business is drone production, has approached Talam Co with an offer to buy the Uwa Project in its entirety from Talam Co, for $30m at the start of the third year of the project's life. Talam Co's finance director has requested that the value of Honua Co's offer is estimated using the real options method.

Additional information

Both Honua Co and Talam Co pay corporation tax at an annual rate of 20%. Talam Co has estimated Uwa Project's and Jigu Project's risk-adjusted cost of capital at 11%, based on Honua Co's asset beta. Talam Co believes that the central bank base rate, which is currently 2.30%, provides a good estimate of the risk-free rate of interest.

Jigu Project as a real option

Talam Co estimates that Jigu Project's cash flows are highly uncertain, and its standard deviation is 50%. It is estimated that $60m will be required at the start of the project in four years' time. Using conventional net present value, Talam Co's best estimate is that net present value of the project will be $10m at the start of the project.

The following figures were estimated for the Jigu Project using the real options method.

Asset value (Pa) = $46.1m (to nearest 100,000)

Exercise price (Pe) = $60m

Exercise date (t) = 4 years

Risk-free rate (r) = 2.30%

Volatility (s) = 50%

d1 = 0.329

d2 = –0.671

N(d1) = 0.6288

N(d2) = 0.2510

Call option value: $15.3m

It can be assumed that the call option value is accurate.

Talam Co's finance director wants to know how the asset value of $46.1m has been estimated.

Biodegradable drones and related issues

At a recent trade show, the biodegradable drones attracted considerable interest from organisations worldwide.

Nevertheless, some expressed concern about the drone price, which they felt was too high.

Talam Co estimates that even a modest reduction in each drone's price would make the projects unprofitable. Therefore, the operations director suggested that costs could be reduced if drone components were produced in Dunia, a country where Talam Co already gets some of its other products made.

However, the public relations director brought up an issue concerning Dunia. He said that several companies in Dunia, which Talam Co trades with, employ young teenage children. These companies pay the education fees for the teenagers and the companies argued that stopping this practice would harm the teenagers' families financially.

Required:

(a) Discuss how incorporating real options into net present value decisions may help Talam Co with its investment appraisal decisions. **(5 marks)**

(b) Prepare a report for the board of directors (BoD) of Talam Co which:

   (i) Estimates, showing all relevant calculations, the net present value of the Uwa Project before considering the offer from Honua Co and the Jigu Project; **(12 marks)**

   (ii) Addresses the requests made by the finance director about the asset value for the Jigu project and estimated value of the offer from Honua Co using the real options method; **(7 marks)**

   Note: in the Computer Based Exam (CBE), the "BSOP calculator" spreadsheet option will be provided to help you to answer this question.

   (iii) Assesses whether the Uwa Project should be undertaken, using the results from, and discusses the assumptions made in, the calculations in (b)(i) and (b)(ii) above. **(8 marks)**

(c)   Discuss the impact on Talam Co and its aims arising from the possible sustainability and ethical issues relating to the biodegradable drones, and advise on how these issues may be addressed.   **(8 marks)**

Professional marks will be awarded for the demonstration of skill in communication, analysis and evaluation, scepticism and commercial acumen in your answer.   (10 marks)

(Total: 50 marks)

 Calculate your allowed time, allocate the time to the separate parts……………

5   ZHICHI CO (SEP/DEC 21)

The following exhibits, available on the left-hand side of the screen (in the CBE exam), provide information relevant to the question.

1   **Zhichi Co policy failures**

2   **New project discount rate**

3   **New project cash flows**

4   **Financing the new project**

This information should be used to answer the question requirements within your chosen response option(s).

Zhichi Co policy failures

Zhichi Co is a large, listed engineering company involved in the development and manufacture of environmentally friendly products for businesses worldwide. Until a few years ago, the value of its shares had been increasing steadily and it regularly outperformed its main rivals.

However, more recently its shares have been underperforming and many financial analysts are recommending that Zhichi Co shares should be sold. Zhichi Co's investors are becoming increasingly concerned.

The analysis concluded that this underperformance was due to three policy failures in the company's financial strategy, as follows:

–   Zhichi Co does not undertake post-completion audits of its investment projects;

–   Zhichi Co has used a fixed discount rate of 10% to assess all investment projects for some years now. None of the company's senior management can remember why this rate was chosen; and

–   Zhichi Co has continually funded new investment projects using equity finance and the analysis concluded that this financing strategy sent the wrong signals to investors.

New project discount rate

Zhichi Co is considering a new project to manufacture environmentally friendly motor scooters which are fully carbon neutral. This is a diversification into a new business area for Zhichi Co in which it has no previous experience. Zhichi Co's chief financial officer is of the opinion that Zhichi Co should determine an appropriate discount rate for the project based on an initial assumption that the project will be all-equity financed.

Liyu Co would be a competitor to Zhichi Co as it manufactures environmentally friendly motor scooters, as well as equipment for wind farms. Approximately 60% of Liyu Co's business is manufacturing motor scooters and the remaining 40% is manufacturing wind farm equipment.

Given below is the most recent financial information relating to Liyu Co.

Share capital ($0.25 nominal value)	$20,000,000
Reserves	$27,436,000
Market value of equity	$172,000,000
Market value of debt	$48,260,000
Equity beta	1.20

Sanwenyu Co is involved in the manufacture of equipment for wind farms. It has estimated its cost of equity as 15.4%, and it is financed 20% by debt and 80% by equity in market value terms.

The estimated risk-free rate is 4.8% and the market risk premium is 8%. The corporation tax rate applicable to all the companies is 20%.

New project cash flows

Zhichi Co expects the new project manufacturing environmentally friendly motor scooters to last for four years. The project will require an immediate expenditure of $70m for plant and machinery. After the project ends in four years' time, it is anticipated that the project will be sold for $42m, inclusive of any inflationary increase.

The following estimates of revenues and costs, relating directly to the project, have been made:

– In the first year, sales revenue is expected to be $10m and then increase to $40m in year two. In the final two years of the project, sales revenue will grow by 20% each year.

– Costs are estimated at 120% of sales revenue for the first year and 80% of sales revenue for the second year before reducing to 40% of sales revenue for each of the final two years.

Substantial initial working capital of $10m will be required at the start of year one of the project. Subsequently, working capital of 15% of sales revenue for that year will be required at the start of years two to four. Any remaining working capital will be released at the end of the project.

Zhichi Co pays corporation tax of 20% every year. Tax is payable with a year's time delay and any tax losses from the project are set against the company's profits from other projects. Tax allowable depreciation is available on the expenditure on the plant and machinery for the project at an annual rate of 15% on a reducing balance basis. It is anticipated that the plant and machinery will have a realisable value of $20m at the end of the project, and this realisable value is included in the project's estimated sale price of $42m.

Financing the new project

Due to the positive environmental nature of the new project, Zhichi Co can obtain the entire funding for the project through a loan at a subsidised interest rate of 180 basis points lower than the estimated risk-free rate of 4.8%. Zhichi Co's normal borrowing rate is 6%.

Zhichi Co has decided that the project should be entirely funded through the subsidised loan.

Issue costs, which need to be paid, are anticipated to be 3% of the gross finance. Issue costs are not allowable as a tax-deductible expense.

Given that the new project is to be funded by the subsidised loan, Zhichi Co's chief financial officer is of the opinion that the adjusted present value of the project would be more appropriate than the conventional net present value, based on a risk-adjusted cost of capital, to evaluate the project. However, he cannot explain why this should be the case.

Required:

(a) **Discuss and justify the actions Zhichi Co should take to address the three financial strategy policy failures.** **(8 marks)**

(b) **Prepare a report for the Board of Directors (BoD) of Zhichi Co which:**

(i) **Estimates an appropriate discount rate to use to determine the net present value of the new project based on all-equity finance.** **(6 marks)**

(ii) **Estimates the net present value of the new project, assuming that it is all-equity financed.** **(9 marks)**

(iii) **Estimates the adjusted present value of the new project.** **(7 marks)**

(iv) **Evaluates whether the new project should be undertaken, and**

– **discusses the assumptions made in the estimates above,**

– **discusses whether the adjusted present value method would be more appropriate than the conventional net present value method to evaluate the new project.** **(10 marks)**

Professional marks will be awarded for the demonstration of skill in communication, analysis and evaluation, scepticism and commercial acumen in your answer. **(10 marks)**

(Total: 50 marks)

ACQUISITIONS AND MERGERS

6 STANZIAL INC (DEC 06)

Stanzial Inc is a listed telecommunications company. The company is considering the purchase of Besserlot Co, an unlisted company that has developed, patented and marketed a secure, medium-range, wireless link to broadband. The wireless link is expected to increase Besserlot's revenue by 25% per year for three years, and by 10% per year thereafter. Besserlot is currently owned 35% by its senior managers, 30% by a venture capital company, 25% by a single shareholder on the board of directors, and 10% by about 100 other private investors.

Summarised accounts for Besserlot for the last two years are shown below:

Statements of profit or loss for the years ended 31 March ($000)

	20X6	20X5
Sales revenue	22,480	20,218
Operating profit before exceptional items	1,302	820
Exceptional items	(2,005)	–
Interest paid (net)	(280)	(228)
Profit before taxation	(983)	592
Taxation	(210)	(178)
Profit after taxation	(1,193)	414
Note: Dividend	200	100

Statements of financial position as at 31 March ($000)

	20X6	20X5
Non-current assets (net)		
Tangible assets	5,430	5,048
Goodwill	170	200
Current assets		
Inventory	3,400	2,780
Receivables falling due within one year	2,658	2,462
Receivables falling due after one year	100	50
Cash at bank and in hand	48	48
Total assets	11,806	10,588
Equity and liabilities		
Called-up share capital (25 cents par)	2,000	1,000
Retained profits	3,037	4,430
Other reserves	1,249	335
Total equity	6,286	5,765
Current liabilities – payables	5,520	4,823
	11,806	10,588

Other information relating to Besserlot:

(i)   Non-cash expenses, including depreciation, were $820,000 in 20X5–6.

(ii)   Corporate taxation is at the rate of 30% per year.

(iii)   Capital investment was $1 million in 20X5–6, and is expected to grow at approximately the same rate as revenue.

(iv)   Working capital, interest payments and non-cash expenses are expected to increase at the same rate as revenue.

(v)   The estimated value of the patent if sold now is $10 million. This has not been included in non-current assets.

(vi)   Operating profit is expected to be approximately 8% of revenue in 20X6–7, and to remain at the same percentage in future years.

(vii)   Dividends are expected to grow at the same rate as revenue.

(viii) The realisable value of existing inventory is expected to be 70% of its book value.

(ix)   The estimated cost of equity of Besserlot is 14%.

Information regarding the industry sector of Besserlot:

(i)   The average PE ratio of listed companies of similar size to Besserlot is 30:1.

(ii)   Average earnings growth in the industry is 6% per year.

Required:

(a)   **Prepare a report that:**

        (i)   **Estimates the value of Besserlot Co using:**

                • **Asset based valuation**

                • **PE ratios**

                • **Dividend based valuation**

                • **The present value of expected future cash flows.**

                State clearly any assumptions that you make.   **(16 marks)**

        (ii)   **Discusses the potential accuracy of each of the methods used and recommends, with reasons, a value, or range of values that Stanzial might bid for Besserlot.**   **(11 marks)**

(b)   **Discuss how the shareholder mix of Besserlot and type of payment used might influence the success or failure of the bid.**   **(8 marks)**

(c)   **Assuming that the bid was successful, discuss other factors that might influence the medium-term financial success of the acquisition.**   **(5 marks)**

Professional marks will be awarded for the demonstration of skill in communication, analysis and evaluation, scepticism and commercial acumen in your answer.   **(10 marks)**

(Total: 50 marks)

7   PURSUIT CO (JUN 11)

Pursuit Co, a listed company which manufactures electronic components, is interested in acquiring Fodder Co, an unlisted company involved in the development of sophisticated but high risk electronic products. The owners of Fodder Co are a consortium of private equity investors who have been looking for a suitable buyer for their company for some time. Pursuit Co estimates that a payment of the equity value plus a 25% premium would be sufficient to secure the purchase of Fodder Co. Pursuit Co would also pay off any outstanding debt that Fodder Co owed. Pursuit Co wishes to acquire Fodder Co using a combination of debt finance and its cash reserves of $20 million, such that the capital structure of the combined company remains at Pursuit Co's current capital structure level.

Information on Pursuit Co and Fodder Co

Pursuit Co

Pursuit Co has a market debt to equity ratio of 50:50 and an equity beta of 1.18. Currently Pursuit Co has a total firm value (market value of debt and equity combined) of $140 million.

Fodder Co, Statement of profit or loss extracts

Year Ended	31 May 20Y1	31 May 20Y0	31 May 20X9	31 May 20X8
All amounts are in $000				
Sales revenue	16,146	15,229	14,491	13,559
Operating profit (after operating costs and tax allowable depreciation)	5,169	5,074	4,243	4,530
Net interest costs	489	473	462	458
Profit before tax	4,680	4,601	3,781	4,072
Taxation (28%)	1,310	1,288	1,059	1,140
After tax profit	3,370	3,313	2,722	2,932
Dividends	123	115	108	101
Retained earnings	3,247	3,198	2,614	2,831

Fodder Co has a market debt to equity ratio of 10:90 and an estimated equity beta of 1.53. It can be assumed that its tax allowable depreciation is equivalent to the amount of investment needed to maintain current operational levels. However, Fodder Co will require an additional investment in assets of 22c per $1 increase in sales revenue, for the next four years. It is anticipated that Fodder Co will pay interest at 9% on its future borrowings.

For the next four years, Fodder Co's sales revenue will grow at the same average rate as the previous years. After the forecasted four-year period, the growth rate of its free cash flows will be half the initial forecast sales revenue growth rate for the foreseeable future.

Information about the combined company

Following the acquisition, it is expected that the combined company's sales revenue will be $51,952,000 in the first year, and its profit margin on sales will be 30% for the foreseeable future. After the first year the growth rate in sales revenue will be 5.8% per year for the following three years. Following the acquisition, it is expected that the combined company will pay annual interest at 6.4% on future borrowings.

The combined company will require additional investment in assets of $513,000 in the first year and then 18c per $1 increase in sales revenue for the next three years. It is anticipated that after the forecasted four-year period, its free cash flow growth rate will be half the sales revenue growth rate.

It can be assumed that the asset beta of the combined company is the weighted average of the individual companies' asset betas, weighted in proportion of the individual companies' market value.

Other information

The current annual government base rate is 4.5% and the market risk premium is estimated at 6% per year. The relevant annual tax rate applicable to all the companies is 28%.

SGF Co's interest in Pursuit Co

There have been rumours of a potential bid by SGF Co to acquire Pursuit Co. Some financial press reports have suggested that this is because Pursuit Co's share price has fallen recently. SGF Co is in a similar line of business as Pursuit Co and until a couple of years ago, SGF Co was the smaller company. However, a successful performance has resulted in its share price rising, and SGF Co is now the larger company.

The rumours of SGF Co's interest have raised doubts about Pursuit Co's ability to acquire Fodder Co. Although SGF Co has made no formal bid yet, Pursuit Co's board is keen to reduce the possibility of such a bid. The Chief Financial Officer has suggested that the most effective way to reduce the possibility of a takeover would be to distribute the $20 million in its cash reserves to its shareholders in the form of a special dividend. Fodder Co would then be purchased using debt finance. He conceded that this would increase Pursuit Co's gearing level but suggested it may increase the company's share price and make Pursuit Co less appealing to SGF Co.

Required:

(a) Discuss the advantages and disadvantages of organic growth and growth by acquisition. **(8 marks)**

(b) Prepare a report to the Board of Directors of Pursuit Co that

(i) Evaluates whether the acquisition of Fodder Co would be beneficial to Pursuit Co and its shareholders. The free cash flow to firm method should be used to estimate the values of Fodder Co and the combined company assuming that the combined company's capital structure stays the same as that of Pursuit Co's current capital structure. Include all relevant calculations. **(16 marks)**

(ii) Discusses the limitations of the estimated valuations in part (i) above. **(4 marks)**

(iii) Estimates the amount of debt finance needed, in addition to the cash reserves, to acquire Fodder Co and concludes whether Pursuit Co's current capital structure can be maintained. **(3 marks)**

(iv) Explains the implications of a change in the capital structure of the combined company, to the valuation method used in part (i) and how the issue can be resolved. **(4 marks)**

(v) Assesses whether the Chief Financial Officer's recommendation would provide a suitable defence against a bid from SGF Co and would be a viable option for Pursuit Co. **(5 marks)**

Professional marks will be awarded for the demonstration of skill in communication, analysis and evaluation, scepticism and commercial acumen in your answer. **(10 marks)**

(Total: 50 marks)

8 NENTE CO (JUN 12)

Nente Co, an unlisted company, designs and develops tools and parts for specialist machinery. The company was formed four years ago by three friends, who own 20% of the equity capital in total, and a consortium of five business angel organisations, who own the remaining 80%, in roughly equal proportions. Nente Co also has a large amount of debt finance in the form of variable rate loans. Initially the amount of annual interest payable on these loans was low and allowed Nente Co to invest internally generated funds to expand its business. Recently though, due to a rapid increase in interest rates, there has been limited scope for future expansion and no new product development.

The Board of Directors, consisting of the three friends and a representative from each business angel organisation, met recently to discuss how to secure the company's future prospects. Two proposals were put forward, as follows:

Proposal 1

To accept a takeover offer from Mije Co, a listed company, which develops and manufactures specialist machinery tools and parts. The takeover offer is for $2.95 cash per share or a share-for-share exchange where two Mije Co shares would be offered for three Nente Co shares. Mije Co would need to get the final approval from its shareholders if either offer is accepted:

Proposal 2

To pursue an opportunity to develop a small prototype product that just breaks even financially, but gives the company exclusive rights to produce a follow-on product within two years.

The meeting concluded without agreement on which proposal to pursue.

After the meeting, Mije Co was consulted about the exclusive rights. Mije Co's directors indicated that they had not considered the rights in their computations and were willing to continue with the takeover offer on the same terms without them.

Currently, Mije Co has 10 million shares in issue and these are trading for $4.80 each. Mije Co's price to earnings (P/E) ratio is 15. It has sufficient cash to pay for Nente Co's equity and a substantial proportion of its debt, and believes that this will enable Nente Co to operate on a P/E level of 15 as well. In addition to this, Mije Co believes that it can find cost-based synergies of $150,000 after tax per year for the foreseeable future. Mije Co's current profit after tax is $3,200,000.

The following financial information relates to Nente Co and to the development of the new product.

Nente Co financial information

Extract from the most recent statement of profit or loss

	$000
Sales revenue	8,780
Profit before interest and tax	1,230
Interest	(455)
Tax	(155)
Profit after tax	620
Dividends	Nil

Extract from the most recent statement of financial position

	$000
Net non-current assets	10,060
Current assets	690
Total Assets	10,750
Share capital (40c per share nominal value)	960
Reserves	1,400
Non-current liabilities: Variable rate loans	6,500
Current liabilities	1,890
Total liabilities and capital	10,750

In arriving at the profit after tax amount, Nente Co deducted tax allowable depreciation and other non-cash expenses totalling $1,206,000. It requires an annual cash investment of $1,010,000 in non-current assets and working capital to continue its operations.

Nente Co's profits before interest and tax in its first year of operation were $970,000 and have been growing steadily in each of the following three years, to their current level. Nente Co's cash flows grew at the same rate as well, but it is likely that this growth rate will reduce to 25% of the original rate for the foreseeable future.

Nente Co currently pays interest of 7% per year on its loans, which is 380 basis points over the government base rate, and corporation tax of 20% on profits after interest. It is estimated that an overall cost of capital of 11% is reasonable compensation for the risk undertaken on an investment of this nature.

New product development (Proposal 2)

Developing the new follow-on product will require an investment of $2,500,000 initially. The total expected cash flows and present values of the product over its five-year life, with a volatility of 42% standard deviation, are as follows:

Year(s)	Now	1	2	3 to 7 (in total)
Cash flows ($000)	–	–	(2,500)	3,950
Present values ($000)	–	–	(2,029)	2,434

Required:

(a) Explain why synergy might exist when one company merges with or takes over another company. (6 marks)

(b) Prepare a report for the Board of Directors of Nente Co that:

(i) Estimates the current value of a Nente Co share, using the free cash flow to firm methodology. (7 marks)

(ii) Estimates the percentage gain in value to a Nente Co share and a Mije Co share under each payment offer. (8 marks)

(iii) Estimates the percentage gain in the value of the follow-on product to a Nente Co share, based on its cash flows and on the assumption that the production can be delayed following acquisition of the exclusive rights of production. (5 marks)

Note: in the Computer Based Exam (CBE), the "BSOP calculator" spreadsheet option will be provided to help you to answer this question.

      (iv)   Discusses the likely reaction of Nente Co and Mije Co shareholders to the takeover offer, including the assumptions made in the estimates above and how the follow-on product's value can be utilised by Nente Co.   **(8 marks)**

(c)   Explain the circumstances in which the Black-Scholes option pricing (BSOP) model could be used to assess the value of a company, including the data required for the variables used in the model.   **(6 marks)**

Professional marks will be awarded for the demonstration of skill in communication, analysis and evaluation, scepticism and commercial acumen in your answer.   **(10 marks)**

(Total: 50 marks)

9   MLIMA CO (JUN 13)

Mlima Co is a private company involved in aluminium mining. About eight years ago, the company was bought out by its management and employees through a leveraged buyout (LBO). Due to high metal prices worldwide, the company has been growing successfully since the LBO. However, because the company has significant debt borrowings with strict restrictive covenants and high interest levels, it has had to reject a number of profitable projects. The company has currently two bonds in issue, as follows:

- A 16% secured bond with a nominal value of $80m, which is redeemable at par in five years. An early redemption option is available on this bond, giving Mlima Co the option to redeem the bond at par immediately if it wants to; and

- A 13% unsecured bond with a nominal value of $40m, which is redeemable at par in ten years.

Mlima Co's Board of Directors (BoD) has been exploring the idea of redeeming both bonds to provide it with more flexibility when making future investment decisions. To do so, the BoD has decided to consider a public listing of the company on a major stock exchange. It is intended that a total of 100 million shares will be issued in the newly-listed company. From the total shares, 20% will be sold to the public, 10% will be offered to the holders of the unsecured bond in exchange for redeeming the bond through an equity-for-debt swap, and the remaining 70% of the equity will remain in the hands of the current owners. The secured bond would be paid out of the funds raised from the listing.

The details of the possible listing and the distribution of equity were published in national newspapers recently. As a result, potential investors suggested that due to the small proportion of shares offered to the public and for other reasons, the shares should be offered at a substantial discount of as much as 20% below the expected share price on the day of the listing.

Mlima Co, financial information

It is expected that after the listing, deployment of new strategies and greater financial flexibility will boost Mlima Co's future sales revenue and, for the next four years, the annual growth rate will be 120% of the previous two years' average growth rate. After the four years, the annual growth rate of the free cash flows to the company will be 3.5%, for the foreseeable future. Operating profit margins are expected to be maintained in the future. Although it can be assumed that the current tax-allowable depreciation is equivalent to the amount of investment needed to maintain the current level of operations, the company will require an additional investment in assets of 30c per $1 increase in sales revenue for the next four years.

Extracts from Mlima Co's past three years' Statement of Profit or Loss

Year ended	31 May 20X3 $ million	31 May 20X2 $ million	31 May 20X1 $ million
Sales revenue	389.1	366.3	344.7
Operating profit	58.4	54.9	51.7
Net interest costs	17.5	17.7	18.0
Profit before tax	40.9	37.2	33.7
Taxation	10.2	9.3	8.4
Profit after tax	30.7	27.9	25.3

Once listed, Mlima Co will be able to borrow future debt at an interest rate of 7%, which is only 3% higher than the risk-free rate of return. It has no plans to raise any new debt after listing, but any future debt will carry considerably fewer restrictive covenants. However, these plans do not take into consideration the Bahari project (see below).

Bahari Project

Bahari is a small country with agriculture as its main economic activity. A recent geological survey concluded that there may be a rich deposit of copper available to be mined in the north-east of the country. This area is currently occupied by subsistence farmers, who would have to be relocated to other parts of the country. When the results of the survey were announced, some farmers protested that the proposed new farmland where they would be moved to was less fertile and that their communities were being broken up. However, the protesters were intimidated and violently put down by the government, and the state-controlled media stopped reporting about them. Soon afterwards, their protests were ignored and forgotten.

In a meeting between the Bahari government and Mlima Co's BoD, the Bahari government offered Mlima Co exclusive rights to mine the copper. It is expected that there are enough deposits to last at least 15 years. Initial estimates suggest that the project will generate free cash flows of $4 million in the first year, rising by 100% per year in each of the next two years, and then by 15% in each of the two years after that. The free cash flows are then expected to stabilise at the year-five level for the remaining 10 years.

The cost of the project, payable at the start, is expected to be $150 million, comprising machinery, working capital and the mining rights fee payable to the Bahari government. None of these costs is expected to be recoverable at the end of the project's 15-year life.

The Bahari government has offered Mlima Co a subsidised loan over 15 years for the full $150 million at an interest rate of 3% instead of Mlima Co's normal borrowing rate of 7%. The interest payable is allowable for taxation purposes. It can be assumed that Mlima Co's business risk is not expected to change as a result of undertaking the Bahari project.

At the conclusion of the meeting between the Bahari government and Mlima Co's BoD, the president of Bahari commented that working together would be like old times when he and Mlima Co's chief executive officer (CEO) used to run a business together.

Other Information

Mlima Co's closest competitor is Ziwa Co, a listed company which mines metals worldwide. Mlima Co's directors are of the opinion that after listing Mlima Co's cost of capital should be based on Ziwa Co's ungeared cost of equity. Ziwa Co's cost of capital is estimated at 9.4%, its geared cost of equity is estimated at 16.83% and its pre-tax cost of debt is estimated at 4.76%. These costs are based on a capital structure comprising of 200 million shares, trading at $7 each, and $1,700 million 5% irredeemable bonds, trading at $105 per $100. Both Ziwa Co and Mlima Co pay tax at an annual rate of 25% on their taxable profits.

It can be assumed that all cash flows will be in $ instead of the Bahari currency and therefore Mlima Co does not have to take account of any foreign exchange exposure from this venture.

Required:

(a) Prepare a report for the Board of Directors (BoD) of Mlima Co that:

    (i) Explains why Mlima Co's directors are of the opinion that Mlima Co's cost of capital should be based on Ziwa Co's ungeared cost of equity and, showing relevant calculations, estimate an appropriate cost of capital for Mlima Co.

        (7 marks)

    (ii) Estimates Mlima Co's value without undertaking the Bahari project and then with the Bahari project. The valuations should use the free cash flow methodology and the cost of capital calculated in part (i). Include relevant calculations.

        (14 marks)

    (iii) Advises the BoD whether or not the unsecured bondholders are likely to accept the equity-for-debt swap offer. Include relevant calculations.

        (4 marks)

    (iv) Advises the BoD on the listing and the possible share price range, if a total of 100 million shares are issued. The advice should also include:

- A discussion of the assumptions made in estimating the share price range

- In addition to the reasons mentioned in the scenario above, a brief explanation of other possible reasons for changing its status from a private company to a listed one; and

- An assessment of the possible reasons for issuing the share price at a discount for the initial listing   **(9 marks)**

(b) Discuss the possible impact on, and response of, Mlima Co to the following ethical issues, with respect to the Bahari project:

    (i) The relocation of the farmers; and

    (ii) The relationship between the Bahari president and Mlima Co's chief executive officer.

Note: The total marks will be split equally between each part in (b).   **(6 marks)**

Professional marks will be awarded for the demonstration of skill in communication, analysis and evaluation, scepticism and commercial acumen in your answer.   **(10 marks)**

        (Total: 50 marks)

10   NAHARA CO AND FUGAE CO (DEC 14)

Nahara Co is a private holding company owned by the government of a wealthy oil-rich country to invest its sovereign funds. Nahara Co has followed a strategy of risk diversification for a number of years by acquiring companies from around the world in many different sectors.

One of Nahara Co's acquisition strategies is to identify and purchase undervalued companies in the airline industry in Europe. A recent acquisition was Fugae Co, a company based in a country which is part of the European Union (EU). Fugae Co repairs and maintains aircraft engines.

A few weeks ago, Nahara Co stated its intention to pursue the acquisition of an airline company based in the same country as Fugae Co. The EU, concerned about this, asked Nahara Co to sell Fugae Co before pursuing any further acquisitions in the airline industry.

Avem Co's acquisition interest in Fugae Co

Avem Co, a UK-based company specialising in producing and servicing business jets, has approached Nahara Co with a proposal to acquire Fugae Co for $1,200 million. Nahara Co expects to receive a premium of at least 30% on the estimated equity value of Fugae Co, if it is sold.

Given below are extracts from the most recent statements of financial position of both Avem Co and Fugae Co.

	Avem Co $ million	Fugae Co $ million
Share capital (50c/share)	800	100
Reserves	3,550	160
Non-current liabilities	2,200	380
Current liabilities	130	30
Total capital and liabilities	6,680	670

Each Avem Co share is currently trading at $7.50, which is a multiple of 7.2 of its free cash flow to equity. Avem Co expects that the total free cash flows to equity of the combined company will increase by $40 million due to synergy benefits. After adding the synergy benefits of $40 million, Avem Co then expects the multiple of the total free cash flow of the combined company to increase to 7.5.

Fugae Co's free cash flow to equity is currently estimated at $76.5 million and it is expected to generate a return on equity of 11%. Over the past few years, Fugae Co has returned 77.3% of its annual free cash flow to equity back to Nahara Co, while retaining the balance for new investments.

Fugae Co's non-current liabilities consist entirely of $100 nominal value bonds which are redeemable in four years at the nominal value, on which the company pays a coupon of 5.4%. The debt is rated at B+ and the credit spread on B+ rated debt is 80 basis points above the risk-free rate of return.

Proposed luxury transport investment project by Fugae Co

In recent years, the country in which Fugae Co is based has been expanding its tourism industry and hopes that this industry will grow significantly in the near future. At present tourists normally travel using public transport and taxis, but there is a growing market for luxury travel. If the tourist industry does expand, then the demand for luxury travel is expected to grow rapidly. Fugae Co is considering entering this market through a four-year project. The project will cease after four years because of increasing competition.

The initial cost of the project is expected to be $42,000,000 and it is expected to generate the following after-tax cash flows over its four-year life:

Year	1	2	3	4
Cash flows ($000s)	3,277.6	16,134.3	36,504.7	35,683.6

The above figures are based on the tourism industry expanding as expected. However, it is estimated that there is a 25% probability that the tourism industry will not grow as expected in the first year. If this happens, then the present value of the project's cash flows will be 50% of the original estimates over its four-year life.

It is also estimated that if the tourism industry grows as expected in the first year, there is still a 20% probability that the expected growth will slow down in the second and subsequent years, and the present value of the project's cash flows would then be 40% of the original estimates in each of these years.

Lumi Co, a leisure travel company, has offered $50 million to buy the project from Fugae Co at the start of the second year. Fugae Co is considering whether having this choice would add to the value of the project.

If Fugae Co is bought by Avem Co after the project has begun, it is thought that the project will not result in any additional synergy benefits and will not generate any additional value for the combined company, above any value the project has already generated for Fugae Co.

Although there is no beta for companies offering luxury forms of travel in the tourist industry, Reka Co, a listed company, offers passenger transportation services on coaches, trains and luxury vehicles. About 15% of its business is in the luxury transport market and Reka Co's equity beta is 1.6. It is estimated that the asset beta of the non-luxury transport industry is 0.80. Reka Co's shares are currently trading at $4.50 per share and its debt is currently trading at $105 per $100. It has 80 million shares in issue and the book value of its debt is $340 million. The debt beta is estimated to be zero.

General information

The corporation tax rate applicable to all companies is 20%. The risk-free rate is estimated to be 4% and the market risk premium is estimated to be 6%.

Required:

(a)   Discuss whether or not Nahara Co's acquisition strategies, of pursuing risk diversification and of purchasing undervalued companies, can be valid.   **(6 marks)**

(b)   Prepare a report for the Board of Directors of Avem Co, which:

  (i)   Estimates the additional value created for Avem Co, if it acquires Fugae Co without considering the luxury transport project   **(10 marks)**

  (ii)   Estimates the additional value of the luxury transport project to Fugae Co, both with and without the offer from Lumi Co   **(18 marks)**

  (iii)   Evaluates the benefit attributable to Avem Co and Fugae Co from combining the two companies with and without the project, and concludes whether or not the acquisition is beneficial. The evaluation should include any assumptions made.   **(6 marks)**

Professional marks will be awarded for the demonstration of skill in communication, analysis and evaluation, scepticism and commercial acumen in your answer.   (10 marks)

(Total: 50 marks)

11   CHIKEPE CO (MAR/JUN 18)

Chikepe Co is a large listed company operating in the pharmaceutical industry with a current market value of equity of $12,600 million and a debt to equity ratio of 30:70, in market value terms. Institutional investors hold most of its equity shares. The company develops and manufactures antibiotics and anti-viral medicines. Both the company and its products have an established positive reputation among the medical profession, and its products are used widely. However, its rate of innovation has slowed considerably in the last few years and it has fewer new medical products coming into the market.

At a recent meeting of the board of directors (BoD), it was decided that the company needed to change its current strategy of growing organically to one of acquiring companies, in order to maintain the growth in its share price in the future. The members of the BoD had different opinions on the type of acquisition strategy to pursue.

Director A was of the opinion that Chikepe Co should follow a strategy of acquiring companies in different business sectors. She suggested that focusing on just the pharmaceutical sector was too risky and acquiring companies in different business sectors will reduce this risk.

Director B was of the opinion that Director A's suggestion would not result in a reduction in risk for shareholders. In fact, he suggested that this would result in agency related issues with Chikepe Co's shareholders reacting negatively and as a result, the company's share price would fall. Instead, Director B suggested that Chikepe Co should focus on its current business and acquire other established pharmaceutical companies. In this way, the company will gain synergy benefits and thereby increase value for its shareholders.

Director C agreed with Director B, but suggested that Chikepe Co should consider relatively new pharmaceutical companies, as well as established businesses. In her opinion, newer companies might be involved in research and development of innovative products, which could have high potential in the future. She suggested that using real options methodology with traditional investment appraisal methods such as net present value could help establish a more accurate estimate of the potential value of such companies.

The company has asked its finance team to prepare a report on the value of a potential target company, Foshoro Co, before making a final decision.

Foshoro Co

Foshoro Co is a non-listed pharmaceutical company established about 10 years ago. Initially Foshoro Co grew rapidly, but this rate of growth slowed considerably three years ago, after a venture capital equity backer exited the company by selling its stake back to the founding directors. The directors had to raise substantial debt capital to buy back the equity stake. The company's current debt to equity ratio is 60:40. This high level of gearing means that the company will find it difficult to obtain funds to develop its innovative products in the future.

The following financial information relates to Foshoro Co:

Extract from the most recent statement of profit or loss

	$ million
Sales revenue	878.1
Profit before interest and tax	192.3
Interest	78.6
Tax	22.7
Profit after tax	91.0

In arriving at the profit before interest and tax, Foshoro Co deducted tax allowable depreciation and other non-cash expenses totalling $112.0 million. It requires a cash investment of $98.2 million in non-current assets and working capital to continue its operations at the current level.

Three years ago, Foshoro Co's profit after tax was $83.3 million and this has been growing steadily to their current level. Foshoro Co's profit before interest and tax and its cash flows grew at the same growth rate as well. It is likely that this growth rate will continue for the foreseeable future if Foshoro Co is not acquired by Chikepe Co. Foshoro Co's cost of capital has been estimated at 10%.

Combined company: Chikepe Co and Foshoro Co

Once Chikepe Co acquires Foshoro Co, it is predicted that the combined company's sales revenue will be $4,200 million in the first year, and its operating profit margin on sales revenue will be 20% for the foreseeable future.

After the first year, the sales revenue is expected to grow at 7% per year for the following three years. It is anticipated that after the first four years, the growth rate of the combined company's free cash flows will be 5.6% per year.

The combined company's tax allowable depreciation is expected to be equivalent to the amount of investment needed to maintain the current level of operations. However, as the company's sales revenue increases over the four-year period, the combined company will require an additional investment in assets of $200 million in the first year and then $0.64 per $1 increase in sales revenue for the next three years.

It can be assumed that the asset beta of the combined company is the weighted average of the individual companies' asset betas, weighted in proportion of the individual companies' value of equity. It can also be assumed that the capital structure of the combined company remains at Chikepe Co's current capital structure level, a debt to equity ratio of 30:70. Chikepe Co pays interest on borrowings at a rate of 5.3% per year.

Chikepe Co estimates that it will be able to acquire Foshoro Co by paying a premium of 30% above its estimated equity value to Foshoro Co's shareholders.

Other financial information

	Equity beta	Asset beta
Chikepe Co	1.074	0.800
Foshoro Co	2.090	0.950

The current annual government borrowing base rate is 2% and the annual market risk premium is estimated at 7%. Both companies pay tax at an annual rate of 20%.

Chikepe Co estimates equity values in acquisitions using the free cash flow to firm method.

Future acquisitions

The BoD agreed that in the future it is likely that Chikepe Co will target both listed and non-listed companies for acquisition. It is aware that when pursuing acquisitions of listed companies, the company would need to ensure that it complied with regulations such as the mandatory bid rule and the principle of equal treatment to protect shareholders.

Required:

(a) Compare and contrast the reasons for the opinions held by Director A and by Director B, and discuss the types of synergy benefits which may arise from the acquisition strategy suggested by Director B. **(7 marks)**

(b) Discuss how using real options methodology in conjunction with net present value could help establish a more accurate estimate of the potential value of companies, as suggested by Director C. **(5 marks)**

(c) Prepare a report for the board of directors of Chikepe Co which:

   (i) Estimates the current equity value of Foshoro Co **(6 marks)**

   (ii) Estimates the equity value arising from combining Foshoro Co with Chikepe Co **(11 marks)**

   (iii) Evaluates whether the acquisition of Foshoro Co would be beneficial to Chikepe Co's shareholders and discusses the limitations of the valuation method used in (c)(i) and (c)(ii) above. **(7 marks)**

(d) Discuss how the mandatory bid rule and the principle of equal treatment protect shareholders in the event of their company facing a takeover bid. **(4 marks)**

Professional marks will be awarded for the demonstration of skill in communication, analysis and evaluation, scepticism and commercial acumen in your answer. **(10 marks)**

(Total: 50 marks)

12   OPAO CO (DEC 18)

Around seven years ago, Opao Co, a private conglomerate company involved in many different businesses, decided to obtain a listing on a recognised stock exchange by offering a small proportion of its equity shares to the public. Before the listing, the company was owned by around 100 shareholders, who were all closely linked to Opao Co and had their entire shareholding wealth invested in the company. However, soon after the listing these individuals started selling their shares in Opao Co, and over a two-year period after the listing, its ownership structure changed to one of many diverse individual and institutional shareholders.

As a consequence of this change in ownership structure, Opao Co's board of directors (BoD) commenced an aggressive period of business reorganisation through portfolio and organisational restructuring. This resulted in Opao Co changing from a conglomerate company to a company focusing on just two business sectors: financial services and food manufacturing. The financial press reported that Opao Co had been forced to take this action because of the change in the type of its shareholders. The equity markets seem to support this action, and Opao Co's share price has grown strongly during this period of restructuring, after growing very slowly initially.

Opao Co recently sold a subsidiary company, Burgut Co, through a management buy-in (MBI), although it also had the option to dispose of Burgut Co through a management buy-out (MBO). In a statement, Opao Co's BoD justified this by stating that Burgut Co would be better off being controlled by the MBI team.

Opao Co is now considering acquiring Tai Co and details of the proposed acquisition are as follows:

Proposed acquisition of Tai Co

Tai Co is an unlisted company involved in food manufacturing. Opao Co's BoD is of the opinion that the range of products produced by Tai Co will fit very well with its own product portfolio, leading to cross-selling opportunities, new innovations, and a larger market share. The BoD also thinks that there is a possibility for economies of scale and scope, such as shared logistic and storage facilities, giving cost saving opportunities. This, the BoD believes, will lead to significant synergy benefits and therefore it is of the opinion that Opao Co should make a bid to acquire Tai Co.

Financial information related to Opao Co, Tai Co and the combined company

Opao Co

Opao Co has 2,000 million shares in issue and are currently trading at $2.50 each.

Tai Co

Tai Co has 263 million shares in issue and the current market value of its debt is $400 million. Its most recent profit before interest and tax was $132.0 million, after deducting tax allowable depreciation and non-cash expenses of $27.4 million. Tai Co makes an annual cash investment of $24.3 million in non-current assets and working capital. It is estimated that its cash flows will grow by 3% annually for the foreseeable future. Tai Co's current cost of capital is estimated to be 11%.

Combined company

If Opao Co acquires Tai Co, it is expected that the combined company's sales revenue will be $7,351 million in the first year and its annual pre-tax profit margin on sales will be 15.4% for the foreseeable future. After the first year, sales revenue will grow by 5.02% every year for the next three years. It can be assumed that the combined company's annual depreciation will be equivalent to the investment required to maintain the company at current operational levels. However, in order to increase the sales revenue levels each year, the combined company will require an additional investment of $109 million in the first year and $0.31 for every $1 increase in sales revenue for each of the next three years.

After the first four years, it is expected that the combined company's free cash flows will grow by 2.4% annually for the foreseeable future. The combined company's cost of capital is estimated to be 10%. It expected that the combined company's debt to equity level will be maintained at 40:60, in market value terms, after the acquisition has taken place.

Both Opao Co and Tai Co pay corporation tax on profits at an annual rate of 20% and it is expected that this rate will not change if Opao Co acquires Tai Co. It can be assumed that corporation tax is payable in the same year as the profits it is charged on.

Possible acquisition price offers

Opao Co's BoD is proposing that Tai Co's acquisition be made through one of the following payment methods:

(i)   A cash payment offer of $4.40 for each Tai Co share, or

(ii)   Through a share-for-share exchange, where a number of Tai Co shares are exchanged for a number of Opao Co shares, such that 55.5% of the additional value created from the acquisition is allocated to Tai Co's shareholders and the remaining 44.5% of the additional value is allocated to Opao Co's shareholders, or

(iii) Through a mixed offer of a cash payment of $2.09 per share and one Opao Co share for each Tai Co share. It is estimated that Opao Co's share price will become $2.60 per share when such a mixed offer is made.

Similar acquisitions in the food manufacturing industry have normally attracted a share price premium of between 15% and 40% previously.

Required:

(a) **Distinguish between a management buy-out (MBO) and a management buy-in (MBI), and discuss why Opao Co's board of directors (BoD) might have sold Burgut Co through an MBI.** **(5 marks)**

(b) **Explain what portfolio restructuring and organisational restructuring involve, and discuss possible reason(s) why the change in the type of shareholders may have made Opao Co change from being a conglomerate to one focusing on just two business sectors.** **(6 marks)**

(c) **Prepare a report for the board of directors of Opao Co which:**

(i) **Estimates the value of equity of Opao Co and of Tai Co before the acquisition, and of the combined company after the acquisition** **(10 marks)**

(ii) **Estimates the percentage gain in value for each Opao Co share and Tai Co share, under each of the cash, the share-for-share, and the mixed offers** **(12 marks)**

(iii) **Evaluates the likely reaction of Opao Co's and Tai Co's shareholders to the acquisition offers.** **(7 marks)**

Professional marks will be awarded for the demonstration of skill in communication, analysis and evaluation, scepticism and commercial acumen in your answer. **(10 marks)**

(Total: 50 marks)

13 WESTPARLEY CO (MAR 20)

Westparley Co is a listed retailer, mainly selling food and small household goods. It has outperformed its competitors over the last few years as a result of providing high quality products at reasonable prices, and also having a stronger presence online. It has kept a control on costs, partly by avoiding operating large stores on expensive city centre sites. Instead, it has had smaller stores on the edge of cities and towns, and a limited number of larger stores on convenient out-of-town sites, aiming at customers who want their journeys to shops to be quick. One of its advertising slogans has been: 'We are where you want us to be.'

Westparley Co's share price has recently performed better than most companies in the retail sector generally. Share prices in the retail sector have been relatively low as a result of poor results due to high competition, large fixed cost base and high interest rates. The exception has been shares in retailers specialising in computer and high-technology goods. These shares appear to have benefited from a boom generally in share prices of high-technology companies. Some analysts believe share prices of many companies in the high-technology sector are significantly higher than a rational analysis of their future prospects would indicate.

Matravers Co

Westparley Co has identified the listed retailer Matravers Co as an acquisition target, because it believes that Matravers Co's shares are currently undervalued and part of Matravers Co's operations would be a good strategic fit for Westparley Co.

Matravers Co operates two types of store:

Matravers Home mainly sells larger household items and home furnishings. These types of retailer have performed particularly badly recently and one major competitor of Matravers Home has just gone out of business. Matravers Home operates a number of city centre sites but has a much higher proportion of out-of-town sites than its competitors.

Matravers Tech sells computers and mobile phones in much smaller outlets than those of Matravers Home.

Extracts from Matravers Co's latest annual report are given below:

	$m
Pre-tax profit	1,950
Long-term loan	6,500
Share capital ($1 shares)	5,000

The share of pre-tax profit between Matravers Home and Matravers Tech was 80:20.

The current market value of Matravers Co's shares is $12,500m and its debt is currently trading at its book value. Westparley Co believes that it will have to pay a premium of 15% to Matravers Co's shareholders to buy the company.

Westparley Co intends to take advantage of the current values attributed to businesses such as Matravers Tech by selling this part of Matravers Co at the relevant sector price earnings ratio of 18, rather than a forecast estimate of Matravers Tech's present value of future free cash flows of $4,500m.

The company tax rate for both companies is 28% per year.

Post-acquisition cost of capital

The post-acquisition cost of capital of the combined company will be based on its cost of equity and cost of debt. The asset beta post-acquisition can be assumed to be both companies' asset betas weighted in proportion to their current market value of equity.

Westparley Co has 4,000 million $1 shares in issue, currently trading at $8.50. It has $26,000m debt in issue, currently trading at $105 per $100 nominal value. Its equity beta is 1.02.

Matravers Co's asset beta is 0.75. The current market value of Matravers Co's shares is $12,500m and its long-term loan is currently trading at its book value of $6,500m.

The risk-free rate of return is estimated to be 3.5% and the market risk premium is estimated to be 8%.

The pre-tax cost of debt of the combined company is expected to be 9.8%. It can be assumed that the debt:equity ratio of the combined company will be the same as Westparley Co's current debt:equity ratio in market values.

The company tax rate for both companies is 28% per year.

Plans for Matravers Co

The offer for Matravers Co will be a cash offer. Any funding required for this offer will be a mixture of debt and equity. Although for the purposes of the calculation it has been assumed that the overall mix of debt and equity will remain the same, the directors are considering various plans for funding the purchase which could result in a change in Westparley Co's gearing.

As soon as it acquires all of Matravers Co's share capital, Westparley Co would sell Matravers Tech as it does not fit in with Westparley Co's strategic plans and Westparley Co wishes to take advantage of the large values currently attributed to high-technology businesses. Westparley Co would then close Matravers Home's worst-performing city centre stores. It anticipates the loss of returns from these stores would be partly compensated by higher online sales by Matravers Co, generated by increased investment in its online operations. The remaining city centre stores and all out-of-town stores would start selling the food and household items currently sold in Westparley Co's stores, and Westparley Co believes that this would increase profits from those stores.

Westparley Co also feels that reorganising Matravers Co's administrative functions and using increased power as a larger retailer can lead to synergies after the acquisition.

Post-acquisition details

Once Matravers Tech has been sold, Westparley Co estimates that sales revenue from the Matravers Home stores which remain open, together with the online sales from its home business, will be $43,260m in the first year post-acquisition, and this figure is expected to grow by 3% per year in years 2 to 4.

The profit margin before interest and tax is expected to be 6% of sales revenue in years 1 to 4.

Tax allowable depreciation is assumed to be equivalent to the amount of investment needed to maintain existing operations. However, an investment in assets (including working capital) will be required of $630m in year 1. In years 2 to 4, investment in assets each year will be $0.50 of every $1 increase in sales revenue.

After four years, the annual growth rate of free cash flows is expected to be 2% for the foreseeable future.

As well as the free cash flows from Matravers Co, Westparley Co expects that post-tax synergies will arise from its planned reorganisation of Matravers Co as follows in the next three years:

Year	1	2	3
	$m	$m	$m
Free cash flows	700	750	780

The current market value of Matravers Co's shares is $12,500m and its debt is currently trading at its book value of $6,500m.

Required:

(a) Discuss the behavioural factors which may have led to businesses such as Matravers Tech being valued highly. **(4 marks)**

(b) Prepare a report for the board of directors of Westparley Co which:

(i) compares the additional value which Westparley Co believes can be generated from the sale of Matravers Tech based on the P/E ratio, with that of the projected present value of its future free cash flows **(4 marks)**

(ii) calculates the weighted average cost of capital for the combined company **(6 marks)**

(iii) estimates the total value which Westparley Co's shareholders will gain from the acquisition of Matravers Co; and **(10 marks)**

(iv) assesses the strategic and financial value to Westparley Co of the acquisition, including a discussion of the estimations and assumptions made. **(10 marks)**

(c) Discuss the factors which may determine how the offer for Matravers Co will be financed and hence the level of gearing which Westparley Co will have. **(6 marks)**

Professional marks will be awarded for the demonstration of skill in communication, analysis and evaluation, scepticism and commercial acumen in your answer. **(10 marks)**

(Total: 50 marks)

CORPORATE RECONSTRUCTION AND REORGANISATION

14   CIGNO CO (SEP/DEC 15)

Cigno Co is a large pharmaceutical company, involved in the research and development (R&D) of medicines and other healthcare products. Over the past few years, Cigno Co has been finding it increasingly difficult to develop new medical products. In response to this, it has followed a strategy of acquiring smaller pharmaceutical companies which already have successful products in the market and/or have products in development which look very promising for the future. It has mainly done this without having to resort to major cost-cutting and has therefore avoided large-scale redundancies. This has meant that not only has Cigno Co performed reasonably well in the stock market, but it has also maintained a high level of corporate reputation.

Anatra Co is involved in two business areas: the first area involves the R&D of medical products, and the second area involves the manufacture of medical and dental equipment. Until recently, Anatra Co's financial performance was falling, but about three years ago a new chief executive officer (CEO) was appointed and she started to turn the company around. Recently, the company has developed and marketed a range of new medical products, and is in the process of developing a range of cancer-fighting medicines. This has resulted in a good performance in the stock market, but many analysts believe that its shares are still trading below their true value. Anatra Co's CEO is of the opinion that the turnaround in the company's fortunes makes it particularly vulnerable to a takeover threat, and she is thinking of defence strategies that the company could undertake to prevent such a threat. In particular, she was thinking of disposing some of the company's assets and focussing on its core business.

Cigno Co is of the opinion that Anatra Co is being held back from achieving its true potential by its equipment manufacturing business and that by separating the two business areas, corporate value can be increased. As a result, it is considering the possibility of acquiring Anatra Co, unbundling the manufacturing business, and then absorbing Anatra Co's R&D of medical products business. Cigno Co estimates that it would need to pay a premium of 35% to Anatra Co's shareholders to buy the company.

Financial information: Anatra Co

Given below are extracts from Anatra Co's latest statement of profit or loss and statement of financial position for the year ended 30 November 20X5.

	20X5
	$ million
Sales revenue	21,400
Profit before interest and tax (PBIT)	3,210
Interest	720
Pre-tax profit	2,490
Non-current liabilities	9,000
Share capital (50c/share)	3,500
Reserves	4,520

Anatra Co's share of revenue and profits between the two business areas are as follows:

	Medical products R&D	Equipment manufacturing
Share of revenue and profit	70%	30%

Post-acquisition benefits from acquiring Anatra Co

Cigno Co estimates that following the acquisition and unbundling of the manufacturing business, Anatra Co's future sales revenue and profitability of the medical R&D business will be boosted. The annual sales growth rate is expected to be 5% and the profit margin before interest and tax is expected to be 17.25% of sales revenue, for the next four years. It can be assumed that the current tax allowable depreciation will remain equivalent to the amount of investment needed to maintain the current level of operations, but that the company will require an additional investment in assets of 40c for every $1 increase in sales revenue.

After the four years, the annual growth rate of the company's free cash flows is expected to be 3% for the foreseeable future.

Anatra Co's unbundled equipment manufacturing business is expected to be divested through a sell-off, although other options such as a management buy-in were also considered. The value of the sell-off will be based on the medical and dental equipment manufacturing industry. Cigno Co has estimated that Anatra Co's manufacturing business should be valued at a factor of 1.2 times higher than the industry's average price-to-earnings ratio. Currently the industry's average earnings-per-share is 30c and the average share price is $2.40.

Possible additional post-acquisition benefits

Cigno Co estimates that it could achieve further cash flow benefits following the acquisition of Anatra Co, if it undertakes a limited business re-organisation. There is some duplication of the R&D work conducted by Cigno Co and Anatra Co, and the costs related to this duplication could be saved if Cigno Co closes some of its own operations. However, it would mean that many redundancies would have to be made including employees who have worked in Cigno Co for many years. Anatra Co's employees are considered to be better qualified and more able in these areas of duplication, and would therefore not be made redundant.

Cigno Co could also move its headquarters to the country where Anatra Co is based and thereby potentially save a significant amount of tax, other than corporation tax. However, this would mean a loss of revenue for the government where Cigno Co is based.

The company is concerned about how the government and the people of the country where it is based might react to these issues. It has had a long and beneficial relationship with the country and with the country's people.

Cigno Co has estimated that it would save $1,600 million after-tax free cash flows to the firm at the end of the first year as a result of these post-acquisition benefits. These cash flows would increase by 4% every year for the next three years.

Estimating the combined company's weighted average cost of capital

Cigno Co is of the opinion that as a result of acquiring Anatra Co, the cost of capital will be based on the equity beta and the cost of debt of the combined company. The asset beta of the combined company is the individual companies' asset betas weighted in proportion of the individual companies' market value of equity. Cigno Co has a market debt to equity ratio of 40:60 and an equity beta of 1.10.

It can be assumed that the proportion of market value of debt to market value of equity will be maintained after the two companies combine.

Currently, Cigno Co's total firm value (market values of debt and equity combined) is $60,000 million and Anatra Co's asset beta is 0.68.

Additional information

- The estimate of the risk free rate of return is 4.3% and of the market risk premium is 7%. The corporation tax rate applicable to all companies is 22%.

- Anatra Co's current share price is $3 per share, and it can be assumed that the book value and the market value of its debt are equivalent.

- The pre-tax cost of debt of the combined company is expected to be 6.0%.

Important note:

Cigno Co's board of directors (BoD) does not require any discussion or computations of currency movements or exposure in this report. All calculations are to be presented in $ millions. Currency movements and their management will be considered in a separate report. The BoD also does not expect any discussion or computations relating to the financing of acquisition in this report, other than the information provided above on the estimation of the cost of capital.

Required:

(a) **Distinguish between a divestment through a sell-off and a management buy-in as forms of unbundling.** **(4 marks)**

(b) **Prepare a report for the board of directors (BoD) of Cigno Co which:**

   (i) **Estimates the value attributable to Cigno Co's shareholders from the acquisition of Anatra Co before taking into account the cash benefits of potential tax savings and redundancies, and then after taking these into account;** **(18 marks)**

   (ii) **Assesses the value created from (b)(i) above, including a discussion of the estimations made and methods used;** **(8 marks)**

   (iii) **Advises the BoD on the key factors it should consider in relation to the redundancies and potential tax savings.** **(4 marks)**

(c) **Discuss whether the defence strategy suggested by Anatra Co's CEO of disposing assets is feasible.** **(6 marks)**

Professional marks will be awarded for the demonstration of skill in communication, analysis and evaluation, scepticism and commercial acumen in your answer. **(10 marks)**

(Total: 50 marks)

15   MORADA CO (SEP/DEC 16)

Morada Co is involved in offering bespoke travel services and maintenance services. In addition to owning a few hotels, it has built strong relationships with companies in the hospitality industry all over the world. It has a good reputation of offering unique, high quality holiday packages at reasonable costs for its clients. The strong relationships have also enabled it to offer repair and maintenance services to a number of hotel chains and cruise ship companies.

Following a long discussion at a meeting of the board of directors (BoD) about the future strategic direction which Morada Co should follow, three directors continued to discuss one particular issue over dinner. In the meeting, the BoD had expressed concern that Morada Co was exposed to excessive risk and therefore its cost of capital was too high. The BoD feared that several good projects had been rejected over the previous two years, because they did not meet Morada Co's high cost of capital threshold. Each director put forward a proposal, which they then discussed in turn. At the conclusion of the dinner, the directors decided to ask for a written report on the proposals put forward by the first director and the second director, before taking all three proposals to the BoD for further discussion.

First director's proposal

The first director is of the opinion that Morada Co should reduce its debt in order to mitigate its risk and therefore reduce its cost of capital. He proposes that the company should sell its repair and maintenance services business unit and focus just on offering bespoke travel services and hotel accommodation. In the sale, the book value of non-current assets will reduce by 30% and the book value of current liabilities will reduce by 10%. It is thought that the non-current assets can be sold for an after-tax profit of 15%.

The first director suggests that the funds arising from the sale of the repair and maintenance services business unit and cash resources should be used to pay off 80% of the long-term debt. It is estimated that as a result of this, Morada Co's credit rating will improve from Baa2 to A2.

Second director's proposal

The second director is of the opinion that risk diversification is the best way to reduce Morada Co's risk and therefore reduce its cost of capital. He proposes that the company raise additional funds using debt finance and then create a new strategic business unit. This business unit will focus on construction of new commercial properties.

The second director suggests that $70 million should be borrowed and used to invest in purchasing non-current assets for the construction business unit. The new debt will be issued in the form of four-year redeemable bonds paying an annual coupon of 6.2%. It is estimated that if this amount of debt is raised, then Morada Co's credit rating will worsen to Ca3 from Baa2. Current liabilities are estimated to increase to $28 million.

Third director's proposal

The third director is of the opinion that Morada Co does not need to undertake the proposals suggested by the first director and the second director just to reduce the company's risk profile. She feels that the above proposals require a fundamental change in corporate strategy and should be considered in terms of more than just tools to manage risk. Instead, she proposes that a risk management system should be set up to appraise Morada Co's current risk profile, considering each type of business risk and financial risk within the company, and taking appropriate action to manage the risk where it is deemed necessary.

Morada Co, extracts from the forecast financial position for the coming year

	$000
Non-current assets	280,000
Current assets	48,000
Total assets	328,000
Equity and liabilities	
Share capital (40c/share)	50,000
Retained earnings	137,000
Total equity	187,000
Non-current liabilities (6.2% redeemable bonds)	120,000
Current liabilities	21,000
Total liabilities	141,000
Total liabilities and equity capital	328,000

Other financial information

Morada Co's forecast after-tax earnings for the coming year are expected to be $28 million. It is estimated that the company will make a 9% return after-tax on any new investment in non-current assets, and will suffer a 9% decrease in after-tax earnings on any reduction in investment in non-current assets.

Morada Co's current share price is $2.88 per share. According to the company's finance division, it is very difficult to predict how the share price will react to either the proposal made by the first director or the proposal made by the second director. Therefore it has been assumed that the share price will not change following either proposal.

The finance division has further assumed that the proportion of the book value of non-current assets invested in each business unit gives a fair representation of the size of each business unit within Morada Co.

Morada Co's equity beta is estimated at 1.2, while the asset beta of the repairs and maintenance services business unit is estimated to be 0.65. The relevant equity beta for the new, larger company including the construction unit relevant to the second director's proposals has been estimated as 1.21.

The bonds are redeemable in four years' time at face value. For the purposes of estimating the cost of capital, it can be assumed that debt beta is zero. However, the four-year credit spread over the risk free rate of return is 60 basis points for A2 rated bonds, 90 basis points for Baa2 rated bonds and 240 basis points for Ca3 rated bonds.

A tax rate of 20% is applicable to all companies. The current risk free rate of return is estimated to be 3.8% and the market risk premium is estimated to be 7%.

Required:

(a) **Prepare a report for the board of directors of Morada Co which:**

(i) **Estimates Morada Co's cost of equity and cost of capital, based on market value of equity and debt, before any changes and then after implementing the proposals put forward by the first and by the second directors.**

(17 marks)

(ii) **Estimates the impact of the first and second directors' proposals on Morada Co's forecast after-tax earnings and forecast financial position for the coming year; and** **(7 marks)**

(iii) **Discusses the impact on Morada Co of the changes proposed by the first and second directors and recommends whether or not either proposal should be accepted. The discussion should include an explanation of any assumptions made in the estimates in (b)(i) and (b)(ii) above.** **(9 marks)**

(b) **Discuss the possible reasons for the third director's proposal that a risk management system should consider each risk, before taking appropriate action.** **(7 marks)**

Professional marks will be awarded for the demonstration of skill in communication, analysis and evaluation, scepticism and commercial acumen in your answer. **(10 marks)**

(Total: 50 marks)

16 CHRYSOS CO (MAR/JUN 17)

The eight-member board of executive directors (BoD) of Chrysos Co, a large private, unlisted company, is considering the company's long-term business and financial future. The BoD is considering whether or not to undertake a restructuring programme. This will be followed a few years later by undertaking a reverse takeover to obtain a listing on the stock exchange in order to raise new finance. However, a few members of the BoD have raised doubts about the restructuring programme and the reverse takeover, not least the impact upon the company's stakeholders. Some directors are of the opinion that an initial public offering (IPO) would be a better option when obtaining a listing compared to a reverse takeover.

Chrysos Co was formed about 15 years ago by a team of five senior equity holders who are part of the BoD and own 40% of the equity share capital in total; 30 other equity holders own a further 40% of the equity share capital but are not part of the BoD; and a consortium of venture capital organisations (VCOs) own the remaining 20% of the equity share capital and have three representatives on the BoD. The VCOs have also lent Chrysos Co substantial debt finance in the form of unsecured bonds due to be redeemed in 10 years' time. In addition to the BoD, Chrysos Co also has a non-executive supervisory board consisting of members of Chrysos Co's key stakeholder groups. Details of the supervisory board are given below.

Chrysos Co has two business units: a mining and shipping business unit, and a machinery parts manufacturing business unit. The mining and shipping business unit accounts for around 80% of Chrysos Co's business in terms of sales revenue, non-current and current assets, and payables. However, it is estimated that this business unit accounts for around 75% of the company's operating costs. The smaller machinery parts manufacturing business unit accounts for the remaining 20% of sales revenue, non-current and current assets, and payables; and around 25% of the company's operating costs.

The following figures have been extracted from Chrysos Co's most recent financial statements:

Profit before depreciation, interest and tax for the year to 28 February 20X7

	$m
Sales revenue	16,800
Operating costs	(10,080)
Profit before depreciation, interest and tax	6,720

Financial position as at 28 February 20X7

	$m
Non-current assets	
Land and buildings	7,500
Equipment	5,400
Current assets	
Inventory	1,800
Receivables	900
Total assets	15,600
Equity	
Share capital ($1 nominal value per share)	1,800
Reserves	5,400
Non-current liabilities	
4.50% unsecured bonds 20Y6 (from the VCOs)	4,800
Other debt	1,050
Current liabilities	
Payables	750
Bank overdraft	1,800
Total equity and liabilities	15,600

Corporate restructuring programme

The purpose of the restructuring programme is to simplify the company's gearing structure and to obtain extra funding to expand the mining and shipping business in the future. At present, Chrysos Co is having difficulty obtaining additional funding without having to pay high interest rates.

Machinery parts manufacturing business unit

The smaller machinery parts manufacturing business unit will be unbundled either by having its assets sold to a local supplier for $3,102 million after its share of payables have been paid; or

The smaller machinery parts manufacturing business unit will be unbundled through a management buy-out by four managers. In this case, it is estimated that its after-tax net cash flows will increase by 8% in the first year only and then stay fixed at this level for the foreseeable future. The cost of capital related to the smaller business unit is estimated to be 10%. The management buy-out team will pay Chrysos Co 70% of the estimated market value of the smaller machinery parts manufacturing business unit.

Mining and shipping business unit

Following the unbundling of the smaller machinery parts manufacturing business unit, Chrysos Co will focus solely on the mining and shipping business unit, prior to undertaking the reverse takeover some years into the future.

As part of the restructuring programme, the existing unsecured bonds lent by the VCOs will be cancelled and replaced by an additional 600 million $1 shares for the VCOs. The VCOs will pay $400 million for these shares. The bank overdraft will be converted into a 15-year loan on which Chrysos Co will pay a fixed annual interest of 4.50%. The other debt under non-current liabilities will be repaid. In addition to this, Chrysos Co will invest $1,200 million into equipment for its mining and shipping business unit and this will result in its profits and cash flows growing by 4% per year in perpetuity.

Additional financial information

Chrysos Co aims to maintain a long-term capital structure of 20% debt and 80% equity in market value terms. Chrysos Co's finance director has assessed that the 4.50% annual interest it will pay on its bank loan is a reasonable estimate of its long-term cost of debt, based on the long-term capital structure above.

Chrysos Co's finance director has determined that the current ungeared cost of equity of Sidero Co, a large quoted mining and shipping company, is 12.46%, and hence that the cost of capital for the mining and shipping business unit is approximately 12%.

The annual corporation tax rate on profits applicable to all companies is 18% and it can be assumed that tax is payable in the year incurred. All the non-current assets are eligible for tax allowable depreciation of 12% annually on the book values. The annual reinvestment needed to keep operations at their current levels is equivalent to the tax allowable depreciation.

Details of the supervisory board

The non-executive supervisory board provides an extra layer of governance over the BoD. It consists of representatives from the company's internal stakeholder groups including the finance providers, employees and the company's management. It ensures that the actions taken by the BoD are for the benefit of all the stakeholder groups and to the company as a whole. Any issues raised in board meetings are resolved through negotiation until an agreed position is reached.

Required:

(a)   Explain what a reverse takeover involves and discuss the relative advantages and disadvantages to a company, such as Chrysos Co, of obtaining a listing through a reverse takeover as opposed to an initial public offering (IPO).   (6 marks)

(b)   Prepare a report for the board of directors of Chrysos Co which includes:

   (i)   An extract of the financial position and an estimate of Chrysos Co's value to the equity holders, after undertaking the restructuring programme.

   (16 marks)

   (ii)   An explanation of the approach taken and assumptions made in estimating Chrysos Co's value to the equity holders, after undertaking the restructuring programme.   (5 marks)

   (iii) A discussion of the impact of the restructuring programme on Chrysos Co and on the venture capital organisations.   (9 marks)

(c) Discuss why the attention Chrysos Co pays to its stakeholders represented on the supervisory board may change once it has obtained a listing. (4 marks)

Professional marks will be awarded for the demonstration of skill in communication, analysis and evaluation, scepticism and commercial acumen in your answer. (10 marks)

(Total: 50 marks)

17 CONEJO CO (SEP/DEC 17)

Conejo Co is a listed company based in Ardilla and uses the $ as its currency. The company was formed around 20 years ago and was initially involved in cybernetics, robotics and artificial intelligence within the information technology industry. At that time due to the risky ventures Conejo Co undertook, its cash flows and profits were very varied and unstable. Around 10 years ago, it started an information systems consultancy business and a business developing cyber security systems. Both these businesses have been successful and have been growing consistently. This in turn has resulted in a stable growth in revenues, profits and cash flows. The company continues its research and product development in artificial intelligence and robotics, but this business unit has shrunk proportionally to the other two units.

Just under eight years ago, Conejo Co was successfully listed on Ardilla's national stock exchange, offering 60% of its share capital to external equity holders, whilst the original founding members retained the remaining 40% of the equity capital. The company remains financed largely by equity capital and reserves, with only a small amount of debt capital. Due to this, and its steadily growing sales revenue, profits and cash flows, it has attracted a credit rating of A from the credit rating agencies.

At a recent board of directors (BoD) meeting, the company's chief financial officer (CFO) argued that it was time for Conejo Co to change its capital structure by undertaking a financial reconstruction, and be financed by higher levels of debt. As part of her explanation, the CFO said that Conejo Co is now better able to bear the increased risk resulting from higher levels of debt finance; would be better protected from predatory acquisition bids if it was financed by higher levels of debt; and could take advantage of the tax benefits offered by increased debt finance. She also suggested that the expected credit migration from a credit rating of A to a credit rating of BBB, if the financial reconstruction detailed below took place, would not weaken Conejo Co financially.

Financial reconstruction

The BoD decided to consider the financial reconstruction plan further before making a final decision. The financial reconstruction plan would involve raising $1,320 million ($1.32 billion) new debt finance consisting of bonds issued at their face value of $100. The bonds would be redeemed in five years' time at their face value of $100 each. The funds raised from the issue of the new bonds would be used to implement one of the following two proposals:

(i) Proposal 1: Either buy back equity shares at their current share price, which would be cancelled after they have been repurchased; or

(ii) Proposal 2: Invest in additional assets in new business ventures.

Conejo Co, Financial information

Extract from the forecast financial position for next year

	$m
Non-current assets	1,735
Current assets	530
Total assets	**2,265**
Equity and liabilities	
Share capital ($1 per share nominal value)	400
Reserves	1,700
Total equity	**2,100**
Non-current liabilities	120
Current liabilities	45
Total liabilities	**165**
Total liabilities and capital	**2,265**

Conejo Co's forecast after-tax profit for next year is $350 million and its current share price is $11 per share.

The non-current liabilities consist solely of 5.2% coupon bonds with a face value of $100 each, which are redeemable at their face value in three years' time. These bonds are currently trading at $107.80 per $100. The bond's covenant stipulates that should Conejo Co's borrowing increase, the coupon payable on these bonds will increase by 37 basis points.

Conejo Co pays tax at a rate of 15% per year and its after-tax return on the new investment is estimated at 12%.

Other financial information

Current government bond yield curve

Year	1	2	3	4	5
	1.5%	1.7%	1.9%	2.2%	2.5%

Yield spreads (in basis points)

	1 year	2 years	3 years	4 years	5 years
A	40	49	59	68	75
BBB	70	81	94	105	112
BB	148	167	185	202	218

The finance director wants to determine the percentage change in the value of Conejo Co's current bonds, if the credit rating changes from A to BBB. Furthermore, she wants to determine the coupon rate at which the new bonds would need to be issued, based on the current yield curve and appropriate yield spreads given above.

Conejo Co's chief executive officer (CEO) suggested that if Conejo Co paid back the capital and interest of the new bond in fixed annual repayments of capital and interest through the five-year life of the bond, then the risk associated with the extra debt finance would be largely mitigated. In this case, it was possible that credit migration, by credit rating companies, from A rating to BBB rating may not happen. He suggested that comparing the duration of the new bond based on the interest payable annually and the face value in five years' time with the duration of the new bond where the borrowing is paid in fixed annual repayments of interest and capital could be used to demonstrate this risk mitigation.

Required:

(a) Discuss the possible reasons for the finance director's suggestions that Conejo Co could benefit from higher levels of debt with respect to risk, from protection against acquisition bids, and from tax benefits. **(5 marks)**

(b) Prepare a report for the board of directors of Conejo Co which:

(i) Estimates, and briefly comments on, the change in value of the current bond and the coupon rate required for the new bond, as requested by the CFO; **(6 marks)**

(ii) Estimates the Macaulay duration of the new bond based on the interest payable annually and face value repayment, and the Macaulay duration based on the fixed annual repayment of the interest and capital, as suggested by the CEO; **(6 marks)**

(iii) Estimates the impact of the two proposals on how the funds may be used on next year's forecast earnings, forecast financial position, forecast earnings per share and on forecast gearing; **(11 marks)**

(iv) Using the estimates from (b)(i), (b)(ii) and (b)(iii), discusses the impact of the proposed financial reconstruction and the proposals on the use of funds on:

• Conejo Co

• Possible reaction(s) of credit rating companies and on the expected credit migration, including the suggestion made by the CEO

• Conejo Co's equity holders

• Conejo Co's current and new debt holders. **(12 marks)**

Professional marks will be awarded for the demonstration of skill in communication, analysis and evaluation, scepticism and commercial acumen in your answer. (10 marks)

(Total: 50 marks)

18 CHAKULA CO (MAR/JUN 21)

 Answer debrief

The following exhibits, available on the left-hand side of the screen (in the CBE exam), provide information relevant to the question.

1 Introduction – about Chakula Co, the demerger of Kawa Co and Lahla Co a prospective buyer of Kawa Co

2 Areas for further clarification – requested by Lahla Co

3 Capital structure details – for all companies

4 Kawa Co as a demerged company

5 Acquisition of Kawa Co by Lahla Co

This information should be used to answer the question requirements within your chosen response option(s).

Introduction

Chakula Co is a large listed company involved in two business sectors. Its main business is in the production of food and drink for supermarkets and other large traders. It also owns a chain of coffee shops nationwide. Chakula Co's board of directors (BoD) thinks that the company is undervalued and is of the opinion that it should focus on the rapid innovation taking place in the food and drink production sector.

Therefore, Chakula Co's BoD has decided to unbundle the coffee shops' business into a company called Kawa Co. Chakula Co will then either demerge Kawa Co through a spin-off or sell Kawa Co. Chakula Co will then turn its full focus on its remaining business of food and drink production. Initially, Chakula Co's shareholders will own Kawa Co on the basis of owning one Kawa Co share for every Chakula Co share owned by them.

Lahla Co is a large unlisted company controlled by 20 shareholders who all have a significant stake in the business. Lahla Co owns a number of hotels around the country and is looking to diversify into the coffee retail business. Lahla Co has approached Chakula Co about the possibility of purchasing Kawa Co. Lahla Co will finance the purchase either through a cash-only offer or a share-for-share offer.

If Kawa Co is demerged, it will be listed on the stock exchange as an independent company. Chakula Co is unsure whether to sell Kawa Co to Lahla Co or to demerge it into an independent company.

Areas for further clarification

Further clarification has been sought by Lahla Co's BoD on the following two areas:

(i)   Lahla Co's chief executive officer (CEO) has determined that a regulatory framework in the area of mergers and acquisitions is designed to protect the interests of shareholders and other stakeholders. She wants to find out why there is a need for a regulatory framework.

(ii) The acquisition of Kawa Co will be a major investment for Lahla Co and its BoD has concerns about how the acquisition will be financed. The BoD has heard that there are several theories explaining the capital structure of a company, including the following two propositions:

  –   A company should maximise its debt financing; and

  –   Too much debt can be harmful to a company and there needs to be a balance between equity and debt financing.

Capital structure details

Extracts from Chakula Co's financial statements are as follows:

	$m
Assets, less current liabilities	5,010
Financed by:	
Share capital (nominal value $0.50 per share)	1,000
Reserves	1,180
Non-current liabilities: Loan notes A (nominal value $100 per loan note)	2,470
Non-current liabilities: Loan notes B (nominal value $100 per loan note)	360

Chakula Co's shares are trading at $2.45 each. The estimated equity value of Kawa Co is $1,200m.

Chakula Co's loan notes A currently have a total market value of $2,100m. Loan notes B currently have a total market value of $400m. After the unbundling, loan notes B will be serviced by Kawa Co and loan notes A will remain with Chakula Co, with the post-tax cost of debt for loan notes B expected to be 3.52%. It is expected that Kawa Co will maintain its capital structure after the unbundling.

Lahla Co's debt to equity ratio is estimated to be 40:60 in equivalent market value terms and it has 1,200 million shares in issue.

The cost of equity for Kawa Co is estimated to be 13.51%.

All companies pay corporation tax at a rate of 20% per year and tax is payable in the same year as the profits it is based on.

Kawa Co as a demerged company

The following estimated information will be applicable to Kawa Co if it is demerged.

Chakula Co's sales revenue is $4,500m currently, of which 20% is attributable to Kawa Co. It is estimated that after Kawa Co is demerged, its annual sales revenue growth rate will be 6% and the profit margin before interest and tax will be 21% of sales revenue, for each of the next four years. It can be assumed that the current tax allowable depreciation will remain equivalent to the amount of investment needed to maintain the current level of operations, but that Kawa Co will require an additional investment in assets of $0.25 for every $1 increase in sales revenue.

After the initial four years, the annual growth rate of the company's free cash flows is expected to be 2.5% for the foreseeable future.

Acquisition of Kawa Co by Lahla Co

The following estimated information applies to the acquisition of Kawa Co by Lahla Co, if Kawa Co is acquired.

The average price to earnings (PE) ratio for the hotel industry is 15.61, however, Lahla Co's PE ratio is estimated to be 10% lower than this.

Extracts from the current statements of profit or loss applicable to Lahla Co and Kawa Co are as follows:

	Lahla Co	Kawa Co
	$m	$m
Profit before interest and tax	305.0	161.2
Interest	(91.2)	(14.8)
Tax 20%	(42.8)	(29.3)
Profit after tax	171.0	117.1

After the acquisition, it is expected that the PE ratio of the combined company will be the midpoint between the two individual companies' PE ratios. The annual after-tax profits will increase by $62m due to combining the two companies.

Lahla Co has proposed to pay for acquiring Kawa Co either through a cash offer of $0.66 for a Kawa Co share, or one Lahla Co share for every three Kawa Co shares. Lahla Co will borrow the money needed to pay for the acquisition.

Required:

(a) Explain why a regulatory framework related to mergers and acquisitions is necessary to protect the interests of shareholders and other stakeholders. (5 marks)

(b) Discuss the two theoretical propositions, as raised by Lahla Co's board of directors (BoD), in relation to a company's capital structure. (6 marks)

(c) Prepare a report for the BoD of Lahla Co which:

   (i) Estimates the value of each Kawa Co share if it is demerged and listed as an independent company; (8 marks)

   (ii) Estimates;

      - the additional equity value created when combining Lahla Co and Kawa Co;

      - the percentage gain to each of Lahla Co's and Kawa Co's shareholder group under each payment method;

      - the impact on Lahla Co's capital structure under each payment method; and (12 marks)

   (iii) Evaluates the financial and other factors that both Lahla Co's shareholders and Kawa Co's shareholders would consider prior to agreeing to the acquisition, and the impact on Lahla Co's capital structure under each payment method.

(9 marks)

Professional marks will be awarded for the demonstration of skill in communication, analysis and evaluation, scepticism and commercial acumen in your answer. (10 marks)

(Total: 50 marks)

 Calculate your allowed time, allocate the time to the separate parts..............

TREASURY AND ADVANCED RISK MANAGEMENT TECHNIQUES

19 LIRIO CO (MAR/JUN 16)

Lirio Co is an engineering company which is involved in projects around the world. It has been growing steadily for several years and has maintained a stable dividend growth policy for a number of years now. The board of directors (BoD) is considering bidding for a large project which requires a substantial investment of $40 million. It can be assumed that the date today is 1 March 20X6.

The BoD is proposing that Lirio Co should not raise the finance for the project through additional debt or equity. Instead, it proposes that the required finance is obtained from a combination of funds received from the sale of its equity investment in a European company and from cash flows generated from its normal business activity in the coming two years. As a result, Lirio Co's current capital structure of 80 million $1 equity shares and $70 million 5% bonds is not expected to change in the foreseeable future.

The BoD has asked the company's treasury department to prepare a discussion paper on the implications of this proposal. The following information on Lirio Co has been provided to assist in the preparation of the discussion paper.

Expected income and cash flow commitments prior to undertaking the large project for the year to the end of February 20X7

Lirio Co's sales revenue is forecast to grow by 8% next year from its current level of $300 million, and the operating profit margin on this is expected to be 15%. It is expected that Lirio Co will have the following capital investment requirements for the coming year, before the impact of the large project is considered:

1   A $0.10 investment in working capital for every $1 increase in sales revenue

2   An investment equivalent to the amount of depreciation to keep its non-current asset base at the present productive capacity. The current depreciation charge already included in the operating profit margin is 25% of the non-current assets of $50 million

3   A $0.20 investment in additional non-current assets for every $1 increase in sales revenue

4    $8 million additional investment in other small projects.

In addition to the above sales revenue and profits, Lirio Co has one overseas subsidiary – Pontac Co, from which it receives dividends of 80% on profits. Pontac Co produces a specialist tool which it sells locally for $60 each. It is expected that it will produce and sell 400,000 units of this specialist tool next year. Each tool will incur variable costs of $36 per unit and total annual fixed costs of $4 million to produce and sell.

Lirio Co pays corporation tax at 25% and Pontac Co pays corporation tax at 20%. In addition to this, a withholding tax of 8% is deducted from any dividends remitted from Pontac Co. A bi-lateral tax treaty exists between the countries where Lirio Co is based and where Pontac Co is based. Therefore corporation tax is payable on profits made by subsidiary companies, but full credit is given for corporation tax already paid.

It can be assumed that receipts from Pontac Co are in $ equivalent amounts and exchange rate fluctuations on these can be ignored.

Sale of equity investment in the European country

It is expected that Lirio Co will receive Euro (€) 20 million in three months' time from the sale of its investment. The € has continued to remain weak, while the $ has continued to remain strong through 20X5 and the start of 20X6. The financial press has also reported that there may be a permanent shift in the €/$ exchange rate, with firms facing economic exposure. Lirio Co has decided to hedge the € receipt using one of currency forward contracts, currency futures contracts or currency options contracts.

The following exchange contracts and rates are available to Lirio Co.

	Per €1
Spot rates	$1.1585–$1.1618
Three-month forward rates	$1.1559–$1.1601

Currency futures (contract size $125,000, quotation: € per $1)

March futures	€0.8638
June futures	€0.8656

Currency options
(contract size $125,000, exercise price quotation € per $1, premium € per $1)

	Calls		Puts	
Exercise price	March	June	March	June
0.8600	0.0255	0.0290	0.0267	0.0319

It can be assumed that futures and options contracts expire at the end of their respective months.

Dividend history, expected dividends and cost of capital, Lirio Co

Year to end of February	20X3	20X4	20X5	20X6
Number of $1 equity shares in issue (000)	60,000	60,000	80,000	80,000
Total dividends paid ($ 000)	12,832	13,602	19,224	20,377

It is expected that dividends will grow at the historic rate, if the large project is not undertaken.

Expected dividends and dividend growth rates if the large project is undertaken.

Year to end of February 20X7	Remaining cash flows after the investment in the $40 million project will be paid as dividends.
Year to end of February 20X8	The dividends paid will be the same amount as the previous year.
Year to end of February 20X9	Dividends paid will be $0.31 per share.
In future years from February 20X9	Dividends will grow at an annual rate of 7%.

Lirio Co's cost of equity capital is estimated to be 12%.

Required:

(a)   With reference to purchasing power parity, explain how exchange rate fluctuations may lead to economic exposure.   **(4 marks)**

(b)   Prepare a discussion paper, including all relevant calculations, for the board of directors (BoD) of Lirio Co which:

(i)   Estimates Lirio Co's dividend capacity as at 28 February 20X7, prior to investing in the large project   **(9 marks)**

(ii)   Advises Lirio Co on, and recommends, an appropriate hedging strategy for the Euro (€) receipt it is due to receive in three months' time from the sale of the equity investment   **(12 marks)**

(iii)   Using the information on dividends provided in the question, and from (b) (i) and (b) (ii) above, assesses whether or not the project would add value to Lirio Co   **(8 marks)**

(iv)   Discusses the issues of proposed methods of financing the project which need to be considered further.   **(7 marks)**

Professional marks will be awarded for the demonstration of skill in communication, analysis and evaluation, scepticism and commercial acumen in your answer.   **(10 marks)**

(Total: 50 marks)

20   WASHI CO (SEP 18)

Washi Co is a large, unlisted company based in Japan and its local currency is the Japanese Yen (JPY). It manufactures industrial equipment and parts. Initially Washi Co's customers consisted of other Japanese companies, but over the last 12 years it has expanded into overseas markets and also sources its materials from around the world. The company's board of directors (BoD) believes that the strategy of overseas investments, through subsidiary companies, branches and joint ventures, has directly led to the company's substantial increase in value in the past few years.

Washi Co's BoD is considering investing in a project based in Airone, whose currency is the Airone Rand (ARD). It believes that the project will be an important addition to the company's portfolio of investments, because Washi Co does not currently have a significant presence in the part of the world where Airone is located. It is intended that the project will commence in one year's time. Details of the project are given below.

Washi Co intends to finance the project through proceeds from an agreed sale of a small European subsidiary, with any remaining funding requirement being met by additional debt finance issued in Japanese Yen. The company is due to receive the proceeds from the sale of a European subsidiary company in six months' time and it will then invest these funds in short-dated Japanese treasury bills for a further six months before they are needed for the project. Washi Co has a centralised treasury department, which hedges expected future cash flows against currency fluctuations.

Funding and financial information

The agreed proceeds from the sale of the European subsidiary company receivable in six months' time are Euro (EUR) 80 million. The BoD is concerned about a negative fluctuation in EUR/JPY rate between now and in six months when the EUR 80 million will be received. Therefore, it has asked Washi Co's treasury department to hedge the expected receipt using one of currency forwards, currency futures or exchange traded currency options. Washi Co's treasury department has obtained the following information:

	JPY per EUR 1	ARD per EUR 1
Spot	129.2–132.4	92.7–95.6
Six-month forward rate	125.3–128.6	

Currency futures (contract size EUR 125,000, quotation JPY per EUR 1)

Four-month expiry	126.9
Seven-month expiry	125.2

Currency options (contract size EUR 125,000, exercise price quotation: JPY per EUR 1, premium quotation: JPY per EUR 1)

At an exercise price of JPY 126.0 per EUR 1

	Four-month expiry	Seven-month expiry
Calls	2.3	2.6
Puts	3.4	3.8

Annualised yield on short-dated Japanese treasury bills	1.20%

Airone's annual inflation rate is 9% currently, but has fluctuated markedly in the last five years. The Japanese annual inflation rate is 1.5% and has been stable for many years.

Airone project information

A member of Washi Co's finance team has produced the following estimates of the Airone project which is expected to last for four years. The estimates are based on the notes given below but not on the further information. The estimates have been checked and verified independently for their numerical accuracy.

All figures are in ARD millions

Project year	0	1	2	3	4
Sales revenue		13,000	30,800	32,300	4,500
Costs		(10,200)	(24,200)	(24,500)	(3,200)
Tax allowable depreciation		(1,000)	(1,000)	(1,000)	(1,000)
Pre-tax profits		1,800	5,600	6,800	300
Tax at 15%		(270)	(840)	(1,020)	(45)
Tax allowable depreciation		1,000	1,000	1,000	1,000
Working capital	(400)				400
Investment in buildings	(5,750)				
Investment in machinery	(4,000)				
Cash flows in ARD	(10,150)	2,530	5,760	6,780	1,655

Notes (incorporated into the estimates above):

1 The estimates are based on using the end of the first year, when the project commences, as the start of the project (year 0). The numbers are given in ARD million (m).

2 The total investment required for the project is ARD 10,150m and separated into buildings, machinery and working capital in the table above. The machinery is eligible for tax allowable depreciation on a straight-line basis and the working capital is redeemable at the end of the project.

3 The impact of inflation has been incorporated into the sales revenue and cost figures, at Airone's current annual inflation figures.

4 Corporation tax has been included based on Airone's annual rate of 15%. The tax is payable in the year that the tax liability arises.

Further information (not incorporated into the estimates above):

1 Undertaking the Airone project will result in lost sales for Washi Co. These sales would have generated a pre-tax contribution of JPY 110m in the first year of the project, rising by the Japanese rate of inflation in the following years 2 to 4 of the project.

2 The Airone project costs include components which are made in Japan by Washi Co and would be imported to the Airone project. The pre-inflation revenues generated from the sale of the components are estimated to be as follows (in JPY millions):

Project year	1	2	3	4
Components revenue	1,200	2,400	2,500	300

These revenues are expected to increase by the Japanese inflation rate in years 2 to 4 of the project. The contribution which Washi Co expects to earn on these components is 25% of revenue.

3   The Japanese annual corporation tax rate is 30% and tax is payable in the year that the tax liability arises. A bilateral tax treaty exists between Japan and Airone, which permits offset of overseas tax against any Japanese tax liability on overseas earnings.

4   Washi Co's finance department has estimated a cost of capital of 12% to be used as a discount rate for the project.

Required:

(a)   Discuss how investing in overseas projects may enable Washi Co to gain competitive advantage over its competitors, who only invest in domestic projects.

(5 marks)

(b)   Prepare a report for the board of directors of Washi Co which:

(i)   Estimates the expected amount of JPY receivable under each hedge choice and the additional debt finance needed to fund the Airone project for the preferred hedge choice;   (12 marks)

(ii)   Estimates the net present value of the Airone project in Japanese Yen, based on the end of year one being the start of the project (year 0);   (9 marks)

(iii)   Evaluates the preferred hedge choice made, the debt finance needed and whether the Airone project should be undertaken, considering both financial and non-financial factors.   (8 marks)

(c)   Washi Co's chief operations officer (COO) has suggested that it would be more beneficial for the company to let its major subsidiary companies have their own individual treasury departments, instead of having one centralised treasury department for the whole company.

Required:

Discuss the validity of the COO's suggestion.   (6 marks)

Professional marks will be awarded for the demonstration of skill in communication, analysis and evaluation, scepticism and commercial acumen in your answer.   (10 marks)

(Total: 50 marks)

21   OKAN CO (SEP/DEC 19)

Okan Co, a large listed company located in Yasailand whose currency is the Y$, manufactures engines and engine parts. It is considering whether or not to invest in one of two new four-year projects: Project Alpha or Project Beta. Details of both projects are given separately. Previously, Okan Co has used relevant risk-adjusted discount rates to calculate the net present value (NPV) of projects. However, the finance director believes that calculating adjusted present values (APV) of projects would be more appropriate. Okan Co wants to base its decision on which project to invest in, on the returns generated by the projects, the projects' risk as measured by their project durations, and important non-financial aspects. Both projects are due to commence in six months' time.

Funding for projects Alpha and Beta

Project Alpha or Project Beta will each require the same amount of initial funding of Y$50,000,000.

Proceeds from the sale of a factory based in Europe in six months' time, for Euro (€)10,000,000, will provide part of the funding and the balance will be financed by debt borrowing.

Okan Co expects to hedge the €10,000,000 using either forward markets or money markets. The following information is available on these markets:

Foreign exchange rates

	Y$/€1
Spot	2.5210–2.5862
Six months forward	2.5462–2.6121

Bank interest rates

	Investing	Borrowing
Yasailand	2.40%	5.00%
Eurozone	1.05%	2.20%

The balance of funding raised by domestic debt borrowing will be through a four-year subsidised loan on which interest is payable at 2.1%, although Okan Co's normal borrowing rate is 5%.

Issue costs related to raising this finance will be 3% of the gross proceeds.

Project Alpha details

Project Alpha's base case NPV and APV, in six months' time when the project will commence, should be estimated using the following information.

The sales revenues and production costs related to Project Alpha in six months' time, before any annual price or cost increases, are estimated as follows:

Year	1	2	3	4
Sales revenue (Y$ 000s)	15,750	28,350	47,250	23,100
Production cost (Y$ 000s)	6,120	10,710	21,420	8,160

It is expected that the sales price will increase at an annual inflation rate of 10%. Domestic production costs are likely to increase at Yasailand's annual inflation rate.

In addition to the above, components will be imported from the UK (currency £), at the following current cost:

Year	1	2	3	4
Component costs (£000s)	1,200	1,800	3,700	1,400

The costs of components from the UK are fixed and not subject to inflation.

The funds of Y$50,000,000 for Project Alpha will be used to purchase plant and equipment needed for manufacturing purposes. Tax allowable depreciation is available on the value of the plant and equipment at 25% per year on a reducing balance basis, with a balancing allowance or charge applicable at the end of the project. The plant and equipment is expected to be sold for Y$10,000,000 (post-inflation) at the end of the project.

At the start of every year, Project Alpha will require working capital. In the first year this will be 10% of the estimated year 1 sales revenue. In subsequent years, the project will require an increase or a reduction in working capital of 15% for every $1 increase or decrease in sales revenue respectively. The working capital is expected to be fully released when Project Alpha ceases.

The expected spot exchange rate between the Y$ and the £, in six months' time, is expected to be Y$3.03 per £1. The annual inflation rates are currently 2% in the UK and 4% in Yasailand. It can be assumed that these inflation rates will not change for the foreseeable future.

The cost of capital for appraising the base case net present value of Project Alpha is 10%. Okan Co pays tax at an annual rate of 20%. Tax is payable in the same year as the profits it is based on. Okan Co makes sufficient profits from its other activities to take advantage of any tax loss relief.

Project Beta details

Given below are Project Beta's base case present values, based on the project start date in six months' time, discounted at the project's relevant risk-adjusted all-equity financed discount rate:

Year	1	2	3	4
Present values (Y$ 000s)	8,450	19,360	22,340	4,950

It can be assumed that any working capital requirements for Project Beta are included in the annual cash flows.

Project Beta's duration has been calculated as 2.43 years, based on its base case present values.

Economic risk and risk categories

One of Okan Co's subsidiary companies in Yasailand, which produces and sells all its products domestically, has still found that it is exposed to economic risk (economic exposure). The directors of the subsidiary believe that this is because Yasailand's government has maintained comparatively higher interest rates, even though the inflation in Yasailand is now under control.

Required:

(a) Discuss why a company may prefer to use the adjusted present value (APV) method, rather than the net present value (NPV) method. **(4 marks)**

(b) Prepare a report for the board of directors (BoD) of Okan Co which:

 (i) Estimates the minimum amount of debt borrowing Okan Co would require
 (4 marks)

 (ii) Estimates

 – Project Alpha's and Project Beta's base case NPV, in six months' time, before considering the financing side effects **(12 marks)**

 – Project Alpha's and Project Beta's APV, in six months' time, and
 (6 marks)

 – Project Alpha's duration based on its base case present values of cash flows **(2 marks)**

 (iii) Evaluates and justifies which project Okan Co should choose, basing the decision on the factors Okan Co considers to be important. The evaluation should include a discussion of the assumptions made. **(8 marks)**

(c) Discuss why Okan Co's subsidiary company may be exposed to economic risk (economic exposure) and how it may be managed. **(4 marks)**

Professional marks will be awarded for the demonstration of skill in communication, analysis and evaluation, scepticism and commercial acumen in your answer. **(10 marks)**

(Total: 50 marks)

Section 2

PRACTICE QUESTIONS – SECTION B

ROLE OF SENIOR FINANCIAL ADVISER IN THE MULTINATIONAL ORGANISATION

22   LAMRI CO (DEC 10)

Lamri Co (Lamri), a listed company, is expecting sales revenue to grow to $80 million next year, which is an increase of 20% from the current year. The operating profit margin for next year is forecast to be the same as this year at 30% of sales revenue. In addition to these profits, Lamri receives 75% of the after-tax profits from one of its wholly owned foreign subsidiaries – Magnolia Co (Magnolia), as dividends. However, its second wholly owned foreign subsidiary – Strymon Co (Strymon) does not pay dividends.

Lamri is due to pay dividends of $7.5 million shortly and has maintained a steady 8% annual growth rate in dividends over the past few years. The company has grown rapidly in the last few years as a result of investment in key projects and this is likely to continue.

For the coming year it is expected that Lamri will require the following capital investment.

1   An investment equivalent to the amount of depreciation to keep its non-current asset base at the present productive capacity. Lamri charges depreciation of 25% on a straight-line basis on its non-current assets of $15 million. This charge has been included when calculating the operating profit amount.

2   A 25% investment in additional non-current assets for every $1 increase in sales revenue.

3     $4.5 million additional investment in non-current assets for a new project.

Lamri also requires a 15% investment in working capital for every $1 increase in sales revenue.

Strymon produces specialist components solely for Magnolia to assemble into finished goods. Strymon will produce 300,000 specialist components at $12 variable cost per unit and will incur fixed costs of $2.1 million for the coming year. It will then transfer the components to Magnolia at full cost price, where they will be assembled at a cost of $8 per unit and sold for $50 per unit. Magnolia will incur additional fixed costs of $1.5 million in the assembly process.

Tax-Ethic (TE) is a charitable organisation devoted to reducing tax avoidance schemes by companies operating in poor countries around the world. TE has petitioned Lamri's Board of Directors to reconsider Strymon's policy of transferring goods at full cost. TE suggests that the policy could be changed to cost plus 40% mark-up. If Lamri changes Strymon's policy, it is expected that Strymon would be asked to remit 75% of its after-tax profits as dividends to Lamri.

Other Information

1   Lamri's outstanding non-current liabilities of $35 million, on which it pays interest of 8% per year, and its 30 million $1 issued equity capital will not change for the coming year.

2   Lamri's, Magnolia's and Strymon's profits are taxed at 28%, 22% and 42% respectively. A withholding tax of 10% is deducted from any dividends remitted from Strymon.

3   The tax authorities where Lamri is based charge tax on profits made by subsidiary companies but give full credit for tax already paid by overseas subsidiaries.

4   All costs and revenues are in $ equivalent amounts and exchange rate fluctuations can be ignored.

Required:

(a)   **Calculate Lamri's dividend capacity for the coming year prior to implementing TE's proposal and after implementing the proposal.**   **(14 marks)**

(b)   **Comment on the impact of implementing TE's proposal and suggest possible actions Lamri may take as a result.**   **(6 marks)**

Professional marks will be awarded for the demonstration of skill in analysis and evaluation, and commercial acumen in your answer.   **(5 marks)**

(Total: 25 marks)

23   LIMNI CO (JUN 13)

Limni Co is a large company manufacturing hand-held electronic devices such as mobile phones and tablet computers. The company has been growing rapidly over the last few years, but it also has high research and development expenditure. It is involved in a number of projects worldwide, developing new and innovative products and systems in a rapidly changing industry. Due to the nature of the industry, this significant growth in earnings has never been stable, but has depended largely on the success of the new innovations and competitor actions. However, in the last two years it seems that the rapid period of growth is slowing, with fewer products coming to market compared to previous years.

Limni Co has never paid dividends and has financed projects through internally generated funds and with occasional rights issues of new share capital. It currently has insignificant levels of debt. The retained cash reserves have recently grown because of a drop in the level of investment in new projects.

The company has an active treasury division which invests spare funds in traded equities, bonds and other financial instruments; and releases the funds when required for new projects. The division also manages cash flow risk using money and derivative markets. The treasury division is currently considering investing in three companies with the following profit after tax (PAT) and dividend history:

Year	Company Theta		Company Omega		Company Kappa	
	PAT	Dividends	PAT	Dividends	PAT	Dividends
	$000	$000	$000	$000	$000	$000
20X3	57,100	22,840	93,300	60,560	162,400	44,100
20X2	54,400	21,760	90,600	57,680	141,500	34,200
20X1	52,800	21,120	88,000	54,840	108,900	26,300
20X0	48,200	19,280	85,400	52,230	105,700	20,250
20W9	45,500	18,200	82,900	49,740	78,300	15,700

All of the three companies' share capital has remained largely unchanged since 20W9.

Recently, Limni Co's Board of Directors (BoD) came under pressure from the company's larger shareholders to start returning some of the funds, currently retained by the company, back to the shareholders. The BoD thinks that the shareholders have a strong case to ask for repayments.

Limni Co is due to prepare its statement of profit or loss shortly and estimates that the annual sales revenue will be $600 million, on which its profit before tax is expected to be 23% of sales revenue. It charges depreciation of 25% on a straight-line basis on its non-current assets of $220 million. It estimates that $67 million investment in current and non-current assets was spent during the year. It is due to receive $15 million in dividends from its subsidiary companies, on which annual tax of 20% on average has been paid. Limni Co itself pays annual tax at 26%, and the tax authorities where Limni Co is based charge tax on dividend remittances made by overseas subsidiary companies, but give full credit on tax already paid on those remittances. In order to fund the new policy of returning funds to shareholders, Limni Co's BoD wants to increase the current estimated dividend capacity by 10%, by asking the overseas subsidiary companies for higher repatriations.

Required:

(a) Discuss Limni Co's current dividend, financing and risk management policies, and suggest how the decision to return retained funds back to the shareholders will affect these policies. (7 marks)

(b) Evaluate the dividend policies of each of the three companies that Limni Co is considering investing in, and discuss which company Limni Co might select. (7 marks)

(c) Calculate, and briefly comment on, how much the dividends from overseas companies need to increase by, to increase Limni Co's dividend capacity by 10%. (6 marks)

Professional marks will be awarded for the demonstration of skill in analysis and evaluation, scepticism and commercial acumen in your answer. (5 marks)

(Total: 25 marks)

24 CHAWAN CO (JUN 15)

The treasury department of Chawan Co, a listed company, aims to maintain a portfolio of around $360 million consisting of equity shares, corporate bonds and government bonds, which it can turn into cash quickly for investment projects. Chawan Co is considering disposing 27 million shares, valued at $2.15 each, which it has invested in Oden Co. The head of Chawan Co's treasury department is of the opinion that, should the decision be made to dispose of its equity stake in Oden Co, this should be sold through a dark pool network and not sold on the stock exchange where Oden Co's shares are listed. In the last few weeks, there have also been rumours that Oden Co may become subject to a takeover bid.

Oden Co operates in the travel and leisure (T&L) sector, and the poor weather conditions in recent years, coupled with a continuing recession, has meant that the T&L sector is under-performing. Over the past three years, sales revenue fell by an average of 8% per year in the T&L sector. However, there are signs that the economy is starting to recover, but this is by no means certain.

Given below are extracts from the recent financial statements and other financial information for Oden Co and the T&L sector.

Oden Co

Year ending 31 May (all amounts in $m)

	20X3	20X4	20X5
Total non-current assets	972	990	980
Total current assets	128	142	126
Total assets	1,100	1,132	1,106
Equity			
Ordinary shares ($0.50)	300	300	300
Reserves	305	329	311
Total equity	605	629	611
Non-current liabilities			
Bank loans	115	118	100
Bonds	250	250	260
Total non-current liabilities	365	368	360
Current liabilities			
Trade and other payables	42	45	37
Bank overdraft	88	90	98
Total current liabilities	130	135	135
Total equity and liabilities	1,100	1,132	1,106

Oden Co

Year ending 31 May (all amounts in $m)

	20X3	20X4	20X5
Sales revenue	1,342	1,335	1,185
Operating profit	218	203	123
Finance costs	(23)	(27)	(35)
Profit before tax	195	176	88
Taxation	(35)	(32)	(16)
Profit for the year	160	144	72

Other financial information (Based on annual figures till 31 May of each year)

	20X2	20X3	20X4	20X5
Oden Co average share price ($)	2.10	2.50	2.40	2.20
Oden Co dividend per share ($)	0.15	0.18	0.20	0.15
T&L sector average share price ($)	3.80	4.40	4.30	4.82
T&L sector average earnings per share ($)	0.32	0.36	0.33	0.35
T&L sector average dividend per share ($)	0.25	0.29	0.29	0.31
Oden Co's equity beta	1.5	1.5	1.6	2.0
T&L sector average equity beta	1.5	1.4	1.5	1.6

The risk-free rate and the market return have remained fairly constant over the last ten years at 4% and 10% respectively.

Required:

(a) Explain what a dark pool network is and why Chawan Co may want to dispose of its equity stake in Oden Co through one, instead of through the stock exchange where Oden Co's shares are listed. **(4 marks)**

(b) Discuss whether or not Chawan Co should dispose of its equity stake in Oden Co. Provide relevant calculations to support the discussion.

Note: Up to 8 marks are available for the calculations. **(16 marks)**

Professional marks will be awarded for the demonstration of skill in analysis and evaluation, scepticism and commercial acumen in your answer. **(5 marks)**

(Total: 25 marks)

25 CHITHURST CO (SEP/DEC 16)

Chithurst Co gained a stock exchange listing five years ago. At the time of the listing, members of the family who founded the company owned 75% of the shares, but now they only hold just over 50%. The number of shares in issue has remained unchanged since Chithurst Co was listed. Chithurst Co's directors have continued the policy of paying a constant dividend per share each year which the company had before it was listed. However, investors who are not family members have become increasingly critical of this policy, saying that there is no clear rationale for it. They would prefer to see steady dividend growth, reflecting the increase in profitability of Chithurst Co since its listing.

The finance director of Chithurst Co has provided its board with details of Chithurst Co's dividends and investment expenditure, compared with two other similar-sized companies in the same sector, Eartham Co and Iping Co. Each company has a 31 December year end.

	Chithurst Co			Eartham Co			Iping Co		
	Profit for year after interest and tax	Dividend paid	New investment expenditure	Profit for year after interest and tax	Dividend paid	New investment expenditure	Profit for year after interest and tax	Dividend paid	New investment expenditure
	$m	$m	$m	$m	$m	$m	$m	$m	$m
20X2	77	33	18	95	38	30	75	35	37
20X3	80	33	29	(10)	15	15	88	17	64
20X4	94	33	23	110	44	42	118	39	75
20X5	97	33	21	120	48	29	132	42	84

Other financial information relating to the three companies is as follows:

	Chithurst Co	Eartham Co	Iping Co
Cost of equity	11%	14%	12%
Market capitalisation $m	608	1,042	1,164
Increase in share price in last 12 months	1%	5%	10%

Chithurst Co's finance director has estimated the costs of equity for all three companies. None of the three companies has taken out significant new debt finance since 20X1.

Required:

(a) **Discuss the benefits and drawbacks of the dividend policies which the three companies appear to have adopted. Provide relevant calculations to support your discussion.**

    Note: Up to 4 marks are available for the calculations. (13 marks)

(b) **Discuss how the market capitalisation of the three companies compares with your valuations calculated using the dividend valuation model. Use the data provided to calculate valuations based on growth rates for the most recent year and for the last three years.**

    Note: Up to 4 marks are available for the calculations. (7 marks)

Professional marks will be awarded for the demonstration of skill in analysis and evaluation, scepticism and commercial acumen in your answer. (5 marks)

(Total: 25 marks)

26   HIGH K CO (SEP/DEC 17)

High K Co is one of the three largest supermarket chains in the country of Townia. Its two principal competitors, Dely Co and Leminster Co, are of similar size to High K Co. In common with its competitors (but see below), High K Co operates three main types of store:

- Town centre stores – these sell food and drink and a range of small household items. High K Co's initial growth was based on its town centre stores, but it has been shutting them over the last decade, although the rate of closure has slowed in the last couple of years.

- Convenience stores – these are smaller and sell food and drink and very few other items. Between 20X3 and 20Y3, High K Co greatly expanded the number of convenience stores it operated. Their performance has varied, however, and since 20Y3, High K Co has not opened any new stores and closed a number of the worst-performing stores.

- Out-of-town stores – these sell food and drink and a full range of household items, including large electrical goods and furniture. The number of out-of-town stores which High K Co operated increased significantly until 20Y0, but has only increased slightly since.

The majority of town centre and out-of-town stores premises are owned by High K Co, but 85% of convenience stores premises are currently leased.

High K Co also sells most of its range of products online, either offering customers home delivery or 'click and collect' (where the customer orders the goods online and picks them up from a collection point in one of the stores).

High K Co's year end is 31 December. When its 20Y6 results were published in April 20Y7, High K Co's chief executive emphasised that the group was focusing on:

- Increasing total shareholder return by improvements in operating efficiency and enhancement of responsiveness to customer needs

- Ensuring competitive position by maintaining flexibility to respond to new strategic challenges

- Maintaining financial strength by using diverse sources of funding, including making use in future of revolving credit facilities

Since April 20Y7, Dely Co and Leminster Co have both announced that they will be making significant investments to boost online sales. Dely Co intends to fund its investments by closing all its town centre and convenience stores, although it also intends to open more out-of-town stores in popular locations.

The government of Townia was re-elected in May 20Y7. In the 18 months prior to the election, it eased fiscal policy and consumer spending significantly increased. However, it has tightened fiscal policy since the election to avoid the economy overheating. It has also announced an investigation into whether the country's large retail chains treat their suppliers unfairly.

Extracts from High K Co's 20Y6 financial statements and other information about it are given below:

High K Co statement of profit or loss extracts

Year ending 31 December (all amounts in $m)

	20Y4	20Y5	20Y6
Sales revenue	23,508	23,905	24,463
Gross profit	1,018	1,211	1,514
Operating profit	204	407	712
Finance costs	(125)	(115)	(100)
Profit after tax	52	220	468
Dividends	150	170	274

High K Co statement of financial position extracts

Year ending 31 December (all amounts in $m)

	20Y4	20Y5	20Y6
Non-current assets	10,056	9,577	8,869
Cash and cash equivalents	24	709	1,215
Other current assets	497	618	747
Total non-current and current assets	10,577	10,904	10,831

Equity

	20Y4	20Y5	20Y6
Ordinary shares ($1)	800	800	800
Reserves	7,448	7.519	7,627
Total equity	8,248	8,319	8,427
Non-current liabilities	1,706	1,556	1,246
Current liabilities	623	1,029	1,158

Other information

	20Y4	20Y5	20Y6
Market price per share (in $, $3.89 at end of 20Y3, $3.17 currently)	3.54	3.34	3.23
Staff working in shops ('000)	78	75	72

Segment information

Revenue ($m)	20Y4	20Y5	20Y6
Town centre stores	5,265	5,189	5,192
Convenience stores	3,786	3,792	3,833
Out-of-town stores	10,220	10,340	10,547
Store revenue	19,271	19,321	19,572
Online sales	4,237	4,584	4,891
Number of stores			
Town centre stores	165	157	153
Convenience stores	700	670	640
Out-of-town stores	220	224	227

Required:

(a) Evaluate High K Co's financial performance. You should indicate in your discussion areas where further information about High K Co would be helpful. Provide relevant calculations for ratios and trends to support your evaluation.

Note: Up to 8 marks are available for calculations. **(16 marks)**

(b) Discuss how High K Co may seek to finance an investment programme. **(4 marks)**

Professional marks will be awarded for the demonstration of skill in analysis and evaluation, scepticism and commercial acumen in your answer. **(5 marks)**

(Total: 25 marks)

27 ARTHURO CO (MAR/JUN 18)

Arthuro Co is based in Hittyland and is listed on Hittyland's stock exchange. Arthuro Co has one wholly-owned subsidiary, Bowerscots Co, based in the neighbouring country of Owlia. Hittyland and Owlia are in a currency union and the currency of both countries is the $.

Arthuro Co purchased 100% of Bowerscots Co's share capital three years ago. Arthuro Co has the power under the acquisition to determine the level of dividend paid by Bowerscots Co. However, Arthuro Co's board decided to let Bowerscots Co's management team have some discretion when making investment decisions. Arthuro Co's board decided that it should receive dividends of 60% of Bowerscots Co's post-tax profits and has allowed Bowerscots Co to use its remaining retained earnings to fund investments chosen by its management. A bonus linked to Bowerscots Co's after-tax profits is a significant element of Bowerscots Co's managers' remuneration.

Bowerscots Co operates in a very competitive environment. Recently, a senior member of its management team has left to join a competitor.

Arthuro Co's dividend policy

Until three months ago, Arthuro Co had 90 million $2 equity shares in issue and $135 million 8% bonds. Three months ago it made a 1 for 3 rights issue. A number of shareholders did not take up their rights, but sold them on, so there have been changes in its shareholder base. Some shareholders expressed concern about dilution of their dividend income as a result of the rights issue. Therefore, Arthuro Co's board felt it had to promise, for the foreseeable future, at least to maintain the dividend of $0.74 per equity share (so $88.8 million in total now), which it paid for the two years before the rights issue.

Arthuro Co's board is nevertheless concerned about whether it will have sufficient funds available to fulfil its promise about the dividend. It has asked the finance director to forecast its dividend capacity based on assumptions about what will happen in a 'normal' year. The finance director has made the following assumptions in the forecast:

1   Sales revenue can be assumed to be 4% greater than the most recent year's of $520 million.

2   The operating profit margin can be assumed to be 20%.

3   Operating profit can be assumed to be reported after charging depreciation of $30 million and profit on disposal of non-current assets of $5.9 million. The cost of the non-current assets sold can be assumed to be $35 million and its accumulated depreciation to be $24.6 million. Depreciation is allowable for tax and the profit on disposal is fully chargeable to tax.

4   The net book value of non-current assets at the year-end in the most recent accounts was $110 million. To maintain productive capacity, sufficient investment to increase this net book value figure 12 months later by 4% should be assumed, in line with the increase in sales. The calculation of investment required for the year should take into account the depreciation charged of $30 million, and net book value of the non-current assets disposed of during the year.

5   A $0.15 investment in working capital can be assumed for every $1 increase in sales revenue.

6   Bowerscots Co's pre-tax profits can be assumed to be $45 million.

Arthuro Co's directors have decided that if there is a shortfall of dividend capacity, compared with the dividends required to maintain the current dividend level, the percentage of post-tax profits of Bowerscots Co paid as dividend should increase, if necessary up to 100%.

Taxation

Arthuro Co pays corporation tax at 30% and Bowerscots Co pays corporation tax at 20%. A withholding tax of 5% is deducted from any dividends remitted by Bowerscots Co. There is a bilateral tax treaty between Hittyland and Owlia. Corporation tax is payable by Arthuro Co on profits declared by Bowerscots Co, but Hittyland gives full credit for corporation tax already paid in Owlia. Hittyland gives no credit for withholding tax paid on dividends in Owlia.

Required:

(a)   Estimate Arthuro Co's forecast dividend capacity for a 'normal' year.   (11 marks)

(b)   Arthuro Co has decided to increase its level of dividend from Bowerscots Co if its dividend capacity is insufficient.

   Required:

   (i)   From Arthuro Co's viewpoint, discuss the financial benefits of, and problems with, this decision.   (4 marks)

   (ii)   Discuss the agency problems, and how they might be resolved, with this decision.   (5 marks)

Professional marks will be awarded for the demonstration of skill in analysis and evaluation, scepticism and commercial acumen in your answer.   (5 marks)

(Total: 25 marks)

28 TILLINTON CO (SEP 18)

 Answer debrief

Tillinton Co is a listed company which has traditionally manufactured children's clothing and toys with long lives. Five years ago, it began manufacturing electronic toys and has since made significant investment in development and production facilities. The first electronic toys which Tillinton Co introduced into the market were received very well, partly as it was seen to be ahead of its competitors in making the most of the technology available.

The country where Tillinton Co is listed has seen a significant general increase in share prices over the last three years, with companies in the electronic goods sector showing particularly rapid increases.

Statement by Tillinton Co's chief executive

Assume it is now September 20X3. Tillinton Co's annual report for the year ended 31 March 20X3 has just been published. Its chief executive commented when announcing the company's results:

'I am very pleased to report that revenue and gross profits have shown bigger increases than in 20X2, resulting in higher post-tax earnings and our company being able to maintain increases in dividends. The sustained increase in our share price clearly demonstrates how happy investors are with us. Our cutting-edge electronic toys continue to perform well and justify our sustained investment in them. Our results have also benefited from improvements in operational efficiencies for our older ranges and better working capital management. We are considering the development of further ranges of electronic toys for children, or developing other electronic products for adults. If necessary, we may consider scaling down or selling off our operations for some of our older products.'

Steph Slindon represents an institutional investor who holds shares in Tillinton Co. Steph is doubtful whether its share price will continue to increase, because she thinks that Tillinton Co's situation may not be as good as its chief executive suggests and because she believes that current share price levels generally may not be sustainable.

Financial information

Extracts from Tillinton Co's financial statements for the last three years and other information about it are given below.

Tillinton Co statement of profit or loss in years ending 31 March (all amounts in $m)

	20X1	20X2	20X3
Sales revenue	1,385	1,636	1,914
Gross profit	381	451	528
Operating profit	205	252	300
Finance costs	(46)	(50)	(66)
Profit before tax	159	202	234
Taxation	(40)	(51)	(65)
Profit after tax	119	151	169
Dividends	(60)	(72)	(84)

Tillinton Co statement of financial position in years ending 31 March (all amounts in $m)

	20X1	20X2	20X3
Non-current assets	2,070	2,235	2,449
Cash and cash equivalents	10	15	15
Other current assets	150	130	125
Total non-current and current assets	2,230	2,380	2,589
Equity			
Ordinary shares ($0.50)	400	400	400
Reserves	805	884	969
Total equity	1,205	1,284	1,369
Non-current liabilities	920	970	1,000
Current liabilities	105	126	220
Total equity and liabilities	2,230	2,380	2,589

Other information

	20X1	20X2	20X3
Market price per $0.50 share (in $, $2.50 at 31 March 20X0, $5.06 in September 20X3)	2.76	3.49	4.44
Earnings per share ($)	0.15	0.19	0.21
Dividend per share ($)	0.075	0.09	0.105

Analysis of revenue

	20X1	20X2	20X3
Electronic toys	249	319	390
Non-electronic toys	302	350	404
Clothing	834	967	1,120
	1,385	1,636	1,914

Analysis of gross profit

	20X1	20X2	20X3
Electronic toys	100	112	113
Non-electronic toys	72	88	105
Clothing	209	251	310
	381	451	528

Note: None of Tillinton Co's loan finance in 20X3 is repayable within one year.

Required:

(a)   **Evaluate Tillinton Co's performance and business prospects in the light of the chief executive's comments and Steph Slindon's concerns. Provide relevant calculations for ratios and trends to support your evaluation.**

Note: 8 marks are available for the calculations.   **(16 marks)**

(b)   **Discuss how behavioural factors may have resulted in Tillinton Co's share price being higher than is warranted by a rational analysis of its position.**   **(4 marks)**

Professional marks will be awarded for the demonstration of skill in analysis and evaluation, scepticism and commercial acumen in your answer.   **(5 marks)**

(Total: 25 marks)

     Calculate your allowed time, allocate the time to the separate parts...............

---

29   CADNAM CO (SEP/DEC 19)

Cadnam Co is a large company in the support services sector.

Cadnam Co's most recent annual report, for the year ended 31 December 20X5, acknowledged challenges for the company, including financing the major investment programme required to meet its clients' increasing expectations. Cadnam Co also faced upward pressure on employment costs, fuelled by a 'fair wage' campaign which adversely compared wage rises in the support services sector with increases in dividends and directors' remuneration, and a consequent government enquiry into low pay in the sector.

Cadnam Co's board, however, was confident that the company would be able to renew a number of large contracts which were coming up for review. The report stressed the strength of Cadnam Co's senior management team as a vital success factor. Directors' remuneration packages thus reflected the need to retain its directors in a competitive labour market at senior level.

In the stakeholder engagement section of its annual report, Cadnam Co highlighted that it had fulfilled its aim of guaranteeing investors a consistent rise in dividends and its board was confident that Cadnam Co would be able to maintain the recent rate of dividend increase.

Dividend policy

At Cadnam Co's last annual general meeting, there were no questions about the level of profits, dividends or directors' remuneration. However, a recent investment analysts' report on the support services sector highlighted Cadnam Co as a company which might have problems in the next few years. The report suggested that Cadnam Co's investment and dividend policies could not both be maintained. It highlighted one of Cadnam Co's principal competitors, Holmsley Co, as a company whose policies it believed would sustain long-term growth. It highlighted directors' remuneration as an area where Holmsley Co's policies were more likely to encourage long-term value creation and share price increases than Cadnam Co's policies.

Cadnam Co's board is currently considering the comments made by the investment analysts, and also assessing what the dividend for 20X6 should be.

Cadnam Co

	20X2	20X3	20X4	20X5
	$m	$m	$m	$m
Profit after tax	1,380	1,490	1,550	1,580
Dividends	765	840	925	1,020
Investment in additional assets	282	312	584	864
Share price ($)	$4.88	$5.35	$5.61	$5.75
Gearing (debt/(debt + equity)) (market value) × 100%	33.0%	33.2%	35.0%	38.8%

Holmsley Co

	20X2	20X3	20X4	20X5
	$m	$m	$m	$m
Profit after tax	1,485	1,590	1,700	1,830
Dividends	560	590	621	654
Investment in additional assets	595	625	660	690
Share price	$5.04	$5.23	$5.55	$5.93
Gearing (debt/(debt + equity)) (market value) × 100%	35.1%	35.2%	34.9%	34.7%

Average gearing in the support services sector since 20X1 has been stable at around 34%. There have been no changes in the issued share capital of Cadnam Co and Holmsley Co since 20X1.

Directors' remuneration

	Cadnam Co	Holmsley Co
Average salary executive director	$550,000	$550,000
Performance bonus	Maximum 25% of salary	Maximum 30% of salary
Loyalty bonus	Maximum 10% of salary	None
Share options	None	Options to be exercised on 31 December 20X8 at an exercise price of $7.00

Cadnam Co 20X6 forecast

Forecasts prepared by Cadnam Co's finance director for 20X6 predict that:

- Cadnam Co's pre-tax operating profit for 20X6 will be $2,678m, an increase of 3% compared with 20X5. The operating profit margin will be 2%, the same as for 20X5.

- The tax rate will be 30%.

- Average debt in 20X6 will be $10,250m and predicted year-end gearing will be 41.3%. The average pre-tax interest rate on the debt will be 8%.

- The investment required to keep the non-current asset base at its present productive capacity in 20X6 will be $2,430m, which has been included in the calculation of operating profit as depreciation.

- Investment required in additional assets in 20X6 will be $0.25 for every $1 increase in revenue.

Required:

(a)   Calculate the forecast dividend capacity of Cadnam Co for 20X6.   **(5 marks)**

(b)   Discuss the viability and financial impacts of Cadnam Co seeking to maintain its current dividend policy, supporting your answers with relevant calculations.

   Note: 5 marks are available for calculations in part (b).   **(10 marks)**

(c)   Discuss the governance and ethical issues associated with Cadnam Co's dividend and directors' remuneration policies.   **(5 marks)**

Professional marks will be awarded for the demonstration of skill in analysis and evaluation, scepticism and commercial acumen in your answer.   **(5 marks)**

(Total: 25 marks)

ADVANCED INVESTMENT APPRAISAL

30   FUBUKI CO (DEC 10)

Fubuki Co, an unlisted company based in Megaera, has been manufacturing electrical parts used in mobility vehicles for people with disabilities and the elderly, for many years. These parts are exported to various manufacturers worldwide but at present there are no local manufacturers of mobility vehicles in Megaera. Retailers in Megaera normally import mobility vehicles and sell them at an average price of $4,000 each. Fubuki Co wants to manufacture mobility vehicles locally and believes that it can sell vehicles of equivalent quality locally at a discount of 37.5% to the current average retail price.

Although this is a completely new venture for Fubuki Co, it will be in addition to the company's core business. Fubuki Co's directors expect to develop the project for a period of four years and then sell it for $16 million to a private equity firm. Megaera's government has been positive about the venture and has offered Fubuki Co a subsidised loan of up to 80% of the investment funds required, at a rate of 200 basis points below Fubuki Co's borrowing rate. Currently Fubuki Co can borrow at 300 basis points above the five-year government debt yield rate.

A feasibility study commissioned by the directors, at a cost of $250,000, has produced the following information.

1   Initial cost of acquiring suitable premises will be $11 million, and plant and machinery used in the manufacture will cost $3 million. Acquiring the premises and installing the machinery is a quick process and manufacturing can commence almost immediately.

2   It is expected that in the first year 1,300 units will be manufactured and sold. Unit sales will grow by 40% in each of the next two years before falling to an annual growth rate of 5% for the final year. After the first year the selling price per unit is expected to increase by 3% per year.

3   In the first year, it is estimated that the total direct material, labour and variable overheads costs will be $1,200 per unit produced. After the first year, the direct costs are expected to increase by an annual inflation rate of 8%.

4   Annual fixed overhead costs would be $2.5 million of which 60% are centrally allocated overheads. The fixed overhead costs will increase by 5% per year after the first year.

5 Fubuki Co will need to make working capital available of 15% of the anticipated sales revenue for the year, at the beginning of each year. The working capital is expected to be released at the end of the fourth year when the project is sold.

Fubuki Co's tax rate is 25% per year on taxable profits. Tax is payable in the same year as when the profits are earned. Tax allowable depreciation is available on the plant and machinery on a straight-line basis. It is anticipated that the value attributable to the plant and machinery after four years is $400,000 of the price at which the project is sold. No tax allowable depreciation is available on the premises.

Fubuki Co uses 8% as its discount rate for new projects but feels that this rate may not be appropriate for this new type of investment. It intends to raise the full amount of funds through debt finance and take advantage of the government's offer of a subsidised loan. Issue costs are 4% of the gross finance required. It can be assumed that the debt capacity available to the company is equivalent to the actual amount of debt finance raised for the project.

Although no other companies produce mobility vehicles in Megaera, Haizum Co, a listed company, produces electrical-powered vehicles using similar technology to that required for the mobility vehicles. Haizum Co's cost of equity is estimated to be 14% and it pays tax at 28%. Haizum Co has 15 million shares in issue trading at $2.53 each and $40 million bonds trading at $94.88 per $100. The five-year government debt yield is currently estimated at 4.5% and the market risk premium at 4%.

Required:

(a) **Evaluate, on financial grounds, whether Fubuki Co should proceed with the project.**
(15 marks)

(b) **Briefly explain the appropriateness of the evaluation method used, and any assumptions made in part (a) above.**
(5 marks)

Professional marks will be awarded for the demonstration of skill in analysis and evaluation, and commercial acumen in your answer.
(5 marks)

(Total: 25 marks)

31 MMC (JUN 11)

MesmerMagic Co (MMC) is considering whether to undertake the development of a new computer game based on an adventure film due to be released in 22 months. It is expected that the game will be available to buy two months after the film's release, by which time it will be possible to judge the popularity of the film with a high degree of certainty. However, at present, there is considerable uncertainty about whether the film, and therefore the game, is likely to be successful. Although MMC would pay for the exclusive rights to develop and sell the game now, the directors are of the opinion that they should delay the decision to produce and market the game until the film has been released and the game is available for sale.

MMC has forecast the following end of year cash flows for the four-year sales period of the game.

Year	1	2	3	4
Cash flows ($ million)	25	18	10	5

MMC will spend $12 million immediately to develop the game, the gaming platform, and to pay for the exclusive rights to develop and sell the game. Following this, the company will require $35 million for production, distribution and marketing costs at the start of the four-year sales period of the game.

It can be assumed that all the costs and revenues include inflation. The relevant cost of capital for this project is 11% and the risk free rate is 5%. MMC has estimated the likely volatility of the cash flows at a standard deviation of 50%.

Required:

(a) **Estimate the financial impact of the directors' decision to delay the production and marketing of the game. The Black-Scholes Option Pricing model may be used, where appropriate. All relevant calculations should be shown.** **(8 marks)**

Note: in the Computer Based Exam (CBE), the "BSOP calculator" spreadsheet option will be provided to help you to answer this question.

(b) **Briefly discuss the implications of the answer obtained in part (a) above.** **(6 marks)**

(c) MMC is funded partly by equity and partly by debt. The yield on its five year debt is 5.2% and the yield on its ten year debt is 5.4% i.e. MMC faces an upward sloping yield curve.

Required:

Explain the possible reasons for an upward sloping yield curve. **(6 marks)**

Professional marks will be awarded for the demonstration of skill in analysis and evaluation, and commercial acumen in your answer. **(5 marks)**

(Total: 25 marks)

32 TISA CO (JUN 12)

Tisa Co is considering an opportunity to produce an innovative component which, when fitted into motor vehicle engines, will enable them to utilise fuel more efficiently. The component can be manufactured using either process Omega or process Zeta. Although this is an entirely new line of business for Tisa Co, it is of the opinion that developing either process over a period of four years and then selling the productions rights at the end of four years to another company may prove lucrative.

The annual after-tax cash flows for each process are as follows:

Process Omega

Year	0	1	2	3	4
After-tax cash flows ($000)	(3,800)	1,220	1,153	1,386	3,829

Process Zeta

Year	0	1	2	3	4
After-tax cash flows ($000)	(3,800)	643	546	1,055	5,990

Tisa Co has 10 million 50c shares trading at 180c each. Its loans have a current value of $3.6 million and an average after-tax cost of debt of 4.50%. Tisa Co's capital structure is unlikely to change significantly following the investment in either process.

Elfu Co manufactures electronic parts for cars including the production of a component similar to the one being considered by Tisa Co. Elfu Co's equity beta is 1.40, and it is estimated that the equivalent equity beta for its other activities, excluding the component production, is 1.25. Elfu Co has 400 million 25c shares in issue trading at 120c each. Its debt finance consists of variable rate loans redeemable in seven years. The loans paying interest at base rate plus 120 basis points have a current value of $96 million. It can be assumed that 80% of Elfu Co's debt finance and 75% of Elfu Co's equity finance can be attributed to other activities excluding the component production.

Both companies pay annual corporation tax at a rate of 25%. The current base rate is 3.5% and the market risk premium is estimated at 5.8%.

Required:

(a) **Provide a reasoned estimate of the cost of capital that Tisa Co should use to calculate the net present value of the two processes. Include all relevant calculations.**

(8 marks)

(b) **Calculate the internal rate of return (IRR) and the modified internal rate of return (MIRR) for Process Omega. Given that the IRR and MIRR of Process Zeta are 26.6% and 23.3% respectively, recommend which process, if any, Tisa Co should proceed with and explain your recommendation.** (8 marks)

(c) Elfu Co has estimated an annual standard deviation of $800,000 on one of its other projects, based on a normal distribution of returns. The average annual return on this project is $2,200,000.

Required:

Estimate the project's Value at Risk (VAR) at a 99% confidence level for one year and over the project's life of five years. Explain what is meant by the answers obtained. (4 marks)

Professional marks will be awarded for the demonstration of skill in analysis and evaluation, scepticism and commercial acumen in your answer. (5 marks)

(Total: 25 marks)

33 COEDEN CO (DEC 12)

Coeden Co is a listed company operating in the hospitality and leisure industry. Coeden Co's board of directors met recently to discuss a new strategy for the business. The proposal put forward was to sell all the hotel properties that Coeden Co owns and rent them back on a long-term rental agreement. Coeden Co would then focus solely on the provision of hotel services at these properties under its popular brand name. The proposal stated that the funds raised from the sale of the hotel properties would be used to pay off 70% of the outstanding non-current liabilities and the remaining funds would be retained for future investments.

The board of directors are of the opinion that reducing the level of debt in Coeden Co will reduce the company's risk and therefore its cost of capital. If the proposal is undertaken and Coeden Co focuses exclusively on the provision of hotel services, it can be assumed that the current market value of equity will remain unchanged after implementing the proposal.

Coeden Co: Extract from the most recent Statement of Financial Position

	$000
Non-current assets (re-valued recently)	42,560
Current assets	26,840
Total assets	69,400
Share capital (25c per share nominal value)	3,250
Reserves	21,780
Non-current liabilities (5.2% redeemable bonds)	42,000
Current liabilities	2,370
Total capital and liabilities	69,400

Coeden Co's latest free cash flow to equity of $2,600,000 was estimated after taking into account taxation, interest and reinvestment in assets to continue with the current level of business. It can be assumed that the annual reinvestment in assets required to continue with the current level of business is equivalent to the annual amount of depreciation. Over the past few years, Coeden Co has consistently used 40% of its free cash flow to equity on new investments while distributing the remaining 60%. The market value of equity calculated on the basis of the free cash flow to equity model provides a reasonable estimate of the current market value of Coeden Co.

The bonds are redeemable at par in three years and pay the coupon on an annual basis. Although the bonds are not traded, it is estimated that Coeden Co's current debt credit rating is BBB but would improve to A+ if the non-current liabilities are reduced by 70%.

Other Information

Coeden Co's current equity beta is 1.1 and it can be assumed that debt beta is 0. The risk free rate is estimated to be 4% and the market risk premium is estimated to be 6%.

There is no beta available for companies offering just hotel services, since most companies own their own buildings. The average asset beta for property companies has been estimated at 0.4. It has been estimated that the hotel services business accounts for approximately 60% of the current value of Coeden Co and the property company business accounts for the remaining 40%.

Coeden Co's corporation tax rate is 20%. The three-year borrowing credit spread on A+ rated bonds is 60 basis points and 90 basis points on BBB rated bonds, over the risk free rate of interest.

Required:

(a)   Calculate, and comment on, Coeden Co's cost of equity and weighted average cost of capital before and after implementing the proposal. State any assumptions made. **(16 marks)**

(b)   Discuss the validity of the assumption that the market value of equity will remain unchanged after the implementation of the proposal. **(4 marks)**

Professional marks will be awarded for the demonstration of skill in analysis and evaluation, scepticism and commercial acumen in your answer. **(5 marks)**

(Total: 25 marks)

34 BURUNG CO (JUN 14)

You have recently commenced working for Burung Co and are reviewing a four-year project which the company is considering for investment. The project is in a business activity which is very different from Burung Co's current line of business.

The following net present value estimate has been made for the project:

All figures are in $ million

Year	0	1	2	3	4
Sales revenue		23.03	36.60	49.07	27.14
Direct project costs		(13.82)	(21.96)	(29.44)	(16.28)
Interest		(1.20)	(1.20)	(1.20)	(1.20)
Profit		8.01	13.44	18.43	9.66
Tax (20%)		(1.60)	(2.69)	(3.69)	(1.93)
Investment/sale	(38.00)				4.00
Cash flows	(38.00)	6.41	10.75	14.74	11.73
Discount factors (7%)	1	0.935	0.873	0.816	0.763
Present values	(38.00)	5.99	9.38	12.03	8.95

Net present value is negative $1.65 million, and therefore the recommendation is that the project should not be accepted.

Notes to NPV appraisal

In calculating the net present value of the project, the following notes were made:

(i) Since the real cost of capital is used to discount cash flows, neither the sales revenue nor the direct project costs have been inflated. It is estimated that the inflation rate applicable to sales revenue is 8% per year and to the direct project costs is 4% per year.

(ii) The project will require an initial investment of $38 million. Of this, $16 million relates to plant and machinery, which is expected to be sold for $4 million when the project ceases, after taking any taxation and inflation impact into account.

(iii) Tax allowable depreciation is available on the plant and machinery at 50% in the first year, followed by 25% per year thereafter on a reducing balance basis. A balancing adjustment is available in the year the plant and machinery is sold. Burung Co pays 20% tax on its annual taxable profits. No tax allowable depreciation is available on the remaining investment assets and they will have a nil value at the end of the project.

(iv) Burung Co uses either a nominal cost of capital of 11% or a real cost of capital of 7% to discount all projects, given that the rate of inflation has been stable at 4% for a number of years.

(v) Interest is based on Burung Co's normal borrowing rate of 150 basis points over the 10-year government yield rate.

(vi) Depreciation has not been taken into account in the net present value calculation above, since depreciation is not a cash flow.

Further financial information

It is anticipated that the project will be financed entirely by debt, 60% of which will be obtained from a subsidised loan scheme run by the government, which lends money at a rate of 100 basis points below the 10-year government debt yield rate of 2.5%. Issue costs related to raising the finance are 2% of the gross finance required. The remaining 40% will be funded from Burung Co's normal borrowing sources. It can be assumed that the debt capacity available to Burung Co is equal to the actual amount of debt finance raised for the project.

Burung Co has identified a company, Lintu Co, which operates in the same line of business as that of the project it is considering. Lintu Co is financed by 40 million shares trading at $3.20 each and $34 million debt trading at $94 per $100. Lintu Co's equity beta is estimated at 1.5. The current yield on government treasury bills is 2% and it is estimated that the market risk premium is 8%. Lintu Co pays tax at an annual rate of 20%.

Both Burung Co and Lintu Co pay tax in the same year as when profits are earned.

Required:

(a) Calculate the adjusted present value (APV) for the project, correcting any errors made in the net present value estimate above, and conclude whether the project should be accepted or not. Show all relevant calculations. **(13 marks)**

(b) Comment on the corrections made to the original net present value estimate and explain the APV approach taken in part (a), including any assumptions made. **(7 marks)**

Professional marks will be awarded for the demonstration of skill in analysis and evaluation, scepticism and commercial acumen in your answer. **(5 marks)**

(Total: 25 marks)

35 RIVIERE CO (DEC 14)

Riviere Co is a small company based in the European Union (EU). It produces high quality frozen food which it exports to a small number of supermarket chains located within the EU as well.

Riviere Co finds it difficult to obtain bank finance and relies on a long-term strategy of using internally generated funds for new investment projects. This constraint means that it cannot accept every profitable project and often has to choose between them.

Riviere Co is currently considering investment in one of two mutually exclusive food production projects: Privi and Drugi. Privi will produce and sell a new range of frozen desserts exclusively within the EU. Drugi will produce and sell a new range of frozen desserts and savoury foods to supermarket chains based in countries outside the EU. Each project will last for five years and the following financial information refers to both projects.

Project Drugi, annual after-tax cash flows expected at the end of each year (€000s)

Year	Current	1	2	3	4	5
Cash flows (€000s)	(11,840)	1,230	1,680	4,350	10,240	2,200

	Privi	Drugi
Net present value	€2,054,000	€2,293,000
Internal rate of return	17.6%	Not provided
Modified internal rate of return	13.4%	Not provided
Value at risk (over the project's life)		
95% confidence level	€1,103,500	Not provided
90% confidence level	€860,000	Not provided

Both projects' net present values have been calculated based on Riviere Co's nominal cost of capital of 10%. It can be assumed that both projects' cash flow returns are normally distributed and the annual standard deviation of project Drugi's present value of after-tax cash flows is estimated to be €400,000. It can also be assumed that all sales are made in € (Euro) and therefore the company is not exposed to any foreign exchange exposure.

Notwithstanding how profitable project Drugi may appear to be, Riviere Co's board of directors is concerned about the possible legal risks if it invests in the project because they have never dealt with companies outside the EU before.

Required:

(a)   Calculate the figures which have not been provided for project Drugi and recommend which project should be accepted. Provide a justification for the recommendation and explain what the value at risk measures.   **(13 marks)**

(b)   Discuss the possible legal risks of investing in project Drugi which Riviere Co may be concerned about and how these may be mitigated.   **(7 marks)**

Professional marks will be awarded for the demonstration of skill in analysis and evaluation, scepticism and commercial acumen in your answer.   **(5 marks)**

(Total: 25 marks)

36   FURLION CO (MAR/JUN 16)

Furlion Co manufactures heavy agricultural equipment and machinery which can be used in difficult farming conditions. Furlion Co's chief executive has been investigating a significant opportunity in the country of Naswa, where Furlion Co has not previously sold any products. The government of Naswa has been undertaking a major land reclamation programme and Furlion Co's equipment is particularly suitable for use on the reclaimed land. Because of the costs and other problems involved in transporting its products, Furlion Co's chief executive proposes that Furlion Co should establish a plant for manufacturing machinery in Naswa. He knows that the Naswan government is keen to encourage the development of sustainable businesses within the country.

Initial calculations suggest that the proposed investment in Naswa would have a negative net present value of $1.01 million. However, Furlion Co's chief executive believes that there may be opportunities for greater cash flows in future if the Naswan government expands its land reclamation programme. The government at present is struggling to fund expansion of the programme out of its own resources and is looking for other funding. If the Naswan government obtains this funding, the chief executive has forecast that the increased demand for Furlion Co's products would justify $15 million additional expenditure at the site of the factory in three years' time. The expected net present value for this expansion is currently estimated to be $0.

It can be assumed that all costs and revenues include inflation. The relevant cost of capital is 12% and the risk free rate is 4%. The chief executive has estimated the likely volatility of cash flows at a standard deviation of 30%.

One of Furlion Co's non-executive directors has read about possible changes in interest rates and wonders how these might affect the investment appraisal.

Required:

(a)   **Assess, showing all relevant calculations, whether Furlion Co should proceed with the significant opportunity. Discuss the assumptions made and other factors which will affect the decision of whether to establish a plant in Naswa. The Black Scholes pricing model may be used, where appropriate.**   **(12 marks)**

   Note: in the Computer Based Exam (CBE), the "BSOP calculator" spreadsheet option will be provided to help you to answer this question.

(b)   **Discuss the impact of changes in interest rates on the appraisal of the investment.**
                                                                          (3 marks)

(c)   **Discuss the possibility of the Naswan government obtaining funding for further land reclamation from the World Bank, referring specifically to the International Development Association.**   **(5 marks)**

Professional marks will be awarded for the demonstration of skill in analysis and evaluation, scepticism and commercial acumen in your answer.   **(5 marks)**

                                                                    (Total: 25 marks)

37   FERNHURST CO (SEP/DEC 16)

Fernhurst Co is a manufacturer of mobile communications technology. It is about to launch a new communications device, the Milland, which its directors believe is both more technologically advanced and easier to use than devices currently offered by its rivals.

Investment in the Milland

The Milland will require a major investment in facilities. Fernhurst Co's directors believe that this can take place very quickly and production be started almost immediately.

Fernhurst Co expects to sell 132,500 units of the Milland in its first year. Sales volume is expected to increase by 20% in Year 2 and 30% in Year 3, and then be the same in Year 4 as Year 3, as the product reaches the end of its useful life. The initial selling price in Year 1 is expected to be $100 per unit, before increasing with the rate of inflation annually.

The variable cost of each unit is expected to be $43.68 in year 1, rising by the rate of inflation in subsequent years annually. Fixed costs are expected to be $900,000 in Year 1, rising by the rate of inflation in subsequent years annually.

The initial investment in non-current assets is expected to be $16,000,000. Fernhurst Co will also need to make an immediate investment of $1,025,000 in working capital. The working capital will be increased annually at the start of each of Years 2 to 4 by the inflation rate and is fully recoverable at the end of the project's life. Fernhurst Co will also incur one-off marketing expenditure of $1,500,000 post inflation after the launch of the Milland. The marketing expenditure can be assumed to be made at the end of Year 1 and be a tax allowable expense.

Fernhurst Co pays company tax on profits at an annual rate of 25%. Tax is payable in the year that the tax liability arises. Tax allowable depreciation is available at 20% on the investment in non-current assets on a reducing balance basis. A balancing adjustment will be available in Year 4. The realisable value of the investment at the end of Year 4 is expected to be zero.

The expected annual rate of inflation in the country in which Fernhurst Co is located is 4% in Year 1 and 5% in Years 2 to 4.

The applicable cost of capital for this investment appraisal is 11 %.

Other calculations

Fernhurst Co's finance director has indicated that besides needing a net present value calculation based on this data for the next board meeting, he also needs to know the figure for the project's duration, to indicate to the board how returns from the project will be spread over time.

Assessment of new products

Fernhurst Co's last board meeting discussed another possible new product, the Racton, and the finance director presented a range of financial data relating to this product, including the results of net present value and payback evaluations. One of the non-executive directors, who is not a qualified accountant, stated that he found it difficult to see the significance of the different items of financial data. His understanding was that Fernhurst Co merely had to ensure that the investment had a positive net present value and shareholders were bound to be satisfied with it, as it would maximise their wealth in the long term. The finance director commented that, in reality, some shareholders looked at the performance of the investments which Fernhurst Co made over the short term, whereas some were more concerned with the longer term. The financial data he presented to board meetings included both short and long-term measures.

Required:

(a) Evaluate the financial acceptability of the investment in the Milland and, calculate and comment on the investment's duration. **(15 marks)**

(b) Discuss the non-executive director's understanding of net present value and explain the importance of other measures in providing data about an investment's short and long-term performance. **(5 marks)**

Professional marks will be awarded for the demonstration of skill in analysis and evaluation, scepticism and commercial acumen in your answer. **(5 marks)**

(Total: 25 marks)

38 TIPPLETINE CO (MAR/JUN 18)

Tippletine Co is based in Valliland. It is listed on Valliland's stock exchange but only has a small number of shareholders. Its directors collectively own 45% of the equity share capital.

Tippletine Co's growth has been based on the manufacture of household electrical goods. However, the directors have taken a strategic decision to diversify operations and to make a major investment in facilities for the manufacture of office equipment.

Details of investment

The new investment is being appraised over a four-year time horizon. Revenues from the new investment are uncertain and Tippletine Co's finance director has prepared what she regards as cautious forecasts. These predicted operating cash flows are as follows:

$000	1	2	3	4
Net operating cash flows before marketing costs	2,000	14,500	15,225	15,834
Marketing costs	9,000	2,000	2,000	2,000

The new investment will require immediate expenditure on facilities of $30.6 million. Tax allowable depreciation will be available on the new investment at an annual rate of 25% reducing balance basis. It can be assumed that there will either be a balancing allowance or charge in the final year of the appraisal. The finance director believes the facilities will remain viable after four years, and therefore a realisable value of $13.5 million can be assumed at the end of the appraisal period.

The new facilities will also require an immediate initial investment in working capital of $3 million. Working capital requirements will increase by the rate of inflation for the next three years and any working capital at the start of Year 4 will be assumed to be released at the end of the appraisal period.

Tippletine Co pays tax at an annual rate of 30%. Tax is payable with a year's time delay. Any tax losses on the investment can be assumed to be carried forward and written off against future profits from the investment.

Predicted inflation rates are as follows:

Year	1	2	3	4
	8%	6%	5%	4%

Financing the investment

Tippletine Co has been considering two choices for financing all of the $30.6 million needed for the initial investment in the facilities:

– A subsidised loan from a government loan scheme, with the loan repayable at the end of the four years. Issue costs of 4% of the gross finance would be payable. Interest would be payable at a rate of 30 basis points below the risk free rate of 2.5%. In order to obtain the benefits of the loan scheme, Tippletine Co would have to fulfil various conditions, including locating the facilities in a remote part of Valliland where unemployment is high.

– Convertible loan notes, with the subscribers for the notes including some of Tippletine Co's directors. The loan notes would have issue costs of 4% of the gross finance. If not converted, the loan notes would be redeemed in six years' time. Interest would be payable at 5%, which is Tippletine Co's normal cost of borrowing. Conversion would take place at an effective price of $2.75 per share. However, the loan note holders could enforce redemption at any time from the start of Year 3 if Tippletine Co's share price fell below $1.50 per share. Tippletine Co's current share price is $2.20 per share.

Issue costs for the subsidised loan and convertible loan notes would be paid out of available cash reserves. Issue costs are not allowable as a tax-deductible expense.

In initial discussions, the majority of the board favoured using the subsidised loan. The appraisal of the investment should be prepared on the basis that this method of finance will be used. However, the chair argued strongly in favour of the convertible loan notes, as, in his view, operating costs will be lower if Tippletine Co does not have to fulfil the conditions laid down by the government of Valliland. Tippletine Co's finance director is sceptical, however, about whether the other shareholders would approve the issue of convertible loan notes on the terms suggested. The directors will decide which method of finance to use at the next board meeting.

Other information

Humabuz Co is a large manufacturer of office equipment in Valliland. Humabuz Co's geared cost of equity is estimated to be 10.5% and its pre-tax cost of debt to be 5.4%. These estimates are based on a capital structure comprising $225 million 6% irredeemable bonds, trading at $107 per $100, and 125 million $1 equity shares, trading at $3.20 per share. Humabuz Co also pays tax at an annual rate of 30% on its taxable profits.

Required:

(a)   Calculate the adjusted present value for the investment on the basis that it is financed by the subsidised loan and conclude whether the project should be accepted or not. Show all relevant calculations.   **(15 marks)**

(b)   Discuss the issues which Tippletine Co's shareholders who are not directors would consider if its directors decided that the new investment should be financed by the issue of convertible loan notes on the terms suggested.

      Note: You are not required to carry out any calculations when answering part (b).

      (5 marks)

Professional marks will be awarded for the demonstration of skill in analysis and evaluation, scepticism and commercial acumen in your answer.   **(5 marks)**

(Total: 25 marks)

39   AMBERLE CO (DEC 18)

Amberle Co is a listed company with divisions which manufacture cars, motorbikes and cycles. Over the last few years, Amberle Co has used a mixture of equity and debt finance for its investments. However, it is about to make a new investment of $150 million in facilities to produce electric cars, which it proposes to finance solely by debt finance.

Project information

Amberle Co's finance director has prepared estimates of the post-tax cash flows for the project, using a four-year time horizon, together with the realisable value at the end of four years:

Year	1	2	3	4
	$m	$m	$m	$m
Post-tax operating cash flows	28.50	36.70	44.40	50.90
Realisable value				45.00

Working capital of $6 million, not included in the estimates above and funded from retained earnings, will also be required immediately for the project, rising by the predicted rate of inflation for each year. Any remaining working capital will be released in full at the end of the project.

Predicted rates of inflation are as follows:

Year	1	2	3	4
	8%	6%	5%	4%

The finance director has proposed the following finance package for the new investment:

	$m
Bank loan, repayable in equal annual instalments over the project's life, interest payable at 8% per year	70
Subsidised loan from a government loan scheme over the project's life on which interest is payable at 3.1% per year	80
	————
	150
	————

Issue costs of 3% of gross proceeds will be payable on the subsidised loan. No issue costs will be payable on the bank loan. Issue costs are not allowable for tax.

Financial information

Amberle Co pays tax at an annual rate of 30% on profits in the same year in which profits arise.

Amberle Co's asset beta is currently estimated at 1.14. The current return on the market is estimated at 11%, and the current risk-free rate is 4% per year, so a suitable all-equity discount rate for the project is 12%.

Amberle Co's chair has noted that all of the company's debt, including the new debt, will be repayable within three to five years. He is wondering whether Amberle Co needs to develop a longer term financing policy in broad terms and how flexible this policy should be.

Required:

(a) **Calculate the adjusted present value (APV) for the project and conclude whether the project should be accepted or not.** **(13 marks)**

(b) **Discuss the factors which may determine the long-term finance policy which Amberle Co's board may adopt and the factors which may cause the policy to change.** **(7 marks)**

Professional marks will be awarded for the demonstration of skill in analysis and evaluation, scepticism and commercial acumen in your answer. **(5 marks)**

(Total: 25 marks)

40 HATHAWAY CO (MAR 20)

Hathaway Co operates in the aviation industry, manufacturing safety equipment for commercial aircraft. The company has a policy of carefully appraising new investment opportunities, including the detailed analysis of all cost and revenue assumptions prior to their approval.

Project chi

Hathaway Co's board is reviewing a potential investment, project chi. The company's engineers have developed a new technology which can detect the potential for mechanical failure with a greater degree of accuracy than has previously been the case. Early test results have been extremely encouraging.

If the board accepts the engineers' proposal, Hathaway Co would need to submit an application to the relevant regulatory authority. It is expected regulatory approval would be granted in one year's time. Manufacturing and sales would commence immediately after being granted regulatory approval. Hathaway Co's chief engineer presented an investment case for project chi to the board, including a summary of the following cost and revenue forecasts and assumptions.

Hathaway Co is expected to sell 3,000 units in the first year of production with demand increasing by 5% in each subsequent year of its four-year life. These sales forecasts are based on a contribution of $5,000 per unit in the first year of production and increasing at 2% per year in subsequent years. Annual fixed costs of $8.7m are expected in the first year of production, increasing at 3% per year throughout the life of the project.

An investment in plant and machinery of $12m will be required as soon as regulatory approval has been granted. Tax allowable depreciation is available on the plant and machinery at an annual rate of 20% on a straight-line basis. A balancing adjustment is expected at the end of the project when the plant and machinery will be scrapped.

Tax is payable at 20% in the year in which profits are made. The relevant cost of capital to be used in the appraisal is 12%.

Project chi extra information

The finance director, however, raised the following objections and consequences to the chief engineer's presentation.

The chief engineer's cost and revenue assumptions ignore the possibility of a recession, which has a 20% probability of occurring. In a recession, the total present values for the four years of production are likely to be 40% lower. The finance director also believes there is an alternative, mutually exclusive, development opportunity based on the new technology although this would still depend on it being granted regulatory approval. This alternative option would incur an identical investment cost of $12m but generate annual, inflation adjusted, post-tax cash flows of $3.43m over its seven-year life from year two onwards.

The investment case assumes regulatory approval is certain whereas historically only 70% of Hathaway Co's applications have been approved. In one year's time, if the regulatory application is not approved, it is assumed that the concept can be sold to Gepe Co for $1.0m at that time. If the board rejects the proposal now, assume the concept can be sold for $4.3m immediately.

Projects lambda and kappa

A recent board meeting discussed two recent investments, projects lambda and kappa, both involving the construction of new manufacturing plants for safety equipment. Both projects are now operational although project lambda experienced significant time delays and cost overruns while project kappa was under budget and within schedule. One of the directors suggested the company could benefit from the introduction of a capital investment monitoring system and post-completion audit. The directors agreed to discuss this in greater depth at the next board meeting.

Required:

(a) (i) Evaluate the financial acceptability of the project chi investment proposal based on the chief engineer's forecasts, assuming regulatory approval is granted in one year's time. **(6 marks)**

(ii) Calculate the expected net present value of the proposal based on the finance director's assumptions about the likelihood of a recession and the potential impact on project chi's cash flows. **(2 marks)**

(iii) Calculate the net present value of the finance director's alternative option for the technology and advise the board whether this is worth pursuing. **(3 marks)**

(iv) Recommend whether the board should proceed with the application for regulatory approval after taking into consideration Hathaway Co's 70% approval rate with its regulatory applications or to sell the concept now to Gepe Co. Include in your analysis any comments on your findings. **(5 marks)**

(b) Explain the rationale for implementing capital investment monitoring systems and post-completion audits. **(4 marks)**

Professional marks will be awarded for the demonstration of skill in analysis and evaluation, scepticism and commercial acumen in your answer. **(5 marks)**

(Total: 25 marks)

41 ROBSON CO (MAR/JUN 21)

The following exhibits, available on the left-hand side of the screen (in the CBE exam), provide information relevant to the question.

1 **Robson Co and project information**

2 **Further information on project finance**

This information should be used to answer the question requirements within your chosen response option(s).

Robson Co and project information

Robson Co is a food manufacturer with a portfolio of well-known brands. The founding directors retain a significant minority shareholding in the company and continue to serve on the board following a successful listing ten years ago. After obtaining the listing, Robson Co's gearing ratio increased significantly above the sector average as the result of a poorly timed expansion strategy, mainly financed by debt. Earnings became increasingly volatile and the debt burden triggered a decline in the company's financial performance. The board responded to these problems five years ago by pursuing a debt-reduction turnaround strategy, which has been financed by a series of rights issues and asset disposals.

Even though this strategy successfully reduced the gearing ratio, which is now equal to the industry average, the share price remains depressed due to competitive pressures within the industry. The company's credit rating has recently been downgraded once again. Robson Co's chief executive officer (CEO) has identified an opportunity to relocate the manufacturing plant and develop a state-of-the-art automated production line, which will reduce the underlying cost base and be a source of competitive advantage.

Project information

Robson Co's finance director has prepared estimates of the free cash flows generated by the project, based on a four-year time horizon:

Year	0	1	2	3	4
	$m	$m	$m	$m	$m
Free cash flows		20.9	20.6	28.7	104.6

The investment cost is $120m, which Robson Co's CEO proposes to finance as follows:

	$m
Disposal of existing manufacturing plant	20
Rights issue	10
Subsidised loan, 3.5% annual interest rate	40
Bank loan, 9% annual interest rate	50
Total	**120**

The bank loan is repayable in equal annual instalments over four years. Issue costs of 2% are payable on gross external financing and are not allowable for corporation tax. Issue costs are payable out of available cash reserves. The finance director has asked you to ignore underwriting costs relating to the rights issue.

Additional information

Robson Co's current asset beta is 1.222. The risk free rate is 3% and the market risk premium is 9%. The CEO expects the business risk of the company to remain unchanged as a result of the investment.

Corporation tax is payable at an annual rate of 20%.

Further information on project finance

The board discussed the financing of the project at a recent meeting. Robson Co's corporate bankers have already approved the funding decision for the $50m bank loan but the finance director is concerned about the following capital providers:

External shareholders

The last rights issue took place 18 months ago and there were two others in the previous five years. A group of shareholders have formed an action group to exert pressure on the board for more drastic change. This included a campaign to replace the CEO, which was only narrowly avoided when the shareholders voted at the most recent annual general meeting. The CEO is optimistic about the prospects of a rights issue but suggested underwriting the issue to reduce the risk of failure.

Subsidised loan provider

The government funds the subsidised loan programme to boost job creation in the economically deprived northern region of the country, which is where the new automated manufacturing plant is to be located. Although the loan has yet to be approved, the chief executive is optimistic about the outcome of their application. One feature of the loan programme is that it is open to applicants without assets available to provide security although other restrictions may be imposed. This is relevant to Robson Co since surplus assets were disposed of during the turnaround strategy and those which remain will be used to secure the new bank loan.

Required:

(a) Calculate the adjusted present value of the investment and recommend whether the project should be accepted or not. **(13 marks)**

(b) Discuss the factors the capital providers, excluding the bank, will consider before deciding whether or not to approve the funding decision for Robson Co's investment in a new manufacturing plant. **(7 marks)**

Professional marks will be awarded for the demonstration of skill in analysis and evaluation, scepticism and commercial acumen in your answer. **(5 marks)**

(Total: 25 marks)

42 MOONSTAR CO (SEP/DEC 15)

Moonstar Co is a property development company which is planning to undertake a $200 million commercial property development. Moonstar Co has had some difficulties over the last few years, with some developments not generating the expected returns and the company has at times struggled to pay its finance costs. As a result Moonstar Co's credit rating has been lowered, affecting the terms it can obtain for bank finance. Although Moonstar Co is listed on its local stock exchange, 75% of the share capital is held by members of the family who founded the company. The family members who are shareholders do not wish to subscribe for a rights issue and are unwilling to dilute their control over the company by authorising a new issue of equity shares. Moonstar Co's board is therefore considering other methods of financing the development, which the directors believe will generate higher returns than other recent investments, as the country where Moonstar Co is based appears to be emerging from recession.

Securitisation proposals

One of the non-executive directors of Moonstar Co has proposed that it should raise funds by means of a securitisation process, transferring the rights to the rental income from the commercial property development to a special purpose vehicle. Her proposals assume that the leases will generate an income of 11% per year to Moonstar Co over a ten-year period. She proposes that Moonstar Co should use 90% of the value of the investment for a collateralised loan obligation which should be structured as follows:

- 60% of the collateral value to support a tranche of A-rated floating rate loan notes offering investors SOFR plus 150 basis points

- 15% of the collateral value to support a tranche of B-rated fixed rate loan notes offering investors 12%

- 15% of the collateral value to support a tranche of C-rated fixed rate loan notes offering investors 13%

- 10% of the collateral value to support a tranche as subordinated certificates, with the return being the excess of receipts over payments from the securitisation process

The non-executive director believes that there will be sufficient demand for all tranches of the loan notes from investors. Investors will expect that the income stream from the development to be low risk, as they will expect the property market to improve with the recession coming to an end and enough potential lessees to be attracted by the new development.

The non-executive director predicts that there would be annual costs of $200,000 in administering the loan. She acknowledges that there would be interest rate risks associated with the proposal, and proposes a fixed for variable interest rate swap on the A-rated floating rate notes, exchanging SOFR for 9.5%.

However the finance director believes that the prediction of the income from the development that the non-executive director has made is over-optimistic. He believes that it is most likely that the total value of the rental income will be 5% lower than the non-executive director has forecast. He believes that there is some risk that the returns could be so low as to jeopardise the income for the C-rated fixed rate loan note holders.

Islamic finance

Moonstar Co's chair has pointed out that a major bank in the country where Moonstar Co is located has begun to offer a range of Islamic financial products. The chair has suggested that a Mudaraba contract would be the most appropriate method of providing the funds required for the investment.

Required:

(a)   Calculate the amounts in $ which each of the tranches can expect to receive from the securitisation arrangement proposed by the non-executive director and discuss how the variability in rental income affects the returns from the securitisation.

(11 marks)

(b)   Discuss the benefits and risks for Moonstar Co associated with the securitisation arrangement that the non-executive director has proposed.   (5 marks)

(c)   Discuss whether a Mudaraba contract would be an appropriate method of financing the investment and discuss why the bank may have concerns about providing finance by this method.   (4 marks)

Professional marks will be awarded for the demonstration of skill in analysis and evaluation, and commercial acumen in your answer.   (5 marks)

(Total: 25 marks)

43   GNT CO (JUN 11)

GNT Co is considering an investment in one of two corporate bonds. Both bonds have a nominal value of $1,000 and pay coupon interest on an annual basis. The market price of the first bond is $1,079·68. Its coupon rate is 6% and it is due to be redeemed at par in five years. The second bond is about to be issued with a coupon rate of 4% and will also be redeemable at par in five years. Both bonds are expected to have the same gross redemption yields (yields to maturity).

GNT Co considers duration of the bond to be a key factor when making decisions on which bond to invest.

Required:

(a)   Estimate the Macaulay duration of the two bonds GNT Co is considering for investment.   (8 marks)

(b)   Discuss how useful duration is as a measure of the sensitivity of a bond price to changes in interest rates.   (6 marks)

(c)   Among the criteria used by credit agencies for establishing a company's credit rating are the following: industry risk, earnings protection and evaluation of the company's management.

        Briefly explain each criterion and suggest factors that could be used to assess it.

(6 marks)

Professional marks will be awarded for the demonstration of skill in analysis and evaluation, and commercial acumen in your answer.   (5 marks)

(Total: 25 marks)

44   TOLTUCK CO (MAR/JUN 17)

Toltuck Co is a listed company in the building industry which specialises in the construction of large commercial and residential developments. Toltuck Co had been profitable for many years, but has just incurred major losses on the last two developments which it has completed in its home country of Arumland. These developments were an out-of-town retail centre and a major residential development. Toltuck Co's directors have blamed the poor results primarily on the recent recession in Arumland, although demand for the residential development also appears to have been adversely affected by it being located in an area which has suffered serious flooding over the last two years.

As a result of returns from these two major developments being much lower than expected, Toltuck Co has had to finance current work-in-progress by a significantly greater amount of debt finance, giving it higher gearing than most other construction companies operating in Arumland. Toltuck Co's directors have recently been alarmed by a major credit agency's decision to downgrade Toltuck Co's credit rating from AA to BBB. The directors are very concerned about the impact this will have on the valuation of Toltuck Co's bonds and the future cost of debt.

The following information can be used to assess the consequences of the change in Toltuck Co's credit rating.

Toltuck Co has issued an 8% bond, which has a face or nominal value of $100 and a premium of 2% on redemption in three years' time. The coupon on the bond is payable on an annual basis.

The government of Arumland has three bonds in issue. They all have a face or nominal value of $100 and are all redeemable at par. Taxation can be ignored on government bonds. They are of the same risk class and the coupon on each is payable on an annual basis. Details of the bonds are as follows:

Bond	Redeemable	Coupon	Current market value $
1	1 year	9%	104
2	2 years	7%	102
3	3 years	6%	98

Credit spreads, published by the credit agency, are as follows (shown in basis points):

Rating	1 year	2 years	3 years
AA	18	31	45
BBB	54	69	86

Toltuck Co's shareholder base can be divided broadly into two groups. The majority of shareholders are comfortable with investing in a company where dividends in some years will be high, but there will be low or no dividends in other years because of the cash demands facing the business. However, a minority of shareholders would like Toltuck Co to achieve at least a minimum dividend each year and are concerned about the company undertaking investments which they regard as very speculative. Shareholders from both groups have expressed some concerns to the board about the impact of the fall in credit rating on their investment.

Required:

(a) Calculate the valuation and yield to maturity of Toltuck Co's $100 bond under its old and new credit ratings. **(9 marks)**

(b) Discuss the factors which may have affected the credit rating of Toltuck Co published by the credit agency. **(6 marks)**

(c) Discuss the impact of the fall in Toltuck Co's credit rating on its ability to raise financial capital and on its shareholders' return. **(5 marks)**

Professional marks will be awarded for the demonstration of skill in analysis and evaluation, and commercial acumen in your answer. **(5 marks)**

(Total: 25 marks)

ACQUISITIONS AND MERGERS

45 KODIAK COMPANY (DEC 09)

Kodiak Company is a small software design business established four years ago. The company is owned by three directors who have relied upon external accounting services in the past. The company has grown quickly and the directors have appointed you as a financial consultant to advise on the value of the business under their ownership.

The directors have limited liability and the bank loan is secured against the general assets of the business. The directors have no outstanding guarantees on the company's debt.

The company's latest statement of profit or loss and the extracted balances from the latest statement of financial position are as follows:

	$000	Financial Position	$000
Revenue	5,000	Opening non-current assets	1,200
Cost of Sales	3,000	Additions	66
Gross profit	2,000	Non-current assets (gross)	1,266
Other operating costs	1,877	Accumulated depreciation	367
Operating profit	123	Net book value	899
Interest on loan	74	Net current assets	270
Profit before tax	49	Loan	(990)
Income tax expense	15	Net Assets Employed	179
Profit for the period	34		

During the current year:

1   Depreciation is charged at 10% per year on the year end non-current asset balance before accumulated depreciation, and is included in other operating costs in the statement of profit or loss.

2   The investment in net working capital is expected to increase in line with the growth in gross profit.

3   Other operating costs consisted of:

	$000
Variable component at 15% of sales	750
Fixed costs	1,000
Depreciation on non-current assets	127

4   Revenue and variable costs are projected to grow at 9% per year and fixed costs are projected to grow at 6% per year.

5   The company pays interest on its outstanding loan of 7.5% per year and incurs tax on its profits at 30%, payable in the following year. The company does not pay dividends.

6   The net current assets reported in the statement of financial position contain $50,000 of cash.

One of your first tasks is to prepare for the directors a forward cash flow projection for three years and to value the firm on the basis of its expected free cash flow to equity. In discussion with them you note the following:

*   The company will not dispose of any of its non-current assets but will increase its investment in new non-current assets by 20% per year. The company's depreciation policy matches the currently available tax allowable depreciation. This straight-line write off policy is not likely to change.

*   The directors will not take a dividend for the next three years but will then review the position taking into account the company's sustainable cash flow at that time.

*   The level of the loan will be maintained at $990,000 and, on the basis of the forward yield curve, interest rates are not expected to change.

*   The directors have set a target rate of return on their equity of 10% per year which they believe fairly represents the opportunity cost of their invested funds.

Required:

(a)   Prepare a three-year cash flow forecast for the business on the basis described above highlighting the free cash flow to equity in each year.   (12 marks)

(b)   Estimate the value of the business based upon the expected free cash flow to equity and a terminal value based upon a sustainable growth rate of 3% per year thereafter.   (3 marks)

(c)   Advise the directors on the assumptions and the uncertainties within your valuation.   (5 marks)

Professional marks will be awarded for the demonstration of skill in analysis and evaluation, scepticism and commercial acumen in your answer.   (5 marks)

(Total: 25 marks)

46 SIGRA CO (DEC 12)

Sigra Co is a listed company producing confectionary products which it sells around the world. It wants to acquire Dentro Co, an unlisted company producing luxury chocolates. Sigra Co proposes to pay for the acquisition using one of the following three methods:

Method 1

A cash offer of $5.00 per Dentro Co share; or

Method 2

An offer of three of its shares for two of Dentro Co's shares; or

Method 3

An offer of a 2% coupon bond in exchange for 16 Dentro Co's shares. The bond will be redeemed in three years at its nominal value of $100.

Extracts from the latest financial statements of both companies are as follows:

	Sigra Co	Dentro Co
	$000	$000
Sales revenue	44,210	4,680
Profit before tax	6,190	780
Taxation	(1,240)	(155)
Profit after tax	4,950	625
Dividends	(2,700)	(275)
Retained earnings for the year	2,250	350

	Sigra Co	Dentro Co
Non-current assets	22,450	3,350
Current assets	3,450	247
Non-current liabilities	9,700	873
Current liabilities	3,600	436
Share capital (40c per share)	4,400	500
Reserves	8,200	1,788

Sigra Co's current share price is $3.60 per share and it has estimated that Dentro Co's price to earnings ratio is 12.5% higher than Sigra Co's current price to earnings ratio. Sigra Co's non-current liabilities include a 6% bond redeemable in three years at par which is currently trading at $104 per $100 nominal value. Sigra Co estimates that it could achieve synergy savings of 30% of Dentro Co's estimated equity value by eliminating duplicated administrative functions, selling excess non-current assets and through reducing the workforce numbers, if the acquisition were successful.

Required:

(a) **Estimate the percentage gain on a Dentro Co share under each of the above three payment methods. Comment on the answers obtained.** **(16 marks)**

(b) In relation to the acquisition, the board of directors of Sigra Co are considering the following two proposals:

Proposal 1

Once Sigra Co has obtained agreement from a significant majority of the shareholders, it will enforce the remaining minority shareholders to sell their shares.

Proposal 2

Sigra Co will offer an extra 3 cents per share, in addition to the bid price, to 30% of the shareholders of Dentro Co on a first-come, first-serve basis, as an added incentive to make the acquisition proceed more quickly.

Required:

With reference to the key aspects of the global regulatory framework for mergers and acquisitions, briefly discuss the above proposals. **(4 marks)**

Professional marks will be awarded for the demonstration of skill in analysis and evaluation, scepticism and commercial acumen in your answer. **(5 marks)**

(Total: 25 marks)

47 HAV CO (JUN 13)

The following exhibits, available on the left-hand side of the screen (in the CBE exam), provide information relevant to the question.

1 **Hav Co**

2 **Strand Co - information about Strand Co an acquisition target**

3 **Financial information – relating to both companies and the suggested acquisition methods**

This information should be used to answer the question requirements within your chosen response option(s).

Hav Co

Hav Co is a publicly listed company involved in the production of highly technical and sophisticated electronic components for complex machinery. It has a number of diverse and popular products, an active research and development department, significant cash reserves and a highly talented management who are very good in getting products to market quickly.

A new industry that Hav Co is looking to venture into is biotechnology, which has been expanding rapidly and there are strong indications that this recent growth is set to continue. However, Hav Co has limited experience in this industry. Therefore it believes that the best and quickest way to expand would be through acquiring a company already operating in this industry sector.

Strand Co

Strand Co is a private company operating in the biotechnology industry and is owned by a consortium of business angels and company managers. The owner-managers are highly skilled scientists who have developed a number of technically complex products, but have found it difficult to commercialise them. They have also been increasingly constrained by the lack of funds to develop their innovative products further.

Discussions have taken place about the possibility of Strand Co being acquired by Hav Co. Strand Co's managers have indicated that the consortium of owners is happy for the negotiations to proceed. If Strand Co is acquired, it is expected that its managers would continue to run the Strand Co part of the larger combined company.

Strand Co is of the opinion that most of its value is in its intangible assets, comprising intellectual capital. Therefore, the premium payable on acquisition should be based on the present value to infinity of the after tax excess earnings the company has generated in the past three years, over the average return on capital employed of the biotechnological industry. However, Hav Co is of the opinion that the premium should be assessed on synergy benefits created by the acquisition and the changes in value, due to the changes in the price-to-earnings (PE) ratio before and after the acquisition.

Financial information

Given below are extracts of financial information for Hav Co for 20X3 and Strand Co for 20X1, 20X2 and 20X3:

	Hav Co		Strand Co	
Year ended 30 April	20X3	20X3	20X2	20X1
	$ million	$ million	$ million	$ million
Earnings before tax	1,980	397	370	352
Non-current assets	3,965	882	838	801
Current assets	968	210	208	198
Share capital ($0.25/share)	600	300	300	300
Reserves	2,479	183	166	159
Non-current liabilities	1,500	400	400	400
Current liabilities	354	209	180	140

The current average PE ratio of the biotechnology industry is 16.4 times and it has been estimated that Strand Co's PE ratio is 10% higher than this. However, it is thought that the PE ratio of the combined company would fall to 14.5 times after the acquisition. The annual after tax earnings will increase by $140m due to synergy benefits resulting from combining the two companies.

Both companies pay tax at 20% per year and Strand Co's annual cost of capital is estimated at 7%. Hav Co's current share price is $9.24 per share. The biotechnology industry's pre-tax return on capital employed is currently estimated to be 20% per year.

Hav Co has proposed to pay for the acquisition using one of the following methods:

(i)   A cash offer of $5.72 for each Strand Co share; or

(ii)   A cash offer of $1.25 for each Strand Co share plus one $100 3% convertible bond for every $5 nominal value of Strand Co shares. In six years, the bond can be converted into 12 Hav Co shares or redeemed at nominal value.

Required:

(a) Distinguish between the different types of synergy and discuss possible sources of revenue synergy based on the above scenario. **(6 marks)**

(b) Based on the two different opinions expressed by Hav Co and Strand Co, calculate the maximum acquisition premium payable in each case. **(7 marks)**

(c) Calculate the percentage premium per share that Strand Co's shareholders will receive under each acquisition payment method and justify, with explanations, which payment method would be most acceptable to them. **(7 marks)**

Professional marks will be awarded for the demonstration of skill in analysis and evaluation, scepticism and commercial acumen in your answer. **(5 marks)**

(Total: 25 marks)

48 VOGEL CO (JUN 14)

Vogel Co, a listed engineering company, manufactures large scale plant and machinery for industrial companies. Until ten years ago, Vogel Co pursued a strategy of organic growth. Since then, it has followed an aggressive policy of acquiring smaller engineering companies, which it feels have developed new technologies and methods, which could be used in its manufacturing processes. However, it is estimated that only between 30% and 40% of the acquisitions made in the last ten years have successfully increased the company's shareholder value.

Vogel Co is currently considering acquiring Tori Co, an unlisted company, which has three departments. Department A manufactures machinery for industrial companies, Department B produces electrical goods for the retail market, and the smaller Department C operates in the construction industry. Upon acquisition, Department A will become part of Vogel Co, as it contains the new technologies which Vogel Co is seeking, but Departments B and C will be unbundled, with the assets attached to Department C sold and Department B being spun off into a new company called Ndege Co.

Given below are extracts of financial information for the two companies for the year ended 30 April 20X4.

	Vogel Co $ million	Tori Co $ million
Sales revenue	790.2	124.6
Profit before depreciation, interest and tax (PBDIT)	244.4	37.4
Interest	13.8	4.3
Depreciation	72.4	10.1
Pre-tax profit	158.2	23.0
Non-current assets	723.9	98.2
Current assets	142.6	46.5
7% unsecured bond	–	40.0
Other non-current and current liabilities	212.4	20.2
Share capital (50c/share)	190.0	20.0
Reserves	464.1	64.5

Share of current and non-current assets and profit of Tori Co's three departments:

	Department A	Department B	Department C
Share of current and non-current assets	40%	40%	20%
Share of PBDIT and pre-tax profit	50%	40%	10%

Other information

(i)   It is estimated that for Department C, the realisable value of its non-current assets is 100% of their book value, but its current assets' realisable value is only 90% of their book value. The costs related to closing Department C are estimated to be $3 million.

(ii)   The funds raised from the disposal of Department C will be used to pay off Tori Co's other non-current and current liabilities.

(iii)   The 7% unsecured bond will be taken over by Ndege Co. It can be assumed that the current market value of the bond is equal to its book value.

(iv)   At present, around 10% of Department B's PBDIT come from sales made to Department C.

(v)   Ndege Co's cost of capital is estimated to be 10%. It is estimated that in the first year of operation Ndege Co's free cash flows to firm will grow by 20%, and then by 5.2% annually thereafter.

(vi)   The tax rate applicable to all the companies is 20%, and Ndege Co can claim 10% tax allowable depreciation on its non-current assets. It can be assumed that the amount of tax allowable depreciation is the same as the investment needed to maintain Ndege Co's operations.

(vii)   Vogel Co's current share price is $3 per share and it is estimated that Tori Co's price-to-earnings (PE) ratio is 25% higher than Vogel Co's PE ratio. After the acquisition, when Department A becomes part of Vogel Co, it is estimated that Vogel Co's PE ratio will increase by 15%.

(viii) It is estimated that the combined company's annual after-tax earnings will increase by $7 million due to the synergy benefits resulting from combining Vogel Co and Department A.

Required:

(a)   **Discuss the possible actions Vogel Co could take to reduce the risk that the acquisition of Tori Co fails to increase shareholder value.   (6 marks)**

(b)   **Estimate, showing all relevant calculations, the maximum premium Vogel Co could pay to acquire Tori Co, explaining the approach taken and any assumptions made.   (14 marks)**

Professional marks will be awarded for the demonstration of skill in analysis and evaluation, scepticism and commercial acumen in your answer.   (5 marks)

(Total: 25 marks)

49   LOUIEED CO (MAR/JUN 16)

Louieed Co, a listed company, is a major supplier of educational material, selling its products in many countries. It supplies schools and colleges and also produces learning material for business and professional exams. Louieed Co has exclusive contracts to produce material for some examining bodies. Louieed Co has a well-defined management structure with formal processes for making major decisions.

Although Louieed Co produces online learning material, most of its profits are still derived from sales of traditional textbooks. Louieed Co's growth in profits over the last few years has been slow and its directors are currently reviewing its long-term strategy. One area in which they feel that Louieed Co must become much more involved is the production of online testing materials for exams and to validate course and textbook learning.

Bid for Tidded Co

Louieed Co has recently made a bid for Tidded Co, a smaller listed company. Tidded Co also supplies a range of educational material, but has been one of the leaders in the development of online testing and has shown strong profit growth over recent years. All of Tidded Co's initial five founders remain on its board and still hold 45% of its issued share capital between them. From the start, Tidded Co's directors have been used to making quick decisions in their areas of responsibility. Although listing has imposed some formalities, Tidded Co has remained focused on acting quickly to gain competitive advantage, with the five founders continuing to give strong leadership.

Louieed Co's initial bid of five shares in Louieed Co for three shares in Tidded Co was rejected by Tidded Co's board. There has been further discussion between the two boards since the initial offer was rejected and Louieed Co's board is now considering a proposal to offer Tidded Co's shareholders two shares in Louieed Co for one share in Tidded Co or a cash alternative of $22.75 per Tidded Co share.

It is expected that Tidded Co's shareholders will choose one of the following options:

(i)   To accept the two-shares-for-one-share offer for all the Tidded Co shares; or,

(ii)   To accept the cash offer for all the Tidded Co shares; or,

(iii)   60% of the shareholders will take up the two-shares-for-one-share offer and the remaining 40% will take the cash offer.

In case of the third option being accepted, it is thought that three of the company's founders, holding 20% of the share capital in total, will take the cash offer and not join the combined company. The remaining two founders will probably continue to be involved in the business and be members of the combined company's board.

Louieed Co's finance director has estimated that the merger will produce annual post-tax synergies of $20 million. He expects Louieed Co's current price-earnings (P/E) ratio to remain unchanged after the acquisition.

Extracts from the two companies' most recent accounts are shown below:

	Louieed	Tidded
	$m	$m
Profit before finance cost and tax	446	182
Finance costs	(74)	(24)
Profit before tax	372	158
Tax	(76)	(30)
Profit after tax	296	128
Issued $1 nominal shares	340 million	90 million
P/E ratios, based on most recent accounts	14	15.9
Long-term liabilities (market value) ($m)	540	193
Cash and cash equivalents ($m)	220	64

The tax rate applicable to both companies is 20%.

Assume that Louieed Co can obtain further debt funding at a pre-tax cost of 7.5% and that the return on cash surpluses is 5% pre-tax.

Assume also that any debt funding needed to complete the acquisition will be reduced instantly by the balances of cash and cash equivalents held by Louieed Co and Tidded Co.

Required:

(a) Discuss the advantages and disadvantages of the acquisition of Tidded Co from the viewpoint of Louieed Co. **(6 marks)**

(b) Calculate, and comment on, the funding required for the acquisition of Tidded Co and the impact on Louieed Co's earnings per share and gearing, for each of the three options given above.

Note: Up to 10 marks are available for the calculations. **(14 marks)**

Professional marks will be awarded for the demonstration of skill in analysis and evaluation, scepticism and commercial acumen in your answer. **(5 marks)**

(Total: 25 marks)

50 SELORNE CO (SEP 18)

Selorne Co is one of the biggest removal companies in Pauland, offering home and business removals. It has a number of long-term contracts with large businesses, although it has not won any new major contracts in the last two years. Selorne Co is listed on Pauland's stock market for smaller companies. Selorne Co is financed by a mixture of equity and short and long-term debt, but its gearing level is below the average for its sector.

Selorne Co has four executive directors, who each own 20% of the company's share capital, with the other 20% owned by external shareholders. Selorne Co has paid a constant dividend since it has been listed and its share price has risen slightly over the last three years.

Selorne Co is based in a number of the large cities and towns in Pauland and owns the majority of the sites where it is located. Many of its employees have worked for the company for a long time. Drivers of the lorries used by Selorne Co are required to have a special, heavy vehicles licence. Salary levels at Selorne Co are relatively high compared with other companies in the sector.

Chawon Co

Selorne Co is currently considering making a bid for Chawon Co, an unlisted company specialising in distribution and delivery services. Chawon Co is owned 100% by its founder, Chris Chawon. Chawon Co has built up a portfolio of small contracts over time. It has made unsuccessful bids for two larger contracts over the last 12 months, the bids being rejected primarily because Chawon Co was not felt to be big enough to be able to guarantee the level of service required.

Chawon Co is based in many of the same cities and towns where Selorne Co is located, although Chawon's premises are all rented. The drivers of Chawon's vehicles do not require a heavy vehicles licence. Chawon Co has a few long-serving employees who are mostly centre managers. Most of its drivers and staff, however, stay at Chawon Co for only a short time. Salary levels are low, although Chawon Co pays high levels of overtime and high bonuses if target profit levels are achieved. Chawon Co is highly geared, leading to recent media speculation about its financial viability.

Terms of bid for Chawon Co

In initial discussions about the acquisition, Chris Chawon indicated that he would prefer the consideration to be a share-for-share exchange, the terms being one Chawon Co share for five Selorne Co shares.

Chawon Co has 2 million $1 shares in issue, and Selorne Co has 50 million $0.50 shares in issue. Each Selorne Co share is currently trading at $6.50, which is a multiple of 8 of its free cash flow to equity. The multiple of 8 can be assumed to remain unchanged if the acquisition takes place. Chawon Co's free cash flow to equity is currently estimated at $7 million, with an expected annual growth rate of 3%, and it is expected to generate a return on equity of 15%.

Chris Chawon expects that the total free cash flows to equity of the combined company will increase by $5 million due to synergy benefits. He believes that Selorne Co will be able to win more contracts because it is larger and because it will be diversifying the services which it offers. He also believes that significant operational synergies can be achieved, pointing out the time Selorne Co drivers spend idle during the winter months when removal activity is traditionally lower. Chris Chawon believes that he can achieve the synergies if he is given management responsibility for the operational reorganisation, including dealing with the staff employment and retention issues. Chris Chawon thinks that synergies could also be achieved in central administration and in premises costs.

The chief executive and the finance director of Selorne Co are in favour of bidding for Chawon Co. However, one of the other executive directors is opposed to the bid. He is sceptical about the level of synergies which can be achieved and does not want Chris Chawon to be brought into the management of Selorne Co. He suggests that if the bid is to go ahead, it should be a cash offer rather than a share exchange. Selorne Co's chief executive has responded that Chris Chawon is likely to ask for a higher equivalent price if the purchase is for cash.

Required:

(a) (i) **Estimate the equity value of the combined company and the expected additional value arising from the combination of Selorne Co and Chawon Co.**

(6 marks)

(ii) **Estimate the share of the gain from the combination created for Chris Chawon and the share of the gain created for Selorne Co's shareholders and comment on your results.**

(6 marks)

(b) **Evaluate how reliable the estimates of the synergies for the combined company are likely to be and discuss the factors which may prevent the forecast synergies from being achieved.**

(8 marks)

Professional marks will be awarded for the demonstration of skill in analysis and evaluation, scepticism and commercial acumen in your answer.

(5 marks)

(Total: 25 marks)

51   KERRIN CO (SEP/DEC 19)

   Answer debrief

A new client has approached you for advice on a potential acquisition. Kerrin Co is a consumer electronics manufacturer and retailer. The company obtained a listing eight years ago with the founders retaining a 20% stake in the business. Whilst Kerrin Co had previously experienced rapid growth in earnings before tax, problems arose soon after the listing as competition intensified. Although the company remains profitable, annual growth has declined significantly and is currently 3%.

The board is concerned by the lack of future growth opportunities. The current share price reflects these concerns, trading well below the offer price of eight years ago. In response, the directors have decided to invest in a market development strategy for future growth, utilising significant cash reserves to acquire companies in other areas of the country where competition is less intense. The board has identified a potential target, Danton Co.

Danton Co

Danton Co is a privately owned consumer electronics company, established ten years ago. Significant unrelieved losses were incurred in the early years of development although the company is now profitable and achieving growth in earnings before tax of 6% per year. However, cash reserves are low. Access to capital has acted as a severe constraint on Danton Co's reinvestment potential throughout this period. The founders and their families own 60% of the shares with the balance held by a venture capitalist organisation, which acquired its equity stake around six years ago.

Acquisition information

Kerrin Co's board is keen to ensure that Danton Co's founders remain as directors after the acquisition and the company has sufficient cash reserves to purchase Danton Co outright.

Early discussions between the directors of both companies suggest Danton Co's shareholders would approve a cash offer of $13.10 per share. As an alternative, the board is considering a share-for-share exchange to fund the acquisition in order to preserve cash for future acquisitions and dividend payments. Recent mergers have attracted an acquisition premium of around 25%–30% and Danton Co's directors indicated their shareholders would be expecting a premium towards the higher end of this scale for a share-for-share offer. Kerrin Co has therefore asked you to design a share-for-share offer scheme which will allow for a 30% acquisition premium. You have been provided with extracts from the latest financial statements for both companies.

Extracts from the most recent financial statements

	Kerrin Co	Danton Co
	$m	$m
Operating profit	448.6	201.8
Earnings before tax	381.9	116.3

Additional financial information

The book value of Kerrin Co's $0.50 ordinary shares is $375m. These shares are currently trading at $5.28 and the finance director expects the price earnings (PE) ratio to increase by 10% if the acquisition proceeds.

Danton Co upgraded its main manufacturing facility during the previous year and expects to make annual pre-tax cost savings of $2.5m from the start of the current financial year. The book value of Danton Co's $0.25 ordinary shares is $35m. Based on an analysis of companies of a comparable size and cost structure, it is estimated that Danton Co's PE ratio is 20% higher than Kerrin Co's current PE ratio.

Kerrin Co's chief executive officer estimates annual pre-tax revenue and cost synergies of $15.2m to arise as a result of the acquisition. In addition, the finance director anticipates annual pre-tax financial synergies of $5.3m.

The rate of corporation tax relevant to both companies is 20%.

Required:

(a)   **Discuss possible sources of financial synergy arising from Kerrin Co's acquisition of Danton Co.** **(4 marks)**

(b)   **Advise the directors on a suitable share-for-share exchange offer which meets the criteria specified by Danton Co's shareholders and calculate the effect of the cash and share-for-share offers on the post-acquisition wealth of both Kerrin Co's and Danton Co's shareholders.** **(12 marks)**

(c)   **Discuss the likely reaction of Kerrin Co's and Danton Co's shareholders to the cash and share-for-share offers.** **(4 marks)**

Professional marks will be awarded for the demonstration of skill in analysis and evaluation, scepticism and commercial acumen in your answer. **(5 marks)**

(Total: 25 marks)

 Calculate your allowed time, allocate the time to the separate parts...............

CORPORATE RECONSTRUCTION AND REORGANISATION

52   ALASKA SALVAGE (DEC 09)

Alaska Salvage is in discussion with potential lenders about financing an ambitious five-year project searching for lost gold in the central Atlantic. The company has had great success in the past with its various salvage operations and is now quoted on the London Alternative Investment Market. The company is currently financed by 120,000 equity shares trading at $85 per share. It needs to borrow $1.6 million and is concerned about the level of the fixed rates being suggested by the lenders. After lengthy discussions the lenders are prepared to offer finance against a mezzanine issue of fixed rate five-year notes with warrants attached. Each $10,000 note, repayable at par, would carry a warrant for 100 equity shares at an exercise price of $90 per share. The estimated volatility of the returns on the company's equity is 20% and the risk free rate of interest is 5%. The company does not pay dividends to its equity investors.

You may assume that the issue of these loan notes will not influence the current value of the firm's equity. The issue will be made at par.

Required:

(a)   Estimate, using Black-Scholes Option Pricing Model as appropriate, the current value of each warrant to the lender noting the assumptions that you have made in your valuation.   **(6 marks)**

Note: in the Computer Based Exam (CBE), the "BSOP calculator" spreadsheet option will be provided to help you to answer this question.

(b)   Estimate the coupon rate that would be required by the lenders if they wanted a 13% rate of return on their investment.   **(4 marks)**

(c)   Discuss the advantages and disadvantages of issuing mezzanine debt in the situation outlined in the case.   **(6 marks)**

(d)   Explain how sukuk bonds could be used (instead of more conventional loan notes) to fund the project being considered by Alaska Salvage.   **(4 marks)**

Professional marks will be awarded for the demonstration of skill in analysis and evaluation, and commercial acumen in your answer.   **(5 marks)**

(Total: 25 marks)

53   ENNEA CO (JUN 12)

Three proposals were put forward for further consideration after a meeting of the executive directors of Ennea Co to discuss the future investment and financing strategy of the business. Ennea Co is a listed company operating in the haulage and shipping industry.

Proposal 1

To increase the company's level of debt by borrowing a further $20 million and use the funds raised to buy back share capital.

Proposal 2

To increase the company's level of debt by borrowing a further $20 million and use these funds to invest in additional non-current assets in the haulage strategic business unit.

Proposal 3

To sell excess non-current haulage assets with a net book value of $25 million for $27 million and focus on offering more services to the shipping strategic business unit. This business unit will require no additional investment in non-current assets. All the funds raised from the sale of the non-current assets will be used to reduce the company's debt.

Financial information: Extracts from the forecast financial position for the coming year

	$m
Non-current assets	282
Current assets	66
Total assets	348

Equity and liabilities

Share capital (40c per share nominal value)	48
Retained earnings	123
	——
Total equity	171
	——
Non-current liabilities	140
Current liabilities	37
	——
Total liabilities	177
	——
Total liabilities and capital	348
	——

Ennea Co's forecast after tax profit for the coming year is expected to be $26 million and its current share price is $3.20 per share. The non-current liabilities consist solely of a 6% medium term loan redeemable within seven years. The terms of the loan contract stipulates that an increase in borrowing will result in an increase in the coupon payable of 25 basis points on the total amount borrowed, while a reduction in borrowing will lower the coupon payable by 15 basis points on the total amount borrowed. Ennea Co's effective tax rate is 20%. The company's estimated after tax rate of return on investment is expected to be 15% on any new investment. It is expected that any reduction in investment would suffer the same rate of return.

Required:

Estimate and discuss the impact of each of the three proposals on the forecast statement of financial position, the earnings and earnings per share, and gearing of Ennea Co.

(20 marks)

Professional marks will be awarded for the demonstration of skill in analysis and evaluation, and commercial acumen in your answer. **(5 marks)**

(Total: 25 marks)

54 NUBO CO (DEC 13)

Nubo Co has divisions operating in two diverse sectors: production of aircraft parts and supermarkets. Whereas the aircraft parts production division has been growing rapidly, the supermarkets division's growth has been slower. The company is considering selling the supermarkets division and focusing solely on the aircraft parts production division.

Extracts from Nubo Co's most recent financial statements are as follows:

Year ended 30 November	20X3
	$m
Profit after tax	166
Non-current assets	550
Current assets	122
Non-current liabilities	387
Current liabilities	95

About 70% of Nubo Co's non-current assets and current assets are attributable to the supermarkets division and the remainder to the aircraft parts production division. Each of the two divisions generates roughly half of the total profit after tax. The market value of the two divisions is thought to be equivalent to the price-to-earnings (PE) ratios of the two divisions' industries. The supermarket industry's PE ratio is 7 and the aircraft parts production industry's PE ratio is 12.

Nubo Co can either sell the supermarkets division as a going concern or sell the assets of the supermarkets division separately. If the assets are sold separately, Nubo Co believes that it can sell the non-current assets for 115% of the book value and the current assets for 80% of the book value. The funds raised from the sale of the supermarkets division will be used to pay for all the company's current and non-current liabilities.

Following the sale of the supermarkets division and paying off the liabilities, Nubo Co will raise additional finance for new projects in the form of debt. It will be able to borrow up to a maximum of 100% of the total asset value of the new downsized company.

One of the new projects which Nubo Co is considering is a joint venture with Pilvi Co to produce an innovative type of machinery which will be used in the production of light aircraft and private jets. Both companies will provide the expertise and funding required for the project equally. Representatives from both companies will make up the senior management team and decisions will be made jointly. Legal contracts will be drawn up once profit-sharing and other areas have been discussed by the companies and agreed on.

Pilvi Co has approached Ulap Bank for the finance it requires for the venture, based on Islamic finance principles. Ulap Bank has agreed to consider the request from Pilvi Co, but because the financing requirement will be for a long period of time and because of uncertainties surrounding the project, Ulap Bank wants to provide the finance based on the principles of a Musharaka contract, with Ulap Bank requiring representation on the venture's senior management team. Normally Ulap Bank provides funds based on the principles of a Mudaraba contract, which the bank provides for short-term, low-risk projects, where the responsibility for running a project rests solely with the borrower.

Required:

(a) **Advise Nubo Co whether it should sell the supermarkets division as a going concern or sell the assets separately and estimate the additional cash and debt funds which could be available to the new, downsized company. Show all relevant calculations.**

(8 marks)

(b) **Discuss why Ulap Bank may want to consider providing the finance based on a Musharaka contract instead of a Mudaraba contract, and the key concerns Nubo Co may have from the arrangement between Pilvi Co and Ulap Bank.** (12 marks)

Professional marks will be awarded for the demonstration of skill in analysis and evaluation, scepticism and commercial acumen in your answer. (5 marks)

(Total: 25 marks)

55 BENTO CO (JUN 15)

In order to raise funds for future projects, the management of Bento Co, a large manufacturing company, is considering disposing of one of its subsidiary companies, Okazu Co, which is involved in manufacturing rubber tubing. They are considering undertaking the disposal through a management buy-out (MBO). Bento Co wants $60 million from the sale of Okazu Co.

Given below are extracts from the most recent financial statements for Okazu Co:

Year ending 30 April (all amounts in $000)

	20X5
Total non-current assets	40,800
Total current assets	12,300
Total assets	53,100
Equity	24,600
Non-current liabilities	16,600
Current liabilities	
Trade and other payables	7,900
Bank overdraft	4,000
Total current liabilities	11,900
Total equity and liabilities	53,100

Year ending 30 April (all amounts in $000)

	20X5
Sales revenue	54,900
Operating profit	12,200
Finance costs	1,600
Profit before tax	10,600
Taxation	2,120
Profit for the year	8,480

Notes relating to the financial statements above:

(i)   Current assets, non-current assets and the trade and other payables will be transferred to the new company when Okazu Co is sold. The bank overdraft will be repaid by Bento Co prior to the sale of Okazu Co.

(ii) With the exception of the bank overdraft, Bento Co has provided all the financing to Okazu Co. No liabilities, except the trade and other payables specified above, will be transferred to the new company when Okazu Co is sold.

(iii) It is estimated that the market value of the non-current assets is 30% higher than the book value and the market value of the current assets is equivalent to the book value.

(iv) The group finance costs and taxation are allocated by Bento Co to all its subsidiaries in pre-agreed proportions.

Okazu Co's senior management team has approached Dofu Co, a venture capital company, about the proposed MBO. Dofu Co has agreed to provide leveraged finance for a 50% equity stake in the new company on the following basis:

(i) $30 million loan in the form of an 8% bond on which interest is payable annually, based on the loan amount outstanding at the start of each year. The bond will be repaid on the basis of fixed equal annual payments (constituting of interest and principal) over the next four years

(ii) $20 million loan in the form of a 6% convertible bond on which interest is payable annually. Conversion may be undertaken on the basis of 50 equity shares for every $100 from the beginning of year five onwards

(iii) 5,000,000 $1 equity shares for $5,000,000.

Okazu Co's senior management will contribute $5,000,000 for 5,000,000 $1 equity shares and own the remaining 50% of the equity stake.

As a condition for providing the finance, Dofu Co will impose a restrictive covenant that the new company's gearing ratio will be no higher than 75% at the end of its first year of operations, and then fall to no higher than 60%, 50% and 40% at the end of year two to year four respectively. The gearing ratio is determined by the book value of debt divided by the combined book values of debt and equity.

After the MBO, it is expected that earnings before interest and tax will increase by 11% per year and annual dividends of 25% on the available earnings will be paid for the next four years. It is expected that the annual growth rate of dividends will reduce by 60% from year five onwards following the MBO. The new company will pay tax at a rate of 20% per year. The new company's cost of equity has been estimated at 12%.

Required:

(a) **Estimate, showing all relevant calculations, whether the restrictive covenant imposed by Dofu Co is likely to be met.** **(12 marks)**

(b) **Discuss, with supporting calculations, whether or not an MBO would be beneficial for Dofu Co and Okazu Co's senior management team.** **(8 marks)**

Professional marks will be awarded for the demonstration of skill in analysis and evaluation, scepticism and commercial acumen in your answer. **(5 marks)**

(Total: 25 marks)

56 FLUFFTORT CO (SEP/DEC 15)

Five years ago the Patel family invested in a new business, Flufftort Co, which manufactures furniture. Some family members became directors of Flufftort Co; others have not been actively involved in management. A venture capital firm, Gupte VC, also made a 20% investment in Flufftort Co. A representative of Gupte VC was appointed to Flufftort Co's board. Flufftort Co also took out a long-term 8.5% bank loan.

Sales have generally been disappointing. As a result, members of the Patel family have been reluctant to invest further in Flufftort Co. Over the last year Gupte VC has taken a tougher attitude towards Flufftort Co. Gupte VC pressurised Flufftort Co to pay a dividend of $2 million for the year ended 30 June 20X5. Gupte VC has also said that if Flufftort Co's financial results do not improve, Gupte VC may exercise its right to compel Flufftort Co to buy back its shares at par on 30 June 20X6.

However, Flufftort Co's most recent product, the Easicushion chair, has been a much bigger success than expected. In order to produce enough Easicushion chairs to affect its results substantially, Flufftort Co will need to make significant expenditure on manufacturing facilities and additional working capital.

Extracts from the statement of profit or loss for year ended 30 June 20X5, and the forecast statement of profit or loss for year ended 30 June 20X6 are presented below:

	20X5	20X6 Forecast
	$m	$m
Operating profit	8.0	6.0
Finance cost	(3.0)	(3.0)
Profit before tax	5.0	3.0
Tax on profits (20%)	(1.0)	(0.6)
Profit for the period	4.0	2.4
Dividends	(2.0)	–
Retained earnings	2.0	2.4

Note: The forecast statement of profit or loss for the year ended 30 June 20X6 is not affected by the proposed investment. This can be assumed only to affect results after 30 June 20X6. The figure shown for retained earnings in the 20X6 forecast can be assumed to be the net increase in cash for the year ended 30 June 20X6.

Summarised statement of financial position as at 30 June 20X5

Assets	$m
Non-current assets	69.0
Current assets excluding cash	18.0
Cash	7.6
Total assets	94.6

Equity and liabilities	
Share capital ($1 shares)	50.0
Retained earnings	2.6
Total equity	52.6

Long-term liabilities	
8.5% Bank loan	30.0
9% Loan note	5.0
Total long-term liabilities	35.0
Current liabilities	7.0
Total liabilities	42.0
Total equity and liabilities	94.6

Notes:

1   55% of shares are owned by the members of the Patel family who are directors, 25% by other members of the Patel family and 20% by Gupte VC.

2   The bank loan is secured on the non-current assets of Flufftort and is due for repayment on 31 December 20X9. The loan is subject to a covenant that the ratio of equity to non-current liabilities should be greater than 1.3 on a book value basis. Flufftort has also been granted an overdraft facility of up to $5 million by its bank.

3   The loan note is held by Rajiv Patel, a member of the Patel family who is not a director. The loan note is unsecured, is subordinated to the bank loan and has no fixed date for repayment.

4   If no finance is available for investment in manufacturing facilities, non-current assets, current assets excluding cash, the bank loan, loan note and current liabilities can be assumed to be the same at 30 June 20X6 as at 30 June 20X5.

However, the chief executive and finance director of Flufftort Co intend to propose that the company should be refinanced to fund the expanded production of the Easicushion chair. They have not yet consulted anyone else about their proposals.

Details of the proposed refinancing are as follows:

1   The members of the Patel family who are directors would subscribe to an additional 15 million $1 shares at par.

2   Gupte VC would subscribe to an additional 20 million $1 shares at par.

3   The 8.5% bank loan would be renegotiated with the bank and the borrowing increased to $65 million, to be repaid on 30 June 2022. The expected finance cost of the loan would be 10% per year.

4   Rajiv Patel's loan note would be replaced by 5 million $1 shares.

5   The refinancing would mean non-current assets would increase to $125 million, current assets other than cash would increase to $42 million and current liabilities would increase to $12 million.

6   Operating profits would be expected to increase to $20 million in the first full year after the facilities are constructed (year ended 30 June 20X7) and $25 million in the second year (year ended 30 June 20X8). No dividends would be paid for these two years, as cash surpluses would be used for further investment as required. Tax on company profits can be assumed to remain at 20%.

Required:

(a)   (i)   Prepare a projected statement of financial position as at 30 June 20X6, on the assumption that Gupte VC exercises its rights and Gupte VC's shares are repurchased and cancelled by Flufftort Co.   (4 marks)

(ii)   Prepare a projected statement of financial position as at 30 June 20X6 on the assumption that the proposed refinancing and investment take place.

(4 marks)

(iii)   Prepare projected statements of profit or loss for the years ended 30 June 20X7 and 30 June 20X8 on the basis that the profit forecasts are correct.

(2 marks)

(b)   Evaluate whether the suggested refinancing scheme is likely to be agreed by all finance providers. State clearly any assumptions which you make.   (10 marks)

Professional marks will be awarded for the demonstration of skill in analysis and evaluation, scepticism and commercial acumen in your answer.   (5 marks)

(Total: 25 marks)

57   STAPLE GROUP (MAR/JUN 16)

Staple Group is one of Barland's biggest media groups. It consists of four divisions, organised as follows:

- **Staple National** – the national newspaper, the Daily Staple. This division's revenues and operating profits have decreased for the last two years.

- **Staple Local** – a portfolio of 18 local and regional newspapers. This division's operating profits have fallen for the last five years and operating profits and cash flows are forecast to be negative in the next financial year. Other newspaper groups with local titles have also reported significant falls in profitability recently.

- **Staple View** – a package of digital channels showing sporting events and programmes for a family audience. Staple Group's board has been pleased with this division's recent performance, but it believes that the division will only be able to sustain a growth rate of 4% in operating profits and cash flows unless it can buy the rights to show more major sporting events. Over the last year, Staple View's biggest competitor in this sector has acquired two smaller digital broadcasters.

- **Staple Investor** – established from a business which was acquired three years ago, this division offers services for investors including research, publications, training events and conferences. The division gained a number of new clients over the last year and has thus shown good growth in revenues and operating profits.

Some of Staple Group's institutional investors have expressed concern about the fall in profitability of the two newspaper divisions.

The following summarised data relates to the group's last accounting year. The % changes in pre-tax profits and revenues are changes in the most recent figures compared with the previous year.

		Division			
	Total	National	Local	View	Investor
Revenues ($m)	1,371.7	602.4	151.7	496.5	121.1
Increase/(decrease) in revenues (%)		(5.1)	(14.7)	8.2	16.5
Pre-tax profits ($m)	177.3	75.6	4.5	73.3	23.9
Increase/(decrease) in pre-tax profits (%)		(4.1)	(12.6)	7.4	19.1
Post-tax cash flows ($m)	120.2	50.7	0.3	53.5	15.7
Share of group net assets ($m)	635.8	267.0	66.6	251.2	51.0
Share of group long-term liabilities ($m)	230.9	104.4	23.1	93.4	10.0

Staple Group's board regards the *Daily Staple* as a central element of the group's future. The directors are currently considering a number of investment plans, including the development of digital platforms for the *Daily Staple*. The finance director has costed the investment programme at $150 million. The board would prefer to fund the investment programme by disposing parts or all of one of the other divisions. The following information is available to help assess the value of each division:

- One of Staple Group's competitors, Postway Co, has contacted Staple Group's directors asking if they would be interested in selling 15 of the local and regional newspapers for $60 million. Staple Group's finance director believes this offer is low and wishes to use the net assets valuation method to evaluate a minimum price for the Staple Local division.

- Staple Group's finance director believes that a valuation using free cash flows would provide a fair estimate of the value of the Staple View division. Over the last year, investment in additional non-current assets for the Staple View division has been $12.5 million and the incremental working capital investment has been $6.2 million. These investment levels will have to increase at 4% annually in order to support the expected sustainable increases in operating profit and cash flow.

- Staple Group's finance director believes that the valuation of the Staple Investor division needs to reflect the potential it derives from the expertise and experience of its staff. The finance director has calculated a value of $118.5 million for this division, based on the earnings made last year but also allowing for the additional earnings which he believes that the expert staff in the division will be able to generate in future years.

Assume a risk-adjusted, all-equity financed, cost of capital of 12% and a tax rate of 30%. Goodwill should be ignored in any calculations.

Staple Group's finance and human resources directors are looking at the staffing of the two newspaper divisions. The finance director proposes dismissing most staff who have worked for the group for less than two years, two years' employment being when staff would be entitled to enhanced statutory employment protection. The finance director also proposes a redundancy programme for longer-serving staff, selecting for redundancy employees who have complained particularly strongly about recent changes in working conditions. There is a commitment in Staple Group's annual report to treat employees fairly, communicate with them regularly and enhance employees' performance by structured development.

Required:

(a) **Evaluate the options for disposing of parts of Staple Group, using the financial information to assess possible disposal prices. The evaluation should include a discussion of the benefits and drawbacks to Staple Group from disposing of parts of the Staple Group.** **(16 marks)**

(b) **Briefly discuss the significance of the finance director's proposals for reduction in staff costs for Staple Group's relationships with its shareholders and employees, and discuss the ethical implications of the proposals.** **(4 marks)**

Professional marks will be awarded for the demonstration of skill in analysis and evaluation, scepticism and commercial acumen in your answer. **(5 marks)**

(Total: 25 marks)

58 EVIEW CINEMAS CO (SEP/DEC 17)

Eview Cinemas Co is a long-established chain of cinemas in the country of Taria. Twenty years ago Eview Cinemas Co's board decided to convert some of its cinemas into sports gyms, known as the EV clubs. The number of EV clubs has expanded since then. Eview Cinemas Co's board brought in outside managers to run the EV clubs, but over the years there have been disagreements between the clubs' managers and the board. The managers have felt that the board has wrongly prioritised investment in, and refurbishment of, the cinemas at the expense of the EV clubs.

Five years ago, Eview Cinemas Co undertook a major refurbishment of its cinemas, financing this work with various types of debt, including loan notes at a high coupon rate of 10%. Shortly after the work was undertaken, Taria entered into a recession which adversely affected profitability. The finance cost burden was high and Eview Cinemas Co was not able to pay a dividend for two years.

The recession is now over and Eview Cinemas Co has emerged in a good financial position, as two of its competitors went into insolvency during the recession. Eview Cinemas Co's board wishes to expand its chain of cinemas and open new, multiscreen cinemas in locations which are available because businesses were closed down during the recession.

In two years' time Taria is due to host a major sports festival. This has encouraged interest in sport and exercise in the country. As a result, some gym chains are looking to expand and have contacted Eview Cinemas Co's board to ask if it would be interested in selling the EV clubs. Most of the directors regard the cinemas as the main business and so are receptive to selling the EV clubs.

Valuation of the EV clubs

The finance director has recommended that the sales price of the EV clubs be based on predicted free cash flows.

The current value, using the current weighted average cost of capital of 12%, and based on an assumption that cash flows will grow at 5.2% per year in perpetuity, is $6,139 million. The finance director believes that the result of the free cash flow valuation will represent a fair value of the EV clubs' business, but Eview Cinemas Co is looking to obtain a 25% premium on the fair value as the expected sales price.

Other information

Other information supplied by the finance director is as follows:

1   The predicted after-tax profits of the EV clubs are $454 million in Year 1. This can be assumed to be 40% of total after-tax profits of EV Cinemas Co.

2   The expected proceeds which Eview Cinemas Co receives from selling the EV clubs will be used firstly to pay off the 10% loan notes. Part of the remaining amount from the sales proceeds will then be used to enhance liquidity by being held as part of current assets, so that the current ratio increases to 1.5. The rest of the remaining amount will be invested in property, plant and equipment. The current net book value of the non-current assets of the EV clubs to be sold can be assumed to be $3,790 million. The profit on the sale of the EV clubs should be taken directly to reserves.

3   Eview Cinemas Co's asset beta for the cinemas can be assumed to be 0.952.

4   Eview Cinemas Co currently has 1,000 million $1 shares in issue. These are currently trading at $15.75 per share. The finance director expects the share price to rise by 10% once the sale has been completed, as he thinks that the stock market will perceive it to be a good deal.

5   Tradeable debt is currently quoted at $96 per $100 for the 10% loan notes and $93 per $100 for the other loan notes. The value of the other loan notes is not expected to change once the sale has been completed. The overall pre-tax cost of debt is currently 9% and can be assumed to fall to 8% when the 10% loan notes are redeemed.

6   The current tax rate on profits is 20%.

7   Additional investment in current assets is expected to earn a 7% pre-tax return and additional investment in property, plant and equipment is expected to earn a 12% pre-tax return.

8   The current risk-free rate is 4% and the return on the market portfolio is 10%.

Eview Cinemas Co's current summarised statement of financial position is shown below. The CEO wants to know the impact the sale of the EV clubs would have immediately on the statement of financial position, the impact on the Year 1 forecast earnings per share and on the weighted average cost of capital.

Assets	$m
Non-current assets	15,621
Current assets	2,347
Total assets	17,968
Equity and liabilities	
Called up share capital	1,000
Retained earnings	7,917
Total equity	8,917
Non-current liabilities	
10% loan notes	3,200
Other loan notes	2,700
Bank loans	985
Total non-current liabilities	6,885
Current liabilities	2,166
Total liabilities	9,051
Total equity and liabilities	17,968

Required:

(a) Calculate the expected sales price of the EV clubs and demonstrate its impact on Eview Cinemas Co's statement of financial position, forecast earnings per share and weighted average cost of capital. **(13 marks)**

(b) Evaluate the decision to sell the EV clubs. **(7 marks)**

Professional marks will be awarded for the demonstration of skill in analysis and evaluation, scepticism and commercial acumen in your answer. **(5 marks)**

(Total: 25 marks)

59 NEWIMBER CO (MAR/JUN 19)

Newimber Co is a listed company which has always manufactured formal clothing for adults and children. It obtained a listing ten years ago after years of steady growth. 70% of shares in the company are owned by its directors or their relatives, with the remaining 30% owned by external investors, including institutional investors.

Sportswear division

Eight years ago it set up a division to manufacture sportswear. This investment has been very successful and the sportswear division now accounts for 40% of total group revenue, having grown much quicker than the original formal clothing division.

Newimber Co's board has given divisional management at the sportswear division more authority over time, although the board has continued to make major policy and investment decisions relating to the division. Initially, relations between Newimber Co's board and management of the sportswear division were good, but there have been problems over the last couple of years. The sportswear division's management has been frustrated by the board's refusal to approve their recent investment plans on the grounds that they were too risky. In order to achieve operational efficiencies, the sportswear division's management would also like to pursue stricter policies for managing operational staff and suppliers than Newimber Co's board has so far allowed.

Restructuring

A few months ago, the management of the sportswear division approached Newimber Co's board with a proposal for a management buyout of the sportswear division. However, the price the sportswear division's management was able to offer was insufficient to persuade Newimber Co's board to sell the sportswear division to them.

Newimber Co's board has, subsequently, decided that the sportswear division should be demerged into a new company, Poynins Co. The shareholders and proportion of shares held would be the same for Poynins Co as currently for Newimber Co. The sportswear division's senior management team would become the board of Poynins Co and Poynins Co would seek an immediate listing on the same stock exchange as Newimber Co.

Financial information

The market capitalisation of Newimber Co's share capital is currently $585 million. Newimber Co also currently has $200 million 5.9% loan notes, whose market value is $220 million. The loan notes are redeemable in five years' time at a premium of 5%. Newimber Co's equity beta is currently estimated at 1.4. Newimber Co's current cost of equity is 11.8% and its current before-tax cost of debt is 4.5%.

The asset beta of the formal clothing division is estimated to be 1.21. The weighting in estimating Newimber Co's overall asset beta is 60% for the formal clothing division to 40% for the sportswear division. The debt beta can be assumed to be zero.

In return for 40% of the issued share capital of Newimber Co, its current shareholders will receive 100% of the issued share capital of Poynins Co, corresponding to the assets and liabilities being transferred. The shares in Newimber Co which shareholders have given up will be cancelled. After the demerger, Newimber Co's new market capitalisation can be assumed to be $351 million. Poynins Co will have no long-term debt, the liability for the $200 million loan notes remaining with Newimber Co.

The current risk-free rate of return is estimated to be 3.4%. The market risk premium is estimated to be 6%. A tax rate of 28% is applicable to all companies.

The sportswear division currently has $36 million operating cash flows. Its managers believe that operating cash flows can increase by the following rates once Poynins Co has been listed:

Year	%
1	25
2	20
3	15
4 onwards	2

The sportswear division's managers believe that Poynins Co will require a $20 million investment of additional assets in Year 1, rising to $22 million in each of Years 2 and 3, and to $25 million annually from Year 4 onwards.

Required:

(a) Discuss the advantages and disadvantages of demerging the sportswear division into a new company. **(4 marks)**

(b) Calculate:

– The change in the weighted average cost of capital of Newimber Co if the demerger of the sportswear division takes place

– The valuation of Poynins Co using free cash flows, based on the information and assumptions given and briefly discuss your results. **(12 marks)**

(c) Discuss the factors which may determine the policies Poynins Co should adopt for communication of information to its shareholders and other significant stakeholders. **(4 marks)**

Professional marks will be awarded for the demonstration of skill in analysis and evaluation, and commercial acumen in your answer. **(5 marks)**

(Total: 25 marks)

60 HANWOOD SHOES CO (SEP/DEC 21)

The following exhibits, available on the left-hand side of the screen (in the CBE exam), provide information relevant to the question.

1 **Hanwood Shoes Co**

2 **Sale of children's shoes division**

3 **Impact and consequences of sale**

4 **Hanwood Shoes Co's SOFP**

This information should be used to answer the question requirements within your chosen response option(s).

Hanwood Shoes Co

Hanwood Shoes Co started trading 40 years ago, manufacturing and selling children's shoes in shops. The shoes have been of higher quality than shoes produced by its competitors, although also more expensive. School shoe sales in particular have been a consistent large generator of cash, helping to fund the company's expansion.

About 15 years ago, Hanwood Shoes Co started manufacturing and selling adults' shoes. Hanwood Shoes Co's adults' shoes are currently sold at a higher profit margin than children's shoes. Adults' shoe sales now generate the majority of Hanwood Shoes Co's profits. The adults' shoes sold are a mixture of formal types with a long lifespan and some fashionable shoes. The inventory turnover period for adults' shoes is, on average, significantly higher than for children's shoes.

Hanwood Shoes Co is organised on the basis of two separate divisions for children's and adults' shoes. Its shops sell either children's shoes or adults' shoes, but not both. Hanwood Shoes Co also sells adult shoes to other retailers.

Five years ago, Hanwood Shoes Co restructured its cost base. It moved production of children's shoes to new facilities in its home country and outsourced the production of adults' shoes to foreign suppliers. However, Hanwood Shoes Co's board now predicts that profits from children's shoes will increase at a slower rate than adults' shoes. It expects that in the next few years, a greater share of the children's shoes market will be taken by companies with a lower cost base.

Hanwood Shoes Co's board is aware that it must convince investors that any major strategic changes it makes will result in an increase in earnings per share. Investors will also consider a change in earnings per share against any change in the business risk profile of the company.

Sale of children's shoes division

Hanwood Shoes Co's board wishes to improve the company's cash position for two reasons. First, loan notes of $175m nominal value are due to be redeemed in just over a year's time. The board is unwilling to seek renewed loan funding because the terms would not be favourable and some investors have expressed concern about gearing levels. Second, Hanwood Shoes Co has recently been slow to pay some of its suppliers of adults' shoes. One major supplier recently delayed delivery of shoes to Hanwood Shoes Co until it was paid for previous deliveries.

Hanwood Shoes Co's chief executive proposed that the company should in future only sell adults' shoes and should sell the children's shoes division. He believed from industry contacts that at least three children's clothing manufacturers, looking to expand their product range, would be interested. The finance director suggested that the proceeds from the sale of the division could first be used to pay off the loan notes. It would then be used to increase cash held and thus improve liquidity. The remaining proceeds would be invested in the adults' shoes division to improve earnings per share.

Impact and consequences of sale

1. The sales price of the children's shoes division will be the sum of the present value of predicted future free cash flows. The discount rate to be used is 10%.

2. The predicted after-tax free cash flows of the children's shoes division ($m) are as follows:

Year	1	2	3	4
	$m	$m	$m	$m
	76	81	85	88

3. The predicted after-tax profits of the children's shoes division in Year 1 can be assumed to be $76m. The total after-tax profits for Hanwood Shoes Co for Year 1 if the children's shoe division is not sold is predicted to be $217m.

4. After Year 4, free cash flows for the children's shoes division should be assumed to increase at a rate of 3.5% per year.

5. The proceeds received for selling the children's shoes division would be used first to pay off the 9% loan notes. Part of the remaining amount from the sales proceeds will be held as part of current assets, so that the current ratio increases to 1.4. The rest of the sale proceeds will be invested in non-current assets.

6. The profit on the sale of the children's shoes division should be taken directly to reserves.

7. The non-current assets of the children's shoes division can be assumed to be $608m and the current assets can be assumed to be $349m.

8. Additional investment in non-current assets is expected to earn an 18% pre-tax return and additional investment in current assets is expected to earn a 6% pre-tax return.

9. Tax is payable at an annual rate of 20% on profits.

Hanwood Shoes Co's SOFP

Hanwood Shoes Co's current statement of financial position:

	$m
Non-current assets	1,200
Current assets	909
	————
Total assets	2,109
	————
Called up share capital	50
Reserves	737
	————
Total equity	787
	————
Non-current liabilities	
9% loan notes	175
7% loan notes	145
Bank loans	108
	————
Total non-current liabilities	428
	————
Current liabilities	894
	————
Total equity and liabilities	2,109
	————

Required:

(a)   Calculate the expected sales price of the children's shoes division and demonstrate its impact on Hanwood Shoes Co's statement of financial position and forecast earnings per share.   **(13 marks)**

(b)   Discuss whether Hanwood Shoes Co's investors are likely to be satisfied with the proposed sale of the children's shoes division and its consequences for profits and funding.   **(7 marks)**

Professional marks will be awarded for the demonstration of skill in analysis and evaluation, scepticism and commercial acumen in your answer.   **(5 marks)**

(Total: 25 marks)

TREASURY AND ADVANCED RISK MANAGEMENT TECHNIQUES

61 LEVANTE CO (DEC 11)

Levante Co has identified a new project for which it will need to increase its long-term borrowings from $250 million to $400 million. This amount will cover a significant proportion of the total cost of the project and the rest of the funds will come from cash held by the company.

The current $250 million borrowing is in the form of a 4% bond which is trading at $98.71 per $100 and is due to be redeemed at par in three years. The issued bond has a credit rating of AA. The new borrowing will also be raised in the form of a traded bond with a nominal value of $100 per unit. It is anticipated that the new project will generate sufficient cash flows to be able to redeem the new bond at $100 nominal value per unit in five years. It can be assumed that coupons on both bonds are paid annually.

Both bonds would be ranked equally for payment in the event of default and the directors expect that as a result of the new issue, the credit rating for both bonds will fall to A. The directors are considering the following two alternative options when issuing the new bond:

(i)   Issue the new bond at a fixed coupon of 5% but at a premium or discount, whichever is appropriate to ensure full take up of the bond; or

(ii)   Issue the new bond at a coupon rate where the issue price of the new bond will be $100 per unit and equal to its nominal value.

The following extracts are provided on the current government bond yield curve and yield spreads for the sector in which Levante Co operates:

Current Government Bond Yield Curve

Years	1	2	3	4	5
	3.2%	3.7%	4.2%	4.8%	5.0%

Yield spreads (in basis points)

Bond Rating	1 year	2 years	3 years	4 years	5 years
AAA	5	9	14	19	25
AA	16	22	30	40	47
A	65	76	87	100	112
BBB	102	121	142	167	193

Required:

(a)   Calculate the expected percentage fall in the market value of the existing bond if Levante Co's bond credit rating falls from AA to A.   **(3 marks)**

(b)   Advise the directors on the financial implications of choosing each of the two options when issuing the new bond. Support the advice with appropriate calculations.   **(8 marks)**

(c)   Among the criteria used by credit agencies for establishing a company's credit rating are the following: industry risk, earnings protection, financial flexibility and evaluation of the company's management.

Briefly explain each criterion and suggest factors that could be used to assess it.   **(9 marks)**

Professional marks will be awarded for the demonstration of skill in analysis and evaluation, and commercial acumen in your answer.   **(5 marks)**

(Total: 25 marks)

62 SEMBILAN CO (JUN 12)

Sembilan Co, a listed company, recently issued debt finance to acquire assets in order to increase its activity levels. This debt finance is in the form of a floating rate bond, with a face value of $320 million, redeemable in four years. The bond interest, payable annually, is based on the spot yield curve plus 60 basis points. The next annual payment is due at the end of year one.

Sembilan Co is concerned that the expected rise in interest rates over the coming few years would make it increasingly difficult to pay the interest due. It is therefore proposing to either swap the floating rate interest payment to a fixed rate payment, or to raise new equity capital and use that to pay off the floating rate bond. The new equity capital would either be issued as rights to the existing shareholders or as shares to new shareholders.

Ratus Bank has offered Sembilan Co an interest rate swap, whereby Sembilan Co would pay Ratus Bank interest based on an equivalent fixed annual rate of 3.76¼% in exchange for receiving a variable amount based on the current yield curve rate. Payments and receipts will be made at the end of each year, for the next four years. Ratus Bank will charge an annual fee of 20 basis points if the swap is agreed.

The current annual spot yield curve rates are as follows:

Year	One	Two	Three	Four
Rate	2.5%	3.1%	3.5%	3.8%

The current annual forward rates for years two, three and four are as follows:

Year	Two	Three	Four
Rate	3.7%	4.3%	4.7%

Required:

(a) Based on the above information, calculate the amounts Sembilan Co expects to pay or receive every year on the swap (excluding the fee of 20 basis points). Explain why the fixed annual rate of interest of 3.76¼% is less than the four-year yield curve rate of 3.8%. **(6 marks)**

(b) Demonstrate that Sembilan Co's interest payment liability does not change, after it has undertaken the swap, whether the interest rates increase or decrease.

(5 marks)

(c) Discuss the factors that Sembilan Co should consider when deciding whether it should raise equity capital to pay off the floating rate debt. **(9 marks)**

Professional marks will be awarded for the demonstration of skill in analysis and evaluation, and commercial acumen in your answer. **(5 marks)**

(Total: 25 marks)

63 PAULT CO (SEP/DEC 16)

Pault Co is currently undertaking a major programme of product development. Pault Co has made a significant investment in plant and machinery for this programme. Over the next couple of years, Pault Co has also budgeted for significant development and launch costs for a number of new products, although its finance director believes there is some uncertainty with these budgeted figures, as they will depend upon competitor activity amongst other matters.

Pault Co issued floating rate loan notes, with a face value of $400 million, to fund the investment in plant and machinery. The loan notes are redeemable in ten years' time. The interest on the loan notes is payable annually and is based on the spot yield curve, plus 50 basis points.

Pault Co's finance director has recently completed a review of the company's overall financing strategy. His review has highlighted expectations that interest rates will increase over the next few years, although the predictions of financial experts in the media differ significantly.

The finance director is concerned about the exposure Pault Co has to increases in interest rates through the loan notes. He has therefore discussed with Millbridge Bank the possibility of taking out a four-year interest rate swap. The proposed terms are that Pault Co would pay Millbridge Bank interest based on an equivalent fixed annual rate of 4.847%. In return, Pault Co would receive from Millbridge Bank a variable amount based on the forward rates calculated from the annual spot yield curve rate at the time of payment minus 20 basis points. Payments and receipts would be made annually, with the first one in a year's time. Millbridge Bank would charge an annual fee of 25 basis points if Pault Co enters the swap.

The current annual spot yield curve rates are as follows:

Year	One	Two	Three	Four
Rate	3.70%	4.25%	4.70%	5.10%

A number of concerns were raised at the recent board meeting when the swap arrangement was discussed.

- Pault Co's chair wondered what the value of the swap arrangement to Pault Co was, and whether the value would change over time.

- One of Pault Co's non-executive directors objected to the arrangement, saying that in his opinion the interest rate which Pault Co would pay and the bank charges were too high. Pault Co ought to stick with its floating rate commitment. Investors would be critical if, at the end of four years, Pault Co had paid higher costs under the swap than it would have done had it left the loan unhedged.

Required:

(a) (i) Using the current annual spot yield curve rates as the basis for estimating forward rates, calculate the amounts Pault Co expects to pay or receive each year under the swap (excluding the fee of 25 basis points). **(6 marks)**

(ii) Calculate Pault Co's interest payment liability for Year 1 if the yield curve rate is 4.5% or 2.9%, and comment on your results. **(6 marks)**

(b) Advise the chair on the current value of the swap to Pault Co and the factors which would change the value of the swap. **(3 marks)**

(c) Briefly discuss the disadvantages and advantages to Pault Co of not undertaking a swap and being liable to pay interest at floating rates. **(5 marks)**

Professional marks will be awarded for the demonstration of skill in analysis and evaluation, and commercial acumen in your answer. **(5 marks)**

(Total: 25 marks)

64 LIGNUM CO (DEC 12)

Lignum Co, a large listed company, manufactures agricultural machines and equipment for different markets around the world. Although its main manufacturing base is in France and it uses the Euro (€) as its base currency, it also has a few subsidiary companies around the world. Lignum Co's treasury division is considering how to approach the following three cases of foreign exchange exposure that it faces.

Case One

Lignum Co regularly trades with companies based in Zuhait, a small country in South America whose currency is the Zupesos (ZP). It recently sold machinery for ZP140 million, which it is about to deliver to a company based there. It is expecting full payment for the machinery in four months. Although there are no exchange traded derivative products available for the Zupesos, Medes Bank has offered Lignum Co a choice of two over-the-counter derivative products.

The first derivative product is an over-the-counter forward rate determined on the basis of the Zuhait base rate of 8.5% plus 25 basis points and the French base rate of 2.2% less 30 basis points.

Alternatively, with the second derivative product Lignum Co can purchase either Euro call or put options from Medes Bank at an exercise price equivalent to the current spot exchange rate of ZP142 per €1. The option premiums offered are: ZP7 per €1 for the call option or ZP5 per €1 for the put option.

The premium cost is payable in full at the commencement of the option contract. Lignum Co can borrow money at the base rate plus 150 basis points and invest money at the base rate minus 100 basis points in France.

Case Two

Namel Co is Lignum Co's subsidiary company based in Maram, a small country in Asia, whose currency is the Maram Ringit (MR). The current pegged exchange rate between the Maram Ringit and the Euro is MR35 per €1. Due to economic difficulties in Maram over the last couple of years, it is very likely that the Maram Ringit will devalue by 20% imminently. Namel Co is concerned about the impact of the devaluation on its Statement of Financial Position.

Given below is an extract from the current Statement of Financial Position of Namel Co.

	MR '000
Non-current assets	179,574
Current assets	146,622
Total assets	326,196
Share capital and reserves	102,788
Non-current liabilities	132,237
Current liabilities	91,171
Total capital and liabilities	326,196

The current assets consist of inventories, receivables and cash. Receivables account for 40% of the current assets. All the receivables relate to sales made to Lignum Co in Euro. About 70% of the current liabilities consist of payables relating to raw material inventory purchased from Lignum Co and payable in Euro. 80% of the non-current liabilities consist of a Euro loan and the balance are borrowings sourced from financial institutions in Maram.

Case Three

Lignum Co manufactures a range of farming vehicles in France which it sells within the European Union to countries which use the Euro. Over the previous few years, it has found that its sales revenue from these products has been declining and the sales director is of the opinion that this is entirely due to the strength of the Euro. Lignum Co's biggest competitor in these products is based in the USA and US$ rate has changed from almost parity with the Euro three years ago, to the current value of US$1.47 for €1. The agreed opinion is that the US$ will probably continue to depreciate against the Euro, but possibly at a slower rate, for the foreseeable future.

Required:

(a) Explain briefly the type of currency exposure Lignum Co faces for each of the above cases. **(3 marks)**

(b) Recommend which of the two derivative products Lignum Co should use to manage its exposure in case one and advise on alternative hedging strategies that could be used. Show all relevant calculations. **(10 marks)**

(c) Compute the gain or loss on Namel Co's Statement of Financial Position, due to the devaluation of the Maram Ringit in case two, and discuss whether and how this exposure should be managed. **(7 marks)**

Professional marks will be awarded for the demonstration of skill in analysis and evaluation, and commercial acumen in your answer. **(5 marks)**

(Total: 25 marks)

65 ALECTO CO (DEC 11)

Alecto Co, a large listed company based in Europe, is expecting to borrow €22,000,000 in four months' time on 1 May 20X2. It expects to make a full repayment of the borrowed amount nine months from now. Currently there is some uncertainty in the markets, with higher than normal rates of inflation, but an expectation that the inflation level may soon come down. This has led some economists to predict a rise in interest rates and others suggesting an unchanged outlook or maybe even a small fall in interest rates over the next six months.

Although Alecto Co is of the opinion that it is equally likely that interest rates could increase or fall by 0.5% in four months, it wishes to protect itself from interest rate fluctuations by using derivatives. The company can borrow at ESTER plus 80 basis points and ESTER is currently 3.3%. The company is considering using interest rate futures, options on interest rate futures or interest rate collars as possible hedging choices.

The following information and quotes from an appropriate exchange are provided on Euro futures and options. Margin requirements may be ignored.

Three month Euro futures, €1,000,000 contract, tick size 0.01% and tick value €25.

March 96.27

June 96.16

September 95.90

Options on three month Euro futures, €1,000,000 contract, tick size 0.01% and tick value €25. Option premiums are in annual %.

	Calls		Strike		Puts	
March	June	September		March	June	September
0.279	0.391	0.446	96.00	0.006	0.163	0.276
0.012	0.090	0.263	96.50	0.196	0.581	0.754

It can be assumed that settlement for both the futures and options contracts is at the end of the month. It can also be assumed that basis diminishes to zero at contract maturity at a constant rate and that time intervals can be counted in months.

Required:

(a) **Briefly discuss the main advantage and disadvantage of hedging interest rate risk using an interest rate collar instead of options.** **(4 marks)**

(b) **Based on the three hedging choices Alecto Co is considering and assuming that the company does not face any basis risk, recommend a hedging strategy for the €22,000,000 loan. Support your recommendation with appropriate comments and relevant calculations in €.** **(16 marks)**

Professional marks will be awarded for the demonstration of skill in analysis and evaluation, and commercial acumen in your answer. **(5 marks)**

(Total: 25 marks)

66   KENDURI CO (JUN 13)

Kenduri Co is a large multinational company based in the UK with a number of subsidiary companies around the world. Currently, foreign exchange exposure as a result of transactions between Kenduri Co and its subsidiary companies is managed by each company individually. Kenduri Co is considering whether or not to manage the foreign exchange exposure using multilateral netting from the UK, with the Sterling Pound (£) as the base currency. If multilateral netting is undertaken, spot mid-rates would be used.

The following cash flows are due in three months between Kenduri Co and three of its subsidiary companies. The subsidiary companies are Lakama Co, based in the United States (currency US$), Jaia Co, based in Canada (currency CAD) and Gochiso Co, based in Japan (currency JPY).

Owed by	Owed to	Amount
Kenduri Co	Lakama Co	US$ 4.5 million
Kenduri Co	Jaia Co	CAD 1.1 million
Gochiso Co	Jaia Co	CAD 3.2 million
Gochiso Co	Lakama Co	US$ 1.4 million
Jaia Co	Lakama Co	US$ 1.5 million
Jaia Co	Kenduri Co	CAD 3.4 million
Lakama Co	Gochiso Co	JPY 320 million
Lakama Co	Kenduri Co	US$ 2.1 million

Exchange rates available to Kenduri Co

	US$/£1	CAD/£1	JPY/£1
Spot	1.5938–1.5962	1.5690–1.5710	131.91–133.59
3-month forward	1.5996–1.6037	1.5652–1.5678	129.15–131.05

Therefore, the spot mid-rates which should be used in the multilateral netting calculations are: US$1.5950/£1; CAD1.5700/£1; JPY132.75/£1

Currency options available to Kenduri Co Contract size £62,500, Exercise price quotation: US$/£1, Premium: cents per £1

	Call Options		Put Options	
Exercise price	3-month expiry	6-month expiry	3-month expiry	6-month expiry
1.60	1.55	2.25	2.08	2.23
1.62	0.98	1.58	3.42	3.73

It can be assumed that option contracts expire at the end of the relevant month

Annual interest rates available to Kenduri Co and subsidiaries

	Borrowing rate	Investing rate
UK	4.0%	2.8%
United States	4.8%	3.1%
Canada	3.4%	2.1%
Japan	2.2%	0.5%

Required:

(a)   Advise Kenduri Co on, and recommend, an appropriate hedging strategy for the US$ cash flows it is due to receive or pay in three months, from Lakama Co. Show all relevant calculations to support the advice given.   **(11 marks)**

(b)   Calculate, using a tabular format (transactions matrix), the impact of undertaking multilateral netting by Kenduri Co and its three subsidiary companies for the cash flows due in three months. Briefly discuss why some governments allow companies to undertake multilateral netting, while others do not.   **(9 marks)**

Professional marks will be awarded for the demonstration of skill in analysis and evaluation, scepticism and commercial acumen in your answer.   **(5 marks)**

(Total: 25 marks)

67   AWAN CO (DEC 13)

Awan Co is expecting to receive $48,000,000 on 1 February 20X4, which will be invested until it is required for a large project on 1 June 20X4. Due to uncertainty in the markets, the company is of the opinion that it is likely that interest rates will fluctuate significantly over the coming months, although it is difficult to predict whether they will increase or decrease.

Awan Co's treasury team want to hedge the company against adverse movements in interest rates using either forward rate agreements (FRAs), interest rate futures or options on interest rate futures.

Awan Co can invest funds at the relevant inter-bank rate less 20 basis points. The current inter-bank rate is 4.09%. However, Awan Co is of the opinion that interest rates could increase or decrease by as much as 0.9% over the coming months.

The following information and quotes are provided from an appropriate exchange on $ futures and options. Margin requirements can be ignored.

Three-month $ futures, $2,000,000 contract size

Prices are quoted in basis points at 100 – annual % yield

December 20X3:   94.80
March 20X4:   94.76
June 20X4:   94.69

Options on three-month $ futures, $2,000,000 contract size, option premiums are in annual %

Calls			Strike	Puts		
December	March	June		December	March	June
0.342	0.432	0.523	94.50	0.090	0.119	0.271
0.097	0.121	0.289	95.00	0.312	0.417	0.520

Voblaka Bank has offered the following FRA rates to Awan Co:

1–7: 4.37%

3–4: 4.78%

3–7: 4.82%

4–7: 4.87%

It can be assumed that settlement for the futures and options contracts is at the end of the month and that basis diminishes to zero at contract maturity at a constant rate, based on monthly time intervals. Assume that it is 1 November 20X3 now and that there is no basis risk.

Required:

Based on the three hedging choices Awan Co is considering, recommend a hedging strategy for the $48,000,000 investment, if interest rates increase or decrease by 0.9%. Support your answer with appropriate calculations and discussion. (20 marks)

Professional marks will be awarded for the demonstration of skill in analysis and evaluation, scepticism and commercial acumen in your answer. (5 marks)

(Total: 25 marks)

68 CMC CO (JUN 14)

Cocoa-Mocha-Chai (CMC) Co is a large listed company based in Switzerland and uses Swiss Francs as its currency. It imports tea, coffee and cocoa from countries around the world, and sells its blended products to supermarkets and large retailers worldwide. The company has production facilities located in two European ports where raw materials are brought for processing, and from where finished products are shipped out. All raw material purchases are paid for in US dollars (US$), while all sales are invoiced in Swiss Francs (CHF).

The company's board of directors (BoD) has been reviewing its risk management strategies, and is considering hedging the following two transactions:

(i)   a payment of US$5,060,000 which is due in four months' time; and

(ii)   a four-year CHF60,000,000 loan taken out to fund the setting up of four new production facilities. Interest will be payable on the loan at a fixed annual rate of 2.2% or a floating annual rate based on the yield curve rate plus 0.40%. The loan's principal amount will be repayable in full at the end of the fourth year.

Additional information

The current spot rate is US$1.0635 per CHF1. The current annual inflation rate in the USA is three times higher than Switzerland.

The following derivative products are available to CMC Co to manage the exposures of the US$ payment and the interest on the loan:

Exchange-traded currency futures

Contract size CHF125,000 price quotation: US$ per CHF1

3-month expiry   1.0647

6-month expiry   1.0659

Exchange-traded currency options

Contract size CHF125,000, exercise price quotation: US$ per CHF1, premium: cents per CHF1

	Call Options		Put Options	
Exercise price	3-month expiry	6-month expiry	3-month expiry	6-month expiry
1.06	1.87	2.75	1.41	2.16
1.07	1.34	2.22	1.88	2.63

It can be assumed that futures and option contracts expire at the end of the month and transaction costs related to these can be ignored.

Over-the-counter products

In addition to the exchange-traded products, Pecunia Bank is willing to offer the following over-the-counter derivative products to CMC Co:

(i)   A forward rate between the US$ and the CHF of US$ 1.0677 per CHF1.

(ii)   An interest rate swap contract with a counterparty, where the counterparty can borrow at an annual floating rate based on the yield curve rate plus 0.8% or an annual fixed rate of 3.8%. Pecunia Bank would charge a fee of 20 basis points each to act as the intermediary of the swap. Both parties will benefit equally from the swap contract.

Required:

(a)   **Advise CMC Co on an appropriate hedging strategy to manage the foreign exchange exposure of the US$ payment in four months' time. Show all relevant calculations, including the number of contracts bought or sold in the exchange-traded derivative markets.** (14 marks)

(b)   **Demonstrate how CMC Co could benefit from the swap offered by Pecunia Bank.**
(6 marks)

Professional marks will be awarded for the demonstration of skill in analysis and evaluation, scepticism and commercial acumen in your answer. (5 marks)

(Total: 25 marks)

69 KESHI CO (DEC 14)

Keshi Co is a large multinational company with a number of international subsidiary companies. A centralised treasury department manages Keshi Co and its subsidiaries' borrowing requirements, cash surplus investment and financial risk management. Financial risk is normally managed using conventional derivative products such as forwards, futures, options and swaps.

Assume it is 1 December 20X4 today and Keshi Co is expecting to borrow $18,000,000 on 1 February 20X5 for a period of seven months. It can either borrow the funds at a variable rate of SOFR plus 40 basis points or a fixed rate of 5.5%. SOFR is currently 3.8% but Keshi Co feels that this could increase or decrease by 0.5% over the coming months due to increasing uncertainty in the markets.

The treasury department is considering whether or not to hedge the $18,000,000, using either exchange-traded March options or over-the-counter swaps offered by Rozu Bank.

The following information and quotes for $ March options are provided from an appropriate exchange. The options are based on three-month $ futures, $1,000,000 contract size and option premiums are in annual %.

March calls	Strike price	March puts
0.882	95.50	0.662
0.648	96.00	0.902

Option prices are quoted in basis points at 100 minus the annual % yield and settlement of the options contracts is at the end of March 20X5. The current basis on the March futures price is 44 points; and it is expected to be 33 points on 1 January 20X5, 22 points on 1 February 20X5 and 11 points on 1 March 20X5.

Rozu Bank has offered Keshi Co a swap on a counterparty variable rate of SOFR plus 30 basis points or a fixed rate of 4.6%, where Keshi Co receives 70% of any benefits accruing from undertaking the swap, prior to any bank charges. Rozu Bank will charge Keshi Co 10 basis points for the swap.

Suisen Co is a subsidiary of Keshi Co. It operates in a country where most companies conduct business activities based on Islamic finance principles. It produces confectionery products including chocolates. It wants to use Salam contracts instead of commodity futures contracts to hedge its exposure to price fluctuations of cocoa. Salam contracts involve a commodity which is sold based on currently agreed prices, quantity and quality. Full payment is received by the seller immediately, for an agreed delivery to be made in the future.

Required:

(a)   **Based on the two hedging choices Keshi Co is considering, recommend a hedging strategy for the $18,000,000 borrowing. Support your answer with appropriate calculations and discussion.**   **(16 marks)**

(b)   **Discuss the key differences between a Salam contract, under Islamic finance principles, and futures contracts.**   **(4 marks)**

Professional marks will be awarded for the demonstration of skill in analysis and evaluation, scepticism and commercial acumen in your answer.   **(5 marks)**

(Total: 25 marks)

70   DAIKON CO (JUN 15)

For a number of years Daikon Co has been using forward rate agreements to manage its exposure to interest rate fluctuations. Recently its chief executive officer (CEO) attended a talk on using exchange-traded derivative products to manage risks. She wants to find out by how much the extra cost of the borrowing detailed below can be reduced, when using interest rate futures, options on interest rate futures, and a collar on the options, to manage the interest rate risk. She asks that detailed calculations for each of the three derivative products be provided and a reasoned recommendation to be made.

Daikon Co is expecting to borrow $34,000,000 in five months' time. It expects to make a full repayment of the borrowed amount in 11 months' time. Assume it is 1 June 20X5 today. Daikon Co can borrow funds at SOFR plus 70 basis points. SOFR is currently 3.6%, but Daikon Co expects that interest rates may increase by as much as 80 basis points in five months' time.

The following information and quotes from an appropriate exchange are provided on SOFR based $ futures and options.

Three-month $ December futures are currently quoted at 95.84. The contract size is $1,000,000, the tick size is 0.01% and the tick value is $25.

Options on three-month $ futures, $1,000,000 contract, tick size 0.01% and tick value $25. Option premiums are in annual %.

December calls	Strike price	December puts
0.541	95.50	0.304
0.223	96.00	0.508

Initial assumptions

It can be assumed that settlement for both the futures and options contracts is at the end of the month; that basis diminishes to zero at a constant rate until the contract matures and time intervals can be counted in months; that margin requirements may be ignored; and that if the options are in-the-money, they will exercised at the end of the hedge instead of being sold.

Further issue – marking to market

In the talk, the CEO was also informed of the following issue.

Futures contracts will be marked-to-market daily. The CEO wondered what the impact of this would be if 50 futures contracts were bought at 95.84 on 1 June and 30 futures contracts were sold at 95.61 on 3 June, based on the $ December futures contract given above. The closing settlement prices are given below for four days:

Date	Settlement price
1 June	95.84
2 June	95.76
3 June	95.66
4 June	95.74

Required:

(a)   Based on the three hedging choices available to Daikon Co and the initial assumptions given above, draft a response to the chief executive officer's (CEO) request made in the first paragraph of the question.   **(15 marks)**

(b)   Discuss the impact on Daikon Co of the further issue detailed above. As part of the discussion, include the calculations of the daily impact of the mark-to-market closing prices on the transactions specified by the CEO.   **(5 marks)**

Professional marks will be awarded for the demonstration of skill in analysis and evaluation, scepticism and commercial acumen in your answer.   **(5 marks)**

(Total: 25 marks)

71   THE ARMSTRONG GROUP (SEP/DEC 15)

The Armstrong Group is a multinational group of companies. Today is 1 September. The treasury manager at Massie Co, one of Armstrong Group's subsidiaries based in Europe, has just received notification from the group's head office that it intends to introduce a system of netting to settle balances owed within the group every six months. Previously inter-group indebtedness was settled between the two companies concerned.

The predicted balances owing to, and owed by, the group companies at the end of February are as follows:

Owed by	Owed to	Local currency million (m)
Armstrong (USA)	Horan (South Africa)	US $12.17
Horan (South Africa)	Massie (Europe)	SA R42.65
Giffen (Denmark)	Armstrong (USA)	D Kr21.29
Massie (Europe)	Armstrong (USA)	US $19.78
Armstrong (USA)	Massie (Europe)	€1.57
Horan (South Africa)	Giffen (Denmark)	D Kr16.35
Giffen (Denmark)	Massie (Europe)	€1.55

The predicted exchange rates, used in the calculations of the balances to be settled, are as follows:

	D Kr	US$	SAR	€
1 D Kr =	1.0000	0.1823	1.9554	0.1341
1 US $ =	5.4855	1.0000	10.7296	0.7358
1 SA R =	0.5114	0.0932	1.0000	0.0686
1 € =	7.4571	1.3591	14.5773	1.0000

Settlement will be made in dollars, the currency of Armstrong Group, the parent company. Settlement will be made in the order that the company owing the largest net amount in dollars will first settle with the company owed the smallest net amount in dollars.

Note: D Kr is Danish Krone, SA R is South African Rand, US $ is United States dollar and € is Euro.

Required:

(a)   Calculate the inter-group transfers which are forecast to occur for the next period.
                                                                                    (7 marks)

The most significant transaction which Massie Co is due to undertake with a company outside the Armstrong Group in the next six months is that it is due to receive €25 million from Bardsley Co on 30 November. Massie Co's treasury manager intends to invest this money for the six months until 31 May, when it will be used to fund some major capital expenditure. However, the treasury manager is concerned about changes in interest rates. Predictions in the media range from a 0.5% rise in interest rates to a 0.5% fall.

Because of the uncertainty, the treasury manager has decided to protect Massie Co by using derivatives. The treasury manager wishes to take advantage of favourable interest rate movements. Therefore she is considering options on interest rate futures or interest rate collars as possible methods of hedging, but not interest rate futures. Massie Co can invest at ESTER minus 40 basis points and ESTER is currently 3.6%.

The treasury manager has obtained the following information on Euro futures and options. She is ignoring margin requirements.

Three-month Euro futures, €1,000,000 contract, tick size 0.01% and tick value €25.

September	95.94
December	95.76
March	95.44

Options on three-month Euro futures, €1,000,000 contract, tick size 0.01% and tick value €25. Option premiums are in annual %.

Calls			Strike	Puts		
September	December	March		September	December	March
0.113	0.182	0.245	96.50	0.002	0.123	0.198
0.017	0.032	0.141	97.00	0.139	0.347	0.481

It can be assumed that settlement for the contracts is at the end of the month. It can also be assumed that basis diminishes to zero at contract maturity at a constant rate and that time intervals can be counted in months.

Required:

(b)   Based on the choice of options on futures or collars which Massie Co is considering and assuming the company does not face any basis risk, recommend a hedging strategy for the €25 million receipt. Support your recommendations with appropriate comments and relevant calculations.
                                                                                    (13 marks)

Professional marks will be awarded for the demonstration of skill in analysis and evaluation, scepticism and commercial acumen in your answer.
                                                                                    (5 marks)

                                                                                    (Total: 25 marks)

72   BURYECS CO (MAR/JUN 17)

Buryecs Co is an international transport operator based in the Eurozone which has been invited to take over a rail operating franchise in Wirtonia, where the local currency is the dollar ($). Previously this franchise was run by a local operator in Wirtonia but its performance was unsatisfactory and the government in Wirtonia withdrew the franchise.

Buryecs Co will pay $5,000 million for the rail franchise immediately. The government has stated that Buryecs Co should make an annual income from the franchise of $600 million in each of the next three years. At the end of the three years the government in Wirtonia has offered to buy the franchise back for $7,500 million if no other operator can be found to take over the franchise. Today's spot exchange rate between the Euro and Wirtonia $ is €0.1430 = $1. The predicted inflation rates are as follows:

Year	1	2	3
Eurozone	6%	4%	3%
Wirtonia	3%	8%	11%

Buryecs Co's finance director (FD) has contacted its bankers with a view to arranging a currency swap, since he believes that this will be the best way to manage financial risks associated with the franchise. The swap would be for the initial fee paid for the franchise, with a swap of principal immediately and in three years' time, both these swaps being at today's spot rate. Buryecs Co's bank would charge an annual fee of 0.5% in € for arranging the swap. Buryecs Co would take 60% of any benefit of the swap before deducting bank fees, but would then have to pay 60% of the bank fees.

Relevant borrowing rates are:

	Buryecs Co	Counterparty
Eurozone	4.0%	5.8%
Wirtonia	Wirtonia bank rate + 0.6%	Wirtonia bank rate + 0.4%

In order to provide Buryecs Co's board with an alternative hedging method to consider, the FD has obtained the following information about over-the-counter options in Wirtonia $ from the company's bank.

The exercise price quotation is in Wirtonia $ per €1, premium is % of amount hedged, translated at today's spot rate.

Exercise price	Call options	Put options
7.75	2.8%	1.6%
7.25	1.8%	2.7%

Assume a discount rate of 14%.

Required:

(a) (i)   Calculate the annual percentage interest saving which Buryecs Co could make from using a currency swap, compared with borrowing directly in Wirtonia, demonstrating how the currency swap will work.   **(4 marks)**

(ii)   Evaluate, using net present value, the financial acceptability of Buryecs Co operating the rail franchise under the terms suggested by the government of Wirtonia and calculate the gain or loss in € from using the swap arrangement.

(8 marks)

(b)   Calculate the results of hedging the receipt of $7,500 million using the currency options and discuss whether currency options would be a better method of hedging this receipt than a currency swap.   **(8 marks)**

Professional marks will be awarded for the demonstration of skill in analysis and evaluation, and commercial acumen in your answer.   **(5 marks)**

(Total: 25 marks)

73 THE ADVERANE GROUP (MAR/JUN 18)

The Adverane Group is a multinational group of companies with its headquarters in Switzerland. The Adverane Group consists of a number of fully-owned subsidiaries and Elted Co, an associate company based in the USA in which Adverane Group owns 30% of the ordinary equity share capital. Balances owing between the parent, Adverane Co, and its subsidiaries and between subsidiaries are settled by multilateral netting. Transactions between the parent and Elted Co are settled separately.

Transactions with Elted Co

Adverane Co wishes to hedge transactions with Elted Co which are due to be settled in four months' time in US$. Adverane Co will owe Elted Co US$3.7 million for a major purchase of supplies and Elted Co will owe Adverane Co US$10.15 million for non-current assets. Adverane Group's treasury department is considering whether to use money markets or exchange-traded currency futures for hedging.

Annual interest rates available to Adverane Co

	Investing rate	Borrowing rate
Switzerland	2.7%	3.9%
USA	2.5%	3.7%

Exchange traded currency futures

Contract size CHF125,000, price quotation US$ per CHF1

Three-month expiry: 1.1213

Six-month expiry: 1.1204

Netting

The balances owed to and owed by members of Adverane Group when netting is to take place are as follows:

Owed by	Owed to	Local currency
		m
Adverane (Switzerland)	Bosha (Eurozone)	CHF15.90
Adverane (Switzerland)	Diling (Brazil)	CHF4.46
Bosha (Eurozone)	Cogate (USA)	€24.89
Bosha (Eurozone)	Diling (Brazil)	€18.57
Cogate (USA)	Adverane (Switzerland)	US$27.08
Cogate (USA)	Diling (Brazil)	US$5.68
Diling (Brazil)	Adverane (Switzerland)	BRL38.80
Diling (Brazil)	Bosha (Eurozone)	BRL51.20

Spot rates are currently as follows:

	CHF	€	US$	BRL
1 CHF =	1.0000	0.9347–0.9369	1.1196–1.1222	3.1378–3.1760

The group members will make settlement in Swiss francs. Spot mid-rates will be used in calculations. Settlement will be made in the order that the company owing the largest net amount in Swiss francs will first settle with the company owed the smallest net amount in Swiss francs.

Transfer price arrangements

The Adverane Group board has been reviewing the valuation of inter-group transactions, as it is concerned that the current system is not working well. Currently inter-group transfer prices are mostly based on fixed cost plus a mark-up negotiated by the buying and selling divisions. If they cannot agree a price, either the sale does not take place or the central treasury department determines the margin. The board has the following concerns:

–   Both selling and buying divisions have claimed that prices are unfair and distort the measurement of their performance.

–   Significant treasury department time is being taken up dealing with disputes and then dealing with complaints that the price it has imposed is unfair on one or the other division.

–   Some parts of the group are choosing to buy from external suppliers rather than from suppliers within the group.

As a result of the review, the Adverane Group board has decided that transfer prices should in future be based on market prices, where an external market exists.

Note: CHF is Swiss Franc, € is Euro, US$ is United States dollar and BRL is Brazilian Real.

Required:

(a)   **Advise Adverane Co on, and recommend, an appropriate hedging strategy for the US$ cash flows it is due to receive from, or pay to, Elted Co.**   **(8 marks)**

(b)   **Calculate the inter-group transfers which are forecast to take place.**   **(7 marks)**

(c)   **Evaluate the extent to which changing to a market-price system of transfer pricing will resolve the concerns of the Adverane Group board.**   **(5 marks)**

Professional marks will be awarded for the demonstration of skill in analysis and evaluation, scepticism and commercial acumen in your answer.   **(5 marks)**

(Total: 25 marks)

74   LURGSHALL CO (MAR/JUN 19)

The following exhibits, available on the left-hand side of the screen (in the CBE exam), provide information relevant to the question.

1   **Lurgshall Co**

2   **Hedging information**

3   **Chief executive's views**

This information should be used to answer the question requirements within your chosen response option(s).

Lurgshall Co

Lurgshall Co is a listed electronics company. Lurgshall Co has recently appointed a new chief executive, who has a number of plans to expand the company. The chief executive also plans to look carefully at the costs of all departments in Lurgshall Co's head office, including the centralised treasury department.

The first major investment which the chief executive will oversee is an investment in facilities to produce applications-specific components. To finance the planned investment, it is likely that Lurgshall Co will have to borrow money.

Hedging information

It is now 1 May. At present, it seems that Lurgshall Co will need to borrow $84 million on 1 September, for a period of six months, though both the amount and the period of borrowing are subject to some uncertainty. The treasurer plans to borrow the funds at a variable rate of central bank base rate plus 50 basis points. The central bank base rate is currently 4.5% but is expected to rise by up to 0.6% between now and 1 September.

So far, the possibility of hedging a rise in the base rate of 0.6% using a forward rate agreement or September $ futures has been investigated. The results of the calculations for these instruments were as follows:

4–10 Forward rate agreement from Birdam Bank:	5.38%
Three-month traded September $ futures:	5.36%

Lurgshall Co's treasurer also wants to consider using options on futures to hedge loans.

Although Lurgshall Co has not previously used swaps for hedging purposes, the treasurer has asked Birdam Bank to find a counterparty for a potential swap arrangement.

Relevant information about options and swaps is as follows:

Options

The current price for three-month $ September futures, $2 million contract size is 95.05. The price is quoted in basis points at 100 – annual % yield.

Options on three-month September $ futures, $2 million contract size, option premiums are in annual %

September calls	Strike price	September puts
0.132	95.25	0.411

It can be assumed that futures and options contracts are settled at the end of each month. Basis can be assumed to diminish to zero at contract maturity at a constant rate, based on monthly time intervals. It can also be assumed that there is no basis risk and there are no margin requirements.

Swap

Birdam Bank has found a possible counterparty to enter into a swap with Lurgshall Co. The counterparty can borrow at an annual floating rate of central bank base rate + 1.5% or a fixed rate of 6.1%. Birdam Bank has quoted Lurgshall Co a notional fixed rate of 5.6% for it to borrow. Birdam Bank would charge a fee of 10 basis points to each party individually to act as the intermediary of the swap. Both parties would share equally the potential gains from the swap contract.

Chief executive's views

Lurgshall Co's new chief executive has made the following comments: 'I understand that the treasury department has a number of day-to-day responsibilities, including investing surplus funds for the short-term liquidity management and hedging against currency and interest rates. However, these tasks could all be carried out by the junior, less experienced, members of the department. I do not see why the department needs to employ experienced, expensive staff, as it does not contribute to the strategic success of the company.'

Required:

(a) Compare the results of hedging the $84 million, using the options and the swap, with the results already obtained using the forward rate agreement and futures, and comment on the results. Show all relevant calculations, including how the interest rate swap would work. **(15 marks)**

Note: Up to 4 marks are available for discussion.

(b) Criticise the views of the chief executive about the work carried out by the treasury department and the staff required to do this work. **(5 marks)**

Professional marks will be awarded for the demonstration of skill in analysis and evaluation, scepticism and commercial acumen in your answer. **(5 marks)**

(Total: 25 marks)

75 FITZHARRIS CO (SEP/DEC 20)

Fitzharris Co is a large construction company. Its treasury department uses a variety of derivatives regularly to manage interest rate and commodity price risk.

Transaction to be hedged

Today's date is 1 August. Fitzharris Co plans to borrow an amount of $48m on 1 December, to finance a major construction project, for a period of up to three years. Its treasury department has decided to hedge the risk associated with this borrowing, as there is some uncertainty about how interest rates will move over the rest of this year. The current central bank base rate is 3.7%, but predictions in the media suggest that it could rise or fall by 0.4% by 1 December. Fitzharris Co can currently borrow funds at a floating rate of central bank base rate plus 50 basis points.

Fitzharris Co's treasury department is considering hedging the interest rate risk by using:

– An interest rate swap arranged through Fitzharris Co's bank.

– A collar on options on interest rate futures.

Swap

Fitzharris Co's bank has found a possible counterparty for a swap with Fitzharris Co. The counterparty can borrow at an annual floating rate of base rate plus 130 basis points, or a fixed rate of 4.8%. Fitzharris Co's bank has quoted it a nominal fixed rate of 4.6% for it to borrow. The bank would charge a fee of 5 basis points to each party individually to act as the intermediary of the swap. Both parties would share equally the potential gains from the swap.

Collar

Options on three-month December $ futures, $1,000,000 contract size, option premiums are in annual %

Strike price	Calls	Puts
96.25	0.198	
95.75		0.211

The current three-month $ futures price for December futures is 95.85.

Futures and options contracts are assumed to be settled at the end of each month. Basis is assumed to diminish to zero at contract maturity at a constant rate, based on monthly time intervals. It is also assumed that there is no basis risk and there are no margin requirements.

Required:

(a)   Calculate, in % terms, the results of the hedging strategies that are being considered for the $48m loan, if the central bank base rate increases to 4.1% or falls to 3.3%. Your calculations should demonstrate the rates at which payments between counterparties should be made.   **(13 marks)**

(b)   Comment on the results of your calculations in (a), and discuss the advantages and drawbacks for Fitzharris Co of interest rate swaps compared with traded collars.

(7 marks)

Professional marks will be awarded for the demonstration of skill in analysis and evaluation, and commercial acumen in your answer.   **(5 marks)**

(Total: 25 marks)

76   GOGARTH CO (MAR/JUN 21)

    Answer debrief

The following exhibits, available on the left-hand side of the screen (in the CBE exam), provide information relevant to the question.

1   Gogarth Co's currency risk management

2   Board queries about risk management

This information should be used to answer the question requirements within your chosen response option(s).

Gogarth Co's currency risk management

Gogarth Co is an electrical equipment manufacturer, based in Malaysia, looking to develop its operations abroad. One of its biggest sales markets is the USA and Gogarth Co also imports components from the USA. Gogarth Co regularly hedges transactions in foreign currencies.

It is currently 1 May. On 31 August, Gogarth Co is due to pay $14,500,000 to an American supplier and receive $37,400,000 from an American customer.

The following quotations have been obtained:

Exchange rates (quoted as US dollar per Malaysian Ringgit US$/MR1)

Spot:	0.2355 – 0.2358
Four months forward:	0.2370 – 0.2374

Currency futures (contract size MR500,000, futures price quoted as US$/MR1)

Futures price	
June	0.2366
September	0.2378

Currency options (contract size MR500,000, exercise price quoted as US$/MR1, premium: US cents/MR1)

Exercise price	Calls		Puts	
	June	September	June	September
0.2368	0.11	0.14	0.19	0.23

Futures and options contracts mature at the month end. The number of contracts to be used should be rounded to the nearest whole number in calculations. If the amount cannot be hedged using an exact number of futures or options contracts, the amount unhedged or over-hedged should be hedged using the forward market. For the purposes of the calculations, it should be assumed that the options are exercised.

Board queries about risk management

The head of Gogarth Co's treasury function gave a presentation about the treasury function and what it does to manage foreign exchange risk at the last board meeting.

A new non-executive director has stated that he understands what the treasury function does in relation to the management of transaction risk, but is unclear on the treasury function's role in the management of economic risk.

Required:

(a) Advise Gogarth Co on, and recommend, an appropriate hedging strategy for its US$ cash flows on 31 August. Include relevant calculations. **(15 marks)**

(b) Discuss the role of Gogarth Co's treasury function in relation to the management of economic risk in relation to foreign exchange. **(5 marks)**

Professional marks will be awarded for the demonstration of skill in analysis and evaluation, and commercial acumen in your answer. **(5 marks)**

(Total: 25 marks)

 Calculate your allowed time, allocate the time to the separate parts...............

77 BRANDON CO (SEP/DEC 21)

The following exhibits, available on the left-hand side of the screen (in the CBE exam), provide information relevant to the question.

1 Brandon Co

2 Transaction to be hedged

This information should be used to answer the question requirements within your chosen response option(s).

Brandon Co

Brandon Co is a holding company, operating a small chain of luxury department stores in city centre locations throughout the eurozone. Under the existing structure, the stores are grouped into a number of regional subsidiaries, each with their own head office and treasury function.

The board plans to undertake a restructuring exercise in response to a significant decline in revenue over recent years. This will involve closing unprofitable stores within the eurozone whilst expanding into other more profitable locations worldwide. The proposal represents a significant expansion for the company and will be financed by a combination of debt and equity.

The restructuring is due to be discussed at the upcoming board meeting, including the possibility of centralising the treasury function.

Transaction to be hedged

Assume today's date is 1 November. Brandon Co's treasury manager predicts a short-term loan of $36m will be required next year on 31 January to fund an investment in non-current assets as part of the overseas expansion. The loan will be repaid on 31 May.

Brandon Co can borrow at the central bank base rate plus 40 basis points. The central bank base rate is currently 5.7%. Interest rates have been relatively volatile over the last few years and the finance director is concerned that the central bank could increase the base rate to 6.6% between now and 31 January in response to expectations about inflationary pressures within the economy. Recent media reports have also speculated on the possibility of a reduction in the base rate.

Hedging

Brandon Co's treasury manager is considering the following hedging possibilities with the objective of minimising exposure to interest rate risk:

–   Forward rate agreements (FRAs)

–   Interest rate futures

–   Options on interest rate futures

The following data is available for each of the above:

FRAs

The following FRA rates are available:

3–4   5.82%

3–7   5.90%

4–8   5.99%

Three-month $ futures, $500,000 contract size

Prices are quoted in basis points at 100 – annual % yield.

Dec: 94.07

Mar: 93.95

June: 93.82

Options on three-month $ futures, $500,000 contract size, option premiums are in annual %.

Calls			Strike price	Puts		
December	March	June		December	March	June
0.168	0.238	0.323	93.75	0.025	0.087	0.163

Assume futures and options contracts are settled at the end of each month. Basis is assumed to diminish to zero at contract maturity at a constant rate, based on monthly time intervals. It is also assumed that there is no basis risk and there are no margin requirements.

Required:

(a)   Explain how the functional areas of a treasury department could add value to Brandon Co's restructuring plans and, for each functional area, discuss the advantages of a centralised treasury department.   **(6 marks)**

(b)   Recommend a hedging strategy for the $36m loan based on the hedging choices the treasury manager is considering, if the central bank base rate increases to 6.6%. Support your answer with appropriate calculations.   **(14 marks)**

Professional marks will be awarded for the demonstration of skill in analysis and evaluation, and commercial acumen in your answer.   **(5 marks)**

(Total: 25 marks)

Section 3

ANSWERS TO PRACTICE QUESTIONS – SECTION A

ADVANCED INVESTMENT APPRAISAL

1   TRAMONT CO (DEC 11)

Key answer tips

This was the first 50-mark question published by the examiner when the format of the exam changed. It is important to note that the examiner's 50 mark questions are always split into several different parts, so don't allow yourself to get bogged down in any one part. The key to success is to attempt the easier parts of the question first and to leave sufficient time to attempt all parts of the question.

REPORT TO THE BOARD OF DIRECTORS, TRAMONT CO

EVALUATION OF WHETHER THE PRODUCTION OF X-IT SHOULD MOVE TO GAMALA

This report evaluates the possibility of moving the production of the X-IT to Gamala from the USA. Following the initial evaluation the report discusses the key assumptions made, the possible impact of a change in the government in Gamala after the elections due to take place shortly and other business factors that should be considered before a final decision is made.

Initially a base case net present value calculation is conducted to assess the impact of the production in Gamala. This is then adjusted to show the impact of cash flows in the USA as a result of the move, the immediate impact of ceasing production and the impact of the subsidy and the tax shield benefits from the loan borrowing.

Based on the calculations presented in the appendix, the move will result in a positive adjusted present value of just over $2.4 million. On this basis, the initial recommendation is that the production of X-IT should cease in the USA and the production moved to Gamala instead.

Assumptions

It is assumed that the borrowing rate of 5% is used to calculate the benefits from the tax shield. It could be argued that the risk free rate of 3% could be used as the discount rate instead of 5% to calculate the present value of benefits from the tax shields and the subsidies.

In adjusted present value calculations, the tax shield benefit is normally related to the debt capacity of the investment, not the actual amount of debt finance used. Since this is not given, it is assumed that the increase in debt capacity is equal to the debt finance used.

It has been assumed that many of the input variables, such as for example the tax and tax allowable depreciation rates, the various costs and prices, units produced and sold, the rate of inflation and the prediction of future exchange rates based on the purchasing power parity, are accurate and will change as stated over the four-year period of the project. In reality any of these estimates could be subject to change to a greater or lesser degree and it would appropriate for Tramont Co to conduct uncertainty assessments like sensitivity analysis to assess the impact of the changes to the initial predictions.

Government change

From the facts of the case it would seem that a change of government could have a significant impact on whether or not the project is beneficial to Tramont Co. The threat to raise taxes may not be too significant as the tax rates would need to increase to more than 30% before Tramont Co would lose money. However, the threat by the opposition party to review 'commercial benefits' may be more significant.

Just over 40% of the present value comes from the tax shield and subsidy benefits. If these were reneged then Tramont Co would lose a significant of the value attached to the project. Also the new government may not allow remittances every year, as is assumed in part (i). However this may not be significant since the largest present value amount comes from the final year of operation.

Other business factors

Tramont Co should consider the possibility of becoming established in Gamala, and this may lead to follow-on projects. The real options linked to this should be included in the analysis.

Tramont Co's overall corporate strategy should be considered. Does the project fit within this strategy? Even if the decision is made to close the operation in the USA, there may be other alternatives and these need to be assessed.

The amount of experience Tramont Co has in international ventures needs to be considered. For example, will it be able to match its systems to the Gamalan culture? It will need to develop strategies to deal with cultural differences. This may include additional costs such as training which may not have been taken into account.

Tramont Co needs to consider if the project can be delayed at all. From part (i), it can be seen that a large proportion of the opportunity cost relates to lost contribution in years 1 and 2. A delay in the commencement of the project may increase the overall value of the project.

Tramont Co needs to consider the impact on its reputation due to possible redundancies. Since the production of X-IT is probably going to be stopped in any case, Tramont Co needs to communicate its strategy to the employees and possibly other stakeholders clearly so as to retain its reputation. This may make the need to consider alternatives even more important.

Conclusion

Following from a detailed sensitivity analysis, analysis of a possible change in the government and an evaluation of the financial benefits accruing from the other business factors discussed above, the BoD can make a decision of whether to move the production to Gamala or not. This initial evaluation suggests that moving the production of the X-IT to Gamala would be beneficial.

Appendix

Gamalan Project Operating Cash Flows

(All amounts in GR/$000s)

Year	Now	1	2	3	4
Sales revenue (w2)		48,888	94,849	214,442	289,716
Local variable costs (w3)		(16,200)	(32,373)	(75,385)	(104,897)
Imported component (w4)		(4,889)	(9,769)	(22,750)	(31,658)
Fixed costs		(30,000)	(32,700)	(35,643)	(38,851)
Profits before tax		(2,201)	20,007	80,664	114,310
Taxation (w5)		0	0	(7,694)	(18,862)
Investment	(230,000)				450,000
Working capital	(40,000)	(3,600)	(3,924)	(4,277)	51,801
Cash flows (GR)	(270,000)	(5,801)	16,083	68,693	597,249
Exchange rate (w1)	55.00	58.20	61.59	65.18	68.98
Cash flows ($)	(4,909)	(100)	261	1,054	8,658
Discount factor for 9.6% (w6)		0.912	0.832	0.760	0.693
(Full credit given if 10% is used as the discount rate)					
Present values ($)	(4,909)	(91)	217	801	6,000

Net present value (NPV) of the cash flows from the project is approx. $2,018,000.

Tutorial note

When attempting a question like this in the Computer Based Exam (CBE), make your answer look like a professional document by writing the report in the word processor but putting your numbers (appendix) in a spreadsheet.

When preparing your calculations, use the spreadsheet functions SUM and NPV to save time. Be careful when using the NPV function to enter =NPV, then a bracket containing the discount rate, a comma, and then the cells containing the cash flows from year 1 onwards. The initial investment then needs to be subtracted separately.

Adjusted present value (APV)	$000
NPV of cash flows	2,018
Additional USA tax,	
opportunity cost (revenues foregone from current operations) and	
additional contribution from component exported to project (net of tax) (w7)	(1,237)
Closure revenues and costs ($2,300,000 – $1,700,000)	600
Tax shield and benefit of subsidy (w8)	1,033
Total APV	2,414

Workings:

(W1) Exchange rates

Year	1	2	3	4
GR/$1	55 × 1.09/1.03 = 58.20	58.20 × 1.09/ 1.03 = 61.59	61.59 × 1.09/ 1.03 = 65.18	65.18 × 1.09/ 1.03 = 68.98

(W2) Sales revenue (GR 000s)

Year	1	2	3	4
Price × units × exchange rate	70 × 12,000 × 58.20 = 48,888	70 × 22,000 × 61.59 = 94,849	70 × 47,000 × 65.18 = 214,442	70 × 60,000 × 68.98 = 289,716

(W3) Local variable costs (GR 000s)

Year	1	2	3	4
Cost × units × inflation after yr 1	1,350 × 12,000 = 16,200	1,350 × 22,000 × 1.09 = 32,373	1,350 × 47,000 × 1.09^2 = 75,385	1,350 × 60,000 × 1.09^3 = 104,897

(W4) Imported component (GR 000s)

Year	1	2	3	4
Price × units × inflation after year 1 × exchange rate	7 × 12,000 × 58.20 = 4,889	7 × 22,000 × 1.03 × 61.59 = 9,769	7 × 47,000 × 1.03^2 × 65.18 = 22,750	70 × 60,000 × 1.03^3 × 68.98 = 31,658

(W5) Local variable costs (GR 000s)

Year	1	2	3	4
Profits before tax	(2,201)	20,007	80,664	114,310
Tax allowable depreciation	(20,000)	(20,000)	(20,000)	(20,000)
Profit/(loss) after depreciation	(22,201)	7	60,664	94,310
Taxable profits	0	0	38,470	94,310
Taxation (20%)	0	0	(7,694)	(18,862)

(W6) Gamala project all-equity financed discount

Tramont Co equity beta = 1.17

MVe = $2.40 × 25m shares = $60m

MVd = $40m × $1,428/$1,000 = $57.12m

Tramont Co asset beta (assuming debt is rate risk free)

1.17 × 60m/(60m + 57.12m × 0.7) = 0.70

Project asset beta = 0.70 + 0.40 = 1.10

Project all-equity financed discount rate = 3% + 6% × 1.1 = 9.6%

(W7) **Additional tax, additional contribution and opportunity cost ($000s)**

Year	1	2	3	4
Additional tax				
Taxable profits × 1/exchange rate × 10%	0	0	38,470 × 1/65.18 × 10% = (59)	94,310 × 1/68.98 × 10% = (137)
Opportunity cost				
Units × contribution × (1 – tax)	40 × $20 × 0.7 = (560)	32 × $20 × 0.7 = (448)	25.6 × $20 × 0.7 = (358)	20.48 × $20 × 0.7 = (287)
Additional Contribution				
Units × contribution × inflation × (1 – tax)	12 × $4 × 0.7 = 34	22 × $4 × 1.03 × 0.7 = 63	47 × $4 × 1.032 × 0.7= 140	60 × $4 × 1.033 × 0.7 = 184
Total cash flows	(526)	(385)	(277)	(240)
PV of cash flows				
Discount at 7%	(492)	(336)	(226)	(183)
NPV is approx. $(1,237,000)				

(W8) **Tax shield and subsidy benefits** ($/GR 000s)

Year	1	2	3	4
Interest × loan × tax rate	6% × 270m × 20% = 3,240	3,240	3,240	3,240
Annual subsidy benefit (GR)				
Interest gain × loan × (1 – tax rate)	7% × 270m × 0.8 = 15,120	15,120	15,120	15,120
Total tax shield + subsidy benefits (GR)	18,360	18,360	18,360	18,360
Exchange rate (GR/$1)	58.20	61.59	65.18	68.98
Cash flows ($)	**315**	**298**	**282**	**266**
PV of cash flows				
Discount at 5%	**300**	**270**	**244**	**219**

NPV of tax shield and subsidy benefit is approx. $1,033,000

(b) A triple bottom line (TBL) report provides a quantitative summary of performance in terms of economic or financial impact, impact on the environment and impact on social performance. TBL provides the measurement tool to assess a corporation's or project's performance against its objectives.

The principle of TBL reporting is that true performance should be measured in terms of a balance between economic (profits), environmental (planet) and social (people) factors; with no one factor growing at the expense of the others. The contention is that a corporation that accommodates the pressures of all the three factors in its strategic investment decisions will enhance shareholder value, as long as the benefits that accrue from producing such a report exceeds the costs of producing it.

For example, in the case of the X-IT, reporting on the impact of moving the production to Gamala, in terms of the impact on the employees and environment in the USA and in Gamala will highlight Tramont Co as a good corporate citizen, and thereby increase its reputation and enable it to attract and retain high performing, high calibre employees. It can also judge the impact on the other business factors mentioned in the report above.

Note: Credit will be given for alternative relevant answers.

Marking scheme		Marks
(a)(i)	Estimated future rates based on PPP	1
	Sales revenue, VC, component cost, FC (in GR) – 1 mark each	4
	Taxable profits and taxation	2
	Investment, terminal value and WC	2
	Cash flows in GR	1
	Cash flows in $	1
	Discount rate for all equity financed project	2
	Base case PVs and NPV	2
	PV of additional contribution, additional tax and opportunity cost	4
	PV of tax shield and subsidy benefits	4
	Closure costs and benefits	1
	Initial comments and conclusion	1–2
	Assumptions and sensitivity analysis	2–3
	Maximum	27
(a)(ii)	Implications of change of government	2–3
	Other business factors (1 to 2 marks per factor)	5–6
	Maximum	8
(b)	1–2 marks per issue discussed	5
	Maximum	5
	Professional skills marks (see below)	10
Total		50

Professional skills marks

Communication

General report format and structure (use of headings/sub-headings and an introduction)

Style, language and clarity (appropriate layout and tone of report response, presentation of calculations, appropriate use of the tools)

Effectiveness of communication (answer is relevant, specific rather than general and focused to the requirement)

Analysis and Evaluation

Appropriate use of the data to determine suitable calculations

Appropriate use of the data to support discussion and draw appropriate conclusions

Identification of further analysis, which could be carried out to enable an appropriate recommendation to be made

Demonstration of ability to consider relevant factors applicable to Tramont Co's choices

Scepticism

Effective challenge of information and assumptions supplied and techniques carried out to support any investment decision

Demonstration of the ability to probe into the reasons for issues and problems, including the identification of missing information or additional information, which would alter the decision reached

Commercial acumen

Recognition of external constraints and opportunities as necessary

Maximum 10 marks

2   CHMURA CO (DEC 13)

Key answer tips

Investment appraisal and option pricing are very commonly tested syllabus areas. Note that in this question there were lots of easy discussion marks (e.g. assumptions, role of WTO) as well as the many complex calculations. In order to guarantee success, you must attempt all parts of the question, both calculations and discussion.

(a)   The World Trade Organisation (WTO) was set up to continue to implement the General Agreement on Tariffs and Trade (GATT), and its main aims are to reduce the barriers to international trade. It does this by seeking to prevent protectionist measures such as tariffs, quotas and other import restrictions. It also acts as a forum for negotiation and offering settlement processes to resolve disputes between countries.

The WTO encourages free trade by applying the most favoured nation principle between its members, where reduction in tariffs offered to one country by another should be offered to all members.

Whereas the WTO has had notable success, some protectionist measures between groups of countries are nevertheless allowed and some protectionist measures, especially non-tariff based ones, have been harder to identify and control.

Mehgam could benefit from reducing protectionist measures because its actions would make other nations reduce their protectionist measures against it. Normally countries retaliate against each other when they impose protectionist measures. A reduction in these may allow Mehgam to benefit from increased trade and economic growth. Such a policy may also allow Mehgam to specialise and gain competitive advantage in certain products and services, and compete more effectively globally. Its actions may also gain political capital and more influence worldwide.

Possible drawbacks of reducing protectionist policies mainly revolve around the need to protect certain industries. It may be that these industries are developing and in time would be competitive on a global scale. However, inaction to protect them now would damage their development irreparably. Protection could also be given to old, declining industries, which, if not protected, would fail too quickly due to international competition, and would create large scale unemployment making such inaction politically unacceptable. Certain protectionist policies are designed to prevent 'dumping' of goods at a very cheap price, which hurt local producers.

Note: Credit will be given for alternative relevant discussion.

(b)   **Report to the Board of Directors (BoD), Chmura Co**

This report recommends whether or not Chmura Co should invest in a food packaging project in Mehgam, following Mehgam reducing its protectionist measures. It initially considers the value of the project without taking into account the offer made by Bulud Co to purchase the project after two years. Following this, Bulud Co's offer is considered. The report concludes by recommending a course of action for the BoD to consider further.

Estimated value of the Mehgam project and initial recommendation

The initial net present value of the project is negative at approximately $(451,000) [see Appendix 1]. This would suggest that Chmura Co should not undertake the project.

Bulud Co's offer is considered to be a real option for Mehgam Co. Since it is an offer to sell the project as an abandonment option, a put option value is calculated based on the finance director's assessment of the standard deviation and using the Black-Scholes option pricing (BSOP) model. The value of the put option is added to the initial net present value of the project without the option, to give the value of the project. Although Chmura Co will not actually obtain any immediate cash flow from Bulud Co's offer, the real option computation indicates that the project is worth pursuing because the volatility may result in increases in future cash flows.

After taking account of Bulud Co's offer and the finance director's assessment, the net present value of the project is positive at approximately $2,996,000 [see Appendix 2]. This would suggest that Chmura Co should undertake the project.

Assumptions

It is assumed that all the figures relating to variables such as revenues, costs, taxation, initial investments and their recovery, inflation figures and cost of capital are accurate. There is considerable uncertainty surrounding the accuracy of these, and in addition to the assessments of value conducted in appendices one and two, sensitivity analysis and scenario analysis are probably needed to assess the impact of these uncertainties.

It is assumed that future exchange rates will reflect the differential in inflation rates between the two countries. It is, however, unlikely that exchange rates will move fully in line with the inflation rate differentials.

It is assumed that the value of the land and buildings at the end of the project is a relevant cost, as it is equivalent to an opportunity benefit, even if the land and buildings are retained by Chmura Co.

It is assumed that Chmura Co will be given and will utilise the full benefit of the bi-lateral tax treaty and therefore will not pay any additional tax in the country where it is based.

It is assumed that the short-dated $ treasury bills are equivalent to the risk-free rate of return required for the BSOP model.

And it is assumed that the finance director's assessment of the 35% standard deviation of cash flows is accurate.

It is assumed that Bulud Co will fulfil its offer to buy the project in two years' time and there is no uncertainty surrounding this. Chmura Co may want to consider making the offer more binding through a legal contract.

The BSOP model makes several assumptions such as perfect markets, constant interest rates and lognormal distribution of asset prices. It also assumes that volatility can be assessed and stays constant throughout the life of the project, and that the underlying asset can be traded. Neither of these assumptions would necessarily apply to real options. Therefore the BoD needs to treat the value obtained as indicative rather than definitive.

Additional business risks

Before taking the final decision on whether or not to proceed with the project, Chmura Co needs to take into consideration additional risks, including business risks, and where possible mitigate these as much as possible. The main business risks are as follows:

Investing in Mehgam may result in political risks. For example, the current government may be unstable and if there is a change of government, the new government may impose restrictions, such as limiting the amount of remittances which can be made to the parent company. Chmura Co needs to assess the likelihood of such restrictions being imposed in the future and consider alternative ways of limiting the negative impact of such restrictions.

Chmura Co will want to gain assurance that the countries to which it will sell the packaged food batches remain economically stable and that the physical infrastructure such as railways, roads and shipping channels are maintained in good repair. Chmura Co will want to ensure that it will be able to export the special packaging material into Mehgam. Finally, it will need to assess the likelihood of substantial protectionist measures being lifted and not re-imposed in the future.

As much as possible, Chmura Co will want to ensure that fiscal risks such as imposition of new taxes and limits on expenses allowable for taxation purposes do not change. Currently, the taxes paid in Mehgam are higher than in Chmura Co's host country, and even though the bi-lateral tax treaty exists between the countries, Chmura Co will be keen to ensure that the tax rate does not change disadvantageously.

Chmura Co will also want to protect itself, as much as possible, against adverse changes in regulations. It will want to form the best business structure, such as a subsidiary company, joint venture or branch, to undertake the project. Also, it will want to familiarise itself on regulations such as employee health and safety law, employment law and any legal restrictions around land ownership.

Risks related to the differences in cultures between the host country, Mehgam, and the countries where the batches will be exported to would be a major concern to Chmura Co. For example, the product mix in the batches which are suitable for the home market may not be suitable for Mehgam or where the batches are exported. It may contain foods which would not be saleable in different countries and therefore standard batches may not be acceptable to the customers. Chmura Co will also need to consider the cultural differences and needs of employees and suppliers.

The risk of the loss of reputation through operational errors would need to be assessed and mitigated. For example, in setting up sound internal controls, segregation of duties is necessary. However, personal relationships between employees in Mehgam may mean that what would be acceptable in another country may not be satisfactory in Mehgam. Other areas where Chmura Co will need to focus on are the quality control procedures to ensure that the quality of the food batches is similar to the quality in the host country.

Recommendation

With Bulud Co's offer, it is recommended that the BoD proceed with the project, as long as the BoD is satisfied that the offer is reliable, the sensitivity analysis/scenario analysis indicates that any negative impact of uncertainty is acceptable and the business risks have been considered and mitigated as much as possible.

If Bulud Co's offer is not considered, then the project gives a marginal negative net present value, although the results of the sensitivity analysis need to be considered. It is recommended that, if only these results are taken into consideration, the BoD should not proceed with the project. However, this decision is marginal and there may be other valid reasons for progressing with the project such as possibilities of follow-on projects in Mehgam.

Report compiled by:

Date:

APPENDICES

Appendix 1: Estimated value of the Mehgam project excluding the Bulud Co offer

(Cash flows in MP, millions)

Year	1	2	3	4	5
Sales revenue (w2)	1,209.6	1,905.1	4,000.8	3,640.7	2,205.4
Production and selling costs (w3)	(511.5)	(844.0)	(1,856.7)	(1,770.1)	(1,123.3)
Special packaging costs (w4)	(160.1)	(267.0)	(593.7)	(572.0)	(366.9)
Training and development costs	(409.2)	(168.8)	0	0	0
Tax allowable depreciation	(125)	(125)	(125)	(125)	(125)
Balancing allowance					(125)
Taxable profits/(loss)	3.8	500.3	1,425.4	1,173.6	465.2
Taxation (25%)	(1.0)	(125.1)	(356.4)	(293.4)	(116.3)
Add back depreciation	125	125	125	125	250
Cash flows (MP, millions)	127.8	500.2	1,194.0	1,005.2	598.9

(All amounts in $, 000s)

Year	1	2	3	4	5
Exchange rate (w1)	76.24	80.72	85.47	90.50	95.82
Cash flows ($ 000s)	1,676.3	6,196.7	13,969.8	11,107.2	6,250.3
Discount factor for 12%	0.893	0.797	0.712	0.636	0.567
Present values ($ 000s)	1,496.9	4,938.8	9,946.5	7,064.2	3,543.9

Present value of cash flows approx. = $26,990,000

PV of value of land, buildings and machinery in year 5 = (80% × MP1,250m + MP500m)/95.82 × 0.567 approx. = $8,876,000

PV of working capital = MP200m/95.82 × 0.567 approx. = $1,183,000

Cost of initial investment in $ = (MP2,500 million + MP200 million)/72 = $37,500,000

NPV of project = $26,990,000 + $8,876,000 + $1,183,000 – $37,500,000 = $(451,000)

Tutorial note

When attempting a question like this in the Computer Based Exam (CBE), make your answer look like a professional document by writing the report in the word processor but putting your numbers (appendix) in a spreadsheet.

When preparing your calculations, use the spreadsheet functions SUM and NPV to save time. Be careful when using the NPV function to enter =NPV, then a bracket containing the discount rate, a comma, and then the cells containing the cash flows from year 1 onwards. The initial investment then needs to be subtracted separately.

Workings:

(W1) Exchange rates

Year	1	2	3	4	5
MP/$1	72 × 1.08/1.02 = 76.24	76.24 × 1.08/1.02 = 80.72	80.72 × 1.08/1.02 = 85.47	85.47 × 1.08/1.02 = 90.50	90.50 × 1.08/1.02 = 95.82

(W2) Sales revenue (MP million)

Year	1	2	3	4	5
	10,000 × 115,200 × 1.05 = 1,209.6	15,000 × 115,200 × 1.05^2 = 1,905.1	30,000 × 115,200 × 1.05^3 = 4,000.8	26,000 × 115,200 × 1.05^4 = 3,640.7	15,000 × 115,200 × 1.05^5 = 2,205.4

(W3) Production and selling (MP million)

Year	1	2	3	4	5
	10,000 × 46,500 × 1.1 = 511.5	15,000 × 46,500 × 1.1^2 = 844.0	30,000 × 46,500 × 1.1^3 = 1,856.7	26,000 × 46,500 × 1.1^4 = 1,770.1	15,000 × 46,500 × 1.1^5 = 1,123.3

(W4) Special packaging (MP million)

Year	1	2	3	4	5
	10,000 × 200 × 76.24 × 1.05 = 160.1	15,000 × 200 × 80.72 × 1.05^2 = 267.0	30,000 × 200 × 85.47 × 1.05^3 = 593.7	26,000 × 200 × 90.50 × 1.05^4 = 572.0	15,000 × 200 × 95.82 × 1.05^5 = 366.9

Appendix 2: Estimated value of the Mehgam project including the Bulud Co offer

Present value of underlying asset (Pa) = $30,613,600 (approximately)

(This is the sum of the present values of the cash flows foregone in years 3, 4 and 5)

Price offered by Bulud Co (Pe) = $28,000,000

Risk free rate of interest (r) = 4% (assume government treasury bills are valid approximation of the risk free rate of return)

Volatility of underlying asset (s) = 35%

Time to expiry of option (t) = 2 years

Tutorial note

Look out for the BSOP calculator spreadsheet response option in the exam. You'll need to enter the above five key variables in the spreadsheet to generate the answers shown below.

From the BSOP calculator spreadsheet, we can read off the following values:

d_1 = 0.5894

d_2 = 0.0944

$N(d_1)$ = 0.7222

$N(d_2)$ = 0.5376

Call value = $8,213,394

Put value = $3,447,051

Net present value of the project with put option = $3,447,000 – $451,000 = approx. $2,996,000

		Marking scheme	
			Marks
(a)		Role of the World Trade Organisation	2–3
		Benefits of reducing protectionist measures	2–3
		Drawbacks of reducing protectionist measures	2–3
		Maximum	**7**
(b)	(i)	Future exchange rates predicted on inflation rate differential	1
		Sales revenue	1
		Production and selling costs	1
		Special packaging costs	2
		Training and development costs	1
		Correct treatment of tax and tax allowable depreciation	2
		Years 1 to 5 cash flows in $ and present values of cash flows	2
		Ignoring initial investigation cost and additional taxation in Chmura Co host country	1
		Correct treatment of land, buildings, machinery and working capital	2
		Net present value of the project	1
		Maximum	**14**
	(ii)	Pa value	1
		Other four BSOP input variables	1
		Correct use of BSOP calculator	1
		Correctly identifying this is a put option	1
		Value of the project	1
			5
	(iii)	Estimated value and initial recommendation	2–3
		Up to 2 marks per assumption discussed	5–6
		Up to 2 marks per additional business risk discussed	5–6
		Overarching recommendation(s)	1–2
		Maximum	**14**
		Professional skills marks (see below)	**10**
Total			**50**

Professional skills marks

Communication

General report format and structure (use of headings/sub-headings and an introduction)

Style, language and clarity (appropriate layout and tone of report response, presentation of calculations, appropriate use of the tools)

Effectiveness of communication (answer is relevant, specific rather than general and focused to the requirement)

Analysis and Evaluation

Appropriate use of the data to determine suitable calculations

Appropriate use of the data to support discussion and draw appropriate conclusions

Identification of further analysis, which could be carried out to enable an appropriate recommendation to be made

Demonstration of ability to consider relevant factors applicable to Chmura Co's choices

Scepticism

Effective challenge of information and assumptions supplied and techniques carried out to support any investment decision

Demonstration of the ability to probe into the reasons for issues and problems, including the identification of missing information or additional information, which would alter the decision reached

Commercial acumen

Recognition of external constraints and opportunities as necessary

Maximum 10 marks

3   YILANDWE (JUN 15)

Key answer tips

Investment appraisal, with foreign currencies, is a commonly tested topic.

It is critical to lay out your numerical answer clearly, keeping cash flows in different currencies separate.

Also, leave plenty of time for the written parts. Half of the marks here were for discussion/written points, but many students will have spent the vast majority of their time attacking the numbers.

(a)   **Benefits of own investment as opposed to licensing**

Imoni Co may be able to benefit from setting up its own plant as opposed to licensing in a number of ways. Yilandwe wants to attract foreign investment and is willing to offer a number of financial concessions to foreign investors which may not be available to local companies. The company may be able to control the quality of the components more easily, and offer better and targeted training facilities if it has direct control of the labour resources. The company may also be able to maintain the confidentiality of its products, whereas assigning the assembly rights to another company may allow that company to imitate the products more easily. Investing internationally may provide opportunities for risk diversification, especially if Imoni Co's shareholders are not well-diversified internationally themselves. Finally, direct investment may provide Imoni Co with new opportunities in the future, such as follow-on options.

Drawbacks of own investment as opposed to licensing

Direct investment in a new plant will probably require higher, upfront costs from Imoni Co compared to licensing the assembly rights to a local manufacturer. It may be able to utilise these saved costs on other projects. Imoni Co will most likely be exposed to higher risks involved with international investment such as political risks, cultural risks and legal risks. With licensing these risks may be reduced somewhat. The licensee, because it would be a local company, may understand the operational systems of doing business in Yilandwe better. It will therefore be able to get off-the-ground quicker. Imoni Co, on the other hand, will need to become familiar with the local systems and culture, which may take time and make it less efficient initially. Similarly, investing directly in Yilandwe may mean that it costs Imoni Co more to train the staff and possibly require a steeper learning curve from them. However, the scenario does say that the country has a motivated and well-educated labour force and this may mitigate this issue somewhat.

Note: Credit will be given for alternative, relevant suggestions.

(b)   **Report on the proposed assembly plant in Yilandwe**

This report considers whether or not it would be beneficial for Imoni Co to set up a parts assembly plant in Yilandwe. It takes account of the financial projections, presented in detail in appendices 1 and 2, discusses the assumptions made in arriving at the projections and discusses other non-financial issues which should be considered. The report concludes by giving a reasoned recommendation on the acceptability of the project.

Assumptions made in producing the financial projections

It is assumed that all the estimates such as sales revenue, costs, royalties, initial investment costs, working capital, and costs of capital and inflation figures are accurate. There is considerable uncertainty surrounding the accuracy of these and a small change in them could change the forecasts of the project quite considerably. A number of projections using sensitivity and scenario analysis may aid in the decision making process.

It is assumed that no additional tax is payable in the USA for the profits made during the first two years of the project's life when the company will not pay tax in Yilandwe either. This is especially relevant to year 2 of the project.

No details are provided on whether or not the project ends after four years. This is an assumption which is made, but the project may last beyond four years and therefore may yield a positive net present value. Additionally, even if the project ceases after four years, no details are given about the sale of the land, buildings and machinery. The residual value of these non-current assets could have a considerable bearing on the outcome of the project.

It is assumed that the increase in the transfer price of the parts sent from the USA directly increases the contribution which Imoni Co earns from the transfer. This is probably not an unreasonable assumption. However, it is also assumed that the negotiations with Yilandwe's government will be successful with respect to increasing the transfer price and the royalty fee. Imoni Co needs to assess whether or not this assumption is realistic.

The basis for using a cost of capital of 12% is not clear and an explanation is not provided about whether or not this is an accurate or reasonable figure. The underpinning basis for how it is determined may need further investigation.

Although the scenario states that the project can start almost immediately, in reality this may not be possible and Imoni Co may need to factor in possible delays.

It is assumed that future exchange rates will reflect the differential in inflation rates between the respective countries. However, it is unlikely that the exchange rates will move fully in line with the inflation rate differentials.

Other risks and issues

Investing in Yilandwe may result in significant political risks. The scenario states that the current political party is not very popular in rural areas and that the population remains generally poor. Imoni Co needs to assess how likely it is that the government may change during the time it is operating in Yilandwe and the impact of the change. For example, a new government may renege on the current government's offers and/or bring in new restrictions. Imoni Co will need to decide what to do if this happens.

Imoni Co needs to assess the likelihood that it will be allowed to increase the transfer price of the parts and the royalty fee. Whilst it may be of the opinion that currently Yilandwe may be open to such suggestions, this may depend on the interest the government may get from other companies to invest in Yilandwe. It may consider that agreeing to such demands from Imoni Co may make it obligated to other companies as well.

The financial projections are prepared on the basis that positive cash flows from Yilandwe can be remitted back to the USA. Imoni Co needs to establish that this is indeed the case and that it is likely to continue in the future.

Imoni Co needs to be careful about its ethical stance and its values, and the impact on its reputation, given that a school is being closed in order to provide it with the production facilities needed. Whilst the government is funding some of the transport costs for the children, the disruption this will cause to the children and the fact that after six months the transport costs become the parents' responsibility, may have a large, negative impact on the company's image and may be contrary to the ethical values which the company holds. The possibility of alternative venues should be explored.

Imoni Co needs to take account of cultural risks associated with setting up a business in Yilandwe. The way of doing business in Yilandwe may be very different and the employees may need substantial training to adapt to Imoni Co's way of doing business. On the other hand, the fact that the population is well educated, motivated and keen may make this process easier to achieve.

Imoni Co also needs to consider fiscal and regulatory risks. The company will need to assess the likelihood of changes in tax rates, laws and regulations, and set up strategies to mitigate eventualities which can be predicted. In addition to these, Imoni Co should also consider and mitigate as far as possible, operational risks such as the quality of the components and maintenance of transport links.

Imoni Co should assess and value alternative real options which it may have. For example, it could consider whether licensing the production of the components to a local company may be more financially viable; it could consider alternative countries to Yilandwe, which may offer more benefits; it could consider whether the project can be abandoned if circumstances change against the company; entry into Yilandwe may provide Imoni Co with other business opportunities.

Recommendation

The result from the financial projections is that the project should be accepted because it results in a positive net present value. It is recommended that the financial projections should be considered in conjunction with the assumptions, the issues and risks, and the implications of these, before a final decision is made.

There is considerable scope for further investigation and analysis. It is recommended that sensitivity and scenario analysis be undertaken to take into consideration continuing the project beyond four years and so on. The value of any alternative real options should also be considered and incorporated into the decision.

Consideration must also be given to the issues, risks and factors beyond financial considerations, such as the impact on the ethical stance of the company and the impact on its image, if the school affected is closed to accommodate it.

Report compiled by: AN Accountant

Date: XX/XX/XXXX

APPENDICES

Appendix 1

(all amounts in YR, millions)

Year	0	1	2	3	4
Sales revenue (w2)		18,191	66,775	111,493	60,360
Parts costs (w2)		(5,188)	(19,060)	(31,832)	(17,225)
Variable costs (w2)		(2,921)	(10,720)	(17,901)	(9,693)
Fixed costs		(5,612)	(6,437)	(7,068)	(7,760)
Royalty fee (w3)		(4,324)	(4,813)	(5,130)	(5,468)
Tax allowable depreciation		(4,500)	(4,500)	(4,500)	(4,500)
Taxable profits/(loss)		(4,354)	21,245	45,062	15,714
Tax loss carried forward				(4,354)	
				40,708	
Taxation (40%)		0	0	(16,283)	(6,286)
Add back loss carried fwd				4,354	
Add back depreciation		4,500	4,500	4,500	4,500
Cash flows after tax		146	25,745	33,279	13,928
Working capital	(9,600)	(2,112)	(1,722)	(1,316)	14,750
Land, buildings and machinery	(39,000)				
Cash flows (YR, millions)	(48,600)	(1,966)	24,023	31,963	28,678

(All amounts in $000s)

Year	0	1	2	3	4
Exchange rate	101.4	120.1	133.7	142.5	151.9
Remittable flows	(479,290)	(16,370)	179,678	224,302	188,795
Contribution (parts sales) ($120 + inflation per unit)		18,540	61,108	95,723	48,622
Royalty (w3)		36,000	36,000	36,000	36,000
Tax on contribution and royalty (20%)		(10,908)	(19,422)	(26,345)	(16,924)
Cash flows	(479,290)	27,262	257,364	329,680	256,493
Discount factors (12%)	1	0.893	0.797	0.712	0.636
Present values	(479,290)	24,345	205,119	234,732	163,130

Net present value project before considering the impact of the lost contribution and redundancy is approximately $148.0 million.

Tutorial note

When attempting a question like this in the Computer Based Exam (CBE), make your answer look like a professional document by writing the report in the word processor but putting your numbers (appendix) in a spreadsheet.

When preparing your calculations, use the spreadsheet functions SUM and NPV to save time. Be careful when using the NPV function to enter =NPV, then a bracket containing the discount rate, a comma, and then the cells containing the cash flows from year 1 onwards. The initial investment then needs to be subtracted separately.

Lost contribution and redundancy cost

The lost contribution and redundancy costs are small compared to the net present value and would therefore have a minimal impact of reducing the net present value by $0.1 million approximately.

Note: Full credit will be given if the assumption is made that the amounts are in $000s instead of $.

Appendix 2: Workings

(W1) Unit prices and costs including inflation

Year	1	2	3	4
Selling price (€)	735	772	803	835
Parts ($)	288	297	306	315
Variable costs (YR)	19,471	22,333	24,522	26,925

(W2) Sales revenue and costs

In YR millions Year

Year	1	2	3	4
Sales revenue	150 × 735 × 165 = 18,191	480 × 772 × 180.2 = 66,775	730 × 803 × 190.2 = 111,493	360 × 835 × 200.8 = 60,360
Parts costs	150 × 288 × 120.1 = 5,188	480 × 297 × 133.7 = 19,060	730 × 306 × 142.5 = 31,832	360 × 315 × 151.9 = 17,225
Variable costs	150 × 19,471 = 2,921	480 × 22,333 = 10,720	730 × 24,522 = 17,901	360 × 26,925 = 9,693

(W3) Royalty fee

$20 million × 1.8 = $36 million

This is then converted into YR at the YR/$ rate for each year: 120.1, 133.7, 142.5 and 151.9 for years 1 to 4 respectively.

Note: Credit will be given for alternative, relevant approaches to the calculations, and to the discussion of the assumptions, risks and issues.

Marking scheme			
			Marks
(a)		Benefits	2–3
		Drawbacks	2–3
			—
		Maximum	**4**
			—
(b)	(i)	Sales revenue	3
		Parts costs	3
		Variable costs	2
		Fixed costs	1
		Royalty fee	1
		Tax payable in Yilandwe	3
		Working capital	2
		Remittable flows ($)	1
		Contribution from parts ($)	2
		Tax on parts' contribution and royalty	1
		Impact of lost contribution and redundancy	1
		NPV of project	1
			—
		Maximum	**20**
			—
			Marks
	(ii)	Up to 2 marks per assumption discussed	8
		2–3 marks per issue/risk discussed	8
			—
		Maximum	**14**
			—
		Note: For (b)(ii), where points can be made either as assumptions or as issues, marks will be allocated to either area as relevant.	
	(iii)	Reasoned recommendation	**2**
			—
		Professional skills marks (see below)	**10**
			—
Total			**50**
			—

Professional skills marks

Communication

General report format and structure (use of headings/sub-headings and an introduction)

Style, language and clarity (appropriate layout and tone of report response, presentation of calculations, appropriate use of the tools)

Effectiveness of communication (answer is relevant, specific rather than general and focused to the requirement)

Analysis and Evaluation

Appropriate use of the data to determine suitable calculations

Appropriate use of the data to support discussion and draw appropriate conclusions

Identification of further analysis, which could be carried out to enable an appropriate recommendation to be made

Demonstration of ability to consider relevant factors applicable to Imoni Co's choices

Scepticism

Effective challenge of information and assumptions supplied and techniques carried out to support any investment decision

Demonstration of the ability to probe into the reasons for issues and problems, including the identification of missing information or additional information, which would alter the decision reached

Commercial acumen

Recognition of external constraints and opportunities as necessary

Maximum 10 marks

4   TALAM CO (MAR/JUN 19)

Key answer tips

The examiner tries to help candidates in his section A questions by setting a small part (a) in each question to start you thinking about some of the key issues that will be covered in more detail later in the question.

For example, here you are asked to discuss real options in general terms in part (a), so it was no surprise to find detailed calculations and discussions of real options in the report.

(a)   When making decisions, following investment appraisals of projects, net present value assumes that a decision must be made immediately or not at all, and once made, it cannot be changed. Real options, on the other hand, recognise that many investment appraisal decisions have some flexibility.

For example, decisions may not have to be made immediately and can be delayed to assess the impact of any uncertainties or risks attached to the projects. Alternatively, once a decision on a project has been made, to change it, if circumstances surrounding the project change. Finally, to recognise the potential future opportunities, if the initial project is undertaken, like the Jigu Project.

Real options give managers choices when making decisions about whether or not to undertake projects, by estimating the value of this flexibility or choice. Real options take into account the time available before a decision, on a project, has to be made, and the risks and uncertainties attached to the project. It uses these factors to estimate an additional value which can be attributable to the project. Real options view risks and uncertainties as opportunities, where upside outcomes can be exploited, and a company has the option to disregard any downside impact.

By incorporating the value of any real options available into an investment appraisal decision, Talam Co will be able to assess the full value of a project.

(b) **Report to the board of directors (BoD), Talam Co**

Introduction

This report assesses whether or not the Uwa Project should be undertaken based on its value from an initial net present value (NPV) calculation, and then taking into account the options provided by the offer from Honua Co and the Jigu Project. As part of the assessment, a discussion of the assumptions and their impact on the assessment is provided.

Assessment

The value of the Uwa Project based on just the initial NPV is a small negative amount of $(6,000) approximately (appendix 1). This would indicate that the project is not worth pursuing, although the result is very marginal. The offer from Honua Co, and the Jigu Project, using the real options method, gives an estimated value of $17.71m (appendix 2), which is positive and substantial. This indicates that the Uwa Project should be undertaken.

Assumptions

The following assumptions have been made when calculating the values in appendices 1 and 2.

Since the Uwa Project is in a different industry to Talam Co's current activities, the project-specific, risk-adjusted cost of capital of 11% based on Honua Co's asset beta is used. It is assumed that Honua Co's asset beta would provide a good approximation of the business risk inherent in drone production.

It is assumed that all the variables used to calculate the values of the projects in appendices 1 and 2 are correct and accurate. Furthermore, it is assumed all the variables such as inflation rates, tax rates, interest rates and volatility figures, remain as forecast through the period of each project. It is also assumed that the time periods related to the projects and the offer from Honua is accurate and/or reasonable.

The Black-Scholes option pricing (BSOP) model is used to estimate the real option values of the Jigu Project and the Honua Co offer. The BSOP model was developed for financial products and not for physical products, on which real options are applied. The BSOP model assumes that a market exists to trade the underlying project or asset without restrictions, within frictionless financial and product markets.

The BSOP model assumes that the volatility or risk of the underlying asset can be determined accurately and readily. Whereas for traded financial assets this would most probably be reasonable, as there is likely to be sufficient historical data available to assess the underlying asset's volatility, this is probably not going to be the case for real options. For large, one-off projects, there would be little or no historical data available. Volatility in such situations would need to be estimated using simulation models, such as the Monte-Carlo simulation, with the need to ensure that the model is developed accurately and the data input used to generate outcomes reasonably reflects what is likely to happen in practice.

The BSOP model assumes that the real option is a European-style option which can only be exercised on the date when the option expires. In some cases, it may make more strategic sense to exercise an option earlier. The real option is more representative of an American-style option which can be exercised before expiry. Therefore, the BSOP model may underestimate the true value of an option.

Real options models assume that any contractual obligations involving future commitments made between parties will be binding, and will be fulfilled. For example, it is assumed that Honua Co will fulfil its commitment to purchase the project from Talam Co at the start of the third year for $30 million and there is therefore no risk of non-fulfilment of that commitment.

The BSOP model does not take account of behavioural anomalies which may be displayed by managers when making decisions.

Conclusion

The initial recommendation is that the Uwa Project should be undertaken when the offer from Honua Co and going ahead with the Jigu Project are included. Taken together, these result in a significant positive NPV. However, one or more of the above assumptions may not apply and therefore NPV value is not a 'correct' value. Instead, the appendices provide indicative value which can be attached to the flexibility of a choice of possible future actions which are embedded with the Uwa Project and indicate that it should be undertaken.

Report compiled by:

Date

Note: Credit will be given for alternative and valid discussion comments.

Tutorial note

When attempting a question like this in the Computer Based Exam (CBE), make your answer look like a professional document by writing the report in the word processor but putting your numbers (appendix) in a spreadsheet.

When preparing your calculations, use the spreadsheet functions SUM and NPV to save time. Be careful when using the NPV function to enter =NPV, then a bracket containing the discount rate, a comma, and then the cells containing the cash flows from year 1 onwards. The initial investment then needs to be subtracted separately.

APPENDICES:

Appendix 1 (Part (b) (i)):

Net present value computation of the Uwa Project before incorporating the offer from Honua Co and the financial impact of the Jigu Project. All figures are in $000s.

Year	0	1	2	3	4
Sales revenue (w1)		5,160	24,883	49,840	38,405
Less:					
Variable costs (w2)		2,064	9,581	18,476	13,716
Fixed costs		2,700	2,970	3,267	3,594
Training costs		4,128	5,749	1,848	1,372
Cash flows before tax		(3,732)	6,583	26,249	19,723
Tax (w3)		1,796	(267)	(4,200)	(1,495)
Working capital	(1,032)	(1,972)	(2,496)	1,144	4,356
Machinery purchase and sale	(35,000)				7,000
Net cash flows	(36,032)	(3,908)	3,820	23,193	29,584
Present value of cash flows (discounted at 11%)	(36,032)	(3,521)	3,100	16,959	19,488

Approximate net present value of the project = $(6,000)

Workings:

Working 1 (w1): Sales revenue

Year	1	2	3	4
Units produced and sold	4,300	19,200	35,600	25,400
Selling price ($) (inflated at 8%)	1,200	1,296	1,400	1,512
Sales revenue ($000s)	5,160	24,883	49,840	38,405

Working 2 (w2): Variable costs

Year	1	2	3	4
Units produced and sold	4,300	19,200	35,600	25,400
Variable costs per unit ($) (inflated at 4%)	480	499	519	540
Total variable costs ($000s)	2,064	9,581	18,476	13,716

Working 3 (w3): Tax

Year	1	2	3	4
Cash flows before tax	(3,732)	6,583	26,249	19,723
Tax allowable depreciation	(5,250)	(5,250)	(5,250)	(12,250)
Taxable cash flows	(8,982)	1,333	20,999	7,473
Tax payable (20%)	(1,796)	267	4,200	1,495

Appendix 2 (Part (b) (ii)):

Jigu Project: Asset value

Asset value of Jigu Project of $46.1m is estimated as present value of future cash flows related to the project:

$70m × 1.11^–4, where $70m = $60m + $10m.

Honua Co offer, initial variables used to calculate the d1, d2, N(d1) and N(d2) figures:

Asset value (Pa) = $16,959,000 + $19,488,000 = $36,447,000 (cash flows foregone)

Exercise price (Pe) = $30m

Exercise date (t) = 2 years

Risk-free rate (r) = 2.30%

Volatility (s) = 30%

Tutorial note

Look out for the BSOP calculator spreadsheet response option in the exam. You'll need to enter the above five key variables in the spreadsheet to generate the answers shown below.

From the BSOP calculator spreadsheet, we can read off the following values:

	A	B	C	D	E
1					
2	Pa	Pe	r	t	s
3	36.447	30.000	0.023	2	0.30
4					
5	d1	0.7794			
6	d2	0.3551			
7	Nd1	0.7821			
8	Nd2	0.6387			
9	c	10.21			
10	p	2.41			
11					

Value of put = $2.41m

Estimated total value arising from the two real options

Value of Jigu Project: $15.3m

Value of Honua Co's offer: $2.41m

Estimated total value from the two real options: $2.41m + $15.3m = $17.71m

(c) The overarching issue is that of conflict between the need to satisfy shareholders and the financial markets, and Talam Co's stated aims of bringing affordable environmentally friendly products to market and maintaining high ethical standards. This overarching issue can be broken down into smaller related issues.

Producing profitable products will presumably result in positive NPV projects, thus ensuring a continued strong share price performance. This should satisfy the markets and shareholders. However, if the products cannot be sold at a reasonable selling price because some farmers are not able to afford the higher prices, then this may compromise Talam Co's aim of bringing environmentally friendly products to market and making them affordable.

A possible solution is to lower production costs, by shifting manufacturing to locations where such costs are lower. Talam Co's BoD thus considered the move to Dunia, to lower production costs. This presumably would allow Talam Co to reduce prices and make the drones more affordable, but at the same time ensure that the projects result in positive NPVs. However, the issue here is that supplier companies in Dunia whom Talam Co trades with use young teenage children as part of their workforce. This may impact negatively on Talam Co's stated aim of maintaining high ethical standards. In fact, Talam Co may need to rethink its links with companies it trades with in Dunia entirely. Otherwise there is a real risk that Talam Co could suffer from long-term loss of reputation, and this may cause substantial and sustained financial damage to the company.

Talam Co may decide that maintaining its share price and its reputation should take the highest priority and therefore it may reach a decision that the best way to address the issue(s) is to not try to reduce costs, and to withdraw from Dunia completely. But this would prevent many agriculturalists from taking advantage of the biodegradable drones. Therefore, Talam Co may want to explore alternative ways to meet all the aims.

Talam Co could consider moving to another location, if this was feasible. It is not known from the narrative whether or not viable alternatives are available, but Talam Co would need to ensure that possible alternative locations would have the infrastructure to produce the components at the same or lower costs. Talam Co may also want to consider the softer issues; for example, it will want a good working relationship and network in the new locations which it has with the companies in Dunia. These may need to be developed and would take time and probably incur additional costs.

For these reasons, Talam Co may decide to explore the existing production facilities in Dunia further. It is possible that the supplier companies are not exploiting the young teenage children, but are supporting their education and their families in a positive way. Stopping the relationship may jeopardise this support. Talam Co would need to investigate the working conditions of the children and the manner in which they are rewarded and supported. It may want to consult the guardians of the young teenage children and see if there are other feasible solutions. For example, could the guardians be employed instead of the young teenage children or are they already engaged in alternative employment?

After all factors are considered, Talam Co may conclude that the best way to achieve all its aims is to continue in Dunia and also have the production of drone components located there. If this is the case and young teenage children continue to be employed there, then Talam Co would need a sustained public relations campaign to defend its position and demonstrate how it ensures that the teenage children have not been exploited, but are gainfully employed and receiving a good education to help them progress in life.

Note: Credit will be given for alternative and valid discussion comments.

			Marking guide			*Marks*
(a)			1–2 marks per well-discussed comment			
					Maximum	**5**
(b)	**(i)**		**(Appendix 1)**			
			Sales revenue			2
			Variable costs			2
			Fixed costs			1
			Training costs Tax			2
			Tax			2
			Working capital			2
			Uwa Project net present value			1
						12
	(ii)		**(Appendix 2)**			
			Jigu Project: underlying asset value			2
			Honua Co offer: exercise price			1
			Honua Co offer: underlying asset value			2
			Honua Co offer: other variables used in option calculation			1
			Honua Co offer: choose put value			1
						7
	(iii)		Initial assessment of value of Uwa Project			2–3
			Up to 2 marks per well-discussed assumption			
			(Max 3 marks if assumptions related to real options are not discussed)			6
					Maximum	**8**
(c)			Discussion of the issues			4–5
			Discussion of how the issues may be addressed			4-5
					Maximum	**8**
			Professional skills marks (see below)			**10**
Total						**50**

Professional skills marks

Communication

General report format and structure (use of headings/sub-headings and an introduction)

Style, language and clarity (appropriate layout and tone of report response, presentation of calculations, appropriate use of the tools)

Effectiveness of communication (answer is relevant, specific rather than general and focused to the requirement)

Analysis and Evaluation

Appropriate use of the data to determine suitable calculations

Appropriate use of the data to support discussion and draw appropriate conclusions

Identification of further analysis, which could be carried out to enable an appropriate recommendation to be made

Demonstration of ability to consider relevant factors applicable to Talam Co's choices

Scepticism

Effective challenge of information and assumptions supplied and techniques carried out to support any investment decision

Commercial acumen

Effective use of examples and/or calculations from the scenario information and other practical considerations related to the context to illustrate points being made in respect of options and sustainability/ethics

Recognition of external constraints and opportunities as necessary

Maximum 10 marks

5   ZHICHI CO (SEP/DEC 21)

Key answer tips

This is a very good question on cost of capital and investment appraisal – key parts of the syllabus.

Note that although 6% (normal borrowing rate) is used as the discount rate to calculate the present value of the tax shield and subsidised loan benefits, the risk-free rate of 4.8%, could have been used as an alternative.

(a)   Post-completion audits

A post completion audit is a part of monitoring and appraising capital investment projects. Its aims are to compare income, costs and timing of projects against the original budget and any subsequent changes to the budget as more information becomes known. It can be a useful learning tool to help Zhichi Co manage projects more effectively and efficiently in the future. This can lead to setting realistic budget targets, better control of costs and reduction of bottlenecks to help complete projects on time. This is especially so for similar projects. It can be an expensive process and its usefulness may be limited to projects which are unique. In order to maximise the effectiveness of post completion audits, Zhichi Co would need to ensure that sufficient resources are provided to undertake the audit and the aims of the audit are clear and achievable.

Fixed discount rate

A fixed discount rate to appraise new investment projects, which Zhichi Co uses, can be ineffective when a decision is being made whether or not to undertake the project. This is because projects will have different risks attached to them and therefore the returns required from these projects would differ. This could result in low-risk projects being rejected which could have added to Zhichi Co's corporate value, and high-risk projects being accepted which could reduce corporate value. Zhichi Co should instead estimate an appropriate discount (or hurdle) rate which accounts for the risk of the project. In this way, the company can assess the value of projects more accurately and thereby add to its corporate value.

New project finance

Observations of how companies raise new finance for projects show that they typically prefer internal funds before accessing external markets. If new finance is raised through external markets then companies prefer debt to equity. Debt finance may have advantages such as tax benefits and controlling the actions of managers. Investors have less information compared to managers and directors in a company, and use companies' actions on raising finance as a signal. Issuing debt finance also can be seen as a sign of confidence that the company can fulfil its interest payment commitments, and can therefore be considered to be stable and less risky by investors. Information asymmetry between investors and a company's managers sends signals that the company is only raising equity finance when share prices have peaked or shares are over-valued. This causes share prices to fall following announcements that a company is raising new equity finance. It is likely that Zhichi Co has experienced this. Therefore, Zhichi Co should finance through a long-term strategy of internal finance, followed by debt issues and then equity issues as a last resort.

(b) REPORT TO THE BOARD OF DIRECTORS (BoD), ZHICHI CO

Introduction

This report evaluates whether or not the new motor scooter project should be undertaken. It discusses the assumptions made in estimating the value of the project and whether the adjusted present value (APV) method, which is used to estimate the value of the project, is more appropriate than the conventional net present value (NPV) method.

Evaluation

Although the NPV based on an all-equity financed discount rate is negative $0.9m (appendix 2), when the impact of the financing side effects is taken into account the APV is positive $4.9m (appendix 3). On that basis the project should be accepted if the project is funded using the subsidised loan, but not necessarily without it.

However, both values are marginal and a small change in the variables (see below) could easily mean that the project is no longer viable. In addition to this, it should be noted that a large proportion of the present value of cash inflows from the project, $51.5m (appendix 2) occur in the fourth year of the project. Projections further into the future tend to be more uncertain.

Zhichi Co may benefit from undertaking sensitivity and scenario analysis to assess the impact of changes in the input variables instead relying solely on the results of appendices 2 and 3.

Assumptions

The assumptions made in each of the three appendices are discussed in turn.

In appendix one, Liyu Co's and Sanwenyu Co's asset betas are calculated, by degearing each company's equity beta to eliminate the company specific financial risk. The asset betas of both companies represent just the business risk element. It is assumed that Sanwenyu Co's asset beta represents the business risk of the wind farm business and Liyu Co's asset beta represents the business risks of both the wind farm and the environmentally friendly motor scooter businesses. From these it is assumed that the asset beta, representing a suitable proxy for the business risk of environmentally friendly motor scooters, can be computed and used to estimate the all-equity financed discount rate.

In appendix two, it is assumed that all input variables are known with certainty or reasonable accuracy. It is also assumed that these variables, and the factors which determine the variables, do not change in the future. Uncertainty increases as cash flows are predicted further into the future, and the majority of the positive cash flows for the new project occur in year 4.

In appendix three, it is assumed that the interest rates of the subsidised loan and the corporate tax rates remain unchanged for the period of the project. The normal borrowing rate of 6% is used to determine the present value of the financing side effects, although the risk-free rate could also be used and this will give a higher APV. The debt capacity of Zhichi Co could change as a result of undertaking the project.

In the computations, debt beta is assumed to be zero, although in practice, corporate debt is not free of default risk.

Adjusted present value or net present value

With NPV, future cash flows are discounted using Zhichi Co's average cost of capital (discount rate) since a positive NPV will ensure that the minimum return requirement of all Zhichi Co's investors is met. However, the discount rate often does not take into account (i) the changing business risk profile (since the project is a diversification) nor (ii) the changing financial risk profile (since the new project will be entirely financed by debt). With the new project, both these risks are changing and the APV method takes both changes into account.

Furthermore, the APV method will provide significantly more information about the sources of value and also about the different levels of risk applicable to different cash flows. When using the average cost of capital as the discount rate to generate the NPV, it is not possible to tell where the project's value is generated from, whether the value is from undertaking the project or from the changing capital structure. It also assumes that all cash flows have the same risk profile and should therefore be discounted at the same rate. The adjusted present value method considers the risk elements separately and considers the cash flow impact of each. It also assigns a suitable cost of capital which is relevant to each cash flow (for example, the ungeared cost of equity to base case NPV and the cost of debt to the financing side effects).

APV does not normally take into account costs of financial distress, possibility of tax exhaustion and agency costs related to financing using debt. However, in Zhichi Co's case none of these is likely to be an issue because it has only used equity financing previously and therefore the impact of the above is likely to be minimal.

For these reasons, APV is the more appropriate method to use to evaluate Zhichi Co's new project.

Conclusion

After considering the assumptions made in the calculations and discussing why the APV is the more appropriate method, the recommendation is that the new project is undertaken because it generates a positive APV. However, sensitivity and scenario analysis should be undertaken because of the assumptions made and because the decision to accept is marginal.

Report compiled by:

Date

APPENDICES:

Appendix 1: (Part (b)(i)):

Liyu Co

Asset beta = 1.2 × $172m/($172m + $48.26m × 0.8) = 0.98

Sanwenyu Co

Equity beta = (15.4% - 4.8%)/8% = 1.325

Asset beta = 1.325 × 0.8/(0.8 + 0.2 × 0.8) = 1.1 approx.

[Assumption: asset beta of 1.1 reflects the business risk attributable to manufacturing wind farms and related equipment]

Asset beta attributable to business risk of manufacturing motor scooters

0.98 = 0.6 × [asset beta, motor scooters] + 0.4 × 1.1

Asset beta = (0.98 – 0.44)/0.6 = 0.9

Base case discount rate = 4.8% + 8% × 0.9 = 12%

Appendix 2: (Part (b)(ii)): Motor scooter project, all-equity financed

Year	0	1	2	3	4	5
	$m	$m	$m	$m	$m	$m
Sales revenue		10.0	40.0	48.0	57.6	
Costs		(12.0)	(32.0)	(19.2)	(23.0)	
Cash flow before tax		(2.0)	8.0	28.8	34.6	
Taxation (w1)			2.5	0.2	(4.2)	(2.3)
Investment	(70.0)				42.0	
Working capital (w2)	(10.0)	4.0	(1.2)	(1.4)	8.6	
Cash flows	(80.0)	2.0	9.3	27.6	81.0	(2.3)
Discounted at 12% (app. 1)	1	0.893	0.797	0.712	0.636	0.567
Present value of cash flows	(80.0)	1.8	7.4	19.7	51.5	(1.3)

All-equity financed net present value is approximately $(0.9)m

Working 1 (w1): Taxation

Year	TAD (Tax allowable depreciation) ($m)	Balance ($m)
	Investment	70.0
1	TAD (15%)	(10.5)
		59.5
2	TAD (15%)	(8.9)
		50.6
3	TAD (15%)	(7.6)
		43.0
4	Balancing allowance	(23.0)
		20.0

Year	1 $m	2 $m	3 $m	4 $m
Cash flow before tax	(2.0)	8.0	28.8	34.6
TAD	(10.5)	(8.9)	(7.6)	(23.0)
Taxable cash flows	(12.5)	(0.9)	21.2	11.6
Tax (20%)	(2.5)	(0.2)	4.2	2.3
Year payable	2	3	4	5

Working 2 (w2) Working capital

Year	0 $m	1 $m	2 $m	3 $m	4 $m
Required		10	6.0	7.2	8.6
Invested/(Released)	10	(4)	1.2	1.4	(8.6)

Appendix 3: (Part (b)(iii): Motor scooter project, adjusted present value

Issue Costs

3/97 × $80m = $2.5m

Tax shield

Annual interest payable = $80m × 0.03 × 0.2 = $0.5m

Present value of interest payable = $0.5m × (4.212 – 0.943) = $1.6m

Subsidised loan benefit and cost

Present value of subsidised loan benefit = $80m × 0.03 × 3.465 = $8.3m

Present value of tax shield lost = $80m × 0.03 × 0.2 × (4.212 – 0.943) = $1.6m

Adjusted present value

$(0.9)m (from appendix 2) + $(2.5)m + $1.6m + $8.3m + $(1.6)m = $4.9m

		Marking guide	Marks

(a) 2-3 marks per policy failure (For example, post-completion audits: compare to budget, useful for future budget development, can be expensive and needs sufficient resources, all projects can be unique and different so not universal. Fixed discount rate: need project specific discount rate to take account of project risk, otherwise low-risk projects can be rejected and high-risk projects might be accepted. Using equity finance. Not observed in practice. Instead pecking order of internal, then debt, then equity sources of finance. Due to information asymmetry, signalling and tax advantage of debt) — **8**

Maximum — **8**

(b) **(i)** **Appendix 1**
Liyu Co, asset beta — 1
Sanwenyu Co, equity beta — 2
Sanwenyu Co, asset beta — 1
Asset beta for business risk of motor scooter manufacturing — 1
Cost of equity/discount rate — 1
— **6**

(ii) **Appendix 2**
Sales revenue — 1
Costs — 2
TAD — 1
Tax and timing — 2
Working capital invested/released: years 0 and 1 — 1
Working capital invested/released: years 2-4 — 1
Cash flows and all-equity financed NPV — 1
— **9**

(iii) **Appendix 3**
Issue costs — 1
PV tax shield — 2
PV loan subsidy benefit and cost — 3
APV — 1
— **7**

(iv) **Report**
Evaluation — 2 – 3
Discussion of assumptions — 4 – 5
(For example, rival companies' asset betas represent business risk, all-equity financed project from asset beta, variable known with certainty and will not change, interest rates will not change, debt capacity is sufficient, cost of debt represents appropriate discount rate)
Discussion of appropriateness of APV — 4 – 5
(For example, limitations of cost of capital re changes in business and financial risk, APV takes account of both risks, APV separates out areas where value is derived from, APV takes into account different levels of risk and required return, but APV does not consider financial distress, tax exhaustion or agency issues)

Maximum — **10**

Professional skills marks (see below) — **10**

Total — **50**

Professional skills marks

Communication

General report format and structure (use of headings/sub-headings and an introduction)

Style, language and clarity (appropriate layout and tone of report response, presentation of calculations, appropriate use of the tools)

Effectiveness of communication (answer is relevant, specific rather than general and focused to the requirement)

Analysis and Evaluation

Appropriate use of the data to determine suitable calculations

Appropriate use of the data to support discussion and draw appropriate conclusions

Identification of further analysis, which could be carried out to enable an appropriate recommendation to be made

Demonstration of ability to consider relevant factors applicable to Zhichi Co

Scepticism

Effective challenge of information and assumptions supplied and techniques carried out to support any investment decision

Commercial acumen

Effective use of examples and/or calculations from the scenario information and other practical considerations related to the context to illustrate points being made in respect of options and sustainability/ethics

Recognition of external constraints and opportunities as necessary

Maximum 10 marks

ACQUISITIONS AND MERGERS

6   STANZIAL INC (DEC 06)

Key answer tips

This is a very good question on business valuation, one of the most important syllabus topics.

Notice that in part (a) you are expected to calculate the value using four different valuation methods, but also to comment on the methods and state your assumptions. Unless you attempt all these different elements, you'll struggle to score a pass mark here.

(a) **REPORT**

The valuation of private companies involves considerable subjectivity. Many alternative solutions to the one presented below are possible and equally valid.

As Stanzial is considering the purchase of Besserlot, this will involve gaining ownership through the purchase of Stanzial's shares, hence an equity valuation is required.

Before undertaking any valuations it is advisable to recalculate the earnings for 20X6 without the exceptional item. It is assumed that this is a one-off expense, which was not fully tax allowable.

The revised statement of profit or loss is:

	20X6
	$000
Sales revenue	22,480
Operating profit before exceptional items	1,302
Interest paid (net)	280
Profit before taxation	1,022
Taxation (30%)	307
Profit after tax	715
Dividend	200
Change in equity	515

Asset-based valuation

An asset valuation might be regarded as the absolute minimum value of the company. Asset-based valuations are most useful when the company is being liquidated and the assets disposed of. In an acquisition, where the company is a going concern, asset-based values do not fully value future cash flows, or items such as the value of human capital, market position, etc.

Asset values may be estimated using book values, which are of little use, replacement cost values, or disposal values. The information provided does not permit a full disposal value, although some adjustments to book value are possible. In this case an asset valuation might be:

	$000
Net assets	6,286
Patent	10,000
Inventory adjustment	(1,020)
	15,266 or $15,266,000

This value is not likely to be accurate as it assumes the economic value of non-current assets is the same as the book value, which is very unlikely. The same argument may also be related to current assets and liabilities other than inventory.

P/E ratios

P/E ratios of competitors are sometimes used in order to value unlisted companies. This is problematic as the characteristics of all companies differ, and a P/E ratio valid for one company might not be relevant to another.

There is also a question of whether or not the P/E ratio should be adjusted downwards for an unlisted company, and how different expected growth rates should be allowed for.

Expected earnings growth for Besserlot is much higher than the average for the industry, especially during this next three years. In view of this it might be reasonable to apply a P/E ratio of at least the industry average when attempting to value Besserlot.

The after-tax earnings of Besserlot, based upon the revised statement of profit or loss, are:

$$1,022 - 307 = 715$$

Using a P/E ratio of 30:1, this gives an estimated value of $715 \times 30 = \$21,450,000$.

This is a very subjective estimate, and it might be wise to use a range of P/E ratio values, for example from 25:1 to 35:1, which would result in a range of values from $17,875,000 to $25,025,000.

It could also be argued that the value should be based upon the anticipated next earnings rather than the past earnings several months ago.

This is estimated to be:

	20X7
	$000
Sales revenue	28,100
Operating profit before exceptional items	2,248
Interest paid (net)	350
Profit before taxation	1,898
Taxation	569
	1,329

$1,329 \times 30$ gives a much higher estimate of $39,870,000

PE-based valuation might also be criticised as it is based upon profits rather than cash flows.

Dividend-based valuation

Dividend-based valuation assumes that the value of the company may be estimated from the present value of future dividends paid. In this case the expected dividend growth rates are different during the next three years and the subsequent period.

The estimated dividend valuation is:

Year	1	2	3	After Year 3	
Expected dividend				$\dfrac{391\ (1.1)}{0.14 - 0.10}$	Using $P_o = \dfrac{D_o(1+g)}{(r_e - g)}$
	250	313	391		
Discount factors (14%)	0.877	0.769	0.675	0.675	
Present values	219	241	264	7,258	

The estimated value is $7,982,000.

This is a rather low estimated value and might be the result of Besserlot having a relatively low dividend pay-out ratio, and no value being available for a final liquidating dividend.

The present value of expected future cash flows

The present value of future cash flows will be estimated using the expected free cash flow to equity. In theory, this is probably the best valuation method, but in reality it is impossible for an acquiring company to make accurate estimates of these cash flows. The data below relies upon many assumptions about future growth rates and relationships between variables.

	20X7	20X8	20X9	After 20X9
Sales revenue	28,100	35,125	43,906	
Operating profit	2,248	2,810	3,512	
Interest paid (net)	350	438	547	
Profit before taxation	1,898	2,372	2,965	
Taxation	569	712	890	
	1,329	1,660	2,075	
Add back non-cash expenses	1,025	1,281	1,602	
Less increase in working capital	(172)	(214)	(268)	
Less capital investment	(1,250)	(1,562)	(1,953)	
Free cash flow to equity	932	1,165	1,456	40,040
Discount factors (14%)	0.877	0.769	0.675	0.675
Present values	817	896	983	27,027

The estimated present value of free cash flows to equity is $29,723,000

Note: Free cash flow after 20X9 is estimated by $\dfrac{1.456\,(1.1)}{0.14-0.10} = 40{,}040$

This valuation also ignores any real options that arise as a result of the acquisition.

Recommended valuation

It is impossible to produce an accurate valuation. The valuation using the dividend growth model is out of line with all others and will be ignored.

On the basis of this data, the minimum value should be the adjusted asset value, a little over $15,000,000, and the maximum approximately $30,000,000.

All of the above valuations may be criticised as they are based upon the value of Besserlot as a separate entity, not the valuation as part of Stanzial Inc. There might be synergies, such as economies of scale, savings in duplicated facilities, processes, etc, as a result of the purchase, which would increase the above estimates.

(b) The success of the purchase would depend upon enticing the existing shareholders to sell their shares. The most important shareholders are the senior managers, the venture capital company, and the single shareholder holding 25% of the shares. If any two of these types of shareholder can be persuaded to sell, Stanzial can gain control of Besserlot.

If the shareholders of a private company do not want to sell, there is little Stanzial can do. However, most shareholders will sell if the price or other conditions are attractive enough.

The venture capital company will probably have invested in Besserlot with a view to making a large capital gain, possibly if Besserlot was itself to seek a listing on a stock market. Stanzial will have to offer a sum large enough to satisfy the venture capital company relative to possible alternatives such as the listing.

Similarly, the managers and major shareholder would need to be satisfied. In the case of the managers it might also be necessary to provide some guarantee that they would continue to have managerial positions with attractive contracts within Stanzial, and the large single shareholder might insist on continued representation on the Board of Directors.

The nature of payment might also be important. The managers and single investor could be liable to immediate capital gains tax if payment was to be made in cash. They might have a preference for shares in Stanzial. The venture capital company might prefer cash rather than maintain an equity stake in a different company.

(c) Factors that might influence the medium-term success of the acquisition include:

(i) The thoroughness of the planning of the acquisition. This would include establishing key reporting relationships and control of key factors.

(ii) Corporate objectives and plans should be harmonised. Effective integration will require mutual respect for the different cultures and systems of the two companies.

(iii) Human resource issues are important, such as how any redundancies are dealt with, and the role of the managers of the acquired company in the new organisation.

(iv) Effective post-acquisition audit. Monitoring of whether or not the post-acquisition performance is as expected, and implementation of any necessary action to remedy problems and under-performance.

(v) The reaction of competitors; in particular, can they produce alternative wireless links that would adversely affect Stanzial's market share?

(vi) Maintenance of the pension rights of existing employees post-acquisition.

7 PURSUIT CO (JUN 11)

Key answer tips

Business valuation, especially using free cash flows, is very commonly tested. Lay out your forecast free cash flows neatly, and leave time to also attempt all the discussion parts of the question.

(a) **Organic growth** permits an organisation to carefully plan its strategic growth in line with specified objectives.

However, when entering new markets there may be a substantial cost involved with researching markets and/or buying-in expertise.

Lead-times in establishing production facilities are relatively long in comparison with growth by acquisition, which may be a significant factor when trying to establish or to consolidate market share.

Growth by acquisition is often not as carefully planned, and may be a rapid reaction to a perceived market opportunity.

It permits quick access to new markets or new technology, or the elimination of a competitor.

Information about the financial and other attributes of a potential acquisition target is inevitably less complete than a company's own internal management information.

This makes the valuation of a potential acquisition target difficult, and projections of future cash flows less precise.

The potential for significant savings is often not fully known until after the acquisition, when attempts are made to rationalise and integrate the operations of the two companies.

Growth by acquisition may be the only way to achieve very rapid growth.

(b) **REPORT**

Prepared by AN Accountant

(i) The calculations and estimations for part (i) are given in the appendix. To assess whether or not the acquisition would be beneficial to Pursuit's shareholders, the additional synergy benefits after the acquisition has been paid for need to be ascertained.

The estimated synergy benefit from the acquisition is approximately $9,074,000 (see Appendix), which is the post-acquisition value of the combined company less the values of the individual companies. However, once Fodder Co's debt obligations and the equity shareholders have been paid, the benefit to Pursuit Co's shareholders reduces to approximately $52,000 (see Appendix), which is minimal. Even a small change in the variables and assumptions could negate it. It is therefore doubtful that the shareholders would view the acquisition as beneficial to themselves or the company.

(ii) The limitations of the estimates stem from the fact that although the model used is theoretically sound, it is difficult to apply it in practice for the following reasons.

The calculations in part (i) are based on a number of assumptions such as the growth rate in the next four years, the perpetual growth rate after the four years, additional investment in assets, stable tax rates, discount rates and profit margins, assumption that debt is risk free when computing the asset beta. All these assumptions would be subject to varying margins of error.

It may be difficult for Pursuit Co to assess the variables of the combined company to any degree of accuracy, and therefore the synergy benefits may be hard to predict.

No information is provided about the pre-acquisition and post-acquisition costs.

Although it may be possible to estimate the equity beta of Pursuit Co, being a listed company, to a high level of accuracy, estimating Fodder Co's equity beta may be more problematic, because it is a private company.

Given the above, it is probably more accurate to present a range of possible values for the combined company depending on different scenarios and the likelihood of their occurrence, before a decision is made.

(iii) The current value of Pursuit Co is $140,000,000, of which the market value of equity and debt are $70,000,000 each. The value of the combined company before paying Fodder Co shareholders is approximately $189,169,000, and if the capital structure is maintained, the market values of debt and equity will be approximately $94,584,500 each. This is an increase of approximately $24,584,500 in the debt capacity.

The amount payable for Fodder Co's debt obligations and to the shareholders including the premium is approximately $49,116,500 [4,009 + 36,086 × 1.25]. If $24,584,500 is paid using the extra debt capacity and $20,000,000 using cash reserves, an additional amount of approximately $4,532,000 will need to be raised. Hence, if only debt finance and cash reserves are used, the capital structure cannot be maintained.

(iv) If Pursuit Co aims to acquire Fodder Co using debt finance and cash reserves, then the capital structure of the combined company will change. It will also change if they adopt the Chief Financial Officer's recommendation and acquire Fodder Co using only debt finance.

Both these options will cause the cost of capital of the combined company to change. This in turn will cause the value of the company to change. This will cause the proportion of market value of equity to market value of debt to change, and thus change the cost of capital. Therefore the changes in the market value of the company and the cost of capital are interrelated.

To resolve this problem, an iterative procedure needs to be adopted where the beta and the cost of capital are recalculated to take account of the changes in the capital structure, and then the company is re-valued. This procedure is repeated until the assumed capital structure is closely aligned to the capital structure that has been re-calculated. This process is normally done using a spreadsheet package such as Excel. This method is used when both the business risk and the financial risk of the acquiring company change as a result of an acquisition (referred to as a type III acquisition).

Alternatively an adjusted present value approach may be undertaken.

(v) The Chief Financial Officer's suggestion appears to be a disposal of 'crown jewels'. Without the cash reserves, Pursuit Co may become less valuable to SGF Co. Also, the reason for the depressed share price may be because Pursuit Co's shareholders do not agree with the policy to retain large cash reserves. Therefore returning the cash reserves to the shareholders may lead to an increase in the share price and make a bid from SGF Co more unlikely. This would not initially contravene the regulatory framework as no formal bid has been made. However, Pursuit Co must investigate further whether the reason for a possible bid from SGF Co might be to gain access to the large amount of cash or it might have other reasons. Pursuit Co should also try to establish whether remitting the cash to the shareholders would be viewed positively by them.

Whether this is a viable option for Pursuit Co depends on the bid for Fodder Co. In part (iii) it was established that more than the expected debt finance would be needed even if the cash reserves are used to pay for some of the acquisition cost. If the cash is remitted, a further $20,000,000 would be needed, and if this was all raised by debt finance then a significant proportion of the value of the combined company would be debt financed. The increased gearing may have significant implications on Pursuit Co's future investment plans and may result in increased restrictive covenants. Ultimately gearing might have to increase to such a level that this method of financing might not be possible. Pursuit Co should investigate the full implications further and assess whether the acquisition is worthwhile given the marginal value it provides for the shareholders (see part (i)).

Tutorial note

When attempting a question like this in the Computer Based Exam (CBE), make your answer look like a professional document by writing the report in the word processor but putting your numbers (appendix) in a spreadsheet.

When preparing your calculations, use the spreadsheet functions SUM and NPV to save time. Be careful when using the NPV function to enter =NPV, then a bracket containing the discount rate, a comma, and then the cells containing the cash flows from year 1 onwards. The initial investment then needs to be subtracted separately.

APPENDIX

Part (i)

Interest is ignored as its impact is included in the companies' discount rates

Fodder cost of capital

Ke = 4.5% + 1.53 × 6% = 13.68%

Cost of capital = 13.68% × 0.9 + 9% × (1 – 0.28) × 0.1 = 12.96% assume 13%

Fodder

Sales revenue growth rate = $(16,146/13,559)^{1/3} - 1 \times 100\%$ = 5.99% assume 6%
Operating profit margin = approx. 32% of sales revenue

Fodder Co cash flow and value computation ($000)

Year	1	2	3	4
Sales revenue	17,115	18,142	19,231	20,385
Operating profit	5,477	5,805	6,154	6,523
Less tax (28%)	(1,534)	(1,625)	(1,723)	(1,826)
Less additional investment (22c/$1 of sales revenue increase)	(213)	(226)	(240)	(254)
Free cash flows	3,730	3,954	4,191	4,443
PV (13%)	3,301	3,097	2,905	2,725

	$(000)
PV (first 4 years)	12,028
PV (after 4 years) $[4,443 \times 1.03/(0.13 - 0.03)] \times 1.13^{-4}$	28,067
Firm value	40,095

Combined Company: Cost of capital calculation

Asset beta (Pursuit Co) = 1.18 × 0.5/(0.5 + 0.5 × 0.72) = 0.686

Asset beta (Fodder Co) = 1.53 × 0.9/(0.9 + 0.1 × 0.72) = 1.417

Asset beta of combined co.

= (0.686 × 140,000 + 1.417 × 40,095)/(140,000 + 40,095) = 0.849

Equity beta of combined company = 0.849 × (0.5 + 0.5 × 0.72)/0.5 = 1.46

Ke = 4.5% + 1.46 × 6% = 13.26%

Cost of capital = 13.26% × 0.5 + 6.4% × 0.5 × 0.72 = 8.93%, assume 9%

Combined Co cash flow and value computation ($000)

Sales revenue growth rate = 5.8%, operating profit margin = 30% of sales revenue

Year	1	2	3	4
Sales revenue	51,952	54,965	58,153	61,526
Operating profit	15,586	16,490	17,446	18,458
Less tax (28%)	(4,364)	(4,617)	(4,885)	(5,168)
Less additional investment (18c/$1 of sales revenue increase)	(513)	(542)	(574)	(607)
Free cash flows	10,709	11,331	11,987	12,683
PV (9%)	9,825	9,537	9,256	8,985

	$(000)
PV (first 4 years)	37,603
PV (after 4 years) [12,683 × 1.029/(0.09 – 0.029)] × 1.09^{-4}	151,566
Firm value	189,169

Synergy benefits = 189,169,000 – (140,000,000 + 40,095,000) = $9,074,000

Estimated premium required to acquire Fodder Co = 0.25 × 36,086,000 = $9,022,000

Net benefit to Pursuit Co shareholders = $52,000

		Marking scheme		Marks
(a)		1-2 marks per sensible, well explained point		8
				—
			Maximum	8
				—
(b)	(i)	Ignore interest in calculations		1
		Estimate of cost of capital of Fodder Co		1
		Estimates of growth rates and profit margins for Fodder Co		2
		Estimate of intrinsic value of Fodder Co		3
		Equity beta of combined co		3
		Cost of capital of combined co		1
		Estimate of value of combined co		3
		Synergy benefits, value to Pursuit Co shareholders, and conclusion		2-3
				—
			Maximum	16
				—
	(ii)	1-2 marks per each point discussed		4
		(Credit will be given for alternative relevant points)		
				—
			Maximum	4
				—
	(iii)	Estimate of the increase in debt capacity after acquisition		1
		Estimate of the funds required to acquire Fodder Co		1
		Conclusion		1
				—
				3
				—
	(iv)	Explanation of the problem of the changing capital structure		2
		Explanation of the resolution of the problem using the iterative process		2
				—
				4
				—
	(v)	Assessment of suitable defence		2-3
		Assessment of viability		2-3
		(Credit will be given for alternative relevant points)		
				—
				5
				—
		Professional skills marks (see below)		10
Total				50

Professional skills

Communication

General report format and structure (use of headings/sub-headings and an introduction)

Style, language and clarity (appropriate layout and tone of report response, presentation of calculations, appropriate use of the tools)

Effectiveness of communication (answer is relevant, specific rather than general and focused to the requirement)

Analysis and Evaluation

Appropriate use of the data to determine suitable calculations

Appropriate use of the data to support discussion and draw appropriate conclusions

Demonstration of reasoned judgement when considering key matters for this specific company

Demonstration of ability to consider relevant factors applicable to increasing the level of debt finance

Scepticism

Effective challenge of information and assumptions supplied and, techniques carried out to support any decision

Commercial acumen

Effective use of examples and/or calculations from the scenario information and other practical considerations related to the context to illustrate points being made

Recognition of external constraints and opportunities as necessary

Maximum 10 marks

8 NENTE CO (JUN 12)

Key answer tips

Always make sure that you use a report format in the section A question, with your report in the word processor and appendices in the spreadsheet. Presenting your answer professionally will enable you to score the 'professional marks' relating to "Communication" – the easiest marks on the whole paper.

(a) Synergy might exist for several reasons, including:

Economic efficiency gains

Gains might relate to economies of scale or scope.

Economies of scale occur through such factors as fixed operating costs being spread over a larger production volume, equipment being used more efficiently with higher volumes of production, or bulk purchasing reducing costs.

Economies of scope may arise from reduced advertising and distribution costs when companies have complementary resources. Economies of scale and scope relate mainly to horizontal acquisitions and mergers. Economic efficiency gains may also occur with backward or forward vertical integration which might reduce production costs as the 'middle man' is eliminated, improve control of essential raw materials or other resources that are needed for production, or avoid disputes with what were previously suppliers or customers.

Economic efficiency gains might also result from replacing inefficient management as the result of a merger/takeover.

Financial synergy

Financial synergy might involve a reduction in the cost of capital and risk.

The variability (standard deviation) of returns of a combined entity is usually less than the weighted average of the risk of the individual companies. This is a reduction in total risk, but does not affect systematic risk, and hence might not be regarded as a form of synergy by shareholders. However, reduced variability of returns might improve a company's credit rating making it easier and/or cheaper to obtain a loan.

Another possible financial synergy exists when one company in an acquisition or merger is able to use tax shields, or accumulated tax losses, which would otherwise have been unavailable to the other company.

Market power

A large organisation, particularly one which has acquired competitors, might have sufficient market power to increase its profits through price leadership or other monopolistic or oligopolistic means.

(b) **REPORT TO THE BOARD OF DIRECTORS, NENTE CO**

IMPACT OF THE TAKEOVER PROPOSAL FROM MIJE CO AND PRODUCTION RIGHTS OF THE FOLLOW-ON PRODUCT

The report considers the value of the takeover to Nente Co and Mije Co shareholders based on a cash offer and on a share-for-share offer. It discusses the possible reaction of each group of shareholders to the two offers and how best to utilise the follow-on product opportunity. The significant assumptions made in compiling the report are also explained.

The appendices to the report show the detailed calculations in estimating the equity value of Nente Co, the value to Nente Co and Mije Co shareholders of acquiring Nente Co by cash and by a share-for-share exchange, and the value to Nente Co of the exclusive rights to the follow-on product. The results of the calculation are summarised below:

Estimated price of a Nente Co share before the takeover offer and follow-on product is £2.90/share (Appendix i)

Estimated increase in share price	Nente Co	Mije Co
Cash offer (Appendix ii)	1.7%	9.4%
Share-for-share offer (Appendix ii)	17.9%	6.9%

Estimate of the value per share of the follow-on product to Nente Co is 8.7% (Appendix iii)

It is unlikely that Nente Co shareholders would accept the cash offer because it is little more than the estimated price of a Nente Co share before the takeover offer. However, the share-for-share offer gives a larger increase in value of a share of 17.9%. Given that the normal premium on acquisitions ranges from 20% to 40%, this is closer to what Nente Co shareholders would find acceptable. It is also greater than the additional value from the follow-on product. Therefore, based on the financial figures, Nente Co's shareholders would find the offer of a takeover on a share-for-share exchange basis the most attractive option. The other options considered here yield lower expected percentage increase in share price.

Mije Co shareholders would prefer the cash offer so that they can maximise the price of their shares and also not dilute their shareholding, but they would probably accept either option because the price of their shares increases. However, Mije Co shareholders would probably assess whether or not to accept the acquisition proposal by comparing it with other opportunities that the company has available to it and whether this is the best way to utilise its spare cash flows.

The calculations and analysis in each case is made on a number of assumptions. For example, in order to calculate the estimated price of a Nente Co share, the free cash flow valuation model is used. For this, the growth rate, the cost of capital and effective time period when the growth rate will occur (perpetuity in this instance) are all estimates or based on assumptions. For the takeover offer, the synergy savings and P/E ratio value are both assumptions. For the value of the follow-on product and the related option, the option variables are estimates and it is assumed that they would not change during the period before the decision. The value of the option is based on the possibility that the option will only be exercised at the end of the two years, although it seems that the decision can be made any time within the two years.

The follow-on product is initially treated separately from the takeover, but Nente Co may ask Mije Co to take the value of the follow-on product into consideration in its offer. The value of the rights that allow Nente Co to delay making a decision are themselves worth $603,561 (Appendix iii) and add just over 25c or 8.7% to the value of a Nente Co share. If Mije Co can be convinced to increase their offer to match this or the rights could be sold before the takeover, then the return for Nente Co's shareholders would be much higher at 26.6% (17.9% + 8.7%).

In conclusion, the most favourable outcome for Nente Co shareholders would be to accept the share-for-share offer, and try to convince Mije Co to take the value of the follow-on product into consideration. Prior to accepting the offer Nente Co shareholders would need to be assured of the accuracy of the results produced by the computations in the appendices.

Report compiled by: XXX

Date: XXX

Note: Credit will be given for alternative relevant discussion and suggestions.

APPENDICES

Appendix i: Estimate of Nente Co Equity Value Based on Free Cash Flows

Company value = Free cash flows (FCF) × (1 + growth rate (g))/(cost of capital (k) – g)

k = 11%

Past g = (latest profit before interest and tax (PBIT)/earliest PBIT)$^{1/\text{no. of years of growth}}$ – 1

Past g = $(1,230/970)^{1/3}$ – 1 = 0.0824

Future g = 0.25 × 0.0824 = 0.0206

FCF Calculation

FCF = PBIT + non-cash flows – cash investment – tax

FCF = $1,230,000 + $1,206,000 – $1,010,000 – ($1,230,000 × 20%) = $1,180,000

Company value = $1,180,000 × 1.0206/(0.11 – 0.0206) = $13,471,000

Equity value = $13,471,000 – $6,500,000 = $6,971,000

Per share = $6,971,000/2,400,000 shares = $2.90

Appendix ii: Estimated Returns to Nente Co and Mije Co Shareholders

Cash Offer

Gain in value to a Nente Co share = ($2.95 – $2.90)/$2.90 = 1.7%

Additional earnings after acquisition = $620,000 + $150,000 = $770,000

Additional EPS created from acquisition = $770,000/10,000,000 = 7.7c/share

Increase in share price based on P/E of 15 = 7.7c × 15 = $1.16

Additional value created = $1.16 × 10,000,000 =	$11,600,000
Less: paid for Nente Co acquisition = ($2.95 × 2.4m shares)	$(7,080,000)
Value added for Mije shareholders =	$4,520,000
Gain in value to a Mije Co share = $4,520,000/10,000,000 =	45.2c
or 45.2c/480c =	9.4%

Share-for-share Offer

Earnings combined company = $620,000 + $150,000 + $3,200,000 = $3,970,000

Shares in combined company = 10,000,000 + 2,400,000 × 2/3 = 11,600,000

EPS = 34.2c/share [$3,970,000/11,600,000]

Expected share price = 34.2c × 15 = 513c or $5.13/share

Three Nente Co shares = $2.90 × 3 = $8.70

Gain in value to a Mije Co share = ($5.13 – $4.80)/$4.80	=	6.9%
Gain in value to a Nente Co share = ($10.26 – $8.70)/$8.70	=	17.9%

Appendix iii: Increase in Value of Follow-On Product

Present value of the positive cash flows	=	$2,434,000
Present value of the cash outflow	=	$(2,029,000)
Net present value of the new product	=	$405,000

Based on conventional NPV, without considering the value of the option to delay the decision, the project would increase the value of the company by $405,000.

Considering the value of the option to delay the decision

Price of asset (PV of future positive cash flows)	=	$2,434,000
Exercise price (initial cost of project, not discounted)	=	$2,500,000
Time to expiry of option	=	2 years
Risk free rate (estimate)	=	3.2%
Volatility	=	42%

Tutorial note

Look out for the BSOP calculator spreadsheet response option in the exam. You'll need to enter the above five key variables in the spreadsheet to generate the answers shown below.

From the BSOP calculator spreadsheet, we can read off the following values:

d_1 = 0.3597

d_2 = -0.2343

$N(d_1)$ = 0.6405

$N(d_2)$ = 0.4074

Call value = $603,561

The project increases the value of the company by $603,561 or 25.1c per share ($603,561/2,400,000 shares). In percentage terms this is an increase of about 8.7% (25.1c/290c).

(c) Using the BSOP model in company valuation rests upon the idea that equity is a call option, written by the lenders, on the underlying assets of the business. If the value of the company declines substantially then the shareholders can simply walk away, losing the maximum of their investment. On the other hand, the upside potential is unlimited once the interest on debt has been paid.

The BSOP model can be helpful in circumstances where the conventional methods of valuation do not reflect the risks fully or where they cannot be used. For example if we are trying to value an unlisted company with unpredictable future growth.

There are five variables which are input into the BSOP model to determine the value of the option. Proxies need to be established for each variable when using the BSOP model to value a company. The five variables are: the value of the underlying asset, the exercise price, the time to expiry, the volatility of the underlying asset value and the risk free rate of return.

For the exercise price, the debt of the company is taken. In its simplest form, the assumption is that the borrowing is in the form of zero coupon debt, i.e., a discount bond. In practice such debt is not used as a primary source of company finance and so we calculate the value of an equivalent bond with the same yield and term to maturity as the company's existing debt. The exercise price in valuing the business as a call option is the value of the outstanding debt calculated as the present value of a zero coupon bond offering the same yield as the current debt.

The proxy for the value of the underlying asset is the fair value of the company's assets less current liabilities on the basis that if the company is broken up and sold, then that is what the assets would be worth to the long-term debt holders and the equity holders.

The time to expiry is the period of time before the debt is due for redemption. The owners of the company have that time before the option needs to be exercised, that is when the debt holders need to be repaid.

The proxy for the volatility of the underlying asset is the volatility of the business' assets.

The risk-free rate is usually the rate on a riskless investment such as a short-term government bond.

		Marking scheme		Marks
(a)		1-2 marks per sensible, well-explained point		6
			Maximum	6
(b)	(i)	Based on PBIT, calculation of the growth rate		2
		Calculation of free cash flows		2
		Calculation of company value, equity value and value of each share		3
				7
	(ii)	**Cash offer**		
		Additional value created for Mije Co shareholders		3
		Value created per share for Nente Co shareholders		1
		Share for share offer		
		Expected share price for the combined company		2
		Value created for Nente Co share		1
		Value created for Mije Co share		1
				8
	(iii)	PV of underlying asset		1
		Value of exercise price		1
		Other three BSOP variables (r,s and t)		1
		Value of call option		1
		Value added to Nente Co share		1
				5
	(iv)	Nente Co shareholders		2–3
		Mije Co shareholders		2–3
		Assumptions		2–3
		Use of value of follow-on product		2–3
			Maximum	8
(a)		1-2 marks per sensible, well-explained point		6
			Maximum	6
		Professional skills marks (see below)		10
Total				50

Professional skills

Communication

General report format and structure (use of headings/sub-headings and an introduction)

Style, language and clarity (appropriate layout and tone of report response, presentation of calculations, appropriate use of the tools)

Effectiveness of communication (answer is relevant, specific rather than general and focused to the requirement)

Analysis and Evaluation

Appropriate use of the data to determine suitable calculations

Appropriate use of the data to support discussion and draw appropriate conclusions

Demonstration of reasoned judgement when considering key matters for this specific company

Demonstration of ability to consider relevant factors applicable to this specific scenario

Scepticism

Effective challenge of information and assumptions supplied and, techniques carried out to support any decision

Commercial acumen

Effective use of examples and/or calculations from the scenario information and other practical considerations related to the context to illustrate points being made

Recognition of external constraints and opportunities as necessary

Maximum 10 marks

9   MLIMA CO (JUN 13)

Key answer tips

Notice that part (b) of this question is totally independent of part (a). Feel free to attempt part (b) first if you feel that it is easier than part (a).

(a)   **Report to the Board of Directors, Mlima Co Initial public listing: price range and implications**

This report considers a range of values of Mlima Co and possible share price, based on 100 million issued shares in preparation of the initial public listing. The assumptions made in determining the value range and the likelihood of the unsecured bond holders accepting the 10% equity-for-debt swap offer are discussed. Alternative reasons for the listing and reasons for issuing the share at a discount are evaluated.

Mlima Co cost of capital explanation

Ziwa Co's ungeared cost of equity represents the return Ziwa Co's shareholders would require if Ziwa Co was financed entirely by equity and had no debt. The return would compensate them for the business risk undertaken by the company.

This required rate of return would compensate Mlima Co's shareholders as well because, since both companies are in the same industry, they face the same business risk. This rate is then used as Mlima Co's cost of capital because of the assumption that Mlima Co will not issue any debt and faces no financial risk. Therefore its cost of equity (ungeared) is its cost of capital.

Mlima Co Estimated Value

Based on a cost of capital of 11% (Appendix 1), the value of Mlima Co is estimated at $564.3m (Appendix 2), prior to considering the impact of the Bahari project. The value of the Bahari project, without taking into account the benefits of the tax shield and the subsidies, does not exceed the initial investment. With the benefits of the tax shield and subsidies, it is estimated that the project will generate a positive net present value of $21.5m (Appendix 3). Taking the Bahari project into account gives a value for Mlima Co at just under $586m.

Possible share price *(100m shares)*	Without the Bahari project	With the Bahari project
At full value	$5.64/share	$5.86/share
With 20% discount	$4.51/share	$4.69/share

Unsecured bondholders (equity-for-debt swap)

The current value of the unsecured bond is estimated at $56.8m (Appendix 4) and if the unsecured bondholders are to be offered a 10% equity stake in Mlima Co post-listing, then only the share price at $5.86 would be acceptable to them. If the listing is made at the lowest price of $4.51/share, then they would need to be offered around a 12.6% equity stake ($56.8m/$4.51 = 12.594m).

The value of the bond is based on a flat yield curve (or yield to maturity) of 7%, which is the rate at which Mlima Co can borrow funds and therefore its current yield. A more accurate method would be to assess the yield curve based on future risk-free rates and credit spreads for the company.

Assumptions

The main assumptions made are around the accuracy of the information used in estimating the values of the company and the project. For example, the value of the company is based on assumptions of future growth rates, profit margins, future tax rates and capital investment. The basis for estimating the future growth rates and profit margins on past performance may not be accurate. With the Bahari project, for example, projections of future cash flows are made for 15 years and the variability of these has been estimated. Again, the reasonableness of these estimates needs to be assessed. Are they, for example, based on past experience and/or have professional experts judged the values?

The cost of capital is estimated based on a competitor's ungeared cost of equity, on the basis that Mlima Co is in a similar line of business and therefore faces similar business risk. The financial risk element has been removed since it has been stated that Mlima Co is not looking to raise extra debt finance. However, it is possible that the business risks faced by Mlima Co and that faced by Ziwa Co, the competitor, are not the same. Accepting the Bahari project would also change the risk profile of Mlima Co and therefore its discount rate.

The values are based on the Bahari government fulfilling the subsidised loan concession it has offered. Mlima Co needs to consider the likelihood of this concession continuing for the entire 15 years and whether a change of government may jeopardise the agreement. The political and other risks need to be assessed and their impact assessed.

It has been assumed that the underwriting and other costs involved with the new listing are not significant or have been catered for, before the assessment of the cash flows. This assumption needs to be reviewed and its accuracy assessed.

Reasons for the public listing

The main reason given for the public listing is to use the funds raised to eliminate the debt in the company. There are other reasons why a company may undertake a public listing. These include: gaining a higher reputation by being listed on a recognised stock exchange and therefore reducing the costs of contracting with stakeholders; being able to raise funds more easily in the future to undertake new projects; the listing will provide the current owners with a value for their equity stake; and the listing may enable the current owners to sell their equity stakes and gain from the value in the organisation.

Issuing shares at a discount

Issuing only 20% of the share capital to the public at the initial listing would make them minority shareholders effectively. As such, their ability to influence the decision-making process in the company would be severely curtailed, since even if all the new investors voted as a bloc against a decision, they would not be able to overturn it. The discounted share price would reflect the additional risk of investing in a company as a minority shareholder. In this case, the position of the unsecured bondholders is important. If the unsecured bondholders, holding between 10% and 12.6% of the share capital in an equity-for-debt swap, are included with the new investors, then the equity stake rises to 30%–32.6%. In such a case, shareholders, as a bloc, would have a significant influence on the company's decisions. The question that should be asked is whether the current unsecured bondholders are more closely aligned to the interests of the current owners or to the interests of the new investors.

The second reason for issuing shares at a discount is to ensure that they do all get sold and as a reward for the underwriters. Research suggests that, normally, for new listings, shares are issued at a discount and the price of such shares rises immediately after launch.

Conclusion

The report and the calculations in the appendices suggest a price range for the listing of between $4.51 and $5.86 per share, depending on whether or not the Bahari project is undertaken, the discount at which the shares are issued and the assumptions made. It is recommended that Mlima Co should consult its underwriters and potential investors about the possible price they would be willing to pay before making a final decision (known as book-building).

If 20 million shares are offered to the public for $4.51 each, this will result in total funds raised of just over $90 million. If the $80 million are spent in paying for the secured bond, just over $10 million liquid funds remain. Therefore, Mlima Co needs to consider whether issuing the shares at a discount would ensure sufficient liquid funds are available for it to continue its normal business. In addition to this, the Bahari investment may result in a change in the desired capital structure of the company and have an impact on the cost of capital. Finally, being listed will result in additional listing costs and annual costs related to additional reporting requirements.

These factors should be balanced against the benefits of undertaking the new listing before a final decision is made.

Report compiled by: XXX

Date: XXX

Tutorial note

When attempting a question like this in the Computer Based Exam (CBE), make your answer look like a professional document by writing the report in the word processor but putting your numbers (appendix) in a spreadsheet.

When preparing your calculations, use the spreadsheet functions SUM and NPV to save time. Be careful when using the NPV function to enter =NPV, then a bracket containing the discount rate, a comma, and then the cells containing the cash flows from year 1 onwards. The initial investment then needs to be subtracted separately.

APPENDICES

Appendix 1: Mlima Co, cost of capital

Ziwa Co

MV debt = $1,700m × 1.05 = $1,785m MV equity = 200m × $7 = $1,400m

Ziwa Co, ungeared Ke

$Ke_g = Ke_u + (1 - t)(Ke_u - K_d) D/E$

$16.83\% = Ke_u + 0.75 \times (Ke_u - 4.76\%) \times 1,785/1,400$

$16.83\% + 4.55\% = 1.9563 \times Ke_u$

$Ke_u = 10.93\%$ (say 11%)

Appendix 2: Mlima Co, estimate of value prior to Bahari project

Value based on future free cash flows

Historic mean sales revenue growth = $(389.1/344.7)^{1/2} - 1 = 0.625$ or 6.25%

Next four years annual growth rate of sales revenue = 120% of 6.25% = 7.5%

Thereafter 3.5% of cash flows per year

Operating profit margin (approx) = 58.4/389.1 = 54.9/366.3 = 51.7/344.7 = 15%

Year (in $ millions)	1	2	3	4
Sales revenue	418.3	449.7	483.4	519.7
Operating profit	62.7	67.5	72.5	78.0
Less taxation (25%)	(15.7)	(16.9)	(18.1)	(19.5)
Less additional capital investment				
(30c per $1 change in sales revenue)	(8.8)	(9.4)	(10.1)	(10.9)
Free cash flows	38.2	41.2	44.3	47.6
PV of free cash flows (11%)	34.4	33.4	32.4	31.4

PV first four years $131.6m

PV after four years $(47.6 \times 1.035)/(0.11 - 0.035) \times 1.11^{-4}$ $432.7m

Value of company $564.3m

Appendix 3: Value of the Bahari project Base case present value

Year	Free Cash flows (in $ millions)	PV (11%) (in $ millions)
1	4.0	3.6
2	8.0	6.5
3	16.0	11.7
4	18.4	12.1
5	21.2	12.6
6 to 15	21.2	**74.0
Total		120.5

** The free cash flows in years 6 to 15 are an annuity for 10 years at 11%, then discounted back for five years: $21.2 \times 5.889 \times 0.593 = 74.0$

PV of the tax shield and subsidy

Annuity factor (7%, 15 years) = 9.108

Annual tax shield benefit interest paid = 3% × $150m × 25% = $1.1m Subsidy benefit = 4% × $150m × (1 – 25%) = $4.5m PV of tax shield and subsidy benefit = 5.6 × 9.108 = $51.0m

Adjusted present value = $120.5m + $51.0m – $150.0m = $21.5m

Appendix 4: Estimated value of the unsecured bond

Assume a flat yield or yield to maturity of 7%

Annual coupon interest = $5.2m (13% × $40m)

10-year annuity at 7% = 7.024; Discount factor (10 years, 7%) = 0.508

Bond value = $5.2m × 7.024 + $40m × 0.508 = $56.8m

(b) It is likely that Mlima Co's actions will be scrutinised more closely in the run up to the listing and once it has been listed. In both the situations, the company should consider the action it should take based on its ethical and accountability code. Most major corporations now publicise such codes of behaviour and would consult these in cases of ethical and/or accountability difficulties.

With the first situation concerning the relocation of the farmers, Mlima Co would consult its ethical code to judge how far its responsibility lay. It may take the view that the matter is between the farmers and the government, and it is not directly or indirectly responsible for the situation. In any case, it is likely that the mining rights will be assigned to another company, should Mlima Co decide to walk away from the deal. It is unlikely that, even if Mlima Co did not agree to the offer, the plight of the farmers would cease.

Instead, Mlima Co may decide to try to influence the government with respect to the farmers by urging the government to keep the community together and offer the farmers better land. Mlima Co may also decide to offer jobs and training to farmers who decide not to leave.

With the second situation concerning the Bahari president and Mlima Co's CEO, whilst it would make good business sense to forge strong relationships as a means of competitive advantage, Mlima Co should ensure that the negotiation was transparent and did not involve any bribery or illegal practice. If both the company and Bahari government can demonstrate that they acted in the best interests of the company and the country respectively, and individuals did not benefit as a result, then this should not be seen in a negative light.

Mlima Co needs to establish a clear strategy of how it would respond to public scrutiny of either issue. This may include actions such as demonstrating that it is acting according to its ethical code, pre-empting media scrutiny by releasing press statements, and using its influence to ensure the best and correct outcome in each case for the stakeholders concerned.

Tutorial note (from the examiner's model answer)

Credit will be given for alternative, relevant approaches to the calculations, comments and suggestions/recommendations.

				Marks
		Marking scheme		
(a)	(i)	Explanation of Mlima Co's cost of capital based on Ziwa Co's ungeared cost of equity		3
		Ziwa Co, cost of ungeared equity		4
			Maximum	7
	(ii)	Sales revenue growth rates		1
		Operating profit rate		1
		Estimate of free cash flows and PV of free cash flows for years 1 to 4		4
		PV of free cash flows after year 4		2
		Base case Bahari project value		2
		Annual tax shield benefit		1
		Annual subsidy benefit		1
		PV of the tax shield and subsidy benefits		1
		Value of the Bahari project		1
			Maximum	14
	(iii)	Calculation of unsecured bond value		2
		Comment		1
		Limitation		1
			Maximum	4
	(iv)	Comments on the range of values/prices with and without the project, and concluding statement		3–4
		Discussion of assumptions		2–3
		Explanation for additional reasons for listing		1–2
		Assessment of reasons for discounted share price		1–2
			Maximum	9
(b)		Discussion of relocation of farmers		3–4
		Discussion of relationship between Bahari president and Mlima Co CEO		3–4
			Maximum	6
		Professional skills marks (see below)		10
Total				50

Professional skills

Communication

General report format and structure (use of headings/sub-headings and an introduction)

Style, language and clarity (appropriate layout and tone of report response, presentation of calculations, appropriate use of the tools)

Effectiveness of communication (answer is relevant, specific rather than general and focused to the requirement)

Analysis and Evaluation

Appropriate use of the data to determine suitable calculations

Appropriate use of the data to support discussion and draw appropriate conclusions

Demonstration of reasoned judgement when considering key matters for this specific company

Demonstration of ability to consider relevant factors applicable to this specific scenario

Scepticism

Effective challenge of information and assumptions supplied and, techniques carried out to support any decision

Commercial acumen

Effective use of examples and/or calculations from the scenario information and other practical considerations related to the context to illustrate points being made

Recognition of external constraints and opportunities as necessary

Maximum 10 marks

10 NAHARA CO AND FUGAE CO (DEC 14)

Key answer tips

All the section A questions are very time pressured, with lots of parts to complete in the time.

It is therefore critically important to attempt the easier parts of the question first and leave the more difficult parts until the end.

(a) Risk diversification, especially into diverse business sectors, has often been stated as a reason for undertaking mergers and acquisitions (M&As). Like individuals holding well-diversified portfolios, a company with a number of subsidiaries in different sectors could reduce its exposure to unsystematic risk. Another possible benefit of diversification is sometimes argued to be a reduction in the volatility of cash flows, which may lead to a better credit rating and a lower cost of capital.

The argument against this states that since individual investors can undertake this level of risk diversification both quickly and cheaply themselves, there is little reason for companies to do so. Indeed, research suggests that markets do not reward this risk diversification.

Nevertheless, for Nahara Co, undertaking M&As may have beneficial outcomes, especially if the sovereign fund has its entire investment in the holding company and is not well-diversified itself. In such a situation unsystematic risk reduction can be beneficial. The case study does not state whether or not the sovereign funds are invested elsewhere and therefore a definitive conclusion cannot be reached.

If Nahara Co is able to identify undervalued companies and after purchasing the company can increase the value for the holding company overall, by increasing the value of the undervalued companies, then such M&As activity would have a beneficial impact on the funds invested. However, for this strategy to work, Nahara Co must:

(i)   Possess a superior capability or knowledge in identifying bargain buys ahead of its competitor companies. To achieve this, it must have access to better information, which it can tap into quicker, and/or have superior analytical tools. Nahara Co should assess whether or not it does possess such capabilities, otherwise its claim is not valid.

(ii)   Ensure that it has quick access to the necessary funds to pursue an undervalued acquisition. Even if Nahara Co possesses superior knowledge, it is unlikely that this will last for a long time before its competitors find out; therefore it needs to have the funds ready, to move quickly. Given that it has access to sovereign funds from a wealthy source, access to funds is probably not a problem.

(iii)   Set a maximum ceiling for the price it is willing to pay and should not go over this amount, or the potential value created will be reduced.

If, in its assessment, Nahara Co is able to show that it meets all the above conditions, then the strategy of identifying and pursuing undervalued companies may be valid.

(b)   Report to the Board of Directors, Avem Co

Proposed acquisition of Fugae Co

This report evaluates whether or not it is beneficial for Avem Co to acquire Fugae Co. Initially the value of the two companies is determined separately and as a combined entity, to assess the additional value created from bringing the two companies together. Following this, the report considers how much Nahara Co and Avem Co will gain from the value created. The assumptions made to arrive at the additional value are also considered. The report concludes by considering whether or not the acquisition will be beneficial to Avem Co and to Nahara Co.

Appendix 1 shows that the additional value created from combining the two companies is approximately $451.5 million, of which $276.8 million will go to Nahara Co, as the owner of Fugae Co. This represents a premium of about 30% which is the minimum acceptable to Nahara Co. The balance of the additional value will go to Avem Co which is about $174.7 million, representing an increase in value of 1.46% [$174.7m/$12,000m].

Appendix 2 shows that accepting the project would increase Fugae Co's value as the expected net present value is positive. After taking into account Lumi Co's offer, the expected net present value is higher. Therefore, it would be beneficial for Fugae Co to take on the project and accept Lumi Co's offer, if the tourism industry does not grow as expected, as this will increase Fugae Co's value.

Assumptions

It is assumed that all the figures relating to synergy benefits, betas, growth rates, multipliers, risk adjusted cost of capital and the probabilities are accurate. There is considerable uncertainty surrounding the accuracy of these, and in addition to the probability analysis conducted in Appendix 2 and the assessments of value conducted in Appendix 1, a sensitivity analysis is probably needed to assess the impact of these uncertainties.

It is assumed that the rb model provides a reasonably good estimate of the growth rate, and that perpetuity is not an unreasonable assumption when assessing the value of Fugae Co.

It is assumed that the capital structure would not change substantially when the new project is taken on. Since the project is significantly smaller than the value of Fugae Co itself, this is not an unreasonable assumption.

When assessing the value of the project, the outcomes are given as occurring with discrete probabilities and the resulting cash flows from the outcomes are given with certainty. There may be more outcomes in practice than the ones given and financial impact of the outcomes may not be known with such certainty. The Black-Scholes Option Pricing model may provide an alternative and more accurate way of assessing the value of the project.

It is assumed that Fugae Co can rely on Lumi Co paying the $50m at the beginning of year two with certainty. Fugae Co may want to assess the reliability of Lumi Co's offer and whether formal contracts should be drawn up between the two companies. Furthermore, Lumi Co may be reluctant to pay the full amount of money once Fugae Co becomes a part of Avem Co.

Concluding comments

Although Nahara Co would gain more than Avem Co from the acquisition both in percentage terms and in monetary terms, both companies benefit from the acquisition. If Fugae Co were to take on the project, although it is value-neutral to the acquisition, Nahara Co could ask for an additional 30% of $12.3 million value to be transferred to it, which is about $3.7 million. Hence the return to Avem Co would reduce by a small amount, but not significantly.

As long as all the parties are satisfied that the value is reasonable despite the assumptions highlighted above, it would appear that the acquisition should proceed.

Report compiled by: AN Accountant

Date: XX/XX/XXXX

APPENDICES

Appendix 1: Additional value created from combining Avem Co and Fugae Co

Avem Co, current value = $7.5/share × 1,600 million shares = $12,000m

Avem Co, free cash flow to equity = $12,000 million/7.2 = $1,666.7m

The growth rate is calculated on the basis of the rb model.

Fugae Co, estimate of growth rate = 0.227 × 0.11 = 0.025 = 2.5%

Fugae Co, current value estimate = $76.5 million × 1.025/(0.11 – 0.025) = $922.5m

Combined company, estimated additional value created =

([$1,666.7m + $76.5m + $40m] × 7.5) − ($12,000m + $922.5m) = $451.5m

Gain to Nahara for selling Fugae Co, 30% × $922.5m = $276.8m

Avem Co will gain $174.7 million of the additional value created, $451.5m − $276.8m = $174.7m

Appendix 2: Value of project to Fugae Co

Appendix 2.1

Estimate of risk-adjusted cost of capital to be used to discount the project's cash flows

The project value is calculated based on its cash flows which are discounted at the project's risk adjusted cost of capital, to reflect the business risk of the project.

Reka Co's asset beta

Reka Co equity value = $4.50 × 80 million shares = $360m

Reka Co debt value = 1.05 × $340 million = $357m

Asset beta = 1.6 × $360m/($360m + $357m × 0.8) = 0.89

Project's asset beta (PAB)

0.89 = PAB × 0.15 + 0.80 × 0.85

PAB = 1.4

Fugae Co

MVe = $922.5m

MVd

Cost of debt = Risk free rate of return plus the credit spread

= 4% + 0.80% = 4.80%

Current value of a $100 bond: $5.4 × 1.048^{-1} + $5.4 × 1.048^{-2} + $5.4 × 1.048^{-3} + $105.4 × 1.048^{-4} = $102.14 per $100

MVd = 1.0214 × $380m = $388.1 m

Project's risk adjusted equity beta

1.4 × ($922.5m + $388.1m × 0.8)/$922.5m = 1.87

Project's risk adjusted cost of equity

4% + 1.87 × 6% = 15.2%

Project's risk adjusted cost of capital

(15.2% × $922.5m + 4.8% × 0.8 × $388.1m)/($922.5m + $388.1m) = 11.84%, say 12%

Appendix 2.2

Estimate of expected value of the project without the offer from Lumi Co

(All amounts in $000s)

Year	1	2	3	4
Cash flows	3,277.6	16,134.3	36,504.7	35,683.6
Discount factor for 12%	0.893	0.797	0.712	0.636
Present values	2,926.9	12,859.0	25,991.3	22,694.8

Probabilities are assigned to possible outcomes based on whether or not the tourism market will grow. The expected net present value (PV) is computed on this basis.

PV year 1: $2,926,900

50% of PV years 1 to 4: $32,236,000

PV years 2 to 4: $61,545,100

40% PV years 2 to 4: $24,618,040

Expected present value of cash flows

$= [0.75 \times (2,926,900 + (0.8 \times 61,545,100 + 0.2 \times 24,618,040))] + [0.25 \times 32,236,000]$

$= [0.75 \times (2,926,900 + 54,159,688)] + [0.25 \times 32,236,000] = 42,814,941 + 8,059,000$

$= \$50,873,941$

Expected NPV of project = $50,873,941 − $42,000,000 = $8,873,941

Estimate of expected value of the project with the offer from Lumi Co

PV of $50m = $50,000,000 × 0.893 = $44,650,000

If the tourism industry does not grow as expected in the first year, then it is more beneficial for Fugae Co to exercise the offer made by Lumi Co, given that Lumi Co's offer of $44.65 million (PV of $50 million) is greater than the PV of the years two to four cash flows ($30.8 million approximately) for that outcome. This figure is then incorporated into the expected net present value calculations.

50% of year 1 PV: $1,463,450

Expected present value of project

$= [0.75 \times (2,926,900 + 54,159,688)] + [0.25 \times (1,463,450 + 44,650,000)]$

$= 42,814,941 + 11,528,363 = \$54,343,304$

Expected NPV of project = $54,343,304 − $42,000,000 = $12,343,304

		Marking scheme		
				Marks
(a)		Risk diversification		2–3
		Purchasing undervalued companies		3–4
				───
			Maximum	**6**
				───
(b)	(i)	Avem Co, current value		1
		Avem Co, free cash flows to equity		1
		Fugae Co, estimate of growth rate		2
		Fugae Co, current value estimate		2
		Combined company, estimated additional value created		2
		Gain to Nahara Co when selling Fugae Co		1
		Gain to Avem Co		1
				───
			Maximum	**10**
				───
	(ii)	Reka Co asset beta		2
		Project asset beta		1
		Fugae Co's market value of debt		2
		Project's risk adjusted equity beta		1
		Project's risk adjusted cost of equity		1
		Project's risk adjusted cost of capital		1
		Annual PVs of project		1
		Different outcomes PVs (year 1, years 2 to 4, 50% and 40%)		2
		Expected NPV of project before Lumi Co offer		3
		PV of Lumi Co offer		1
		Expected NPV of project with Lumi Co's offer		3
				───
			Maximum	**18**
				───
	(iii)	Presentation of benefits to each group of equity holders		
		With and without the project		2–3
		Assumptions made		2–3
		Concluding comments		1–2
				───
			Maximum	**6**
				───
		Note: Maximum 5 marks if no concluding comments given		
		Professional skills marks (see below)		10
				───
Total				**50**
				───

Professional skills

Communication

General report format and structure (use of headings/sub-headings and an introduction)

Style, language and clarity (appropriate layout and tone of report response, presentation of calculations, appropriate use of the tools)

Effectiveness of communication (answer is relevant, specific rather than general and focused to the requirement)

Analysis and Evaluation

Appropriate use of the data to determine suitable calculations

Appropriate use of the data to support discussion and draw appropriate conclusions

Demonstration of reasoned judgement when considering key matters for this specific company

Demonstration of ability to consider relevant factors applicable to this specific scenario

Scepticism

Effective challenge of information and assumptions supplied and, techniques carried out to support any decision

Demonstration of the ability to probe into the reasons for issues and problems, including the identification of missing information or additional information, which would alter the decision reached

Commercial acumen

Effective use of examples and/or calculations from the scenario information and other practical considerations related to the context to illustrate points being made

Recognition of external constraints and opportunities as necessary

Maximum 10 marks

11 CHIKEPE CO (MAR/JUN 18)

Key answer tips

This was a question that cleverly pulled in several areas of the syllabus, and struck a nice balance between knowledge and application. There was a lot to do in the time available, but a student with good exam technique might have chosen to do the written parts of (a), (b) and (d) first, to get plenty of easy marks before starting the lengthy calculations in part (c).

(a) Director A's focus is on reducing the risk in the business through diversification and thereby increasing its value. A strategy of risk diversification resulting in greater value can work in situations where the equity holders are exposed to both unsystematic and systematic risks, for example, when their investment is concentrated in one company. In such situations, the shareholders would be subject to unsystematic risk and diversification would reduce this risk.

In the case of Chikepe Co, this is unlikely to be the case as a large proportion of shares are owned by institutional shareholders and it is likely that their investment portfolios are already well-diversified and therefore they are not exposed to unsystematic risk. Further diversification will be of no value to them. In fact, it may be construed that managers are only taking this action for their own benefit, as they may be closely tied to the company and therefore be exposed to total risk (both unsystematic and systematic risks). This may then become a source of agency related conflict between the management and the shareholders.

However, diversification overseas into markets which have some barriers to entry might reduce both systematic and unsystematic risks as well.

Director B, on the other hand, seems to be suggesting that Chikepe Co should focus on its core business and increase value through identifying areas of synergy benefits. It may be the case that Chikepe Co's management and directors are well placed to identify areas where the company can gain value by acquiring companies with potential synergy benefits.

The types of synergy benefits, which may arise in established pharmaceutical companies, can include:

Identifying undervalued companies, where the management is not effective in unlocking the true value of company. By replacing the existing management, Chikepe Co may be able to unlock the value of the company.

Acquiring companies which have strategic assets or product pipelines. Chikepe Co may be well placed to identify companies which have a number of product pipelines, which those companies are not exploiting fully. By acquiring such companies, Chikepe Co may be able to exploit the product pipelines.

Through acquisitions, Chikepe Co may be able to exploit economies of scope by eliminating process duplication or economies of scale where its size may enable it to negotiate favourable terms.

Foshoro Co may benefit if Chikepe Co acquires it because it is struggling to raise funding for its innovative products. Chikepe Co is an established company but has few new product innovations coming in the future. Therefore, it may have spare cash resources which Foshoro Co may be able to utilise.

Tutorial note

The marking scheme here allowed for credit to be given for any alternative but relevant discussion.

(b)   Traditional investment appraisal methods such as net present value assume that an investment needs to be taken on a now or never basis, and once undertaken, it cannot be reversed. Real options take into account the fact that in reality, most investments have within them certain amounts of flexibility, such as whether or not to undertake the investment immediately or to delay the decision; to pursue follow-on opportunities; and to cancel an investment opportunity after it has been undertaken. Where there is increasing uncertainty and risk, and where a decision can be changed or delayed, this flexibility has value, known as the time value of an option.

Net present value captures just the intrinsic value of an investment opportunity, whereas real options capture both the intrinsic value and the time value, to give an overall value for an opportunity. When a company still has time available to it before a decision needs to be made, it may have opportunities to increase the intrinsic value of the investment through the strategic decisions it makes.

Investing in new companies with numerous potential innovative product pipelines may provide opportunities for flexibility where decisions can be delayed and the intrinsic value can be increased through strategic decisions and actions taken by the company. Real options try to capture the value of this flexibility within companies with innovative product pipelines, whereas net present value does not.

(c)   **Report to the board of directors**

(BoD), Chikepe Co Introduction

This report evaluates whether the acquisition of Foshoro Co would be beneficial to Chikepe Co's shareholders by estimating the additional equity value created from the synergies resulting when the two companies are combined. The market values of equity of the two companies as separate entities are considered initially and then compared with the equity value of the two companies together. The free cash flow to firm valuation method is used to estimate the values of the companies and the limitations of this method are discussed.

The market value of equity of Chikepe Co is given as $12,600 million.

Based on the free cash flow to firm valuation method:

The current market value of equity of Foshoro Co is estimated at $986 million (appendix 1), and

The market value of equity of the combined company is estimated at $14,993 million (appendix 2).

Therefore, the additional market value of equity arising from synergy benefits when the two companies are combined is estimated at $1,407 million (appendix 3), which is then split between Foshoro Co's shareholders receiving $296 million (a 30% premium) and Chikepe Co's shareholders receiving the balance of $1,111 million, which is approximately 8.8% excess over the original equity value (appendix 3).

However, the valuation method used has a number of limitations, as follows:

–   The values of both Foshoro Co and the combined company are based on estimations and assumptions, for example,

–   Foshoro Co's future growth rate of free cash flows is based on past growth rates and it is assumed that this will not change in the future;

–   It is not explained how Foshoro Co's cost of capital is estimated/calculated. Such an estimate may be more difficult to make for private companies;

–   The assumption of perpetuity is made when estimating the values of Foshoro Co and the combined company, and this may not be valid.

–   The basis for the synergy benefits such as higher growth rates of sales revenue and profit margins needs to be explained and justified. It is not clear how these estimates have been made.

–   Whereas it may be possible to estimate the asset beta of a listed company such as Chikepe Co, it may be more difficult to provide a reasonable estimate for the asset beta of Foshoro Co. Therefore, the estimate of the cost of capital of the combined company may not be accurate.

–   The costs related to the acquisition process would need to be factored in.

Therefore, whereas the free cash flow method of estimating corporate values is theoretically sound, using it in practice to estimate values is open to errors and judgements.

Conclusion

The valuations indicate that Chikepe Co's shareholders would benefit from the acquisition of Foshoro Co and the value of their shares should increase by 8.8%. However, the method used to estimate the value created makes a number of estimates and assumptions. It is therefore recommended that a range of valuations is made under different assumptions and estimates, through a process of sensitivity analysis, before a final decision is made. As well as this, the limitations of the valuation method used should be well understood and taken into account.

Tutorial note

When attempting a question like this in the Computer Based Exam (CBE), make your answer look like a professional document by writing the report in the word processor but putting your numbers (appendix) in a spreadsheet.

When preparing your calculations, use the spreadsheet functions SUM and NPV to save time. Be careful when using the NPV function to enter =NPV, then a bracket containing the discount rate, a comma, and then the cells containing the cash flows from year 1 onwards. The initial investment then needs to be subtracted separately.

APPENDICES:

Appendix 1 (Part (c) (i)): Foshoro Co, estimate of current value

Cost of capital = 10%

Growth rate of profits and free cash flows = $(\$91.0m/\$83.3m)^{1/3} - 1 = 0.03 = 3\%$

Free cash flow to firm (FCFF) = PBIT + non-cash expenses − additional cash investment − tax FCFF = $192.3m + $112.0m − $98.2m − (20% × $192.3m) = $167.6m

Foshoro Co, estimated value = ($167.6m × 1.03)/(0.10 − 0.03) = $2,466.1m

Current estimated market value of equity of Foshoro Co = $2,466.1m × 40% = $986.4m, say $986m approximately.

Appendix 2 (Part (c) (ii)): Estimate of value created from combining Chikepe Co and Foshoro Co

Asset beta of combined company =

(0.800 × $12,600m + 0.950 × $986.4m)/($12,600m + $986.4m) = 0.811

Equity beta of combined company = 0.811 × (0.70 + 0.30 × 0.80)/0.70 = 1.089

Cost of equity, combined company = 2% + 1.089 × 7% = 9.6% approx.

Cost of capital, combined company = 9.6% × 0.7 + 5.3% × 0.3 × 0.8 = 8% approx.

Combined company, free cash flows and value computation ($ millions)

Sales growth rate, years 2 to 4 = 7% per year; operating profit margin = 20%

Year	1	2	3	4
Sales revenue	4,200	4,494	4,809	5,146
Operating profit	840	899	962	1,029
Less tax (20%)	(168)	(180)	(192)	(206)
Less additional investment in assets	(200)	(188)	(202)	(216)
Free cash flows	472	531	568	607
PV of free cash flows (8%)	437	455	451	446

	$ millions
Present value (first four years)	1,789
Present value (after four years)	
$607 \times 1.056/(0.08 - 0.056) \times 0.735$	19,630
Estimated market value of the combined company	21,419

Market value of equity of the combined company = 70% × $21,419m = $14,993m

Appendix 3: Synergy benefits and their distribution

Additional market equity value created by combining the two companies

$14,993m – ($12,600m + $986m) = $1,407m

Therefore, synergy benefits resulting from combining the two companies: $1,407m

Premium payable to Foshoro Co shareholders: 30% × $986m = $296m

Balance of synergy benefits going to Chikepe Co's shareholders: $1,111 m

As a percentage of current value: $1,111m/$12,600m × 100% = 8.8%

(d) Both the mandatory bid rule and the principle of equal treatment are designed to protect minority shareholders, where an acquirer has obtained a controlling interest of the target company.

The mandatory bid rule provides minority shareholders with the opportunity to sell their shares and exit the target company at a specified fair share price. This price should not be lower than the highest price paid for shares, which have already been acquired within a specified period.

The principle of equal treatment requires the acquiring company to offer the same terms to minority shareholders as were offered to the earlier shareholders from whom the controlling interest was acquired. Both these regulatory devices are designed to ensure that the minority shareholders are protected financially and are not exploited by the acquirer.

Marking guide

				Marks
(a)		Compare and contrast the two directors' opinions		3–4
		Discussion of types of synergy benefits		3–4
			Maximum	**7**
(b)		1–2 marks per point		
			Maximum	**5**
(c)	(i)	(Appendix 1)		
		Estimate of future growth rate		1
		Exclude interest from free cash flows		1
		Estimate of free cash flows		2
		Estimate of Foshoro Co's value		1
		Estimate of equity value of Foshoro Co		1
				6
	(ii)	(Appendix 2)		
		Combined company asset beta		1
		Combined company equity beta		1
		Combined company cost of equity		1
		Combined company cost of capital		1
		Combined company sales revenue (or operating profits) (years 1 to 4)		1
		Combined company taxation amounts (years 1 to 4)		1
		Combined company additional asset investment (years 1 to 4)		1
		Combined company total value (years 1 to 4)		1
		Combined company value after first four years		1
		Combined company total market value		1
		Combined company market value of equity		1
				11
	(iii)	(Discussion in report and appendix 3)		
		Evaluation of benefit to Chikepe Co shareholders		3–4
		Discussion of the limitations of the valuation method used		4
				7
(d)		Discussion of mandatory-bid rule		2–3
		Discussion of principle of equal treatment		2–3
			Maximum	**4**
		Professional skills marks (see below)		**10**
Total				**50**

Professional skills

Communication

General report format and structure (use of headings/sub-headings and an introduction)

Style, language and clarity (appropriate layout and tone of report response, presentation of calculations, appropriate use of the tools)

Effectiveness of communication (answer is relevant, specific rather than general and focused to the requirement)

Analysis and Evaluation

Appropriate use of the data to determine suitable calculations

Appropriate use of the data to support discussion and draw appropriate conclusions

Demonstration of reasoned judgement when considering key matters for this specific company

Demonstration of ability to consider relevant factors applicable to this specific scenario

Scepticism

Effective challenge of information and assumptions supplied and, techniques carried out to support any decision

Demonstration of the ability to probe into the reasons for issues and problems, including the identification of missing information or additional information, which would alter the decision reached

Commercial acumen

Effective use of examples and/or calculations from the scenario information and other practical considerations related to the context to illustrate points being made

Recognition of external constraints and opportunities as necessary

Maximum 10 marks

12   OPAO CO (DEC 18)

Key answer tips

There were lots of easy marks in parts (a) and (b) available to those students who had learned the AFM syllabus thoroughly. As long as you label your answer clearly, you can answer the questions in any order, so always focus on the easier parts first.

(a)   A management buy-out (MBO) involves the purchase of a company by the management running that company. Hence Burgut Co's current management team would be buying Burgut Co from Opao Co. A management buy-in (MBI) involves selling Burgut Co to a management team brought in from outside the company.

Opao Co may have sold Burgut Co through a MBI for the following reasons. Opao Co's BoD may have felt that Burgut Co's current management team lacked fresh ideas and strategies which could have driven Burgut Co forward successfully. Instead, it may have felt that a fresh team, with skills and expertise gained externally, would have had the required innovative ideas and skills. It may be that the external team of managers may have had the finance available to move quickly, whereas the internal team of managers may not have had the finance in place to purchase Burgut Co at that time. It is also possible that the management teams within Burgut Co and Opao Co had disagreements in the past, and Opao Co's BoD may have believed the two management teams would not be able to work together in the future, if needed. Thus, the BoD may have felt that a fresh management team was the better option going forwards.

(b) Portfolio restructuring involves the acquisition of companies, or disposals of assets, business units and/or subsidiary companies through divestments, demergers, spin-offs, MBOs and MBIs. Organisational restructuring involves changing the way a company is organised. This may involve changing the structure of divisions in a business, business processes and other changes such as corporate governance.

The aim of either type of restructuring is to increase the performance and value of the business.

Opao Co, in going from a conglomerate business to one focusing on just two business areas, can be seen as restructuring its portfolio, as businesses and assets which are not part of financial services and food manufacturing are disposed of, and businesses focusing on these areas are acquired. Financial markets may take the view that focusing on food manufacturing and financial services has enabled Opao Co's senior management to concentrate on areas in which they have expertise. Whereas other businesses in which the senior management are not experts are disposed of. This activity leads to the maximisation of business value.

Shareholders are interested in maximising returns from their investments, which companies achieve through maximising business value, whilst minimising the risks inherent in their investment activity. Shareholders who are closely linked to a particular business do not hold diversified investment portfolios, and therefore benefit from diversification of risk undertaken by a company, investing in many different areas. On the other hand, institutional shareholders and other shareholders, who hold diversified portfolios, would not benefit from a company undertaking risk management through diversification by becoming a conglomerate. Instead, such companies would increase value by focusing on areas in which they have relative expertise, as Opao Co seems to do. So Opao Co's changing owner clientele has forced it to change its overall strategy. This strategy change was implemented through portfolio restructuring.

(c) **Report to the board of directors (BoD), Opao Co**

Introduction

This report provides an estimate of the additional value created if Opao Co were to acquire Tai Co, and the gain for each company's shareholders based on a cash offer, a share-for-share offer and a mixed offer. It evaluates the likely reaction of the two companies' shareholders to each payment method.

Summary of the estimates from the appendices

From appendix 1

Opao Co equity value pre-acquisition: $5,000m

Tai Co equity value pre-acquisition: $1,000m

Combined company equity value post-acquisition: $6,720m

From appendix 2

Therefore, additional value based on synergy benefits is $720m or 12% ($720m/$6,000m)

Estimated percentage gain in value

	Opao Co	Tai Co
Cash offer	11.2%	15.8%
Share-for-share offer	6.4%	40.0%
Mixed offer	9.7%	23.4%

Likely reactions

Tai Co's shareholders are likely to consider all the offers made, because they all fall within the range of premiums paid in previous acquisitions of 15% to 40%. The cash offer is at the lower end of the range, the share-for-share offer at the top end of the range and the mixed offer in between. It is likely that Tai Co's shareholders will be more attracted to the share-for-share offer as it maximises their return. However, this offer is reliant on the fact that the expected synergy benefits will be realised and Tai Co will probably need to analyse the likelihood of this. Cash payment, although much lower, gives a certainty of return. The mixed offer provides some of the certainty of a cash payment, but also offers a higher return compared to the cash offer. This return is roughly in the middle of the premium range. It may therefore prove to be the better option for Tai Co's shareholders.

Opao Co's shareholders benefit less from the acquisition compared to Tai Co's shareholders. In each case, they get less than the additional value created of 12%, with the cash payment offering the highest return of 11.2%, which is just below the 12% overall return. The share-for-share offer gives the least return at just over half (6.4%) of the overall return of 12%. Nevertheless, with this option, cash is retained within Opao Co and can be used for other value creating projects. Opao Co's shareholders may also prefer the mixed offer, because the return they are expecting to receive is between the cash and share-for-share offers. Also, less cash resources are used compared to the cash offer, and they still benefit from a significant proportion of the additional value created.

Conclusion

Based on the benefits accruing to both sets of shareholders, it is not possible to conclusively say that one method of acquisition payment would be acceptable to both sets of shareholders. However, both sets of shareholders may be persuaded that the mixed offer provides a reasonable compromise between the wholly cash and the wholly share-for-share prices. Given that synergy benefits are shared (even if not equally), both companies' share prices should increase if the acquisition proceeds, as long as the estimates when estimating the valuations are reasonably accurate.

Report compiled by:

Date

Tutorial note

When attempting a question like this in the Computer Based Exam (CBE), make your answer look like a professional document by writing the report in the word processor but putting your numbers (appendix) in a spreadsheet.

When preparing your calculations, use the spreadsheet functions SUM and NPV to save time. Be careful when using the NPV function to enter =NPV, then a bracket containing the discount rate, a comma, and then the cells containing the cash flows from year 1 onwards. The initial investment then needs to be subtracted separately.

APPENDICES:

Appendix 1 (Part (c) (i)):

Equity value of Opao Co prior to acquisition

$2.50/share × 2,000m shares = $5,000m

Equity value of Tai Co prior to acquisition

Free cash flows to firm = $132.0m + $27.4m − $24.3m − ($132.0m × 0.2) = $108.7m

Company value = $108.7m × 1.03/(0.11 − 0.03) = $1,399.5m, say $1,400m

Equity value = $1,400m − $400m = $1,000m

Equity value of combined company post acquisition

All amounts in $ millions

Year	1	2	3	4
Sales revenue (5.02% growth, yrs 2 to 4)	7,351	7,720	8,108	8,515
Pre-tax profit (15.4% of sales revenue)	1,132	1,189	1,249	1,311
Less: Tax (20%)	(226)	(238)	(250)	(262)
Less: Additional investment ($0.31 per $1, yrs 2 to 4)	(109)	(114)	(120)	(126)
Free cash flows	797	837	879	923
Present value of free cash flows (10%)	724	691	660	630

Combined company value: years 1 to 4 = $2,705m

Combined company value: after year 4 = $923 \times 1.024/(0.1 - 0.024) \times 1.1^{-4}$ = $8,494m

Total combined company value = $11,199m

Equity value (60% × $11,199m) = $6,719.4m, say $6,720m

Tutorial note

Your answer to part (c) (ii) depends on the numbers calculated in part (c) (i). The markers are told to be aware of this when they are marking the real exam. As long as your method is correct, you will score full marks in part (c) (ii) even if your numbers are incorrect due to errors made in part (c) (i).

Appendix 2 (Part (c) (ii): Percentage gains for Tai Co and Opao Co shareholders under each payment method

Estimate of additional value created from acquisition due to synergy benefits $6,720m – ($5,000m + $1,000m) = $720m

Tai Co, value per share = $1,000m/263m shares = $3.80/share approx.

Cash offer

Tai Co shareholders, percentage gain

($4.40 – $3.80)/$3.80 = $0.60/$3.80 = 15.8%

Opao Co shareholders, percentage gain

Amount of additional value created going to Tai Co shareholders = $0.60 × 263m shares = $157.8m
Amount of additional value created going to Opao Co shareholders = $720m – $157.8m = $562.2m
As a percentage = ($562.2m/2,000m shares)/$2.50 = 11.2%.

Share-for-share offer

Share of additional value to Tai Co shareholders = $720m × 0.555 = $399.6m
Share of additional value to Opao Co shareholders = $720m × 0.445 = $320.4m

Opao Co equity value after acquisition = $5,320.4m

Opao Co, estimated share price after acquisition = $5,320.4m/2,000m shares = $2.66/share

Opao Co shares to be allocated to Tai Co shareholders = ($1,000m + $399.6m)/$2.66 = 526m shares approximately

Therefore, share-for-share offer will be 2 Opao Co shares for 1 Tai Co share [526/263 = 2]

Tai Co shareholders, percentage gain

($2.66 × 2 shares – $3.80 × 1 share)/($3.80 × 1 share) = 40%

Opao Co shareholders, percentage gain

($2.66 – $2.50)/$2.50 = 6.4%

Mixed offer

Tai Co shareholders, percentage gain

(($2.60 + $2.09) – $3.80)/$3.80 = $0.89/$3.80 = 23.4%

Opao Co shareholders, percentage gain

Amount of additional value going to Tai Co shareholders = $0.89 × 263m = $234.1m

Amount of additional value created going to Opao Co shareholders = $720m – $234.1m = $485.9m

As a percentage = ($485.9m/2,000m shares)/$2.50 = 9.7%

			Marks
	Marking guide		*Marks*
(a)	Distinguishing between MBO and MBI		1–2
	Discussion of choice of MBI		2–3
		Maximum	**5**
(b)	Explanation of portfolio restructuring and organisational restructuring		3
	Discussion of reason(s) for change in business focus		3
		Maximum	**6**
(c) (i)	(Appendix 1)		
	Equity value of Opao Co		1
	Tai Co, free cash flow to firm		2
	Estimate of value of Tai Co		1
	Estimate of equity value of Tai Co		1
	Combined company, free cash flows		2
	Value of combined company, years 1 to 4		1
	Value of combined company, after year 4		1
	Equity value of combined company		1
			10
(ii)	(Appendix 2)		
	Cash offer, percentage gain, Tai Co		1
	Cash offer, percentage gain, Opao Co		2
	Share-for-share offer, share of additional value		1
	Share-for-share offer, Opao Co share value		1
	Share-for-share offer, total shares allocated to Tai Co		1
	Share-for-share offer, 2 Opao Co shares for 1 Tai Co share		1
	Share-for-share offer, percentage gain, Tai Co		1
	Share-for-share offer, percentage gain, Opao Co		1
	Mixed offer, percentage gain, Tai Co		1
	Mixed offer, percentage gain, Opao Co		2
			12
(iii)	(Report on proposed acquisition)		
	Evaluation: Opao Co		3–4
	Evaluation: Tai Co		3–4
		Maximum	**7**
	Professional skills marks (see below)		**10**
Total			**50**

Professional skills

Communication

General report format and structure (use of headings/sub-headings and an introduction)

Style, language and clarity (appropriate layout and tone of report response, presentation of calculations, appropriate use of the tools)

Effectiveness of communication (answer is relevant, specific rather than general and focused to the requirement)

Analysis and Evaluation

Appropriate use of the data to determine suitable calculations

Appropriate use of the data to support discussion and draw appropriate conclusions

Demonstration of reasoned judgement when considering key matters for this specific company

Demonstration of ability to consider relevant factors applicable to this specific scenario

Scepticism

Effective challenge of information and assumptions supplied and, techniques carried out to support any decision

Commercial acumen

Effective use of examples and/or calculations from the scenario information and other practical considerations related to the context to illustrate points being made

Recognition of external constraints and opportunities as necessary

Maximum 10 marks

13 WESTPARLEY CO (MAR 20)

Key answer tips

There is lots to do here, and some of the calculations are quite tricky.

But notice that only 20 marks are available for the calculations and 30 marks for discussion. Much of the discussion was independent of the numbers, so it should have been easy enough to pass this question even if you struggled with the calculations.

(a) **Individual business**

A number of behavioural factors, to do with the individual company as well as the sector as a whole, may lead to Matravers Tech being valued higher than appears to be warranted by rational analysis of its future prospects. One possible factor is the asking price, even if it is not a fair one, may provide a reference point which significantly influences the purchaser's valuation of the business.

The fact that Matravers Tech is available for purchase may help raise its price. Purchasers may see this as a rare opportunity to buy an attractive business in this retail sector. This will be made more likely if investors have loss aversion bias, a desire to buy Matravers Tech now because otherwise the opportunity will be lost.

Matravers Tech being offered for sale will mean that information about the company, showing it in a positive light, will be available for purchasers. This could result in availability bias, investors taking particular note of this information because they can readily obtain it, rather than other information which may be more difficult or costly to find.

Sector

There are a number of possible behavioural reasons why share prices in this sector appear generally higher than rational analysis indicates. One is the herd instinct, investing in the sector because other investors have also been buying shares, not wishing to make judgements independently of other investors.

The herd instinct may be generated by previous share price movements. Investors may believe once prices start rising in the sector, they will continue to do so indefinitely.

Following fashion may also be a factor. Fund managers who wish to give the impression that they are actively managing their portfolio by making regular changes to it, may have a preference for companies which appear up-to-date and are currently popular. This may be linked to an expectation that sales of technologically-advanced goods are likely to generate high returns.

There is also confirmation bias, the idea that investors will pay attention to evidence which confirms their views that the sector is a good one in which to invest, and ignore evidence which contradicts their beliefs. In the past, technology companies have been valued using methods which support the beliefs of investors that they are of high value, rather than traditional methods, such as cash flow analysis, which suggest a lower business value is more realistic.

(b)   (iv)   Report to the board of directors, Westparley Co

This report evaluates whether the acquisition of Matravers Co would be beneficial to Westparley Co's shareholders by estimating the future value generated by Matravers Co (i.e. Matravers Home currently), the proceeds from selling Matravers Tech and the additional value created from synergies immediately after the companies are combined.

Strategic fit

The strategic case for taking over the business appears to be strongest for the out-of-town stores and the online business. The acquisition would provide an additional out-of-town presence for Westparley Co. Better usage in the out-of-town stores could generate higher returns. Having the food and home businesses on the same site could generate some cross-sales between the two. Possibly combining the two companies' online presence and investing further could mean Matravers Home benefiting from the factors which have driven strong performance by Westparley Co.

Taking over the city centre stores, even the successful ones, seems to have less strategic logic, however. Westparley Co would be taking on a high cost burden. The success of the food business in city centres is doubtful, as food shops sited there will be less convenient for customers who do not live in the city centres, and Westparley Co has marketed itself as being easily accessible for customers. There is, perhaps, wider incompatibility between the two businesses. The food business is characterised by quick shopping for often a limited number of items, whereas purchases in the home business, particularly of larger items, are likely to take longer and site convenience be less of an issue.

Financial aspects

Based on the predictions for future cash flows and required premiums from Matravers Co's shareholders, the acquisition would add value to Westparley Co's shareholders, if, and only if, the excess value on selling Matravers Tech and the synergies are both largely achieved. Together they add up to $2,400m ($558m + $1,842m) compared with total added value of $1,897m. There are questions about the estimates for these figures and also the estimates for the future free cash flows of the current Matravers Home business.

Synergies

Most of the additional value is due to synergies and it is difficult to see how the synergies are calculated. There is likely to be scope for some administrative savings. However, operational cost synergies appear less obvious as the two companies are operating in different retail sectors. Any synergy figures will also have to take account of costs in achieving synergies, such as store closure costs, and also commitments such as leases which may be a burden for some time. Synergies may also not be achieved because of lack of co-operation by staff or problems integrating the two businesses.

Current Matravers Home business

The suggested increase in cash flows appears doubtful for a number of reasons. If stores being closed are making positive cash flow contributions, these will have to be replaced. Whether they can be is doubtful given the problems in this part of the retail sector. It may be a more profitable use of store space to have an area for food sales, but the food sales generated in Matravers Co's shops may take business from Westparley Co's existing shops. Similarly, increased online sales may be at the expense of sales in stores.

Sale of Matravers Tech

There is no indication of how interested buyers will be in the business. The industry price-earnings (P/E) ratio used may be an average which does not reflect Matravers Tech's circumstances. It would be better to find a P/E ratio for a proxy company with similar financial and business risk. As Matravers Tech would not be listed, this would suggest a discount to the P/E ratio should be applied. Since also Westparley Co has an estimate of future free cash flow, potential buyers may be able to come up with their own estimates and base the price they are prepared to pay on their estimates.

Other assumptions

One important assumption is the 15% premium expected to be required by Matravers Co's shareholders. Other assumptions made in the calculations include operating profit margin and tax rates remaining constant and cash flows being assumed to increase to perpetuity. Incremental capital investment is assumed to be accurate. It is assumed that the cost of debt will remain unchanged and that the asset beta, cost of equity and cost of debt can be determined accurately. Given all the assumptions, Westparley Co should carry out sensitivity analysis using different assumptions and obtaining a range of values.

Conclusion

On the assumptions made, the acquisition appears to add financial value for the shareholders of Westparley Co. However, the figures are subject to a significant number of uncertainties and the strategic logic for buying the whole Matravers business appears unclear. On balance, Westparley Co may want to consider a more limited acquisition of just the out-of-town stores if these are available, as their acquisition appears to make better strategic sense.

Tutorial note

When attempting a question like this in the Computer Based Exam (CBE), make your answer look like a professional document by writing the report in the word processor but putting your numbers (appendix) in a spreadsheet.

When preparing your calculations, use the spreadsheet functions SUM and NPV to save time. Be careful when using the NPV function to enter =NPV, then a bracket containing the discount rate, a comma, and then the cells containing the cash flows from year 1 onwards. The initial investment then needs to be subtracted separately.

Appendix 1 Estimate of additional value created from sell-off of Matravers Tech (b) (i)

Share of pre-tax profit = 20% × $1,950m = $390m

After-tax profit = $390m × (1 − 0.28) = $281m

Proceeds from sell-off based on P/E ratio = $281m × 18 = $5,058m

Excess value from sell-off = $5,058m − $4,500m = $558m

Appendix 2 Estimate of combined company cost of capital (b) (ii)

Matravers Co asset beta = 0.75

Westparley Co asset beta

Market value of debt = 1.05 × $26,000m = $27,300m
Market value of equity = 4,000 million × $8.50 = $34,000m
Asset beta = 1.02 × (34,000)/(34,000 + (27,300 × 0.72)) = 0.65

Combined company, asset beta

Market value of Matravers Co equity = $12,500m

Asset beta = ((0.75 × 12,500) + (0.65 × 34,000))/(12,500 + 34,000) = 0.68
Equity beta = 0.68 ((34,000 + (27,300 × 0.72))/34,000) = 1.07

Combined company cost of equity = 3.5% + (1.07 × 8%) = 12.1%

Combined company cost of capital =

((34,000 × 12.1%) + (27,300 × 9.8% × 0.72))/(34,000 + 27,300) = 9.9%, say 10%

Appendix 3 Estimate of the value created for Westparley Co's shareholders (b) (iii)

Cash flows, years 1 to 4

Year	1	2	3	4
	$m	$m	$m	$m
Sales revenue	43,260	44,558	45,895	47,272
Profit before interest and tax	2,596	2,673	2,754	2,836
Tax	(727)	(748)	(771)	(794)
Additional capital investment	(630)	(649)	(669)	(689)
Free cash flows	1,239	1,276	1,314	1,353
Discount factor	0.909	0.826	0.751	0.683
Present value of free cash flows	1,126	1,054	987	924

Present value years 1 to 4 = $4,091m

Present value year 5 onwards $(($1,353m \times 1.02)/(0.1 - 0.02)) \times 1.10^{-4}$ = $11,781m

Total present value = $4,091m + $11,781m = $15,872m

Synergies

Year	1	2	3
	$m	$m	$m
Free cash flows	700	750	780
Discount factor	0.909	0.826	0.751
Present value of cash flows	636	620	586

Present value of synergies = $1,842m

Amount payable for Matravers Co's shares = $12,500m × 1.15 = $14,375m

Value attributable to Matravers Co's investors = $14,375m + $6,500m = $20,875m

Value attributable to Westparley Co shareholders = present value of cash flows + proceeds from sell-off + value of synergies – value to Matravers Co's investors

= $15,872m + $5,058m + $1,842m – $20,875m = $1,897m

(c) **Calculation of gearing**

If gearing is calculated on the basis of market values, a fall in the share price will result in the level of gearing rising. Westparley Co's board may be worried about a fall in the share price given the problems affecting many companies' share prices in the retail sector and the possibility that the stock market may react adversely to the acquisition.

Directors' preferences

Directors may have their own preferences about financing. They may be able to choose a mix of sources and a level of gearing which reflects these preferences. Directors may be concerned about too high a burden of payment to finance providers, in terms of cost or ultimately repayment of debt. They may not wish to commit the company to conditions imposed by finance providers. By contrast, they may be concerned about how a change in the shareholder base as a result of a share issue may impact upon their own position. Directors may also be concerned about the impression given by their choice of finance. Pecking order theory states that equity issue is seen as the last resort for financing, so if the purchase is financed by an equity issue, it may be seen as a sign of a lack of confidence by directors that Westparley Co can sustain its current share price.

Costs and cash flows

Gearing decisions may not just be determined by their own preferences but by external conditions or constraints. Choosing more debt could lower the overall cost of capital, due to lower cost and tax relief, making investments such as Matravers Co appear more profitable. Higher levels of debt may result in the cost of equity rising, reducing the overall impact on the cost of capital. Against that, higher levels of debt mean increased finance cost commitments, even though Westparley Co may need further cash for investment in stores. This may be an important concern if interest rates are high. By contrast, dividends to shareholders do not have to be paid when returns are low or money is required for investment, although failure to meet dividend expectations may result in the board being pressurised by shareholders.

Availability

The availability of finance may also be a significant issue, particularly if an acquisition has to be completed quickly. An equity issue may take time to arrange and require shareholder approval. Sufficient debt finance may be difficult to obtain if lenders feel that Westparley Co already has significant commitments to debt finance providers. The timescale over which finance is available may be significant. Westparley Co may seek longer-term finance if existing debt finance is due to be repaid soon or if significant cash is needed for short-term investment, not just in Matravers Co's stores, but also in Westparley Co's existing stores.

Mix

Other external factors may influence the mix of finance chosen. Westparley Co's directors may be concerned about keeping the level of gearing at or below the industry average, because of finance providers becoming worried if gearing exceeds industry levels. Keeping debt as a significant element in overall finance may act as a deterrent to acquirers becoming interested in making a bid for Westparley Co. Directors may also not have a target figure in mind but be content if gearing is within a range of values.

				Marks
		Marking guide		
(a)		1–2 marks per relevant point (e.g. asking price, herd instinct, following fashion and confirmation bias)		
			Maximum	**4**
(b)	(i)	Share of pre-tax profit		1
		After-tax profit		1
		Proceeds from sell-off		1
		Comparison with free cash flow valuation		1
				4
	(ii)	Westparley Co MV debt and equity		1
		Westparley Co asset beta		1
		Combined company asset beta and equity beta (1 each)		2
		Combined company cost of equity and WACC (1 each)		2
				6
	(iii)	Sales revenue		1
		Profit before interest and tax		1
		Tax		1
		Additional capital investment		1
		PV of free cash flows years 1–4		1
		PV of free cash flows year 5 onwards		2
		Present value of synergies		1
		Premium payable		1
		Value attributable to Westparley Co's shareholders		1
				10
	(iv)	Strategic value		2–3
		Financial value		2–3
		Estimations made		2–3
		Assumptions made		2–3
			Maximum	**10**
(c)		1–2 marks per relevant point (e.g. security, tax relief, industry norms)		
			Maximum	**6**
		Professional skills marks (see below)		**10**
Total				**50**

Professional skills

Communication

General report format and structure (use of headings/sub-headings and an introduction)

Style, language and clarity (appropriate layout and tone of report response, presentation of calculations, appropriate use of the tools)

Effectiveness of communication (answer is relevant, specific rather than general and focused to the requirement)

Analysis and Evaluation

Appropriate use of the data to determine suitable calculations

Appropriate use of the data to support discussion and draw appropriate conclusions

Demonstration of reasoned judgement when considering key matters for this specific company

Demonstration of ability to consider relevant factors applicable to this specific scenario

Scepticism

Effective challenge of information and assumptions supplied and, techniques carried out to support any decision

Commercial acumen

Effective use of examples and/or calculations from the scenario information and other practical considerations related to the context to illustrate points being made

Recognition of external constraints and opportunities as necessary

Maximum 10 marks

CORPORATE RECONSTRUCTION AND REORGANISATION

14   CIGNO CO (SEP/DEC 15)

Key answer tips

This question contained lots of loosely connected parts.

Many students are drawn to the numbers first, but notice that parts (a), (b)(iii) and (c) can be answered independently of the numerical section.

To make sure that you don't over-run on time in a question like this, attack these independent written bits first before starting on the numbers.

(a)   Both forms of unbundling involve disposing the non-core parts of the company.

The divestment through a sell-off normally involves selling part of a company as an entity or as separate assets to a third party for an agreed amount of funds or value. This value may comprise of cash and non-cash based assets. The company can then utilise the funds gained in alternative, value-enhancing activities.

The management buy-in is a particular type of sell-off which involves selling a division or part of a company to an external management team, who will take up the running of the new business and have an equity stake in the business. A management buy-in is normally undertaken when it is thought that the division or part of the company can probably be run better by a different management team compared to the current one.

(b) **Report to the board of directors (BoD), CIGNO CO**

This report assesses the potential value of acquiring Anatra Co for the equity holders of Cigno Co, both with and without considering the benefits of the reduction in taxation and in employee costs. The possible issues raised by reduction in taxation and in employee costs are discussed in more detail below. The assessment also discusses the estimates made and the methods used.

Assessment of value created

Cigno Co estimates that the premium payable to acquire Anatra Co largely accounts for the benefits created from the acquisition and the divestment, before considering the benefits from the tax and employee costs' saving. As a result, before these savings are considered, the estimated benefit to Cigno Co's shareholders of $128 million (see Appendix 3) is marginal. Given that there are numerous estimations made and the methods used make various assumptions, as discussed below, this benefit could be smaller or larger. It would appear that without considering the additional benefits of cost and tax reductions, the acquisition is probably too risky and would probably be of limited value to Cigno Co's shareholders.

If the benefits of the taxation and employee costs saved are taken into account, the value created for the shareholders is $5,609 million (see Appendix 4), and therefore significant. This would make the acquisition much more financially beneficial. It should be noted that no details are provided on the additional pre-acquisition and post-acquisition costs or on any synergy benefits that Cigno Co may derive in addition to the cost savings discussed. These should be determined and incorporated into the calculations.

Basing corporate value on the price-earnings (PE) method for the sell-off, and on the free cash flow valuation method for the absorbed business, is theoretically sound. The PE method estimates the value of the company based on its earnings and on competitor performance. With the free cash flow method, the cost of capital takes account of the risk the investors want to be compensated for and the non-committed cash flows are the funds which the business can afford to return to the investors, as long as they are estimated accurately.

However, in practice, the input factors used to calculate the organisation's value may not be accurate or it may be difficult to assess their accuracy. For example, for the free cash flow method, it is assumed that the sales growth rate, operating profit margin, the taxation rate and incremental capital investment can be determined accurately and remain constant. It is assumed that the cost of capital will remain unchanged and it is assumed that the asset beta, the cost of equity and cost of debt can be determined accurately. It is also assumed that the length of the period of growth is accurate and that the company operates in perpetuity thereafter. With the PE model, the basis for using the average competitor figures needs to be assessed, for example, have outliers been ignored; and the basis for the company's higher PE ratio needs to be justified as well. The uncertainties surrounding these estimates would suggest that the value is indicative, rather than definitive, and it would be more prudent to undertake sensitivity analysis and obtain a range of values.

Key factors to consider in relation to the redundancies and potential tax savings

It is suggested that the BoD should consider the impact of the cost-savings from redundancies and from the tax payable in relation to corporate reputation and ethical considerations.

At present, Cigno Co enjoys a good reputation and it is suggested that this may be because it has managed to avoid large scale redundancies. This reputation may now be under threat and its loss could affect Cigno Co negatively in terms of long-term loss in revenues, profits and value; and it may be difficult to measure the impact of this loss accurately.

Whilst minimising tax may be financially prudent, it may not be considered fair. For example, currently there is ongoing discussion and debate from a number of governments and other interested parties that companies should pay tax in the countries they operate and derive their profits, rather than where they are based. Whilst global political consensus in this area seems some way off, it is likely that the debate in this area will increase in the future. Companies that are seen to be operating unethically with regard to this, may damage their reputation and therefore their profits and value.

Nonetheless, given that Cigno Co is likely to derive substantial value from the acquisition, because of these savings, it should not merely disregard the potential savings. Instead it should consider public relations exercises it could undertake to minimise the loss of reputation, and perhaps meet with the government to discuss ways forward in terms of tax payments.

Conclusion

The potential value gained from acquiring and unbundling Anatra Co can be substantial if the potential cost savings are taken into account. However, given the assumptions that are made in computing the value, it is recommended that sensitivity analysis is undertaken and a range of values obtained. It is also recommended that Cigno Co should undertake public relations exercises to minimise the loss of reputation, but it should probably proceed with the acquisition, and undertake the cost saving exercise because it is likely that this will result in substantial additional value.

Report compiled by: AN Accountant

Date: XX/XX/XXXX

Tutorial note

When attempting a question like this in the Computer Based Exam (CBE), make your answer look like a professional document by writing the report in the word processor but putting your numbers (appendix) in a spreadsheet.

When preparing your calculations, use the spreadsheet functions SUM and NPV to save time. Be careful when using the NPV function to enter =NPV, then a bracket containing the discount rate, a comma, and then the cells containing the cash flows from year 1 onwards. The initial investment then needs to be subtracted separately.

Appendix 1: Estimate of value created from the sell-off of the equipment manufacturing business

Average industry PE ratio = $2.40/$0.30 = 8

Anatra Co's equipment manufacturing business PE ratio = 8 × 1.2 = 9.6

Value from sell-off of equipment manufacturing business

Share of pre-tax profit = 30% × $2,490 million = $747m

After tax profit = $747 million × (1 – 0.22) = $582.7m

Value from sell-off = $582.7 million × 9.6 = $5,594m (approximately)

Appendix 2: Estimate of the combined company cost of capital

Anatra Co, asset beta = 0.68

Cigno Co, asset beta:

Equity beta =1.10

Proportion of market value of debt = 40%; Proportion of market value of equity = 60%

Asset beta = 1.10 × 0.60/(0.60 + 0.40 × 0.78) = 0.72

Combined company, asset beta

Market value of equity, Anatra Co = $3 × 7,000 million shares = $21,000m

Market value of equity, Cigno Co = 60% × $60,000 million = $36,000m

Asset beta = (0.68 × 21,000 + 0.72 × 36,000)/(21,000 + 36,000) = 0.71 (approximately)

Combined company equity beta = 0.71 × (0.6 + 0.4 × 0.78)/0.6 = 1.08

Combined company, cost of equity = 4.3% + 1.08 × 7% = 11.86%

Combined company, cost of capital = 11.86% × 0.6 + 6.00% × 0.78 × 0.4 = 8.99, say 9%

Appendix 3: Estimate of the value created for Cigno Co's equity holders from the acquisition

Anatra Co, Medical R&D value estimate:

Sales revenue growth rate = 5%

Operating profit margin = 17.25%

Tax rate = 22%

Additional capital investment = 40% of the change in sales revenue Cost of capital = 9% (Appendix 2)

Free cash flow growth rate after four years = 3%

Current sales revenue = 70% × $21,400m = $14,980m

Cash flows, years 1 to 4 ($ millions)

Year	1	2	3	4
Sales revenue	15,729	16,515	17,341	18,208
Profit before interest and tax	2,713	2,849	2,991	3,141
Tax	597	627	658	691
Additional capital investment	300	314	330	347
Free cash flows	1,816	1,908	2,003	2,103
Present value of cash flows (9% discount)	1,666	1,606	1,547	1,490

Value, years 1 to 4: $6,309m

Value, year 5 onwards: $[\$2{,}103 \times 1.03/(0.09 - 0.03)] \times 1.09^{-4} = \$25{,}575m$

Total value of Anatra Co's medical R&D business area = $31,884m

Total value of Anatra Co following unbundling of equipment manufacturing business and absorbing medical R&D business: $5,594m (Appendix 1) + $31,884m = $37,478m (approximately)

Anatra Co, current market value of equity = $21,000m Anatra Co, current market value of debt = $9,000m Premium payable = $21,000m × 35% = $7,350m

Total value attributable to Anatra Co's investors = $37,350m

Value attributable to Cigno Co's shareholders from the acquisition of Anatra Co before taking into account the cash benefits of potential tax savings and redundancies = $128m

Appendix 4: Estimate of the value created from savings in tax and employment costs following possible redundancies

Cash flows, years 1 to 4 ($ millions)

Year	1	2	3	4
Cash flows (4% increase p.a.)	1,600	1,664	1,731	1,800
Present value of cash flows (9%)	1,468	1,401	1,337	1,275

Total value = $5,481m

Value attributable to Cigno Co's shareholders from the acquisition of Anatra Co after taking into account the cash benefits of potential tax savings and redundancies = $5,609m

(c) The feasibility of disposing of assets as a defence tool against a possible acquisition depends upon the type of assets sold and how the funds generated from the sale are utilised.

If the type of assets are fundamental to the continuing business then this may be viewed as disposing of the corporation's 'crown-jewels'. Such action may be construed as being against protecting the rights of shareholders. In order for key assets to be disposed of, the takeover regulatory framework may insist on the corporation obtaining permission from the shareholders first before carrying it out.

On the other hand, the assets may be viewed as not being fundamental to the core business and may be disposed of to generate extra funds through a sell-off (see part (a) above). This may make sense if the corporation is undertaking a programme of restructuring and re-organisation.

In addition to this, the company needs to consider what it intends to do with the funds raised from the sale of assets. If the funds are used to grow the core business and therefore enhancing value, then the shareholders would see this positively and the value of the corporation will probably increase. Alternatively, if there are no profitable alternatives, the funds could be returned to the shareholders through special dividends or share buy-backs. In these circumstances, disposing of assets may be a feasible defence tactic.

However, if the funds are retained but not put to value-enhancing use or returned to shareholders, then the share price may continue to be depressed. And the corporation may still be an attractive takeover target for corporations which are in need of liquid funds. In these circumstances, disposing of assets would not be a feasible defence tactic.

Marking scheme				
				Marks
(a)			Up to 2 marks for distinguishing the two forms of unbundling	4
(b)	(i)		Appendix 1	
			Anatra Co, Manufacturing business, PE ratio	1
			Estimate of the value created from sell-off	3
			Appendix 2	
			Cigno Co asset beta	1
			Combined company asset beta	1
			Combined company equity beta	1
			Combined company cost of capital	1
			Appendix 3	
			Sales revenue, years 1 to 4	1
			Operating profit, years 1 to 4	1
			Taxation, years 1 to 4	1
			Capital investment, years 1 to 4	1
			Value from years 1 to 4	1
			Value from year 5 onwards	1
			Value for Cigno Co shareholders before impact of savings from tax and employee cost reduction	2
			Appendix 4	
			Value created from tax and employee cost savings	1
			Value for Cigno Co shareholders after impact of savings from tax and employee cost reduction	1
			Maximum	18
	(ii)		Discussion of values for the equity holders, additional costs/benefits not given	3–4
			Methods used and assumptions made	4–5
			Maximum	8
	(iii)		Reputation factors	1–2
			Ethical factors	1–2
			Comment on value	1–2
			Maximum	4
(c)			1 to 2 marks per point	
			Maximum	6
			Professional skills marks (see below)	10
Total				50

Professional skills

Communication

General report format and structure (use of headings/sub-headings and an introduction)

Style, language and clarity (appropriate layout and tone of report response, presentation of calculations, appropriate use of the tools)

Effectiveness of communication (answer is relevant, specific rather than general and focused to the requirement)

Analysis and Evaluation

Appropriate use of the data to determine suitable calculations

Appropriate use of the data to support discussion and draw appropriate conclusions

Demonstration of reasoned judgement when considering key matters for this specific company

Demonstration of ability to consider relevant factors applicable to this specific scenario

Scepticism

Effective challenge of information and assumptions supplied and, techniques carried out to support any decision

Commercial acumen

Effective use of examples and/or calculations from the scenario information and other practical considerations related to the context to illustrate points being made

Recognition of external constraints and opportunities as necessary

Maximum 10 marks

15 MORADA CO (SEP/DEC 16)

Key answer tips

There are lots of marks here for calculating the company's cost of equity and cost of capital in different scenarios.

However, note that there are also lots of marks available for (easier?) discussion points, such as part (b). This part can be answered independently of the tricky cost of capital calculations, so always try to answer this sort of thing first to build up confidence at the start of the question.

(a) **Report to the board of directors (BoD), Morada Co**

This report provides a discussion on the estimates of the cost of equity and the cost of capital and the impact on the financial position and the earnings after tax, as a result of the proposals put forward by the first director and the second director. The main assumptions made in drawing up the estimates will also be explained. The report concludes by recommending which of the two directors' proposals, if any, should be adopted.

Discussion

The table below shows the revised figures of the cost of equity and the cost of capital (Appendix 1), and the forecast earnings after tax for the coming year (Appendix 2), following each proposal from the first and second directors. For comparison purposes, figures before any changes are given as well.

	Cost of equity	Cost of capital	Earnings after tax
	Appendix 1	Appendix 1	Appendix 2
Current position	12.2%	10.0%	$28.0 million
Following first director's proposal	11.6%	11.1%	$37.8 million
Following second director's proposal	12.3%	9.8%	$30.8 million

Under the first director's proposal, although the cost of equity falls due to the lower financial risk in Morada Co because of less debt, the cost of capital actually increases. This is because, even though the cost of debt has decreased, the benefit of the tax shield is reduced significantly due to the lower amount of debt borrowing. Added to this is the higher business risk, reflected by the asset beta, of Morada Co just operating in the travel services sector. This higher business risk and reduced tax shield more than override the lower cost of debt resulting in a higher cost of capital.

Under the second director's proposal, the cost of equity is almost unchanged. There has been a significant increase in the cost of debt from 4.7% to 6.2%. However, the cost of capital has not reduced significantly because the benefit of the tax shield is also almost eroded by the increase in the cost of debt.

If no changes are made, then the forecast earnings after tax as a percentage of non-current assets is 10% ($28m/$280m). Under the first director's proposal, this figure almost doubles to 19.3% ($37.8m/$196m), and even if the one-off profit from the sale of non-current assets is excluded, this figure is still higher at 12.9% ($25.2m/$196m). Under the second director's proposal, this figure falls to 8.8% ($30.8m/$350m).

Assumptions

1   It is assumed that the asset beta of Morada Co is a weighted average of the asset betas of the travel services and the maintenance services business units, using non-current assets invested in each business unit as a fair representation of the size of each business unit and therefore the proportion of the business risk which business unit represents within the company.

2   The assumption of the share price not changing after either proposal is not reasonable. It is likely that due to changes in the business and financial risk from implementing either proposal, the risk profile of the company will change. The changes in the risk profile will influence the cost of equity, which in turn will influence the share price.

3   In determining the financial position of Morada Co, it is assumed that the current assets will change due to changes in the profit after tax figure; therefore this is used as the balancing figure for each proposal.

Recommendation

It is recommended that neither the first director's proposal nor the second director's proposal should be adopted. The second director's proposal results in a lower return on investment and a virtually unchanged cost of capital. So there will not be a meaningful benefit for Morada Co. The first director's proposal does increase the return on investment but results in a higher cost of capital. If the reason for adopting either proposal is to reduce risk, then this is not achieved. The main caveat here is that where the assumptions made in the calculations are not reasonable, they will reduce the usefulness of the analysis.

Report compiled by:

Date:

Note: Credit will be given for alternative and relevant points.

Appendix 1: Estimates of cost of equity and cost of capital

Before either proposal is implemented

Cost of equity (Ke) = 3.8% + 1.2 × 7% = 12.2%
Cost of debt (Kd) = 3.8% + 0.9% = 4.7%

Market value of equity (MV$_e$) = $2.88 × 125 million shares = $360m

Market value of debt (MV$_d$)
Per $100 $6.20 × 1.047^{-1} + $6.20 × 1.047^{-2} + $6.20 × 1.047^{-3} + $106.20 × 1.047^{-4}
= $105.36
Total MV$_d$ = $105.36/$100 × $120m = $126.4m

Cost of capital = (12.2% × $360m + 4.7% × 0.8 × $126.4m)/$486.4m = 10.0%

If the first director's proposal is implemented

MV$_e$ = $360m
BV$_d$ = $120m × 0.2 = $24m
Kd = 4.4%

MV$_d$ per $100 $6.20 × 1.044^{-1} + $6.20 × 1.044^{-2} + $6.20 × 1.044^{-3} + $106.20 × 1.044^{-4}
= $106.47
Total MV$_d$ = 106.47/$100 × $24 = $25.6m

Morada Co, asset beta
1.2 × $360m/($360m + $126.4m × 0.8) = 0.94
Asset beta of travel services = [0.94 − (0.65 × 30%)]/70% = 1.06
Equity beta of travel services = 1.06 × ($360m + $25.6m × 0.8)/$360m = 1.12

Ke = 3.8% + 1.12 × 7% = 11.6%
Cost of capital = (11.6% × $360m + 4.4% × 0.8 × $25.6m)/$385.6 = 11.1%

If the second director's proposal is implemented

MV$_e$ = $360m
The basis points for the Ca3 rated bond is 240 basis points higher than the risk free-free rate of interest, giving a cost of debt of 6.2%, therefore:
MV$_d$ = BV$_d$ = $190m

Equity beta of the new, larger company = 1.21

Ke = 3.8% + 1.21 × 7% = 12.3%
Cost of capital = (12.3% × $360m + 6.2% × 0.8 × $190m)/$550m = 9.8%

Appendix 2: Estimates of forecast after-tax earnings and forecast financial position

Morada Co, extracts from the forecast after-tax earnings for the coming year (Amounts in $000)

	Current forecast	Forecast: first director proposal	Forecast: second director proposal
Current forecast after-tax earnings	28,000	28,000	28,000
Interest saved due to lower borrowing ($96m × 6.2% × 0.8)		4,762	
Interest payable on additional borrowing ($70m × 6.2% × 0.8)			(3,472)
Reduction in earnings due to lower investment (9% × $84m)		(7,560)	
Additional earnings due to higher investment (9% × $70m)			6,300
Profit on sale of non-current assets (15% × $84m)		12,600	
Revised forecast after-tax earnings	28,000	37,802	30,828
Increase in after-tax earnings		9,802	2,828

Morada Co, extracts from the forecast financial position for the coming year (Amounts in $000)

	Current forecast	Forecast: first director proposal	Forecast: second director proposal
Non-current assets	280,000	196,000	350,000
Current assets (balancing figure)	48,000	43,702	57,828
Total assets	328,000	239,702	407,828
Equity and liabilities			
Share capital (40c/share)	50,000	50,000	50,000
Retained earnings**	137,000	146,802	139,828
Total equity	187,000	196,802	189,828
Non-current liabilities (6.2% redeemable bonds)	120,000	24,000	190,000
Current liabilities	21,000	18,900	28,000
Total liabilities	141,000	42,900	218,000
Total liabilities and capital	328,000	239,702	407,828

** **Note:** With the two directors' proposals, the retained earnings amount is adjusted to reflect the revised forecast after-tax earnings.

(b) [**Note:** This is an open-ended question and a variety of relevant answers can be given by candidates depending on how the question requirement is interpreted. The following answer is just one possible approach which could be taken. Credit will be given for alternative, but valid, interpretations and answers therein.]

According to the third director, risk management involves more than just risk mitigation or risk diversification as proposed by the first and second directors. The proposals suggested by the first and the second directors are likely to change the makeup of the company, and cause uncertainty amongst the company's owners or clientele. This in turn may cause unnecessary fluctuations in the share price. She suggests that these changes are fundamental and more than just risk management tools.

Instead, it seems that she is suggesting that Morada Co should follow the risk management process suggested in part (a) above, where risks should be identified, assessed and then mitigated according to the company's risk appetite.

The risk management process should be undertaken with a view to increasing shareholder wealth, and therefore the company should consider what drives this value and what are the risks associated with these drivers of value. Morada Co may assess that some of these risks are controllable and some not controllable. It may assess that some are severe and others less so, and it may assess some are likely to occur more frequently than others.

Morada Co may take the view that the non-controllable, severe and/or frequent risks should be eliminated (or not accepted). On the other hand, where Morada Co is of the opinion that it has a comparative advantage or superior knowledge of risks, and therefore is better able to manage them, it may come to the conclusion that it should accept these. For example, it may take the view that it is able to manage events such as flight delays or hotel standards, but would hedge against currency fluctuations and insure against natural disasters due to their severity or non-controllability.

Theory suggests that undertaking risk management may increase the value of a company if the benefits accruing from the risk management activity are more than the costs involved in managing the risks. For example, smoothing the volatility of profits may make it easier for Morada Co to plan and match long-term funding with future projects, it may make it easier for Morada Co to take advantage of market imperfections by reducing the amount of taxation payable, or it may reduce the costs involved with incidences of financial distress. In each case though, the benefits accrued should be assessed against the costs involved.

Therefore, a risk management process is more than just mitigating risk through reducing financial risk as the first director is suggesting or risk diversification as the second director is suggesting. Instead it is a process of risk analysis and then about judgement of which risks to hedge or mitigate, and finally, which risk-reduction mechanisms to employ, depending on the type of risk, the cost of the risk analysis and mitigation, and the benefits accruing from the mitigation.

			Marking scheme		
					Marks
(a)	(i)		**[Appendix 1]**		
			Prior to implementation of any proposal		
			Cost of equity		1
			Cost of debt		1
			Market value of equity		1
			Market value of debt		2
			Cost of capital		1
			After implementing the first director's proposal		
			Market value of debt		2
			Morada Co, asset beta		1
			Asset beta of travel services only		1
			Equity beta of travel services only		1
			Cost of equity		1
			Cost of capital		1
			After implementing the second director's proposal		
			Market value of debt		2
			Cost of equity		1
			Cost of capital		1
					———
					17
					———
	(ii)		**[Appendix 2]**		
			Adjusted earnings, first director's proposal		2
			Financial position, first director's proposal		2
			Adjusted earnings, second director's proposal		2
			Financial position, second director's proposal		1
					———
					7
					———
	(iii)		Discussion		5–6
			Assumptions		2–3
			Reasoned recommendation		1–2
			(**Note:** Maximum 8 marks if no recommendation given)		
					———
				Maximum	9
					———
(b)		1–2 marks per point		Maximum	7
					———
			Professional skills marks (see below)		10
					———
Total					50
					———

Professional skills

Communication

General report format and structure (use of headings/sub-headings and an introduction)

Style, language and clarity (appropriate layout and tone of report response, presentation of calculations, appropriate use of the tools)

Effectiveness of communication (answer is relevant, specific rather than general and focused to the requirement)

Analysis and Evaluation

Appropriate use of the data to determine suitable calculations

Appropriate use of the data to support discussion and draw appropriate conclusions

Demonstration of reasoned judgement when considering key matters for this specific company

Demonstration of ability to consider relevant factors applicable to this specific scenario

Scepticism

Effective challenge of information and assumptions supplied and, techniques carried out to support any decision

Demonstration of the ability to probe into the reasons for issues and problems, including the identification of missing information or additional information, which would alter the decision reached

Commercial acumen

Effective use of examples and/or calculations from the scenario information and other practical considerations related to the context to illustrate points being made

Recognition of external constraints and opportunities as necessary

Maximum 10 marks

16   CHRYSOS CO (MAR/JUN 17)

Key answer tips

There was a lot to do in this question, but students would have been pleased to see that the question was split up into several smaller sub-requirements to help with time management.

A good exam technique would have been critical – the calculations in part (i) of the report were quite tricky (preparing a statement of financial position after the reconstruction, and two business valuations using the FCF method) and it would have been easy to spend too much time on them.

The discussion points in the question were more straightforward though, and the requirements were very clear.

A well prepared student, who presented the answer in a report format and left enough time to answer to both calculations and discussions, should have been able to pass this question.

(a)   A reverse takeover enables a private, unlisted company, like Chrysos Co, to gain a listing on the stock exchange without needing to go through the process of an initial public offering (IPO). The private company merges with a listed 'shell' company. The private company initially purchases equity shares in the listed company and takes control of its board of directors. The listed company then issues new equity shares and these are exchanged for equity shares in the unlisted company, thereby the original private company's equity shares gain a listing on the stock exchange. Often the name of the listed company is also changed to that of the original unlisted company.

Advantages relative to an IPO

1   An IPO can take a long time, typically between one and two years, because it involves preparing a prospectus and creating an interest among potential investors. The equity shares need to be valued and the issue process needs to be administered. Since with the reverse takeover shares in the private company are exchanged for shares in the listed company and no new capital is being raised, the process can be completed much quicker.

2   An IPO is an expensive process and can cost between 3% and 5% of the capital being raised due to involvement of various parties, such as investment banks, law firms, etc, and the need to make the IPO attractive through issuing a prospectus and marketing the issue. A reverse takeover does not require such costs to be incurred and therefore is considerably cheaper.

3   In periods of economic downturn, recessions and periods of uncertainty, an IPO may not be successful. A lot of senior managerial time and effort will be spent, as well as expenditure, with nothing to show for it. On the other hand, a reverse takeover would not face this problem as it does not need external investors and it is not raising external finance, but is being used to gain from the potential benefits of going public by getting a listing.

Disadvantages relative to an IPO

1   The 'shell' listed company being used in the reverse takeover may have hidden liabilities and may be facing potential litigation, which may not be obvious at the outset. Proper and full due diligence is necessary before the process is started. A company undertaking an IPO would not face such difficulties.

2   The original shareholders of the listed company may want to sell their shares immediately after the reverse takeover process has taken place and this may affect the share price negatively. A lock-up period during which shares cannot be sold may be necessary to prevent this. [NB: An IPO may need a lock-up period as well, but this is not usually the case.]

3   The senior management of an unlisted company may not have the expertise and/or understanding of the rules and regulations which a listed company needs to comply with. The IPO process normally takes longer and is more involved, when compared to a reverse takeover. It also involves a greater involvement from external experts. These factors will provide the senior management involved in an IPO, with opportunities to develop the necessary expertise and knowledge of listing rules and regulations, which the reverse takeover process may not provide.

4   One of the main reasons for gaining a listing is to gain access to new investor capital. However, a smaller, private company which has become public through a reverse takeover may not obtain a sufficient analyst coverage and investor following, and it may have difficulty in raising new finance in future. A well-advertised IPO will probably not face these issues and find raising new funding to be easier.

(b)   **Report to the board of directors (BoD), Chrysos Co**

This report provides extracts from the financial position and an estimate of the value of Chrysos Co after it has undertaken a restructuring programme. It also contains an explanation of the process used in estimating the value and of the assumptions made. Finally, the report discusses the impact of the restructuring programme on the company and on venture capital organisations.

It is recommended that the manufacturing business unit is unbundled through a management buy-out, rather than the assets being sold separately, and it is estimated that Chrysos Co will receive $3,289m from the unbundling of the manufacturing business unit (Appendix one). This amount is recorded as a cash receipt in the extract of the financial position given below.

Extract of Chrysos Co's financial position following the restructuring programme

	$m
Non-current assets	
Land and buildings (80% × $7,500m)	6,000
Equipment ((80% × $5,400m) + $1,200m)	5,520
Current assets	
Inventory (80% × $1,800m)	1,440
Receivables (80% × $900m)	720
Cash ($3,289m + $400m – $1,200m – $1,050m)	1,439
Total assets	15,119
Equity	
Share capital ($1,800m + $600m)	2,400
Reserves **	10,319
Non-current liabilities: Bank loan	1,800
Current liabilities: Payables (80% × $750m)	600
Total equity and liabilities	15,119

** Balancing figure

Estimate of Chrysos Co's equity value following the restructuring programme

It is estimated that Chrysos Co's equity value after the restructuring programme has taken place will be just over $46 billion (Appendix three).

Process undertaken in determining Chrysos Co's equity value

The corporate value is based on a growth rate of 4% on cash flows in perpetuity, which are discounted at Chrysos Co's cost of capital (Appendix two). The cash flows are estimated by calculating the profit before depreciation and tax of the unbundled firm consisting of just the mining and shipping business unit and then deducting the depreciation and taxation amounts from this.

The bank loan debt is then deducted from the corporate value to estimate the value of the firm which is attributable to the equity holders (Appendix three).

Assumptions made in determining Chrysos Co's equity value

It is assumed that Sidero Co's ungeared cost of equity is equivalent to Chrysos Co's ungeared cost of equity, given that they are both in the same industry and therefore face the same business risk. Modigliani and Miller's proposition 2 is used to estimate Chrysos Cos's restructured cost of equity and cost of capital.

It is assumed that deducting depreciation and tax from the profit before depreciation, interest and tax provides a reasonably accurate estimate of the free cash flows (Appendix three). Other adjustments such as changes in working capital are reckoned to be immaterial and therefore not considered. Depreciation is not added back because it is assumed to be the same as the capital needed for reinvestment purposes.

It is assumed that the cash flows will grow in perpetuity. The assumption of growth in perpetuity may be over-optimistic and may give a higher than accurate estimate of Chrysos Co's equity value.

Note: Credit will be given for alternative and relevant assumptions.

Impact of the restructuring programme on Chrysos Co and on the venture capital organisations (VCOs)

By acquiring an extra 600 million equity shares, the proportion of the VCOs' equity share capital will increase to 40% ((600m + 20% × 1,800)/(1,800 + 600)) from 20%. Therefore, the share of the equity value the VCOs will hold in Chrysos Co will increase by $9,229m, which is 77.5% more than the total of the value of bonds cancelled and extra payment made (Appendix four). As long as the VCOs are satisfied that the equity value of Chrysos Co after the restructuring programme has been undertaken is accurate, the value of their investment has increased substantially.

The VCOs may want undertake a feasibility study on the annual growth rate in cash flows of 4% and the assumption of growth in perpetuity. However, the extent of additional value created seems to indicate that the impact for the VCOs is positive.

By cancelling the VCOs' unsecured bonds and repaying the other debt in non-current liabilities, an opportunity has been created for Chrysos Co to raise extra debt finance for future projects. Based on a long-term capital structure ratio of 80% equity and 20% debt, and a corporate value of $47,944m (Appendix three), this equates to just under $9,600m of possible debt finance which could be accessed. Since the bank loan has a current value of $1,800m, Chrysos Co could raise just under an extra $7,800m debt funding and it would also have $1,439 million in net cash available from the sale of the machinery parts manufacturing business unit.

Chrysos Co's current value has not been given and therefore it is not possible to determine the financial impact of the equity value after the restructuring has taken place on the company as a whole. Nevertheless, given that the company has access to an extra $7,800m debt funding to expand its investment into new value-creating projects, it is likely that the restructuring programme will be beneficial. However, it is recommended that the company tries to determine its current equity value and compares this with the proposed new value. A concern may be that both the five senior equity holders' group and the 30 other equity holders group's proportion of equity shares will reduce to 30% from 40% each, as a result of the VCOs acquiring an additional 600 million shares. Both these shareholder groups need to be satisfied about the potential negative impact of these situations against the potential additional benefits accruing from the restructuring programme, before the company proceeds with the programme.

Conclusion

The restructuring programme creates an opportunity for Chrysos Co to have access to extra funding and additional cash for investment in projects in the future. The VCOs are likely to benefit financially from the restructuring programme as long as they are satisfied about the assumptions made when assessing the value created. However, Chrysos Co will need to ensure that all equity holder groups are satisfied with the change in their respective equity holdings.

Report compiled by:

Date:

Note: Credit will be given for alternative and relevant points.

APPENDICES

Appendix One: Unbundling the manufacturing business unit

Option 1: Sale of assets

Net proceeds to Chrysos Co from net sale of assets of the manufacturing business unit are $3,102 million.

Option 2: Management buy-out

	$m
Sales revenue (20% × $16,800m)	3,360
Operating costs (25% × 10,080m)	(2,520)
Profit before depreciation, interest and tax	840
Depreciation (12% × 20% × ($7,500m + $5,400m))	(310)
	530
Tax (18% × $530m)	(95)
Cash flows	435

Estimated value = ($435m × 1.08)/0.10 = $4,698m

Amount payable to Chrysos Co = 70% × $4,698m = $3,289m

The option to unbundle through a management buy-out (option 2) is marginally better for Chrysos Co and it will opt for this.

Appendix Two: Calculation of cost of equity and cost of capital

Chrysos Co, estimate of cost of equity (Ke) and cost of capital (CoC)

Ke = 12.46% + [0.82 × (12.46% − 4.5%) × (0.2/0.8)]

Ke = 14.09%

CoC = 0.8 × 14.09% + 0.2 × 4.5% × 0.82 = 12.01, say 12%

Tutorial note

The 12% cost of capital was given in the question, but this working shows how it was calculated. You would not have needed to present these workings in the exam.

Appendix Three: Estimate of value

	$m
Sales revenue (80% × $16,800m)	13,440
Costs prior to depreciation, interest and tax (75% × 10,080m)	(7,560)
	——
Profit before depreciation and tax	5,880
Depreciation (12% × ($6,000m + $5,520m))	(1,382)
	——
	4,498
Tax (18% × $4,498m)	(810)
	——
Cash flows	3,688
	——

Cost of capital to be used in estimating Chrysos Co's value is 12% (Appendix two)

Estimated corporate value = ($3,688m × 1.04)/(0.12 − 0.04) = $47,944m

Estimated equity value = $47,944m − $1,800m = $46,144m

Note: It is also acceptable to calculate cash flows after interest payment and use the cost of equity to estimate the equity value based on cash flows to equity instead of cash flows to firm.

Appendix Four: Value created for VCOs

Value attributable to the VCOs = 40% × $46,144m = $18,458m

Value from increased equity ownership (this has doubled from 20% to 40%)

50% × $18,458m = $9,229m

Value of unsecured bonds foregone by the VCOs = $4,800m

Additional capital invested by the VCOs = $400m

Total of additional capital invested and value of bonds forgone = $5,200m

Additional value = ($9,229m − $5,200m)/$5,200m = 77.5% (or $4,029m)

(c)   As a private company, Chrysos Co is able to ensure that the needs of its primary stakeholder groups – finance providers, managers and employees – are taken into account through the supervisory board. The supervisory board has representatives from each of these groups and each group member has a voice on the board. Each stakeholder group should be able to present its position to the board through its representatives, and decisions will be made after agreement from all group representatives. In this way, no single stakeholder group holds primacy over any other group.

Once Chrysos Co is listed and raises new capital, it is likely that it will have a large and diverse range of equity shareholders, who will likely be holding equity shares in many other companies. Therefore there is likely to be pressure on Chrysos Co to engage in value creating activity aimed at keeping its share price buoyant and thereby satisfying the equity shareholders. It is, therefore, likely that the equity shareholders' needs will hold primacy over the other stakeholder groups and quite possibly the power of the supervisory board will diminish as a result of this.

		Marking scheme		
				Marks
(a)		Explanation of what a reverse takeover involves		2
		Advantages (up to 2 marks per well explained point)		2–3
		Disadvantages (up to 2 marks per well explained point)		2–3
			Maximum	6
(b)	(i)	Extract of financial position after restructuring programme		5
		Appendix 1: Manufacturing business unit unbundled through an MBO		
		Estimate of cash flows		3
		Estimate of amount payable to Chrysos Co		2
		Selection of higher value option		1
		Appendix 3		
		Estimate of cash flows		3
		Estimate of equity value		2
				16
	(ii)	Explanation of approach taken		1–2
		Explanation of assumptions made (up to 2 marks per assumption)		3–4
			Maximum	5
	(iii)	**Appendix 4**		
		Value from increased ownership		1
		Additional value		1
		Discussion of restructuring programme on the VCOs		3–4
		Discussion of restructuring programme on Chrysos Co		3–4
			Maximum	9
(c)		1-2 marks per relevant point		4
			Maximum	4
		Professional skills marks (see below)		10
Total				50

Professional skills

Communication

General report format and structure (use of headings/sub-headings and an introduction)

Style, language and clarity (appropriate layout and tone of report response, presentation of calculations, appropriate use of the tools)

Effectiveness of communication (answer is relevant, specific rather than general and focused to the requirement)

Analysis and Evaluation

Appropriate use of the data to determine suitable calculations

Appropriate use of the data to support discussion and draw appropriate conclusions

Demonstration of reasoned judgement when considering key matters for this specific company

Demonstration of ability to consider relevant factors applicable to this specific scenario

Scepticism

Effective challenge of information and assumptions supplied and, techniques carried out to support any decision

Commercial acumen

Effective use of examples and/or calculations from the scenario information and other practical considerations related to the context to illustrate points being made

Recognition of external constraints and opportunities as necessary

Maximum 10 marks

17 CONEJO CO (SEP/DEC 17)

Key answer tips

A good exam technique would have been critical here – the calculations in part (i) and (ii) of the report were quite tricky and related specifically to a technical article written by the examiner in 2011, and then the calculations in part (iii) (preparing a statement of financial position etc after the reconstruction) could have been very time consuming. It would have been easy to spend too much time on these calculations.

The discussion points in the question were more straightforward though, and the requirements were very clear.

Students understand how important it is to read the examiner's *recent* articles before they attempt the AFM exam, but this question demonstrates how important it is to read all the previous technical articles.

(a) Increasing the debt finance of a company relative to equity finance increases its financial risk, and therefore the company will need to be able to bear the consequences of this increased risk. However, companies face both financial risk, which increases as the debt levels in the capital structure increase, and business risk, which is present in a company due to the nature of its business.

In the case of Conejo Co, it could be argued that as its profits and cash flows have stabilised, the company's business risk has reduced, in contrast to early in its life, when its business risk would have been much higher due to unstable profits and cash flows. Therefore, whereas previously Conejo Co was not able to bear high levels of financial risk, it is able to do so now without having a detrimental impact on the overall risk profile of the company. It could therefore change its capital structure and have higher levels of debt finance relative to equity finance.

The predatory acquisition of one company by another could be undertaken for a number of reasons. One possible reason may be to gain access to cash resources, where a company which needs cash resources may want to take over another company which has significant cash resources or cash generative capability. Another reason may be to increase the debt capacity of the acquirer by using the assets of the target company. Where the relative level of debt finance is increased in the capital structure of a company through a financial reconstruction, like in the case of Conejo Co, these reasons for acquiring a company may be diminished. This is because the increased levels of debt would probably be secured against the assets of the company and therefore the acquirer cannot use them to raise additional debt finance, and cash resources would be needed to fund the higher interest payments.

Many tax jurisdictions worldwide allow debt interest to be deducted from profits before the amount of tax payable is calculated on the profits. Increasing the amount of debt finance will increase the amount of interest paid, reducing the taxable profits and therefore the tax paid. Modigliani and Miller referred to this as the benefit of the tax shield in their research into capital structure, where their amended capital proposition demonstrated the reduction in the cost of capital and increase in the value of the firm, as the proportion of debt in the capital structure increases.

(b) Report to the board of directors (BoD), Conejo Co

Introduction

This report discusses whether the proposed financial reconstruction scheme which increases the amount of debt finance in Conejo Co would be beneficial or not to the company and the main parties affected by the change in the funding, namely the equity holders, the debt holders and the credit rating companies. Financial estimates provided in the appendices are used to support the discussion.

Impact on Conejo Co

Benefits to Conejo Co include the areas discussed in part (a) above and as suggested by the CFO. The estimate in Appendix 3 assumes that the interest payable on the new bonds and the extra interest payable on the existing bonds are net of the 15% tax. Therefore, the tax shield reduces the extra amount of interest paid. Further, it is likely that because of the large amount of debt finance which will be raised, the company's assets would have been used as collateral. This will help protect the company against hostile takeover bids. Additionally, proposal 2 (Appendix 3) appears to be better than proposal 1, with a lower gearing figure and a higher earnings per share figure. However, this is dependent on the extra investment being able to generate an after-tax return of 12% immediately. The feasibility of this should be assessed further.

Conejo Co may also feel that this is the right time to raise debt finance as interest rates are lower and therefore it does not have to offer large coupons, compared to previous years. Appendix 1 estimates that the new bond will need to offer a coupon of 3.57%, whereas the existing bond is paying a coupon of 5.57%.

The benefits above need to be compared with potential negative aspects of raising such a substantial amount of debt finance. Conejo Co needs to ensure that it will be able to finance the interest payable on the bonds and it should ensure it is able to repay the capital amount borrowed (or be able to re-finance the loan) in the future. The extra interest payable (Appendix 3) will probably not pose a significant issue given that the profit after tax is substantially more than the interest payment. However, the repayment of the capital amount will need careful thought because it is significant.

The substantial increase in gearing, especially with respect to proposal 1 (Appendix 3), may worry some stakeholders because of the extra financial risk. However, based on market values, the level of gearing may not appear so high. The expected credit migration from A to BBB seems to indicate some increase in risk, but it is probably not substantial.

The BoD should also be aware of, and take account of, the fact that going to the capital markets to raise finance will require Conejo Co to disclose information, which may be considered strategically important and could impact negatively on areas where Conejo Co has a competitive advantage.

Reaction of credit rating companies

Credit ratings assigned to companies and to borrowings made by companies by credit rating companies depend on the probability of default and recovery rate. A credit migration from A to BBB means that Conejo Co has become riskier in that it is more likely to default and bondholders will find it more difficult to recover their entire loan if default does happen. Nevertheless, the relatively lower increase in yield spreads from A to BBB, compared to BBB to BB, indicates that BBB can still be considered a relatively safe investment.

Duration indicates the time it takes to recover half the repayments of interest and capital of a bond, in present value terms. Duration measures the sensitivity of bond prices to changes in interest rates. A bond with a higher duration would see a greater fluctuation in its value when interest rates change, compared to a bond with a lower duration. Appendix 2 shows that a bond which pays interest (coupon) and capital in equal annual instalments will have a lower duration. This is because a greater proportion of income is received earlier and income due to be received earlier is less risky. Therefore, when interest rates change, this bond's value will change by less than the bond with the higher duration. The CEO is correct that the bond with equal annual payments of interest and capital is less sensitive to interest rate changes, but it is not likely that this will be a significant factor for a credit rating company when assigning a credit rating.

A credit rating company will consider a number of criteria when assigning a credit rating, as these would give a more appropriate assessment of the probability of default and the recovery rate. These criteria include, for example, the industry within which the company operates, the company's position within that industry, the company's ability to generate profits in proportion to the capital invested, the amount of gearing, the quality of management and the amount of financial flexibility the company possesses. A credit rating company will be much less concerned about the manner in which a bond's value fluctuates when interest rates change.

Impact on equity holders

The purpose of the financial reconstruction would be of interest to the equity holders. If, for example, Conejo Co selects proposal 1 (Appendix 3), it may give equity holders an opportunity to liquidate some of their invested capital. At present, the original members of the company hold 40% of the equity capital and proposal 1 provides them with the opportunity to realise a substantial capital without unnecessary fluctuations in the share price. Selling large quantities of equity shares in the stock exchange may move the price of the shares down and cause unnecessary fluctuations in the share price.

If, on the other hand, proposal 2 (Appendix 3) is selected, any additional profits after the payment of interest will benefit the equity holders directly. In effect, debt capital is being used for the benefit of the equity holders.

It may be true that equity holders may be concerned about the increased risk which higher gearing will bring, and because of this, they may need higher returns to compensate for the higher risk. However, in terms of market values, the increased gearing may be of less concern to equity holders. Conejo Co should consider the capital structure of its competitors to assess what should be an appropriate level of gearing.

Equity holders will probably be more concerned about the additional restrictive covenants which will result from the extra debt finance, and the extent to which these covenants will restrict the financial flexibility of Conejo Co when undertaking future business opportunities.

Equity holders may also be concerned that because Conejo Co has to pay extra interest to debt holders, its ability to pay increasing amounts of dividends in the future could be affected. However, Appendix 3 shows that the proportion of interest relative to after-tax profits is not too high and any concern from the equity holders is probably unfounded.

Impact on debt holders

Although the current debt holders may be concerned about the extra gearing which the new bonds would introduce to Conejo Co, Appendix 1 shows that the higher coupon payments which the current debt holders will receive would negate any fall in the value of their bonds due to the credit migration to BBB rating from an A rating. Given that currently Conejo Co is subject to low financial risk, and probably lower business risk, it is unlikely that the current and new debt holders would be overly concerned about the extra gearing. The earnings figures in Appendix 3 also show that the after-tax profit figures provide a substantial interest cover and therefore additional annual interest payment should not cause the debt holders undue concern either.

The current and new debt holders would be more concerned about Conejo Co's ability to pay back the large capital sum in five years' time. However, a convincing explanation of how this can be achieved or a plan to roll over the debt should allay these concerns.

The current and new debt holders may be concerned that Conejo Co is not tempted to take unnecessary risks with the additional investment finance, but sensible use of restrictive covenants and the requirement to make extra disclosures to the markets when raising the debt finance should help mitigate these concerns.

Conclusion

Overall, it seems that the proposed financial reconstruction will be beneficial, as it will provide opportunities for Conejo Co to make additional investments and/or an opportunity to reduce equity capital, and thereby increasing the earnings per share. The increased gearing may not look large when considered in terms of market values. It may also be advantageous to undertake the reconstruction scheme in a period when interest rates are low and the credit migration is not disadvantageous. However, Conejo Co needs to be mindful of how it intends to repay the capital amount in five years' time, the information it will disclose to the capital markets and the impact of any negative restrictive covenants.

Report compiled by:

Date:

APPENDICES

Appendix 1: Change in the value of the current bond from credit migration and coupon rate required from the new bond (Question (b) (i))

Spot yield rates (yield curve) based on BBB rating

1 year: 2.20%

2 year: 2.51%

3 year: 2.84%

4 year: 3.25%

5 year: 3.62%

Bond value based on BBB rating

$\$5.57 \times 1.0220^{-1} + \$5.57 \times 1.0251^{-2} + \$105.57 \times 1.0284^{-3} = \$107.81$

Current bond value = $107.80

Although the credit rating of Conejo Co declines from A to BBB, resulting in higher spot yield rates, the value of the bond does not change very much at all. This is because the increase in the coupons and the resultant increase in value almost exactly matches the fall in value from the higher spot yield rates.

Coupon rate required from the new bond

Take R as the coupon rate, such that:

$(\$R \times 1.0220^{-1}) + (\$R \times 1.0251^{-2}) + (\$R \times 1.0284^{-3}) + (\$R \times 1.0325^{-4}) + (\$R \times 1.0362^{-5}) + (\$100 \times 1.0362^{-5}) = \$100$

4.5665R + 83.71 = 100

R = $3.57

Coupon rate for the new bond is 3.57%.

If the coupon payments on the bond are at a rate of 3.57% on the face value, it ensures that the present values of the coupons and the redemption of the bond at face value exactly equals the bond's current face value, based on Conejo Co's yield curve.

Appendix 2: Macaulay durations (Question (b) (ii))

Macaulay duration based on annual coupon of $3.57 and redemption value of $100 in year 5:

$[(\$3.57 \times 1.0220^{-1} \times 1 \text{ year}) + (\$3.57 \times 1.0251^{-2} \times 2 \text{ years}) + (\$3.57 \times 1.0284^{-3} \times 3 \text{ years}) + (\$3.57 \times 1.0325^{-4} \times 4 \text{ years}) + (\$103.57 \times 1.0362^{-5} \times 5 \text{ years})]/\$100$

= [3.49 + 6.79 + 9.85 + 12.57 + 433.50]/100 = 4.7 years

Macaulay duration based on fixed annual repayments of interest and capital:

Annuity factor: (3.57%, 5 years) = $(1 - 1.0357^{-5})/0.0357$ = 4.51 approximately

Annual payments of capital and interest required to pay back new bond issue = $100/4.51 = $22.17 per $100 bond approximately

$[(\$22.17 \times 1.0220^{-1} \times 1 \text{ year}) + (\$22.17 \times 1.0251^{-2} \times 2 \text{ years}) + (\$22.17 \times 1.0284^{-3} \times 3 \text{ years}) + (\$22.17 \times 1.0325^{-4} \times 4 \text{ years}) + (\$22.17 \times 1.0362^{-5} \times 5 \text{ years})]/\$100$

= [21.69 + 42.20 + 61.15 + 78.03 + 92.79]/100 = 3.0 years

Appendix 3: Forecast earnings, financial position, earnings per share and gearing (Question (b) (iii))

Adjustments to forecast earnings (Amounts in $ millions)

	Current	Proposal 1	Proposal 2
Forecast after-tax profit	350.00	350.00	350.00
Interest payable on additional borrowing (based on a coupon rate of 3.57%) $3.57\% \times \$1,320m \times (1 - 0.15)$		(40.06)	(40.06)
Additional interest payable due to higher coupon $0.37\% \times \$120m \times (1 - 0.15)$		(0.38)	(0.38)
Return on additional investment (after tax) $12\% \times \$1,320m$			158.40
Revised forecast after-tax earnings	350.00	309.56	467.96

Forecast financial position (Amounts in $ millions)

	Current	Proposal 1	Proposal 2
Non-current assets	1,735.00	1,735.00	3,055.00
Current assets	530.00	489.56	647.96
Total assets	2,265.00	2,224.56	3,702.96
Equity and liabilities			
Share capital ($1 per share par)	400.00	280.00	400.00
Reserves	1,700.00	459.56	1,817.96
Total equity	2,100.00	739.56	2,217.96
Non-current liabilities	120.00	1,440.00	1,440.00
Current liabilities	45.00	45.00	45.00
Total liabilities	165.00	1,485.00	1,485.00
Total liabilities and capital	2,265.00	2,224.56	3,702.96

	Current	Proposal 1	Proposal 2
Gearing % (non-current liabilities/equity)	5.7%	194.7%	64.9%
Earnings per share (in cents) (adj profit after tax/no. of shares)	87.5c	110.6c	117.0c

Notes:

If gearing is calculated based on non-current liabilities/(non-current liabilities + equity) and/or using market value of equity, instead of as above, then this is acceptable as well.

Proposal 1

Additional interest payable is deducted from current assets, assuming it is paid in cash and this is part of current assets. Reserves are also reduced by this amount.

Shares repurchased as follows: $1 × 120m shares deducted from share capital and $10 × 120m shares deducted from reserves. $1,320m, consisting of $11 × 120m shares, added to non-current liabilities.

Proposal 2

Treatment of additional interest payable is as per proposal 1.

Additional debt finance raised, $1,320 million, is added to non-current liabilities and to non-current assets, assuming that all this amount is invested in non-current assets to generate extra income.

It is assumed that this additional investment generates returns at 12%, which is added to current assets and to profits (and therefore to reserves).

(Explanations given in notes are not required for full marks, but are included to explain how the figures given in Appendix 3 are derived)

Note: Credit will be given for alternative relevant presentation of financial positions and discussion.

			Marks
		Marking scheme	
(a)		Being able to bear higher levels of financial risk	2–3
		Better protection from predatory takeover bids	2–3
		Tax benefit of higher levels of debt finance	1–2
		Maximum	**5**
(b)	(i)	Conejo Co's yield curve based on BBB rating	1
		Bond value based on BBB rating and spot yield rates	1
		Comment on reason for virtually no change in value	1
		Calculation of coupon rate of new bond	2
		Comment on coupon rate	1
			6
	(ii)	Duration based on annual coupon and balloon payment of $100 in year 5	2
		Amount of fixed annual repayments of capital and interest	2
		Duration based on annual equivalent payments	2
			6
	(iii)	Financial position, proposal 1	3
		Financial position, proposal 2	3
		Interest payable on additional new debt finance	1
		Interest payable on higher coupon for current debt finance	1
		Return on additional investment	1
		Gearing calculations	1
		EPS calculations	1
			11
	(iv)	Impact on Conejo Co	3–4
		Credit migration, credit rating agencies and CEO's opinion	3–4
		Impact on Conejo Co's equity holders	2–3
		Impact on Conejo Co's debt holders: current and new	2–3
		Maximum	**12**
		Professional skills marks (see below)	**10**
Total			**50**

Professional skills

Communication

General report format and structure (use of headings/sub-headings and an introduction)

Style, language and clarity (appropriate layout and tone of report response, presentation of calculations, appropriate use of the tools)

Effectiveness of communication (answer is relevant, specific rather than general and focused to the requirement)

Analysis and Evaluation

Appropriate use of the data to determine suitable calculations

Appropriate use of the data to support discussion and draw appropriate conclusions

Demonstration of reasoned judgement when considering key matters for this specific company

Demonstration of ability to consider relevant factors applicable to increasing the level of debt finance

Scepticism

Effective challenge of information and assumptions supplied and, techniques carried out to support any decision

Commercial acumen

Effective use of examples and/or calculations from the scenario information and other practical considerations related to the context to illustrate points being made

Recognition of external constraints and opportunities as necessary

Maximum 10 marks

18 CHAKULA CO (MAR/JUN 21)

(a)   The key reason for a regulatory framework to exist in merger and acquisition (M&A) activity is to ensure that the interests of stakeholders are protected, and where the natural market forces may not be sufficient on their own to ensure that this happens. The regulatory framework aims to ensure a well-functioning market for corporate control.

With respect to shareholders, as a major stakeholder group, the regulatory framework aims to establish that shareholders of the target company are not affected negatively by ensuring that:

–   minority shareholders' rights are protected;

–   the target company's management cannot block a M&A where it is in commercial and economic interest of shareholders; and,

–   sufficient time is made available for a proposal to be properly scrutinised. The regulatory framework also aims to ensure that sufficient information is provided about the proposed M&A for all investor groups to evaluate the proposed deal properly.

With respect to other stakeholders, the aim of the regulatory framework is to ensure that there is not a substantial lessening of competition after the M&A has taken place. This will protect the choice that consumers, suppliers and employees have in engaging with a range of organisations in that business sector, and within a properly functioning economic market.

(b) The two theoretical propositions are based on the opinion that a company's capital structure does matter to the value of the company. The first proposition posits that since debt is cheaper than equity and there is a 'tax shield' attached to debt finance, it is better for a company to be financed by as much debt as possible. This is the view presented by the Modigliani and Miller with taxes model. Since interest is paid before a company pays corporation tax, but dividends are not, a company does not have to pay taxes on profits used to pay interest. This is referred to as a tax shield. The presence of a tax shield results in the cost of capital reducing as the proportion of debt financing increases.

The second proposition builds on this by arguing that although debt carries with it the advantage of a tax shield, at high levels of gearing this position no longer holds true. Here financial risk increases significantly and the company experiences increasing levels of financial distress, resulting in the cost of equity increasing significantly. This overrides the benefits gained from the tax shield. As a result, the cost of capital increases. At very high levels of gearing, even the cost of debt starts to increase significantly. Hence, there is a trade-off between the benefits of the tax shield and the costs related to financial distress, such that the cost of capital reduces initially but then rises, meaning that there is an optimal, minimum cost of capital where corporate value is maximised.

(c) **REPORT TO THE BOARD OF DIRECTORS (BoD), LAHLA CO**

This report evaluates and discusses the financial and other factors that both Lahla Co's and Kawa Co's shareholders would consider prior to agreeing to the acquisition. It also evaluates and discusses the impact of the acquisition on Lahla Co's capital structure under the two payment methods.

Factors to consider

Demerger (Appendix 2)	Additional value created for Kawa Co's shareholders 18.3%	
Acquisition, cash payment (Appendix 3)	Additional value created for Kawa Co's shareholders 10.0%	Additional value created for Lahla Co's shareholders 22.0%
Acquisition, share-for-share exchange (Appendix 3)	Additional value created for Kawa Co's shareholders 26.7%	Additional value created for Lahla Co's shareholders 14.0%

The initial evaluation would indicate that the demerger is the better option for Kawa Co's shareholders, compared to the acquisition, if the acquisition is paid for by cash. However, the share-for-share exchange gives a higher return compared to the demerger and therefore on purely financial grounds this is the best option for Kawa Co's shareholders. Although Lahla Co's shareholders lose some additional value derived from the acquisition if the share-for-share option is chosen, they would probably still be in favour of the acquisition because the company's value will increase and so will the value of their shares.

However, the following additional factors also need to be considered in the evaluation:

The value estimates are based on predicted variables, both for the demerger valuation and for the acquisition valuations. It is likely that there will be changes to the actual variables, and it is recommended that Lahla Co undertake sensitivity analysis and assess the results of this before making the final acquisition decision.

Kawa Co's shareholders probably have three main areas they would want considered further with respect to the acquisition with the share-for-share exchange.

Firstly, they would become part of a larger company with interests both in hotels and in coffee shops and they would own just under 36% (667m share/ 1,867m shares) of the share capital of the new combined company. However, they would be minority shareholders. As such, they may feel that they do not have sufficient influence in the major decisions the company makes.

Therefore, Kawa Co's shareholders may be of the opinion that operating as a stand-alone demerged independent company may give them a better opportunity to shape the company's strategy. On the other hand, they may equally decide that they would need to be part of a large company to be able to compete effectively against Buni Co.

Secondly, Kawa Co's shareholders cannot be certain whether the 26.7% additional value is realistic or not. This may be especially pertinent because Lahla Co is an unlisted company and therefore may keep proprietary/strategic information private, limiting the ability for external parties to undertake a full and effective evaluation.

Thirdly, because Lahla Co is an unlisted company, Kawa Co's shareholders may be concerned about how they would be able to exit the company, if they want to. For instance, if their investment portfolios become imbalanced when the companies are combined, they may need to sell some shares to rebalance it. Lahla Co should consider the possibility of undertaking a partial listing in order to make the deal more palatable for Kawa Co's shareholders.

In addition to ensuring that the acquisition is financially beneficial for them, Lahla Co's shareholders' main concern would be that Kawa Co's shareholders will own a significant portion of the combined company (just under 36%). This could mean that the new shareholders would have a significant influence on the way the company is run and its strategic direction, which may be different to what Lahla Co's current shareholders want.

Capital structure changes

Capital Structure	Equity %	Debt %
Original: Lahla Co	60.0%	40.0%
Cash payment: Combined company (Appendix 3)	46.9%	53.1%
Share-for-share exchange: Combined company (Appendix 3)	68.0%	32.0%

The cash payment option means that the proportion of market value of debt increases significantly and is higher than the market value of equity. This would probably increase the costs related to financial distress and future borrowing costs would increase as a result.

On the other hand, the share-for-share exchange, increases the proportion of equity compared to debt financing. This may reduce financial distress costs, but also reduce Lahla Co's ability to benefit from the tax shields.

On the face of it, it would appear that Lahla Co would find it difficult to raise the funds needed through just debt financing, although the BoD could explore this option further. Equity finance through a partial listing may be a necessary option which Lahla Co will need to explore as well, although this may require Lahla Co to disclose private information to the markets.

Tutorial note: additional consideration which could be made:

If the cash payment to Kawa Co's shareholders is increased to $0.71/share, to bring it in line with the value obtained from the demerger, and the funding is sought from debt financing, then the debt percentage compared to total firm value will increase to 53.8% (as shown below):

$0.71 × 2,000m shares = $1,420m.

Market value of equity: $2,933.7m, 46.2%

Market value of debt = ($1,601.7m + $1,420m + $400m) = $3,421.7m, 53.8%

Conclusion

The share-for-share exchange gives the highest return for Kawa Co's shareholders and also makes a good return for Lahla Co's shareholders. The impact on capital structure from this method is a higher percentage of equity and therefore scope to raise more finance through debt if required.

However, concerns that Lahla Co is unlisted and complications arising from this, might make the cash payment method the preferred one for Kawa Co shareholders. The current cash offer is less than the value generated from the demerger and therefore unlikely to be accepted. Therefore, a cash offer to match the benefit from the demerger would need to be made. The initial cash offer and a higher revised cash offer would have a significant impact on Lahla Co's capital structure in terms of increased debt. Therefore, it is recommended that Lahla Co should consider equity finance through a partial listing. This would also enable Kawa Co's shareholders to trade their shares and thereby make the deal look better for them.

Report compiled by:

Date

Note: credit will be given for alternative and valid discursive comments.

APPENDICES:

Appendix 1: Estimate of Kawa Co cost of capital (Part (c)(i))

Kawa Co, cost of equity = 13.51%

Kawa Co, post tax cost of debt = 3.52%

Kawa Co, cost of capital =

(13.51% × $1,200m + 3.52% × $400m)/($1,200m + $400m) = 11.01%, say 11%

Appendix 2: Estimate of Kawa Co equity value if demerger is undertaken (Part (c)(i))

Current sales revenue attributable to Kawa Co = 20% × $4,500m = $900m

Per year, sales revenue growth rate = 6%

Profit before interest and tax (PBIT) = 21%

Tax rate = 20%

Additional asset investment = $0.25/$1

Cost of capital (appendix 1) = 11%

Per year, free cash flow growth rate after first four years = 2.5%

Cash flows, years 1 to 4 ($m)

Year	1	2	3	4
Sales revenue	954.0	1,011.2	1,071.9	1,136.2
PBIT	200.3	212.4	225.1	238.6
Tax	40.1	42.5	45.0	47.7
Additional asset investment	13.5	14.3	15.2	16.1
Free cashflows	146.7	155.6	164.9	174.8
Present value of free cashflows (11%)	132.2	126.3	120.6	115.1

Corporate value, years 1 to 4: $494.2m

Corporate value, year 5 onwards:

($174.8m × 1.025/(0.11 − 0.025)) × 1.11^-4 = $1,388.5m

Total corporate value: $1,882.7m

Value attributable to equity: 75% × $1,882.8m = $1,412.0m

Per share value = $1,412.0m/2,000 million shares = $0.71 per share

Kawa Co original value = $1,200m/2,000 million shares = $0.60 per share

Gain = ($0.71 − $0.60)/$0.60 = 18.3%, if Kawa Co gets demerged

Appendix 3: Sale of Kawa Co to Lahla Co (Part (c)(ii)

Lahla Co PE ratio = 90% × 15.61 = 14.05

Lahla Co equity value = 14.05 × $171.0m = $2,402.6m

Kawa Co equity value = $1,200m

Kawa Co estimate of PE ratio = $1,200m/$117.1m = 10.25

Profits after tax of combined company = $171.0m + $117.1m + $62m = $350.1m

Average PE ratio of combined company = (14.05+10.25)/2 = 12.15

Estimate of equity value of combined company = $350.1m × 12.15 = $4,253.7m

Additional equity value created from combining the two companies =

$4,253.7m − ($1,200m + $2,402.6m) = $651.1m

Cash offer

Chakula Co's shareholders will receive $0.66 per share from sale of Kawa Co, or

$0.66 × 2,000 million shares = $1,320m in total

Kawa Co original value per share = $0.60

Gain = $0.06/$0.60 = 10%

Lahla Co's total shareholders' value is estimated at = $4,253.7m − $1,320m = $2,933.7m, or $2,933.7m/1,200 million shares = $2.44 share

Lahla Co estimate of original value = $2,402.6m/1,200 million = $2 per share

Gain = $0.44/$2 = 22%

Share-for-share Offer

Additional shares issued by Lahla Co= 2,000 million/3 = 667 million

Equity value of combined company = $4,253.7m

Per share value = $4,253.7m/1,867 million shares = $2.28

Gain to Kawa Co's shareholders

$2.28 – ($0.60 × 3) = $0.48

$0.48/$1.80 = 26.7%

Gain to Lahla Co's shareholders from combining the company

($2.28 - $2)/$2 = 14.0%

Lahla Co: Impact on capital structure from the two payment methods

Lahla Co, before acquisition

Market value of equity: $2,402.6m (see above)

Market value of debt = 40/60 × $2,402.6m = $1,601.7m

Combined company, cash payment through debt borrowing

Market value of equity: $2,933.7m or 46.9%

Market value of debt = $1,601.7m + $1,320m + $400m* = $3,321.7m or 53.1%

(Note: $2,933.7m + $3,321.7m = $6,255.4m; 46.9% = ($2,933.7m/$6,255.4m) × 100% and 53.1% = ($3,321.7m/$6,255.4m) × 100%)

Combined company, share-for-share exchange

Market value of equity: $4,253.7m or 68.0%

Market value of debt: $1,601.7m + $400m* = $2,001.7m or 32.0%

(Note: $4,253.7m + $2,001.7m = $6,255.4m; 68.0% = ($4,253.7m/$6,255.4m) × 100% and 32.0% = ($2,001.7m/$6,255.4m) × 100%)

* In the above cases when the two companies are combined, it is assumed that Lahla Co will continue to service loan notes B or cancel them by paying them off through an equivalent borrowing.

			Marks
		Marking scheme	
(a)		Shareholders	2-3
		Other stakeholders	2-3
		Other comments	1-2
			5
(b)		3 marks for discussing each of the two propositions	**6**
(c)	(i)	**[Appendices 1 and 2]**	
		Kawa demerged	
		Kawa, Cost of capital	1
		Sales revenue years 1-4	1
		PBIT years 1-4	1
		Taxation years 1-4	1
		Additional asset investment years 1-4	1
		Corporate value	2
		Value per share	1
			8
	(ii)	**[Appendix 3]**	
		Lahla, current equity value	1
		Kawa, estimate of PE ratio	1
		Combined company, current equity value	1
		Estimate of additional value	1
		Cash offer gains (both groups of shareholders)	2
		Share offer gains (both groups of shareholders)	3
		Financing implications	3
			12
	(iii)	**Report**	
		Evaluation of financial and other factors (evaluation report could include, for example, financial returns from demerger and each form of consideration, exit strategies, concerns about becoming minority shareholders, but also concerns for majority shareholders on the impact minority shareholders may have, assumptions made and whether the value created from the share-for-share exchange is realistic)	6-7
		Impact on the capital structure	2-3
		Maximum	**9**
		Professional skills marks (see below)	**10**
Total			**50**

Professional skills marks

Communication

General report format and structure (use of headings/sub-headings and an introduction)

Style, language and clarity (appropriate layout and tone of report response, presentation of calculations, appropriate use of the tools)

Effectiveness of communication (answer is relevant, specific rather than general and focused to the requirement)

Analysis and Evaluation

Appropriate use of the data to determine suitable calculations

Appropriate use of the data to support discussion and draw appropriate conclusions

Demonstration of reasoned judgement when considering key matters for Lahla Co

Demonstration of ability to consider relevant factors applicable to each company's situation

Scepticism

Effective challenge of forecast information supplied and assumptions to support key facts and/or decisions

Commercial acumen

Effective use of examples and/or calculations from the scenario information and other practical considerations related to the context to illustrate points being made

Recognition of external constraints and opportunities as necessary

Maximum 10 marks

TREASURY AND ADVANCED RISK MANAGEMENT TECHNIQUES

19   LIRIO CO (MAR/JUN 16)

Key answer tips

This section A question was a wide ranging question that covered several diverse areas of the syllabus (dividend capacity, foreign currency hedging, discounted cash flow techniques, financing options).

In questions like this it is important to manage time carefully, to avoid running over time on one part and not leaving enough time for the other parts.

Note that there is no requirement to answer the question in the order it is set. So for example if you feel confident with foreign currency hedging, you could start with part (b)(ii) (as long as you label your answer clearly, to avoid confusing the marker).

(a)   Purchasing power parity (PPP) predicts that the exchange rates between two currencies depend on the relative differences in the rates of inflation in each country. Therefore, if one country has a higher rate of inflation compared to another, then its currency is expected to depreciate over time. However, according to PPP the 'law of one price' holds because any weakness in one currency will be compensated by the rate of inflation in the currency's country (or group of countries in the case of the euro).

Economic exposure refers to the degree by which a company's cash flows are affected by fluctuations in exchange rates. It may also affect companies which are not exposed to foreign exchange transactions, due to actions by international competitors.

If PPP holds, then companies may not be affected by exchange rate fluctuations, as lower currency value can be compensated by the ability to raise prices due to higher inflation levels. This depends on markets being efficient.

However, a permanent shift in exchange rates may occur, not because of relative inflation rate differentials, but because a country (or group of countries) lose their competitive positions. In this case the 'law of one price' will not hold, and prices readjust to a new and long-term or even permanent rate. For example, the UK £ to USA $ rate declined in the 20th century, as the USA grew stronger economically and the UK grew weaker. The rate almost reached parity in 1985 before recovering. Since the financial crisis in 2009, it has fluctuated between roughly $1.5 to £1 and $1.7 to £1.

In such cases, where a company receives substantial amounts of revenue from companies based in countries with relatively weak economies, it may find that it is facing economic exposure and its cash flows decline over a long period of time.

(b) Discussion paper to the board of directors (BoD), Lirio Co

Discussion paper compiled by

Date

Purpose of the discussion paper

The purpose of this discussion paper is:

(i) To consider the implications of the BoD's proposal to use funds from the sale of its equity investment in the European company and from its cash flows generated from normal business activity over the next two years to finance a large project, instead of raising funds through equity and/or debt;

(ii) To assess whether or not the project adds value for Lirio Co or not.

Background information

The funds needed for the project are estimated at $40,000,000 at the start of the project. $23,118,000 of this amount is estimated to be received from the sale of the equity investment (appendices 2 and 3). This leaves a balance of $16,882,000 (Appendix 3), which will be obtained from the free cash flows to equity (the dividend capacity) of $21,642,000 (Appendix 1) expected to be generated in the first year. However, this would leave only $4,760,000 available for dividend payments in the first year, meaning a cut in expected dividends from $0.27/share to $0.0595/share (Appendix 3). The same level of dividends will be paid in the second year as well.

Project assessment

Based on the dividend valuation model, Lirio Co's market capitalisation, and therefore its value, is expected to increase from approximately $360 million to approximately $403 million, or by just under 12% (Appendix 3). This would suggest that it would be beneficial for the project to be undertaken.

Possible issues

1 The dividend valuation model is based on a number of factors such as: an accurate estimation of the dividend growth rate, a non-changing cost of equity and a predictable future dividend stream growing in perpetuity. In addition to this, it is expected that the sale of the investment will yield €20,000,000 but this amount could increase or reduce in the next three months. The dividend valuation model assumes that dividends and their growth rate are the sole drivers of corporate value, which is probably not accurate.

2   Although the dividend irrelevancy theory proposed by Modigliani and Miller suggests that corporate value should not be affected by a corporation's dividend policy, in practice changes in dividends do matter for two main reasons. First, dividends are used as a signalling device to the markets and unexpected changes in dividends paid and/or dividend growth rates are not generally viewed positively by them. Changes in dividends may signal that the company is not doing well and this may affect the share price negatively.

3   Second, corporate dividend policy attracts certain groups of shareholders or clientele. In the main this is due to personal tax reasons. For example, higher rate taxpayers may prefer low dividend pay-outs and lower rate taxpayers may prefer higher dividend pay-outs. A change in dividends may result in the clientele changing and this changeover may result in excessive and possibly negative share price volatility.

4   It is not clear why the BoD would rather not raise the required finance through equity and/or debt. The BoD may have considered increasing debt to be risky. However, given that the current level of debt is $70 million compared to an estimated market capitalisation of $360 million (Appendix 3), raising another $40 million through debt finance will probably not result in a significantly higher level of financial risk. The BoD may have been concerned that going into the markets to raise extra finance may result in negative agency type issues, such as having to make proprietary information public; or being forced to give extra value to new equity owners; or sending out negative signals to the markets.

Areas for further discussion by the BoD

Each of these issues should be considered and discussed further by the BoD. With reference to point 1, the BoD needs to discuss whether the estimates and the model used are reasonable in estimating corporate value or market capitalisation. With reference to points 2 and 3, the BoD needs to discuss the implications of such a significant change in the dividend policy and how to communicate Lirio Co's intention to the market so that any negative reaction is minimised. With reference to point 4, the BoD should discuss the reasons for any reluctance to raise finance through the markets and whether any negative impact of this is perhaps less than the negative impact of points 2 and 3.

Tutorial note

When attempting a question like this in the Computer Based Exam (CBE), make your answer looks like a professional document by writing the report in the word processor but putting your numbers (appendix) in a spreadsheet.

Appendix 1: Expected dividend capacity prior to large project investment

	$000
Operating profit (15% × (1.08 × $300 million)	48,600
Less interest (5% of $70 million)	(3,500)
Less taxation (25% × ($48.6 million – 3.5 million))	(11,275)
Less investment in working capital ($0.10 × (0.08 × $300 million)	(2,400)
Less investment in additional non-current assets ($0.20 × (0.08 × $300 million)	(4,800)
Less investment in projects	(8,000)
Cash flows from domestic operations	18,625
Cash flows from Pontac Co's dividend remittances (see Appendix 1.1)	3,297
Additional tax payable on Pontac Co's profits (5% × $5.6 million)	(280)
Dividend capacity	21,642

Appendix 1.1: Dividend remittances expected from Pontac Co

	$000
Total contribution $24 × 400,000 units	9,600
Less fixed costs	(4,000)
Less taxation (20% × $5.6 million)	(1,120)
Profit after tax	4,480
Remitted to Lirio Co (80% × $4.48 million × 92%)	3,297

Appendix 2: Euro (€) investment sale receipt hedge

Lirio Co can use one of forward contracts, futures contracts or option contracts to hedge the € receipt.

Forward contract

Since it is a € receipt, the 1.1559 rate will be used.

€20,000,000 × 1.1559 = $23,118,000

Futures contracts

Go long to protect against a weakening € and use the June contracts to hedge as the receipt is expected at the end of May 20X6 or beginning of June 20X6 (in three months' time).

June contracts will be closed out one month before expiry, therefore expected futures price (based on a linear narrowing of basis) can be calculated as follows:

Spot rate = $1.1585 per €1, or alternatively €0.8632 per $1 (calculated as 1/1.1585)

Current basis = 0.8632 – 0.8656 = -0.0024

Unexpired basis on transaction date = -0.0024 × (1/4) = -0.0006

So predicted lock in rate = 0.8656 – 0.0006 = €0.8650 per $1

Tutorial note

Interpolating between the given futures prices would have also been acceptable, as follows:

Predicted futures rate = 0.8638 + (2/3 × (0.8656 – 0.8638)) = 0.8650.

Expected receipt = €20,000,000/0.8650 = $23,121,387

Number of contracts bought = $23,121,387/$125,000 = approximately 185 contracts (resulting in a very small over-hedge and therefore not material)

[Full credit will be given where the calculations are used to show the correction of the over-hedge using forwards]

Option contracts

Purchase the June call option to protect against a weakening € and because receipt is expected at the end of May 20X6 or beginning of June 20X6.

Exercise price is 0.86, therefore expected receipt is €20,000,000/0.8600 = $23,255,814
Contracts purchased = $23,255,814/$125,000 = 186.05, say 186

Amount hedged = $125,000 × 186 = $23,250,000

Premium payable = 186 × 125,000 × 0.0290 = €674,250

Premium in $ = €674,250 × 1.1618 = $783,344

Amount not hedged = €20,000,000 — (186 × 125,000 × 0.8600) = €5,000

Use forward contracts to hedge €5,000 not hedged. €5,000 × 1.1559 = $5,780

[Full credit will be given if a comment on the under-hedge being immaterial and therefore not hedged is made, instead of calculating the correction of the under-hedge]

Total receipts = $23,250,000 + $5,780 — $783,344 = $22,472,436

Advice and recommendation

Hedging using options will give the lowest receipt at $22,472,436 from the sale of the investment, while hedging using futures will give the highest receipt at $23,127,387, with the forward contracts giving a receipt of $23,118,000.

The lower receipt from the option contracts is due to the premium payable, which allows the option buyer to let the option lapse should the € strengthen. In this case, the option would be allowed to lapse and Lirio Co would convert the € into $ at the prevailing spot rate in three months' time. However, the € would need to strengthen significantly before the cost of the option is covered. Given market expectation of the weakness in the € continuing, this is not likely to be the case.

Although futures and forward contracts are legally binding and do not have the flexibility of option contracts, they both give higher receipts. Hedging using futures gives the higher receipt, but futures require margin payments to be made upfront and contracts are marked-to-market daily. In addition to this, the basis may not narrow in a linear fashion and therefore the amount received is not guaranteed. All these factors create uncertainty in terms of the exact amounts of receipts and payments resulting on a daily basis and the final receipt.

On the other hand, when using forward contracts to hedge the receipt exposure, Lirio Co knows the exact amount it will receive. It is therefore recommended that Lirio Co use the forward markets to hedge the expected receipt.

[**Note:** It could be argued that in spite of the issues when hedging with futures, the higher receipt obtained from using futures markets to hedge mean that they should be used. This is acceptable as well.]

Appendix 3: Estimate of Lirio Co's value based on the dividend valuation model

If the large project is not undertaken and dividend growth rate is maintained at the historic level:

Dividend history

Year to end of February	20X3	20X4	20X5	20X6
Number of $1 equity shares in issue (000)	60,000	60,000	80,000	80,000
Total dividends paid ($000)	12,832	13,602	19,224	20,377
Dividend per share	$0.214	$0.227	$0.240	$0.255

Average dividend growth rate = $(0.255/0.214)^{1/3} - 1 = 1.0602$ (or say 6%) Expected dividend in February 20X7 = $0.255 \times 1.06 = \$0.270$

Lirio Co, estimate of value if large project is not undertaken =

$0.270/(0.12 - 0.06) = \$4.50$ per share or $360 million market capitalisation

If the large project is undertaken

Funds required for project	$40,000,000
Funds from sale of investment (Appendix 2)	$23,118,000
Funds required from dividend capacity cash flows	$16,882,000
Dividend capacity funds before transfer to project (Appendix 1)	$21,642,000
Dividend capacity funds left after transfer	$4,760,000
Annual dividend per share after transfer	$0.0595
Annual dividend paid (end of February 20X7 and February 20X8)	$0.0595
Dividend paid (end of February 20X9)	$0.3100
New growth rate	7%

Lirio Co, estimate of value if large project is undertaken =

$0.0595 \times 1.12^{-1} + \$0.0595 \times 1.12^{-2} + \$0.3100 \times 1.12^{-3}$

+ $[\$0.3100 \times 1.07/(0.12 - 0.07)] \times 1.12^{-3} = \$5.04$ per share or $403 million market capitalisation

---

Tutorial note

A discussion paper can take many formats. The answer provides one possible format. Credit will be given for alternative and sensible formats; and for relevant approaches to the calculations and commentary.)

					Marks
(a)		1-2 marks per well-explained point			
				Maximum	**4**
(b)	(i)	**Appendices 1 and 1.1**			
		Operating profit			1
		Interest paid			1
		Tax paid for normal activities			1
		Investment in working capital			1
		Investment in additional non-current assets			1
		Correct treatment of depreciation			1
		Cash flows remitted from Pontac Co			2
		Additional tax payable			1
				Maximum	**9**
	(ii)	**Appendix 2**			
		Amount received based on forward contracts			1
		Correctly identifying long contracts and purchasing call options			1
		Expected futures price based on linear narrowing of basis			1
		Amount received based on futures contracts			1
		Recognition of small over-hedge when using futures contracts			1
		Option contracts or futures contracts purchased			1
		Premium paid in dollars			1
		Amount received based on options contracts			2
		1 mark for each well-discussed point			2
		Reasonable recommendation			1
				Maximum	**12**
	(iii)	**Appendix 3 and project assessment**			
		Estimate of dividend growth rate (prior to project undertaken)			2
		Estimate of corporate value (prior to project undertaken)			1
		Annual dividend per share after transfer of funds to project			2
		Estimate of value after project is undertaken			2
		Concluding comments on project assessment			1
				Maximum	**8**
	(iv)	**Discussion of issues**			
		Limitations of method used			1–2
		Signalling impact of change in dividend policy			1–2
		Clientele impact of change in dividend policy			1–2
		Rationale for not considering debt or equity			2–3
		Other relevant discussion points			2–3
				Maximum	**7**
		Professional skills marks (see below)			**10**
Total					**50**

Professional skills

Communication

General report format and structure (use of headings/sub-headings and an introduction)

Style, language and clarity (appropriate layout and tone of report response, presentation of calculations, appropriate use of the tools)

Effectiveness of communication (answer is relevant, specific rather than general and focused to the requirement)

Analysis and Evaluation

Appropriate use of the data to determine suitable calculations

Appropriate use of the data to support discussion and draw appropriate conclusions

Demonstration of reasoned judgement when considering key matters for this specific company

Demonstration of ability to consider relevant factors applicable to this specific scenario

Scepticism

Effective challenge of information and assumptions supplied and, techniques carried out to support any decision

Commercial acumen

Effective use of examples and/or calculations from the scenario information and other practical considerations related to the context to illustrate points being made

Recognition of external constraints and opportunities as necessary

Maximum 10 marks

20 WASHI CO (SEP 18)

Key answer tips

The AFM syllabus and study guide promises that "every exam will have question(s) which have a focus on syllabus sections B and E" (investment appraisal and hedging). In this September 2018 exam, the section A question covered both of these syllabus areas in the same question.

Being happy with these two syllabus areas is critical to guarantee success in AFM.

(a) Washi Co may want to invest in overseas projects for a number of reasons which result in competitive advantage for it, for example:

Investing overseas may give Washi Co access to new markets and/or enable it to develop a market for its products in locations where none existed before. Being involved in marketing and selling products in overseas markets may also help it gain an understanding of the needs of customers, which it may not have had if it merely exported its products.

Investing overseas may give Washi Co easier and cheaper access to raw materials it needs. It would therefore make good strategic sense for it to undertake the overseas investment.

Investing in projects internationally may give Washi Co access to cheaper labour resources and/or access to expertise which may not be readily available in Japan. This could therefore lead to reduction in costs and give Washi Co an edge against its competitors.

Closer proximity to markets, raw materials and labour resources may enable Washi Co to reduce its costs. For example, transportation and other costs related to logistics may be reduced if products are manufactured close to the markets where they are sold.

Risk, such as economic risk resulting from long-term currency fluctuations, may be reduced where costs and revenues are matched and therefore naturally hedged.

Washi Co may increase its reputation because it is based in the country within which it trades leading to a competitive edge against its rivals.

International investments might reduce both the unsystematic and systematic risks for Washi Co if its shareholders only hold well diversified portfolios in domestic markets, but not internationally.

(b) **Report to the board of directors (BoD), Washi Co**

Introduction

This report evaluates whether or not Washi Co should invest in the Airone project and the amount of debt finance required of JPY 3,408.6 million (appendix 1) to fund the project. The evaluation considers both the financial and the non-financial factors.

Evaluation of the preferred hedge choice and debt finance required

The income from the sale of the European subsidiary is maximised when futures contracts are used. Therefore, these are chosen as Washi Co will borrow the least amount of debt finance as a result. However, compared to the forward contract, futures are marked-to-market daily and require a margin to be placed with the broker. This could affect Washi Co's liquidity position. The assumption has been made that basis reduces proportionally as the futures contracts approach expiry, but there is no guarantee that this will be the case. Therefore, basis risk still exists with futures contracts. Although forward contracts give a smaller return, there is no basis risk and margin requirements. However, they do contain a higher risk of default as they are not market traded. Options give the lowest return but would give Washi Co the flexibility of not exercising the option should the Euro strengthen against the Yen.

Although the EUR 80 million receipt from the sale of the subsidiary has been agreed, there may be a risk that the sale may fall through and/or the funds or some proportion of the funds are not received. Washi Co may need to assess and factor in this risk, however small it may be.

The amount of interest on deposit is based on the current short-dated Japanese treasury bills and the estimate of the borrowing requirement is computed from the predicted exchange rate between ARD and JPY in a year's time, based on the purchasing power parity. Both these estimates could be inaccurate if changes occur over the coming months. Although insufficient information is provided for a financial assessment, Washi Co should explore the possibility of converting the EUR into ARD immediately on receipt and keeping it in an ARD bank account until needed, instead of first converting EUR into JPY and then into ARD.

Using debt finance to make up any shortfall in the funding requirement may be appropriate for Washi Co given that it is an unlisted company and therefore access to other sources of funding may be limited. Nevertheless, Washi Co should assess how the extra borrowing would affect any restrictive covenants placed on it and the impact on its cost of capital. Since the amount seems to be small in the context of the project as a whole, this may not be a major problem.

Washi Co should also explore whether or not investing in the Airone project restricts its ability to fund other projects or affects its ability to continue normal business activity, especially if Washi Co is facing the possibility of hard capital rationing.

Evaluation of the Airone project

The net present value of the Airone project is estimated to be JPY (457) million (appendix 2). Given the negative net present value, the initial recommendation would be to reject the project. However, given that the result is marginal, Washi Co should consider the following factors before rejecting the project.

At present, Washi Co does not have a significant presence in the part of the world where Airone is located. Taking on the project may make good strategic sense and provide a platform for Washi Co to establish its presence in that part of the world.

Furthermore, once Washi Co has established itself in Airone, it may be able to develop further opportunities and new projects. The value of these follow-on options has not been incorporated into the financial assessment. Washi Co should explore the possibility of such opportunities and their possible value.

The financial assessment ends abruptly at the end of the four years. No indication is given on what would happen to the project thereafter. It may be sold as a going concern or, if closed, its land and assets may be sold. The cash flows from these possible courses of action need to be incorporated into the assessment, and these could make the project worthwhile.

A number of assumptions and estimates would have been made in the financial assessment. For example, the rate of inflation used for future figures is the current rate and the tax rate used is the current rate, these may well change in the coming years. Therefore, it is best to undertake sensitivity analysis and produce a number of financial assessments before making any firm commitment to proceed with the project or deciding to reject it.

Conclusion and recommendation

The income from the sale of the European subsidiary is maximised when futures contracts are used, but Washi Co should weigh this against the benefits and drawbacks of all hedging instruments before making a final decision.

Although the project is currently giving a negative net present value, rejecting it at the outset is premature. A number of factors, discussed above, need to be considered and assessed before a final decision is made. Sensitivity analysis would be very helpful in this respect.

Finally, Washi Co should consider alternative uses for the funding which will be dedicated to the project. These alternative uses for the finance need to be considered before any decision is made, especially if Washi Co is facing the possibility of hard capital rationing.

Report compiled by: XXX

Date XX/XX/XX

APPENDICES:

Appendix 1 (Part (c) (i)): Japanese Yen receivable from sale of European subsidiary under each hedging choice and the additional debt finance needed to fund the Airone project

Forward rate

Since it is a EUR receipt, the lock-in rate of JPY125.3 per EUR will be used. Expected receipt from sale: EUR 80m × 125.3 = JPY 10,024m

Futures contracts

The futures contracts need to show a gain when the Euro depreciates against the Yen, therefore a short position is needed, using the seven-month contracts. It is assumed that basis will depreciate proportionally to the time expired.

Predicted futures rate

Current basis = 129.2 – 125.2 = 4

Unexpired basis on transaction date = 4 × (1/7) = 0.6

So predicted lock in rate = 125.2 + 0.6 = 125.8

Tutorial note

Interpolating between the given futures prices would have also been acceptable, as follows:

Predicted futures rate = 125.2 + 1/3 × (126.9 – 125.2) = 125.8.

Number of contacts sold = EUR 80,000,000/EUR 125,000 = 640 contracts Expected receipt from sale: EUR 125,000 × 640 × 125.8 = JPY 10,064m

Options contracts

640 seven-month put options contracts will be purchased to protect against a depreciation of Euro.

If options are exercised:

EUR 125,000 × 640 × 126 = JPY 10,080m

Premium payable = JPY 3.8 × 125,000 × 640 = JPY 304m

Net income = JPY 10,080m – JPY 304m = JPY 9,776m

Conclusion

Futures contracts give the highest receipt and will, therefore, be used to hedge the expected Euro receipt.

Receipt invested

Invested for further six months till needed for the Airone project. JPY 10,064m × (1 + (0.012/2)) = JPY 10,124.4m

Spot cross rates: 0.70 – 0.74 ARD per JPY 1

calculated as: 92.7/132.4 = 0.70 and 95.6/129.2 = 0.74

Tutorial note

To explain how the cross rates are calculated, consider the following examples:

Assume I have 1 JPY and want to use it to buy ARD. This is a two step process:

1) First use 1 JPY to buy € - rate is 132.4, so 1JPY = 1/132.4€

2) Now use these € to buy ARD - rate is 92.7 so 1/132.4€ becomes (92.7/132.4) ARD

My 1 JPY has therefore bought 0.70 ARD (92.7/132.4).

Now assume I have 1 ARD and want to use it to buy JPY.

1) First use 1 ARD to buy € - rate is 95.6, so 1ARD = 1/95.6€

2) Now use these € to buy JPY - rate is 129.2 so 1/95.6€ becomes (129.2/95.6) JPY

My 1 ARD has therefore bought 1.3515 JPY (129.2/95.6).

(N.B. This is equivalent to 0.74 ARD to 1 JPY for consistency (1/1.3515).

Expected ARD/JPY conversion spot rate in 12 months = 0.70 × 1.09/1.015 = 0.75

Additional debt finance needed to fund Airone project

Investment amount required = ARD 10,150m/0.75 = JPY 13,533m

Debt finance required = JPY 13,533m – JPY 10,124.4m = JPY 3,408.6m

Tutorial note

When attempting a question like this in the Computer Based Exam (CBE), make your answer look like a professional document by writing the report in the word processor but putting your numbers (appendix) in a spreadsheet.

When preparing your calculations, use the spreadsheet functions SUM and NPV to save time. Be careful when using the NPV function to enter =NPV, then a bracket containing the discount rate, a comma, and then the cells containing the cash flows from year 1 onwards. The initial investment then needs to be subtracted separately.

Appendix 2 (Part (c) (ii): Airone project net present value

Project year	0	1	2	3	4
Cash flows in ARD (millions)	(10,150)	2,530	5,760	6,780	1,655
Future exchange rate ARD/JPY (W1)	0.75	0.81	0.87	0.93	1.00

In JPY million

Project year	0	1	2	3	4
Cash flows	(13,533)	3,123	6,621	7,290	1,655
Lost contribution		(110)	(112)	(113)	(115)
Tax saving on lost contribution (30%)		33	34	34	35
Contribution: components (W2)		300	609	644	79
Tax on components cont. (30%)		(90)	(183)	(193)	(24)
Additional tax payable (15%) (W3)		(333)	(966)	(1,097)	(45)
Net cash flows	(13,533)	2,923	6,003	6,565	1,585
Present value (discounted at 12%)	(13,533)	2,610	4,784	4,674	1,008

Expected net present value is JPY (457)m

Workings:

(W1) Predicted future exchange rate (ARD/JPY)

Project year	0	1	2	3	4
	0.70 ×	0.75 ×	0.81 ×	0.87 ×	0.93 ×
	1.09/1.015	1.09/1.015	1.09/1.015	1.09/1.015	1.09/1.015
Exchange rate ARD/JPY	0.75	0.81	0.87	0.93	1.00

(W2) Components contribution

Project year	1	2	3	4
In JPY millions				
Components revenue (post inflation)	1,200	2,436	2,576	314
Contribution (25%)	300	609	644	79

(W3) Additional tax payable

Project year	1	2	3	4
Pre-tax profits (ARD m)	1,800	5,600	6,800	300
Additional tax payable at 15% (JPY m)	1,800/0.81 × 0.15 = 333	5,600/0.87 × 0.15 = 966	6,800/0.93 × 0.15 = 1,097	300/1.0 × 0.15 = 45

(c) It is difficult to conclude definitively whether a centralised treasury department is beneficial or not in all circumstances and for all companies. It depends on each company itself and the circumstances it faces. Washi Co should take this into account before making a final decision.

Benefits of a centralised treasury department

Having a centralised treasury management function avoids the need to have many bank accounts and may therefore reduce transactions costs and high bank charges.

Large cash deposits may give Washi Co access to a larger, diverse range of investment opportunities and it may be able to earn interest on a short-term basis, to which smaller cash deposits do not have access. On the other hand, if bulk borrowings are required, it may be possible for Washi Co to negotiate lower interest rates, which it would not be able to do on smaller borrowings.

A centralised treasury function can offer the opportunity for Washi Co to match income and expenditure and reduce the need for excessive risk management, and thereby reduce costs related to this.

A centralised treasury management department could hire experts, which smaller, diverse treasury management departments may not have access to.

A centralised treasury function may be better able to access what is beneficial for Washi Co as a whole, whereas local treasury functions may lead to dysfunctional behaviour.

Benefits of separate (decentralised) treasury departments

It could be argued that decentralised treasury departments are better able to match and judge the funding required with the need for asset purchases for investment purposes on a local level. Therefore, they may be able to respond quicker when opportunities arise and so could be more effective and efficient.

Individual departments within a subsidiary may have better relationships with the treasury departments of that subsidiary and are therefore able to present their case without lengthy bureaucratic delays.

Ultimately, the benefits may be implicit rather than explicit. Having decentralised treasury departments may make the subsidiary companies' senior management and directors more empowered and have greater autonomy. This in turn may increase their levels of motivation, as they are more in control of their own future, resulting in better decisions being made.

					Marks
Marking guide					
(a)		1–2 marks per valid point			
				Maximum	**5**
(b)	(i)	Amount to be received based on forward rate			1
		Decision to go short on futures			1
		Estimate of futures rate in six months based on basis			1
		Amount to be received based on futures market			1
		Decision to purchase put options			1
		Premium payable			1
		Amount to be received based on options market			1
		Decision: select appropriate hedge instrument			1
		JPY receivable following further six months of investment			1
		Estimate of current cross rate(s)			1
		Estimate of ARD/JPY rate in one year's time			1
		Debt borrowing required			1
				Maximum	**12**
	(ii)	Estimate of future ARD/JPY rates			1
		Lost contribution			1
		Tax saving on lost contribution			1
		Contribution from sales of components			2
		Tax on contribution from components sales			1
		Additional tax payable in Japan			2
		Present values and net present value			1
				Maximum	**9**
	(iii)	Evaluation of hedge choice and debt finance required			3–4
		Evaluation of Airone project			3–4
		Conclusion			1–2
				Maximum	**8**
(c)		Benefits of a centralised treasury department			2–3
		Benefits of decentralised treasury departments			2–3
		Over-arching commentary (Note: Max 6 marks if none)			1
				Maximum	**6**
		Professional skills marks (see below)			**10**
Total					**50**

Professional skills

Communication

General report format and structure (use of headings/sub-headings and an introduction)

Style, language and clarity (appropriate layout and tone of report response, presentation of calculations, appropriate use of the tools)

Effectiveness of communication (answer is relevant, specific rather than general and focused to the requirement)

Analysis and Evaluation

Appropriate use of the data to determine suitable calculations

Appropriate use of the data to support discussion and draw appropriate conclusions

Demonstration of reasoned judgement when considering key matters for this specific company

Demonstration of ability to consider relevant factors applicable to this specific scenario

Scepticism

Effective challenge of information and assumptions supplied and, techniques carried out to support any decision

Commercial acumen

Effective use of examples and/or calculations from the scenario information and other practical considerations related to the context to illustrate points being made

Recognition of external constraints and opportunities as necessary

Maximum 10 marks

21   OKAN CO (SEP/DEC 19)

Key answer tips

Risk management is a key part of the AFM syllabus, so we normally expect to find detailed calculations on hedging methods such as forwards, futures, options etc on each exam. However, there is more to risk management than these calculations, as shown in this question.

Here, there are 4 marks for calculations and then 4 marks (part (c)) for discussion of risk management issues.

When you are preparing for the exam, make sure you revise both the calculations and the discussion elements in this key part of the syllabus.

(a)   Adjusted present values (APVs) separate out a project's cash flows and allocate a specific discount rate to each type of cash flow, dependent on the risk attributable to that particular type of cash flow. Net present value (NPV) discounts all cash flows by the average discount rate attributable to the average risk of a project.

One reason why APV may be preferable to NPV is because by separating out different types of cash flows, the company's managers will be able to see which part of the project generates what proportion of the project's value. Furthermore, allocating a specific discount rate to a cash flow part helps determine the value added or destroyed. In this example, Okan Co is able to determine how much value is being created by the investment and how much by the debt financing. For complex projects, investment related cash flows could be further distinguished by their constituent risk factors, where applicable.

(b)   **Report to the board of directors (BoD), Okan Co**

Introduction

This report evaluates, and provides a justification and decision, on whether Okan Co should pursue Project Alpha or Project Beta, based on the important factors identified by the company, namely the returns generated by the projects, the projects' risks and non-financial aspects.

Evaluation

Financing

Using forward markets to hedge the expected receipt in six months' time results in the higher receipt equalling Y$25,462,000 approximately. If the money markets hedge is used the receipt is Y$25,234,936 (appendix 1).

Using forward markets to hedge the expected receipt would therefore minimise the amount of debt borrowing. However, the amount receivable from the money markets hedge is based on the annual bank investment rate available to Okan Co of 2.4%. Okan Co may be able to use the funds borrowed to generate a higher return than the bank investment and therefore using money markets to undertake the hedge may be financially advisable. Okan Co should investigate any opportunities for higher income, but based on the current results, the forward market hedge is recommended to minimise the amount of debt finance needed.

Minimum amount of debt borrowing required is Y$24,538,000 approximately.

Project returns and risk

	Project Alpha	**Project Beta**
Base case net present value (NPV) (in six months' time)	Y$5,272,000 (appendix 2a)	Y$5,100,000 (appendix 2a)
Adjusted present value (APV)	Y$6,897,218 (appendix 2b)	Y$6,725,218 (appendix 2b)
Project duration	3.04 years (appendix 2c)	2.43 years (given)

Project Alpha's and Project Beta's base case NPVs and APVs are similar to each other, with Project Alpha expected to yield a small amount in excess to the yield expected from Project Beta. However, Project Beta's project duration is significantly lower. This is because a higher proportion of Project Beta's cash flows come earlier in the project's life, compared to Project Alpha. There is more certainty to earlier cash flows and this is reflected in the lower duration for Project Beta. Project Beta's risk is lower than Project Alpha.

In estimating the base case NPV and APV for Project Alpha, it is assumed that the cash flows are known with reasonable certainty and the inflation rates will not change during the life of the project. It is also assumed that the future exchange rate between the Y$ and the £ will change in accordance with the purchasing power parity differential. Furthermore, it is assumed that the prices and costs related to Project Alpha will increase in line with inflation during the six months before the project starts. For Project Alpha, it is assumed that the initial working capital requirement is funded by the company and not from the funds raised from the subsidised loan, similar to the assumption made for Project Beta. However, for both projects, Okan Co needs to consider, and take account of, the opportunity costs related to this.

In terms of the Project Alpha's discount rate, it is assumed that the given discount rate accurately reflects the business risk of the project.

Whilst this level of detail is not provided for Project Beta, it is assumed that similar assumptions will have been made for Project Beta as well. In the case of both projects, Okan Co should assess the accuracy or reasonableness of the assumptions, and if necessary, conduct sensitivity analysis to observe how much the projects' values change if input variables are altered.

Notwithstanding the assumptions and caveats made above, it would appear that Project Beta would be preferable to Project Alpha, given that it has a similar APV but a significantly lower risk.

Nevertheless, there may be good strategic reasons why Okan Co may select Project Alpha over Project Beta. For example, these reasons may include providing access to new markets, enabling Okan Co to erect barriers to entry against competitors or looking at follow-on opportunities as possible real options.

Justification

Due to the substantially lower risk (as measured by the project duration) and similar APV, it is recommended that Project Beta be selected by Okan Co. It is also recommended that forward markets are used to hedge the income expected in six months' time to part fund the project. This would minimise the debt borrowing needed.

However, this decision is predicated on the fact that the implications of the assumptions and the wider strategic reasons discussed above have been carefully considered by Okan Co.

Report compiled by:

Date

Note: Credit will be given for alternative and valid evaluative comments.

Tutorial note

When attempting a question like this in the Computer Based Exam (CBE), make your answer look like a professional document by writing the report in the word processor but putting your numbers (appendix) in a spreadsheet.

When preparing your calculations, use the spreadsheet functions SUM and NPV to save time. Be careful when using the NPV function to enter =NPV, then a bracket containing the discount rate, a comma, and then the cells containing the cash flows from year 1 onwards. The initial investment then needs to be subtracted separately.

Appendices:

Appendix 1 (Part (b) (i)):

Expected receipt in six months' time, using forward markets
€10,000,000 × 2.5462 = Y$25,462,000

Expected receipt in six months' time, using money markets
€10,000,000/(1 + 0.022/2) = €9,891,197
€9,891,197 × 2.5210 = Y$24,935,708
Y$24,935,708 × (1 + 0.024/2) = Y$25,234,936

Minimum amount of debt borrowing Okan Co would require
Y$50,000,000 − Y$25,462,000 = Y$24,538,000

Appendix 2a (Part (b) (ii)): Projects Alpha and Beta, base case net present value, in six months' time

Base case net present value before considering financing side effects. All figures are in Y$000s.

Year	0	1	2	3	4
Sales revenue (w1)		17,325	34,304	62,890	33,821
Less:					
Production costs (w2)		(6,365)	(11,584)	(24,095)	(9,546)
Component costs (w3)		(3,708)	(5,670)	(11,877)	(4,578)
Cash flows before tax		7,252	17,050	26,918	19,697
Tax (w4)		1,050	(1,535)	(3,977)	(1,721)
Working capital	(1,733)	(2,547)	(4,288)	4,360	4,208
Plant purchase and sale	(50,000)				10,000
Net cash flows	(51,733)	5,755	11,227	27,301	32,184
Base case present value of cash flows (discounted at 10%)	(51,733)	5,232	9,279	20,512	21,982

Approximate, base case net present value (NPV) of Project Alpha = Y$5,272,000.

Base case net present value (NPV) of Project Beta = Y$(8,450,000 + 19,360,000 + 22,340,000 + 4,950,000) – Y$50,000,000 = Y$ 5,100,000

Workings:

Working 1 (w1): Sales revenue

Year	1	2	3	4
Pre-inflated revenues (Y$ 000s)	15,750	28,350	47,250	23,100
Inflation	$\times 1.1^1$	$\times 1.1^2$	$\times 1.1^3$	$\times 1.1^4$
Post-inflated revenues (Y$ 000s)	17,325	34,304	62,890	33,821

Working 2 (w2): Production costs

Year	1	2	3	4
Pre-inflated production costs (Y$ 000s)	6,120	10,710	21,420	8,160
Inflation	$\times 1.04^1$	$\times 1.04^2$	$\times 1.04^3$	$\times 1.04^4$
Post-inflated production costs (Y$ 000s)	6,365	11,584	24,095	9,546

Component costs are not inflated, but future exchange rates are based on purchasing power parity (PPP).

Working 3 (w3): Component cost

Year	1	2	3	4
PPP multiplier	3.03 ×	3.09 ×	3.15 ×	3.21 ×
	1.04/1.02	1.04/1.02	1.04/1.02	1.04/1.02
Forecast Y$ per £1	3.09	3.15	3.21	3.27
Component cost (£)	1,200	1,800	3,700	1,400
Component cost (Y$)	3,708	5,670	11,877	4,578

Working 4 (w4): Tax

Year	1	2	3	4
Cash flows before tax	7,252	17,050	26,918	19,697
Tax allowable depreciation	(12,500)	(9,375)	(7,031)	(11,094)
Taxable cash flows	(5,248)	7,675	19,887	8,603
Tax payable (20%)	(1,050)	1,535	3,977	1,721

Appendix 2b (Part (b) (ii)): Projects Alpha and Beta, adjusted present value (APV), in six months' time

Issue costs = 3/97 × Y$24,538,000 = Y$758,907

Annual tax shield = 2.1% × Y$24,538,000 × 20% = Y$103,060
Annual interest saved on subsidised loan = 2.9% × Y$24,538,000 × 80% = Y$569,282

Annuity factor, years 1 to 4 at 5% interest = 3.546

Present value of the tax shield and loan subsidy benefit = (Y$103,060 + Y$569,282) × 3.546 = Y$2,384,125

Project Alpha APV	Y$
Base case NPV of Project Alpha (appendix 2a)	5,272,000
Issue costs	(758,907
Present value of the tax shield and loan subsidy benefit	2,384,125
APV	6,897,218

Project Beta APV	Y$
Base case NPV of Project Beta (appendix 2a)	5,100,000
Issue costs	(758,907
Present value of the tax shield and loan subsidy benefit	2,384,125
APV	6,725,218

Appendix 2c (Part (b) (ii)): Project Alpha's duration based on its base case present values of cash flows

Project Alpha

Year	1	2	3	4
PVs × years	5,232,000 × 1 = 5,232,000	9,279,000 × 2 = 18,558,000	20,512,000 × 3 = 61,536,000	21,982,000 × 4 = 87,928,000

Total PVs × time = 173,254,000 approximately

Total PVs = 57,005,000 approximately

Project Alpha duration = 173,254,000/57,005,000 = 3.04 years

(c)   **Explanation of why the subsidiary company may be exposed to economic risk and how it may be managed**

Companies face economic exposure when their competitive position is affected due to macroeconomic factors such as changes in currency rates, political stability, or changes in the regulatory environment. Long-term economic exposure or economic shocks can cause a permanent shift in the purchasing power and other parity conditions. Normally, companies face economic exposure when they trade internationally. However, even companies which do not trade internationally nor rely on inputs sourced internationally may still face economic exposure.

In the case of Okan Co's subsidiary company, economic risk may have occurred because interest rates have been kept at a high level, causing the original parity conditions to break down. High interest rates will be attractive to international investors, as they can get higher returns and may lead to the Y$ becoming stronger relative to other currencies. This in turn would allow international competitors to produce goods more cheaply than the subsidiary company and thereby enhance their competitive position relative to the subsidiary company.

Managing economic exposure is difficult due to its long-lasting nature and because it can be difficult to identify. Financial instruments, such as derivatives, and money markets cannot normally be used to manage such risks. Okan Co's subsidiary company can try tactics such as borrowing in international or eurocurrency markets, sourcing input products from overseas suppliers and ultimately shifting production facilities overseas. None of these are easy or cheap, and can expose the company to new types of risks. Okan Co would also need to assess that any action it takes to manage economic risk fits into its overall risk management strategy.

Marking guide

				Marks
(a)	1–2 marks per well-discussed comment		Maximum	**4**
(b)	**(i)**	**(Appendix 1)**		
		Forward market hedge		1
		Money markets hedge		2
		Minimum borrowing required		1
				4
	(ii)	**(Appendix 2a)**		
		Sales revenue		2
		Production costs		1
		Component costs		3
		Tax		2
		Working capital		2
		Project Alpha base case NPV		1
		Project Beta base case NPV		1
				12
		(Appendix 2b)		
		Issue costs		1
		Annual tax shield		1
		Annual subsidy		1
		Present value of tax shield and subsidy		1
		Project Alpha adjusted present value		1
		Project Beta adjusted present value		1
				6
		(Appendix 2c)		
		Project Alpha duration		**2**
	(iii)	Discussion of the assumptions made		4–5
		Evaluation and justification		3–4
		(Maximum 7 marks if no considered justification given)	Maximum	**8**
(c)	Explanation of economic risk faced by Okan Co			2–3
	Discussion of management of economic risk			1–2
			Maximum	**4**
	Professional skills marks (see below)			**10**
Total				**50**

Professional skills

Communication

General report format and structure (use of headings/sub-headings and an introduction)

Style, language and clarity (appropriate layout and tone of report response, presentation of calculations, appropriate use of the tools)

Effectiveness of communication (answer is relevant, specific rather than general and focused to the requirement)

Analysis and Evaluation

Appropriate use of the data to determine suitable calculations

Appropriate use of the data to support discussion and draw appropriate conclusions

Demonstration of reasoned judgement when considering key matters for this specific company

Demonstration of ability to consider relevant factors applicable to this specific scenario

Scepticism

Effective challenge of information and assumptions supplied and, techniques carried out to support any decision

Demonstration of the ability to probe into the reasons for issues and problems, including the identification of missing information or additional information, which would alter the decision reached

Commercial acumen

Effective use of examples and/or calculations from the scenario information and other practical considerations related to the context to illustrate points being made

Recognition of external constraints and opportunities as necessary

Maximum 10 marks

Section 4

ANSWERS TO PRACTICE QUESTIONS – SECTION B

ROLE OF SENIOR FINANCIAL ADVISER IN THE MULTINATIONAL ORGANISATION

22   LAMRI CO (DEC 10)

Key answer tips

When asked to calculate dividend capacity, you should try to estimate the amount of cash that the company will generate, after paying any operating expenses and interest, and investing in assets. This is commonly known as the free cash flow to equity.

(a)   Dividend Capacity Prior to TE Proposal Implementation

	$000
Operating profit (30% × $80,000,000)	24,000
Less interest (8% × $35,000,000)	(2,800)
Less taxation (28% × (24,000 – 2,800))	(5,936)
Less investment in working capital (15% × (20/120 × 80,000))	(2,000)
Less investment in additional non-current assets (25% × (20/120 × 80,000))	(3,333)
Less investment in project	(4,500)
	———
Cash flows from domestic operations	5,431
Cash flows from overseas subsidiary dividend remittances (W1)	3,159
Additional tax payable on Magnolia profits (6% × 5,400)	(324)
	———
Dividend capacity	8,266
	———

Dividend Capacity After TE Proposal Implementation

Cash flows from domestic operations (as above)	5,431
Cash flows from overseas subsidiaries dividend remittances (W2)	2,718
Additional tax payable on Magnolia profits (6% × 3,120)	(187)
Dividend capacity	7,962

Estimate of actual dividend for coming year	
(7,500 × 1.08)	8,100

Note: The impact of depreciation is neutral, as this amount will be spent to retain assets at their current productive capability.

Workings:

(W1) Prior to Implementation of TE Proposal

	$000 Strymon	$000 Magnolia
Sales revenue	5,700	15,000
Cost		
Variable	(3,600)	(2,400)
Fixed	(2,100)	(1,500)
Transfer		(5,700)
Profit before tax	Nil	5,400
Tax	Nil	1,188
Profit after tax	Nil	4,212
Remitted	Nil	3,159
Retained	Nil	1,053

(W2) After Implementation of TE Proposal

	$000 Strymon	$000 Magnolia
Sales revenue	7,980	15,000
Cost		
Variable	(3,600)	(2,400)
Fixed	(2,100)	(1,500)
Transfer		(7,980)
Profit before tax	2,280	3,120
Tax (42%, 22%)	958	686
Profit after tax	1,322	2,434
Remitted (75% × 1,322 × 90%)	892	
Remitted		1,826
Retained	331	608
Total remitted	2,718	

(b) Lamri's dividend capacity before implementing TE's proposal ($8,266,000) is more than the dividend required for next year ($8,100,000). If the recommendation from TE is implemented as policy for next year then there is a possibility that Lamri will not have sufficient dividend capacity to make the required dividend payments. It requires $8,100,000 but will have $7,962,000 available. The reason is due to the additional tax that will be paid in the country in which Strymon operates, for which credit cannot be obtained. Effectively 14% additional tax and 10% withholding tax will be paid. Some of this amount is recovered because lower additional tax is paid on Magnolia's profits but not enough.

The difference between what is required and available is small and possible ways of making up the shortfall are as follows. Lamri could lower its growth rate in dividends to approximately 6.2% (7962/7500 – 1 × 100%) and have enough capacity to make the payment. However, if the reasons for the lower growth rate are not explained to the shareholders and accepted by them, the share price may fall.

An alternative could be to borrow the small amount needed possibly through increased overdraft facilities. However, Lamri may not want to increase its borrowings and may be reluctant to take this option. In addition to this, there is a possibility that because of the change of policy this shortfall may occur more often than just one off, and Lamri may not want to increase borrowing regularly.

Lamri may consider postponing the project or part of the project, if that option were available. However, this must be considered in the context of the business. From the question narrative, the suggestion is that Lamri have a number of projects in the pipeline for the future. The option to delay may not be possible or feasible.

Perhaps the most obvious way to get the extra funds required is to ask the subsidiary companies (most probably Strymon) to remit a higher proportion of their profits as dividends. In the past Strymon did not make profits and none were retained hence there may be a case for a higher level of remittance from there. However, this may have a negative impact on the possible benefits, especially manager morale.

Note: Credit will be given for alternative relevant suggestions.

Marking guide		Marks
(a)	Calculation of operating profit, interest and domestic tax	3
	Calculation of investments in working capital and non-current assets (including correct treatment of depreciation)	3
	Calculation of dividend remittance before new policy implementation	2
	Calculation of additional tax payable on Magnolia profits before new policy implementation	1
	Calculation of dividend remittance after new policy implementation	3
	Calculation of additional tax payable on Magnolia profits after new policy implementation	1
	Dividend capacity	1
		14
(b)	Concluding comments and explanation of reason	2
	Possible actions (1 mark per suggestion)	4
	Maximum	6
	Professional skills marks (see below)	5
Total		25

Professional skills marks

Analysis and Evaluation

Appropriate use of the data to determine suitable calculations

Appropriate use of the data to support discussion and draw appropriate conclusions

Appraisal of information objectively to make a recommendation

Commercial acumen

Effective use of examples and/or practical considerations related to the context to illustrate points being made

Maximum 5 marks

23 LIMNI CO (JUN 13)

Key answer tips

This was a very wide-ranging question, covering risk management, dividend policy and financing. Use these three subheadings in your answer to make sure that you are addressing all the necessary issues.

(a) As a high growth company, Limni Co probably requires the cash flows it generates annually for investing in new projects and has therefore not paid any dividends. This is a common practice amongst high-growth companies, many of which declare that they have no intention of paying any dividends. The shareholder clientele in such companies expects to be rewarded by growth in equity value as a result of the investment policy of the company.

Capital structure theory would suggest that because of the benefit of the tax shield on interest payments, companies should have a mix of equity and debt in their capital structure. Furthermore, the pecking order proposition would suggest that companies tend to use internally generated funds before going to markets to raise debt capital initially and finally equity capital. The agency effects of having to provide extra information to the markets and where one investor group benefits at the expense of another have been cited as the main deterrents to companies seeking external sources of finance. To a certain extent, this seems to be the case with Limni Co in using internal finance first, but the pecking order proposition seems to be contradicted in that it seeks to go straight to the equity market and undertake rights issues thereafter. Perhaps the explanation for this can be gained from looking at the balance of business and financial risk. Since Limni Co operates in a rapidly changing industry, it probably faces significant business risk and therefore cannot afford to undertake high financial risk, which a capital structure containing significant levels of debt would entail.

This, together with agency costs related to restrictive covenants, may have determined Limni Co's financing policy.

Risk management theory suggests that managing the volatility of cash flows enables a company to plan its investment strategy better. Since Limni Co uses internally generated funds to finance its projects, it needs to be certain that funds will be available when needed for the future projects, and therefore managing its cash flows will enable this. Moreover, because Limni Co faces high business risk, managing the risk that the company's managers cannot control through their actions, may be even more necessary.

The change to making dividend payments will affect all three policies. The company's clientele may change and this may cause share price fluctuations. However, since the recommendation for the change is being led by the shareholders, significant share price fluctuations may not happen. Limni Co's financing policy may change because having reduced internal funds means it may have to access debt markets and therefore have to look at its balance between business and financial risk. The change to Limni Co's financial structure may result in a change in its risk management policy, because it may be necessary to manage interest rate risk as well.

Note: Credit will be given for alternative relevant comments.

(b)   In the case of company Theta, dividends are growing but not at a stable rate. In fact company Theta is paying out $0.40 in dividends for every $1 in earnings, and has a fixed dividend cover ratio of 2.50. This would be confusing for the shareholders, as they would not know how much dividend they would receive from year to year. Although profits have risen over the past five years, if profits do fall, company Theta may reduce dividends and therefore send the wrong signals to shareholders and investors. This may cause unnecessary fluctuations of the share price or result in a depressed share price.

In the case of company Omega, annual dividends are growing at a stable rate of approximately 5% per year, while the company's earnings are growing steadily at around 3% per year, resulting in an increasing pay-out ratio. Also a high proportion of earnings are paid out as dividends, increasing from 60% in 20W9 to almost 65% in 20X3. This would indicate a company operating in a mature industry, signalling that there are few new projects to invest in and therefore reducing the retention rate. Such an investment would be attractive to investors requiring high levels of dividend returns from their investments.

In the case of company Kappa, although a lower proportion of earnings is paid out as dividends (from about 20% in 20W9 to about 27% in 20X3), they are growing at a higher but stable rate of 29%–30% per year. The company's earnings are growing rapidly but erratically, ranging between 3% and 35% between 20W9 and 20X3. This probably indicates a growing company, possibly similar to Limni Co itself, where perhaps returns to investors having been coming from share price growth, but one where dividends are becoming more prominent. Such an investment would be attractive to investors requiring lower levels of dividend returns, but higher capital returns from their investments.

Due to company Theta's confusing dividend policy, which may lead to erratic dividend pay-outs and a depressed share price, Limni Co would probably not want to invest in that company. The choice between company Omega and company Kappa would depend on how Limni Co wants to receive its return from the investment, maybe taking into account factors such as taxation implications, and the period of time it wishes to invest for, in terms of when the returns from an investment will be maximised and when it will need the funds for future projects.

Note: Credit will be given for alternative relevant comments.

(c)   Limni Co, current dividend capacity

	$000
Profit before tax (23% × $600,000,000)	138,000
Tax (26% × $138,000,000)	(35,880)
Profit after tax	102,120
Add back depreciation (25% × $220,000,000)	55,000
Less investment in assets	(67,000)
Remittances from overseas subsidiaries	15,000
Additional tax on remittances (6% × $15,000,000)	(900)
Dividend capacity	104,220

Increase in dividend capacity = 10% × $104,220,000 = $10,422,000

Gross up for tax = $10,422,000/0.94 = $11,087,234

Percentage increase in remittances from overseas subsidiaries = 73.9% [$11,087,234/ $15,000,000]

Dividend repatriations need to increase by 73.9% from Limni Co's international subsidiaries in order to increase the dividend capacity by 10%. Limni Co would need to consider whether or not it is feasible for its subsidiaries to increase their repatriations to such an extent, and the impact this will have on the motivation of the subsidiaries' managers and on the subsidiaries' ability to operate as normal.

Marking scheme		
		Marks
(a) Discussion of dividend policy		1–2
Discussion of financing policy		2–3
Discussion of risk management policy		1–2
Effect of dividends on the policies		2–3
	Maximum	**7**
(b) 2 marks per evaluation of each of the three companies		6
Conclusion - which company to invest in		2
	Maximum	**7**
c) Calculation of initial dividend capacity		3
Calculation of new repatriation amount		2
Comment		1–2
	Maximum	**6**
Professional skills marks (see below)		**5**
Total		**25**

Professional skills marks

Analysis and Evaluation

Appropriate use of the data to determine suitable calculations

Appropriate use of the data to support discussion and draw appropriate conclusions

Appraisal of information objectively to make a recommendation

Scepticism

Effective challenge of information supplied to support key facts and/or decisions

Demonstration of ability to consider all relevant factors

Commercial acumen

Recommendations are practical and plausible in the context of Limni Co's situation

Effective use of examples from the scenario information and other practical considerations related to the context to illustrate points being made

Maximum 5 marks

24 CHAWAN CO (JUN 15)

Key answer tips

This is a very difficult question, because part (b) is so open-ended.

To assess whether Chawan Co should dispose of its equity stake in Oden Co, you should first assess the performance of Oden Co using ratio analysis.

In order to make your ratio analysis useful, make sure you incorporate trends over time and comparisons with the rest of the industry.

(a)   A dark pool network allows shares to be traded anonymously, away from public scrutiny. No information on the trade order is revealed prior to it taking place. The price and size of the order are only revealed once the trade has taken place. Two main reasons are given for dark pool networks: first they prevent the risk of other traders moving the share price up or down; and second they often result in reduced costs because trades normally take place at the mid-price between the bid and offer; and because broker-dealers try and use their own private pools, and thereby saving exchange fees.

Chawan Co's holding in Oden Co is 27 million shares out of a total of 600 million shares, or 4.5%. If Chawan Co sold such a large holding all at once, the price of Oden Co shares may fall temporarily and significantly, and Chawan Co may not receive the value based on the current price. By utilising a dark pool network, Chawan Co may be able to keep the price of the share largely intact, and possibly save transaction costs.

Although the criticism against dark pool systems is that they prevent market efficiency by not revealing bid-offer prices before the trade, proponents argue that in fact market efficiency is maintained because a large sale of shares will not move the price down artificially and temporarily.

(b)   Ratio calculations

Focus on investor and profitability ratios

Oden Co	20X2	20X3	20X4	20X5
Operating profit/sales revenue		16.2%	15.2%	10.4%
Operating profit/capital employed		22.5%	20.4%	12.7%
Earnings per share		$0.27	$0.24	$0.12
Price to earnings ratio		9.3	10.0	18.3
Gearing ratio (debt/(debt + equity))		37.6%	36.9%	37.1%
Interest cover (operating profit/finance costs)		9.5	7.5	3.5
Dividend yield	7.1%	7.2%	8.3%	6.8%

Travel and leisure (T&L) sector

	20X2	20X3	20X4	20X5
Price to earnings ratio	11.9	12.2	13.0	13.8
Dividend yield	6.6%	6.6%	6.7%	6.4%

Other calculations

Oden Co, sales revenue annual growth rate average between 20X3 and 20X5 = $(1,185/1,342)^{1/2} - 1 = -6.0\%$.

Between 20X4 and 20X5 = $(1,185-1,335)/1,335 = -11.2\%$.

Oden Co, average financing cost

20X3:   23/(365 + 88) = 5.1%
20X4:   27/(368 + 90) = 5.9%
20X5:   35/(360 + 98) = 7.6%

Share price changes	20X2–20X3	20X3–20X4	20X4–20X5
Oden Co	19.0%	− 4.0%	− 8.3%
T&L sector	15.8%	− 2.3%	12.1%

Oden Co

Return to shareholders (RTS)	20X3	20X4	20X5
Dividend yield	7.2%	8.3%	6.8%
Share price gain	19.0%	− 4.0%	− 8.3%
Total	26.2%	4.3%	− 1.5%
Average: 9.7%			
Required return (based on capital asset pricing model (CAPM))	13.0%	13.6%	16.0%
Average: 14.2%			

T&L sector (RTS)	20X3	20X4	20X5
Dividend yield	6.6%	6.7%	6.4%
Share price gain	15.8%	− 2.3%	12.1%
Total	22.4%	4.4%	18.5%
Average: 15.1%			
Required return (based on CAPM)	12.4%	13.0%	13.6%
Average: 13.0%			

Note: The averages for Oden Co, RTS and for the T&L sector are the simple averages of the three years: 20X3 to 20X5.

Tutorial note

When attempting a question like this in the Computer Based Exam (CBE), use the spreadsheet to present your calculations but the word processor to present your analysis/discussion.

Discussion

The following discussion compares the performance of Oden Co over time, to the T&L sector and against expectations, in terms of it being a sound investment. It also considers the wider aspects which Chawan Co should take account of and the further information which the company should consider before coming to a final decision.

In terms of Oden Co's performance between 20X3 and 20X5, it is clear from the calculations above, that the company is experiencing considerable financial difficulties. Profit margins have fallen and so has the earnings per share (EPS). Whereas the amount of gearing appears fairly stable, the interest cover has deteriorated. The reason for this is that borrowing costs have increased from an average of 5.1% to an average of 7.6% over the three years. The share price has decreased over the three years as well and in the last year so has the dividend yield. This would indicate that the company is unable to maintain adequate returns for its investors (please also see below).

Although Oden Co has tried to maintain a dividend yield which is higher than the sector average, its price to earnings (PE) ratio has been lower than the sector average between 20X3 and 20X4. It does increase significantly in 20X5, but this is because of the large fall in the EPS, rather than an increase in the share price. This could be an indication that there is less confidence in the future prospects of Oden Co, compared to the rest of the T&L sector. This is further corroborated by the higher dividend yield which may indicate that the company has fewer value-creating projects planned in the future. Finally, whereas the T&L sector's average share price seems to have recovered strongly in 20X5, following a small fall in 20X4, Oden Co's share price has not followed suit and the decline has gathered pace in 20X5. It would seem that Oden Co is a poor performer within its sector.

This view is further strengthened by comparing the actual returns to the required returns based on the capital asset pricing model (CAPM). Both the company and the T&L sector produced returns exceeding the required return in 20X3 and Oden Co experienced a similar decline to the sector in 20X4. However, in 20X5, the T&L sector appears to have recovered but Oden Co's performance has worsened. This has resulted in Oden Co's actual average returns being significantly below the required returns between 20X2 and 20X5.

Taking the above into account, the initial recommendation is for Chawan Co to dispose of its investment in Oden Co. However, there are three important caveats which should be considered before the final decision is made.

The first caveat is that Chawan Co should look at the balance of its portfolio of investments. A sale of $58 million worth of equity shares within a portfolio total of $360 million may cause the portfolio to become unbalanced, and for unsystematic risk to be introduced into the portfolio. Presumably, the purpose of maintaining a balanced portfolio is to virtually eliminate unsystematic risk by ensuring that it is well diversified. Chawan Co may want to re-invest the proceeds from the sale of Oden Co (if it decides to proceed with the disposal) in other equity shares within the same sector to ensure that the portfolio remains balanced and diversified.

The second caveat is that Chawan Co may want to look into the rumours of a takeover bid of Oden Co and assess how realistic it is that this will happen. If there is a realistic chance that such a bid may happen soon, Chawan Co may want to hold onto its investment in Oden Co for the present time. This is because takeover bids are made at a premium and the return to Chawan Co may increase if Oden Co is sold during the takeover.

The third caveat is that Chawan Co may want to consider Oden Co's future prospects. The calculations above are based on past performance between 20X2 and 20X5 and indicate an increasingly poor performance. However, the economy is beginning to recover, albeit slowly and erratically. Chawan Co may want to consider how well placed Oden Co is to take advantage of the improving conditions compared to other companies in the same industrial sector.

If Chawan Co decides that none of the caveats materially affect Oden Co's poor performance and position, then it should dispose of its investment in Oden Co.

Marking scheme		
		Marks
(a) Explanation of a dark pool network		2–3
Explanation of why Chawan Co may want to use one		1–2
	Maximum	**4**
(b) Profitability ratios		1–2
Investor ratios		2–3
Other ratios		1–2
Trends and other calculations		2–3
	Maximum	**8**
Note: Maximum 6 marks if only ratio calculations provided		
Discussion of company performance over time		1–2
Discussion of company performance against competitors		1–2
Discussion of actual returns against expected returns		1–2
Discussion of need to maintain portfolio and alternative investments		1–2
Discussion of future trends and expectations		1–2
Discussion of takeover rumour and action as a result		1–2
Other relevant discussion/commentary		1–2
	Maximum	**8**
Professional skills marks (see below)		**5**
Total		**25**

Professional skills marks

Analysis and Evaluation

Appropriate use of the data to determine suitable calculations

Appropriate use of the data to support discussion and draw appropriate conclusions

Appraisal of information objectively to make a recommendation

Scepticism

Effective challenge of evidence and assumptions supplied

Commercial acumen

Effective use of examples and/or practical considerations related to the context to illustrate points being made

Maximum 5 marks

25   CHITHURST CO (SEP/DEC 16)

Key answer tips

Parts (a) and (b) in this question cover dividend policy and business valuation respectively – but note that they can be answered independently of each other.

In any question like this, start with the part that you feel most confident about, to build up confidence at the start of the question.

(a)   **Dividend pay-out ratio**

	Chithurst Co	Eartham Co	Iping Co
	%	%	%
20X2	42.9	40.0	46.7
20X3	41.3	(150.0)	19.3
20X4	35.1	40.0	33.1
20X5	34.0	40.0	31.8

Residual profit (after-tax profit for the year – dividend – new investment)

	Chithurst Co	Eartham Co	Iping Co
	£m	£m	£m
20X2	26	27	3
20X3	18	(40)	7
20X4	38	24	4
20X5	43	43	6

Tutorial note

When attempting a question like this in the Computer Based Exam (CBE), use the spreadsheet to present your calculations but the word processor to present your analysis/discussion.

Chithurst Co's policy

Benefits

Chithurst Co's policy provides shareholders with a stable, predictable income each year. As profits have grown consistently, dividend cover has increased, which suggests that, for now, dividend levels are sustainable. These are positive signals to the stock market.

Drawbacks

Chithurst Co's dividend policy is unpopular with some of its shareholders. They have indicated a preference for dividend levels to bear a greater relation to profit levels. Although they are still in a minority and cannot force the directors to pay more dividends, they are now possibly a significant minority. Ultimately, Chithurst Co's share price could fall significantly if enough shareholders sell their shares because they dislike the dividend policy.

The dividend policy may also have been established to meet the financial needs of the shareholders when Chithurst Co was unquoted. However, it is now difficult to see how it fits into Chithurst Co's overall financial strategy. The greater proportion of funds retained does not appear to be linked to the levels of investment Chithurst Co is undertaking. Chithurst Co's shareholders may be concerned that best use is not being made of the funds available. If there are profitable investments which Chithurst Co could be making but is not doing so, then Chithurst Co may find it more difficult in future to sustain the levels of profit growth. Alternatively, if profitable investments do not exist, some shareholders may prefer to have funds returned in the form of a special dividend or share repurchase.

Eartham Co

Benefits

For three out of four years, Eartham Co has been paying out dividends at a stable pay-out ratio. This may be attractive to some investors, who have expectations that the company's profits will keep increasing in the longer term and wish to share directly in increases in profitability.

The year when Eartham Co's dividend pay-out ratio differed from the others was 20X3, when Eartham Co made a loss. A dividend of $15 million was paid in 20X3, which may be a guaranteed minimum. This limits the downside risk of the dividend pay-out policy to shareholders, as they know they will receive this minimum amount in such a year.

Drawbacks

Although shareholders are guaranteed a minimum dividend each year, dividends have been variable. Eartham Co's shareholders may prefer dividends to increase at a steady rate which is sustainable over time, even if this rate is lower than the rate of increase in some years under the current policy.

If Eartham Co had another poor year of trading like 20X3, shareholders' expectations that they will be paid a minimum dividend may mean that cash has to be earmarked to pay the minimum dividend, rather than for other, maybe better, uses in the business.

Having a 'normal' dividend policy results in expectations about what the level of dividend will be. Over time Eartham Co's managers may be reluctant to change to a lower pay-out ratio because they fear that this will give shareholders an adverse signal. Even if its directors maintain a constant ratio normally, shareholders may question whether the proportion of funds being retained is appropriate or whether a higher proportion could be paid out as dividends.

Eartham Co appears to be linking investment and dividend policy by its normal policy of allocating a constant proportion of funds for dividends and therefore a constant proportion of funds to invest. However, the actual level of new investments does not seem to bear much relation to the proportion of funds put aside for investment. When deciding on investments, the directors would also take into account the need to take advantage of opportunities as they arise and the overall amount of surplus funds built up over the years, together with the other sources of external finance available.

Iping Co

Benefits

Iping Co seems to have adopted a residual dividend policy, which links investment and dividend decisions. The strategy appears to be to make investments if they offer sufficient return to increase long-term company value and only pay dividends if there are no more profitable investments. They are assuming that internal funds are cheaper than external funds, or maybe Iping Co cannot raise the funds required from external sources.

The policy is likely to appeal to shareholders who are more concerned with capital growth than short-term income.

Drawbacks

Dividend payments are totally unpredictable, as they depend on the investment choices. Shareholders cannot rely on having any dividend income in a particular year.

Many shareholders may be prepared to sacrifice dividends for a while in order for funds to be available for investment for growth. However, at some point they may consider that Iping Co is well established enough to be able to maintain a consistent dividend policy as well as invest sufficiently for future growth.

(b) **Use of dividend valuation model**

Chithurst Co

Valuation = 33/0.11 = $300m

Chithurst Co's market capitalisation of $608m is considerably in excess of the valuation suggested by the dividend valuation model. This may suggest that investors have some positive expectations about the company and the lower cost of equity compared with the other two companies suggests it is regarded as a more stable investment. Investors could also be valuing the company using earnings growth rather than dividend growth. However, the lower market capitalisation compared with the other two companies and the smaller increase in share price suggest that investors have higher expectations of long-term growth from Eartham Co and Iping Co.

Eartham Co

One-year growth rate = (48/44) − 1 = 9.1 %

Valuation using one-year growth rate = 48 (1 + 0.091)/(0.14 − 0.091) = $1,068.7m

Three-year growth rate = $\sqrt[3]{(48/38)}$ − 1 = 8.1%

Valuation using three-year growth rate = 48 (1 + 0.081)/(0.14 − 0.081) = $879m

Eartham Co's market capitalisation is closer to the valuation suggested by the dividend growth model using the one-year growth rate between 20X4 and 20X5 rather than the three-year growth rate between 20X2 and 20X5. This, together with the recent increase in share price, suggests that Eartham Co's shareholders have an optimistic view of its ability to sustain the profit growth and hence the dividend growth of the last two years, although its higher cost of equity than the other companies suggests that they are more wary about the risks of investing in Eartham Co. It indicates confidence in the directors' strategy, including the investments they have made.

Iping Co

One-year growth rate = (42/39) − 1 = 7.7%

Valuation using one-year growth rate = 42 (1 + 0.077)/(0.12 − 0.077) = $1,052.0m

Three-year growth rate = $\sqrt[3]{(42/35)}$ − 1 = 6.3%

Valuation using three-year growth rate = 42 (1 + 0.063)/(0.12 − 0.063) = $783.3m

The market capitalisation of Iping Co is higher than is suggested by the dividend valuation model, but the dividend valuation model may not provide a realistic valuation because dividends payable are dependent on investment opportunities.

The larger increase in share price compared with the other two companies suggests that Iping Co's investors expect its investments to produce high long-term returns and hence are presumably satisfied with its dividend policy.

	Marking scheme		
			Marks
(a)	Benefits of dividend policy – 1–2 marks for each company	Maximum	4
	Drawbacks of dividend policy – 1–2 marks for each company	Maximum	6
	Calculations – Dividend pay-out ratios – 1 mark per company		3
	Other calculations		1
		Maximum	13
(b)	Comments on valuation of each company, max 2 marks per company (max 4 marks for valuation calculation(s))		
		Maximum	7
	Professional skills marks (see below)		5
Total			25

Professional skills marks

Analysis and Evaluation

Appropriate use of the data to determine suitable calculations

Appropriate use of the data to support discussion and draw appropriate conclusions

Appraisal of information objectively to make a recommendation

Scepticism

Effective challenge of information supplied to support key facts and/or decisions

Demonstration of ability to consider all relevant factors

Commercial acumen

Recommendations are practical and plausible in the context of Chithurst Co's situation

Effective use of examples from the scenario information and other practical considerations related to the context to illustrate points being made

Maximum 5 marks

26   HIGH K CO (SEP/DEC 17)

Key answer tips

Part (a) of this question (worth 16 marks) was quite unusual. Previous exam questions had sometimes required students to appraise the performance of a company, to identify whether the company is likely to fail, but rarely for so many marks. Also, the open-ended nature of this requirement may have caused problems.

Given that 8 marks were available for calculations and 8 marks for discussion, it would have been important not to spend too long calculating ratios, and to leave plenty of time for commentary.

Part (b) was a very straightforward discussion of financing options.

(a) Profitability

Revenues from the different types of store and online sales have all increased this year, despite a drop in store numbers. The increase in revenue this year may be largely due, however, to the government-induced pre-election boom in consumer expenditure, which appears unlikely to be sustained. Because the split of profits is not given, it is impossible to tell what has been the biggest contributor to increased profit. Profit as well as revenue details for different types of store would be helpful, also profit details for major product lines.

Improvements in return on capital employed derive from increases in profit margins and asset turnover.

The improvements in gross margins may be due to increased pressure being put on suppliers, in which case they may not be sustainable because of government pressure. The increased sales per store employee figures certainly reflects a fall in staff numbers, improving operating profit, although it could also be due to staff being better utilised or increased sales of higher value items in larger stores. If staff numbers continue to be cut, however, this could result in poorer service to customers, leading ultimately to decreased sales, so again it is questionable how much further High K Co can go.

The asset turnover shows an improvement which partly reflects the increase in sales. There have been only limited movements in the portfolio of the larger stores last year. The fall in non-current assets suggests an older, more depreciated, asset base. If there is no significant investment, this will mean a continued fall in capital employed and improved asset turnover. However, in order to maintain their appeal to customers, older stores will need to be refurbished and there is no information about refurbishment plans. Information about recent impairments in asset values would also be helpful, as these may indicate future trading problems and issues with realising values of assets sold.

Liquidity

The current ratio has improved, although the higher cash balances have been partly reflected by higher current liabilities. The increase in current liabilities may be due to a deliberate policy of taking more credit from suppliers, which the government may take measures to prevent. Being forced to pay suppliers sooner will reduce cash available for short-term opportunities.

Gearing

The gearing level in 20Y6 is below the 20Y4 level, but it would have fallen further had a fall in debt not been partly matched by a fall in High K Co's share price. It seems surprising that High K Co's debt levels fell during 20Y6 at a time of lower interest rates. Possibly lenders were (rightly) sceptical about whether the cut in central bank lending rate would be sustained and limited their fixed rate lending. Interest cover improved in 20Y6 and will improve further if High K Co makes use of revolving credit facilities. However, when High K Co's loans come up for renewal, terms available may not be as favourable as those High K Co has currently.

Investors

The increase in after-tax profits in 20Y5 and 20Y6 has not been matched by an increase in share price, which has continued to fall. The price/earnings ratio has been falling from an admittedly artificially high level, and the current level seems low despite earnings and dividends being higher. The stock market does not appear convinced by High K Co's current strategy. Return to shareholders in 20Y6 has continued to rise, but this has been caused by a significant % increase in dividend and hence increase in dividend yield. The continued fall in share price after the year end suggests that investors are sceptical about whether this increase can be maintained.

Revenue analysis

Town centre stores

High K Co has continued to close town centre stores, but closures have slowed recently and revenue increased in 20Y6. This suggests High K Co may have selected wisely in choosing which stores to keep open, although Dely Co believes there is no future for this type of store. Arguably though, town centre stores appeal to some customers who cannot easily get to out-of-town stores. Town centre stores may also be convenient collection points for customers using online click and collect facilities.

Convenience stores

High K Co has invested heavily in these since 20X3. The figures in 20Y4 suggest it may have over-extended itself or possibly suffered from competitive pressures and saturation of the market. The 20Y6 results show an improvement despite closures of what may have been the worst-performing stores. The figures suggest Dely Co's decision to close its convenience stores may be premature, possibly offering High K Co the opportunity to take over some of its outlets. Maintaining its convenience store presence would also seem to be in line with High K Co's commitment to be responsive to customer needs. Profitability figures would be particularly helpful here, to assess the impact of rental commitments under leases.

Out-of-town stores

Although the revenue per store for out-of-town stores has shown limited improvement in 20Y6, this is less than might have been expected. The recent consumer boom would have been expected to benefit the out-of-town stores particularly, because expenditure on the larger items which they sell is more likely to be discretionary expenditure by consumers which will vary with the business cycle. Where Dely Co sites its new out-of-town stores will also be a major issue for High K Co, as it may find some of its best-performing stores face more competition. High K Co again may need to consider significant refurbishment expenditure to improve the look of these stores and customer experience in them.

Online sales

Online sales have shown steady growth over the last few years, but it is difficult to say how impressive High K Co's performance is. Comparisons with competitors would be particularly important here, looking at how results have changed over the years compared with the level of investment made. It is also impossible to tell from the figures how much increases in online sales have been at the expense of store sales.

Conclusion

If High K Co's share price is to improve, investors need it to make some sort of definite decision about strategy the way its competitors have since its last year end. What the chief executive has been saying about flexibility and keeping a varied portfolio has not convinced investors. If High K Co is to maintain its competitive position, it may well have no choice but to make a significant further investment in online operations. Possibly as well it could review where its competitor is closing convenience stores, as it may be able to open, with limited investment, new stores in locations with potential.

However, it also must decide what to do about the large out-of-town stores, as their performance is already stagnating and they are about to face enhanced competition. High K Co will also need to determine its dividend policy, with maybe a level of dividend which is considered the minimum acceptable to shareholders allowed for in planning cash outflows.

Tutorial note

When attempting a question like this in the Computer Based Exam (CBE), use the spreadsheet to present your calculations but the word processor to present your analysis/discussion.

Appendix

	20Y4	20Y5	20Y6
Profitability			
Gross profit %	4.33	5.07	6.19
Operating profit %	0.87	1.70	2.91
Asset turnover (sales revenue/(total assets – current liabilities))	2.36	2.42	2.53
Return on capital employed % (operating profit % × asset turnover)	2.05	4.11	7.36
Liquidity			
Current ratio	0.84	1.29	1.69
Solvency			
Gearing (non-current liabilities/ non-current liabilities + share capital) (Market values of share capital) %	37.6	36.8	32.5
Interest cover	1.63	3.54	7.12
Investors			
Dividend cover	0.35	1.29	1.71
Price/earnings ratio	54.46	12.15	5.52
Return to shareholders			
Dividend yield %	5.30	6.36	10.60
Share price gain/(loss) %	(9.00)	(5.65)	(3.29)
Total	(3.70)	0.71	7.31

	20Y4	**20Y5**	**20Y6**
Revenue/store ($m)			
Town centre	31.91	33.05	33.93
Convenience	5.41	5.66	5.99
Out-of-town	46.45	46.16	46.46
Store revenue per store staff member ($000)	247	258	272

Note: Credit will be given for alternative relevant calculations and discussion. Candidates are not expected to complete all of the calculations or evaluation above to obtain the available marks.

(b) High K Co has not raised any equity finance over the last five years. Its falling share price means that a new share issue may not be successful. It may not only need debt finance to be renewed, but additional funding to be obtained.

High K Co intends to make more use of revolving credit facilities, which it need not draw on fully, rather than loans, which will mean that its finance costs are lower than on ordinary debt. However, these facilities are likely to be at floating rates, so if the government increases the central bank rate significantly, they could come at significant cost if High K Co decides to utilise them fully.

Finance costs on new debt, whatever form it takes, may therefore be significant and lower interest cover. High K Co may have to investigate selling some of the stores it owns either outright or on a sale or leaseback basis.

Marking scheme		
		Marks
(a)	**Ratios**	
	Profitability	1–2
	Liquidity	1
	Solvency	1–2
	Investor	2–3
	Other ratios and trends	2–3
	Maximum	**8**
	Discussion	
	Profitability	1–2
	Liquidity	1–2
	Gearing	1–2
	Investor	1–2
	Stores and online sales	1–2
	Conclusion	1–2
	Maximum	**8**
(b)	1 mark per relevant point	4
	Maximum	**4**
	Professional skills marks (see below)	**5**
Total		**25**

Professional skills marks

Analysis and Evaluation

Appropriate use of the data to determine suitable calculations

Appropriate use of the data to support discussion and draw appropriate conclusions

Appraisal of information objectively to make a recommendation

Scepticism

Effective challenge of information, evidence and assumptions supplied and, techniques carried out to support key facts and/or decisions

Demonstration of ability to consider all relevant factors applicable to a given course of action

Commercial acumen

Recommendations are practical and plausible in the context of High K Co's situation

Effective use of examples and/or calculations from the scenario information and other practical considerations related to the context to illustrate points being made

Maximum 5 marks

27   ARTHURO CO (MAR/JUN 18)

Key answer tips

When asked to calculate dividend capacity, you should try to estimate the amount of cash that the company will generate, after paying any operating expenses and interest, and investing in assets. This is commonly known as the free cash flow to equity.

Don't spend too long on part (a) though. There are lots of easy discussion marks in part (b).

(a)   **Forecast dividend capacity is as follows:**

	$000
Operating profit (20% × 1.04 × $520 million)	108,160
Less: Interest (8% × $135 million)	(10,800)
Less: Taxation (30% × ($108.16 million – $10.8 million))	(29,208)
Add: Depreciation	30,000
Less: Profit on disposal of NCA	(5,900)
Add: Cash received on disposal of NCA (W1)	16,300
Less: Investment in new NCA (W2)	(44,800)
Less: Investment in working capital (15% × 0.04 × $520 million)	(3,120)
Add: Dividend remittance from Bowerscots Co (W3)	20,520
Less: Additional tax on Bowerscots Co's profits (10% × $45 million)	(4,500)
Forecast dividend capacity	76,652

Workings

1   Disposal of non-current assets

	$000
Profit on disposal	5,900
Cost	35,000
Less: Depreciation	(24,600)
Cash received on disposal	16,300

2   Investment in non-current assets

	$000
Net book value at end of most recent year (start of 'normal' year)	110,000
Less: Depreciation in 'normal' year	(30,000)
Less: Net book value of assets disposed ($35 million – $24.6 million)	(10,400)
Net book value before investment in non-current assets	69,600
Required level of non-current assets ($110 million × 1.04)	114,400
Investment in non-current assets	44,800

3   Dividend remittance from Bowerscots

	$000
Profit before tax	45,000
Less: Tax at 20%	(9,000)
Profit after tax	36,000
Remitted to Arthuro Co (36,000 × 60% × 0.95)	20,520

(b)   (i)   Benefits of policy

The change of policy appears to be viable. Arthuro Co would have had some slack if it had not undertaken the rights issue.

The new policy takes up this slack and effectively tops up the amount required with an increase in dividends.

The new policy appears to ensure that Arthuro Co will have sufficient funds to pay the required level of dividends and fulfil its own investment requirements. It will mean that Bowerscots Co has less retained funds available for investment, but Arthuro Co's investment opportunities may be more profitable.

Problems with policy

Arthuro Co is now taking much more (potentially all) of Bowerscots Co's post-tax earnings as dividends. A limited fall in Bowerscots Co's earnings could lead to its dividends not being enough to sustain Arthuro Co's dividend level. A fall could easily happen given the highly competitive environment in which Bowerscots Co operates. If Arthuro Co wanted to increase its dividends over time, it could not do so by receiving extra dividends from Bowerscots Co.

As mentioned, an increase in dividend will leave Bowerscots Co's management with less retained earnings to invest. The amount of investment they can undertake with the reduced funds available may be insufficient to sustain earnings levels and hence dividends for Arthuro Co.

The tax regime between the two countries means that the group will suffer more tax. The amount of additional tax payable by Arthuro Co on Bowerscots Co's profits will remain unchanged, but the increase in dividends will mean an increase in withholding tax, for which Arthuro Co will receive no credit. Given the lower tax rate in Owlia, for tax purposes higher retained earnings for Bowerscots Co would be preferable, possibly with funds loaned to Arthuro Co rather than paid as dividends.

(ii) Agency problems

An agency situation arises between Arthuro Co's board (the principal) and Bowerscots Co's management (the agent). The proposals are likely to involve agency costs.

The policy limits the discretion of Bowerscots Co's management by restricting the amounts of retained funds available. However, this seems an inefficient way of exercising closer control, with agency costs including the increased liability for withholding tax. If Arthuro Co's board has concerns about Bowerscots Co's management, it would be better to make changes in the management team.

Even if Arthuro Co's board has confidence in Bowerscots Co's management team, it may nevertheless wish to oversee Bowerscots Co more closely, given the dependence of its dividend capacity on the amount received from the subsidiary. Again, increased supervision will involve increased agency costs in terms of time spent by Arthuro Co's management.

Bowerscots Co's management may feel that the new policy threatens their remuneration, as the limited funds available for investment will adversely affect the company's ability to maintain its profit levels. The managers may seek to join competitors, disrupting Bowerscots Co's management, jeopardising its ability to achieve its profit forecasts.

Resolving agency problems

Ways of motivating Bowerscots Co's management include making their remuneration less dependent on Bowerscots Co's results, for example, allowing them share options in Arthuro Co. If more of their remuneration depends on the group's results, Bowerscots Co's management may be happier with the suggested arrangement if they feel it will benefit the group. However, this motivational effect will be limited if Bowerscots Co's management feels that the group results are not influenced much by what they do.

Alternatively, a greater proportion of Bowerscots Co's management's remuneration could be by methods which are not dependent on its results, for example, increased salary or better benefits. However, by weakening the link between results and remuneration, it lessens their incentive to strive to produce the results needed to maintain the required level of dividend.

The decision-making on investments at group level may also have to change. Bowerscots Co will, under the new policy, have insufficient funds for major investments. Its management team should have the opportunity to make a case for retaining a greater percentage of funds, as they may have better investment opportunities than those available to the parent.

			Marks
Marking guide			
(a)	Operating profit		1
	Interest payable		1
	Tax payable for normal activities		1
	Depreciation		1
	Profit on disposal of non-current assets		1
	Cash from disposal of non-current assets		1
	Investment in new non-current assets		2
	Investment in working capital		1
	Dividend remittance from Bowerscots Co		1
	Additional tax payable on Bowerscots Co profits		1
			——
			11
			——
(b)(i)	Benefits of new policy		2–3
	Problems of new policy		2–3
			——
		Maximum	4
			——
(b)(ii)	Agency problems		2–3
	Solutions to problems		2–3
			——
		Maximum	5
			——
	Professional skills marks (see below)		5
			——
Total			25
			——

Professional skills marks

Analysis and Evaluation

Appropriate use of the data to determine suitable calculations

Appropriate use of the data to support discussion and draw appropriate conclusions

Appraisal of information objectively to make a recommendation

Scepticism

Effective challenge of information supplied to support key facts and/or decisions

Demonstration of ability to consider all relevant factors

Commercial acumen

Recommendations are practical and plausible in the context of Arthuro Co's situation

Effective use of examples from the scenario information and other practical considerations related to the context to illustrate points being made

Maximum 5 marks

28 TILLINTON CO (SEP 18)

Key answer tips

The risk in a question like this is that you spend so long calculating ratios that you don't have time to pick up the marks for the discussion. Note that the question tells you that only 8 marks are available for the calculations, so spend no more than about 16 minutes on them before moving on to analyse your figures.

(a) Profitability

Tillinton Co's chief executive is correct in saying that the absolute increase in revenue and gross profits on all products was greater in 20X3 than 20X2, but the % increase in revenue was smaller on all products, and the % increase in gross profit on toys was also lower. The % increase on the electronic toys shows the biggest fall, possibly indicating greater competition.

The improvements in operations mentioned by the chief executive seem to have maintained gross and operating profit margins and resulted in the absolute overall increases in gross and operating profits. However, this aspect of performance is almost all attributable to Tillinton Co's older products. The gross profit on electronic toys has hardly increased and the gross profit margin has fallen over the last two years. Although the margin remains higher than on the other products, even the 20X3 margin may not be sustainable. If competitors are starting to catch up with Tillinton Co, then the profit margin on the current range of electronic toys may continue to fall in future years, as prices fall to maintain market share.

Despite the emphasis on developing the products, the revenue generated by electronic toys is still below the revenue generated by non-electronic toys.

Asset turnover and return on capital employed have risen significantly over the last two years. However, part of the reason for the 20X3 increases was the significant increase in current liabilities. The further amount of investment which the chief executive appears to be contemplating suggests that asset turnover and return on capital employed may fall in future years, particularly if profit margins on electronic toys cannot be sustained.

Liquidity

The figures for other current assets seem to support the chief executive's contention that working capital is being managed better, as other current assets are falling as revenue and gross profits are rising.

However, the fall of the current ratio from 1.52 to 0.64 is significant, and the biggest reason for the fall in 20X3 was the large increase in current liabilities. Cash balances have remained at a low level, despite higher revenues and profit. Possibly there is now a bank overdraft, which could have contributed to the significant increase in finance costs between 20X2 and 20X3. It would seem that cash reserves have been exhausted by the combination of investment in non-current assets and the payments to finance providers (both interest and dividends), and Tillinton Co is more dependent on short-term liability finance. Slowdown in any product area, particularly electronic toys, may result in significant liquidity problems.

Solvency

Gearing has fallen over the last two years, but this is due to share price increases which may not be sustainable. If book values rather than market values are used to calculate gearing, the fall in gearing is much smaller. More information is needed about why finance costs have increased so much, leading to the deterioration in interest rate cover. Tillinton Co has only taken out an additional $30 million in long-term loans. Although costs on these may be higher than on its current loans, this would not account for all the increase in finance costs. As discussed above, Tillinton Co may be making use of overdraft finance. The fact that current liabilities have increased much more than non-current liabilities could be an indication that Tillinton Co is having problems raising all the longer term loan finance which it requires.

The figures suggest that Tillinton Co's board needs to review future financing carefully if the company wants to make further investment in electronic products. At some stage, the board will have to consider raising further finance, either through an issue of shares or through selling off parts of its operations.

Investor ratios

Both earnings and dividends per share have risen since 20X1, which could help explain the significant increase in share price. Dividend cover has remained around 2.0 despite an increase in earnings. Although dividends have increased, dividend yield has fallen since 20X1. The increase in total shareholder return is due solely to the increases in share price, which have also resulted in the price-earnings ratio increasing in 20X3. The current rate of share price increase does not appear to be warranted by the most recent results and may be partly due to generous dividend levels, which may not be sustainable if more cash is required for investment.

Conclusion

Despite the chief executive's optimistic message in the annual report, the benefits from the electronic toys development may be short-lived. There appears to be a mismatch between investment, dividend and financing policies. As discussed, margins on current products may fall further and there is no guarantee that margins on new electronic toys or other products will be higher if competition generally is increasing.

Further significant investment in electronic toys or other goods may be difficult to finance. Increased reliance on short-term finance is clearly not sustainable, but obtaining more debt may be problematic, particularly if gearing levels rise as share prices fall. Tillinton Co seems reluctant to take advantage of high share price levels to issue equity capital. This, plus the increase in dividends, may indicate Tillinton Co's board is unwilling to risk upsetting shareholders, despite the large increases in share price. The chief executive may be right in saying that funds may have to be obtained by selling off one of the other parts of the business, but revenue and profits from the older products may be more sustainable. An increased concentration on electronic products may be a high-risk strategy. Possibly, if investors become less positive towards the electronic goods sector, they may realise this, resulting in an increase in cost of capital and a fall in share price.

Tutorial note

The marking scheme here allowed for credit to be given for any alternative but relevant approaches to the calculations and discussion.

Tutorial note

When attempting a question like this in the Computer Based Exam (CBE), use the spreadsheet to present your calculations but the word processor to present your analysis/discussion.

Appendix

Profitability	20X1	20X2	20X3
% increase in revenue		18.1	17.0
Gross profit %	27.5	27.6	27.6
% increase in gross profit		18.4	17.1
Operating profit %	14.8	15.4	15.7
% increase in operating profit		22.9	19.0
Asset turnover (revenue/(total assets – current liabilities))	0.65	0.73	0.81
Return on capital employed % (operating profit % × asset turnover)	9.6	11.2	12.7
Liquidity			
Current ratio	1.52	1.15	0.64
Solvency			
Gearing (non-current liabilities/(non-current liabilities + market value of share capital)) %	29.4	25.8	22.0
Gearing (non-current liabilities/(non-current liabilities + book value of share capital + reserves)) %	43.3	43.0	42.2
Interest cover	4.5	5.0	4.5
Investors			
Earnings per share ($)	0.15	0.19	0.21
Dividend per share ($)	0.075	0.09	0.105
Dividend cover	1.98	2.10	2.01
Market price per $0.50 share	2.76	3.49	4.44
Price/earnings ratio	18.4	18.4	21.1
Dividend yield % (dividend per share/share price)	2.72	2.58	2.36
Share price gain/(loss) %	10.40	26.45	27.22
Total shareholder return %	13.12	29.03	29.58

Types of product

Electronic toys

% increase in revenue		28.1	22.3
Gross profit %	40.2	35.1	29.0
% increase in gross profit		12.0	1.0

Other toys

% increase in revenue		15.9	15.4
Gross profit %	23.8	25.1	26.0
% increase in gross profit		22.2	19.3

Clothing

% increase in revenue		15.9	15.8
Gross profit %	25.1	26.0	27.7
% Increase in gross profit		20.1	23.5

Tutorial note

Candidates didn't have to complete all the calculations here to obtain 8 marks.

(b) Tillinton Co's shares may be overvalued because share prices generally are too high. The situation may be a stock market bubble. Share prices have been rising consistently recently and this could be encouraging investors to buy more shares, further increasing share prices.

The bubble could be more localised. Tillinton Co seems to be positioning itself as much in terms of producing technologically-advanced electronic products as manufacturing toys. The electronic goods sector may be more likely than other sectors to attract investors on the basis of future profit potential, with investors possibly following a herd instinct, investing because others have been investing in the expectation of future gains.

Possibly, investors are more persuaded by the chief executive's confident language and future promises than they are by the concerns the figures suggest. They may also be paying excessive attention to the most recent set of results, rather than seeing them in the context of whether they can be sustained in the future.

If investors are attempting to make a valuation, they could prefer using a model which confirms what they believe the shares are worth (confirmation bias), rather than one which gives a more reliable indication of value. As discussed above, shareholders may be basing their estimates of value on the recent increases in dividend, even though it may be doubtful whether this is sustainable.

			Marks
Marking guide			
(a)	**Ratios**		
	Profitability		1–2
	Liquidity		1
	Solvency		1–2
	Investor		1–2
	Other ratios and trends including product type split		2–3
		Maximum	8
	Discussion		
	Profitability		1–2
	Liquidity		1–2
	Solvency		1–2
	Investor		1–2
	Conclusion		1–2
		Maximum	8
(b)	Up to 2 marks per relevant point		
		Maximum	4
	Professional skills marks (see below)		5
Total			25

Professional skills marks

Analysis and Evaluation

Appropriate use of the data to determine suitable calculations

Appropriate use of the data to support discussion and draw appropriate conclusions

Appraisal of information objectively to make a recommendation

Scepticism

Effective challenge of evidence and assumptions supplied

Commercial acumen

Effective use of examples and/or practical considerations related to the context to illustrate points being made

Maximum 5 marks

29   CADNAM CO (SEP/DEC 19)

Key answer tips

There is a large amount of information to read in this question, so a good exam technique is critical here.

"Dividend capacity" in part (a) simply means free cash flow to equity, so start with the given operating profit figure and adjust it. Notice that depreciation equals the expected replacement investment in non-current assets, so these two figures net off to zero.

In part (c), make sure you read the question carefully. For full marks you need to address both dividend policy and remuneration policy AND governance and ethical issues.

(a)   Dividend capacity

	$m
Operating profit	2,678
Less: Interest (8% × $10,250m)	(820)
Less: Taxation (30% × ($2,678m – $820m))	(557)
Less: Investment in additional assets (25% × 0.03 × $2,678m/(1.03 × 0.02))	(975)
Forecast dividend capacity	326

(b)   Growth in profit after tax

	20X3	20X4	20X5	Geometric mean annual growth rate
	%	%	%	%
Cadnam	8.0	4.0	1.9	4.6
Holmsley	7.1	6.9	7.6	7.2

Dividend payout ratios

	20X2	20X3	20X4	20X5
	%	%	%	%
Cadnam	55.4	56.4	59.7	64.6
Holmsley	37.7	37.1	36.5	35.7

Growth in dividends

	20X3	20X4	20X5	Geometric mean annual growth rate
	%	%	%	%
Cadnam	9.8	10.1	10.3	10.1
Holmsley	5.4	5.3	5.3	5.3

Residual profit (after tax-profit for the year – dividend – new investment)

	20X2	20X3	20X4	20X5
	$m	$m	$m	$m
Cadnam	333	338	41	(304)
Holmsley	330	375	419	486

Growth in share price

	20X3	20X4	20X5	Geometric mean annual growth rate
	%	%	%	%
Cadnam	9.6	4.9	2.5	5.6
Holmsley	3.8	6.1	6.8	5.6

Tutorial note

When attempting a question like this in the Computer Based Exam (CBE), use the spreadsheet to present your calculations but the word processor to present your analysis/discussion.

Comments

Dividends

Both companies have shown fairly consistent increases over the last three years, with Cadnam Co's dividends increasing at around 10% each year, and Holmsley Co's dividends increasing at around 5% over the last three years. However, Holmsley Co's policy appears to be sustainable at present, whereas it is doubtful whether Cadnam Co's policy is sustainable.

Holmsley Co has managed to increase dividends, gradually also increasing investment in additional assets and residual profits, whilst at the same time having a decreasing dividend pay-out ratio.

In order to maintain its rate of dividend increase, however, Cadnam Co has had to pay out an increasing proportion of earnings each year. It seems that Cadnam Co may have sustained dividend increases up to 20X3 at the expense of additional investment, and is now having to increase additional investment significantly in order to make up for previous under-investment. In 20X5, Cadnam Co's residual profits became negative, and the dividend capacity calculation for 20X6 suggests that a much lower level of dividends would be appropriate.

Gearing

Holmsley Co's gearing appears to be stable at around the average for the industry, suggesting that perhaps it has found its optimum level. Up to 20X4, Cadnam Co could perhaps have been taking advantage of debt capacity to increase its debt towards this level. However, its gearing now appears to be on a rising trend, of necessity increasing significantly in 20X5 to fund both additional investment and increasing dividends, despite the rise in its share price. Cadnam Co's gearing is predicted to increase further in 20X6, but how long this is sustainable is uncertain.

Share price

The average increase for both companies over the last four years has been the same. However, the percentage increases over the last two years for Holmsley Co has been higher than for Cadnam Co. This suggests that the market has placed more significance on the higher % growth in Holmsley Co's after-tax profits than in Cadnam Co's higher % growth in dividends, maybe seeing this as an indication that Holmsley Co's strategy has been more successful and is more likely in future to deliver higher share price growth.

(c)   **Dividend policy**

One possible question is whether the statement in the annual report fairly reflects the likely future dividend policy of Cadnam Co. The report gives the impression that the current dividend policy will be sustained, whereas the figures suggest that this may not be the case. If the policy proves not to be sustainable, it would suggest a failure either of integrity (if the directors made a statement with a high risk that it would not be true) or due care (that they failed to take into account indicators which suggested their policy is not sustainable). The directors may be questioned by the auditors about whether this statement is true and fair.

There is also the question of balancing the interests of different stakeholders. To some degree, criticism of rises in dividend and director remuneration levels versus increases in employee salary levels could be said to be a matter of opinion.

However, the fact that there is a government enquiry into low pay in the sector suggests that pay levels are lower than society deems desirable.

The dividend capacity and gearing figures may also call into question whether Cadnam Co's board is taking excessive risks. Does paying out increasing dividends in future mean that the company is likely to have inadequate resources to sustain its business, and may be jeopardising the interests of lenders and employees as well as stakeholders? Certainly there appears to be doubts about maintenance of future income levels with a number of contracts coming up for renewal and terms possibly being tightened by clients. Clients may be doubtful about renewing contracts if Cadnam Co's solvency appears doubtful.

Directors' remuneration

The directors' remuneration packages also raise concerns. Comparison with Holmsley Co shows that salary, which is not dependent on performance, is a more significant element of the remuneration packages at Cadnam Co than Holmsley Co. Both companies have bonuses which depend to some degree on performance. However, Cadnam Co's directors are also rewarded by loyalty bonuses, which again do not depend on performance but staying with the company. Holmsley Co has a share option scheme in place, which would seem to reward longer-term good performance, although it cannot be determined how significant a part of remuneration share options will be. Cadnam Co's remuneration scheme appears only to reward short-term profitability, possibly meaning that the directors may neglect the longer-term success and possibly even viability of the company.

			Marks
Marking guide			
(a)	Interest		1
	Tax		1
	Investment in additional assets		2
	Depreciation		1
			___
			5
			___
(b)	**Calculations**		
	Growth in PAT		1–2
	Dividend payout ratios		1–2
	Growth in dividends		1–2
	Residual profit		1–2
	Growth in share price		1–2
			___
	Calculations	Maximum	**5**
	Discussion		___
	Dividends		2–3
	Gearing		2
	Share price		2
			___
			10
			___
(c)	Dividend policy statement	Up to	3
	Directors' remuneration	Up to	3
		Maximum	**5**
			___
	Professional skills marks (see below)		**5**
			___
Total			**25**
			___

Professional skills marks

Analysis and Evaluation

Appropriate use of the data to determine suitable calculations

Appropriate use of the data to support discussion and draw appropriate conclusions

Appraisal of information objectively to make a recommendation

Scepticism

Effective challenge of evidence and assumptions supplied with respect to dividend policy and directors' remuneration

Commercial acumen

Effective use of examples and/or practical considerations related to the context to illustrate points being made relating to dividend policy and directors' remuneration

Maximum 5 marks

ADVANCED INVESTMENT APPRAISAL

30   FUBUKI CO (DEC 10)

Key answer tips

APV is very commonly tested. As long as you remember to use the ungeared cost of equity for discounting, the project appraisal is almost identical to a standard NPV question.

In calculating the present values of the tax shield and subsidy benefits in this model answer, the annuity factor used is based on 4.5% debt yield rate for four years. It could be argued that 7.5% may also be used as this reflects the normal borrowing/default risk of the company. Full credit was given where this assumption was made.

(a)   Base Case Net Present Value

Fubuki Co: Project Evaluation

Base Case

Units Produced and sold				1,300	1,820	2,548	2,675
	$000 Unit price/cost	**Inflation**	**Now**	**Year 1**	**Year 2**	**Year 3**	**Year 4**
Sales revenue	2.5	3%		3,250	4,687	6,758	7,308
Direct costs	1.2	8%		1,560	2,359	3,566	4,044
Attributable fixed costs	1,000	5%		1,000	1,050	1,103	1,158
Profits				690	1,278	2,089	2,106
Working capital	15%		(488)	(215)	(311)	(82)	1,096
Taxation (W1)				(10)	(157)	(360)	(364)
Incremental cash flows							
Investment/sale			(14,000)				16,000
Net cash flows			(14,488)	465	810	1,647	18,838
Present Value (10%) (W2)			(14,488)	422	670	1,237	12,867
Base case NPV			708				

Workings:

(W1)

Profits	690	1,278	2,089	2,106
Less: allowances	650	650	650	650
Taxable profits	40	628	1,439	1,456
Tax	10	157	360	364

(W2) Discount rate (Haizum's ungeared Ke)

ke(g) = ke(u) + (1– t)(ke(u) – kd)Vd/Ve

Ve = 2.53 × 15 = 37.95

Vd = 40 × 0.9488 = 37.952

Assume Vd/Ve = 1

14 = ke(u) + 0.72 × (ke(u) – 4.5) × 1

14 = 1.72ke(u) – 3.24

ke(u) = 10.02 assume 10%

Tutorial note

In calculating the ungeared cost of equity, this model answer has used the Modigliani and Miller formula from the formula sheet. The same answer could have been derived using the asset beta formula and the CAPM as follows:

CAPM: $E(r_i) = R_f + \beta_i(E(r_m) – R_f)$

So 14% = 4.5% + (β_i × 4%)

Hence β_i=2.375 (this is the equity beta)

Therefore (since there is no debt beta in this question), the asset beta is:

$$2.375 \times \frac{1}{1+1(1-0.28)} = 1.381$$

Then CAPM can be used again to give the ungeared cost of equity as:

4.5% + (1.381 × 4) = 10.02%

The base case net present value is calculated as approximately $708,000. This is positive but marginal.

The following financing side effects apply

	$000
Issue costs 4/96 × $14,488	(604)
Tax Shield	
Annual tax relief = (14,488 × 80% × 0.055 × 25%)	
+ (14,488 × 20% × 0.075 × 25%)	
= 159.4 + 54.3 = 213.7	
213.7 × 3.588	766
Subsidy benefit	
14,488 × 80% × 0.02 × 75% × 3.588	624
Total benefit of financing side effects	786
Adjusted present value (708 + 786)	1,494

The addition of the financing side effects gives an increased present value and probably the project would not be considered marginal. Once these are taken into account Fubuki Co would probably undertake the project.

(b) The adjusted present value can be used where the impact of using debt financing is significant. Here the impact of each of financing side effects from debt is shown separately rather than being imputed into the weighted average cost of capital. The project is initially evaluated by only taking into account the business risk element of the new venture. This shows that although the project results in a positive net present value, it is fairly marginal and volatility in the input factors could turn the project. Sensitivity analysis can be used to examine the sensitivity of the factors. The financing side effects show that almost 110% value is added when the positive impact of the tax shields and subsidy benefits are taken into account even after the issue costs.

Assumptions (Credit given for alternative, valid assumptions)

1   Haizum Co's ungeared cost of equity is used because it is assumed that this represents the business risk attributable to the new line of business.

2   The ungeared cost of equity is calculated on the assumption that Modigliani and Miller's (MM) proposition 2 applies.

3   It is assumed that initial working capital requirement will form part of the funds borrowed but the subsequent requirements will be available from the funds generated from the project.

4   The feasibility study is ignored as a past cost.

5   It is assumed that the five-year debt yield is equivalent to the risk-free rate,

6   It is assumed that the annual reinvestment needed on plant and machinery is equivalent to the tax allowable depreciation.

Assumptions 4, 5, 6 are standard assumptions made for a question of this nature. Assumptions 1, 2 and 3 warrant further discussion. Taking assumption 3 first, it is reasonable to assume that before the project starts, the company would need to borrow the initial working capital as it may not have access to the working capital needed. In subsequent years, the cash flows generated from the operation of the project may be sufficient to fund the extra working capital required. In the case of Fubuki Co, because of an expected rapid growth in sales in years 2 and 3, the working capital requirement remains high and the management need to assess how to make sufficient funds available.

Considering assumptions 1 and 2, the adjusted present values methodology assumes that MM proposition 2 applies and the equivalent ungeared cost of equity does not take into account the cost of financial distress. This may be an unreasonable assumption. The ungeared cost of equity is based on another company which is in a similar line of business to the new project, but it is not exactly the same. It can be difficult to determine an accurate ungeared cost of equity in practice. However, generally the discount rate (cost of funds) tends to be the least sensitive factor in investment appraisal and therefore some latitude can be allowed.

Marking scheme		Marks
(a)	Sales revenue, direct costs and additional fixed costs	3
	Incremental working capital	1
	Taxation	2
	Estimation of Ke (ungeared)	2
	Base case NPV	1
	Issue costs	1
	Calculation of tax shield impact	2
	Calculation of subsidy impact	1
	Adjusted present value and conclusion	2
		———
	Maximum	15
		———
(b)	Discussion of using APV	1–2
	Assumption about Haizum as proxy and MM proposition 2	1–2
	Other assumptions	1–2
		———
	Maximum	5
		———
	Professional skills marks (see below)	5
		———
Total		25
		———

Professional skills marks

Analysis and Evaluation

Appropriate use of the data to determine suitable calculations

Appropriate use of the data to support discussion and draw appropriate conclusions

Appraisal of information objectively to make a recommendation

Commercial acumen

Effective use of examples and/or practical considerations related to the context to illustrate points being made

Maximum 5 marks

31 MMC (JUN 11)

Key answer tips

Before calculating the value of the real option, it is important to do a basic NPV calculation for the project, in order to identify the value of Pa for the Black-Scholes formula.

(a) The $12 million initial cost will be incurred whether the option to delay is exercised or not. Therefore, since it is common to both scenarios, it can be ignored in the calculations for the moment.

Net Present Value if the project was undertaken immediately (i.e. without the option to delay the decision)

Time	0	1	2	3	4
Cash flows ($)	(35m)	25m	18m	10m	5m
PV (11%) ($)	(35m)	22.52m	14.61m	7.31m	3.29m

Net Present Value = $47.73 million – $35 million = $12.73 million

(or $0.73 million after taking account of the initial $12 million investment).

If the project were to be delayed for 2 years, the cash inflows would now run from year 3 to year 6 inclusive (rather than year 1 to year 4 as above). Therefore, the present value of the cash flows would become:

Time	3	4	5	6
Cash flows ($)	25m	18m	10m	5m
PV (11%) ($)	18.28m	11.86m	5.93m	2.68m

Present value of cash inflows = $38.75 million. This becomes P_a in the Black Scholes Option Pricing model formula.

Tutorial note

The present value of cash inflows could alternatively have been found by simply applying a 2 year discount factor (0.812 at 11%) to the existing figures.

i.e. the present value of cash inflows was $47.73 million in the original calculation, so this becomes $47.73 million × 0.812 = $38.75 million after the 2 year delay.

Value of option to delay the decision until the film is released and its popularity established. Black-Scholes Option Pricing model is used to value the call option.

Variables:

Current price (P_a) = $38.75m (see calculations above)

Exercise price (P_e) = $35m

Exercise date = 2 years

Risk free rate = 5%

Volatility = 50%

Tutorial note

Look out for the BSOP calculator spreadsheet response option in the exam. You'll need to enter the above five key variables in the spreadsheet to generate the answers shown below.

From the BSOP calculator spreadsheet, we can read off the following values:

$d_1 = 0.6389$

$d_2 = -0.0682$

$N(d_1) = 0.7386$

$N(d_2) = 0.4728$

Value of call option = $13.65 million

Value of put option = $6.56 million

The option in this case is a call option.

(b) The option to delay the decision has given MMC's managers the opportunity to monitor and respond to changing circumstances before committing to the project, such as a rise in popularity of this type of genre of films in the next two years or increased competition from similar new releases or a sustained marketing campaign launched by the film's producers before its launch.

Without taking account of the option to delay, the project has an NPV of $12.73 million, which reduces to $0.73 million when the initial $12 million investment is brought in to consideration. Although this is a positive NPV, it is quite a small positive figure, so the project is very sensitive to changes in the cash flows.

By taking account of the option to delay the project, the value of the project increases to $13.65 million (or $1.65 million after bringing in the unavoidable $12 million initial investment).

This shows that the existence of the option to delay makes the project more attractive.

Unfortunately, the option pricing formula requires numerous assumptions to be made about the variables, the primary one being the assumption of volatility. It therefore does not provide a definitive correct value but an indication of the value of the option to delay the decision.

Hence it indicates that the management should consider the project further and not dismiss it, even though current conventional net present value is quite small.

The option to delay the decision may not be the only option within the project. For example, the gaming platform that the company needs to develop for this game may have general programmes which may be used in future projects and MMC should take account of these (options to redeploy). Or if the film is successful, it may lead to follow-on projects involving games based on film sequels.

Note: Credit will be given for alternative relevant comments.

(c) A yield curve may be upward-sloping because of:

(i) **Future expectations**. If future short-term interest rates are expected to increase then the yield curve will be upward sloping.

The greater the expected future rise in interest rates, the steeper the upward-slope of the yield curve will be.

(ii) **Liquidity preference**. It is argued that investors seek extra return for giving up a degree of liquidity with longer-term investments.

Other things being equal, the longer the maturity of the investment, the higher the required return, leading to an upward-sloping yield curve.

(iii) **Preferred habitat/market segmentation**. Different investors are more active in different segments of the yield curve.

For example banks would tend to focus on the short-term end of the curve, whilst pension funds are likely to be more concerned with medium- and long-term segments.

An upward-sloping curve could in part be the result of a fall in demand in the longer-term segment of the yield curve leading to lower bond prices and higher yields.

Marking guide			
			Marks
(a)		Value of project without considering option to delay decision	2
		Pa for BSOP formula	2
		Pe for BSOP formula	1
		Other variables for BSOP formula	1
		Value of the option to delay decision (from BSOP calculator)	2
			8
(b)		1-2 marks for each well explained point	6
		Maximum	6
(c)		1-2 marks for each well explained point	6
		Maximum	6
		Professional skills marks (see below)	5
Total			25

Professional skills marks

Analysis and Evaluation

Appropriate use of the data to determine suitable calculations

Appropriate use of the data to support discussion and draw appropriate conclusions

Appraisal of information objectively to make a recommendation

Commercial acumen

Effective use of examples and/or practical considerations related to the context to illustrate points being made

Maximum 5 marks

32   TISA CO (JUN 12)

Key answer tips

Don't waste time here calculating NPVs, or IRR and MIRR for project Zeta. You are given the IRR and MIRR figures for Zeta to compare with your figures for Omega in part (b).

(a)   Use Elfu Co's information to estimate the component project's asset beta. Then based on Tisa Co's capital structure, estimate the component project's equity beta and weighted average cost of capital. Assume that the beta of debt is zero.

Elfu Co MVe = $1.20 × 400m shares = $480m

Elfu Co MVd = $96m

Elfu Co portfolio asset beta =

$1.40 \times \$480m/(\$480m + \$96m \times (1 - 0.25)) = 1.217$

Elfu Co asset beta of other activities =

$1.25 \times \$360m/(\$360m + \$76.8m \times (1 - 0.25)) = 1.078$

1.217 = component asset beta $\times 0.25 + 1.078 \times 0.75$

Component asset beta = $[1.217 - (1.078 \times 0.75)]/0.25 = 1.634$

Component equity beta based on Tisa Co capital structure =

$1.634 \times [(\$18m + \$3.6m \times 0.75)/\$18m] = 1.879$

Using CAPM, component Ke = $3.5\% + 1.879 \times 5.8\% = 14.40\%$

Component WACC = $(14.40\% \times \$18m + 4.5\% \times \$3.6m)/(\$18m + \$3.6m) = 12.75\%$

Tutorial note

When attempting a question like this in the Computer Based Exam (CBE), make sure you use the spreadsheet functions IRR and MIRR to save time.

The IRR function is especially useful and time-saving. Simply enter =IRR and then brackets containing the spreadsheet cell references of all the project's undiscounted cashflows.

Be careful with the MIRR function though. After =MIRR, the brackets need to contain the spreadsheet cell references of all the project's undiscounted cashflows, and also the company's financing rate and reinvestment rate (usually both the same).

(b) **Process Omega**

Year	0	1	2	3	4
Net cash flows ($000)	(3,800)	1,220	1,153	1,386	3,829
PV 12.75% ($000)	(3,800)	1,082	907	967	2,369
NPV ($000)	1,525				
PV 30%	(3,800)	938	682	631	1,341
NPV ($000)	(208)				

Internal rate of return is approximately 27.3%

Modified internal rate of return (MIRR) is approximately 22.7%

$([[(5,325/3,800)^{1/4} \times (1.1275)] - 1)$

The internal rate of return (IRR) assumes that positive cash flows in earlier years are reinvested at the IRR and therefore process Omega, which has higher initial cash flows when compared to process Zeta, gives a slightly higher IRR.

The modified internal rate of return (MIRR) assumes that positive cash flows are reinvested at the cost of capital. This is a more reasonable assumption and produces a result consistent with the net present value.

Overall, process Zeta should be adopted (although the difference is not significant).

[**Note:** Using 13% instead of 12.75% as the cost of capital is acceptable]

(c) 99% confidence level requires the value at risk (VAR) to be within 2.33 standard deviations from the mean, based on a single tail measure.

Annual VAR = 2.33 × $800,000 = $1,864,000

Five year VAR = $1,864,000 × $5^{1/2}$ approx. = $4,168,000

The figures mean that Elfu Co can be 99% confident that the cash flows will not fall by more than $1,864,000 in any one year and $4,168,000 in total over five years from the average returns. Therefore the company can be 99% certain that the returns will be $336,000 or more every year [$2,200,000 – $1,864,000]. And it can be 99% certain that the returns will be $6,832,000 or more in total over the five-year period [$11,000,000 – $4,168,000]. There is a 1% chance that the returns will be less than $336,000 each year or $6,832,000 over the five-year period.

Marking scheme		Marks
(a)	Reasoning behind cost of capital calculation	2
	Calculation of component asset beta	3
	Calculation of component equity beta, and Ke and WACC	3
		8
(b)	Calculation of IRR for Process Omega	2
	Calculation of MIRR for Process Omega	2
	Recommendation and explanation of the recommendation	4
		8
(c)	Annual and five-year VAR	2
	Explanation	2
		4
	Professional skills marks (see below)	**5**
Total		**25**

Professional skills marks

Analysis and Evaluation

Appropriate use of the data to determine suitable calculations

Appropriate use of the data to support discussion and draw appropriate conclusions

Appraisal of information objectively to make a recommendation

Scepticism

Effective challenge of information, evidence and assumptions supplied and, techniques carried out to support key facts and/or decisions

Demonstration of ability to consider all relevant factors

Commercial acumen

Recommendations are practical and plausible in the context of Tisa Co's situation

Effective use of examples and/or calculations from the scenario information and other practical considerations related to the context to illustrate points being made

Maximum 5 marks

33   COEDEN CO (DEC 12)

Key answer tips

Weighted average cost of capital is a key syllabus area. Invariably, the calculation of cost of capital will involve degearing and/or regearing given beta factors and using the CAPM equation. It is vital that you have practised the calculations so that you are able to manipulate the beta factors quickly.

(a)   Before implementing the proposal

Cost of equity = 4% + 1.1 × 6% = 10.6%

Cost of debt = 4% + 0.9% = 4.9%

Market value of debt (MV$_d$):

Per $100: $5.2 × 1.049^{-1} + $5.2 × 1.049^{-2} + $105.2 × 1.049^{-3} = $100.82

Total value = $42,000,000 × $100.82/$100 = $42,344,400

Market value of equity (MV$_e$):

As share price is not given, use the free cash flow growth model to estimate this. The question states that the free cash flow to equity model provides a reasonable estimate of the current market value of the company.

Assumption 1: Estimate growth rate using the g=rb model. The assumption here is that free cash flows to equity which are retained will be invested to yield at least at the rate of return required by the company's shareholders. This is the estimate of how much the free cash flows to equity will grow by each year.

r = 10.6% and b = 0.4, therefore g is estimated at 10.6% × 0.4 = 4.24%

MV$_e$ = 2,600 × 1.0424/(0.106 – 0.0424) approximately = $42,614,000

The proportion of MV$_e$ to MV$_d$ is approximately 50:50

Therefore, cost of capital:

10.6% × 0.5 + 4.9% × 0.5 × 0.8 = 7.3%

After implementing the proposal

Coeden Co, asset beta estimate

1.1 × 0.5/(0.5 + 0.5 × 0.8) = 0.61

Asset beta, hotel services only

Assumption 2: The question does not provide an asset beta for hotel services only, which is the approximate measure of Coeden Co's business risk once the properties are sold. Assume that Coeden Co's asset beta is a weighted average of the property companies' average beta and hotel services beta.

Asset beta of hotel services only:

0.61 = Asset beta (hotel services) × 60% + 0.4 × 40% Asset beta (hotel services only) approximately = 0.75

Coeden Co, hotel services only, estimate of equity beta:

MV_e = $42,614,000 (Based on the assumption stated in the question)

MV_d = Per $100: 5.2×1.046^{-1} + 5.2×1.046^{-2} + 105.2×1.046^{-3} = $101.65

Total value = $12,600,000 \times $101.65/$100 = $12,807,900 say $12,808,000

0.75 = equity beta $\times$ 42,614/(42,614 + 12,808 $\times$ 0.8)

0.75 = equity beta $\times$ 0.806

Equity beta = 0.93

Coeden Co, hotel services only, weighted average cost of capital

Cost of equity = 4% + 0.93 $\times$ 6% = 9.6%

Cost of capital = 9.6% $\times$ 0.769 + 4.6% $\times$ 0.231 $\times$ 0.8 = 8.2%

Comment:

	Before proposal implementation	**After proposal implementation**
Cost of equity	10.6%	9.6%
WACC	7.3%	8.2%

Implementing the proposal would increase the asset beta of Coeden Co because the hotel services industry on its own has a higher business risk than a business which owns its own hotels as well. However, the equity beta and cost of equity both decrease because of the fall in the level of debt and the consequent reduction in the company's financial risk. The company's cost of capital increases because the lower debt level reduces the extent to which the weighted average cost of capital can be reduced due to the lower cost of debt. Hence the board of directors is not correct in assuming that the lower level of debt will reduce the company's cost of capital.

(b)   It is unlikely that the market value of equity would remain unchanged because of the change in the growth rate of free cash flows and sales revenue, and the change in the risk situation due to the changes in the business and financial risks of the new business.

In estimating the asset beta of Coeden Co as offering hotel services only, no account is taken of the changes in business risk due to renting rather than owning the hotels. A revised asset beta may need to be estimated due to changes in the business risk.

The market value of equity is used to estimate the equity beta and the cost of equity of the business after the implementation of the proposal. But the market value of equity is dependent on the cost of equity, which is, in turn, dependent on the equity beta. Therefore, neither the cost of equity nor the market value of equity is independent of each other and they both will change as a result of the change in business strategy.

Marking guide			
			Marks
(a)	**Before**		
	Cost of equity		1
	Cost of debt		1
	MV debt		2
	MV equity		2
	WACC		1
	After		
	Coeden Co's current asset beta		1
	Asset beta of hotel services business only		2
	Equity beta of hotel services business only		2
	Cost of equity		1
	Cost of capital		1
	1 mark per assumption stated		2-3
	Comments		1-2
		Maximum	16
(b)	Discussion (1–2 marks per point)		4
		Maximum	4
	Professional skills marks (see below)		5
Total			25

Professional skills marks

Analysis and Evaluation

Appropriate use of the data to determine suitable calculations

Appropriate use of the data to support discussion and draw appropriate conclusions

Appraisal of information objectively to make a recommendation

Scepticism

Effective challenge of information supplied to support key facts and/or decisions

Commercial acumen

Effective use of examples and/or practical considerations related to the context to illustrate points being made

Maximum 5 marks

34   BURUNG CO (JUN 14)

Key answer tips

This question presented the investment appraisal as part of the question, and asked for the necessary corrections to be made.

This sort of question is an excellent test of whether you really understand the topic. A student with only a vague understanding of APV would have really struggled to pick out the subtle mistakes.

(a)   All figures are in $ million

Year	0	1	2	3	4
Sales revenue (inflated, 8% p.a.)		24.87	42.69	61.81	36.92
Costs (inflated, 4% p.a.)		(14.37)	(23.75)	(33.12)	(19.05)
		———	———	———	———
Incremental profit		10.50	18.94	28.69	17.87
Tax (W1)		(0.50)	(3.39)	(5.44)	(3.47)
Investment/sale of machinery	(38.00)				4.00
		———	———	———	———
Cash flows	(38.00)	10.00	15.55	23.25	18.40
Discount factors (12%, W2)	1	0.893	0.797	0.712	0.636
		———	———	———	———
Present values	(38.00)	8.93	12.39	16.55	11.70
		———	———	———	———

Base case net present value is approximately $11.57 million.

(W1)   All figures are in $ million

Year	0	1	2	3	4
Incremental profit		10.50	18.94	28.69	17.87
Tax allowable depreciation		8.00	2.00	1.50	0.50
		——	——	——	——
Taxable profit		2.50	16.94	27.19	17.37
		——	——	——	——
Tax (20%)		0.50	3.39	5.44	3.47
		——	——	——	——

(W2) Lintu Co asset beta = 1.5 × $128m/($128m + $31.96m × 0.8) approx. = 1.25

All-equity financed discount rate = 2% + 1.25 × 8% = 12%

Financing side effects

	$000
Issue costs 2/98 × $38,000,000	(775.51)

Tax shield

$$\text{Annual tax relief} = (\$38,000,000 \times 60\% \times 0.015 \times 20\%)$$
$$+ (\$38,000,000 \times 40\% \times 0.04 \times 20\%)$$
$$= 68.40 + 121.60 = 190$$

	$000
The present value of the tax relief annuity = 190 × 3.63	689.70

Annual subsidy benefit

$$\$38,000,000 \times 60\% \times 0.025 \times 80\% = 456$$

	$000
The present value of the subsidy benefit annuity = 456 × 3.63	1,655.28
Total benefit of financing side effects	1,569.47

Financing the project entirely by debt would add just under $1.57 million to the value of the project, or approximately, an additional 13.5% to the all-equity financed project.

The adjusted present value (APV) of the project is $13.14 million and therefore it should be accepted.

Examiner's note

In calculating the present values of the tax shield and subsidy benefits, the annuity factor used is based on 4% to reflect the normal borrowing/default risk of the company.

Alternatively, 2% or 2.5% could be used depending on the assumptions made. Credit will be given where these are used to estimate the annuity factor, where the assumption is explained.

(b)   **Corrections made to the original net present value**

The approach taken to exclude depreciation from the net present value computation is correct, but tax allowable depreciation needs to be taken away from profit estimates before tax is calculated, reducing the profits on which tax is payable.

Interest is not normally included in the net present value calculations. Instead, it is normally imputed within the cost of capital or discount rate. In this case, it is included in the financing side effects.

Cash flows are inflated and the nominal rate based on Lintu Co's all-equity financed rate is used (see below). Where different cash flows are subject to different rates of inflation, applying a real rate to non-inflated amounts would not give an accurate answer.

Approach taken

The value of the project is initially assessed considering only the business risk involved in undertaking the project. The discount rate used is based on Lintu Co's asset beta which measures only the business risk of that company. Since Lintu Co is in the same line of business as the project, it is deemed appropriate to use its discount rate, instead of 11% which Burung Co uses normally.

The impact of debt financing and the subsidy benefit are then considered. In this way, Burung Co can assess the value created from its investment activity and then the additional value created from the manner in which the project is financed.

NSWERS TO PRACTICE QUESTIONS – SECTION B: SECTION 4

Assumptions made

It is assumed that all figures used are accurate and any estimates made are reasonable. Burung Co may want to consider undertaking a sensitivity analysis to assess this.

It is assumed that Lintu Co's asset beta and all-equity financed discount rate represent the business risk of the project. The validity of this assumption needs to be assessed. For example, Lintu Co's entire business may not be similar to the project, and it may undertake other lines of business. In this case, the asset beta would need to be adjusted so that just the project's business risk is considered.

Note: Credit will be given for alternative, relevant explanations.

	Marking scheme	
		Marks
(a)	Inflated incremental profit	2
	Taxation	2
	Estimate of discount rate	2
	Net present value	1
	Issue costs	1
	Tax shield benefit	2
	Subsidy benefit	1
	Adjusted present value and conclusion	2
		───
		13
		───
(b)	Corrections made	2–3
	Approach taken	2–3
	Assumptions made	2–3
		───
		7
		───
	Professional skills marks (see below)	5
		───
Total		**25**
		───

Professional skills marks

Analysis and Evaluation

Appropriate use of the data to determine suitable calculations

Appropriate use of the data to support discussion and draw appropriate conclusions

Appraisal of information objectively to make a recommendation

Scepticism

Demonstration of ability to consider all relevant factors

Commercial acumen

Effective use of examples and/or practical considerations related to the context to illustrate points being made

Maximum 5 marks

35 RIVIERE CO (DEC 14)

Key answer tips

Value at Risk is often perceived to be a tricky topic. Remember to multiply by the square root of 5 to extend your calculation from one year to five years.

Don't worry if you find the mathematics involved in Value at Risk complex. There are plenty of easier, discursive marks in this question if you have a good exam technique.

(a) **Project Drugi**

Internal rate of return (IRR)

10% NPV: €2,293,000 approximately

Year	Current	1	2	3	4	5
Cash flows (€000s)	(11,840)	1,230	1,680	4,350	10,240	2,200
Try 20%		0.833	0.694	0.579	0.482	0.402
	(11,840)	1,025	1,166	2,519	4,936	884

NPV = €(1,310,000)

IRR = 10% + 2,293/(2,293 + 1,310) × 10% approximately = 16.4%

Tutorial note

When attempting a question like this in the Computer Based Exam (CBE), make sure you use the spreadsheet functions IRR and MIRR to save time.

The IRR function is especially useful and time-saving. Simply enter =IRR and then brackets containing the spreadsheet cell references of all the project's undiscounted cashflows.

Be careful with the MIRR function though. After =MIRR, the brackets need to contain the spreadsheet cell references of all the project's undiscounted cashflows, and also the company's financing rate and reinvestment rate (usually both the same).

Modified internal rate of return (MIRR)

Total PVs years 1 to 5 at 10% discount rate = €11,840,000 + €2,293,000 = €14,133,000

MIRR (using formula) = $[(14,133/11,840)^{1/5} \times 1.10] - 1 = 14\%$

Value at risk (VAR)

Based on a single tail test:

A 95% confidence level requires the annual present value VAR to be within approximately 1.645 standard deviations from the mean.

A 90% confidence level requires annual present value VAR to be within approximately 1.282 standard deviations from the mean.

Note: An approximation of standard deviations to two decimal places is acceptable.

95%, five-year present value VAR = $400,000 × 1.645 × 5^{0.5} = approx. €1,471,000

90%, five-year present value VAR = $400,000 × 1.282 × 5^{0.5} = approx. €1,147,000

	Privi	**Drugi**
Net present value (10%)	€2,054,000	€2,293,000
Internal rate of return	17.6%	16.4%
Modified internal rate of return	13.4%	14.0%
VAR (over the project's life)		
95% confidence level	€1,103,500	€1,471,000
90% confidence level	€860,000	€1,147,000

The net present value and the modified internal rate of return both indicate that project Drugi would create more value for Riviere Co. However, the internal rate of return (IRR) for project Privi is higher. Where projects are mutually exclusive, the IRR can give an incorrect answer. This is because the IRR assumes that returns are re-invested at the internal rate of return, whereas net present value and the modified IRR assume that they are re-invested at the cost of capital (discount rate) which in this case is 10%. The cost of capital is a more realistic assumption as this is the minimum return required by investors in a company. Furthermore, the manner in which the cash flows occur will have a bearing on the IRR calculated. For example, with project Drugi, a high proportion of the cash flows occur in year four and these will be discounted by using the higher IRR compared to the cost of capital, thus reducing the value of the project faster. The IRR can give the incorrect answer in these circumstances. Therefore, based purely on cash flows, project Drugi should be accepted due to the higher net present value and modified IRR, as they give the theoretically correct answer of the value created.

The VAR provides an indication of the potential riskiness of a project. For example, if Riviere Co invests in project Drugi then it can be 95% confident that the present value will not fall by more than €1,471,000 over its life. Hence the project will still produce a positive net present value. However, there is a 5% chance that the loss could be greater than €1,471,000. With project Privi, the potential loss in value is smaller and therefore it is less risky. It should be noted that the VAR calculations indicate that the investments involve different risk. However, the cash flows are discounted at the same rate, which they should not be, since the risk differs between them.

Notwithstanding that, when risk is also taken into account, the choice between the projects is not clear cut and depends on Riviere Co's attitude to risk and return. Project Drugi gives the higher potential net present value but is riskier, whereas project Privi is less risky but gives a smaller net present value. This is before taking into account additional uncertainties such as trading in an area in which Riviere Co is not familiar. It is therefore recommended that Riviere Co should only proceed with project Drugi if it is willing to accept the higher risk and uncertainty.

(b)   Possible legal risks

There are a number of possible legal risks which Riviere Co may face, for example:

- The countries where the product is sold may have different legal regulations on food preparation, quality and packaging.

- The company needs to ensure that the production processes and the transportation of the frozen foods comply with these regulations. It also needs to ensure that the promotional material on the packaging complies with regulations in relation to what is acceptable in each country.

- The legal regulations may be more lax in countries outside the EU but Riviere Co needs to be aware that complying only with the minimum standards may impact its image negatively overall, even if they are acceptable in the countries concerned.

- There may be import quotas in the countries concerned or the governments may give favourable terms and conditions to local companies, which may make it difficult for Riviere Co to compete.

- The legal system in some countries may not recognise the trademarks or production patents which the company holds on its packaging and production processes. This may enable competitors to copy the food and the packaging.

- Different countries may have different regulations regarding product liability from poorly prepared and/or stored food which cause harm to consumers. For example, Riviere Co may use other companies to transport its food and different supermarkets may sell its food. It needs to be aware of the potential legal claims on it and its supplier should the food prove harmful to the customers.

Possible mitigation strategies

- Riviere Co needs to undertake sufficient research of the countries' current laws and regulations to ensure that it complies with the standards required. It may even want to ensure that it exceeds the required standards to ensure that it maintains its reputation.

- Riviere Co needs to ensure that it also keeps abreast of potential changes in the law. It may also want to ensure that it complies with best practice, even if it is not the law yet. Often current best practices become enshrined in future legislation.

- Riviere Co needs to investigate the extent to which it may face difficulty in overcoming quota restrictions, less favourable trading conditions and lack of trademark and patent protection. If necessary, these should be factored into the financial analysis. It could be that Riviere Co has already taken these into account.

- Strict contracts need to be set up between Riviere Co and any agents it uses to transport and sell the food. These could be followed up by regular checks to ensure that the standards required are maintained.

- All the above will add extra costs and if these have not been included in the financial analysis, they need to be. These extra costs may mean that the project is no longer viable.

	Marking scheme		
			Marks
(a)	Calculation of IRR and MIRR (2 each)		4
	Determining the two standard deviations (1.645 and 1.282)		1
	Calculations of the two value at risk figures		2
	Explanation of weakness of IRR and why NPV and MIRR are better		2–3
	Explanation of value at risk figures and what they indicate		2–3
	Recommendation		1–2
		Maximum	13
(b)	Discussion of possible legal risks		3–4
	Discussion of how these may be mitigated		3–4
		Maximum	7
	Professional skills marks (see below)		5
Total			25

Professional skills marks

Analysis and Evaluation

Appropriate use of the data to determine suitable calculations

Appropriate use of the data to support discussion and draw appropriate conclusions

Appraisal of information objectively to make a recommendation

Scepticism

Effective challenge of information, evidence and assumptions supplied and, techniques carried out to support key facts and/or decisions

Demonstration of ability to consider all relevant factors

Commercial acumen

Recommendations are practical and plausible in the context of Riviere Co's situation

Effective use of examples and/or calculations from the scenario information and other practical considerations related to the context to illustrate points being made

Maximum 5 marks

36 FURLION CO (MAR/JUN 16)

Key answer tips

The Black-Scholes option pricing model is regularly tested, especially in the context of real options.

Most of the input factors for the model are easy to pick up from the question text, but take care with the Pa ('value of the underlying asset'). In real options theory, the Pa is the present value of all the expected cash flows from the project, excluding the initial investment.

(a) **Value of option to expand**

Variables

Volatility = 30%

Current price (value of project including option exercise price)

= $15m × 0.712 = $10.68m

Exercise price (capital expenditure) = $15m

Exercise date = 3 years

Risk free rate = 4%

Tutorial note

Look out for the BSOP calculator spreadsheet response option in the exam. You'll need to enter the above five key variables in the spreadsheet to generate the answers shown below.

From the BSOP calculator spreadsheet, we can read off the following values:

$d_1 = -0.1630$

$d_2 = -0.6826$

$N(d_1) = 0.4353$

$N(d_2) = 0.2474$

Value of call option = $1.36 million

Value of put option = $3.98 million

The option in this case is a call option.

Overall value = $1.36m – $1.01m = $0.35m

The investment has a positive net present value, so should be accepted on those grounds. Furlion Co should also consider the value of an abandonment option if results turn out to be worse than expected or a delay option if it wants to see how the reclamation programme is going to continue.

Assumptions made and other factors

Using real options for decision-making has limitations. Real options are built around uncertainties surrounding future cash flows, but real option theory is only useful if management can respond effectively to these uncertainties as they evolve. The Black-Scholes model for valuing real options has a number of assumptions which may not be true in practice. It assumes that there is a market for the underlying asset and the volatility of returns on the underlying asset follows a normal distribution. The model also assumes perfect markets, a constant risk-free interest rate and constant volatility.

Furlion Co will also consider expectations about the future of the land reclamation programme. Has the programme been as quick and as effective as the Naswan government originally expected? Furlion Co will also want to consider how the programme will be affected by the amount of funding the government obtains and any conditions attached to that funding.

Furlion Co may also wish to consider whether its investment of this type will be looked on favourably by the Naswan government and whether tax or other concessions will be available. These may come with conditions, given the government's commitment to a sustainable economy, such as the way production facilities operate or the treatment of employees.

Given that this is a market which may expand in the future, Furlion Co should also consider the reaction of competitors. This may be a market where establishing a significant presence quickly may provide a significant barrier if competitors try to enter the market later.

As the investment is for the manufacture of specialist equipment, it is possible that there is insufficient skilled labour in the local labour pool in Naswa. As well as training local labour, supervision is likely to be required, at least initially, from staff based in other countries. This may involve cultural issues such as different working practices.

(b)   Interest rates tend to move quite slowly, so the interest rate is not usually a significant influence on the option's value, particularly for short-term options.

However, many real options are longer term, so the impact of any change will be more significant than for short-term options. A change in interest rates will be more significant the longer the time until expiry of an option.

In addition, there are possible indirect economic effects of interest rate changes, such as on the return demanded by finance providers and hence on the cost of capital.

(c)   The World Bank provides loans, often direct to governments, on a commercial basis, for capital projects. Loans are generally for a long-term period, which may suit the Naswan government. However, the terms of the loan may be onerous, not just the finance costs but the other conditions imposed on the scope of the projects.

Given the circumstances of the investment, Naswa may be able to obtain assistance from the International Development Association, which is part of the World Bank. This provides loans on more generous terms to the poorest countries. However, it is designed for countries with very high credit risk which would struggle to obtain funding by other means, and Naswa may not be eligible.

Marking scheme			
			Marks
(a)	Current price variable (Pa) in BSOP formula		1
	Other variables in BSOP formula		1
	Value of the option to expand decision		1
	Revised value of projects and comments	Max	3
	Assumptions	Max	4
	Other factors	Max	4
		Maximum	**12**
(b)	1-2 marks per well explained relevant point		3
		Maximum	**3**
(c)	Role of World Bank		1
	Usefulness of World Bank as a source of finance		1–2
	Role of IDA		1
	Usefulness of IDA as a source of finance		1–2
		Maximum	**5**
	Professional skills marks (see below)		**5**
Total			**25**

Professional skills marks

Analysis and Evaluation

Appropriate use of the data to determine suitable calculations

Appropriate use of the data to support discussion and draw appropriate conclusions

Appraisal of information objectively to make a recommendation

Scepticism

Effective challenge of information and assumptions supplied and techniques carried out to support any investment decision.

Commercial acumen

Recognition of external constraints and opportunities as necessary.

Maximum 5 marks

37   FERNHURST CO (SEP/DEC 16)

Key answer tips

This is a very standard investment appraisal question.

Note that part (a) requires you to calculate duration as well as NPV, but once you have forecast the free cash flows from the project this should be a simple extra step.

Part (b) covered some important issues relating to investment appraisal too – balancing short term and long term perspectives.

Tutorial note

When attempting a question like this in the Computer Based Exam (CBE), make sure you use the spreadsheet functions SUM and NPV to save time. Be careful when using the NPV function to enter =NPV, then a bracket containing the discount rate, a comma, and then the cells containing the cash flows from year 1 onwards. The initial investment then needs to be subtracted separately.

(a)

	0	1	2	3	4
	$000	$000	$000	$000	$000
Sales revenue (W1)		13,250	16,695	22,789	23,928
Variable costs (W2)		(5,788)	(7,292)	(9,954)	(10,452)
Contribution		7,462	9,403	12,835	13,476
Marketing expenditure		(1,500)			
Fixed costs		(900)	(945)	(992)	(1,042)
Tax-allowable depreciation (W3)		(3,200)	(2,560)	(2,048)	(8,192)
Taxable profits/(losses)		1,862	5,898	9,795	4,242
Taxation (25%)		(466)	(1,475)	(2,449)	(1,061)
Add back tax-allowable depreciation		3,200	2,560	2,048	8,192
Cash flows after tax		4,596	6,983	9,394	11,373
Initial investment	(16,000)				
Working capital	(1,025)	(41)	(53)	(56)	1,175
Cash flows	(17,025)	4,555	6,930	9,338	12,548
Discount factor	1.000	0.901	0.812	0.731	0.659
Present values	(17,025)	4,104	5,627	6,826	8,269
Net present value	7,801				

The NPV is positive, which indicates the project should be undertaken.

Workings:

(W1) Sales revenue

Year

		$000
1	$132{,}500 \times 100$	13,250
2	$132{,}500 \times 100 \times 1.05 \times 1.2$	16,695
3	$132{,}500 \times 100 \times 1.05^2 \times 1.2 \times 1.3$	22,789
4	$132{,}500 \times 100 \times 1.05^3 \times 1.2 \times 1.3$	23,928

(W2) Variable costs

Year

		$m
1	$132{,}500 \times 43.68$	5,788
2	$132{,}500 \times 43.68 \times 1.05 \times 1.2$	7,292
3	$132{,}500 \times 43.68 \times 1.05^2 \times 1.2 \times 1.3$	9,954
4	$132{,}500 \times 43.68 \times 1.05^3 \times 1.2 \times 1.3$	10,452

(W3) Tax allowable depreciation

Year

		$000
		16,000
1	Tax-allowable depreciation	(3,200)
		———
		12,800
2	Tax-allowable depreciation	(2,560)
		———
		10,240
3	Tax-allowable depreciation	(2,048)
		———
		8,192
4	Balancing allowance	(8,192)
		———
		0
		———

Duration

Year	1	2	3	4
Present value $000	4,104	5,627	6,826	8,269
Percentage of total PV	16.5%	22.7%	27.5%	33.3%

Duration = $(1 \times 0.165) + (2 \times 0.227) + (3 \times 0.275) + (4 \times 0.333) = 2.78$ years

The result indicates that it will take approximately 2.78 years to recover half the present value of the project. Duration considers the time value of money and all of the cash flows of a project.

(b) The non-executive director has highlighted the importance of long-term maximisation of shareholders' wealth. The net present value is the most important indicator of whether an investment is likely to do that. However, the assessment of investments using net present value has to be modified if the company is undertaking a number of different investments and capital is rationed. It is not necessarily the case that the investments with the highest net present value will be chosen, as account has to be taken of the amount of capital invested as well.

However, investors are not necessarily concerned solely with the long term. They are also concerned about short-term indicators, such as the annual dividend which the company can sustain. They may be concerned if the company's investment portfolio is weighted towards projects which will produce good long-term returns, but limited returns in the near future.

Risk will also influence shareholders' views. They may prefer investments where a higher proportion of returns are made in the shorter term, if they feel that longer term returns are much more uncertain. The NPV calculation itself discounts longer term cash flows more than shorter term cash flows.

The payback method shows how long an investment will take to generate enough returns to pay back its investment. It favours investments which pay back quickly, although it fails to take into account longer term cash flows after the payback period. Duration is a better measure of the distribution of cash flows, although it may be less easy for shareholders to understand.

Marking scheme		
		Marks
(a)	Sales revenue	2
	Variable costs	2
	Fixed costs	1
	Tax-allowable depreciation	2
	Tax payable	1
	Working capital	2
	NPV of project	1
	Comment on NPV	1
	Duration calculation	2
	Comment on duration	1
		15
		5
(b)	Significance of net present value	1–2
	Shareholders' attitude to the longer and shorter term	2–3
	Timeframe measures	1–2
	Maximum	5
	Professional skills marks (see below)	5
Total		25

Professional skills marks

Analysis and Evaluation

Appropriate use of the data to determine suitable calculations

Appropriate use of the data to support discussion and draw appropriate conclusions

Appraisal of information objectively to make a recommendation

Scepticism

Effective challenge of information, evidence and assumptions supplied and, techniques carried out to support key facts and/or decisions

Demonstration of ability to consider all relevant factors

Commercial acumen

Recommendations are practical and plausible in the context of Fernhurst Co's situation

Effective use of examples and/or calculations from the scenario information and other practical considerations related to the context to illustrate points being made

Maximum 5 marks

38   TIPPLETINE CO (MAR/JUN 18)

Key answer tips

APV is very commonly tested. Make sure that you use the ungeared cost of equity to discount the project cash flows and the risk free rate (or pre-tax cost of debt) to discount the financing cash flows.

(a)

Year	0	1	2	3	4	5
	$000	$000	$000	$000	$000	$000
Operating cash flow excluding marketing costs		2,000	14,500	15,225	15,834	
Marketing costs		(9,000)	(2,000)	(2,000)	(2,000)	
Cash flow before tax		(7,000)	12,500	13,225	13,834	
Taxation (W1)					(310)	(4,328)
Investment	(30,600)				13,500	
Working capital (W2)	(3,000)	(240)	(194)	(172)	3,606	
Cashflows	(33,600)	(7,240)	12,306	13,053	30,630	(4,328)
Discount factor 9% (W3)	1.000	0.917	0.842	0.772	0.708	0.650
Discounted cash flows	(33,600)	(6,639)	10,362	10,077	21,686	(2,813)
Base case NPV	(927)					

1   Taxation

Year	TAD = Tax-allowable depreciation	Balance
		$000
	Investment	30,600
1	TAD 25% reducing balance	(7,650)
		22,950
2	TAD 25% reducing balance	(5,738)
		17,212
3	TAD 25% reducing balance	(4,303)
		12,909
4	Balancing charge	591
		13,500

Year	1	2	3	4
	$000	$000	$000	$000
Cash flow before tax	(7,000)	12,500	13,225	13,834
Tax-allowable depreciation	(7,650)	(5,738)	(4,303)	591
Adjusted cash flow	(14,650)	6,762	8,922	14,425
Offset against previous losses		(14,650)	(7,888)	
Losses carried forward	(14,650)	(7,888)		
Taxable cash flow			1,034	14,425
Taxation at 30%			310	4,328
Year			4	5

2   Working capital

Year	1	2	3	4
	$000	$000	$000	$000
	3,000 × 0.08 = 240	(3,000 + 240) × 0.06 = 194	(3,000 + 240 + 194) × 0.05 = 172	3,000 + 240 + 194 + 172 = 3,606

3   Ungeared cost of equity

Humabuz Co

MV debt = $225 million × 1.07 = $240.8 million

MV equity = 125 million × $3.20 = $400 million

Ungeared cost of equity

$$k_e = k_e^i + (1 - t)\,(k_e^i - k_d)\,V_D/V_E$$

$$10.5\% = k_e^i + (1 - 0.3)\big(k_e^i - 5.4\%\big)\,(240.8/400)$$

$$10.5\% + 2.28\% = 1.42\,k_e^i$$

$$k_e^i = 9\%$$

4   Issue costs

Debt: ($30,600,000/0.96) = $31,875,000

Debt issue costs: $31,875,000 × 0.04 = $1,275,000

5   Tax shield on loan

Use PV of an annuity (PVA) for years 2 – 5 at 5% (assume 5% is cost of debt).

Tutorial note

The risk-free rate of 2.5% could also have been used for discounting the financing cash flows.

Subsidised loan: $30,600,000 × (0.025 − 0.003) × 0.3 × (4.329 − 0.952) = $682,000

6   Subsidy

Benefit = $30,600,000 × (0.05 − 0.022) × 3.546 = $3,038,000

Tax relief lost = $30,600,000 × (0.05 − 0.022) × 0.3 × (4.329 − 0.952) = $868,000

7   Financing side effects

	$000
Issue costs (W4)	(1,275)
Tax shield on loan (W5)	682
Subsidy benefit (W6)	3,038
Tax relief lost on subsidy benefit (W6)	(868)
Total benefit of financing side effects	1,577

Conclusion

If base case net present value is used, the project has a negative net present value of $927,000 and on that basis should be rejected. However, the financing side effects add $1,577,000 to the value of the project, giving a positive adjusted present value of $650,000. On that basis the project should be accepted. The revenues from the project appear to be uncertain and the realisable value at the end of the project may be optimistic. It would be useful to have an indication of the range of outcomes and an idea of the probability that the project will have a negative APV.

Tutorial note

When attempting a question like this in the Computer Based Exam (CBE), make sure you use the spreadsheet functions SUM and NPV to save time. Be careful when using the NPV function to enter =NPV, then a bracket containing the discount rate, a comma, and then the cells containing the cash flows from year 1 onwards. The initial investment then needs to be subtracted separately.

(b)   Advantages of convertible loan notes

The investors may be happy that directors are demonstrating their commitment to the company by subscribing to convertible loan notes. The conversion rights mean that these directors will benefit if the share price increases, aligning their interests with shareholders.

The conversion terms also mean that the loan notes will not necessarily have to be repaid in a few years' time. This may be significant if Tippletine Co does not have the cash available for redemption then.

Drawbacks of convertible loan notes

The convertible loan notes would be treated as debt, increasing Tippletine Co's gearing, which may concern the other shareholders. The interest on the convertible loan notes will be payable before dividends and may leave less money for distribution to shareholders. Shareholders may doubt whether the higher interest burden on the convertible loan notes compared with the subsidised loan is compensated for by the lower costs of Tippletine Co not having to fulfil the government's requirements.

The other shareholders may be concerned by the interest rate on the convertible notes being Tippletine Co's normal cost of borrowing. The option to convert is an advantage for convertible loan note holders. They would often effectively pay for this option by receiving a lower rate of interest on the loan notes.

Shareholders would want to assess how likely conversion would be, that is how likely it would be the share price will rise above $2.75. The option to convert may also change the balance of shareholdings, giving the directors who held the notes a greater percentage of share capital and possibly more influence over Tippletine Co. The other shareholders may be unhappy with this.

The shareholders may also have reservations about the loan note holders having the option to redeem if Tippletine Co's share price is low. This reduces the risk of providing the finance from the loan note holders' viewpoint. However, if the share price is low, Tippletine Co's financial results and cash flows may be poor and it may struggle to redeem the loan notes. Shareholders may also be concerned that there is no cap the other way, allowing Tippletine Co to force conversion if the share price reaches a high enough level.

Tutorial note

The marking scheme here allowed for credit to be given for any alternative but relevant discussion.

Marking guide		
		Marks
(a)	Tax allowable depreciation	1
	Taxation	2
	Working capital	2
	Discount factor	2
	Base case N PV	1
	Issue costs	1
	Tax shield on loan	2
	Subsidy	1
	Tax shield on subsidy	1
	Adjusted present value	1
	Conclusion	1
		15
(b)	1–2 marks per point	
	Maximum	5
	Professional skills marks (see below)	5
Total		25

Professional skills marks

Analysis and Evaluation

Appropriate use of the data to determine suitable calculations

Appropriate use of the data to support discussion and draw appropriate conclusions

Appraisal of information objectively to make a recommendation

Scepticism

Demonstration of ability to consider all relevant factors applicable to the shareholders who are not directors

Commercial acumen

Effective use of examples and/or practical considerations related to the context to illustrate points being made relating to the shareholders who are not directors

Maximum 5 marks

39 AMBERLE CO (DEC 18)

Key answer tips

APV is commonly tested, but this question was a bit unusual. The project appraisal was very straight forward, but the financing side effects were more complex than in other AFM APV questions. Note in particular how to deal with a borrowing that is paid back in equal annual instalments.

(a)

Year	0	1	2	3	4
	$m	$m	$m	$m	$m
Post-tax operating cash flows		28.50	36.70	44.40	50.90
Investment	(150.00)				
Realisable value					45.00
Working capital (W1)	(6.00)	(0.48)	(0.39)	(0.34)	7.21
Cash flows	(156.00)	28.02	36.31	44.06	103.11
Discount factor 12% (given)	1.000	0.893	0.797	0.712	0.636
Present value	(156.00)	25.02	28.94	31.37	65.58
Base case net present value	(5.09)				

Base case net present value is approximately ($5.09 million) and on this basis, the investment should be rejected.

Tutorial note

When attempting a question like this in the Computer Based Exam (CBE), make sure you use the spreadsheet functions SUM and NPV to save time. Be careful when using the NPV function to enter =NPV, then a bracket containing the discount rate, a comma, and then the cells containing the cash flows from year 1 onwards. The initial investment then needs to be subtracted separately.

Workings

1   Working capital

Year	0	1	2	3	4
	$m	$m	$m	$m	$m
Working capital		6.00	6.48	6.87	7.21
Required/(released)	6.00	0.48	0.39	0.34	(7.21)

2   Issue costs

$80 million/0.97 = $82,474,227

Issue costs = 3% × $82,474,227 = $2,474,227

There will be no issue costs for the bank loan.

3   Tax shield on subsidised loan

Use PV of an annuity (PVA) years 1 to 4 at 8% (normal borrowing rate)

$80m × 0.031 × 30% × 3.312 = $2,464,128

Tutorial note

A note to markers here said that full credit should be given if the tax shield was discounted at the government interest rate of 3.1 % rather than the normal borrowing rate of 8%.

4 Tax shield on bank loan

Annual repayment = ($70m/PVA 8% Yr 1 – 4) = ($70m/3.312) = $21,135,266

Year	1	2	3	4
	$000	$000	$000	$000
Opening balance	70,000	54,465	37,687	19,567
Interest at 8%	5,600	4,357	3,015	1,565
Repayment	(21,135)	(21,135)	(21,135)	(21,135)
Closing balance	54,465	37,687	19,567	(3)

Year	1	2	3	4
	$000	$000	$000	$000
Interest cost	5,600	4,357	3,015	1,565
Tax relief at 30%	1,680	1,307	905	470
Discount factor 8%	0.926	0.857	0.794	0.735
Present value	1,556	1,120	719	345
Net present value	3,740			

5 Subsidy benefit

Benefit = $80m × (0.08 – 0.031) × 70% × 3.312 = $9,088,128

6 Financing side effects

	$000
Issue costs (W3)	(2,474)
Tax shield on subsidised loan (W4)	2,464
Tax shield on bank loan (W5)	3,740
Subsidy benefit (W6)	9,088
Total benefit of financing side effects	12,818

Financing the project in this way would add around $12.82 million to the value of the project.

The adjusted present value of the project is around $7.73 million and so the project should be accepted. Sensitivity analysis should be undertaken on all the significant variables. Further analysis may be needed, particularly of the assumptions which lie behind the post-tax cash flows, such as sales and the tax rate. The realisable value of $45 million may be questionable. On the other hand, the time horizon of four years seems low and analysis should be done of potential cash flows beyond that time.

(b) Amberle Co's board can use various principles to determine its long-term finance mix. The directors may aim to follow consistent long-term policies, or they may have preferences which change as circumstances change.

Long-term policy factors

At present Amberle Co is using a mix of finance, raising the question of whether the directors are aiming for an optimal level of gearing, or there is a level which they do not wish gearing to exceed. If the board wishes to maintain gearing at an optimal level, this is likely to be determined by a balance of risks and advantages. The main risks are not being able to maintain the required level of payment to finance providers, interest to debt providers or required level of dividend to shareholders. Advantages may include lower costs of debt, tax relief on finance costs as shown in the APV calculation or, on the other hand, not being legally required to pay dividends in a particular year.

Another issue is whether Amberle Co's board has preferences about what source of finance should be used and in what order. One example of this is following the pecking order of retained earnings, then debt, then equity. The board may prefer this pecking order on the grounds that avoiding a new equity issue means that the composition of shareholdings is unchanged, or because retained earnings and longer term debt are judged low risk, or because the market will assume that an equity issue is being made because directors want to take advantage of Amberle Co's shares being over-priced. Other specific sources of finance may have benefits which attract the directors or drawbacks which deter them.

This investment highlights the aspect of whether the board prefers to match sources of finance with specific investments. Matching arguably gives greater flexibility and avoids committing Amberle Co to a long-term interest burden. However, to adopt this approach, the board will need assurance either that the investment will be able to meet finance costs and ultimately repayment burdens, or these can be met from surpluses from other operations.

Changing long-term financing policy

As well as deciding what financing mix or sources of finance they desire to use, the directors will also need to consider what factors would cause this decision to change.

A major change in the scope of the operations, with investment requirements being paramount, may cause a change in financing policy. Here the $150 million investment has been financed entirely by medium-term debt. Amberle Co may have chosen solely to use debt if it has made a recent equity issue and does not feel it can make another one so soon afterwards. In addition, if Amberle Co expands its manufacture of electric cars, it may decide to sell off its motorbike or cycles divisions if they are performing less well. If part of the business is sold, the sale proceeds could help finance new investment in the cars division.

The board may also be flexible at times and take advantage of whatever source of finance seems to be offering the best terms for Amberle Co. Here the board is taking advantage of loan finance being available at a low cost, thanks to the government loan scheme.

A change in the business or economic environment may also lead to the board rethinking how the company is financed. An economic recession, leading to falling share prices, may mean that the results of a share issue are uncertain. On the other hand, an increase in economic or business risk may mean that lenders are less likely to lend at acceptable rates or will impose greater restrictions. If the directors are risk-averse, they may not seek new finance during a recession but instead rely on retained earnings to finance any expansion.

			Marks
	Marking guide		*Marks*
(a)	Working capital		2
	Base case net present value		1
	Issue costs		1
	Tax shield benefit – subsidised loan		1
	Tax shield benefit – bank loan		4
	Subsidy benefit		1
	Adjusted present value		1
	Comments and conclusion		2
			────
		Maximum	**13**
			────
(b)	Factors determining long-term finance policy		3–4
	Factors which cause policy to change		3–4
			────
		Maximum	**7**
			────
	Professional skills marks (see below)		5
			────
Total			**25**
			────

Professional skills marks

Analysis and Evaluation

Appropriate use of the data to determine suitable calculations

Appropriate use of the data to support discussion and draw appropriate conclusions

Appraisal of information objectively to make a recommendation

Scepticism

Demonstration of ability to consider all relevant factors applicable to the financing policy

Commercial acumen

Effective use of examples and/or practical considerations related to the context to illustrate points being made relating to financing policy

Maximum 5 marks

40   HATHAWAY CO (MAR 20)

Key answer tips

This question covered investment appraisal and incorporated a consideration of options. However, there was insufficient information to use the Black Scholes option pricing model to assess the options so you had to use probability analysis instead.

(a)   (i)   Net present value (NPV): All figures are in $ms unless otherwise indicated

Year	1	2	3	4	5
Contribution (w1)		15.00	16.07	17.21	18.43
Fixed costs		(8.70)	(8.96)	(9.23)	(9.51)
Tax allowable depreciation		(2.40)	(2.40)	(2.40)	(2.40)
Balancing adjustment					(2.40)
Taxable profits		3.90	4.71	5.58	4.12
Taxation (20%)		(0.78)	(0.94)	(1.12)	(0.82)
Add back depreciation		2.40	2.40	2.40	4.80
Investment cost	(12.00)				
Cash flows	(12.00)	5.52	6.17	6.86	8.1
Discount factors (12%)	0.893	0.797	0.712	0.636	0.567
Discounted cash flows	(10.72)	4.40	4.39	4.36	4.59
NPV	7.02				

Tutorial note

When attempting a question like this in the Computer Based Exam (CBE), make sure you use the spreadsheet functions SUM and NPV to save time. Be careful when using the NPV function to enter =NPV, then a bracket containing the discount rate, a comma, and then the cells containing the cash flows from year 1 onwards. The initial investment then needs to be subtracted separately.

Workings

Working 1 (w1): Contribution

Year	2	3	4	5
Volume (000s)	3.00	3.15	3.31	3.47
Contribution per unit ($000s)	5.00	5.10	5.20	5.31
Contribution ($m)	15.00	16.07	17.21	18.43

(ii)   Incorporating finance director's objections

Expected NPV of chief engineer's proposal:

PV of years 2–5 = $17.74m
60% PV of years 2–5 = $10.64m
Expected PV of years 2–5 = (0.8 × $17.74m + 0.2 × $10.64m) = $16.32m
Expected NPV = $16.32m – $10.72m = $5.6m

(iii)   Alternative option NPV

Annuity factor (12%, t2 to t8) = 4.968 – 0.893 = 4.075
PV of years 2–8 = 4.075 × $3.43m = $13.98m
NPV = $13.98m – $10.72m = $3.26m

Therefore, it is more beneficial to follow the chief engineer's proposal.

(iv) Apply for regulatory approval or sell

Next, consider decision to sell to Gepe Co now or continue with application for regulatory approval.

NPV of sale to Gepe Co now = $4.3m

Expected NPV = 0.7 × $5.6m + 0.3 × (0.893 × $1.0m) = $4.19m

Therefore, more beneficial to sell immediately to Gepe Co.

Recommendation:

Immediate sale to Gepe Co for $4.3 million.

Comments

Based on the chief engineer's assumptions, the project generates a positive NPV of $7.02 million and should therefore be accepted in preference to the option to sell the concept for $4.3 million. On the other hand, when the finance director's objections are incorporated into the appraisal, the expected NPV is only $4.19 million and should therefore be rejected in favour of the option to sell.

It should be noted that the expected NPV of $4.19 million is an average. In other words, it is the average NPV if the project is carried out repeatedly which may not be useful in the case of a one-off development opportunity. Based on the calculations above, there is a 30% chance that the NPV will be only $893,000, which may pose a risk the directors are not prepared to take. The directors' attitude to risk will be an important factor in the final decision.

Furthermore, the analysis largely depends upon the values of the probabilities prescribed, the range of possible outcomes and the accuracy of the revenue and cost assumptions. Sensitivity analysis may be useful in testing the impact of variations in each of these variables on the final outcome.

(b) Whilst Hathaway Co's investment plans are based on a detailed analysis of all cost and revenue assumptions, projects lambda and kappa highlight failings in the appraisal and implementation phases.

Capital investment monitoring

Capital investment monitoring involves reviewing the implementation of an investment project to ensure it progresses according to the original investment plan, timescale and budget. This involves assessing the risks associated with the implementation phase and identifying deviations from the investment plan so that remedial action can be taken where necessary. Controls should be established to ensure effective delivery of the project.

Effective investment monitoring may have avoided the cost overruns and time delays experienced by Hathaway Co's project lambda.

Post-completion audit

A post-completion audit is an objective, after the fact, appraisal of all phases of the capital investment process regarding a specific project. Each project is examined from conception until as much as a few years after it has become operational. It examines the rationale behind the initial investment decision, including the strategic fit, and the efficiency and effectiveness of the outcome. The key objective is to improve the appraisal and implementation of future capital investment projects by learning from past mistakes and successes.

An effective post-completion audit may have identified the reasons behind the failure of Hathaway Co's project kappa to achieve its forecast revenues.

Note: Credit will be given for alternative and valid discursive comments.

				Marks
			Marking guide	
(a)	(i)	Contribution		2
		Fixed costs		1
		Tax (including tax allowable depreciation)		2
		NPV		1
				6
	(ii)	Expected NPV		2
	(iii)	Alternative option NPV		2
		Decision outcome		1
				3
	(iv)	Decision		2
		Comments		3
				5
(b)		Capital investment monitoring rationale		2–3
		Post-completion audit rationale		2–3
			Maximum	**4**
		Professional skills marks (see below)		**5**
Total				**25**

Professional skills marks

Analysis and Evaluation

Appropriate use of the data to determine suitable calculations

Appropriate use of the data to support discussion and draw appropriate conclusions

Appraisal of information objectively to make a recommendation

Scepticism

Effective challenge of information, evidence and assumptions supplied and, techniques carried out to support key facts and/or decisions

Demonstration of ability to consider all relevant factors applicable to a given course of action

Commercial acumen

Recommendations are practical and plausible in the context of Hathaway Co's situation

Effective use of examples and/or calculations from the scenario information and other practical considerations related to the context to illustrate points being made

Maximum 5 marks

41   ROBSON CO (MAR/JUN 21)

(a)   Project cash flows: All figures are in $m

Year	0	1	2	3	4
Cash flows	(120.0)	20.9	20.6	28.7	104.6
Discount factors – 14% (w1)	1.000	0.877	0.769	0.675	0.592
Present values	(120.0)	18.3	15.8	19.4	61.9

Base case net present value = ($4.6m)

Base case net present value is negative and on this basis should therefore be rejected.

Financing side effects: All figures are in $m

Issue costs (w2)	(2.0)
Tax shield on subsidised loan (w3)	0.9
Tax shield on bank loan (w4)	2.0
Subsidy benefit (w5)	5.7
Total benefit of financing side effects	6.6

Recommendation

The adjusted present value of the project is $2.0m and so the project should be accepted.

Workings:

Working 1 (w1): Ungeared cost of equity

Asset beta = 1.222

Keu = rf + Asset beta x (rm – rf) = 0.03 + (1.222 x 0.09) = 14%

Working 2 (w2): Issue costs

$100m x 0.02 = $2,000,000

Note: issue costs are payable out of cash reserves, so the finance does not need to be grossed up.

Working 3 (w3): Tax shield on subsidised loan

Annuity factor (9%, 4 years) = 3.240

$40m x 0.035 x 0.20 x 3.240 = $907,200

Note: the risk free rate would also be acceptable as a discount rate.

Working 4 (w4): Tax shield on bank loan

Annual repayment = $50m/3.240 = $15,432,098

Year	1	2	3	4
	$ 000	$ 000	$ 000	$ 000
Opening balance	50,000	39,068	27,152	14,164
Interest at 9%	4,500	3,516	2,444	1,275
Repayment	(15,432)	(15,432)	(15,432)	(15,432)
Closing balance	39,068	27,152	14,164	7
Tax relief on interest (20%)	900	703	489	255
Discount factor (9%)	0.917	0.842	0.772	0.708
Present value	825	592	378	181

Total present value = $1,976,000

Working 5 (w5): Subsidy benefit

Subsidy benefit = $40m x (0.09 – 0.035) x 0.80 x 3.240 = $5,702,400

(b) **Factors each capital provider may consider**

External shareholders

The chief executive's optimism regarding the rights issue may be misplaced. Robson Co's shareholders may question the need for another rights issue so soon after the last one. Nor may they have the funds available to take up their rights, particularly when there has been a series of fund raising exercises in the last six years. Whilst in theory the shareholders are able to sell their rights, this would mean accepting a dilution in their voting power, which may not be acceptable. Therefore it is possible a rights issue could fail. Even if Robson Co has the issue underwritten, failure of the rights issue would have an adverse impact on Robson Co's share price and the market's confidence in the board.

Shareholders may question the logic behind the new project and whether the forecast results can be delivered. They may need reassurance that lessons from the past have been learnt. The underwriting costs have been ignored in the financial appraisal even though these are likely to be significant and may prove fatal to the final outcome, particularly when the project's APV is quite marginal at $2m.

The loan will mean that Robson Co's gearing once again exceeds the average and shareholders will require higher returns to compensate for the increase in financial risk. The shareholders may question whether the commitment to service and repay the new loans may mean that Robson Co will have difficulty paying an acceptable level of dividend.

Subsidised loan provider

The subsidised loan programme provides capital for investment with the objective of boosting employment in a deprived part of the country.   Since the funds ultimately originate from the taxpayer, the government is accountable for any funding decisions made.   Robson Co's ability to service and ultimately repay the debt is therefore paramount. Robson Co's credit rating provides an assessment of the probability of default and the recent downgrade may cause concern. Even though Robson Co is unable to provide assets for security, the directors may still be faced with other covenants, for example restrictions on dividends or further borrowing which may upset shareholders.

The subsidy means demand for such loans is likely to be high and the selection criteria difficult so it is unlikely that the outcome is a foregone conclusion in the way Robson Co's CEO suggests. Based on the information provided it is unclear whether the new project would meet those selection criteria. Although Robson Co's new project is to be located in an area targeted for regeneration, it remains the case that the objective of the move is to automate the production line. Whilst jobs may still be created in a deprived area, net job creation nationwide is still likely to be negative. Whether such a policy would be attractive to the government, or the taxpayer, remains to be seen.

Note: Credit will be given for alternative and valid comments.

Marking guide		
		Marks
(a)	Base case	1
	Ungeared cost of equity	1
	Issue costs	1
	Tax shield on subsidised loan	2
	Tax shield on bank loan	4
	Subsidy benefit	1
	Adjusted present value	1
	Recommendations	2
		___
	Maximum	**13**
		___
(b)	Shareholders (e.g. fund availability, control, track record)	4–5
	Subsidised loan provider (e.g. job creation, default risk, covenants)	3–4
		___
	Maximum	**7**
		___
	Professional skills marks (see below)	5
		___
Total		**25**
		___

Professional skills marks

Analysis and Evaluation

Appropriate use of the data to determine suitable calculations

Appropriate use of the data to support discussion and draw appropriate conclusions

Appraisal of information objectively to make a recommendation

Scepticism

Demonstration of ability to consider all relevant factors applicable to the decisions made by the capital providers

Commercial acumen

Effective use of examples and/or practical considerations related to the context to illustrate points being made relating to capital providers

Maximum 5 marks

42   MOONSTAR CO (SEP/DEC 15)

Key answer tips

In 2014 and 2015, two articles on Islamic Finance and one on securitisation and tranching were published on the ACCA website. Therefore it was no surprise to see these two topics tested here.

Reading the recent articles on the ACCA website is a critical part of preparing properly for the exam.

(a)   An annual cash flow account compares the estimated cash flows receivable from the property against the liabilities within the securitisation process. The swap introduces leverage into the arrangement.

Cash flow receivable	$ million	Cash flow payable	$ million
$200 million × 11%	22.00	A-rated loan notes	
	———	Pay $108 million (W1) × 11% (W2)	11.88
Less: Service charge	(0.20)	B-rated loan notes	
		Pay $27 million (W1) × 12%	3.24
		C-rated loan notes	
		Pay $27 million (W1) × 13%	3.51
	———		———
	21.80		18.63
	———		———
		Balance to the subordinated certificates	3.17

Workings:

(W1) Loan notes

		$million
A	$200m × 0.9 × 0.6	108
B	$200m × 0.9 × 0.15	27
C	$200m × 0.9 × 0.15	27

(W2) Swap

Pay fixed rate under swap	9.5%
Pay floating rate	SOFR + 1.5%
Receive floating rate under swap	(SOFR)
Net payment	11%

The holders of the certificates are expected to receive $3.17million on $18 million, giving them a return of 17.6%. If the cash flows are 5% lower than the non-executive director has predicted, annual revenue received will fall to $20.90 million, reducing the balance available for the subordinated certificates to $2.07 million, giving a return of 11.5% on the subordinated certificates, which is below the returns offered on the B and C-rated loan notes. The point at which the holders of the certificates will receive nothing and below which the holders of the C-rated loan notes will not receive their full income will be an annual income of $18.83 million (a return of 9.4%), which is 14.4% less than the income that the non-executive director has forecast.

(b)   Benefits

The finance costs of the securitisation may be lower than the finance costs of ordinary loan capital. The cash flows from the commercial property development may be regarded as lower risk than Moonstar Co's other revenue streams. This will impact upon the rates that Moonstar Co is able to offer borrowers.

The securitisation matches the assets of the future cash flows to the liabilities to loan note holders. The non-executive director is assuming a steady stream of lease income over the next 10 years, with the development probably being close to being fully occupied over that period.

The securitisation means that Moonstar Co is no longer concerned with the risk that the level of earnings from the properties will be insufficient to pay the finance costs. Risks have effectively been transferred to the loan note holders.

Risks

Not all of the tranches may appeal to investors. The risk-return relationship on the subordinated certificates does not look very appealing, with the return quite likely to be below what is received on the C-rated loan notes. Even the C-rated loan note holders may question the relationship between the risk and return if there is continued uncertainty in the property sector.

If Moonstar Co seeks funding from other sources for other developments, transferring out a lower risk income stream means that the residual risks associated with the rest of Moonstar Co's portfolio will be higher. This may affect the availability and terms of other borrowing.

It appears that the size of the securitisation should be large enough for the costs to be bearable. However Moonstar Co may face unforeseen costs, possibly unexpected management or legal expenses.

(c)   A Mudaraba contract would involve the bank providing capital for Moonstar Co to invest in the development. Moonstar Co would manage the investment which the capital funded. Profits from the investment would be shared with the bank, but losses would be solely borne by the bank. A Mudaraba contract is essentially an equity partnership, so Moonstar Co might not face the threat to its credit rating which it would if it obtained ordinary loan finance for the development. A Mudaraba contract would also represent a diversification of sources of finance. It would not require the commitment to pay interest that loan finance would involve.

Moonstar Co would maintain control over the running of the project. A Mudaraba contract would offer a method of obtaining equity funding without the dilution of control which an issue of shares to external shareholders would bring. This is likely to make it appealing to Moonstar Co's directors, given their desire to maintain a dominant influence over the business.

The bank would be concerned about the uncertainties regarding the rental income from the development. Although the lack of involvement by the bank might appeal to Moonstar Co's directors, the bank might not find it so attractive. The bank might be concerned about information asymmetry – that Moonstar Co's management might be reluctant to supply the bank with the information it needs to judge how well its investment is performing.

	Marking scheme		
			Marks
(a)	Calculation of receivable		1
	Loan note amounts attributable to the A, B and C tranches		1
	Impact of swap		2
	Calculation of interest payable on interest for tranches A, B and C-rated tranches		3
	Estimation of return to subordinated certificates		1
	Comments and calculation relating to sensitivity		3
		Maximum	11
(b)	Benefits of securitisation		2–3
	Risks associated with securitisation		2–3
		Maximum	5
(c)	Explanation/discussion of suitability of Mudaraba contract		2–3
	Discussion of bank's views		1–2
		Maximum	4
	Professional skills marks (see below)		5
Total			25

Professional skills marks

Analysis and Evaluation

Appropriate use of the data to determine suitable calculations

Appropriate use of the data to support discussion and draw appropriate conclusions

Commercial acumen

Effective use of examples and/or practical considerations related to the context to illustrate points being made relating to securitisation and Islamic finance

Maximum 5 marks

43 GNT CO (JUN 11)

Key answer tips

Historically, duration has been more commonly tested in the context of project appraisal, but note that it can also be usefully applied to bonds, to assess the risk associated with different bonds.

(a) In order to calculate the duration of the two bonds, the present value of the annual cash flows and the price or value at which the bonds are trading at need to be determined. To determine the present value of the annual cash flows, they need to be discounted by the gross redemption yield.

Gross Redemption Yield

Tutorial note

When attempting a question like this in the Computer Based Exam (CBE), make sure you use the IRR spreadsheet function to save time. The following detailed workings can then be reduced to a very simple spreadsheet function i.e. =IRR(cash flows from T0 to T5).

Year	Payment ($)	DF 4%	PV @ 4%	DF 5%	PV @ 5%
0	(1,079.68)	1	(1,079.68)	1	(1,079.68)
1-5	60	4.452	267.12	4.329	259.74
5	1,000	0.822	822.00	0.784	784.00
			————		————
			9.44		(35.94)
			————		————

Using IRR approach, yield = 4 + ((9.44/(9.44 + 35.94)) × (5 − 4)) = 4.2%

Bond 1 (PV of cash flows)

$60 \times 1.042^{-1} + 60 \times 1.042^{-2} + 60 \times 1.042^{-3} + 60 \times 1.042^{-4} + 1,060 \times 1.042^{-5}$

PV of cash flows (years 1 to 5) = 57.58 + 55.26 + 53.03 + 50.90 + 862.91 = 1,079.68

Market price = $1,079.68

Duration = [57.58 × 1 + 55.26 × 2 + 53.03 × 3 + 50.90 × 4 + 862.91 × 5]/1,079.68 = 4.49 years

Bond 2 (PV of Coupons and Bond Price)

Price = $40 \times 1.042^{-1} + 40 \times 1.042^{-2} + 40 \times 1.042^{-3} + 40 \times 1.042^{-4} + 1,040 \times 1.042^{-5}$

PV of cash flows (years 1 to 5) = 38.39 + 36.84 + 35.36 + 33.93 + 846.63 = 991.15

Market Price = $991.15

Duration = [38.39 × 1 + 36.84 × 2 + 35.36 × 3 + 33.93 × 4 + 846.63 × 5]/991.15 = 4.63 years

(b) The sensitivity of bond prices to changes in interest rates is dependent on their redemption dates. Bonds which are due to be redeemed at a later date are more price-sensitive to interest rate changes, and therefore are riskier.

Duration measures the average time it takes for a bond to pay its coupons and principal and therefore measures the redemption period of a bond. It recognises that bonds which pay higher coupons effectively mature 'sooner' compared to bonds which pay lower coupons, even if the redemption dates of the bonds are the same. This is because a higher proportion of the higher coupon bonds' income is received sooner. Therefore these bonds are less sensitive to interest rate changes and will have a lower duration.

Duration can be used to assess the change in the value of a bond when interest rates change using the following formula: $\Delta P = [-D \times \Delta i \times P][1 + i]$, where P is the price of the bond, D is the duration and i is the redemption yield.

However, duration is only useful in assessing small changes in interest rates because of convexity. As interest rates increase, the price of a bond decreases and vice versa, but this decrease is not proportional for coupon paying bonds, the relationship is non-linear. In fact, the relationship between the changes in bond value to changes in interest rates is in the shape of a convex curve to origin, see below.

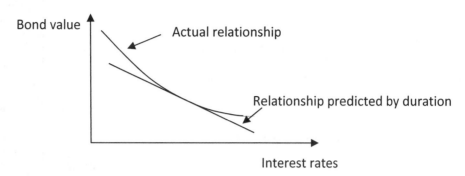

Duration, on the other hand, assumes that the relationship between changes in interest rates and the resultant bond is linear. Therefore duration will predict a lower price than the actual price and for large changes in interest rates this difference can be significant.

Duration can only be applied to measure the approximate change in a bond price due to interest changes, only if changes in interest rates do not lead to a change in the shape of the yield curve. This is because it is an average measure based on the gross redemption yield (yield to maturity). However, if the shape of the yield curve changes, duration can no longer be used to assess the change in bond value due to interest rate changes.

Note: Credit will be given for alternative benefits/limitations of duration.

(c) Industry risk measures the resilience of the company's industrial sector to changes in the economy. In order to measure or assess this, the following factors could be used:

- Impact of economic changes on the industry in terms how successfully the firms in the industry operate under differing economic outcomes;
- How cyclical the industry is and how large the peaks and troughs are;
- How the demand shifts in the industry as the economy changes.

Earnings protection measures how well the company will be able to maintain or protect its earnings in changing circumstances. In order to assess this, the following factors could be used:

- Differing range of sources of earnings growth;
- Diversity of customer base;
- Profit margins and return on capital.

Evaluation of the company's management considers how well the managers are managing and planning for the future of the company. In order to assess this, the following factors could be used:

- The company's planning and control policies, and its financial strategies;
- Management succession planning;
- The qualifications and experience of the managers;
- Performance in achieving financial and non-financial targets.

Marking guide		
		Marks
(a)	Calculation of gross redemption yield	2
	PV of cash flows and duration of bond 1	3
	PV of cash flows, price and duration of bond 2	3
		———
		8
		———
(b)	Duration as a single measure of sensitivity of interest rates	2–3
	Explanation of convexity)	1–2
	Explanation of change in shape of yield curve and other limitations	1–2
		———
	Maximum	**6**
		———
(c)	1 mark for each well explained point	6
		———
	Maximum	**6**
		———
	Professional skills marks (see below)	5
		———
Total		25
		———

Professional skills marks

Analysis and Evaluation

Appropriate use of the data to determine suitable calculations

Appropriate use of the data to support discussion and draw appropriate conclusions

Commercial acumen

Effective use of examples and/or practical considerations related to the context to illustrate points being made relating to credit ratings

Maximum 5 marks

44   TOLTUCK CO (MAR/JUN 17)

Key answer tips

This was a 25 mark question from the June 2017 exam paper, covering bond valuations, bond yields and credit ratings.

The question was based on the topics covered in the examiner's technical article from 2011. (Interestingly there was a question on the September 2016 exam paper that also tested the contents of a 2011 technical article!)

Students understand how important it is to read the examiner's recent articles before they attempt the exam, but this demonstrates how important it is to read all the previous technical articles.

If students were familiar with the content of the 2011 technical article, this question would have been very straight forward.

(a) The government yield curve can be estimated from the data available:

Bond 1: $104 = $109/(1 + r_1)$

$r_1 = ($109/$104) - 1 = 4.81\%$

Bond 2: $102 = $7/1.0481 + $107/(1 + r_2)^2$

$r_2 = [107/(102 - 6.68)]^{1/2} - 1 = 5.95\%$

Bond 3: $98 = $6/1.0481 + $6/1.0595^2 + $106/(1 + r_3)^3$

$r_3 = [106/(98 - 5.72 - 5.35)]^{1/3} - 1 = 6.83\%$

Year	Govt yield curve (%)	Spread old rating (%)	Toltuck Co spot old rating (%)	Spread new rating (%)	Toltuck Co spot new rating (%)
1	4.81	0.18	4.99	0.54	5.35
2	5.95	0.31	6.26	0.69	6.64
3	6.83	0.45	7.28	0.86	7.69

Valuation of bond under old credit rating

Year	Payment ($)	Discount factor	PV
1	8	1/1.0499	7.62
2	8	1/1.0626²	7.09
3	110	1/1.0728³	89.09
			———
			103.80
			———

Valuation of bond under new credit rating

Year	Payment ($)	Discount factor	PV
1	8	1/1.0535	7.59
2	8	1/1.0664²	7.03
3	110	1/1.0769³	88.08
			———
			102.70
			———

Tutorial note

When attempting a question like this in the Computer Based Exam (CBE), make sure you use the IRR spreadsheet function to save time. The following detailed workings can then be reduced to two very simple spreadsheet functions i.e. =IRR(cash flows from T0 to T3) for both the old cash flows and the new cash flows.

Yield to maturity under old credit rating

Year	Payment ($)	DF 8%	PV @ 8%	DF 7%	PV @ 7%
0	(103.80)	1	(103.80)	1	(103.80)
1-3	8.00	2.577	20.62	2.624	20.99
3	102.00	0.794	80.99	0.816	83.23
			_____		_____
			(2.19)		0.42
			_____		_____

Using IRR approach, yield to maturity = 7 + ((0.42/(2.19 + 0.42)) × (8 − 7)) = 7.16%

Yield to maturity under new credit rating

Year	Payment ($)	DF 8%	PV @ 8%	DF 7%	PV @ 7%
0	(102.70)	1	(102.70)	1	(102.70)
1-3	8.00	2.577	20.62	2.624	20.99
3	102.00	0.794	80.99	0.816	83.23
			_____		_____
			(1.09)		1.52
			_____		_____

Using IRR approach, yield to maturity = 7 + ((1.52/(1.09 + 1.52)) × (8 − 7)) = 7.58%
Market value of $100 bond has fallen by $1.10 and the yield to maturity has risen by 0.42%.

(b) The credit agency will have taken the following criteria into consideration when assessing Toltuck C's credit rating:

Country

Toltuck Co's debt would not normally be rated higher than the credit ratings of its country of origin, Arumland. Therefore the credit rating of Arumland should normally be at least AA. The rating will also have depended on Toltuck Co's standing relative to other companies in Arumland. The credit agency may have reckoned that Toltuck Co's recent poor results have weakened its position.

Industry

The credit agency will have taken account of the impact of the recession on property construction companies generally in Arumland. Toltuck Co's position within the industry compared with competitors will also have been assessed. If similar recent developments by competitors have been more successful, this is likely to have had an adverse impact on Toltuck Co's rating.

Management

The credit agency will have made an overall assessment of management and succession planning at Toltuck Co. It will have looked at business and financing strategies and planning and controls. It will also have assessed how successful the management has been in terms of delivering financial results. The credit agency may have believed the poor returns on recent developments show shortcomings in management decision-making processes and it may have rated the current management team poorly.

Financial

The credit agency will have analysed financial results, using measures such as return on capital employed. The agency will also have assessed possible sources of future earnings growth. It may have been sceptical about prospects, certainly for the short term, given Toltuck Co's recent problems.

The credit agency will also have assessed the financial position of Toltuck Co, looking at its gearing and working capital management, and considering whether Toltuck Co has enough cash to finance its needs. The agency will also have looked at Toltuck Co's relationship with its bankers and its debt covenants, to assess how flexible its sources of finances are if it comes under stress. It may well have been worried about Toltuck Co's gearing being higher than the industry average and concerned about the high levels of cash it needs to finance operations. It will also have assessed returns on developments-in-progress compared with commitments to repay loans. Greater doubt about Toltuck Co's ability to meet its commitments is likely to have been a significant factor in the fall in its rating.

The agency will also have needed reassurance about the quality of the financial information it was using, so it will have looked at the audit report and accounting policies.

(c) Toltuck Co may not have increased problems raising debt finance if debtholders do not react in the same way as the credit rating agency. They may attach different weightings to the criteria which they use. They may also come to different judgements about the quality of management and financial stability. Debtholders may believe that the recent problems Toltuck Co has had generating returns may be due more to external factors which its management could not have controlled.

However, it is probable that the fall in Toltuck Co's credit rating will result in it having more difficulty raising debt finance. Banks may be less willing to provide loans and investors less willing to subscribe for bonds. Even if debt finance is available, it may come with covenants restricting further debt or gearing levels. This will mean that if Toltuck Co requires substantial additional finance, it is more likely to have to make a rights issue or issue new equity on the stock market. Shareholders may be faced with the choice of subscribing large amounts for new capital or having their influence diluted. This may particularly worry the more cautious shareholders.

Even if Toltuck Co can obtain the debt it needs, the predicted increase in yield to maturity may be matched by debtholders demanding a higher coupon rate on debt. This will increase finance costs, and decrease profits and earnings per share, with a possible impact on share price. It will also mean that fewer funds are available for paying dividends. Toltuck Co has been faced with difficult decisions on balancing investment expenditure versus paying dividends and these difficulties may well increase.

Additional debt may have other restrictive covenants. They may restrict Toltuck Co's buying and selling of assets, or its investment strategy. Restrictions on Toltuck Co's decisions about the developments it undertakes may impact adversely on shareholder returns.

Loan finance or bonds will also come with repayment covenants. These may require Toltuck Co to build up a fund over time which will be enough to redeem the debt at the end of its life. Given uncertainties over cash flows, this commitment to retain cash may make it more difficult to undertake major developments or pay an acceptable level of dividend.

The fall in Toltuck Co's credit rating may result in its cost of equity rising as well as its cost of debt. In turn, Toltuck Co's weighted average cost of capital will rise. This will affect its investment choices and hence its ability to generate wealth for shareholders. It may result in Toltuck Co prioritising developments offering better short-term returns. This may suit the more cautious shareholders, but the current majority may worry that Toltuck Co will have to turn down opportunities which offer the possibility of high returns.

Marking guide			Marks
(a)	Government yield curve		2
	Toltuck Co spot-curve old and new		2
	Bond valuation – old and new		3
	Yield to maturity – old and news		2
			9
(b)	Financial factors		3
	Other factors		3
	(limit marks to 3 in total if no mention is made of Toltuck Co's position and performance)		
		Maximum	6
(c)	1–2 marks per impact discussed		5
		Maximum	5
	Professional skills marks (see below)		5
Total			25

Professional skills marks

Analysis and Evaluation

Appropriate use of the data to determine suitable calculations

Appropriate use of the data to support discussion and draw appropriate conclusions

Commercial acumen

Effective use of examples and/or practical considerations related to the context to illustrate points being made relating to credit ratings and raising finance

Maximum 5 marks

ACQUISITIONS AND MERGERS

45 KODIAK COMPANY (DEC 09)

Key answer tips

Business valuation is commonly tested, especially using the discounted cash flow method. Be careful to lay out your workings carefully. With lots of forecast figures to derive, it is easy to get in a muddle. A neat columnar format, with references to detailed workings, will ensure that you score well.

(a)   Given the details supplied, a forward forecast of the statement of profit or loss and of the statement of financial position is a precursor to the cash flow forecast. On the assumptions (as stated in the question but not reproduced here) the following projection is obtained (all figures in $000):

Projected statement of profit or loss

	Year 1	Year 2	Year 3
Revenue (9% growth)	5,450	5,941	6,475
Cost of sales (9% growth)	3,270	3,564	3,885
Gross Profit	2,180	2,377	2,590
Operating costs (W1)	2,012	2,159	2,317
Operating profit	168	218	273

Projected cash flows

	Year 1	Year 2	Year 3
Operating profit	168	218	273
Less interest	(74)	(74)	(74)
Less taxation (W4)	(15)	(28)	(43)
Add depreciation (W2)	134	144	155
Less investment in non-current assets (W2)	(79)	(95)	(114)
Less incremental working capital (W3)	(20)	(21)	(24)
Free cash flow to equity	114	144	173

Workings:

(W1) Operating costs

	Year 1	Year 2	Year 3
Variable costs (9% growth)	818	891	971
Fixed costs (6% growth)	1,060	1,124	1,191
Depreciation (W2)	134	144	155
Total operating costs	2,012	2,159	2,317

(W2) Non-current assets and depreciation

Non-current assets at beginning	1,266	1,345	1,440
Additions (20% growth)	79	95	114
Non-current assets	1,345	1,440	1,554
Depreciation (10%)	134	144	155

(W3) Working capital

Working capital (9% growth)	240	261	285
Incremental WC	240 – 220 = 20	261 – 240 = 21	285 – 261 = 24

Initial working capital equals net current assets less cash. Alternatively, the full 270 can be used as working capital as well. Credit will be given for either assumption.

(W4) Taxation

One year in arrears (30%)   15 (given)   30% × (168 – 74) = 28   30% × (218 – 74) = 43

Tutorial note

When attempting a question like this in the Computer Based Exam (CBE), make sure you use the spreadsheet functions SUM and NPV to save time. Be careful when using the NPV function to enter =NPV, then a bracket containing the discount rate, a comma, and then the cells containing the cash flows from year 1 onwards. The initial investment then needs to be subtracted separately.

(b) Our estimate of the value of this business on a going concern basis assumes that cash will be generated and reinvestment made according to the above projection, and that cashflows will grow at 3% per year after year 3.

	0	1	2	3
Free cash flow after reinvestment		114	144	173
Required rate of return	10%			
Present value of cash flows (discounted at 10%)		104	119	130
Value (years 1 to 3)	353			

The value of cashflows from year 4 onwards can be calculated using the growth model formula:

$$PV = (173 \times 1.03)/(0.10 - 0.03) \times 1.10^{-3} = 1,913$$

The total value of the firm, on the basis of the above projections, is $2,266,000 (353 + 1,913).

(c) This valuation is based upon a number of assumptions which you should consider when reviewing this analysis. We have taken your judgement that 10% fairly reflects the market rate of return required for an investment of this type. This rate should compensate you for the business risk to which your firm is exposed. For an investment held within the context of a widely diversified portfolio the rate of return you should expect will only be conditioned by your exposure to market risk. However, in the context of a sole equity investment then the rate of return you may require could be more than that which would be available from the market for an investment of this type.

In generating our projections we have assumed the estimates are certain and that the firm is a going concern. In considering this investment further you may wish to explicitly consider the variability attaching to the underlying variables in the projection and the possible range of values that may result. Of particular importance is the assumption of a three-year forecast. In practice the period chosen does depend upon the nature of the business and in particular the uncertainties to which it is exposed.

Finally we have assumed a terminal value based upon future cash flows from year three forward growing at a compound rate of 3% into the indefinite future. The resulting value will be particularly sensitive to this figure and it may be that you may wish to consider a different rate depending upon what you regard as sustainable in the long term for a business of this type.

Marking scheme		
		Marks
(a)	Estimation of depreciation	1
	Estimation of taxation	1
	Estimation of changes in working capital	2
	Projection of income statements	4
	Projection of cash flows	4
		____
		12
		____
(b)	PV years 1-3	1
	PV of cash flows after year 3	2
		____
		3
		____
(c)	Commentary on required rate of return	1–2
	Assumptions about the growth rates	1–2
	Other relevant points	1–2
		____
	Maximum	**5**
		____
	Professional skills marks (see below)	**5**
		____
Total		**25**
		____

Professional skills marks

Analysis and Evaluation

Appropriate use of the data to determine suitable calculations

Appropriate use of the data to support discussion and draw appropriate conclusions

Scepticism

Effective challenge and critical assessment of the information and assumptions provided

Commercial acumen

Effective use of examples and/or practical considerations related to the context to illustrate points being made

Maximum 5 marks

46   SIGRA CO (DEC 12)

Key answer tips

Different methods of payment (e.g. cash offer, share for share exchange) have been tested frequently in recent sittings. Valuation using P/E ratios is a critical starting point in this question.

(a)   Number of Sigra Co shares = 4,400,000/0.4 = 11,000,000 shares

Sigra Co earnings per share (EPS) = $4,950,000/11,000,000 shares = 45c/share

Sigra Co price to earnings (PE) ratio = $3.6/$0.45 = 8

Dentro PE ratio = 8 × 1.125 = 9

Dentro Co shares = $500,000/0.4 = 1,250,000 shares

Dentro Co EPS = $625,000/1,250,000 = 50c/share

Estimate of Dentro Co value per share = $0.5 × 9 = $4.50/share

Cash offer

Dentro share percentage gain under cash offer

$0.50/$4.50 × 100% = 11.1%

Share-for-share exchange

Equity value of Sigra Co = 11,000,000 × $3.60 =	$39,600,000
Equity value of Dentro Co = 1,250,000 × $4.50 =	$5,625,000
Synergy savings = 30% × $5,625,000 =	$1,688,000
Total equity value of combined company	$46,913,000
Number of shares for share-for-share exchange	
11,000,000 + [1,250,000 × 3/2] =	12,875,000
Expected share price of combined company	$3.644/share

Dentro share percentage gain under share-for-share offer

[($3.644 × 3 − $4.50 × 2)/2]/$4.50 × 100% = 21.5%

Bond offer

First, we need to calculate the yield on the existing bond (and hence assume that the yield on the new bonds will be the same).

Tutorial note

When attempting a question like this in the Computer Based Exam (CBE), make sure you use the IRR spreadsheet function to save time. The following detailed workings can then be reduced to a very simple spreadsheet function i.e. =IRR(cash flows from T0 to T3).

Year	Payment ($)	DF 4%	PV @ 4%	DF 5%	PV @ 5%
0	(104)	1	(104)	1	(104)
1-3	6	2.775	16.65	2.723	16.34
3	100	0.889	88.90	0.864	86.40
			─────		─────
			1.55		(1.26)
			─────		─────

Using IRR approach, yield = 4 + ((1.55/(1.55 + 1.26)) × (5 − 4)) = 4.55%

Price of new bond = future cashflows discounted at yield (4.55%)

$2 × 1.0455^{-1} + $2 × 1.0455^{-2} + $102 × 1.0455^{-3} = 93.00

Value per share = $93.00/16 = $5.81/share

Dentro share percentage gain under bond offer

Bond offer: ($5.81 − $4.50)/$4.50 × 100% = 29.1%

Comments

An initial comparison is made between the cash and the share-for-share offers. Although the share-for-share exchange gives a higher return compared to the cash offer, Dentro Co's shareholders may prefer the cash offer as the gains in the share price are dependent on the synergy gains being achieved. However, purchase for cash may mean that the shareholders face an immediate tax burden. Sigra Co's shareholders would probably prefer the cash option because the premium would only take $625,000 of the synergy benefits ($0.50 × 1,250,000 shares), whereas a share-for-share exchange would result in approximately $1,209,000 of the synergy benefits being given to the Dentro Co shareholders (21.5% × $4.50 × 1,250,000 shares).

The bond offer provides an alternative which may be acceptable to both sets of shareholders. Dentro Co's shareholders receive the highest return for this and Sigra Co's shareholders may be pleased that a large proportion of the payment is deferred for three years. In present value terms, however, a very high proportion of the projected synergy benefits are given to Dentro Co's shareholders (29.1% × $4.50 × $1,250,000 = $1,637,000).

(b) The regulatory framework within the European Union, the EU takeovers directive, will be used to discuss the proposals. However it is acceptable for candidates to refer to other directives and discuss the proposals on that basis.

Proposal 1

With regards to the first proposal, the directive gives the bidder squeeze-out rights, where the bidder can force minority shareholders to sell their shares. However, the limits set for squeeze-out rights are generally high (UK: 90%; Belgium, France, Germany and the Netherlands: 95%; Ireland 80%). It is likely therefore that Sigra Co will need a very large proportion of Dentro Co's shareholders to agree to the acquisition before they can force the rest of Dentro Co's shareholders to sell their shares. Dentro Co's minority shareholders may also require Sigra Co to purchase their shares, known as sell-out rights.

Proposal 2

With regards to the second proposal, the principle of equal treatment in the directive requires that all shareholders should be treated equally. In general terms, the bidder must offer to minority shareholders the same terms as those offered to other shareholders. It could be argued here that the principle of equal treatment is contravened because later shareholders are not offered the extra 3 cents per share, even though the 30% is less than a majority shareholding. It is highly unlikely that Sigra Co will be allowed to offer these terms.

	Marking scheme		
			Marks
(a)	Calculation of Sigra Co PE ratio		2
	Calculation of Dentro Co share value		2
	Calculation of percentage gain under cash offer		1
	Total equity value of combined company		1
	Estimate of per share value of combined company		1
	Calculation of percentage gain under share-for-share offer		1
	Estimation of bond required rate of return		2
	Estimation of value per share under bond offer		2
	Calculation of percentage gain under bond offer		1
	Comments (1 mark per relevant point)		3–4
		Maximum	16
(b)	Discussion of each proposal (2 marks per proposal)		4
		Maximum	4
	Professional skills marks (see below)		5
Total			25

Professional skills marks

Analysis and Evaluation

Appropriate use of the data to determine suitable calculations

Appropriate use of the data to support discussion and draw appropriate conclusions

Appraisal of information objectively to make a recommendation on preferred payment method

Scepticism

Effective challenge and critical assessment of the information and assumptions provided in relation to the valuations

Commercial acumen

Effective use of examples and/or practical considerations related to the context to illustrate points being made

Maximum 5 marks

47 HAV CO (JUN 13)

Key answer tips

In many valuation questions you will also have to address discursive issues such as synergy. Make sure that you allocate your time carefully to enable you to attempt both the calculations and the discussion parts.

(a) An acquisition creates synergy benefits when the value of the combined entity is more than the sum of the two companies' values. Synergies can be separated into three types: revenue synergies which result in higher revenues for the combined entity, higher return on equity and a longer period when the company is able to maintain competitive advantage; cost synergies which result mainly from reducing duplication of functions and related costs, and from taking advantage of economies of scale; financial synergies which result from financing aspects such as the transfer of funds between group companies to where it can be utilised best, or from increasing debt capacity.

Revenue synergies are perhaps where the greatest potential for growth comes from but are also more difficult to identify, quantify and enact. Good post-acquisition planning is essential for these synergies to be realised but they can be substantial and long-lasting. In this case, Hav Co's management can help market Strand Co's products more effectively by using their sales and marketing talents resulting in higher revenues and longer competitive advantage. Research and development activity can be combined to create new products using the technologies in place in both companies, and possibly bringing innovative products to market quicker. The services of the scientists from Strand Co will be retained to drive innovation forward, but these need to be nurtured with care since they had complete autonomy when they were the owners of Strand Co.

The main challenge in ensuring long-lasting benefits is not only ensuring accurate identification of potential synergies but putting into place integration processes and systems to gain full benefit from them. This is probably the greater challenge for management, and, when poorly done, can result in failure to realise the full value of the acquisition. Hav Co needs to be aware of this and make adequate provisions for it.

Note: Credit will be given for alternative relevant comments and suggestions.

(b) **Maximum premium based on excess earnings method**

Average pre-tax earnings: (397 + 370 + 352)/3 = $373.0m

Average capital employed: [(882 + 210 − 209) + (838 + 208 −180) + (801 + 198 − 140)]/3 = $869.3m

Excess annual value/annual premium = 373m − (20% × $869.3m) = $199.1m

After-tax annual premium = $199.1m × 0.8 = $159.3m

PV of annual premium (assume perpetuity) = $159.3m/0.07 = $2,275.7m

According to this method, the maximum premium payable is $2,275.7m in total.

Maximum premium based on price-to-earnings (PE) ratio method

Strand Co estimated PE ratio = 16.4 × 1.10 = 18.0

Strand Co profit after tax: $397m × 0.8 = $317.6m

Hav Co profit after tax = $1,980m × 0.8 =$1,584.0m

Hav Co, current value = $9.24 × 2,400 shares = $22,176.0m

Strand Co, current value = $317.6m × 18.0 = $5,716.8m

Combined company value = ($1,584m + $317.6m + $140.0m) × 14.5 = $29,603.2m

Maximum premium = $29,603.2m − ($22,176.0m + $5,716.8) = $1,710.4m

(c) Strand Co, current value per share = $5,716.8m/1,200m shares = $4.76 per share

Maximum premium % based on PE ratio = $1,710.4m/$5,716.8m x 100% = 29.9%

Maximum premium % based on excess earnings = $2,275.7m/$5,716.8m × 100% = 39.8%

Cash offer: premium (%)

($5.72 −$4.76)/$4.76 × 100% = 20.2%

Cash and bond offer: premium (%)

Each share has a nominal value of $0.25, therefore $5 is $5/$0.25 = 20 shares

Bond value = $100/20 shares = $5 per share

Cash payment = $1.25 per share

Total = $6.25 per share

Premium percentage = ($6.25 −$4.76)/$4.76 = 31.3%

On the basis of the calculations, the cash together with bond offer yields the highest return; in addition to the value calculated above, the bonds can be converted to 12 Hav Co shares, giving them a price per share of $8.33 ($100/12). This price is below Hav Co's current share price of $9.24, and therefore the conversion option is already in-the-money. It is probable that the share price will increase in the 10-year period and therefore the value of the convertible bond should increase. A bond also earns a small coupon interest of $3 per $100 a year. The 31.3% return is the closest to the maximum premium based on the excess earnings method and more than the maximum premium based on the PE ratio method. It would seem that this payment option transfers more value to the owners of Strand Co than the value created based on the PE ratio method.

However, with this option Strand Co shareholders only receive an initial cash payment of $1.25 per share compared to $5.72 per share for the cash payment method. This may make it the more attractive option for the Hav Co shareholders as well, and although their shareholding will be diluted under this option, it will not happen for some time.

The pure cash offer gives an immediate and definite return to Strand Co's shareholders, but is also the lowest offer and may also put a significant burden on Hav Co having to fund so much cash, possibly through increased debt.

It is likely that Strand Co's shareholder/managers, who will continue to work within Hav Co, will accept the mixed cash and bond offer. They, therefore, get to maximise their current return and also potentially gain when the bonds are converted into shares. Different impacts on shareholders' personal taxation situations due to the different payment methods might also influence the choice of method.

It should also be noted that the maximum premiums calculated have used what appears to be subjective adjustments to a PE ratio, or the assumption that annual excess earnings will occur in perpetuity. Neither of these may hold in reality, which would affect the maximum premium payable.

	Marking scheme	
		Marks
(a)	Distinguish between the different synergies	2
	Discuss possible revenue synergy sources	3
	Concluding comments	1
		–––
		6
		–––
(b)	Average earnings	1
	Average capital employed	1
	After-tax annual premium	1
	PV of premium (excess earnings method)	1
	Hav Co and Strand Co values	1
	Combined company value	1
	Value created/premium (PE method)	1
		–––
		7
		–––
(c)	Strand Co, value per share	1
	Cash offer premium (%)	1
	Cash and bond offer premium (%)	2
	Explanation and justification	3
		–––
		7
		–––
	Professional skills marks (see below)	5
		–––
Total		25
		–––

Professional skills marks

Analysis and Evaluation

Appropriate use of the data to determine suitable calculations

Appropriate use of the data to support discussion and draw appropriate conclusions

Appraisal of information objectively to make a recommendation on preferred payment method

Scepticism

Effective challenge and critical assessment of the information and assumptions provided in relation to the valuations

Commercial acumen

Effective use of examples and/or practical considerations related to the context to illustrate points being made relating to synergies or payment methods

Maximum 5 marks

48   VOGEL CO (JUN 14)

Key answer tips

This was a fairly typical question on acquisitions, with a good mix of calculations and discussion.

When asked to perform a valuation calculation, follow the clues in the question to decide which valuation method to use. In this case the given P/E ratios, costs of capital and growth rates meant that DCF and P/E methods should have been used.

(a)   Vogel Co can take the following actions to reduce the risk that the acquisition of Tori Co fails to increase shareholder value.

Since Vogel Co has pursued an aggressive policy of acquisitions, it needs to determine whether or not this has been too aggressive and detailed assessments have been undertaken. Vogel Co should ensure that the valuation is based on reasonable input figures and that proper due diligence of the perceived benefits is undertaken prior to the offer being made. Often it is difficult to get an accurate picture of the target when looking at it from the outside. Vogel Co needs to ensure that it has sufficient data and information to enable a thorough and sufficient analysis to be undertaken.

The sources of synergy need to be properly assessed to ensure that they are achievable and what actions Vogel Co needs to undertake to ensure their achievement. This is especially so for the revenue-based synergies. An assessment of the impact of the acquisition on the risk of the combined company needs to be undertaken to ensure that the acquisition is not considered in isolation but as part of the whole company.

The Board of Directors of Vogel Co needs to ensure that there are good reasons to undertake the acquisition, and that the acquisition should result in an increase in value for the shareholders. Research studies into mergers and acquisitions have found that often companies are acquired not for the shareholders' benefit, but for the benefit or self-interest of the acquiring company's management. The non-executive directors should play a crucial role in ensuring that acquisitions are made to enhance the value for the shareholders. A post-completion audit may help to identify the reasons behind why so many of Vogel Co's acquisitions have failed to create value. Once these reasons have been identified, strategies need to be put in place to prevent their repetition in future acquisitions.

Procedures need to be established to ensure that the acquisition is not overpaid. Vogel Co should determine the maximum premium it is willing to pay and not go beyond that figure. Research indicates that often too much is paid to acquire a company and the resultant synergy benefits are not sufficient to cover the premium paid. Often this is the result of the management of the acquiring company wanting to complete the deal at any cost, because not completing the deal may be perceived as damaging to both their own, and their company's, reputation. The acquiring company's management may also want to show that the costs related to undertaking due diligence and initial negotiation have not been wasted. Vogel Co and its management need to guard against this and maybe formal procedures need to be established which allow managers to step back without loss of personal reputation.

Vogel Co needs to ensure that it has proper procedures in place to integrate the staff and systems of the target company effectively, and also to recognise that such integration takes time. Vogel Co may decide instead to give the target company a large degree of autonomy and thus make integration less necessary; however, this may result in a reduction in synergy benefits. Vogel Co should also have strategies which allow it sufficient flexibility when undertaking integration so that it is able to respond to changing circumstances or respond to inaccurate information prior to the acquisition. Vogel Co should also be mindful that its own and the acquired company's staff and management need to integrate and ensure a good working relationship between them.

Note: The above answer covers more areas than would be needed to achieve full marks for the part. Credit will be given for alternative relevant comments.

(b)   **Approach taken**

The maximum premium payable is equal to the maximum additional benefit created from the acquisition of Tori Co, with no increase in value for the shareholders of Vogel Co (although the shareholders of Vogel Co would probably not approve of the acquisition if they do not gain from it).

The additional benefit can be estimated as the sum of the cash gained (or lost) from selling the assets of Department C, spinning off Department B and integrating Department A, less the sum of the values of Vogel Co and Tori Co as separate companies.

Estimation

Cash gained from selling the assets of Department C = (20% × $98.2m) + (20% × $46.5m × 0.9) – ($20.2 + $3m) = $19.64m + $8.37m – $23.2m = $4.81m

Value created from spinning off Department B into Ndege Co

Free cash flow of Ndege Co	$ million
Current share of PBDIT (0.4 × $37.4m)	14.96
Less: attributable to Department C (10%)	(1.50)
Less: tax allowable depreciation (0.4 × 98.2 × 0.10)	(3.93)
Profits before tax	9.53
Tax (20%)	(1.91)
Free cash flows	7.62

Value of Ndege Co =

Present value of cash flow in year 1: $7.62m × 1.2 × 1.1^{-1} = $8.31m

Add: present value of cash flows from year 2 onwards:

($9.14m × 1.052)/(0.1 – 0.052) × 1.1^{-1} = $182.11m

Less: debt = $40m

Value to shareholders of Ndege Co = $150.42m

Vogel Co's current value = $3 × 380m = $1,140m

Vogel Co, profit after tax = $158.2m × 0.8 = $126.56m

Vogel Co, PE ratio before acquisition = $1,140.0m/$126.56m = 9.01 say 9

Vogel Co, PE ratio after acquisition = 9 × 1.15 = 10.35

Tori Co, PE ratio before acquisition = 9 × 1.25 = 11.25

Tori Co's current value = 11.25 × ($23.0 × 0.8) = $207.0m

Value created from combined company

($126.56m + 0.5 × $23.0m × 0.8 + $7m) × 10.35 = $1,477.57

Maximum premium = ($1,477.57m + $150.42m + $4.81m) − ($1,140m + $207.0m) = $285.80m

Assumptions

Based on the calculations given above, it is estimated that the value created will be 64.9% or $285.80m.

However, Vogel Co needs to assess whether the numbers it has used in the calculations and the assumptions it has made are reasonable. For example, Ndege Co's future cash flows seem to be growing without any additional investment in assets and Vogel Co needs to establish whether or not this is reasonable. It also needs to establish how the increase in its PE ratio was determined after acquisition. Perhaps sensitivity analysis would be useful to show the impact on value changes, if these figures are changed. Given its poor record in generating value previously, Vogel Co needs to pay particular attention to these figures.

Marking scheme			
			Marks
(a)	1–2 marks per point	Maximum	6
(b)	Cash gained from sales of Department C assets		1
	Calculation of free cash flows for Ndege Co		2
	Calculation of present values of Ndege Co cash flows and value		2
	Vogel Co PE ratios before and after acquisition		2
	Tori Co PE ratio and value		1
	Value created from combining Department A with Vogel Co		1
	Maximum premium payable		1
	Approach taken		1–2
	Assumptions made		2–3
		Maximum	14
	Professional skills marks (see below)		5
Total			25

Professional skills marks

Analysis and Evaluation

Appropriate use of the data to determine suitable calculations

Appropriate use of the data to support discussion and draw appropriate conclusions

Appraisal of information objectively

Scepticism

Effective challenge and critical assessment of the information and assumptions provided in relation to the valuation

Commercial acumen

Effective use of examples and/or practical considerations related to the context to illustrate points being made relating to the acquisition

Maximum 5 marks

49   LOUIEED CO (MAR/JUN 16)

Key answer tips

There was a lot to do here in the time available, so strict time management would have been critical.

In part (b) you were asked to calculate and discuss gearing and earnings per share in three alternative scenarios. In questions like this it is very important to present the numbers clearly, so that it is then easy to compare the positions and complete the discussion parts of the question.

(a)   **Advantages of the acquisition**

Louieed Co and Tidded Co appear to be a good strategic fit for a number of reasons. Louieed Co appears to have limited potential for further growth. Acquiring Tidded Co, a company with better recent growth, should hopefully give Louieed Co the impetus to grow more quickly.

Acquiring a company which has a specialism in the area of online testing will give Louieed Co capabilities quicker than developing this function in-house. If Louieed Co does not move quickly, it risks losing contracts to its competitors.

Acquiring Tidded Co will give Louieed Co access to the abilities of some of the directors who have led Tidded Co to becoming a successful company. They will provide continuity and hopefully will help integrate Tidded Co's operations successfully into Louieed Co. They may be able to lead the upgrading of Tidded Co's existing products or the development of new products which ensures that Louieed Co retains a competitive advantage.

It appears that Tidded Co's directors now want to either realise their investment or be part of a larger company, possibly because it will have more resources to back further product development. If Louieed Co does not pursue this opportunity, one of Louieed Co's competitors may purchase Tidded Co and acquire a competitive advantage itself.

There may also be other synergistic benefits, including savings in staff costs and other savings, when the two companies merge.

Disadvantages of the acquisition

It is not known what the costs of developing in-house capabilities will be. Although the process may be slower, the costs may be less and the process less disruptive to Louieed Co than suddenly adding on Tidded Co's operations.

It is not possible to tell which of Tidded Co's directors are primarily responsible for its success. Loss of the three directors may well represent a significant loss of its capability. This will be enhanced if the three directors join a competitor of Louieed Co or set up in competition themselves.

There is no guarantee that the directors who remain will fit into Louieed Co's culture. They are used to working in a less formal environment and may resent having Louieed Co's way of operating imposed upon them. This could result in departures after the acquisition, jeopardising the value which Tidded Co has brought.

Possibly Tidded Co's leadership in the online testing market may not last. If competitors do introduce major advances, this could mean that Tidded Co's current growth is not sustainable.

(b)   Funding of bid

No extra finance will be required if all Tidded Co's shareholders take up the share offer.

All Tidded Co's shareholders take up cash offer

Cash required = 90 million × $22.75 = $2,048m

Extra debt finance required = $2,048m − $220m − $64m = $1,764m

60% share-for-share offer, 40% cash offer

Cash required = 40% × 90m × $22.75 = $819m

Extra debt finance required = $819m − $220m − $64m = $535m

Impact of bid on EPS

Louieed Co's EPS prior to acquisition = $296m/340 = $0.87

All Tidded Co's shareholders take up share offer

Number of shares after acquisition = 340m + (90m × 2) = 520m

EPS after acquisition = ($296m + $128m + $20m)/520m = $0.85

All Tidded Co's shareholders take up cash offer

Number of shares after acquisition = 340m

EPS after acquisition = ($296m + $128m + $20m − $11.36m − $105.84m)/340m = $0.96

$105.84m is the post-tax finance cost on the additional loan finding required of $1,764m. Therefore $1,764m × 7.5% × 80% = $105.84m

$11.36m is the post-tax opportunity cost of interest foregone on the cash and cash equivalents surpluses of the two companies of $220m + $64m = $284m. Therefore $284m × 5% × 80% = $11.36m

60% share-for-share offer, 40% cash offer

Number of shares after acquisition 340m + (90m × 2 × 0.6) = 448m

EPS after acquisition = ($296m + $128m + $20m − $11.36m − $32.1m)/448m = $0.89

$32.1m is the post-tax finance cost on the additional loan funding required of $535m. Therefore $535m × 7.5% × 80% = $32.1 m

Impact of bid on gearing (using market values)

Louieed Co's gearing (debt/(debt + equity)) prior to bid = 540/(540 + (340 × 12.19)) = 11.5%

<u>All Tidded Co's shareholders take up share offer</u>

Debt/(Debt + equity) after bid = (540 + 193)/(540 + 193 + (520 × $0.85 × 14)) = 10.6%

<u>All Tidded Co's shareholders take up cash offer</u>

Debt/(Debt + equity) after anticipated bid

= (540 + 193 + 1,764)/(540 + 193 + 1,764 + (340 × $0.96 × 14)) = 35.3%

<u>60% share-for-share offer, 40% cash offer</u>

Debt/(Debt + equity) after bid

= (540 + 193 + 535)/(540 + 193 + 535 + (448 × $0.89 × 14)) = 18.5%

Comments

The calculations suggest that if Tidded Co's shares are acquired on a share-for-share exchange on the terms required by its shareholders, Louieed Co's shareholders will suffer a fall in earnings per share attributable to them from $0.87 to $0.85. This is because Tidded Co is being bought on a higher price-earnings ratio than Louieed Co and the synergies arising from the acquisition are insufficient to compensate for this.

Use of loan finance to back a cash offer will attract tax relief on interest. The cost of debt will be lower than the cost of equity.

Issuing extra shares will lead to a dilution of the power of Louieed Co's existing shareholders. If all of Tidded Co's shareholders take up the share-for-share offer, they will hold around a third of the shares of the combined company (180m/520m) and this may be unacceptable to Louieed Co's shareholders.

The benefits which Tidded Co's shareholders will gain will be fixed if they take up a cash offer and do not acquire shares in the combined company. If there are significant gains after the acquisition, these will mostly accrue to Louieed Co's existing shareholders if a significant proportion of Tidded Co's shareholders have taken a cash offer.

If the forecast for take up of the offer is correct, even by combining the cash flows of the two companies, the new company will have insufficient funds to be able to pay all the shareholders who are expected to take up the cash offer. Further finance will be required.

The alternative to loan finance is financing the bid by issuing shares. Depending on the method used, this may also result in dilution of existing shareholders' ownership and also there is no guarantee that the issue will be successful.

There is also no guarantee that the forecast of 40% of the shareholders taking up the cash offer is correct. If all five of the major shareholders decide to realise their investment rather than just two, this will increase the cash required by $512 million (25% × $22.75 × 90m), for example.

Gearing will increase if loan finance is needed to finance the cash offer. If the mixed share and cash offer is taken up in the proportions stated, the gearing level of the combined company will increase from 11.5% to 18.5%. Current shareholders may not be particularly concerned about this. However, if all or most of the share capital is bought for cash, the gearing level of the combined company will be significantly greater, at maximum 35.3%, than Louieed Co's current gearing. This may be unacceptable to current shareholders and could mean an increase in the cost of equity, because of the increased risk, and also possibly an increase in the cost of debt, assuming in any case that debt finance at the maximum level required will be available. To guard against this risk, Louieed Co's board may want to limit the cash offer to a certain percentage of share value.

	Marking scheme		
			Marks
(a)	Reasons for acquisition		3
	Reasons against acquisition		3
			—
		Maximum	**6**
			—
(b)	Funding of bid: 1 mark for cash option, 1 mark for mixed option		2
	Earnings per share: 1 mark for share-for-share option, 2 marks for cash option, 2 marks for mixed option		5
	Gearing: 1 mark for each option		3
	Comments		4–5
			—
		Maximum	**14**
			—
	Professional skills marks (see below)		**5**
			—
Total			**25**
			—

Professional skills marks

Analysis and Evaluation

Appropriate use of the data to determine suitable calculations

Appropriate use of the data to support discussion and draw appropriate conclusions

Appraisal of information objectively

Scepticism

Effective challenge and critical assessment of the information and assumptions provided in relation to the acquisition offers

Commercial acumen

Effective use of examples and/or practical considerations related to the context to illustrate points being made relating to the acquisition and funding requirements

Maximum 5 marks

50 SELORNE CO (SEP 18)

Key answer tips

It is very important to read the requirements carefully and answer the requirement that is given rather than the one you were hoping for. In this question, many students lost marks in part (b) by listing out examples of synergies. That is not what the requirement is asking for!

(a) **(i)** Selorne Co current equity value = 50m shares × $6.50 = $325m

Chawon Co current equity value = $7 million × 1.03/(0.15 – 0.03) = $60.1m

Selorne Co free cash flow to equity = $325m/8 = $40.6m

Combined company valuation = ($40.6m + $7m + $5m) × 8 = $420.8m

Additional value created = $420.8m – $325m – $60.1 m = $35.7m

Tutorial note

Your answer to part (a) (ii) depends on the numbers calculated in part (a) (i). The markers are told to be aware of this when they are marking the real exam. As long as your method is correct, you will score full marks in part (a) (ii) even if your numbers are incorrect due to errors made in part (a) (i).

(ii) Chris Chawon will hold 2m × 5 = 10m shares in combined company

Value per share in combined company = $420.8m/(50m + 10m) = $7.01

Value of Chris Chawon's shareholding = 10m × $7.01 = $70.1m

Gain created for Chris Chawon = $70.1m - $60.1m = $10m

Gain created for Selorne Co shareholders = $35.7m – $10m = $25.7m

Chris Chawon will have a 16.7% (10m/(50m + 10m)) shareholding in the combined company but 28.0% ($10m/$35.7m) of the gain on the combination will be attributable to him. Shareholders who are doubtful about the merger may question whether this is excessive, as possibly Chawon Co's desire to sell is being prompted by the company struggling to remain solvent.

(b) **Reliability of synergy estimates**

The reliability of the estimates may vary depending on the synergies involved.

The synergies relating to size and services offered will depend on the ability to gain large contracts and neither company has had recent success in doing this. However, the contracts recently bid for by Chawon Co might have been won if the larger combined company had bid.

The synergies relating to operations and working practices may be difficult to obtain if it is difficult to change the employment conditions of Selorne Co drivers. Claims that improved driver utilisation may reduce spare capacity may be true, but there is likely to be less spare capacity anyway if more contracts are won.

Other synergies may be easier to obtain. Duplication of premises in some locations should be eliminated easily, providing Chawon Co does not have onerous rental contracts and there is space on Selorne Co's sites.

Combining central administrative functions should reduce some staffing costs, although these are likely to be smaller synergies than the potential operational synergies.

Problems with achieving synergies

A significant problem may be lack of unity at the top of the company. Selorne Co's directors are not all keen on the acquisition and this may spill over into being unable to agree on a clear post-acquisition plan. If lack of unity at board level becomes apparent to staff, it may be difficult to achieve unity at employee level.

Chris Chawon's role in the combined company may also make synergies difficult to achieve. He will have a significant shareholding and a place on the board, so it will be difficult for him not to be involved. Possibly he has the abilities and desire to achieve changes in operational practices which other board members lack. However, if Chris is given the leading role he requires, there may be a change in management style which may upset long-serving Selorne Co staff. Some may leave, jeopardising the continuity which seems to have been an important part of Selorne Co's success.

Another reason for possible problems with staff is the differing remuneration arrangements. Selorne Co's staff may have stayed with the company because both their job prospects and their remuneration have been safe. Attempts to change their employment conditions may lead to resistance and employee departures. Ex-Chawon Co employees who have been with the company for a while may expect salaries to be increased to be more in line with Selorne Co's employees, particularly if bonus arrangements become less generous.

The success of the acquisition may also depend on how well the staff of the two businesses integrate. Integration may be difficult to achieve. Many of Chawon Co's staff will not have the necessary licence to drive the Selorne Co lorries and may not wish to go through the process of obtaining this licence. Selorne Co drivers may be reluctant to drive the smaller vehicles. Staff sticking to what they have been used to driving is likely to prolong a 'them and us' culture.

Marking guide			
			Marks
(a)	(i)	Valuation of Selorne Co	1
		Valuation of Chawon Co	2
		Valuation of Selorne Co FCFE	1
		Valuation of combined company	1
		Additional value created	1
			6
	(ii)	Value per share combined company	1
		Value of Chris Chawon's shareholding in combined company	1
		Share of gain created for Chris Chawon	1
		Share of gain created for Selorne Co shareholders	1
		Comments	2
			6
(b)		Up to 2 marks per relevant point discussed. Discussion must be related to Selorne Co to obtain 2 marks for a point.	
		Reliability of estimates	3–4
		Problems with achieving synergies	4–5
		Maximum	**8**
		Professional skills marks (see below)	**5**
Total			**25**

Professional skills marks

Analysis and Evaluation

Appropriate use of the data to determine suitable calculations

Appropriate use of the data to support discussion and draw appropriate conclusions

Appraisal of information objectively

Scepticism

Effective challenge and critical assessment of the information and assumptions provided in relation to the valuation and synergies

Commercial acumen

Effective use of examples and/or practical considerations related to the context to illustrate points being made relating to synergies

Maximum 5 marks

51   KERRIN CO (SEP/DEC 19)

Key answer tips

In part (a) here you are being asked to identify financial synergies, so no marks were available for cost synergies or revenue synergies. Read the requirements carefully!

Some of the calculations in part (b) were quite tricky, but a student with good exam technique would still score well in part (c) by making generic points that do not depend on the specific calculations from part (b).

(a)   Financial synergies

Many acquisitions are justified on the basis that the combined organisation will be more profitable or grow at a faster rate than the companies operating independently. The expectation is that the acquisition will generate higher expected cash flows or a lower cost of capital, creating value for shareholders. The additional value created is known as synergy, the sources of which can be categorised into three types: revenue, cost and financial synergies.

Based on the scenario, there are a number of possible sources of financial synergy. As a private company, Danton Co is experiencing a funding constraint whereas Kerrin Co has significant cash reserves but limited growth opportunities. The combination of the two can create additional value since Danton Co may be able to utilise Kerrin Co's cash resources to fund its expansion in a way which would not have been possible otherwise, leading to an increase in the expected cash flows.

Assuming both companies' cash flows are less than perfectly correlated, those of the combined company will be less volatile than the individual companies operating independently. This reduction in volatility enables the combined company to borrow more and possibly cheaper financing than would otherwise have been possible. This increase in debt capacity, and therefore the present value of the tax shield, increases the value of the combined company in the form of a lower cost of capital.

Further benefits may arise if Kerrin Co is able to utilise Danton Co's unrelieved tax losses. Whilst Danton is no longer loss making and could offset these tax losses independently, the combined company may be able to obtain tax relief earlier since the acquisition increases the availability of profits against which carried forward tax losses can be offset. The present value of the tax saved will therefore be greater in the combined company.

If both companies were publicly traded, there would be no benefit from diversification since investors are capable of diversifying at a lower cost and with greater ease than the company. However, Danton Co is privately owned and the shareholders are therefore exposed to diversifiable unsystematic risk. Therefore the acquisition may lead to potential diversification and risk reduction benefits. The reduction in the cost of the capital increases the value of the combined company.

(b) **Pre-acquisition valuations**

Kerrin Co number of shares = 375m/0.5 = 750m

Kerrin Co market value = 750m × $5.28 = $3,960m

Future maintainable earnings (FME) = ($381.9) × 0.8 = $305.5m

Price earnings (PE) ratio = $3,960m/$305.5m = 12.96

Danton Co future maintainable earnings = ($116.3m + $2.5m) × 0.8 = $95.0m

Danton Co PE ratio = 12.96 × 1.20 = 15.55

Danton Co PE valuation = 15.55 × $95m = $1,477.3m

Combined Co pre-acquisition valuation = $3,960m + $1,477.3m = $5,437.3m

Post-acquisition valuation including synergies

Combined Co FME = $305.5m + $95m + ($20.5m × 0.8) = $416.9m

Combined Co PE ratio 12.96 × 1.1 = 14.3

Combined Co post-merger valuation = 14.3 × $416.9m = $5,961.7m

Value created based on synergies = $5,961.7m – $5,437.3m = $524.4m

Share-for-share offer

	Kerrin Co $m	Danton Co $m
Pre-acquisition valuation	3,960.0	1,477.3
Add premium ($1,477.3m × 0.3)		443.2
Balance of excess value to Kerrin Co:		
$524.4m – $443.2m	81.2	
Post-merger valuation	4,041.2	1,920.5
Relative valuation	2.1	1

Kerrin Co new share issue = 750m/2.1 = 357.14m

Number of existing Danton Co shares = 35m × 4 = 140m

Therefore share-for-share offer = 357.14/140, i.e. approximately 18 Kerrin Co shares for every 7 Danton Co old shares

Advice on terms of share-for-share offer

Danton Co shareholders would receive 140m × (18/7) = 360m new Kerrin Co shares. Total Kerrin Co shares = 750m + 360m = 1,110m.

Kerrin Co shareholders own 67.6% (750m/1,110m) and Danton Co shareholders 32.4% (360m/1,110m) of the post-acquisition company.

Impact on shareholder wealth

	Kerrin Co $m	Danton Co $m
Pre-acquisition valuation	3,960.0	1,477.3
Cash offer		
Danton Co shareholders cash received:		
$13.10 × 140m shares		1,834.0
Kerrin Co post-acquisition equity valuation:		
$5,961.7m less acquisition cost of $1,834.0m	4,127.7	
Increase in shareholder wealth	4.2%	24.1%
Share-for-share offer		
Post-acquisition value		
Kerrin Co: (750/1,110) × $5,961.7	4,028.2	
Danton Co (360/1,110) × $5,961.7		1,933.5
Increase in shareholder wealth	1.7%	30.9%

The terms of the share-for-share offer meet the criteria specified by Danton Co's directors.

(c) Cash offer

The main advantage of a cash offer is that it provides Danton Co's shareholders with a certain and immediate return. However, the premium is lower compared to the share-for-share offer and may be reduced even further if the realised gain gives rise to a tax liability. By indicating their preferred premium under both offers, it is possible the shareholders have priced in the risks associated with an uncertain share-for-share offer and on this basis may be indifferent between the two. The cash offer may give rise to agency issues since Danton Co's founders no longer have a stake in the business even though Kerrin Co's board is keen to ensure the founders remain in position after the acquisition. The information provided is too limited to read too much into the intentions of the venture capitalist. However, typically a venture capitalist would be expected to exit within three to five years. In this case, they may prefer the certainty of the cash offer.

The cash offer transfers more of the added value to Kerrin Co without the need for dilution, which may appeal to the shareholders. As indicated in the question, Kerrin Co's existing reserves are sufficient to fund the cash offer although this may constrain future dividends and/or investment decisions.

Share-for-share offer

Both sets of shareholders benefit from increased wealth as a result of the share offer, albeit only marginally so in the case of Kerrin Co's shareholders. Another drawback is that Kerrin Co's shareholders' percentages are also diluted under this method. However, a share-for-share offer would ensure that Danton Co's founders' interests are aligned with Kerrin Co's shareholders, reducing possible agency costs. It also provides Danton Co's shareholders with the right to participate in the future growth of the larger company, which the cash offer would prevent.

No basis has been provided for the synergistic benefits; the increase in shareholder wealth is so marginal even a minor deviation from the estimates could result in a reduction in shareholder wealth for the owners of Kerrin Co. On this basis, it is quite likely they will not approve a share-for-share offer without further negotiation around the acquisition premium.

Note: Credit will be given for alternative and valid comments.

	Marking guide		
			Marks
(a)	Financial synergies 1–2 marks per relevant point		4
		Maximum	**4**
(b)	Kerrin PE ratio		2
	Danton valuation		2
	Post-acquisition valuation		3
	Share-for-share offer terms		2
	Advice		1
	Impact on shareholder wealth		3
		Maximum	**12**
(c)	Cash offer		2–3
	Share-for-share offer		2–3
		Maximum	**4**
	Professional skills marks (see below)		**5**
Total			**25**

Professional skills marks

Analysis and Evaluation

Appropriate use of the data to determine suitable calculations

Appropriate use of the data to support discussion and draw appropriate conclusions

Appraisal of information objectively to make a recommendation on suitable share exchange terms

Scepticism

Effective challenge and critical assessment of the information and assumptions provided in relation to the different offers

Commercial acumen

Effective use of examples and/or practical considerations related to the context to illustrate points being made relating to financial synergies

Maximum 5 marks

CORPORATE RECONSTRUCTION AND REORGANISATION

52 ALASKA SALVAGE (DEC 09)

Key answer tips

The examiner is constantly trying to think of new ways to test the application of the Black-Scholes model. In previous exams, the application of the model to warrants had never been tested, so many students found this a very difficult question.

However, as with any Black-Scholes question, the key thing is to pick out the five key input factors at the start and to list them out. This will ensure that you are awarded all the available method marks even if you make an error with one or more of the input factors.

(a)   A warrant is an option attached to another financial instrument on issue which can be detached and negotiated independently of the underlying issue. Warrants are usually exercised over a longer term than traded options but can be valued in exactly the same way using the Black Scholes Option Pricing Model by inserting into the standard formula.

Volatility = 20%

Current price = $85

Exercise price = $90

Time = 5 years

Risk free rate = 5%

Tutorial note

Look out for the BSOP calculator spreadsheet response option in the exam. You'll need to enter the above five key variables in the spreadsheet to generate the answers shown below.

From the BSOP calculator spreadsheet, we can read off the following values:

d_1 = 0.6548

d_2 = 0.2076

$N(d_1)$ = 0.7437

$N(d_2)$ = 0.5822

Value of call option = $22.41

The option in this case is a call option.

Given that each warrant represents an option on 100 equity shares the value of each warrant is $2,241.

The Black Scholes model makes a number of restrictive assumptions:

1   The warrant is a 'European' style option.

2   The share price follows a log-normal distribution and is continuously traded.

3   Unrestricted short selling of the underlying security is permitted.

4   There are no market frictions such as taxes or transaction costs.

5   No dividends are paid during the life of the warrant.

These assumptions are less realistic with a company such as Alaska Salvage than with a large enterprise with a full listing. It is unlikely, for example, that the company's shares will be actively traded or that the share market is efficient in its pricing of the equity.

(b)   The coupon rate is derived from the cash flow to the lender as follows:

1   Lay out the cash flow to the lender showing the value of the warrant as a benefit accruing immediately to the lender.

	0	1	2	3	4	5
Coupon	(10,000)	100 × c%	100 × c%	100 × c%	100 × c%	100 × c%
Repayment						10,000
Call value	2,241					
Cash flow to lender	(7,759)	100 × c%	100 × c%	100 × c%	100 × c%	10,000 +
						100 × c%

2   Solve the following equation where c% is the coupon rate and A and V are the five-year annuity and discount factors at 13% respectively:

7,759 = 100 × c% × A + 10,000 × V

Therefore:

7,759 = 100 × c% × 3.517 + 10,000 × 0.543

By rearrangement:

$$c\% = \frac{7,759 - 10,000 \times 0.543}{100 \times 3.517}$$

Therefore a 6.62% coupon rate will give an effective rate of return on the investment to the lender of 13%.

(c)   Mezzanine debt such as this is one mechanism by which a small, high growth firm such as Alaska Salvage can raise debt finance where the risk of default is high and/or there is a low level of asset coverage for the loan. In this case raising a loan of $1.6 million would raise the market gearing of the firm from zero (assuming there is no current outstanding debt) to 13.6% (debt to total capitalisation). This increase in borrowing against what might be presumed to be specialised salvaging equipment and the forward cost of operation may not be attractive to the commercial banking sector and may need specialised venture finance. The issue of warrants gives the lender the opportunity to participate in the success of the venture but with a reasonable level of coupon assured. However, the disadvantage for the current equity investors is that the value of their investment will be reduced by the value of the warrants issued. The extent to which this will be worthwhile depends upon the value of the firm on the assumption that the project proceeds and is financed in the way described. This should ultimately decide the maximum value that they would be prepared to pay to finance the new project.

(d) Sukuk bonds

Sukuk bonds are a type of Islamic financing method.

At the moment, Alaska Salvage intends to issue loan notes to raise debt finance. The loan note holder will receive interest (to be paid before dividends).

This is prohibited under Islamic law.

Instead, Islamic bonds (or sukuk) are linked to an underlying asset, such that a sukuk holder is a partial owner in the underlying assets and profit is linked to the performance of the underlying asset. So, for example, a sukuk holder will participate in the ownership of the company issuing the sukuk and has a right to profits (but will equally bear their share of any losses).

There are two types of sukuk bonds:

- Asset based – raising finance where the principal is covered by the capital value of the asset but the returns and repayments to sukuk holders are not directly financed by these assets.

- Asset backed – raising finance where the principal is covered by the capital value of the asset but the returns and repayments to sukuk holders are directly financed by these assets.

Asset backed sukuk bonds are often considered to be more akin to equity finance, so Alaska Salvage would be best advised to issue asset based sukuk bonds here, to provide the investors with an investment more similar to the conventional loan notes.

Marking scheme		Marks
(a) Correct input factors		1
Correct use of BSOP calculator		2
Value of the warrant		1
Assumptions (one each to a maximum of 3)		3
	Maximum	6
(b) Estimation of the coupon rate (2 marks for deducting option value from face value of warrant and 2 marks for calculation of coupon using annuity and discount factors)		4
	Maximum	4
(c) Identification of mezzanine debt as a source of high risk finance		2
Disadvantage for equity investors (reduction in equity value on exercise)		2
Advantages: low coupon, additional equity participation		2
	Maximum	6
(d) 1–2 marks per sensible, well-explained point		4
Professional skills marks (see below)		5
Total		25

Professional skills marks

Analysis and Evaluation

Appropriate use of the data to determine suitable calculations

Appropriate use of the data to support discussion and draw appropriate conclusions

Appraisal of information objectively

Commercial acumen

Effective use of examples and/or practical considerations related to the context to illustrate points being made

Maximum 5 marks

53   ENNEA CO (JUN 12)

Key answer tips

Notice how this model answer is presented in a very efficient way. The use of columns to show the current position and then the three proposals side by side makes it easy to identify the differences and similarities between the proposals.

Forecast financial position

Amounts in $000	Current	Proposal 1	Proposal 2	Proposal 3
Non-current assets	282,000	282,000	302,000	257,000
Current assets	66,000	64,720	67,720	63,682
Total assets	348,000	346,720	369,720	320,682
Current liabilities	37,000	37,000	37,000	37,000
Non-current liabilities	140,000	160,000	160,000	113,000
Total liabilities	177,000	197,000	197,000	150,000
Share capital (40c/share)	48,000	45,500	48,000	48,000
Retained earnings	123,000	104,220	124,720	122,682
Total equity	171,000	149,720	172,720	170,682
Total liabilities and capital	348,000	346,720	369,720	320,682

Adjustments to forecast earnings

Amounts in $000	Current	Proposal 1	Proposal 2	Proposal 3
Initial profit after tax	26,000	26,000	26,000	26,000
Interest payable on additional borrowing				
($20m × 6% × (1 – 0.2))		(960)	(960)	
Additional interest payable on extra coupon				
($160m × 0.25% × (1 – 0.2))		(320)	(320)	
Interest saved on less borrowing				
($27m × 6% × (1 – 0.2))				1,296
Interest saved on lower coupon				
($113m × 0.15% × (1 – 0.2))				136
Return on additional investment				
($20m × 15%)			3,000	
Return lost on less investment				
($25m × 15%)				(3,750)
Profit on sale of non-current assets				2,000
	————	————	————	————
Adjusted profit after tax	26,000	24,720	27,720	25,682
	————	————	————	————

	Current	Proposal 1	Proposal 2	Proposal 3
Gearing % (non-current liabilities/equity)	81.9%	106.9%	92.6%	66.2%
Number of shares ('000)	120,000	113,750	120,000	120,000
Earnings per share (adjusted profit after tax/number of shares)	21.67c	21.73c	23.10c	21.40c

Note: Gearing defined as non-current liabilities/(non-current liabilities + equity) and/or using market value of equity is acceptable as well.

Tutorial note

Explanations are not required for the answer but are included to explain the approach taken.

Explanations of the financial position based on the three proposals

Proposal 1

Debt is increased by $20m and share capital reduced by the same amount as follows: from nominal value = $20m × 40c/320c = $2.5m; from retained earnings = $20m × 280c/320c = $17.5m.

Additional interest payable totalling $1,280,000 ($960,000 + $320,000) is taken off retained earnings due to reduction in profit after tax and taken off current assets because presumably it is paid from cash. Note that an alternative answer would be to add the additional interest payable to current liabilities.

Proposal 2

Debt and non-current assets are increased by $20m.

Additional interest payable as above, plus the additional investment of $20 million will generate a rate of return of 15%, which is $3,000,000 income. Net impact is $1,720,000 income which is added to retained earnings as an addition to profit after tax and added to current assets as a cash income (presumably).

Proposal 3

Net non-current assets are reduced by the $25 million, their value at disposal. Since they were sold for $27 million, this is how much the non-current liabilities are reduced by and the profit of $2 million is included in the retained earnings.

Interest saved totals $1,432,000 ($1,296,000 + $136,000). The reduction in investment of $25 million will lose $3,750,000, at a rate of return of 15%. Net impact is $2,318,000 loss which is subtracted from earnings as a reduction from profit after tax and deducted from current assets as a cash expense (presumably).

Discussion

Proposals 1 and 3 appear to produce opposite results to each other. Proposal 1 would lead to a small increase in the earnings per share (EPS) due to a reduction in the number of shares although profits would decrease by approximately 5%, due to the increase in the amount of interest payable as a result of increased borrowings. However, the level of gearing would increase substantially (by about 30%).

With proposal 3, although the overall profits would fall, because of the lost earnings due to downsizing being larger than the gain in interest saved and profit made on the sale of assets, this is less than proposal 1 (1.2%). Gearing would reduce substantially (19.2%).

Proposal 2 would give a significant boost in the EPS from 21.67c/share to 23.10c/share, which the other two proposals do not. This is mainly due to increase in earnings through extra investment. However, the amount of gearing would increase by more than 13%.

Overall proposal 1 appears to be the least attractive option. The choice between proposals 2 and 3 would be between whether the company would prefer larger EPS or less gearing. This would depend on factors such as the capital structure of the competitors, the reaction of the equity market to the proposals, the implications of the change in the risk profile of the company and the resultant impact on the cost of capital. Ennea Co should also bear in mind that the above are estimates and the actual results will probably differ from the forecasts.

Note: Credit will be given for alternative relevant comments and suggestions.

Marking scheme	
	Marks
Financial position calculations: proposal 1	3
Financial position calculations: proposal 2	2
Financial position calculations: proposal 3	3
Adjustments to forecast earnings	
Interest payable on additional borrowing and higher coupon	2
Interest saved lower borrowing and lower coupon	1
Return on additional investment	1
Return lost on less investment and profit on sale of non-current assets	1
Gearing and EPS calculations	2
Discussion of the results of the proposals	2–3
Discussion of the implications (e.g. risk, market reaction, etc.)	2–3
Maximum	20
Professional skills marks (see below)	5
Total	25

Professional skills marks

Analysis and Evaluation

Appropriate use of the data to determine suitable calculations

Appropriate use of the data to support discussion and draw appropriate conclusions

Appraisal of information objectively

Commercial acumen

Effective use of examples and/or practical considerations related to the context to illustrate points being made

Maximum 5 marks

54 NUBO CO (DEC 13)

Key answer tips

Islamic finance came into the syllabus in 2013 and it was tested here for the first time. Make sure that you understand the different Islamic financing methods and how they differ from the more traditional financing options.

(a) Current and non-current liabilities = $387m + $95m = $482m

Sale of assets of supermarkets division

Proportion of assets to supermarkets division

Non-current assets = 70% × $550m = $385m; Current assets = 70% × $122m = $85.4m

Sale of assets = $385m × 1.15 + $85.4m × 0.80 = $511.07m

Sale of supermarkets division as a going concern

Profit after tax attributable to the supermarkets division: $166m/2 = $83m

Estimate of value of supermarkets division based on the PE ratio of supermarket industry: $83 × 7 = $581m

Although both options generate sufficient funds to pay for the liabilities, the sale of the supermarkets division as a going concern would generate higher cash flows and the spare cash of $99m [$581m − $482m] can be used by Nubo Co for future investments. This is based on the assumption that the value based on the industries' PE ratios is accurate.

Proportion of assets remaining within Nubo Co

30% × ($550m + $122m) = $201.6m

Add extra cash generated from the sale of $99m

Maximum debt capacity = $300.6m

Total additional funds available to Nubo Co for new investments = $300.6m + $99m = $399.6m

(b) With a Mudaraba contract, the profits which Pilvi Co makes from the joint venture would be shared according to a pre-agreed arrangement when the contract is constructed between Pilvi Co and Ulap Bank. Losses, however, would be borne solely by Ulap Bank as the provider of the finance, although provisions can be made where losses can be written off against future profits. Ulap Bank would not be involved in the executive decision-making process. In effect, Ulap Bank's role in the relationship would be similar to an equity holder, holding a small number of shares in a large organisation.

With a Musharaka contract, the profits which Pilvi Co makes from the joint venture would still be shared according to a pre-agreed arrangement similar to a Mudaraba contract, but losses would also be shared according to the capital or other assets and services contributed by both the parties involved in the arrangement. Therefore a value could be put to the contribution-in-kind made by Pilvi Co and any losses would be shared by Ulap Bank and Pilvi Co accordingly. Within a Musharaka contract, Ulap Bank can also take the role of an active partner and participate in the executive decision-making process. In effect, the role adopted by Ulap Bank would be similar to that of a venture capitalist.

With the Mudaraba contract, Pilvi Co would essentially be an agent to Ulap Bank, and many of the agency issues facing corporations would apply to the arrangement, where Pilvi Co can maximise its own benefit at the expense of Ulap Bank. Pilvi Co may also have a propensity to undertake excessive risk because it is essentially holding a long call option with an unlimited upside and a limited downside.

Ulap Bank may prefer the Musharaka contract in this case, because it may be of the opinion that it needs to be involved with the project and monitor performance closely due to the inherent risk and uncertainty of the venture, and also to ensure that the revenues, expenditure and time schedules are maintained within initially agreed parameters. In this way, it may be able to monitor and control agency related issues more effectively and control Pilvi Co's risky actions and decisions. Being closely involved with the venture would change both Pilvi Co's and Ulap Bank's roles and make them more like stakeholders rather than principals and agents, with a more equitable distribution of power between the two parties.

Nubo Co's concerns would mainly revolve around whether it can work with Ulap Bank and the extra time and cost which would need to be incurred before the joint venture can start. If Pilvi Co had not approached Ulap Bank for funding, the relationship between Nubo Co and Pilvi Co would be less complex within the joint venture. Although difficulties may arise about percentage ownership and profit sharing, these may be resolved through negotiation and having tight specific contracts. The day-to-day running, management and decision-making process could be resolved through negotiation and consensus. Therefore having a third party involved in all aspects of the joint venture complicates matters.

Nubo Co may feel that it was not properly consulted about the arrangements between Pilvi Co and Ulap Bank, and Pilvi Co would need to discuss the involvement of Ulap Bank with Nubo Co and gets its agreement prior to formalising any arrangements. This is to ensure a high level of trust continues to exist between the parties, otherwise the venture may fail.

Nubo Co may want clear agreements on ownership and profit-sharing. They would want to ensure that the contract clearly distinguishes them as not being part of the Musharaka arrangement which exists between Pilvi Co and Ulap Bank. Hence negotiation and construction of the contracts may need more time and may become more expensive.

Nubo Co may have felt that it could work with Pilvi Co on a day-to-day basis and could resolve tough decisions in a reasonable manner. It may not feel the same about Ulap Bank initially. Clear parameters would need to be set up on how executive decision making will be conducted by the three parties. Therefore, the integration process of bringing a third partner into the joint venture needs to be handled with care and may take time and cost more money.

The above issues would indicate that the relationship between the three parties is closer to that of stakeholders, with different levels of power and influence, at different times, as opposed to a principal–agent relationship. This would create an environment which would need ongoing negotiation and a need for consensus, which may make the joint venture hard work. Additionally, it would possibly be more difficult and time consuming to accomplish the aims of the joint venture.

Note: Credit will be given for alternative relevant comments and suggestions for part (b) of the question.

Marking scheme		Marks
(a)	Sale of supermarkets division's assets	2
	Sale of supermarkets division as going concern	1
	Advice	2
	Extra cash after liabilities are paid	1
	Maximum debt which can be borrowed	1
	Additional funds available to Nubo Co	1
		8
(c)	Discussion of why Ulap Bank might prefer a Musharaka contract	6–7
	Discussion of the key concerns of the joint venture relationship	5–6
	Maximum	12
	Professional skills marks (see below)	5
Total		25

Professional skills marks

Analysis and Evaluation

Appropriate use of the data to determine suitable calculations

Appropriate use of the data to support discussion and draw appropriate conclusions

Appraisal of information objectively to make a recommendation

Scepticism

Effective challenge of information, evidence and assumptions supplied and, techniques carried out to support key facts and/or decisions

Demonstration of ability to consider all relevant factors applicable to a given course of action

Commercial acumen

Recommendations are practical and plausible in the context of Nubo Co's situation

Effective use of examples and/or calculations from the scenario information and other practical considerations related to the context to illustrate points being made relating to unbundling and Islamic finance

Maximum 5 marks

55   BENTO CO (JUN 15)

Key answer tips

Achievement of a covenant on a management buyout has been tested several times in recent years.

Make sure you read the specific terms of the covenant carefully before presenting your answer.

(a)   Annuity (8%, 4 years) = 3.312

Annuity payable per year on loan = $30,000,000/3.312 = $9,057,971

Interest payable on convertible loan, per year = $20,000,000 × 6% = $1,200,000

Annual interest on 8% bond

(All amounts in $000s)

Year end	1	2	3	4
Opening loan balance	30,000	23,342	16,151	8,385
Interest at 8%	2,400	1,867	1,292	671
Annuity	(9,058)	(9,058)	(9,058)	(9,058)
Closing loan balance	23,342	16,151	8,385	(2)*

*The loan outstanding in year 4 should be zero. The small negative figure is due to rounding.

Estimate of profit and retained earnings after MBO

(All amounts in $000s)

Year end	1	2	3	4
Operating profit	13,542	15,032	16,686	18,521
Finance costs	3,600	3,067	2,492	1,871
Profit before tax	9,942	11,965	14,194	16,650
Taxation	1,988	2,393	2,839	3,330
Profit for the year	7,954	9,572	11,355	13,320
Dividends	1,989	2,393	2,839	3,330
Retained earnings	5,965	7,179	8,516	9,990

Estimate of gearing

(All amounts in $000s)

Year end	1	2	3	4
Book value of equity	15,965*	23,144	31,660	41,650
Book value of debt	43,342	36,151	28,385	20,000
Gearing	73%	61%	47%	32%
Covenant	75%	60%	50%	40%
Covenant breached?	No	Yes	No	No

*The book value of equity consists of the sum of the 5,000,000 equity shares which Dofu Co and Okazu Co's senior management will each invest in the new company (total 10,000,000), issued at their nominal value of $1 each, and the retained earnings from year 1. In subsequent years the book value of equity is increased by the retained earnings from that year.

The gearing covenant is forecast to be breached in the second year only, and by a marginal amount. It is forecast to be met in all the other years. It is unlikely that Dofu Co will be too concerned about the covenant breach.

(b)   Net asset valuation

Based on the net asset valuation method, the value of the new company is approximately: 1.3 × $40,800,000 + $12,300,000 − $7,900,000 approx. = $57,440,000

Dividend valuation model

Year	Dividend ($000s)	DF (12%)	PV ($000s)
1	1,989	0.893	1,776
2	2,393	0.797	1,907
3	2,839	0.712	2,021
4	3,330	0.636	2,118
Total			7,822

Annual dividend growth rate, years 1 to 4 = $(3{,}330/1{,}989)^{1/3} - 1 = 18.7\%$

Annual dividend growth rate after year 4 = 7.5% [40% × 18.7%]

Value of dividends after year 4 = ($3,330,000 × 1.075)/(0.12 − 0.075) × 0.636 = $50,594,000 approximately

Based on the dividend valuation model, the value of new company is approximately:

$7,822,000 + $50,594,000 = $58,416,000

The $60 million asked for by Bento Co is higher than the current value of the new company's net assets and the value of the company based on the present value of future dividends based on the dividend valuation model. Although the future potential of the company represented by the dividend valuation model, rather than the current value of the assets, is probably a better estimate of the potential of the company, the price of $60 million seems excessive.

Nevertheless, both the management team and Dofu Co are expected to receive substantial dividends during the first four years and Dofu Co's 8% bond loan will be repaid within four years.

Furthermore, the dividend valuation model can produce a large variation in results if the model's variables are changed by even a small amount. Therefore, the basis for estimating the variables should be examined carefully to judge their reasonableness, and sensitivity analysis applied to the model to demonstrate the impact of the changes in the variables. The value of the future potential of the new company should also be estimated using alternative valuation methods including free cash flows and price-earnings methods.

It is therefore recommended that the MBO should not be rejected at the outset but should be considered further. It is also recommended that the management team and Dofu Co try to negotiate the sale price with Bento Co.

Note: Credit will be given for alternative, relevant discussion for part (b).

Marking scheme		
		Marks
(a)	Amount of annual annuity of 8% bond	1
	Annual split between interest and capital repayment of 8% bond	2
	Operating profit for first four years	1
	Finance costs	2
	Tax payable for the first four years	1
	Dividend payable for the first four years	1
	Book values of debt and of equity in years 1 to 4	2
	Gearing levels and concluding comment	2
		–––
		12
		–––
(b)	Company value based on net asset valuation method	1
	Company value based on the dividend valuation method	3
	Discussion (1 to 2 marks per point)	4
		–––
	Maximum	8
		–––
	Professional skills marks (see below)	5
		–––
Total		25
		–––

Professional skills marks

Analysis and Evaluation

Appropriate use of the data to determine suitable calculations

Appropriate use of the data to support discussion and draw appropriate conclusions

Appraisal of information objectively

Scepticism

Effective challenge of information, evidence and assumptions supplied and, techniques carried out to support key facts and/or decisions

Demonstration of ability to consider all relevant factors applicable to a given course of action

Commercial acumen

Effective use of examples and/or calculations from the scenario information and other practical considerations related to the context to illustrate points being made relating to financing and unbundling

Maximum 5 marks

56   FLUFFTORT CO (SEP/DEC 15)

Key answer tips

Notice that the discussion of whether the scheme will be acceptable to the various stakeholders accounts for a significant number of the marks in this question.

It is therefore critical that you don't spend too long on the numerical forecasts in part (a).

(a)   (i)   **SOFP if Gupfe VC shares are purchased by Flufftort Co and cancelled.**

	$m
Assets	
Non-current assets	69
Current assets excluding cash	18
Cash	–
	———
Total assets	87
	———

Equity and liabilities

Share capital	40
Retained earnings	5
Total equity	45
Long-term liabilities	
Bank loan	30
Loan note	5
Total long-term liabilities	35
Current liabilities	7
Total liabilities	42
Total equity and liabilities	87

(ii)   SOFP if full refinancing takes place

	$m
Assets	
Non-current assets	125
Current assets excluding cash	42
Cash (balancing figure)	5
Total assets	172
Equity and liabilities	
Share capital	90
Retained earnings	5
Total equity	95
Long-term liabilities	
Bank loan	65
Loan note	–
Total long-term liabilities	65
Current liabilities	12
Total liabilities	77
Total equity and liabilities	172

(iii)   Projected SOPL

	20X7 $m	20X8 $m
Operating profit	20.0	25.0
Finance cost	(6.5)	(6.5)
Profit before tax	13.5	18.5
Taxation 20%	(2.7)	(3.7)
Profit after tax	10. 8	14.8
Dividends	–	–
Retained earnings	10.8	14.8

(b)   Current situation

Initial product developments have not generated the revenues required to sustain growth. The new Easicushion chair appears to offer Flufftort Co much better prospects of commercial success. At present, however, Flufftort Co does not have the resources to make the investment required.

Purchase of Gupte VC's shares

In the worst case scenario, Gupte VC will demand repayment of its investment in a year's time. The calculations in (a) show the financial position in a year's time, assuming that there is no net investment in non-current assets or working capital, the purchase of shares is financed solely out of cash reserves and the shares are cancelled. Repayment by this method would mean that the limits set out in the covenant would be breached (45/35 = 1.29) and the bank could demand immediate repayment of the loan.

The directors can avoid this by buying some of Gupte VC's shares themselves, but this represents money which is not being put into the business. In addition, the amount of shares which the directors would have to purchase would be greater if results, and therefore reserves, were worse than expected.

Financing the investment

The calculations in (a) show that the cash flows associated with the refinancing would be enough to finance the initial investment. The ratio of equity to non-current liabilities after the refinancing would be 1.46 (95/65), in line with the current limits in the bank's covenant. However, financing for the subsequent investment required would have to come from surplus cash flows.

Shareholdings

The disposition of shareholdings will change as follows:

	Current shareholdings		Shareholdings after refinancing	
	Number in million	%	Number in million	%
Directors	27.5	55.0	42.5	47.2
Other family members	12.5	25.0	12.5	13.9
Gupte VC	10.0	20.0	30.0	33.3
Loan note holder	–	–	5.0	5.6
	50.0	100.0	90.0	100.0

Gupte VC's percentage shareholding will rise from 20% to 33.3%, enough possibly to give it extra rights over the company. The directors' percentage shareholding will fall from 55% to 47.2%, which means that collectively they no longer have control of the company. The percentage of shares held by family members who are not directors falls from 25% to around 19.5%, taking into account the conversion of the loan note. This will mean, however, that the directors can still maintain control if they can obtain the support of some of the rest of the family.

Position of finance providers

The refinancing has been agreed by the chief executive and finance director. At present, it is not clear what the views of the other directors are, or whether the $15 million contributed by directors will be raised from them in proportion to their current shareholdings. Some of the directors may not be able to, or wish to, make a significant additional investment in the company. On the other hand, if they do not, their shareholdings, and perhaps their influence within the company, will diminish. This may be a greater concern than the board collectively losing control over the company, since it may be unlikely that the other shareholders will combine to outvote the board.

The other family shareholders have not been actively involved in Flufftort Co's management out of choice, so a reduction in their percentage shareholdings may not be an issue for them. They may have welcomed the recent dividend payment as generating a return on their investment. However, as they appear to have invested for the longer term, the new investment appears to offer much better prospects in the form of a capital gain on listing or buy-out than an uncertain flow of dividends. The new investment appears only to have an upside for them in the sense that they are not being asked to contribute any extra funding towards it.

Rajiv Patel is unlikely to be happy with the proposed scheme. He is exchanging a guaranteed flow of income for an uncertain flow of future dividends sometime after 20X8. On the other hand, his investment may be jeopardised by the realisation of the worst case scenario, since his debt is subordinated to the bank's debt.

The most important issue from Gupte VC's viewpoint is whether the extra investment required is likely to yield a better outcome than return of its initial investment in a year's time. The plan that no dividends would be paid until after 20X8 is a disadvantage. On the other hand, the additional investment seems to offer the only prospect of realising a substantial gain either by Flufftort Co being listed or sold.

The arrangement will mean that Gupte VC may be able to exercise greater influence over Flufftort Co, which may provide it with a greater sense of reassurance about how Flufftort Co is being run. The fact that Gupte VC has a director on Flufftort Co's board should also give it a clear idea of how successful the investment is likely to be.

The bank will be concerned about the possibility of Flufftort Co breaching the covenant limits and may be concerned whether Flufftort Co is ultimately able to repay the full amount without jeopardising its existence. The bank will be concerned if Flufftort Co tries to replace loan finance with overdraft finance. The refinancing provides reassurance to the bank about gearing levels and a higher rate of interest. The bank will also be pleased that the level of interest cover under the refinancing is higher and increasing (from 2.0 in 20X6 to 3.1 in 20X7 and 3.8 in 20X8). However, it will be concerned about how Flufftort Co finances the additional investment required if cash flows from the new investment are lower than expected. In those circumstances Flufftort Co may seek to draw on its overdraft facility.

Conclusion

The key players in the refinancing are Gupte VC, the bank and the directors other than the chief executive and the finance director. If they can be persuaded, then the scheme has a good chance of being successful. However, Rajiv Patel could well raise objections. He may be pacified if he retains the loan note. This would marginally breach the current covenant limit (90/70 = 1.29), although the bank may be willing to overlook the breach as it is forecast to be temporary. Alternatively, the refinancing would mean that Flufftort Co just had enough spare cash initially to redeem the loan note, although it would be more dependent on cash surpluses after the refinancing to fund the additional investment required.

		Marking scheme		
				Marks
(a)	(i)	SOFP if shares purchased and cancelled		
		Cash and other assets		2
		Equity		1
		Liabilities		1
				4
	(ii)	SOFP if full refinancing takes place		
		Cash and other assets		2
		Equity		1
		Liabilities		1
				4
	(iii)	20X7 forecast		1
		20X8 forecast		1
				2
(b)		Up to 2 marks for each well discussed point	**Maximum**	10
		Professional skills marks (see below)		5
Total				25

Professional skills marks

Analysis and Evaluation

Appropriate use of the data to determine suitable calculations

Appropriate use of the data to support discussion and draw appropriate conclusions

Appraisal of information objectively to make a recommendation

Scepticism

Effective challenge of information, evidence and assumptions supplied and, techniques carried out to support key facts and/or decisions

Demonstration of ability to consider all relevant factors applicable to the refinancing scheme

Commercial acumen

Recommendations are practical and plausible in the context of Flufftort Co's situation

Effective use of examples and/or calculations from the scenario information and other practical considerations related to the context to illustrate points being made

Maximum 5 marks

57   STAPLE GROUP (MAR/JUN 16)

Key answer tips

In all corporate reconstruction questions, it is very important to read the company's plans carefully, and to follow them specifically when presenting the answer.

There were plenty of easy discussion marks in both parts (a) and (b) for students with a good exam technique.

(a)   Staple Local

Net assets valuation = 15/18 × $66.6m = $55.5m.

It is assumed that the titles in this division are equal in size.

The division's pre-tax profits are $4.5m and post-tax cash flows $0.3m, with losses forecast for the next year. Therefore any valuation based on current or future expected earnings is likely to be lower than the net assets valuation.

Benefits of selling Staple Local

The local newspapers seem to have the poorest prospects of any part of the group. Further investment may not make a big difference, if the market for local newspapers is in long-term decline.

The offer from Postway Co gives Staple Group the chance to gain cash immediately and to dispose of the papers. The alternative of selling the titles off piecemeal is an uncertain strategy, both in terms of the timescale required and the amounts which can be realised for individual titles. It is very likely that the titles with the best prospects would be sold first, leaving Staple Group with a remaining portfolio which is of very little value.

Drawbacks of selling Staple Local

The offer is not much more than a net asset valuation of the titles. The amount of cash from the sale to Postway Co will be insufficient for the level of investment required in the Daily Staple.

The digital platforms which will be developed for the Daily Staple could also be used to boost the local papers. Staff on the local titles could have an important role to play in providing content for the platforms.

Loss of the local titles may mean loss of economies of size. In particular, printing arrangements may be more economic if both national and local titles are printed at the same locations.

Staple View

Free cash flows to equity = $53.5m – $12.5m – $6.2m = $34.8m

Free cash flow valuation to equity = $34.8m (1.04)/(0.12 – 0.04) = $452.4m

The assumption of constant growth is most important in this valuation. It is possibly fairly conservative, but just as faster growth could be achieved by gaining the rights to broadcast more sporting events, results may be threatened if Staple View loses any of the rights which it currently has.

Benefits of selling Staple View

Present circumstances may be favourable for selling the television channels, given their current profitability. Staple Group may be able to obtain a better offer from a competitor than in the future, given recent acquisition activity in this sector.

Selling Staple View will certainly generate more cash than selling either of the smaller divisions. This will allow investment not only in the Daily Staple, but also investment in the other divisions, and possibly targeted strategic acquisitions.

Drawbacks of selling Staple View

The television channels have become a very important part of the Staple Group. Investors may believe that the group should be focusing on further investment in this division rather than investing in the Daily Staple, which may be in decline.

Selling the television channels removes an important opportunity for cross-selling. Newspaper coverage can be used to publicise important programmes on the television channels and the television channels can be used for advertising the newspaper.

Staple View is a bigger part of the group than the other two divisions and therefore selling it is likely to mean a bigger reduction in the group's borrowing capacity.

Staple Investor

The valuation made by the finance director is questionable as it is based on one year's profits, which may not be sustainable. There is no information about how the additional earnings have been calculated, whether the finance director has used a widely-accepted method of valuation or just used a best estimate. If a premium for additional earnings is justified, there is also no information about whether the benefit from staff's expertise and experience is assumed to be perpetual or just to last for a certain number of years.

Benefits of selling Staple Investor

This division appears to have great potential. Staple Group will be able to sell this division from a position of strength, rather than it being seen as a forced sale like selling the Staple Local division might be.

The division is in a specialist sector which is separate from the other areas in which Staple Group operates. It is not an integral part of the group in terms of the directors' current core strategy.

Drawbacks of selling Staple Investor

The division currently has the highest profit margin at 19.7% compared with Staple National 12.5%, Staple Local 3.0% and Staple View 14.8%. It seems likely to continue to deliver good results over the next few years. Investors may feel that it is the part of the group which offers the safest prospect of satisfactory returns.

Investors may be happy with the structure of the group as it is, as it offers them some diversification. Selling the Staple Investor division and focusing more on the newspaper parts of the group may result in investors seeking diversification by selling some of the shareholding in Staple Group and investing elsewhere.

Although Staple Group's management may believe that the valuation gives a good indication of the division's true value, they may not be able to sell the division for this amount now. If the division remains within the group, they may achieve a higher price in a few years' time. Even if Staple Investor could be sold for the $118.5 million valuation, this is less than the $150 million required for the planned investment.

Conclusion

Selling the Staple View division offers the directors the best chance to obtain the funds they require for their preferred strategy of investment in the Daily Staple. However, the directors are not considering the possibility of selling the Daily Staple, perhaps in conjunction with selling the local newspapers as well. Although this could be seen as selling off the part of the group which has previously been essential to its success, it would allow Staple Group to raise the funds for further investment in the television channels and the Staple Investor division. It could allow the directors to focus on the parts of the group which have been the most successful recently and offer the best prospects for future success.

(b) **Stakeholder conflicts**

If Staple Group takes a simple view of the role of stakeholders, it will prioritise the interest of shareholders over other stakeholders, particularly employees here, and take whatever actions are required to maximise profitability. However, in Staple Group's position, there may be a complication because of the differing requirements of shareholders. Some may want high short-term profits and dividends, which may imply significant cost cutting in under-performing divisions. Other shareholders may wish to see profits maximised over the long term and may worry that short-term cost cutting may result in a reduction of investment and adversely affect staff performance at an important time.

Transformational change of the newspaper business is likely to require the co-operation of at least some current employees. Inevitably redundancy will create uncertainty and perhaps prompt some staff to leave voluntarily. Staple Group's management may want to identify some key current employees who can lead the change and try to retain them.

Also the policy of making employees who have not been with the group very long redundant is likely to make it difficult to recruit good new employees. The group will probably create new roles as a result of its digital investment, but people may be unwilling to join the group if it has a reputation for bad faith and not fulfilling promises to develop its staff.

Ethical issues

The significance of what the firm's annual report says about its treatment of employees may depend on how specific it is. A promise to treat employees fairly is rather vague and may not carry much weight, although it broadly commits the firm to the ethical principle of objectivity. If, however, the policy makes more specific statements about engaging with employees and goes in the statement beyond what is required by law, then Staple Group is arguably showing a lack of honesty if it does not fulfil the commitments it has made.

The suggestion that managers should ensure that employees who are perceived to be 'troublemakers' should be first to be chosen for redundancy is dubious ethically. If managers do this, then they may be breaking the law, and would certainly be acting with a lack of honesty and transparency.

Marking scheme		Marks
(a) Sale of Staple Local		
Calculations/comments on figures		2
Discussion of benefits/drawbacks		2–3
Sale of Staple View		
Calculations/comments on figures		3
Discussion of benefits/drawbacks		2–3
Sale of Staple Investor		
Comments on figures		2
Discussion of benefits/drawbacks		2–3
Other points/conclusion		2–3
	Maximum	16
(b) Discussion of importance of different stakeholders and possible conflicts		2–3
Discussion of other ethical issues		2–3
	Maximum	4
Professional skills marks (see below)		5
Total		25

Professional skills marks

Analysis and Evaluation

Appropriate use of the data to determine suitable calculations

Appropriate use of the data to support discussion and draw appropriate conclusions

Appraisal of information objectively to make a recommendation

Scepticism

Effective challenge of information, evidence and assumptions supplied and, techniques carried out to support key facts and/or decisions

Demonstration of ability to consider all relevant factors applicable to each given proposal

Commercial acumen

Recommendations are practical and plausible in the context of The Staple Group's situation

Effective use of examples and/or calculations from the scenario information and other practical considerations related to the context to illustrate points being made

Maximum 5 marks

58 EVIEW CINEMAS CO (SEP/DEC 17)

Key answer tips

This question very cleverly integrated lots of separate bits of the syllabus.

The downside of this is that there was an awful lot to do in the time available, but the upside is that a well prepared student with a good exam technique has a wide choice of topics to attempt in order to grab enough marks to ensure a pass.

To be sure of a pass on this question, it would have been vital to leave enough time to attempt the discursive part of the question too, to comment on the figures obtained.

(a) **Proceeds from sales of EV clubs**

Current free cash flow valuation (given) = $6,139m

Desired sales proceeds (25% premium) = $6,139m × 1.25 = $7,674m

Impact on statement of financial position ($m)

Profit on sale = $7,674m – $3,790m = $3,884m

Current assets adjustment = $2,347m + $7,674m – ($2,166m × 1.5) = $6,772m

PPE adjustment = $6,772m – $3,200m = $3,572m

$m	Original	Sale proceeds	Adjust-ments	Final
Non-current assets	15,621	(3,790)	3,572	15,403
Current assets	2,347	7,674	(6,772)	3,249
Total assets	17,968			18,652
Equity and liabilities				
Called up share capital	1,000			1,000
Retained earnings	7,917	3,884		11,801
Total equity	8,917			12,801
Non-current liabilities				
10% loan notes	3,200		(3,200)	0
Other loan notes	2,700			2,700
Bank loans	985			985
Current liabilities	2,166			2,166
Total equity and liabilities	17,968			18,652

Impact on EPS ($m)

	Current	Revised
Predicted post-tax profits	1,135	1,135
Less: profits from EV clubs		(454)
Add: interest saved, net of tax ($3,200m × 10% × (1 – 0.2))		256
Add: return on additional non-current assets ($3,572m × 12% × (1 – 0.2))		343
Add: return on additional current assets ($902m × 7% × (1 – 0.2))		51
Adjusted profits	1,135	1,331
Number of shares	1,000m	1,000m
Adjusted EPS	$1.135	$1.331

Impact on WACC

Equity beta

Ve = $15,750m × 1.1 = $17,325m

Vd = ($2,700 × 0.93) + $985m = $3,496m

βe = 0.952 ((17,325 + 3,496 (1 – 0.2))/17,325 = 1.106

Revised cost of equity

ke = 4 + (10 – 4)1.106 = 10.64%

Revised WACC

WACC = 10.64 x (17,325/ (17,325 + 3,496)) + 8 x (1 – 0.2) (3,496/ (17,325 + 3,496)) = 9.93%

(b) Shareholders would appear to have grounds for questioning the sale of the EV clubs. It would mean that Eview Cinemas Co was no longer diversified into two sectors. Although shareholders can achieve diversification themselves in theory, in practice transaction costs and other issues may mean they do not want to adjust their portfolio.

The increase in gym membership brought about by the forthcoming sports festival could justify the predicted increases in free cash flows made in the forecasts. Although increased earnings per share are forecast once the EV clubs are sold, these are dependent on Eview Cinemas Co achieving the sales price which it desires for the EV clubs and the predicted returns being achieved on the remaining assets.

The proposed expansion of multiscreen cinemas may be a worthwhile opportunity, but the level of demand for big cinema complexes may be doubtful and there may also be practical problems like negotiating change of use. In Year 1 the EV clubs would be forecast to make a post-tax return on assets of (454/3,790) = 12.0% compared with 9.6% (12% × 0.8) on the additional investment in the cinemas.

Investors may also wonder about the motives of Eview Cinemas Co's board. Selling the EV clubs offers the board a convenient way of resolving the conflict with the management team of the EV clubs and investors may feel that the board is trying to take an easy path by focusing on what they are comfortable with managing.

There may be arguments in favour of the sale, however. The lower WACC will be brought about by a fall in the cost of equity as well as the fall in the cost of debt. A reduction in the complexity of the business may result in a reduction in central management costs.

Eview Cinemas Co may also be selling at a time when the EV clubs chain is at its most attractive as a business, in the period before the sports festival. The premium directors are hoping to obtain (on top of a valuation based on free cash flow figures which may be optimistic) suggest that they may be trying to realise maximum value while they can.

	Marking scheme		
			Marks
(a)	Desired sales proceeds (25% premium)		1
	Impact on statement of financial position		4
	Impact on EPS		4
	Impact on WACC		
	Equity beta - cinemas		2
	Revised cost of equity cinemas		1
	Revised WACC		1
			___
			13
			___
(b)	Arguments against sale		3–4
	Arguments for sale		3–4
			___
		Maximum	7
			___
	Professional skills marks (see below)		5
			___
Total			25
			___

Professional skills marks

Analysis and Evaluation

Appropriate use of the data to determine suitable calculations

Appropriate use of the data to support discussion and draw appropriate conclusions

Appraisal of information objectively to make a recommendation

Scepticism

Effective challenge of information, evidence and assumptions supplied and, techniques carried out to support key facts and/or decisions

Demonstration of ability to consider all relevant factors applicable to a given course of action

Commercial acumen

Recommendations are practical and plausible in the context of Eview Cinemas Co's situation

Effective use of examples and/or calculations from the scenario information and other practical considerations related to the context to illustrate points being made

Maximum 5 marks

AFM: ADVANCED FINANCIAL MANAGEMENT

59   NEWIMBER CO (MAR/JUN 19)

Key answer tips

WACC calculations often cause real problems for students.

Here you were asked to calculate the change in Newimber's WACC, so a calculation of WACC before the acquisition and then after the acquisition was required.

The best approach is to focus on calculating k_e and k_d (1-T), and also V_e and V_d, both before the acquisition and then afterwards (eight figures to calculate). Even if you struggle to identify one or two of these eight figures, you'll still score most of the marks.

(a)   Advantages of demerger

If the managers of the sportswear division's belief that they can run the division better without the interventions of senior management at Newimber Co is well-founded, the business may be able to achieve operational efficiencies and increases in value.

The new company is not tied to the financial commitments associated with the formal clothing division in terms of finance cost and loan repayment. Its management will have the ability to determine the finance structure which best suits the new business.

Newimber Co's shareholders will continue to own both companies. If shareholders are concerned about the diversification of their portfolio, this will remain unchanged.

The demerger may allow Newimber Co's management team to focus on the formal clothing division. They should not need to spend time dealing with disagreements with the sportswear division's management team.

Disadvantages of demerger

There will be legal costs associated with the demerger, such as the cost of obtaining a listing for the new company arising out of the sportswear division. Also setting up the new company and establishing the new structure looks likely to take up significant management time. This may mean that neither company is focused on external opportunities and challenges for some time, maybe impacting results and competitive position.

Both the new companies may suffer adverse effects through being smaller entities. Economies of scale may be lost and the companies may find it less easy to raise new finance. Looking at the position across both companies in total, distributable profits may fall because of a rise of overheads as each company will need its separate infrastructure and service departments.

The current arrangement may frustrate the management of the sportswear division but the command structure is clear. Once the director-shareholders of Newimber Co merely become shareholders of the new company, they will not be able to intervene actively in its management and overrule its management team. Agency problems may arise if these shareholders have different attitudes to risk to Poynins Co's board or different views on the importance of short-term versus long-term objectives.

400   KAPLAN PUBLISHING

(b) **Current WACC Newimber Co**

k_e is 11.8% and k_d is 4.5%

MV_e = $585 million

MV_d = $220 million

WACC = ((585 × 11.8%) + (220 × 4.5% × 0.72))/805 = 9.5%

New WACC Newimber Co

MV_e is $351 million

β_e = 1.21 ((351 + (220 (1 − 0.28)))/351) = 1.76

k_e = 3.4% + (1.76 × 6%) = 14.0%

WACC = ((351 × 14.0%) + (220 × 4.5% × 0.72))/571 = 9.9%, an increase of 0.4%

WACC Poynins Co

Current β_a of Newimber Co = 1.4(585/(585 + (220 (1 − 0.28)))) = 1.10

β Poynins Co = (1.10 − (0.6 × 1.21))/0.4 = 0.935

WACC Poynins Co = 3.4% + (0.935 × 6%) = 9.0%

Tutorial note

When attempting a question like this in the Computer Based Exam (CBE), make sure you use the spreadsheet functions SUM and NPV to save time. Be careful when using the NPV function to enter =NPV, then a bracket containing the discount rate, a comma, and then the cells containing the cash flows from year 1 onwards. The initial investment then needs to be subtracted separately.

Free cash flows Poynins Co

Year	1	2	3
	$m	$m	$m
Operating cash flows	45.0	54.0	62.1
Tax	(12.6)	(15.1)	(17.4)
	———	———	———
Post-tax cash flows	32.4	38.9	44.7
Investment in assets	(20.0)	(22.0)	(22.0)
	———	———	———
Free cash flows	12.4	16.9	22.7
Discount factor (9%)	0.917	0.842	0.772
	———	———	———
Discounted cash flows	11.4	14.2	17.5
	———	———	———

Discounted free cash flows Years 1 to 3 = $43.1m

Discounted post-tax cash flows Year 4 onwards = $44.7m (1 + 0.02)/(0.09 − 0.02) = $651.3m × 0.772 = $502.8m

---

Discounted investment in assets Year 4 onwards = (25/0.09) = $277.8m × 0.772 = $214.5m

Poynins Co's valuation = $43.1m + $502.8m – $214.5m = $331.4m

Discussion

If the managers' estimates of the sportswear division's future free cash flows are realistic, then the valuation using free cash flows ($331.4m) exceeds the current valuation ($585m – $351m = $234m).

The valuation is dependent upon achieving ambitious growth targets in Years 1 to 3, particularly given the loss of economies of scale discussed above. The board and shareholders of Newimber Co would want details about the assumptions behind these figures, particularly as growth after that is only assumed to be 2%. The valuation is also dependent upon the investment figures being accurate, so directors and shareholders would again need more detail of these so that they can decide whether the extra investment is likely to generate the increased cash flows predicted.

They would also want to determine how the managers of the sportswear division plan to fund the investments, particularly if initial operating cash flows are not as high as expected.

The restructuring will lead to a marginal increase in the WACC of Newimber Co, as its financial risk increases with more gearing. The directors may be worried that Newimber Co's credit rating will fall.

(c) **Requirement for business review**

The directors of Poynins Co will have to fulfil the same statutory and listing requirements as Newimber Co currently fulfils. These are likely to include the requirements for a business review.

Investors are likely to be particularly interested in how future strategies for Poynins Co may differ from those which have been pursued recently. They are also likely to want to know about attitudes to risk management and risk management policies, as the new company appears to be likely to be more risk-seeking than the old division. They will also want to know about changes in finance policy, particularly if dividend policies are likely to differ.

Communication with stakeholders

Poynins Co's directors are likely to communicate with major shareholders on a regular basis, more than once a year. These will include the director-shareholders actively involved in Newimber Co and external investors. Poynins Co's directors will need to ensure that what they communicate keeps both sets of shareholders happy if the two groups have different priorities.

Poynins Co's directors will also have to be mindful of the need to communicate what their plans are to other important stakeholders. Employees and suppliers are particularly important here, as Poynins Co's board has plans for operational efficiencies. Employees may be interested in being informed about changes in working conditions. Attempts to impose tougher conditions on employees without communication or consultation may lead to employee departures or other disruptions. Suppliers will be interested in changes to payment arrangements. Suppliers may be concerned anyway about dealing with a new, smaller company, so may seek to impose shorter credit periods or lower credit limits if they do not have sufficient information.

Note: Credit will be given for alternative, valid comments.

	Marking guide		Marks
(a)	Advantages of demerger		2–3
	Disadvantages of demerger		2–3
		Maximum	**4**
(b)	Pre demerger WACC		1
	New β_e and k_e Newimber Co		1
	New WACC Newimber Co		1
	Pre demerger β_a		1
	β Poynins Co		1
	WACC Poynins Co		1
	Discounted free cash flows Poynins Co Years 1 to 3		2
	Discounted free cash flow Poynins Co Year 4 onwards		2
	Discussion		2–3
		Maximum	**12**
(c)	1–2 marks per relevant point		
		Maximum	**4**
	Professional skills marks (see below)		**5**
Total			**25**

Professional skills marks

Analysis and Evaluation

Appropriate use of the data to determine suitable calculations

Appropriate use of the data to support discussion and draw appropriate conclusions

Appraisal of information objectively to make a recommendation

Commercial acumen

Effective use of examples and/or practical considerations related to the context to illustrate points being made

Maximum 5 marks

60   HANWOOD SHOES CO (SEP/DEC 21)

Key answer tips

Corporate reconstruction questions will often ask you to calculate and discuss the impact of a proposal on a business's likely performance, such as statement of financial position and earnings per share here.

A clear layout for your calculations, such as the one shown in this model answer, is critical.

(a)   Proceeds from sales of children's shoes division

Year	1	2	3	4
	$m	$m	$m	$m
Free cash flows	76	81	85	88
Discount factor 10%	0.909	0.826	0.751	0.683
Present value	69	67	64	60
Total	260			

Growth rate year 5 onwards = 3.5%

Present value in Year 5 onwards = ($88m × 1.035/(0.10 − 0.035) × 0.683 = $957m

Total present value = $260m + $957m = $1,217m

Impact on statement of financial position ($m)

Profit on sale = $1,217m − $608m − $349m = $260m

Current assets receipt from sale = $1,217m

Current assets adjustment = ($894m × 1.4) − ($909m − $349m) − $1,217m = ($525m)

Gain in current assets = $1,217m − $525m = $692m

Alternative working

Gain in current assets = ($894m × 1.4) − ($909m − $349m) = $692m

Non-current asset adjustment = $525m − $175m = $350m

	Original $m	Sales $m	Adjustments $m	Final $m
Assets				
Non-current assets	1,200	(608) 1,217	350	942
Current assets	909	(349)	(525)	1,252
Total assets	2,109			2,194
Equity and liabilities				
Called-up share capital	50			50
Reserves	737	260		997
Total equity	787			1,047
Non-current liabilities				
9% loan notes	175		(175)	0
7% loan notes	145			145
Bank loans	108			108
Total non-current liabilities	428			253
Current liabilities	894			894
Total equity and liabilities	2,109			2,194

Impact on eps ($m)

	Current forecast	Revised forecast
Predicted post tax profits	217	217
Less: profits from children shoes		(76)
Add: interest saved, net of tax		
($175m × 9% × (1 – 0.2))		13
Add: Return on additional non-current assets		
($350m × 18% × (1 – 0.2))		50
Add: Return on additional current assets		
($692m × 6% × (1 – 0.2))		33
	———	———
Adjusted profits	217	237
Number of shares	50m	50m
Adjusted eps	$4.34	$4.74

(b) **Sale**

Investors may query the need for the sale at this time. Although the board expects the children's shoes market to become more competitive in a few years' time, this has not yet happened. Investors may wonder if a better sales price could be obtained in a few years' time with a few more years' growth. Although some investors are concerned about gearing, a sale to reduce debt funding may seem to be a forced sale, and investors may ask whether alternative strategies could resolve the problems.

Investors may also wonder why Hanwood Shoes Co is not exploring the possibility of selling the production facilities (if sale proceeds equalled net book value that would be enough to pay off the 9% loan notes). Hanwood Shoes Co could then use the same outsourcing business model for producing children's shoes that it does for adults' shoes.

Investors may also be concerned whether Hanwood Shoes Co is achieving best value from the sale if the company is going to be selling the division at $1,217m. Assuming a higher growth rate (perhaps by taking the geometric average of growth over the next four years) would give a higher selling price. Hanwood Shoes Co could also be expected to ask for a premium on the sale, given that a number of companies looking to develop their sales of children's shoes may be interested. That said, the cash flows in the calculation are taken to infinity, which is optimistic.

Investors would also wonder about the decreased diversification that the sale would mean. Although adults' shoes achieve higher margins than children's shoes, they may need more investment to maintain their position, and the appeal of fashionable ranges may be uncertain. Children's school shoes have been a reliable cash generator. Ultimately also the investors may feel that they are investing in a smaller company, given the decrease in the non-current base and range of products, and may want to invest elsewhere in a company offering better growth prospects.

Profits

The forecast increase in earnings per share is 9.2%, but investors will question whether the assumptions on which the forecast is based are optimistic. They will also take into account the risks of the business being less diversified as it will solely be selling adult shoes. However, part of the increase in profits is a fall in the commitment to paying interest, which investors may view positively if they are concerned about gearing.

Funding

The sale will help fund an improvement in the gearing of the company. The funds will not only be available to pay off the 9% loan notes immediately, they could also be used to pay off the bank loan and/or the other loan notes in time, or reduce trade payables as they may be being used as a source of short-term funding. However, investors might also wonder how future investment in adults' shoe shops would be funded, particularly if future sales did not meet current expectations. Current lenders may have placed restrictions on Hanwood Shoes Co seeking new borrowing from other sources. If Hanwood Shoes Co was able to seek additional loan capital, it would have a smaller non-current asset base to offer as security, which may affect lenders' attitudes.

Marking guide		Marks
(a)	PV of free cash flows Years 1–4	2
	PV of free cash flows Year 5 onwards	2
	Revised statement of financial position	4
	Revised eps	5
		13
(b)	Up to 2 marks per relevant point	7
	(relevant points can include need to sell, timing, amount, less diversification, alternative strategies, impact on eps impact on funding)	
	Maximum	7
	Professional skills marks (see below)	5
Total		25

Professional skills marks

Analysis and Evaluation

Appropriate use of the data to determine suitable calculations

Appropriate use of the data to support discussion and draw appropriate conclusions

Appraisal of information objectively to make a recommendation

Scepticism

Effective challenge of evidence and assumptions supplied

Commercial acumen

Effective use of examples and/or practical considerations related to the context to illustrate points being made

Maximum 5 marks

TREASURY AND ADVANCED RISK MANAGEMENT TECHNIQUES

61   LEVANTE CO (DEC 11)

Key answer tips

This question (from the December 2011 exam) tested the contents of a technical article written by the examiner and published in September 2011. It is common for the examiner to test topics covered in recent articles, so keep an eye on the ACCA website for any new articles published.

(a)   Spot yield rates applicable to Levante Co (based on A credit rating)

1 year	3.85%
2 year	4.46%
3 year	5.07%
4 year	5.80%
5 year	6.12%

Bond value based on A rating =

$\$4 \times 1.0385^{-1} + \$4 \times 1.0446^{-2} + \$104 \times 1.0507^{-3} = \$97.18$ per $100

Current price based on AA rating = $98.71

Fall in value = $(97.18 - 98.71)/98.71 \times 100\% = 1.55\%$

(b)   Spot rates applicable to Levante Co (based on A credit rating) [from above]

1 year	3.85%
2 year	4.46%
3 year	5.07%
4 year	5.80%
5 year	6.12%

(i)   Value of 5% coupon bond

$\$5 \times 1.0385^{-1} + \$5 \times 1.0446^{-2} + \$5 \times 1.0507^{-3} + \$5 \times 1.0580^{-4} + \$105 \times 1.0612^{-5}$
= $95.72

Hence the bond will need to be issued at a discount if only a 5% coupon is offered.

(ii)   New coupon rate for bond valued at $100 by the markets

Since the 5% coupon bond is only valued at $95.72, a higher coupon needs to be offered. This coupon amount can be calculated by finding the yield to maturity of the 5% coupon bond discounted at the above yield curve. This yield to maturity will be the coupon amount for the new bond such that its face value will be $100.

Therefore, if the yield to maturity is denoted by YTM then

$5 \times (1 + \text{YTM})^{-1} + \$5 \times (1 + \text{YTM})^{-2} + \$5 \times (1 + \text{YTM})^{-3} + \$5 \times (1 + \text{YTM})^{-4} + \$105 \times (1 + \text{YTM})^{-5} = \$95.72$

Solve by trial and error, assume YTM is 5.5%. This gives the bond value as $97.86.

Assume YTM is 6%; this gives the bond value as $95.78, which is close enough to $95.72

$\$5 \times (1.06)^{-1} + \$5 \times (1.06)^{-2} + \$5 \times (1.06)^{-3} + \$5 \times (1.06)^{-4} + \$105 \times (1.06)^{-5} = \$95.78$

Hence if the coupon payment is 6% or $6 per $100 bond unit then the bond market value will equal the nominal value at $100.

$\$6 \times (1.06)^{-1} + \$6 \times (1.06)^{-2} + \$6 \times (1.06)^{-3} + \$6 \times (1.06)^{-4} + \$106 \times (1.06)^{-5} = \$100$

Alternatively:

Take R as the coupon rate, such that:

$(R \times 1.0385^{-1}) + (R \times 1.0446^{-2}) + (R \times 1.0507^{-3}) + (R \times 1.0580^{-4}) + (R \times 1.0612^{-5}) + (100 \times 1.0612^{-5}) = \$100$

$4.2826R + 74.30 = \$100$

$R = 6\%$ or $6 per $100

Advice:

If only a 5% coupon is offered, the bonds will have to be issued at just under a 4.3% discount. To raise the full $150 million, if the bonds are issued at a 4.3% discount, then 1,567,398 $100 bond units need to be issued, as opposed to 1,500,000. This is an extra 67,398 bond units for which Levante Co will need to pay an extra $6,739,800 when the bonds are redeemed in five years.

On the other hand, paying a higher coupon every year of 6% instead of 5% will mean that an extra $1,163,010 is needed for each of the next five years (being 1,500,000 × $100 × 6% compared with 1,567,398 × $100 × 5%).

If the directors feel that the drain in resources of $1,163,010 every year is substantial and that the project's profits will cover the extra $6,739,800 in five years' time, then they should issue the bond at a discount and at a lower coupon rate. On the other hand, if the directors feel that they would like to spread the amount payable then they should opt for the higher coupon alternative.

(c) Industry risk measures the resilience of the company's industrial sector to changes in the economy. In order to measure or assess this, the following factors could be used:

Impact of economic changes on the industry in terms of how successfully the firms in the industry operate under differing economic outcomes;

How cyclical the industry is and how large the peaks and troughs are;

How the demand shifts in the industry as the economy changes.

Earnings protection measures how well the company will be able to maintain or protect its earnings in changing circumstances. In order to assess this, the following factors could be used:

Differing range of sources of earnings growth

Diversity of customer base

Profit margins and return on capital.

Financial flexibility measures how easily the company is able to raise the finance it needs to pursue its investment goals. In order to assess this, the following factors could be used:

Evaluation of plans for financing needs and range of alternatives available;

Relationships with finance providers, e.g. banks

Operating restrictions that currently exist as debt covenants.

Evaluation of the company's management considers how well the managers are managing and planning for the future of the company. In order to assess this, the following factors could be used:

The company's planning and control policies, and its financial strategies;

Management succession planning;

The qualifications and experience of the managers

Performance in achieving financial and non-financial targets.

Note: Credit will be given for alternative relevant comments and suggestions.

Marking scheme		
		Marks
(a)	Calculation of company specific yield curve	1
	Calculation bond value based on credit rating of A	1
	Calculation of percentage fall in the value of the bond	1
		——
		3
		——
(b)	Calculation of bond value based on 5% coupon	1
	Calculation of new coupon rate	4
	Advice on which type of bond to issue	3–4
		——
	Maximum	**8**
		——
(c)	2-3 marks (for each criteria) for explanation and suggestion of factors per relevant discussion point	
	Maximum	**9**
		——
	Professional skills marks (see below)	**5**
		——
Total		**25**
		——

Professional skills marks

Analysis and Evaluation

Appropriate use of the data to determine suitable calculations

Appropriate use of the data to support discussion and draw appropriate conclusions

Appraisal of information objectively to make a recommendation

Commercial acumen

Effective use of examples and/or practical considerations related to the context to illustrate points being made relating to establishing a credit rating

Maximum 5 marks

62   SEMBILAN CO (JUN 12)

Key answer tips

This question (from the June 2012 exam) tested the contents of a technical article written by the examiner and published in November 2011. It is common for the examiner to test topics covered in recent articles, so keep an eye on the ACCA website for any new articles published.

(a) Gross amounts of annual interest receivable by Sembilan Co from Ratus Bank based on year 1 spot rate and years 2, 3 and 4 forward rates:

Year 1	$0.025 \times \$320m = \$8m$
Year 2	$0.037 \times \$320m = \$11.84m$
Year 3	$0.043 \times \$320m = \$13.76m$
Year 4	$0.047 \times \$320m = \$15.04m$

Gross amount of annual interest payable by Sembilan Co to Ratus Bank: 3.76¼% × $320m = $12.04m

At the start of the swap, Sembilan Co will expect to receive or (pay) the following net amounts at the end of each of the next four years:

Year 1:	$\$8m - \$12.04m = \$(4.04m)$ payment
Year 2:	$\$11.84m - \$12.04m = \$(0.20m)$ payment
Year 3:	$\$13.76m - \$12.04m = \$1.72m$ receipt
Year 4:	$\$15.04m - \$12.04m = \$3m$ receipt

Tutorial note

At the commencement of the swap contract the net present value of the net annual flows, discounted at the yield curve rates, is zero.

The reason the equivalent fixed rate of 3.76¼% is less than the 3.8% four-year yield curve rate, is because the 3.8% rate reflects the zero-coupon rate with only one payment made in year four. Here the bond pays coupons at different time periods when the yield curve rates are lower. Therefore the fixed rate is lower.

(b) After taking the swap, Sembilan Co's net effect is as follows:

	% Impact	Yield Interest 3%	Yield Interest 4%
Borrow at yield interest + 60bp	(Yield + 0.6)%	$(11.52m)	$(14.72m)
Receive yield	Yield	$9.6m	$12.8m
Pay fixed 3.76¼%	(3.76¼)%	$(12.04m)	$(12.04m)
Fee 20bp	(0.2)%	$(0.64m)	$(0.64m)
Net Cost	(4.56¼)%	$(14.6m)	$(14.6m)

The receipt and payment based on the yield curve cancels out interest rate fluctuations, fixing the rate at 3.76¼% + 0.6% + 0.2% = 4.56¼%

(c) Reducing the amount of debt by issuing equity and using the cash raised from this to reduce the amount borrowed changes the capital structure of a company and Sembilan Co needs to consider all the possible implications of this

As the proportion of debt increases in a company's financial structure, the level of financial distress increases and with it the associated costs. Companies with high levels of financial distress would find it more costly to contract with their stakeholders. For example, they may have to pay higher wages to attract the right calibre of employees, give customers longer credit periods or larger discounts, and may have to accept supplies on more onerous terms. Furthermore, restrictive covenants may make it more difficult to borrow funds (debt and equity) for future projects. On the other hand, because interest is payable before tax, larger amounts of debt will give companies greater taxation benefits, known as the tax shield. Presumably, Sembilan Co has judged the balance between the levels of equity and debt finance, such that the positive and negative effects of gearing result in minimising the required rate of return and maximising the value of the company.

By replacing debt with equity the balance may no longer be optimal and therefore the value of Sembilan Co may not be maximised. However, reducing the amount of debt would result in a higher credit rating for the company and reduce the scale of restrictive covenants. Having greater equity would also increase the company's debt capacity. This may enable the company to raise additional finance and undertake future profitable projects more easily. Less financial distress may also reduce the costs of contracting with stakeholders.

The process of changing the financial structure can be expensive. Sembilan Co needs to determine the costs associated with early redemption of debt. The contractual clauses of the bond should indicate the level and amount of early redemption penalties. Issuing new equity can be expensive especially if the shares are offered to new shareholders, such as costs associated with underwriting the issue and communicating or negotiating the share price. Even raising funds by issuing rights can be expensive.

As well as this, Sembilan Co needs to determine the extent to which the current shareholders will be able to take up the rights and the amount of discount that needs to be given on the rights issue to ensure 100% take up. The impact on the current share price from the issue of rights needs to be considered as well. Studies on rights issues seem to indicate that the markets view the issue of rights as a positive signal and the share price does not reduce to the expected theoretical ex-rights price. However, this is mainly because the markets expect the funds raised to be used on new, profitable projects. Using funds to reduce the debt amount may not be viewed so positively.

Sembilan Co may also have to provide information and justification to the market because both the existing shareholders and any new shareholders will need to be assured that the company is not benefiting one group at the expense of the other. If sufficient information is not provided then either shareholder group may discount the share price due to information asymmetry. However, providing too much information may reduce the competitive position of the company.

Note: Credit will be given for alternative relevant comments and suggestions.

	Marking scheme		
			Marks
(a)	Gross amount receivable by Sembilan Co		1
	Gross amounts payable by Sembilan Co		1
	Net amounts receivable or payable every year		2
	Explanation of why fixed rate is less than the four-year yield curve rate		2
		Maximum	6
(b)	Demonstration of impact of interest rate changes		4
	Explanation and conclusion		1
		Maximum	5
(c)	1–2 marks per relevant discussion point	Maximum	9
	Professional skills marks (see below)		5
Total			25

Professional skills marks

Analysis and Evaluation

Appropriate use of the data to determine suitable calculations

Appropriate use of the data to support discussion and draw appropriate conclusions

Appraisal of information objectively

Commercial acumen

Effective use of examples and/or practical considerations related to the context to illustrate points being made relating to hedging and financing

Maximum 5 marks

63 PAULT CO (SEP/DEC 16)

Key answer tips

This was a question from the September 2016 exam paper, covering interest rate swaps. The question was based on the topics covered in an examiner's technical article from 2011.

This shows how important it is to read all the examiner's articles to prepare for the exam, not just the most recent ones.

(a) **(i)** Gross amount of annual interest paid by Pault Co to Millbridge Bank = 4.847% × $400m = $19.39m.

Gross amounts of annual interest receivable by Pault Co from Millbridge Bank, based on Year 1 spot rates and Years 2–4 forward rates:

Year			
1	0.0350 × $400m	=	$14m
2	0.0460 × $400m	=	$18.4m
3	0.0541 × $400m	=	$21.64m
4	0.0611 × $400m	=	$24.44m

Working:

Year 2 forward rate: $(1.0425^2/1.037) - 1 = 4.80\%$

Year 3 forward rate: $(1.0470^3/1.0425^2) - 1 = 5.61\%$

Year 4 forward rate: $(1.0510^4/1.0470^3) - 1 = 6.31\%$

Rates are reduced by 20 basis points in calculation.

At the start of the swap, Pault will expect to pay or receive the following net amounts at each of the next four years:

Year			
1	$14m – $19.39m	=	$(5.39m) payment
2	$18.4m – $19.39m	=	$(0.99m) payment
3	$21.64m – $19.39m	=	$2.25m receipt
4	$24.44m – $19.39m	=	$5.05m receipt

(ii) **Interest payment liability**

	Impact %	Yield interest 2.9%	Yield interest 4.5%
		$m	$m
Borrow at yield interest + 50 bp	(Yield + 0.5)	(13.60)	(20.00)
Receive yield – 20 bp	Yield – 0.2	10.80	17.20
Pay fixed 4.847%	(4.847)	(19.39)	(19.39)
Bank fee – 25 bp	(0.25)	(1.00)	(1.00)
	─────	─────	─────
	(5.797)	(23.19)	(23.19)
	─────	─────	─────

The interest payment liability will be $23.19m, whatever the yield interest, as the receipt and payment are based on the yield curve net of interest rate fluctuations.

(b) At the start of the contract, the value of the swap will be zero. The terms offered by Millbridge Bank equate the discounted value of the fixed rate payments by Pault Co with the variable rate payments by Millbridge Bank.

However, the value of the swap will not remain at zero. If interest rates increase more than expected, Pault Co will benefit from having to pay a fixed rate and the value of the swap will increase. The value of the swap will also change as the swap approaches maturity, with fewer receipts and payments left.

(c)   Disadvantages of swap arrangement

The swap represents a long-term commitment at a time when interest rates appear uncertain. It may be that interest rates rises are lower than expected. In this case, Pault Co will be committed to a higher interest rate and its finance costs may be higher than if it had not taken out the finance arrangements. Pault Co may not be able to take action to relieve this commitment if it becomes clear that the swap was unnecessary.

On the basis of the expected forward rates, Pault Co will not start benefiting from the swap until Year 3. Particularly during Year 1, the extra commitment to interest payments may be an important burden at a time when Pault Co will have significant development and launch costs.

Pault Co will be liable for an arrangement fee. However, other methods of hedging which could be used will have a cost built into them as well.

Advantages of swap arrangement

The swap means that the annual interest payment liability will be fixed at $23.19m over the next four years. This is a certain figure which can be used in budgeting. Having a fixed figure may help planning, particularly as a number of other costs associated with the investment are uncertain.

The directors will be concerned not just about the probability that floating rates will result in a higher commitment than under the swap, but also be concerned about how high this commitment could be. The directors may feel that rates may possibly rise to a level which would give Pault Co problems in meeting its commitments and regard that as unacceptable.

Any criticism after the end of the loan period will be based on hindsight. What appeared to be the cheapest choice at that stage may not have been what appeared most likely to be the cheapest choice when the loan was taken out. In addition, criticism of the directors for not choosing the cheapest option fails to consider risk. The cheapest option may be the most risky. The directors may reasonably take the view that the saving in cost is not worth the risks incurred.

The swap is for a shorter period than the loan and thus allows Pault Co to reconsider the position in four years' time. It may choose to take out another swap then on different terms, or let the arrangement lapse and pay floating rate interest on the loan, depending on the expectations at that time of future interest rates.

		Marking scheme	
			Marks
(a)	(i)	Gross amount payable by Pault Co	1
		Calculation of forward rates	3
		Basis point reduction	1
		Net amounts receivable or payable each year	1
			6
	(ii)	Yield interest calculations	5
		Comment on interest payment liability	1
			6
(b)	1-2 marks per point **Maximum**		3
(c)	Advantages		2-3
	Disadvantages		2-3
	Maximum		5
	Professional skills marks (see below)		5
Total			25

Professional skills marks

Analysis and Evaluation

Appropriate use of the data to determine suitable calculations

Appropriate use of the data to support discussion and draw appropriate conclusions

Appraisal of information objectively

Commercial acumen

Effective use of examples and/or practical considerations related to the context to illustrate points being made

Maximum 5 marks

64 LIGNUM CO (DEC 12)

Key answer tips

Currency risk is most commonly tested in the context of transaction risk. However, this question also covered economic risk and translation risk. Make sure that you understand all three types of risk and how they can be managed.

(a) Foreign exchange exposures

With case one, Lignum Co faces a possible exposure due to the receipt it is expecting in four months in a foreign currency, and the possibility that the exchange rates may move against it between now and in four months' time. This is known as transaction exposure.

With case two, the exposure is in the form of translation exposure, where a subsidiary's assets are being translated from the subsidiary's local currency into Euro. The local currency is facing an imminent depreciation of 20%.

Finally in the third case, the present value of future sales of a locally produced and sold good is being eroded because of overseas products being sold for a relatively cheaper price. The case seems to indicate that because the US$ has depreciated against the Euro, it is possible to sell the goods at the same dollar price but at a lower Euro price. This is known as economic exposure.

(b) **Case One**

Workings:

Using forward rate

Forward rate = 142 × (1 + (0.085 + 0.0025)/3)/(1 + (0.022 − 0.0030)/3) = 145.23

Income in Euro fixed at ZP145.23 = ZP140,000,000/145.23 = €963,988

Using OTC options

Purchase call options to cover for the ZP rate depreciating

Gross income from option = ZP140,000,000/142 = €985,915

Cost

€985,915 × ZP7 = ZP6,901,405

In € = ZP6,901,405/142 = €48,601

€48,601 × (1 + 0.037/3) = €49,200

(Use borrowing rate on the assumption that extra funds to pay costs need to borrowed initially; investing rate can be used if that is the stated preference)

Net income = €985,915 − €49,200 = €936,715

Hedging strategies

Transactions exposure, as faced by Lignum Co in situation one, lasts for a short while and is easier to manage by means of derivative products or more conventional means. Here Lignum Co has access to two derivative products: an OTC forward rate and OTC option. Using the forward rate gives a higher return of €963,988, compared to options where the return is €936,715 (see workings. However, with the forward rate, Lignum Co is locked into a fixed rate (ZP145.23 per €1) whether the foreign exchange rates move in its favour or against it. With the options, the company has a choice and if the rate moves in its favour, that is if the Zupeso appreciates against the Euro, then the option can be allowed to lapse. Lignum Co needs to decide whether it is happy receiving €963,988, no matter what happens to the exchange rate over the four months or whether it is happy to receive at least €936,715 if the ZP weakens against the €, but with a possibility of higher gains if the Zupeso strengthens.

Lignum Co should also explore alternative strategies to derivative hedging. For example, money markets, leading and lagging, and maintaining a Zupeso account may be possibilities. If information on the investment rate in Zupesos could be obtained, then a money market hedge could be considered. Maintaining a Zupeso account may enable Lignum Co to offset any natural hedges and only convert currency periodically to minimise transaction costs.

(c)   **Case Two**

Workings: Financial impact of the devaluation of the Maram Ringit

MR devalued rate = MR35 × 1.20 = MR42 per €1

	MR 000	Exposed?	€000 at current rate MR35 per €1	€000 at devalued rate MR42 per €1
Non-current assets	179,574	Yes	5,131	4,276
Current assets	146,622	60%	2,514	2,095
Non-current liabilities	(132,237)	20%	(756)	(630)
Current liabilities	(91,171)	30%	(781)	(651)
Share capital and reserves	102,788		6,108	5,090

Translation loss = €6,108,000 – €5,090,000 = €1,018,000

Hedging strategies

Hedging translation risk may not be necessary if the stock market in which Lignum Co's shares are traded is efficient. Translation of currency is an accounting entry where subsidiary accounts are incorporated into the group accounts. No physical cash flows in or out of the company. In such cases, spending money to hedge such risk means that the group loses money overall, reducing the cash flows attributable to shareholders. However, translation losses may be viewed negatively by the equity holders and may impact some analytical trends and ratios negatively. In these circumstances, Lignum Co may decide to hedge the risk.

The most efficient way to hedge translation exposure is to match the assets and liabilities. In Namel Co's case the assets are more exposed to the Maram Ringit compared to the liabilities, hence the weakening of the Maram Ringit from MR35 per €1 to MR42 per €1 would make the assets lose more (accounting) value than the liabilities by €1,018,000 (see workings). If the exposure for the assets and liabilities were matched more closely, for example by converting non-current liabilities from loans in Euro to loans in MR, translation exposure would be reduced.

Marking scheme		
		Marks
(a)	1 mark per exposure explained	**3**
(b)	Calculation of forward rate	1
	Calculation of income using the forward rate	1
	Calculation of cash flows using option contracts	3
	Discussion of relative merits of forwards and options	3
	Discussion of alternative hedging possibilities and conclusion	2
	Maximum	**10**
(c)	Calculation of devalued rate	1
	Calculation of translation loss	3
	Discussion of whether risk of translation loss should be managed	1–2
	Discussion of how risk of translation loss should be managed	1–2
	Maximum	**7**
	Professional skills marks (see below)	**5**
Total		**25**

Professional skills marks

Analysis and Evaluation

Appropriate use of the data to determine suitable calculations

Appropriate use of the data to support discussion and draw appropriate conclusions

Appraisal of information objectively

Commercial acumen

Effective use of examples and/or practical considerations related to the context to illustrate points being made relating to transaction, translation and economic risk

Maximum 5 marks

65 ALECTO CO (DEC 11)

Key answer tips

In any interest rate hedging question, be prepared to comment on the advantages and disadvantages of setting up a collar. This question also covers the calculations on the two most commonly tested hedging methods (futures and traded options) in a very typical way.

(a) The main advantage of using a collar instead of options to hedge interest rate risk is lower cost. A collar involves the simultaneous purchase and sale of both call and put options at different exercise prices. The option purchased has a higher premium when compared to the premium of the option sold, but the lower premium income will reduce the higher premium payable. With a normal uncovered option, the full premium is payable.

However, the main disadvantage is that, whereas with a hedge using options the buyer can get full benefit of any upside movement in the price of the underlying asset, with a collar hedge the benefit of the upside movement is limited or capped as well.

(b) **Using Futures**

Need to hedge against a rise in interest rates, therefore go short in the futures market. Alecto Co needs June contracts as the loan will be required on 1 May.

No. of contracts needed = €22,000,000/€1,000,000 × 5 months/3 months = 36.67 say 37 contracts.

Basis

Current price (on 1/1) – futures price = total basis

$(100 - 3.3) - 96.16 = 0.54$

Unexpired basis = $2/6 \times 0.54 = 0.18$

If interest rates increase by 0.5% to 3.8%

Cost of borrowing funds = 4.6% × 5/12 × €22,000,000 = €421,667

Expected futures price = 100 – 3.8 – 0.18 = 96.02

Gain on the futures market = (9,616 – 9,602) × €25 × 37 = €12,950

Net cost = €408,717

Effective interest rate = 408,717/22,000,000 × 12/5 = 4.46%

If interest rates decrease by 0.5% to 2.8%

Cost of borrowing funds = 3.6% × 5/12 × €22,000,000 = €330,000

Expected futures price = 100 – 2.8 – 0.18 = 97.02

Loss on the futures market = (9,616 – 9,702) × €25 × 37 = €79,550

Net cost = €409,550

Effective interest rate = 409,550/22,000,000 × 12/5 = 4.47%

Note: Net cost should be the same. Difference is due to rounding the number of contracts.

Using Options on Futures

Need to hedge against a rise in interest rates, therefore buy put options. As before, Alecto Co needs 37 June put option contracts (€22,000,000/€1,000,000 × 5 months/ 3 months).

If interest rates increase by 0.5% to 3.8%

Exercise Price	96.00	96.50
Futures Price	96.02	96.02
Exercise?	No	Yes
Gain in basis points	0	48
Underlying cost of borrowing (from above)	€421,667	€421,667
Gain on options (0 and €25 × 48 × 37)	€0	€44,400
Premium		
16.3 × €25 × 37	€15,078	
58.1 × €25 × 37		€53,743
Net cost	€436,745	€431,010
Effective interest rate	4.76%	4.70%

If interest rates decrease by 0.5% to 2.8%

Exercise Price	96.00	96.50
Futures Price	97.02	97.02
Exercise?	No	No
Gain in basis points	0	0
Underlying cost of borrowing (from above)	€330,000	€330,000
Gain on options	€0	€0
Premium		
16.3 × €25 × 37	€15,078	
58.1 × €25 × 37		€53,743
Net cost	€345,078	€383,743
Effective interest rate	3.76%	4.19%

Using a collar

Buy June put at 96.00 for 0.163 and sell June call at 96.50 for 0.090.

Premium payable = 0.073

If interest rates increase by 0.5% to 3.8%

	Buy put	Sell Call
Exercise Price	96.00	96.5
Futures Price	96.02	96.02
Exercise?	No	No
Underlying cost of borrowing (from above)	€421,667	
Premium		
7.3 × €25 × 37	€6,753	
Net cost	€428,420	
Effective interest rate	4.67%	

If interest rates decrease by 0.5% to 2.8%

	Buy put	Sell Call
Exercise Price	96.00	96.50
Futures Price	97.02	97.02
Exercise?	No	Yes
Underlying cost of borrowing (from above)	€330,000	
Premium		
7.3 × €25 × 37	€6,753	
Loss on exercise (52 × €25 × 37)	€48,100	
Net cost	€384,853	
Effective interest rate	4.20%	

Tutorial note

The amount of detail shown in this model answer might look overwhelming at first glance.

But bear in mind that using the COPY/PASTE functions in the Computer Based Exam (CBE) will enable you present information like this quite quickly.

Hedging using the interest rate futures market fixes the rate at 4.47%, whereas with options on futures or a collar hedge, the net cost changes. If interest rates fall in the future then a hedge using options gives the most favourable rate. However, if interest rates increase then a hedge using futures gives the lowest interest payment cost and hedging with options give the highest cost, with the cost of the collar hedge being in between the two. If Alecto Co's aim is to fix its interest rate whatever happens to future rates then the preferred instrument would be futures.

This recommendation is made without considering margin and other transactional costs, and basis risk, which is discussed below. These need to be taken into account before a final decision is made.

Note: Credit will be given for alternative approaches to the calculations in part (b).

Marking scheme			
			Marks
(a)	Discussion of the main advantage		2
	Discussion of the main disadvantage		2
		Maximum	4
(b)	Recommendation to go short if futures are used and purchase puts if options are used		1
	Calculation of number of contracts and remaining basis		2
	Futures contracts calculations		4
	Options contracts calculations		4
	Collar approach and calculations		4
	Supporting comments and conclusion		2–3
		Maximum	16
	Professional skills marks (see below)		5
Total			25

Professional skills marks

Analysis and Evaluation

Appropriate use of the data to determine suitable calculations

Appropriate use of the data to support discussion and draw appropriate conclusions

Appraisal of information objectively to make a hedging recommendation

Commercial acumen

Effective use of examples and/or practical considerations related to the context to illustrate points being made relating to hedging

Maximum 5 marks

66   KENDURI CO (JUN 13)

(a)   Only the transactions resulting in cash flows between Kenduri Co and Lakama Co are considered for hedging. Other transactions are not considered.

Net flow in US$: US$4.5m payment – US$2.1m receipt = US$2.4m payment

Hedge the US$ exposure using the forward market, the money market and options.

Forward market

US$ hedge: 2,400,000/1.5996 = £1,500,375 payment

Money market

US$ hedge

Invest in US$: 2,400,000/(1 + 0.031/4) = US$2,381,543

Convert into £ at spot: US$2,381,543/1.5938 = £1,494,255

Borrow in £: £1,494,255 × (1 + 0.040/4) = £1,509,198

Note: Full credit will be given to candidates who use the investing rate of 2.8% instead of the borrowing rate of 4%, where this approach has been explained and justified.

The forward market is preferred due to lower payment costs.

Options

Kenduri Co would purchase Sterling three-month put options to protect itself against a strengthening US$ to £.

Exercise price: $1.60/£1

£ payment = 2,400,000/1.60 = 1,500,000 or 24 contracts

24 put options purchased

Premium payable = 24 × 0.0208 × 62,500 = US$31,200

Premium in £ = 31,200/1.5938 = £19,576

Total payments = £1,500,000 + £19,576 = £1,519,576

Exercise price: $1.62/£1

£ payment = 2,400,000/1.62 = 1,481,481 or 23.7 contracts

23 put options purchased

£ payment = 23 × 62,500 = £1,437,500

Premium payable = 23 × 0.0342 × 62,500 = US$49,163

Premium in £ = 49,163/1.5938 = £30,846

Amount not hedged = US$2,400,000 − (23 × 62,500 × 1.62) = US$71,250

Use forwards to hedge amount not hedged = US$71,250/1.5996 = £44,542

Total payments = 1,437,500 + 30,846 + 44,542 = £1,512,888

Tutorial note

The amount of detail shown in this model answer might look overwhelming at first glance.

But bear in mind that using the COPY/PASTE functions in the Computer Based Exam (CBE) will enable you present information like this quite quickly.

Both these hedges are worse than the hedge using forward or money markets. This is due to the premiums payable to let the option lapse if the prices move in Kenduri Co's favour. Options have an advantage over forwards and money markets because the prices are not fixed and the option buyer can let the option lapse if the rates move favourably. Hence options have an unlimited upside but a limited downside. With forwards and money markets, Kenduri Co cannot take advantage of the US$ weakening against the £.

Conclusion

The forward market minimises the payment and is therefore recommended over the money market. However, options give Kenduri Co the choice of an unlimited upside, although the cost is higher. Therefore the choice between the forward market and the option market depends on the risk preference of the company.

(b) Based on spot mid-rates: US$1.5950/£1; CAD1.5700/£1; JPY132.75/£1 **In £000**

		\multicolumn{5}{c}{**Payments from**}
		UK	**USA**	**Canada**	**Japan**	**Total**
Receipts to	UK		1,316.6	2,165.6		3,482.2
	USA	2,821.3		940.4	877.7	4,639.4
	Canada	700.6			2,038.2	2,738.8
	Japan		2,410.5			2,410.5
	Total payments	3,521.9	3,727.1	3,106.0	2,915.9	
	Total receipts	3,482.2	4,639.4	2,738.8	2,410.5	
	Net receipt/(payment)	(39.7)	912.3	(367.2)	(505.4)	

Each of Kenduri Co, Jaia Co and Gochiso Co will make payments of £ equivalent to the amount given above to Lakama Co. Multilateral netting involves minimising the number of transactions taking place through each country's banks. This would limit the fees that these banks would receive for undertaking the transactions and therefore governments who do not allow multilateral netting want to maximise the fees their local banks receive. On the other hand, some countries allow multilateral netting in the belief that this would make companies more willing to operate from those countries and any banking fees lost would be more than compensated by the extra business these companies and their subsidiaries bring into the country.

\multicolumn{3}{c}{**Marking scheme**}	
		Marks
(a)	Calculation of net US$ amount	1
	Calculation of forward market US$ amount	1
	Calculation of US$ money market amount	2
	Calculation of one put option amount (1.60 or 1.62)	3
	Calculation of the second put option amount or if the preferred exercise price choice is explained	2
	Advice and recommendation	2–3
	Maximum	**11**
(b)	Calculation of the £ equivalent amounts of US$, CAD and JPY	4
	Calculation of the net receipt/payment	2
	Explanation of government reaction to multilateral hedging	3
	Maximum	**9**
	Professional skills marks (see below)	**5**
Total		**25**

Professional skills marks

Analysis and Evaluation

Appropriate use of the data to determine suitable calculations

Appropriate use of the data to support discussion and draw appropriate conclusions

Appraisal of information objectively to make a recommendation

Scepticism

Effective challenge of information supplied to support key facts and/or decisions

Demonstration of ability to consider relevant factors applicable to hedging options

Commercial acumen

Recommendations are practical and plausible in the context of Kenduri Co's situation

Effective use of examples from the scenario information and other practical considerations related to the context to illustrate points being made

Maximum 5 marks

67   AWAN CO (DEC 13)

Key answer tips

This was a very typical question on interest rate hedging. With any hedging question, make sure that you identify the transaction correctly at the start. In this question, you were asked to hedge the interest receipts on a deposit (rather than the more commonly tested interest payments on a borrowing).

Using forward rate agreements (FRAs)

FRA rate 4.82% (3–7), since the investment will take place in three months' time for a period of four months.

If interest rates increase by 0.9% to 4.99%

Investment return = 4.79% × 4/12 × $48,000,000 =	$766,400
Payment to Voblaka bank = (4.99% – 4.82%) × $48,000,000 × 4/12 =	$(27,200)
Net receipt =	$739,200
Effective annual interest rate = 739,200/48,000,000 × 12/4 =	4.62%

If interest rates decrease by 0.9% to 3.19%

Investment return = 2.99% × 4/12 × $48,000,000 =	$478,400
Receipt from Voblaka Bank = (4.82% – 3.19%) × $48,000,000 × 4/12 =	$260,800
Net receipt =	$739,200
Effective annual interest rate (as above)	4.62%

Using futures

Need to hedge against a fall in interest rates, therefore go long in the futures market. Awan Co needs March contracts as the investment will be made on 1 February.

No. of contracts needed = $48,000,000/$2,000,000 × 4 months/3 months = 32 contracts.

Basis

Current price (on 1/11) – futures price = total basis

(100 – 4.09) – 94.76 = 1.15

Unexpired basis = 2/5 × 1.15 = 0.46

If interest rates increase by 0.9% to 4.99%

Investment return (from above) =	$766,400
Expected futures price = 100 – 4.99 – 0.46 = 94.55	
Loss on the futures market	
(0.9455 – 0.9476) × $2,000,000 × 3/12 × 32	$(33,600)
Net return =	$732,800
Effective annual interest rate = $732,800/$48,000,000 × 12/4 =	4.58%

If interest rates decrease by 0.9% to 3.19%

Investment return (from above) =	$478,400
Expected futures price = 100 – 3.19 – 0.46 = 96.35	
Gain on the futures market	$254,400
(0.9635 – 0.9476) × $2,000,000 × 3/12 × 32	
Net return =	$732,800
Effective annual interest rate (as above) =	4.58%

Using options on futures

Need to hedge against a fall in interest rates, therefore buy call options. As before, Awan Co needs 32 March call option contracts

($48,000,000/$2,000,000 × 4 months/3 months).

If interest rates increase by 0.9% to 4.99%

Exercise price	94.50	95.00
Futures price	94.55	94.55
Exercise?	Yes	No
Gain in basis points	5	0
Underlying investment return (from above)	$766,400	$766,400
Gain on options (0.0005 × 2,000,000 × 3/12 × 32, 0)	$8,000	$0
Premium		
0.00432 × $2,000,000 × 3/12 × 32	$(69,120)	
0.00121 × $2,000,000 × 3/12 × 32		$(19,360)
Net return	$705,280	$747,040
Effective interest rate	4.41%	4.67%

If interest rates decrease by 0.9% to 3.19%

Exercise price	94.50	95.00
Futures price	96.35	96.35
Exercise?	Yes	Yes
Gain in basis points	185	135
Underlying investment return (from above)	$478,400	$478,400
Gain on options		
(0.0185 × 2,000,000 × 3/12 × 32)	$296,000	
(0.0135 × 2,000,000 × 3/12 × 32)		$216,000
Premium		
As above	$(69,120)	
As above		$(19,360)
Net return	$705,280	$675,040
Effective interest rate	4.41%	4.22%

Discussion

The FRA offer from Voblaka Bank gives a slightly higher return compared to the futures market; however, Awan Co faces a credit risk with over-the-counter products like the FRA, where Voblaka Bank may default on any money owing to Awan Co if interest rates should fall.

The March call option at the exercise price of 94.50 seems to fix the rate of return at 4.41%, which is lower than the return on the futures market and should therefore be rejected. The March call option at the exercise price of 95.00 gives a higher return compared to the FRA and the futures if interest rates increase, but does not perform as well if the interest rates fall.

If Awan Co takes the view that it is more important to be protected against a likely fall in interest rates, then that option should also be rejected.

The choice between the FRA and the futures depends on Awan Co's attitude to risk and return, the FRA gives a small, higher return, but carries a credit risk. If the view is that the credit risk is small and it is unlikely that Voblaka Bank will default on its obligation, then the FRA should be chosen as the hedge instrument.

Tutorial note

The amount of detail shown in this model answer might look overwhelming at first glance.

But bear in mind that using the COPY/PASTE functions in the Computer Based Exam (CBE) will enable you present information like this quite quickly.

Marking scheme	
	Marks
Calculation of impact of FRA for interest rate increase and decrease	2
Decision to go long on futures	1
Selection of March futures and options	1
Unexpired basis calculation	1
Impact of interest rates increase/decrease with futures	4
Decision to buy call options	1
Impact of interest rates increase/decrease with options	5
Discussion (up to 2 marks available for general explanation of the products' features)	5–6
Maximum	20
Professional skills marks (see below)	5
Total	25

Professional skills marks

Analysis and Evaluation

Appropriate use of the data to determine suitable calculations

Appropriate use of the data to support discussion and draw appropriate conclusions

Appraisal of information objectively to make a recommendation

Scepticism

Effective challenge of information supplied to support key facts and/or decisions

Demonstration of ability to consider relevant factors applicable to hedging options

Commercial acumen

Recommendations are practical and plausible in the context of Awan Co's situation

Effective use of examples from the scenario information and other practical considerations related to the context to illustrate points being made

Maximum 5 marks

68   CMC CO (JUN 14)

(a)   The foreign exchange exposure of the dollar payment due in four months can be hedged using the following derivative products:

- Forward rate offered by Pecunia Bank
- Exchange-traded futures contracts; and
- Exchange-traded options contracts

Using the forward rate

Payment in Swiss Francs = US$5,060,000/1.0677 = CHF4,739,159

Using futures contract

Since a dollar payment needs to be made in four months' time, CMC Co needs to hedge against Swiss Francs weakening.

Hence, the company should go short and the six-month futures contract is undertaken. It is assumed that the basis differential will narrow in proportion to time.

Current basis = 1.0635 – 1.0659 = -0.0024

Unexpired basis on transaction date = -0.0024 × (2/6) = -0.0008

So predicted lock in rate = 1.0659 – 0.0008 = 1.0651

Tutorial note

Interpolating between the given futures prices would have also been acceptable, as follows:

Predicted futures rate = 1.0647 + [(1.0659 — 1.0647) × 1/3] = 1.0651.

Expected payment = US$5,060,000/1.0651 = CHF4,750,728

No. of contracts sold = CHF4,750,728/CHF125,000 = approx. 38 contracts

Using options contracts

Since a dollar payment needs to be made in four months' time, CMC Co needs to hedge against Swiss Francs weakening. Hence, the company should purchase six-month put options.

Exercise price US$1.06/CHF1

Payment = US$5,060,000/1.06 = CHF4,773,585

Buy 4,773,585/125,000 = 38.19 put contracts, say 38 contracts

CHF payment = CHF4,750,000

Premium payable = 38 × 125,000 × 0.0216 = US$102,600

In CHF = 102,600/1.0635 = CHF96,474

Amount not hedged = US$5,060,000 — (38 × 125,000 × 1.06) = US$25,000

Use forward contracts to hedge this = US$25,000/1.0677 = CHF23,415

Total payment = CHF4,750,000 + CHF96,474 + CHF23,415 = CHF4,869,889

Exercise price US$1.07/CHF1

Payment = US$5,060,000/1.07 = CHF4,728,972

Buy 4,728,972/125,000 = 37.83 put contracts, say 38 contracts (but this is an over-hedge)

CHF payment = CHF4,750,000

Premium payable = 38 × 125,000 × 0.0263 = US$124,925

In CHF = 124,925/1.0635 = CHF117,466

Amount over-hedged = US$5,060,000 – (38 × 125,000 × 1.07) = US$22,500

Using forward contracts to show benefit of this = US$22,500/1.0677 = CHF21,073

Total payment = CHF4,750,000 + CHF117,466 – CHF21,073 = CHF4,846,393

Advice

Forward contracts minimise the payment and option contracts would maximise the payment, with the payment arising from the futures contracts in between these two. With the option contracts, the exercise price of US$1.07/CHF1 gives the lower cost. Although transaction costs are ignored, it should be noted that with exchange-traded futures contracts, margins are required and the contracts are marked-to-market daily.

It would therefore seem that the futures contracts and the option contract with an exercise price of US$1.06/CHF1 should be rejected. The choice between forward contracts and the 1.07 options depends on CMC Co's attitude to risk. The forward rate is binding, whereas option contracts give the company the choice to let the option contract lapse if the CHF strengthens against the US$. Observing the rates of inflation between the two countries and the exchange-traded derivatives this is likely to be the case, but it is not definite. Moreover, the option rates need to move in favour considerably before the option is beneficial to CMC Co, due to the high premium payable.

It would therefore seem that forward markets should be selected to minimise the amount of payment, but CMC Co should also bear in mind that the risk of default is higher with forward contracts compared with exchange-traded contracts.

(b)

	CMC Co	Counterparty	Interest rate differential
Fixed rate	2.2%	3.8%	1.6%
Floating rate	Yield rate + 0.4%	Yield rate + 0.8%	0.4%

CMC Co has a comparative advantage in borrowing at the fixed rate and the counterparty has a comparative advantage in borrowing at the floating rate. Total possible benefit before Pecunia Bank's fee is 1.2%, which if shared equally results in a benefit of 0.6% each, for both CMC Co and the counterparty.

	CMC Co	Counterparty
CMC Co borrows at	2.2%	
Counterparty borrows at		Yield rate + 0.8%
Advantage	60 basis points	60 basis points
Net result	Yield rate − 0.2%	3.2%
SWAP		
Counterparty receives		Yield rate
CMC Co pays	Yield rate	
Counterparty pays		2.4%
CMC Co receives	2.4%	

After paying the 20 basis point fee, CMC Co will effectively pay interest at the yield curve rate and benefit by 40 basis points or 0.4%, and the counterparty will pay interest at 3.4% and benefit by 40 basis points or 0.4% as well.

Examiner's note

Full marks will be given where the question is answered by estimating the arbitrage gain of 1.2% and deducting the fees of 0.4%, without constructing the above table.

Marking scheme		
		Marks
(a)	Calculation of payment using the forward rate	1
	Going short on futures and purchasing put options	2
	Predicted futures rate based on basis reduction	1
	Futures: expected payment and number of contracts	2
	Options calculation using either 1.06 or 1.07 rate	3
	Options calculation using the second rate (or explanation)	2
	Advice (1 to 2 marks per point)	3
		14
(b)	Comparative advantage and recognition of benefit as a result	2
	Initial decision to borrow fixed by CMC Co and floating by counterparty	1
	Swap impact	2
	Net benefit after bank charges	1
		6
	Professional skills marks (see below)	**5**
Total		**25**

Professional skills

Analysis and Evaluation

Appropriate use of the data to determine suitable calculations

Appropriate use of the data to support discussion and draw appropriate conclusions

Demonstration of reasoned judgement when considering key matters for this specific company

Scepticism

Effective challenge of information and assumptions supplied and, techniques carried out to support any decision

Commercial acumen

Effective use of examples and/or calculations from the scenario information and other practical considerations related to the context to illustrate points being made

Maximum 5 marks

69 KESHI CO (DEC 14)

Key answer tips

Plenty of the marks in the marking scheme for this question are for discussion points rather than calculations. Unfortunately, many students in the real exam focussed on the numbers exclusively so were unable to score a pass mark.

Always make sure that you attempt all parts of all questions in order to maximise your chances of passing the exam.

(a) **Using traded options**

Need to hedge against a rise in interest rates, therefore buy put options.

Keshi Co needs 42 March put option contracts ($18,000,000/$1,000,000 × 7 months/ 3 months).

Expected futures price on 1 February if interest rates increase by 0.5%

= 100 – (3.8 + 0.5) – 0.22 = 95.48

Expected futures price on 1 February if interest rates decrease by 0.5%

= 100 – (3.8 – 0.5) – 0.22 = 96.48

Tutorial note

The amount of detail shown in this model answer might look overwhelming at first glance.

But bear in mind that using the COPY/PASTE functions in the Computer Based Exam (CBE) will enable you present information like this quite quickly.

If interest rates increase by 0.5% to 4.3%

Exercise price	95.50	96.00
Futures price	95.48	95.48
Exercise?	Yes	Yes
Gain in basis points	2	52
Underlying cost of borrowing		
4.7% × 7/12 × $18,000,000	$493,500	$493,500
Gain on options		
0.0002 × $1,000,000 × 3/12 × 42	$2,100	
0.0052 × $1,000,000 × 3/12 × 42		$54,600
Premium		
0.00662 × $1,000,000 × 3/12 × 42	$69,510	
0.00902 × $1,000,000 × 3/12 × 42		$94,710
Net cost	$560,910	$533,610
Effective interest rate	5.34%	5.08%

If interest rates decrease by 0.5% to 3.3%

Exercise price	95.50	96.00
Futures price	96.48	96.48
Exercise?	No	No
Gain in basis points	0	0
Underlying cost of borrowing		
3.7% × 7/12 × $18,000,000	$388,500	$388,500
Gain on options	$0	$0
Premium	$69,510	$94,710
Net cost	$458,010	$483,210
Effective interest rate	4.36%	4.60%

Using swaps

	Keshi Co	Rozu Bank offer	Basis differential
Fixed rate	5.5%	4.6%	0.9%
Floating rate	SOFR + 0.4%	SOFR + 0.3%	0.1%

Prior to the swap, Keshi will borrow at SOFR + 0.4% and swaps this rate to a fixed rate. Total possible benefit is 0.8% before Rozu Bank's charges.

Keshi Co borrows at	SOFR + 0.4%
From swap Keshi Co receives	SOFR
Keshi Co gets 70% of the benefit	
Advantage (70% × 0.8 – 0.10)	0.46%
Keshi Co's effective borrowing rate (after swap)	5.04%

Alternatively (Swap)

From swap Keshi Co receives	SOFR
Keshi Co pays	4.54%
Effective borrowing rate (as above)	4.54% + 0.4% + 0.10% = 5.04%

Discussion and recommendation

Under each choice the interest rate cost to Keshi Co will be as follows:

	Doing nothing	95.50 option	96.00 option	Swap
If rates increase by 0.5%	4.7% floating; 5.5% fixed	5.34%	5.08%	5.04%
If rates decrease by 0.5%	3.7% floating; 5.5% fixed	4.36%	4.60%	5.04%

Borrowing at the floating rate and undertaking a swap effectively fixes the rate of interest at 5.04% for the loan, which is significantly lower than the market fixed rate of 5.5%.

On the other hand, doing nothing and borrowing at the floating rate minimises the interest rate at 4.7%, against the next best choice which is the swap at 5.04% if interest rates increase by 0.5%. And should interest rates decrease by 0.5%, then doing nothing and borrowing at a floating rate of 3.7% minimises cost, compared to the next best choice which is the 95.50 option.

On the face of it, doing nothing and borrowing at a floating rate seems to be the better choice if interest rates increase or decrease by a small amount, but if interest rates increase substantially then this choice will no longer result in the lowest cost.

The swap minimises the variability of the borrowing rates, while doing nothing and borrowing at a floating rate maximises the variability. If Keshi Co wants to eliminate the risk of interest rate fluctuations completely, then it should borrow at the floating rate and swap it into a fixed rate.

(b)   Islamic principles stipulate the need to avoid uncertainty and speculation. In the case of Salam contracts, payment for the commodity is made at the start of the contract. The buyer and seller of the commodity know the price, the quality and the quantity of the commodity and the date of future delivery with certainty. Therefore, uncertainty and speculation are avoided.

On the other hand, futures contracts are marked-to-market daily and this could lead to uncertainty in the amounts received and paid every day. Furthermore, standardised futures contracts have fixed expiry dates and pre-determined contract sizes. This may mean that the underlying position is not hedged or covered completely, leading to limited speculative positions even where the futures contracts are used entirely for hedging purposes. Finally, only a few commodity futures contracts are offered to cover a range of different quality grades for a commodity, and therefore price movement of the futures market may not be completely in line with the price movement in the underlying asset.

Note: Credit will be given for alternative, relevant discussion for part (b).

	Marking scheme		Marks
(a)	Buy put options and number of contracts		1
	Futures prices if interest rates increase or decrease		1
	Option contracts calculations: either exercise price		3
	Option contract calculations: second exercise price (or justification for calculations of just one exercise price)		2
	Swap: Keshi Co initially borrows at the floating rate and resulting advantage		2
	Swap impact		2
	Effective borrowing rate		1
	Discussion and recommendation		4–5
		Maximum	16
(b)	1–2 marks per point	**Maximum**	4
	Professional skills marks (see below)		5
Total			25

Professional skills marks

Analysis and Evaluation

Appropriate use of the data to determine suitable calculations

Appropriate use of the data to support discussion and draw appropriate conclusions

Appraisal of information objectively to make a recommendation

Scepticism

Effective challenge of information supplied to support key facts and/or decisions

Demonstration of ability to consider relevant factors applicable to hedging options

Commercial acumen

Recommendations are practical and plausible in the context of Keshi Co's situation

Effective use of examples from the scenario information and other practical considerations related to the context to illustrate points being made

Maximum 5 marks

70 DAIKON CO (JUN 15)

Key answer tips

In 2014, an article published on the ACCA website covered the market terminology associated with foreign exchange derivative products.

Therefore it was no surprise to see the topic tested in part (b) here.

Reading recent articles on the ACCA website is a critical part of preparing properly for the exam.

(a) Borrowing period is 6 months (11 months – 5 months)

Current borrowing cost = $34,000,000 × 6 months/12 months × 4.3% = $731,000

Borrowing cost if interest rates increase by 80 basis points (0.8%)

= $34,000,000 × 6/12 × 5.1% = $867,000

Additional cost = $136,000 [$34,000,000 × 6/12 × 0.8%]

Using futures to hedge

Need to hedge against a rise in interest rates, therefore go short in the futures market.

Borrowing period is 6 months

No. of contracts needed = $34,000,000/ $1,000,000 × 6 months/3 months

= 68 contracts.

Basis

Current price (on 1 June 20X5) – futures price = total basis

(100 – 3.6) – 95.84 = 0.56

Unexpired basis (at beginning of November) = 2/7 × 0.56 = 0.16

Assume that interest rates increase by 0.8% (80 basis points) to 4.4%

Expected futures price = 100 – 4.4 – 0.16 = 95.44

Gain on the futures market = (95.84 – 95.44) × $25 × 68 =	$68,000
Net additional cost = ($136,000 – $68,000)	$68,000

Using options on futures to hedge

Need to hedge against a rise in interest rates, therefore buy put options. As before, 68 put option contracts are needed ($34,000,000/$1,000,000 × 6 months/3 months).

Assume that interest rates increase by 0.8% (80 basis points) to 4.4%

Exercise price	95.50	96.00
Futures price	95.44	95.44
Exercise?	Yes	Yes
Gain in basis points	6	56
Gain on options		
6 × $25 × 68	$10,200	
56 × $25 × 68		$95,200
Premium		
30.4 × $25 × 68	$51,680	
50.8 × $25 × 68		$86,360
Option benefit/(cost)	$(41,480)	$8,840
Net additional cost		
($136,000 + $41,480)	$177,480	
($136,000 − $8,840)		$127,160

Using a collar on options to hedge

Buy put options at 95.50 for 0.304 and sell call at 96.00 for 0.223

Net premium payable = 0.081

Assume that interest rates increase by 0.8% (80 basis points) to 4.4%

	Buy put	Sell call
Exercise price	95.50	96.00
Futures price	95.44	95.44
Exercise?*	Yes	No

(*The put option is exercised, since by exercising the option, the option holder has the right to sell the instrument at 95.50 instead of the market price of 95.44 and gain 6 basis points per contract. The call option is not exercised, since by not exercising the option, the option holder can buy the instrument at a lower market price of 95.44 instead of the higher option exercise price of 96.00)

Gain on options	
6 × $25 × 68	$10,200
Premium payable	
8.1 × $25 × 68	$13,770
Net cost of the collar	$3,570
Net additional cost	
($136,000 + $3,570)	$139,570

Based on the assumption that interest rates increase by 80 basis points in the next five months, the futures hedge would lower the additional cost by the greatest amount and is significantly better than either of the options hedge or the collar hedge. In addition to this, futures fix the amount which Daikon Co is likely to pay, assuming that there is no basis risk. The benefits accruing from the options are lower, with the 95.50 option and the collar option actually increasing the overall cost. In each case, this is due to the high premium costs. However, if interest rates do not increase and actually reduce, then the options (and to some extent the collar) provide more flexibility because they do not have to be exercised when interest rates move in the company's favour. But the movement will need to be significant before the cost of the premium is covered.

On that basis, on balance, it is recommended that hedging using futures is the best choice as they will probably provide the most benefit to Daikon Co.

However, it is recommended that the points made in part (b) are also considered before a final conclusion is made.

(b)   Mark-to-market: Daily settlements

2 June:

8 basis points (95.76 – 95.84) × $25 × 50 contracts = $10,000 loss

3 June:

10 basis points (95.66 – 95.76) × $25 × 50 contracts

+ 5 basis points (95.61 — 95.66) × $25 × 30 contracts = $16,250 loss

[Alternatively: 15 basis points (95.61 – 95.76) × $25 × 30 contracts + 10 basis points (95.66 – 95.76) × $25 × 20 contracts = $16,250 loss]

4 June:

8 basis points (95.74 – 95.66) × $25 × 20 contracts = $4,000 profit

Both mark-to-market and margins are used by markets to reduce (eliminate) the risk of non-payment by purchasers of the derivative products if prices move against them.

Mark-to-market closes all the open deals at the end of each day at that day's settlement price, and opens them again at the start of the following day. The notional profit or loss on the deals is then calculated and the margin account is adjusted accordingly on a daily basis. The impact on Daikon Co is that if losses are made, then the company may have to deposit extra funds with its broker if the margin account falls below the maintenance margin level. This may affect the company's ability to plan adequately and ensure it has enough funds for other activities. On the other hand, extra cash accruing from the notional profits can be withdrawn from the broker account if needed.

Marking scheme		
		Marks
(a)	Additional interest cost	1
	Recommendation to go short if futures are used and purchase puts if options are used	1
	Calculation of number of contracts and remaining basis	2
	Futures contracts calculation	1
	Options contracts calculations	4
	Collar on options calculations	4
	Supporting comments and conclusion	2–3
	Maximum	15
(b)	Mark-to-market calculations (1 mark each for 2, 3 and 4 June)	3
	Impact of the daily mark-to-market	2–3
	Maximum	5
	Professional skills marks (see below)	5
Total		25

Professional skills marks

Analysis and Evaluation

Appropriate use of the data to determine suitable calculations

Appropriate use of the data to support discussion and draw appropriate conclusions

Appraisal of information objectively to make a recommendation

Scepticism

Effective challenge of information supplied to support key facts and/or decisions

Demonstration of ability to consider relevant factors applicable to hedging options

Commercial acumen

Recommendations are practical and plausible in the context of Daikon Co's situation

Effective use of examples from the scenario information and other practical considerations related to the context to illustrate points being made

Maximum 5 marks

71 THE ARMSTRONG GROUP (SEP/DEC 15)

Key answer tips

One of interest rate hedging or foreign currency hedging has been tested on every one of the AFM exams.

In this question, the examiner cleverly worked in both topics.

In order to guarantee success in the AFM exam, you cannot afford to question spot. The examiner tries very hard to avoid setting questions according to any logical pattern.

(a)

Owed by	Owed to	Local currency	$
		m	m
Armstrong (USA)	Horan (South (Africa)	US $12.17	12.17
Horan (South Africa)	Massie (Europe)	SA R42.65	3.97
Giffen (Denmark)	Armstrong (USA)	D Kr21.29	3.88
Massie (Europe)	Armstrong (USA)	US $19.78	19.78
Armstrong (USA)	Massie (Europe)	€1.57	2.13
Horan (South Africa)	Giffen (Denmark)	D Kr16.35	2.98
Giffen (Denmark)	Massie (Europe)	€1.55	2.11

Owed to			Owed by		
	Giffen (De)	Armtg (US)	Horan (SA)	Massie (Eu)	Total
	$m	$m	$m	$m	$m
Giffen (De)			2.98		2.98
Armtg (US)	3.88			19.78	23.66
Horan (SA)		12.17			12.17
Massie (Eu)	2.11	2.13	3.97		8.21
	———	———	———	———	
Owed by	(5.99)	(14.30)	(6.95)	(19.78)	
Owed to	2.98	23.66	12.17	8.21	
Net	(3.01)	9.36	5.22	(11.57)	

Under the terms of the arrangement, Massie, as the company with the largest debt, will pay Horan $5.22m, as the company with the smallest amount owed. Then Massie will pay Armstrong $6.35m and Giffen will pay Armstrong $3.01 m.

(b) Need to hedge against a fall in interest rate, therefore buy call options. Require 50 contracts (25,000,000/1,000,000) × 6/3. As Massie is looking to invest on 30 November, December contracts are needed.

Basis

Current price (1 September) – futures price = basis

$(100 - 3.6) - 95.76 = 0.64$

Unexpired basis = $1/4 \times 0.64 = 0.16$

Option

Amount received will be (ESTER – 0.4%) × 25,000,000 × 6/12

If interest rates increase by 0.5% to 4.1%

Expected futures price = $(100 - 4.1) - 0.16 = 95.74$

Exercise price	97.00	96.50
Futures price	95.74	95.74
Exercise option?	No	No
Gain in basis points	–	–
	€	€
Interest received		
(€25m × 6/12 × (4.1 – 0.4)%)	462,500	462,500
Gain on options	–	–
Premium		
(3.2 × €25 × 50)	(4,000)	
(18.2 × €25 × 50)		(22,750)
	———	———
Net receipt	458,500	439,750
	———	———
Effective interest rates	3.67%	3.52%

If interest rates fall by 0.5% to 3.1%

Expected futures price = (100 – 3.1) – 0.16 = 96.74

Exercise price	97.00	96.50
Futures price	96.74	96.74
Exercise option?	No	Yes
Gain in basis points	–	24
	€	€
Interest received		
(€25m × 6/12 × (3.1 – 0.4)%)	337,500	337,500
Gain on options		
(0 and 24 × €25 × 50)	–	30,000
Premium		
(3.2 × €25 × 50)	(4,000)	
(18.2 × €25 × 50)		(22,750)
Net receipt	333,500	344,750
Effective interest rates	2.67%	2.76%

Using a collar

Buy December call at 97.00 for 0.032 and sell December put at 96.50 for 0.123. Net premium received = 0.091.

Tutorial note

The amount of detail shown in this model answer might look overwhelming at first glance.

But bear in mind that using the COPY/PASTE functions in the Computer Based Exam (CBE) will enable you present information like this quite quickly.

If interest rates increase to 4.1%

	Buy call	Sell put
Exercise price	97.00	96.50
Futures price	95.74	95.74
Exercise option?	No	Yes
	€	
Interest received	462,500	
Loss on exercise		
(76 × €25 × 50)	(95,000)	
Premium		
(9.1 × €25 × 50)	11,375	
Net receipt	378,875	
Effective interest rate	3.03%	

If interest rates fall to 3.1%

	Buy call	Sell put
Exercise price	97.00	96.50
Futures price	96.74	96.74
Exercise option?	No	No
	€	
Interest received	337,500	
Loss on exercise	–	
Premium		
(9.1 × €25 × 50)	11,375	
	_____	
Net receipt	348,875	
Effective interest rate	2.79%	

Summary

	97.00	96.50	Collar
Interest rates rise to 4.1%	3.67%	3.52%	3.03%
Interest rates fall to 3.1%	2.67%	2.76%	2.79%

The option with the 97.00 exercise price has a higher average figure than the option with the 96.50 exercise price, and can be recommended on that basis, as its worst result is only marginally worse than the 96.50 option. There is not much to choose between them. The collar gives a significantly worse result than either of the options if interest rates rise, because Massie cannot take full advantage of the increase. It is marginally the better choice if interest rates fall. The recommendation would be to choose the option with the 97.00 exercise price, unless interest rates are virtually certain to fall.

Marking scheme		Marks
(a)	Dollar amounts owed and owing	2
	Totals owed and owing	2
	Net amounts owed	1
	Payments and receipts	2
		—
		7
		—
(b)	Recommendation to purchase calls	1
	Number and month of contracts	1
	Calculation of basis	1
	Options contracts calculations	4
	Collars approach and calculations	5
	Comments and conclusion	1–2
		—
	Maximum	**13**
		—
	Professional skills marks (see below)	5
		—
Total		**25**
		—

Professional skills marks

Analysis and Evaluation

Appropriate use of the data to determine suitable calculations

Appropriate use of the data to support discussion and draw appropriate conclusions

Appraisal of information objectively to make a recommendation

Scepticism

Effective challenge of information supplied to support key facts and/or decisions

Demonstration of ability to consider relevant factors applicable to hedging options

Commercial acumen

Recommendations are practical and plausible in the context of The Armstrong Group's situation

Effective use of examples from the scenario information and other practical considerations related to the context to illustrate points being made

Maximum 5 marks

72 BURYECS CO (MAR/JUN 17)

Key answer tips

Currency swaps are rarely tested, but well prepared students would have read the recent examiner's technical article and so should have expected this question. It was pleasing to see that the question covered the topic in a very similar way to the article.

The currency options were 'over the counter' options so it would have been important to realise that (unlike with traded options) there was no need to calculate the number of contracts.

As ever, students may have struggled to complete everything in the time available, but there were some easy marks throughout for students with a good exam technique.

(a)   (i)

	Buryecs	Counterparty	Interest rate benefit
Eurozone	4.0%	5.8%	1.8%
Wirtonia	Bank rate + 0.6%	Bank rate + 0.4%	0.2%
			———
Gain on swap (60:40)	1.2%	0.8%	2.0%
Bank fee (60:40)	(0.3%)	(0.2%)	(0.5%)
	———	———	———
Gain on swap after fee	0.9%	0.6%	1.5%
	———	———	———

The swap arrangement will work as follows:

	Buryecs	Counterparty
Buryecs borrows at	4.0%	
Counterparty borrows at		Bank rate + 0.4%
Counterparty receives		(Bank rate)
Buryecs pays	Bank rate	
Counterparty pays		4.6%
Buryecs receives	(4.6%)	
Advantage	120 basis points	80 basis points
Net result	Bank rate − 0.6%	5.0%

After paying the 30 point basis fee, Buryecs Co will effectively pay interest at the bank rate − 0.3% and benefit by 90 basis points or 0.9%. The counterparty will effectively pay interest at 5.2% and benefit by 60 basis points or 0.6%.

(ii) Using the purchasing power parity formula to calculate exchange rates:

$S_1 = S_0 \times (1 + h_c)/ (1 + h_b)$

Year	1	2	3
	$0.1430 \times 1.06/1.03$	$0.1472 \times 1.04/ 1.08$	$0.1417 \times 1.03/ 1.11$
	= 0.1472	= 0.1417	= 0.1315

At Year 3, $5,000 million will be exchanged at the original spot rate as per the agreement and the remaining inflows will be exchanged at the Year 3 rate.

Year	0	1	2	3
	$m	$m	$m	$m
Initial fee	(5,000)			
Payment at end of franchise				7,500
Annual income		600	600	600
Exchange rates	0.1430	0.1472	0.1417	0.1315
	€m	€m	€m	€m
Swap translated at 0.1430	(715)			715
Amount not covered by swap (7,500 – 5,000) translated at 0.1315				329
Annual income		88	85	79
Cash flows in home currency	(715)	88	85	1,123
Discount factors at 14%	1	0.877	0.769	0.675
Present value	(715)	77	65	758

The net present value of the project is €185 million, indicating that it should go ahead. However, the value is dependent on the exchange rate, which is worsening for the foreign income. If there are also uncertainties about the variability of returns during the three years, the directors may consider the project to be in excess of their risk appetite and decline the opportunity.

As a result of the exchange rates on the initial fee being fixed at the year 0 spot rate, Buryecs Co has gained $5,000 million × (0.1430 − 0.1315) × 0.675 = €39 million.

(b)   Receipt using swap arrangement = €715m + €329m = €1,044m

Receipt if transaction unhedged = $7,500m × 0.1315 = €986m

Predicted exchange rate at year 3 is €0.1315 = $1 or $7.6046 = €1

Options

Buy $ put options as receiving $.

$7.75 exercise price

Do not exercise

Net receipt = €986m – (1.6% × $7,500m × 0.1430) = €969m

$7.25 exercise price

Exercise

Receipt from government = $7,500m/7.25 = €1,034m

Net receipt = €1,034m – (2.7% × $7,500m × 0.1430) = €1,005m

The $7.25 option gives a better result than not hedging, given the current expectations of the exchange rate. However, it gives a worse result than the swap even before the premium is deducted, because of the exchange rate being fixed on the swap back of the original amount paid. These calculations do not take into account possible variability of the finance costs associated with the swap, caused by swapping into floating rate borrowing.

Marking guide			
			Marks
(a)	(i)	Recognition that swap gives advantage	1
		Swap mechanism	2
		Net benefit after bank charges	1
			4
	(ii)	Exchange rates	2
		Correct translation of amounts swapped	1
		Correct translation of other amounts	1
		Net present value	1
		Gain in € from the swap of the original fee amount	1
		Comments	2–3
		Maximum	8
(b)		Put option	1
		$7.25 option calculations	2
		$7.75 option calculations	2
		Comments	3–4
		Maximum	8
		Professional skills marks (see below)	5
Total			25

Professional skills marks

Analysis and Evaluation

Appropriate use of the data to determine suitable calculations

Appropriate use of the data to support discussion and draw appropriate conclusions

Appraisal of information objectively to make a hedging recommendation

Commercial acumen

Effective use of examples and/or practical considerations related to the context to illustrate points being made relating to hedging the transaction or economic risk

Maximum 5 marks

73 THE ADVERANE GROUP (MAR/JUN 18)

Key answer tips

Hedging questions won't always tell you specifically which calculations to perform, so look out for clues in the question. This question didn't give you a forward rate so it was impossible to use a forward contract. However, it did give futures prices to enable you to calculate the result of a futures hedge, and also borrowing and depositing rates to enable you to use a money market hedge.

(a) Net receipt = $10,150,000 – $3,700,000 = $6,450,000

Adverane Co will have a net dollar receipt in four months' time and needs to hedge against the Swiss Franc strengthening.

Money market

Borrow US$: US$6,450,000/(1 + [0.037/3]) = US$6,371,419

Convert into CHF at spot rate: US$6,371,419/1.1222 = CHF5,677,615

Invest in CHF: CHF5,677,615 × (1 + [0.027/3]) = CHF5,728,714

Futures

Buy Swiss Franc futures and use six-month futures contracts.

Basis

Assume that basis reduces to zero at contract maturity in a linear fashion.

Current basis = 1.1222 – 1.1204 = 0.0018

Unexpired basis on transaction date = 0.0018 × (2/6) = 0.0006

So predicted lock in rate = 1.1204 + 0.0006 = 1.1210

Tutorial note

Interpolating between the given futures prices would have also been acceptable, as follows:

Predicted futures rate = 1.1213 – ([1.1213 – 1.1204] × 1/3) = 1.1210.

Expected receipt = $6,450,000/1.1210 = CHF5,753,791

Number of contracts = CHF5,753,791/125,000 = 46.03 contracts, approximately 46 contracts

On the basis that futures give the higher expected receipt, they should be chosen, but Adverane Co should assess whether basis risk is likely to be significant. Adverane Co should also consider, as regards money market hedging, that CHF receipts could be used to pay off any existing CHF loans, or for other investment purposes, in which case the benefit to Adverane Co could be greater than hedging using futures.

(b) Use mid-spot rates to translate amounts.

Owed by	Owed to	Local currency	CHF
		m	m
Adverane (Switzerland)	Bosha (Eurozone)	CHF15.90	15.90
Adverane (Switzerland)	Diling (Brazil)	CHF4.46	4.46
Bosha (Eurozone)	Cogate (USA)	€24.89	26.60
Bosha (Eurozone)	Diling (Brazil)	€18.57	19.84
Cogate (USA)	Adverane (Switzerland)	US$27.08	24.16
Cogate (USA)	Diling (Brazil)	US$5.68	5.07
Diling (Brazil)	Adverane (Switzerland)	BRL38.80	12.29
Diling (Brazil)	Bosha (Eurozone)	BRL51.20	16.22

Owed to			Owed by		
	Adverane (Sw)	Bosha (Eu)	Cogate (US)	Diling (Br)	Total
	CHFm	CHFm	CHFm	CHFm	CHFm
Adverane (Sw)			24.16	12.29	36.45
Bosha (Eu)	15.90			16.22	32.12
Cogate (US)		26.60			26.60
Diling (Br)	4.46	19.84	5.07		29.37
Owed by	(20.36)	(46.44)	(29.23)	(28.51)	
Owed to	36.45	32.12	26.60	29.37	
Net	16.09	(14.32)	(2.63)	0.86	

Under the terms of the arrangement, Bosha, the company with the largest debt, will pay Diling, the company with the smallest amount owed to it, CHF0.86 million. Bosha will pay Adverane CHF13.46 million and Cogate will pay Adverane CHF2.63 million.

(c) Setting the transfer price at market price should enable a fair assessment of the performance of both the buying and selling divisions. Both internal and external sales will be accounted for at the same price. However, this may distort performance in that the costs of internal sales may be lower than external sales. For example, administration costs should be lower and there should be no costs of bad debts. These cost savings should be shared between the two divisions to give a fair picture. If the selling division has spare capacity, selling at incremental cost rather than market price may provide greater certainty that the buying division will use the selling division.

In theory, using market price should mean that the central treasury function has to intervene less. Simple market price provides an objective measure over which the divisions should agree. However, in reality, there may be complications that require central intervention. The market price may be difficult to determine or may fluctuate wildly, and central treasury may have to decide which price to use. If it is decided that an allowance should be made for costs of internal transfer being lower, central treasury may have to determine what this should be as it may vary significantly between products and divisions.

Specifying the transaction takes place at market price is designed to ensure that the buying division buys from the selling division, rather than an external supplier if the buying and selling division have failed to agree a price. The implicit assumption is that the buying division will use the selling division because of better service from, and greater dependability of, dealing within the group. This may not necessarily be the case. If the buying division previously purchased internally as a result of a low transfer price, forcing it to pay market price may mean it chooses an external supplier for non-price reasons.

Marking guide		Marks
(a) Calculation of net US$ receipt		1
Money market hedge		2
Futures		
Buy futures		1
Predicted futures rate based on basis reduction		2
Expected receipt		1
Number of contracts		1
Conclusion		1
	Maximum	8
(b) CHF amounts owed and owing		2
Totals owed and owing		2
Net amounts owed		1
Payments and receipts		2
		7
(c) Performance assessment		1–2
Work of central treasury		1–2
Buying internally		1–2
	Maximum	5
Professional skills marks (see below)		5
Total		25

Professional skills marks

Analysis and Evaluation

Appropriate use of the data to determine suitable calculations

Appropriate use of the data to support discussion and draw appropriate conclusions

Appraisal of information objectively to make a hedging recommendation

Scepticism

Effective challenge of evidence and assumptions supplied to support key facts and/or decisions

Commercial acumen

Effective use of examples and/or practical considerations related to the context to illustrate points being made relating to hedging the transactions and transfer pricing

Maximum 5 marks

74   LURGSHALL CO (MAR/JUN 19)

Key answer tips

Don't waste time here performing any calculations on futures or forwards – the results of those hedges are already provided. Instead, calculate the results of the options and swaps hedges and then discuss these calculations AND the given forwards and futures information.

(a)   **Options**

Buy put options as need to hedge against a rise in interest rates.

Number of contracts required: $84,000,000/$2,000,000 x 6/3 = 84

Total basis = current price (1 May) – futures price = (100 – 4.50) – 95.05 = 0.45

Unexpired basis on 1 September = 0.45 x 1/5 = 0.09

Expected futures price = 100 – 5.1 – 0.09 = 94.81

Exercise price	95.25
Futures price as above	94.81
Exercise?	Yes
Gain in basis points	44

	$
Interest paid ($84,000,000 × 5.6% × 6/12)	2,352,000
Gain from options	
0.0044 × $2,000,000 × 3/12 × 84	(184,800)
Premium	
0.00411 × $2,000,000 × 3/12 × 84	172,620
Net payment	2,339,820
Effective annual interest rate	
2,339,820/84,000,000 × 12/6	5.57%

Swaps

	Lurgshall Co	Counterparty	Interest rate differential
Fixed rate	5.60%	6.10%	0.50%
Floating rate	Base rate + 0.50%	Base rate + 1.50%	1.00%

Lurgshall Co has an advantage in borrowing at both fixed and floating rates, but the floating rate advantage is larger.

Gain % for Lurgshall Co = 50% (1 − 0.5 − 0.2) = 0.15

	Lurgshall Co	Counterparty
Rate without swap	(5.60%)	(Base rate + 1.50%)
Benefit	0.15%	0.15%
Net result	(5.45%)	(Base rate + 1.35%)
Swap		
Borrows at	(Base rate + 0.50%)	(6.10)
Lurgshall Co pays	(4.85%)	4.85%
Counterparty pays	Base rate	(Base rate)
Bank fee	(0.10%)	(0.10%)
Net result	(5.45%)	(Base rate + 1.35%)

Comments

The swap gives a result which is marginally worse than the forward rate agreement and the futures. The options give a worse result than the other choices.

Risks which might be considered include counterparty risk for the forward rate agreement and swap. Using Birdam Bank should mean that this risk is low for forward rate agreements, and also for swaps, assuming that the bank bears the risk of the counterparty defaulting.

Basis risk should be considered for the traded futures. Here, because the differences between the instruments are small, a failure to estimate basis accurately may mean that futures are chosen when they do not offer the lowest borrowing cost. For the swaps, if Lurgshall Co swaps into fixed rate debt, it faces the market risk of an unexpected fall in interest rates.

Other factors to consider include the possibility that rates will increase rather less than forecast, meaning that the option would not be exercised and at some point would be the lowest cost choice. The length of time of the swap also needs to be considered. Although it commits Lurgshall Co to the fixed rate, if the borrowing turns out to be longer than the six months, the swap may provide a better time match than the other hedging opportunities.

(b)   The chief executive appears to underestimate the degree of knowledge required for day-to-day work. Less experienced staff may be able to arrange borrowing if the lender has already been chosen or, for example, arrange forward rate agreements to be used if they are prescribed.

However, if judgement is required as to, for example, which lender or hedging instrument to use, using less experienced staff may mean that a sub-optimal decision is taken. Poor decisions may result in opportunity costs, for example, not using the lender who gives the best deal or being committed to a fixed forward rate agreement when an option would have allowed the business to take advantage of favourable rate movements. These opportunity costs may not be as clear as the salary costs of experienced staff.

As the business operates internationally, the treasury department will need to monitor financial market conditions and exchange rates, and other issues which may be significant such as political developments. Because of their previous experiences, longer-serving staff are more likely to appreciate the implications of developments and whether treasury policies and decisions need to change in response to changes in risk. Senior staff are also needed to manage the work of less experienced staff to prevent or mitigate the effect of mistakes which may be costly.

Experienced staff are also needed to establish overall guidelines and policies for treasury activities. Their judgement will be required to establish principles which will mean that actions taken by staff are in line with the risk appetite of the business and are sufficiently prudent from the viewpoint of risk management. Experienced staff will also have greater knowledge of law, accounting standards and tax regulations, which can help the business avoid penalties and perhaps structure its dealings so that it can, for example, minimise the level of tax paid.

The chief executive has plans for a major expansion of the business, involving significant investment and financing decisions. Advice from experienced treasury staff will be invaluable in supporting the decisions required. If Lurgshall Co is planning a major acquisition, the treasury function can provide advice on the structure of consideration and financing implications. If, as here, a major investment is being contemplated, experienced staff can advise on translating views on risk into a relevant cost of capital, which will help ensure that the financial appraisal of the investment is realistic.

	Marking guide		
			Marks
(a)	**Options**		
	Buy put options		1
	Number of contracts		1
	Basis calculation		1
	Premium calculation		1
	Exercise option?		1
	Final outcome		1
	Swaps		
	Comparative advantage and recognition of benefit		2
	Initial decision to borrow floating by Lurgshall Co and fixed by counterparty		1
	Swap impact		2
	Net benefit after bank charges		1
	Comments		3–4
		Maximum	**15**
(b)	1–2 marks per relevant point		5
		Maximum	**5**
	Professional skills marks (see below)		5
Total			**25**

Professional skills marks

Analysis and Evaluation

Appropriate use of the data to determine suitable calculations

Appropriate use of the data to support discussion and draw appropriate conclusions

Appraisal of information objectively to make a hedging recommendation

Scepticism

Effective challenge of evidence and assumptions supplied with respect to the chief executive's view on the treasury department

Commercial acumen

Effective use of examples and/or practical considerations related to the context to illustrate points being made relating to hedging the transaction or treasury discussion

Maximum 5 marks

75   FITZHARRIS CO (SEP/DEC 20)

Key answer tips

Don't waste time here performing any calculations on futures or options – the question only wanted you to look at collars and swaps.

Although these two interest rate hedging methods are examined less frequently than FRAs, futures and options, they are still a very important part of the AFM syllabus, so don't neglect them as you prepare for your exam.

(a)   Swap

	Fitzharris Co	Counterparty	Interest rate differential
Fixed rate	4.60%	4.80%	0.20%
Floating rate	Base rate + 0.50%	Base rate + 1.30%	0.80%

Fitzharris Co has an advantage in borrowing at both fixed and floating rates, but the floating rate advantage is larger.

Gain % for Fitzharris Co = 50% (0.8 – 0.2 – 0.1) = 0.25

	Fitzharris Co	Counterparty
Rate without swap	(4.60%)	(Base rate + 1.30%)
Benefit	0.25%	0.25%
Net result	(4.35%)	(Base rate + 1.05%)

Swap

Borrows at	(Base rate + 0.50%)	(4.80%)
Fitzharris Co pays	(3.80%)	3.80%
Counterparty pays	Base rate	(Base rate)
Bank fee	(0.05%)	(0.05%)
Net result	(4.35%)	(Base rate + 1.05%)

Collar

Buy December put options at 95.75 for 0.211 and sell December call options at 96.25 for 0.198

Number of contracts = ($48,000,000/$1,000,000) × (36 months/3 months) = 576 (see note below)

Tutorial note (extracted from the examiner's comments)

It is possible to justify a range of different hedging periods for this situation. Any justified hedging period from the four-month period of uncertainty, outlined in the question, up to 36 months was awarded credit. It was recognised that in reality a collar for 36 months would not happen and instead there would be a rolling series of hedges.

Answers which calculated costs in dollar amounts based on their number of contracts and then calculated an effective annual rate, were also eligible for full credit.

Basis = Current price (1 August) – futures price

$(100 - 3.70) - 95.85 = 0.45$

Unexpired basis on 1 December = $1/5 \times 0.45 = 0.09$

Premium = $(0.00211 - 0.00198) = 0.013\%$

If base rate rises by 0.4% to 4.1 %

Futures price = $100 - 4.1 - 0.09 = 95.81$

	Buy put	Sell call
Exercise price	95.75	96.25
Futures price	95.81	95.81
Exercise?*	No	No
Loss in basis points	–	–

*The put option is not exercised, because Fitzharris Co can sell the futures at the futures market price of 95.81 rather than the option exercise price of 95.75. The call option is not exercised, as the option holder can buy the futures at the lower futures market price of 95.81 rather than the exercise price of 96.25.

	%
Borrowing cost (4.1% + 0.5%)	4.600
Premium	0.013
Total payment	4.613

If base rate falls by 0.4% to 3.3%

Futures price = $100 - 3.3 - 0.09 = 96.61$

	Buy put	Sell call
Exercise price	95.75	96.25
Futures price	96.61	96.61
Exercise?*	No	Yes
Loss in basis points	–	36

* The put option is not exercised, as by not exercising the option Fitzharris Co can sell the futures at the higher futures market price of 96.61 rather than the lower exercise price of 95.75. The call option is exercised, because the option holder can buy the futures at the option exercise price of 96.25 rather than the futures market price of 96.61.

	%
Borrowing cost (3.3% + 0.5%)	3.800
Loss on options (0.0036 × 100)	0.360
Premium	0.013
	———
Effective annual interest rate	4.173
	———

Tutorial note

The amount of detail shown in this model answer might look overwhelming at first glance.

But bear in mind that using the COPY/PASTE functions in the Computer Based Exam (CBE) will enable you present information like this quite quickly.

(b)   Comment

The calculations do not give a clear indication of which strategy should be chosen. The swap gives a better result if base rate rises by 0.4%, the options if base rate falls by 0.4%. The decision may be determined by whether the company views a rise or fall in interest rates as being more likely, or how it views the advantages and disadvantages of the strategies.

Advantages of swaps

As swaps are over-the counter arrangements, they can be arranged in any size. The amount covered by collars based on traded options is determined by the size of the option contract. There may be over and under hedging.

The traded options available may last for a short period, perhaps up to two years, less maybe than the period of the loan. Swaps can be arranged for a much longer period.

Fitzharris Co is swapping here a commitment to pay a variable rate of interest that is uncertain with a guaranteed fixed rate of interest. This allows Fitzharris Co to forecast finance costs on the loan with certainty. The net payments on the collar will depend on how interest rates move.

Unlike collars, swaps make use of the principle of comparative advantage. Fitzharris Co can borrow in the market where the best deal is available to it.

Disadvantages of swaps

Swaps are subject to counterparty risk, the risk that the other party may default on the arrangement. This should not generally be a problem if Fitzharris Co arranges the swap through the bank. It may, however, be a problem if it arranges the swap itself. As the options that the collar is based on are traded on the derivatives markets, this should guarantee there will be no counterparty risk.

As Fitzharris Co is swapping into a fixed rate commitment, it cannot take advantage of favourable interest rate changes as it could, to some extent, if it used collars. Here the swap results in a lower cost than the collar if interest rates rise, but the collar is better if interest rates fall.

As swaps are over-the-counter instruments, they cannot be traded or allowed to lapse if they are not needed. The options can be traded on a derivative market.

	Marking guide		Marks
(a)	**Swaps**		
	Comparative advantage of 0.6%		1
	Initial decision to borrow floating by Fitzharris Co and fixed by counterparty		1
	Advantage of 0.25% per party after the bank fee		1
	Suitable swap rates		1
	Final rate to be paid by Fitzharris Co		1
	Collars		
	Number of contracts		1
	Basis calculation		1
	Buy put and sell call options		1
	Premium calculation		1
	Exercise options?		2
	Impact of interest rate increase/decrease with collars		2
			____
			13
			____
(b)	Comment on calculations		1
	Advantages of swaps compared with collars		3 – 4
	(advantages could include flexibility, longer time period, certainty of finance costs, comparative advantage)		
	Disadvantages of swaps compared with collars		3 – 4
	(disadvantages could include counterparty risk, inability take advantage of favourable rate movements, swaps cannot be traded)		
			____
		Maximum	**7**
			____
	Professional skills marks (see below)		**5**
			____
Total			**25**
			____

Professional skills marks

Analysis and Evaluation

Appropriate use of the data to determine suitable calculations

Appropriate use of the data to support discussion and draw appropriate conclusions

Appraisal of information objectively to make a hedging recommendation

Commercial acumen

Effective use of examples and/or practical considerations related to the context to illustrate points being made relating to hedging the transaction

Maximum 5 marks

76   GOGARTH CO (MAR/JUN 21)

(a)   **Net receipt**

$37,400,000 − $14,500,000 = $22,900,000

Forward contract

$22,900,000/0.2374 = MR96,461,668

Futures

Buy MR September futures

Basis

Assume that basis reduces to zero at contract maturity in a linear fashion.

Current basis = 0.2358 − 0.2378 = -0.0020

Unexpired basis on transaction date = -0.0020 × (1/5) = -0.0004

So predicted lock in rate = 0.2378 - 0.0004 = 0.2374

Tutorial note

Interpolating between the given futures prices would have also been acceptable, as follows:

Predicted futures rate = 0.2366 + ([0.2378 − 0.2366] × 2/3) = 0.2374.

Expected receipt = $22,900,000/0.2374 = MR96,461,668

Number of contracts = MR96,461,668/MR500,000 = 192.9, say 193

Amount over-hedged = (500,000 × 193 × $0.2374) − $22,900,000 = $9,100

Payment at forward rate = $9,100/0.2370 = MR38,397

Outcome

	MR
Futures (500,000 × 193)	96,500,000
Payment on forward market	(38,397)
Total (net)	96,461,603

Options

Purchase MR September call options

Receipt = $22,900,000/0.2368 = MR96,706,081

Number of contracts = MR96,706,081/MR500,000 = 193.4 contracts, approximately 193 contracts

Premium = 193 × $0.0014 × 500,000 = $135,100

Premium in MR, translated at spot rate = $135,100/0.2355 = MR573,673

Amount under-hedged = $22,900,000 − (193 × 500,000 × $0.2368) = $48,800

Translated at forward rate = $48,800/0.2374 = MR205,560

Outcome, assuming options are exercised

	MR
Options (500,000 × 193)	96,500,000
Receipt on forward market	205,560
Premium	(573,673)
Total (net)	96,131,887

Recommendations

The forward contract give a marginally higher receipt than the futures. Futures would be subject to basis risk, the risk that the difference between the futures price and spot rate does not decrease linearly towards the maturity of futures. This means that the receipt may be uncertain. Futures also require a margin payment, an initial payment of cash into a margin account operated by the futures exchange, with further payments if losses are made on contracts.

Options give a lower receipt, because of the need to pay a premium. Gogarth Co may consider options if it considers there is a chance that the dollar will be in a stronger position against the Malaysian ringgit than suggested by the forward rate, or if one or other transaction is likely to fall through.

Overall, Gogarth Co should choose the forward contract as it offers the marginally higher receipt and is not subject to basis risk.

Note: Other valid recommendations could be made.

(b) Economic risk is the longer-term risk that the present value of future cash flows may be increased or reduced by exchange rate movements. The treasury function will be involved in the development of longer-term responses, as the derivatives the treasury function will use for hedging of short-term exchange risk will not be appropriate.

Risk analysis

The treasury function needs to identify the cash flows that may be affected by exchange rate movements. These may not just include transactions with overseas customers and suppliers. Home market sales can also be affected if, for example, the currency of the country where a foreign competitor is based weakens against the ringgit and the competitor can then afford to charge cheaper ringgit prices.

The treasury function must also identify the factors affecting exchange rate movements in the longer term and assess what their impact is likely to be. This could include predicted movements, for example changes in the economic cycle, and also the impact of sudden economic shocks. The treasury function will need to assess the impact of these exchange rate movements on Gogarth Co. This will include consideration of the other impacts that the factors affecting exchange rates will have, for example a change in interest rate policy affecting demand for electrical equipment directly as well as influencing exchange rate levels.

Risk management

The treasury function will be particularly involved in determining funding policy in the context of the need to manage economic risk. One aspect of economic risk management is matching any assets held in a foreign country with a loan in that country's currency. The treasury function will determine the suitability of borrowing abroad and the best possible arrangement if foreign currency loans are required.

Economic risk can also be managed by diversifying customer, supplier and operational bases and changing pricing policy. The treasury function will be involved in assessing the possible impacts of policy changes. However, the decisions will be taken in the context of operational considerations, such as supplier management, and wider strategic considerations, such as scope of operations.

Marking guide		
		Marks
(a)	Netting of receipt and payment	1
	Forward contract	1
	Futures	
	Buy/Sept/No. of contracts	1
	Lock in rate	2
	Expected receipt	1
	Receipt from under/over hedge	1
	Options	
	Number of contracts	1
	Premium	2
	Forward hedge	1
	Outcome	1
	Discussion	3-4
	Maximum	**15**
(b)	Understanding of economic risk	1
	Up to 2 marks for each well developed point (points could include identification of cash flows affected, identification of influences on exchange rate, role in implementing economic risk management, role in advising on economic risk management)	5
	Maximum	**5**
	Professional skills marks (see below)	**5**
Total		**25**

Professional skills marks

Analysis and Evaluation

Appropriate use of the data to determine suitable calculations

Appropriate use of the data to support discussion and draw appropriate conclusions

Appraisal of information objectively to make a hedging recommendation

Commercial acumen

Effective use of examples and/or practical considerations related to the context to illustrate points being made relating to hedging the transaction or economic risk

Maximum 5 marks

77 BRANDON CO (SEP/DEC 21)

> **Key answer tips**
>
> The most common type of interest rate hedging question covers FRAs, futures and options, so well-prepared students would have enjoyed part (b) of this question.
>
> Treasury is also a commonly tested area, but be careful here to talk about adding value in your answer as required. A generic answer explain the role of treasury would not have been sufficient.

(a) There are a number of ways the functional areas of a treasury department could add value to Brandon Co's expansion plans.

Liquidity management

As Brandon Co expands, the increase in the volume of transactions across the group will require a greater emphasis on liquidity management, including the need to support Brandon Co's working capital requirement. A centralised treasury department could add value by netting off subsidiaries' debit and credit balances, which would reduce the number of transactions and hence transaction costs.

Currency management

The expansion outside the eurozone introduces foreign exchange risk into the group and the need to manage the impact of currency flows on Brandon Co's earnings and shareholder value. Effective currency management, including the use of derivatives, can have a significant impact on shareholder value for companies with overseas assets. A centralised treasury department will have the resources to employ experts with the knowledge required to manage these risks. It would also be possible to employ techniques across the group, such as matching income earned by one subsidiary with expenditure by another subsidiary in the same currency, reducing risk and the need for external hedging methods.

Funding

The treasury department will pay a role in sourcing the appropriate debt instruments and matching maturities to the time horizon of the investment as well as managing the relationship with lenders. A centralised treasury department could add value by pooling funding requirements across the group to achieve better rates by borrowing in bulk.

Corporate finance

The corporate finance function would undertake the equity issue(s) to raise part of the funds required for the overseas expansion and be involved with the strategic decision-making such as formulating a dividend policy that meets the needs of shareholders. A centralised treasury department would have the appropriate level of oversight of Brandon Co's group activities to provide operational, strategic and corporate finance advice to enhance value. It can advise on short-term investment strategies, evaluate subsidiary performance and manage Brandon Co's financial structure to minimise the cost of capital.

(b)   FRAs

FRA rate 5.90% (3 - 7) since the funds will be required in three months' time for a period of four months.

If central bank rate increases to 6.6%

	$
Interest payment: (6.6% + 0.4%) × 4/12 × $36,000,000	840,000
Receipt from bank: (6.6% - 5.9%) × 4/12 × $36,000,000	(84,000)
	———
Net borrowing cost	756,000
	———
Effective annual interest rate: 756,000/36,000,000 × 12/4	6.3%

Futures

Hedge against an increase in interest rates, therefore go short in futures market. Use March contracts, as funds will be required on 31 January.

Number of contracts = $36,000,000/$500,000 × 4 months/3 months = 96 contracts

Basis

Spot price (1 Nov) – futures price = basis

(100 – 5.70) – 93.95 = 0.35

Unexpired basis on 31 Jan = 2/5 × 0.35 = 0.14

If central bank rate increases to 6.6%

	$
Interest payment as above	840,000
Expected futures price: 100 – 6.6 – 0.14 = 93.26	
Profit on the futures market: (0.9395 – 0.9326) × $500,000 × 3/12 × 96	(82,800)
	———
Net borrowing cost	757,200
	———
Effective annual interest rate: 757,200/ 36,000,000 x 12/4	6.31%

Options on interest rate futures

Buy March put options to hedge against an increase in interest rates. As above, 96 contracts are required.

Premium = 0.00087 × $500,000 × 3/12 × 96 = $10,440

If central bank base rate increases to 6.6%

	Buy put
Exercise price	93.75
Expected futures price, as above	93.26
Exercise?	Yes
Gain in basis points	49

	$
Interest payment as above	840,000
Profit on options 0.0049 × $500,000 × 3/12 × 96	(58,800)
Premium	10,440
Net borrowing cost	791,640

Effective annual interest rate: 791,640/36,000,000 × 12/4   6.60%

Advice

The forward rate agreement and futures market provide broadly similar results. The outcome of the forward rate agreement hedge is marginally lower and may be the preferred choice. In theory, both methods provide a fixed interest payment and a certain cash outflow but futures contracts are subject to basis risk and margin requirements.

If the central bank rate increases to 6.6%, the option is the least attractive hedging method due to the expensive premium. Unlike forward rate agreements and futures contracts, however, options do not have to be exercised and allow Brandon Co to benefit from upside potential if the central bank base rate falls. Treasury staff would need to assess the likelihood and amount of a possible reduction in interest rates when assessing the viability of the option.

If the board is to achieve its objective of minimising risk exposure, the certain cash flow associated with the forward rate agreement will be more attractive than the variable outcome associated with the options.

Marking guide		
		Marks
(a)	Functional areas (e.g. liquidity management, currency management, funding and corporate finance)	3 – 4
	Advantages of centralised treasury (e.g. netting off, expertise, pooling, strategic oversight and dividend policy)	3 – 4
	Maximum	**6**
(b)	FRA	2
	Go short on March futures	1
	Number of contracts	1
	Basis	1
	Impact of IR increase with futures	2
	Buy March puts	1
	Premium calculation	1
	Exercise	1
	Impact of IR increase with options	2
	Discussion	2 – 3
	Maximum	**14**
	Professional skills marks (see below)	**5**
Total		**25**

Professional skills marks

Analysis and Evaluation

Appropriate use of the data to determine suitable calculations

Appropriate use of the data to support discussion and draw appropriate conclusions

Appraisal of information objectively to make a hedging recommendation

Commercial acumen

Effective use of examples and/or practical considerations related to the context to illustrate points being made relating to the treasury function and hedging the transaction risk

Maximum 5 marks

Section 5

AFM SPECIMEN EXAM QUESTIONS

1 KINGTIM CO (SPECIMEN EXAM 2022)

The following exhibits, available on the left-hand side of the screen (in the CBE exam), provide information relevant to the question.

1 **Kingtim Co**

2 **Takeover defences – to be used by Kingtim**

3 **Financial details – relating to cost of capital and bond information**

4 **Employee remuneration**

This information should be used to answer the question requirements within your chosen response option(s).

Kingtim Co

Kingtim Co is a nationwide chain of garden centres, selling products such as plants, fertilisers, tools and garden furniture. It was established 20 years ago by the current team of executive directors, and achieved a listing on its local stock market four years ago. Since listing, the company has made consistent profits and has been able to increase its dividends each year. The executive directors collectively own between them 25% of issued share capital. The remaining shares are held by a number of investors, with none of them owning more than 10% of issued share capital.

Two of Kingtim Co's major competitors have been taken over in the last two years. Media coverage suggests that further takeovers are possible. Potential acquirers include other chains of garden centres, property developers and supermarket chains looking to diversify their business into the profitable garden centre sector. As yet, no potential acquirer has approached Kingtim Co to buy the whole chain, although Kingtim Co has had enquiries from other businesses wanting to purchase individual garden centres. Kingtim Co can sell a number of individual garden centres without threatening its continued existence.

Takeover defences

Kingtim Co's executive directors remain committed to the business. They are fearful of a takeover, believing that the new owners will want some, or all of them, to leave the company. They have therefore been considering possible defences against a takeover bid. Kingtim Co's chief executive has received two proposals from directors:

– Sell individual garden centres which would be particularly attractive to purchasers. Disposal of these centres would make Kingtim Co, overall, a less attractive purchase.

– Pay the executive directors higher remuneration and change their contracts so that they would receive much higher compensation for loss of office if their contracts were terminated early.

Kingtim Co's chief executive believes, however, that any defence Kingtim Co adopts should also strengthen the company's future. She is therefore proposing to expand the company's current limited sales of camping products in its garden centres by establishing a chain of Kingtim outdoor shops, selling camping, walking and other outdoor equipment. The outdoor retail sector is competitive, but the chief executive believes that Kingtim Co will be successful. The establishment of the chain of outdoor shops would be funded solely by debt, the idea being that changing Kingtim Co's finance structure by having significantly more debt would make it less attractive to acquirers.

Financial details

Kingtim Co currently has 25 million $1 shares in issue, with a current share price of $5.56 per share. It also has 0.45 million 6.5% bonds in issue. Each 6.5% bond has a nominal value of $100, and is currently trading at $104 per $100. The premium on redemption of the bonds in three years' time is 2%. Based on a yield to maturity approach, the after-tax cost of the bonds is 4.1 %.

Kingtim Co's quoted equity beta for its existing garden centre business is 0.9.

Kingtim Co plans to issue 0.6 million, 7.5%, new bonds, each with a nominal value of $100. These bonds will be redeemable in four years' time at a premium of 8%. The coupon on these bonds will be payable on an annual basis. These bonds are anticipated to have a credit rating of BBB–. The issue of the new 7.5% bonds will not affect the market value of Kingtim Co's shares or the existing 6.5% bonds.

The market value of the new bonds will be determined by using information relating to Kingtim Co's credit rating and the four bonds which the government has issued to estimate Kingtim Co's yield curve. All the bonds are of the same risk class. Details of the bonds are as follows:

Bond	Annual yield (based on spot rate)	Redeemable in
Ga	4%	1 year
Th	4.3%	2 years
De	4.7%	3 years
Ro	5.2%	4 years

Credit spreads, shown in basis points, are as follows:

Rating	1 year	2 years	3 years	4 years
BBB–	56	78	106	135

Kingtim Co plans to invest $60m in non-current assets for the outdoor shops (working capital requirements can be ignored). Currently, Kingtim Co's non-current assets have a net book value of $150m. It is assumed that the proportion of the book value of non-current assets which will be invested in the outdoor shops and the garden centres will give a fair representation of the size of each business within Kingtim Co. The asset beta of similar companies in the outdoor retail sector is assumed to be 0.88.

Before taking into consideration the impact of this new investment, Kingtim Co's forecast pre-tax earnings for the coming year is $24m. It is estimated that the new investment will make a 10% pre-tax return and after tax earnings will increase by $1.125m.

The corporation tax rate applicable to all companies is 25% per year. The current risk-free rate of return is estimated to be 4% and the market risk premium is estimated to be 9%.

Employee remuneration

Kingtim Co's annual report contains a general commitment to act with social responsibility, in line with society's expectations. It also commits to paying its staff fairly in accordance with their responsibilities and states that its staff are vital to its success.

To try to improve the situation of low-paid employees, the government has recommended a basic hourly wage as the minimum level employees should be paid, although this minimum is not legally enforceable. A newspaper investigation has revealed that some staff in Kingtim Co's garden centres in the northern region of the country are paid up to 15% less per hour than the recommended minimum wage. Most of these staff are part-time staff, working limited hours each week.

The manager of Kingtim Co's northern region centres, when asked to comment, stated that Kingtim Co had obligations to its shareholders to control staff costs. Lower pay levels were necessary to differentiate between staff, ensuring that managers and staff with experience and expertise were appropriately rewarded. The manager commented that pay levels also reflected the lower commitment to Kingtim Co which part-time staff made compared with full-time staff.

Required:

(a) **Discuss the feasibility and effectiveness of the defence strategies of selling off individual garden centres and enhancing directors' remuneration.** **(7 marks)**

(b) **Prepare a report for the board of directors of Kingtim Co which:**

(i) **estimates the company's cost of capital before the new bonds are issued**
(4 marks)

(ii) **estimates the market value and post tax cost of debt of the new bonds**
(7 marks)

(iii) **estimates the revised cost of equity and revised cost of capital if the new bonds are issued** **(7 marks)**

(iv) **discusses the impact on Kingtim Co's cost of capital and the reaction of equity and bondholders to the chief executive's proposal. The discussion should include an explanation of any assumptions made in the estimates in (b) (i) – (iii) above.** **(9 marks)**

(c) **Discuss the approach taken to employee remuneration by Kingtim Co's Northern region and the issues associated with it.** **(6 marks)**

Professional marks will be awarded for the demonstration of skill in communication, analysis and evaluation, scepticism and commercial acumen in your answer. **(10 marks)**

(Total: 50 marks)

2 COLVIN CO (SPECIMEN EXAM 2022)

The following exhibits, available on the left-hand side of the screen (in the CBE exam), provide information relevant to the question.

1 **Colvin Co**

2 **Project information**

3 **Discount rate**

This information should be used to answer the question requirements within your chosen response option(s).

Colvin Co

Colvin Co is based in the eurozone region and was established ten years ago to manufacture competition standard bicycles for professional road racers. When the company obtained a listing five years ago, the founder retained a small minority shareholding. The remaining shares are held by a number of institutional investors.

The board recently decided to expand the range of models and to look for new growth opportunities abroad. Whilst manufacturing is currently restricted to the eurozone, the board of directors has identified Canvia as a key growth market and is considering a potential investment project to manufacture and sell a new model there. This would involve establishing a subsidiary in Canvia.

Project information

The currency in Canvia is the Canvian lira (CL) and the current exchange rate is CL9.91 per euro (€). The annual rate of inflation in Canvia is expected to remain at 10% throughout the four-year duration of the project.

The finance director estimates the project's sales volumes, inflation-adjusted, pre-tax contribution and fixed costs as follows:

Year	1	2	3	4
Sales volume (units)	109,725	121,795	148,590	197,624
Pre-tax contribution (CLm)	419.4	500.2	671.3	961.2
Fixed costs (CLm)	270.0	291.6	314.9	340.1

The project will require an immediate investment of CL75m in land and buildings and CL700m in plant and machinery. Tax allowable depreciation is available on plant and machinery on a straight-line basis at an annual rate of 25% on cost. Colvin Co's finance director believes the plant and machinery will have a zero residual value at the end of the four years. The land and buildings will be disposed of at the end of the project and their tax exempt value is expected to increase at an annual rate of 30% throughout the four-year life of the investment.

The project will also require an immediate investment in working capital of CL25m. The annual working capital requirements are expected to be as follows:

Year	1	2	3	4
CLm	(25.0)	(2.5)	(2.8)	(3.0)

Working capital will be released back in full at the end of the project. Colvin Co has a policy of extracting remittable cash flows as dividends at the earliest possible opportunity.

All components for the new bicycle will be produced or purchased in Canvia except for a gearing system component which will be manufactured by Colvin Co in the eurozone. The cost of acquiring this component from the eurozone is already included in the pre-tax contribution estimates, based on a transfer price of €10 per component. The finance director estimates a manufacturing cost of €2 per component. Both the transfer price and manufacturing cost are expected to increase in line with eurozone annual inflation of 4% in the first two years of the project and 2% in years three and four.

Corporation tax in Canvia is payable annually at 25% and companies are allowed to carry losses forward to be offset against future trading profits. Colvin Co pays corporation tax in its home country at an annual rate of 20%. Taxes are payable in both countries in the year the liability is incurred. A bi-lateral tax treaty exists between the two countries, which permits the offset of overseas tax against any domestic tax liability incurred on overseas earnings.

Discount rate

The board proposes financing the project with a mix of equity and debt in such a way that the existing capital structure remains unchanged. For the purposes of this project, the chief executive believes Colvin Co's weighted average cost of capital of 13% should be adjusted to include a country risk premium on the basis that Canvia is a developing economy and appears to be economically less stable than the eurozone countries. She made this decision after consulting a country risk index, which compares the standard deviation of market returns in various countries.

Additional factors taken into consideration include foreign exchange risk, the fact that there have been frequent changes of government, and hence economic policies, in Canvia. You have therefore been asked to use a discount rate of 16% to appraise this investment project.

Required:

(a)   **Evaluate the suitability of the investment proposal in Canvia, including the impact of the country risk premium on the net present value of the project.   (14 marks)**

(b)   **Discuss the validity of the chief executive's reasons for adjusting the discount rate used in appraising the project in Canvia.   (6 marks)**

Professional marks will be awarded for the demonstration of skill in analysis and evaluation, scepticism and commercial acumen in your answer.   (5 marks)

(Total: 25 marks)

3 BOULLAIN CO (SPECIMEN EXAM 2022)

The following exhibits, available on the left-hand side of the screen (in the CBE exam), provide information relevant to the question.

1 **Boullain Co and its hedging policy**

2 **Hedging products**

This information should be used to answer the question requirements within your chosen response option(s).

Boullain Co

Boullain Co is based in the Eurozone and manufactures components for agricultural machinery. The company is financed by a combination of debt and equity, having obtained a listing five years ago. In addition to the founder's equity stake, the shareholders consist of pension funds and other institutional investors. Until recently, sales have been generated exclusively within the Eurozone area but the directors are keen to expand and have identified North America as a key export market. The company recently completed its first sale to a customer based in the United States, although payment will not be received for another six months.

At a recent board meeting, Boullain Co's finance director argued that the expansion into foreign markets creates the need for a formal hedging policy and that shareholder value would be enhanced if this policy was communicated to the company's other stakeholders. However, Boullain Co's chief executive officer disagreed with the finance director on the following grounds. First, existing shareholders are already well diversified and would therefore not benefit from additional risk reduction hedging strategies. Second, there is no obvious benefit to shareholder value by communicating the hedging policy to other stakeholders such as debt providers, employees, customers and suppliers. You have been asked to provide a rationale for the finance director's comments in advance of the next board meeting.

Hedging products

Assume today's date is 1 March 20X0. Boullain Co is due to receive $18,600,000 from the American customer on 31 August 20X0. The finance director is keen to minimise the company's exposure to foreign exchange risk and has identified forward contracts, exchange traded futures and options as a way of achieving this objective.

The following quotations have been obtained.

Exchange rates (quoted as €/US$1)

Spot	0.8707–0.8711
Six months forward	0.8729–0.8744

Currency futures (contract size €200,000; exercise price quoted as US$ per €1)

	Exercise price
March	1.1476
June	1.1449
September	1.1422

Currency options (contract size €200,000; exercise price quoted as US$ per €1, premium: US cents per €1)

	Calls			Puts		
Exercise price	**March**	**June**	**September**	**March**	**June**	**September**
1.1420	0.43	0.59	0.77	0.62	0.78	0.89

Assume futures and options contracts mature at the month end and that there is no basis risk. The number of contracts to be used should be rounded down to the nearest whole number in calculations. If the full amount cannot be hedged using an exact number of futures or options contracts, the balance is hedged using the forward market.

Once the position is open, the euro futures contract outlined above will be marked-to-market on a daily basis. The terms of the contract require Boullain Co to deposit an initial margin per contract with the clearing house. Assume the maintenance margin is equivalent to the initial margin.

Your manager is concerned about the impact of an open futures position on Boullain Co's cash flow and has asked you to explain the impact of the margin requirements and their significance for the hedging decision.

Required:

(a) Explain the rationale for the policy of hedging Boullain Co's foreign exchange risk and the potential benefits to shareholder value if that policy is effectively communicated to the company's key stakeholders. **(6 marks)**

(b) Recommend a hedging strategy for Boullain Co's foreign currency receipt in six months' time based on the hedging choices the finance director is considering. Support your recommendation with relevant calculations and appropriate discussion including the impact of the margin requirements. **(14 marks)**

Professional marks will be awarded for the demonstration of skill in analysis and evaluation, scepticism and commercial acumen in your answer. **(5 marks)**

(Total: 25 marks)

Section 6

ANSWERS TO AFM SPECIMEN EXAM

1 KINGTIM CO (SPECIMEN EXAM 2022)

Key answer tips

One of the most challenging things about AFM is the fact that the section A questions often cover different topics from various parts of the syllabus.

To be successful at this question, you had to have a good knowledge of mergers and acquisitions (in particular strategic defences), cost of capital and bond yields, and corporate reconstruction.

Having said that, all the topics were tested in very similar ways to several previous questions, showing how important it is to prepare for the exam by attempting as many past exam questions as possible.

(a) Sell-off of garden centres

Selling some of the most desirable garden centres, known as selling the crown jewels, may deter some acquirers looking to buy the whole chain if Kingtim Co sells the assets they most desire. Kingtim Co could take this option if it is able to sell off individual centres without jeopardising its overall existence.

However if no particular use is made of the cash raised from the sales, Kingtim Co would still remain a tempting takeover target due to its cash surpluses. Returning the surplus cash to shareholders in the form of a one-off dividend might be popular with shareholders, but equally they might be concerned about their future returns given the sale of assets generating significant income. Shareholders and others interested in Kingtim Co might also question what future strategies the board had in mind if it did not use these cash surpluses for investment.

Also, if the money was distributed to shareholders, Kingtim Co would become a smaller company and perhaps more affordable to some potential acquirers.

Enhanced directors' remuneration and contracts

The enhanced commitments to the directors would represent an increased burden for acquirers, either the costs of honouring them, or the cost and the time involved in terminating the directors' employment and compensating them. This burden may deter acquirers, particularly if the decision to acquire is marginal.

However, enhancing the commitments to the directors could be ineffective. The acquirer could decide to keep the directors on and pay the increased remuneration.

Alternatively, the acquirer may feel that buying out the directors' contracts and compensating them is a necessary cost that it is prepared to bear.

Corporate governance aspects are also important. As a listed company, Kingtim Co should have a remuneration committee made up of non-executive directors, who should be reviewing the executive directors' remuneration packages. Kingtim Co may have to publish a remuneration report to explain the rationale for directors' remuneration, and to allow shareholders to discuss and perhaps vote on the report.

Shareholders may believe that the directors are being given a better compensation package without having earned it, and for no other reason than to try to protect their own positions. They may doubt whether directors are acting in the best interests of the company and its shareholders.

(b) **Report to board of directors, Kingtim Co (part iv)**

Introduction

This report indicates the impact of the proposed investment in outdoor shops and the consequent increase in debt finance. It also discusses the possible reactions of equity and bondholders to the proposals. Financial estimates provided in the appendices are used to support the discussion and assumptions underlying the estimates are set out below.

Cost of capital

There are two impacts, in opposite directions, on the weighted average cost of capital.

Kingtim Co's cost of equity has risen significantly. This is due to increased business risk, resulting from the investment in the outdoor shops and increased financial risk from the additional debt. The increase in the cost of equity has pushed the weighted average cost of capital upwards.

However, the higher proportion of debt in the company's finance structure, with debt having a lower cost than equity and also being tax-deductible, has pushed the weighted average cost of capital downwards.

Overall, however, the weighted average cost of capital has risen, meaning the increase in the cost of equity has had the greater impact.

Assumptions

The assumptions about the returns from the new investment may depend on how much Kingtim Co can attract customers away from competitors rather than finding a new market niche itself. Competitor reaction may also impact upon returns.

The CAPM model used is assumed to be a good predictor of equity returns, although some published evidence suggests that it may not be.

The asset beta used for the outdoor shops is a representative beta for similar companies and may not be accurate for Kingtim Co. The asset beta used to calculate the revised cost of equity is a weighted average of the asset betas of the two businesses. The weighting used is the non-current assets in each business, which is assumed to approximate to the size of each business. This assumes that non-current assets currently held are valued fairly, and that their valuation represents their income-generating potential and the proportion of business risk that each business represents.

The share price and price of the existing bonds are assumed to remain unchanged when the new investment is made. As discussed below, there is a strong possibility of changes in the shareholder base leading to changes in the share price and hence in the cost of capital.

Equity holders

Equity holders may consider the returns from the new investment to be insufficient. The pre-tax return of 10% is lower than the 16% pre-tax return ($24m/$150m) on the existing garden centres, and is not much above the 7.5% pre-tax finance cost of the bonds used to finance the investment.

Equity holders are likely to be concerned about the increases in both business and financial risks. The increase in business risk is due to the higher business risk for the outdoor shops, due to the competition in that sector. Equity holders will be concerned about the possible variability of returns and also of dividends, as the company is committed to an increased operating cost burden in terms of extra premises and increased finance costs. Variability of returns may also result in the share price becoming more volatile.

Other aspects concerning equity holders might be any restrictive covenants attached to the new bonds that affect payment of dividends and also the planned repayment of the bonds. Kingtim Co already has a significant commitment to repay the $45m bonds in three years' time. The new bonds would mean an additional commitment to repay $60m just a year later. The alternative is refinancing, but the terms that would be available are currently unknown,

These risks may mean that equity holders reconsider their investment in Kingtim Co, if they are risk-averse and do not feel that the additional returns compensate for the risk. They will take into account that the return on investment in the new business is lower than the current return on investment in the garden centres, although they are not required to make any additional investment themselves for the return on the outdoor shops. The share price will fall if a significant number of shareholders decide to sell their shares, although Kingtim Co may attract a new clientele of shareholders who are more risk-seeking.

Bondholders

Bondholders are likely to be most concerned about Kingtim Co's ability to meet its interest and repayment commitments. Holders of the new bonds are particularly likely to be concerned about the ability to repay their capital, given the commitment to repay existing bondholders. Bondholders may also be concerned about whether the financing of the investment allows Kingtim Co to take undue risks. They may wonder about the motivation for undertaking the new investment using debt finance, particularly if they are not convinced about its business case.

Conclusion

Assuming a strong business case can be made for the investment and the estimates are robust, Kingtim Co may be able to justify financing it solely by debt and claim that the increase in financial risk is within acceptable levels. However, before committing to further debt, Kingtim Co must provide a clear plan for repayment of both the current and new bonds, or offer sufficient assurance that it will be able to refinance its debt when it is due for repayment.

Tutorial note

When attempting a question like this in the Computer Based Exam (CBE), make your answer look like a professional document by writing the report in the word processor but putting your numbers (appendix) in a spreadsheet.

When preparing your calculations, use the spreadsheet functions SUM and IRR to save time.

Appendix 1 Estimate of existing cost of capital (b) (i)

Cost of equity

$k_e = 4.0\% + (0.9 \times 9.0\%) = 12.1\%$

Value of equity (V_e) = $\$5.56 \times 25$ million shares = $\$139$m

Value of existing bonds

$V_d = \$104 \times 0.45$ million = $\$46.8$m

Current WACC

WACC = $((12.1\% \times 139) + (4.1\% \times 46.8))/(139 + 46.8) = 10.1\%$

Appendix 2 Estimate of cost of new bonds (b) (ii)

Annual yield curve

Bond	Government annual yield curve	Credit spread	Kingtim Co annual yield curve
Ga	4%	56	4.56%
Th	4.3%	78	5.08%
De	4.7%	106	5.76%
Ro	5.2%	135	6.55%

Value of new bonds based on annual yield curve

$\$7.50 \times 1.0456^{-1} + \$7.50 \times 1.0508^{-2} + \$7.50 \times 1.0576^{-3} + \$115.50 \times 1.0655^{-4} = \$109.92$

Market value of new bonds

$\$109.92 \times 0.6$m = $\$65.952$m

Post-tax cost of debt of new bonds

Year		$	5%	$	3%	$
0	Market value	(109.92)	1.000	(109.92)	1.000	(109.92)
1 – 4	Interest (post-tax)	5.63	3.546	19.96	3.717	20.93
4	Redemption	108.00	0.823	88.88	0.888	95.90
				–––––		–––––
				(1.08)		6.91
				–––––		–––––

Post-tax cost of debt = $3\% + ((6.91/(6.91 + 1.08)) \times (5\% - 3\%)) = 4.7\%$

Appendix 3 Revised cost of equity and WACC (b) (iii)

β_a garden centre business = 0.9 × (139/(139 + (46.8 × 0.75))) = 0.72

Weighted average β_a = (0.72 × (150/(150 + 60))) + (0.88 × (60/(150 + 60))) = 0.77

β_e = 0.77 × ((139 + ((46.8 + 65.952) × 0.75))/139) = 1.24

k_e = 4.0% + (1.24 × 9.0%) = 15.2%

WACC = ((15.2% × 139) + (4.1 % × 46.8) + (4.7% × 65.952))/(139 + 46.8 + 65.952) = 10.4%

(c) **Approach taken**

The stated approach to employee remuneration has some business logic. Expertise, experience, seniority and commitment are all attributes that staff have that could be reflected in extra rewards for them, not only out of fairness to the staff but also because of their value to the business. If staff with these attributes believe they are not being rewarded fairly, they may leave and perhaps join a competitor.

Kingtim Co also has a duty to enhance the wealth of its shareholders and has raised expectations by recently increasing dividends. There is a stakeholder conflict, as increasing the wages of many employees would lead to lower profits and less money available for distribution to shareholders.

Issues with approach

The statement about part-time staff not having the same level of commitment may well be unjust, as they may be as committed as full-time staff during the hours they work.

The current approach raises a number of ethical issues, which may also harm Kingtim Co's reputation. It has made commitments to act in accordance with society's expectations and to treat its staff fairly. Although the basic wage is not legally enforceable, it does represent society's expectations about what employees should be paid. Limiting rewards to staff who may only be able to work part-time because of other commitments could also be something that society judges to be discriminatory and may be against the law.

In addition, if Kingtim Co's directors are given more lucrative contracts as a takeover defence mechanism, this undermines the argument for limiting staff costs in order to maintain shareholder returns.

The consequences of these threats to reputation might again be that lower-paid staff eventually decide to leave. A high staff turnover will mean few staff develop experience and expertise over time, which may impact on customer quality. Kingtim Co may also have problems recruiting staff for its new outdoor business. Customers may also stop shopping at Kingtim Co in protest at the poor treatment of staff.

			Marks
Marking guide			
(a)	Sell-off assets (examples of points could include company less appealing, use of proceeds from sell-off, how Kingtim Co will be viewed, smaller company being more affordable)		3 – 4
	Onerous contracts (examples of points could include cost burden, acquirer may be prepared to bear it, corporate governance requirements, shareholder reaction)		3 – 4
		Maximum	**7**
(b)	(i)	Cost of equity and value of equity (1 each)	2
		Value of existing bonds and WACC (1 each)	2
			4
	(ii)	Annual spot yield curve	1
		Value of new bonds	3
		Total market value of new bonds	1
		Post-tax cost of debt of proposed bonds	2
			7
	(iii)	Asset beta garden centre business	1
		Weighted asset beta	2
		Revised equity beta	1
		Revised cost of equity	1
		Revised WACC	2
			7
	(iv)	Cost of capital	1 – 2
		Assumptions	2 – 3
		Equity holders	2 – 3
		Bond holders	2 – 3
		Maximum	**9**
(c)	Up to 2 marks for each well-explained issue (issues could include rewarding expertise/seniority fairly, balancing shareholder and employee interests, unfair to question staff's commitment, society's expectations/law, expectations raised by Kingtim Co's statements, employee/customer reaction to poor practices)		6
		Maximum	**6**
	Professional skills marks (see below)		**10**
Total			**50**

Professional skills marks

Communication

General report format and structure (use of headings/sub-headings and an introduction)

Style, language and clarity (appropriate layout and tone of report response, presentation of calculations, appropriate use of the tools)

Effectiveness of communication (answer is relevant, specific rather than general and focused to the requirement)

Adherence to the details of the Chief Executive's proposal in the scenario

Analysis and Evaluation

Appropriate use of the data to determine suitable calculations

Appropriate use of the data to support discussion and draw appropriate conclusions

Demonstration of reasoned judgement when considering key matters for Kingtim Co

Demonstration of ability to consider relevant factors applicable to increasing the level of debt finance

Scepticism

Effective challenge of information, evidence and assumptions supplied and, techniques carried out to support key facts and/or decisions

Demonstration of the ability to probe into the reasons for issues and problems, including the identification of missing information or additional information, which would alter the decision reached by Kingtim Co

Commercial acumen

Recommendations are practical and plausible in the context of Kingtim Co's situation

Effective use of examples and/or calculations from the scenario information and other practical considerations related to the context to illustrate points being made

Recognition of external constraints and opportunities as necessary

Maximum 10 marks

2 COLVIN CO (SPECIMEN EXAM 2022)

Key answer tips

International investment appraisal is a very commonly tested topic.

Make sure you deal with all the foreign currency cash flows first, then convert them to the home currency and add any extra home currency cash flows.

Keeping the different currency cash flows separate is key to success in a question like this.

(a)

Project cash flows: All figures are in CL millions

Year	0	1	2	3	4
Contribution		419.4	500.2	671.3	961.2
Fixed costs		(270.0)	(291.6)	(314.9)	(340.1)
Tax allowable depreciation		(175.0)	(175.0)	(175.0)	(175.0)
		———	———	———	———
Taxable profit/(loss)		(25.6)	33.6	181.4	446.1
Tax loss carried forward		25.6	(25.6)		
		———	———	———	———
Adjusted taxable profit		0.0	8.0	181.4	446.1
Taxation (25%)			(2.0)	(45.4)	(111.5)
Add loss carried forward		(25.6)	25.6		
Add depreciation		175.0	175.0	175.0	175.0
		———	———	———	———
Cash flows after tax		149.4	206.6	311.0	509.6
Working capital	(25.0)	(2.5)	(2.8)	(3.0)	33.3
Investment cost	(775.0)				214.2
	———	———	———	———	———
Cash flows	(800.0)	146.9	203.8	308.0	757.1
	———	———	———	———	———

Cash flows: All figures are in € millions

Year	0	1	2	3	4
Exchange rate (w1)	9.91	10.48	11.09	11.96	12.89
Total investment cost	(80.7)				
Remittable cash flows		14.0	18.4	25.8	58.7
Component contribution (w2)		0.9	1.1	1.3	1.8
Tax on net contribution (20%)		(0.2)	(0.2)	(0.3)	(0.4)
		———	———	———	———
Cash flows	(80.7)	14.7	19.3	26.8	60.1

Net present value using 16% discount rate: All figures are in € millions

Year	0	1	2	3	4
Cash flows	(80.7)	14.7	19.3	26.8	60.1
Discount rate (16%)	1.000	0.862	0.743	0.641	0.552
Present values	(80.7)	12.7	14.3	17.2	33.2

Net present value (€3.3m)

Net present value using 13% discount rate: All figures are in € millions

Year	0	1	2	3	4
Cash flows	(80.7)	14.7	19.3	26.8	60.1
Discount rate (13%)	1.000	0.885	0.783	0.693	0.613
Present values	(80.7)	13.0	15.1	18.6	36.8

Net present value €2.8m

Tutorial note

When attempting a question like this in the Computer Based Exam (CBE), make sure you use the spreadsheet functions SUM and NPV to save time.

Workings

Working 1 (w1): Exchange rates

Year	1	2	3	4
CL/€	9.91 × 1.10/1.04 =10.48	10.48 × 1.10/1.04 = 11.09	11.09 × 1.10/1.02 = 11.96	11.96 × 1.10/1.02 = 12.89

Working 2 (w2): Component contribution (€)

Year	1	2	3	4
Contribution	109,725 × 8 × 1.04 = 0.9m	121,795 × 8 × 1.04^2 = 1.1m	148,590 × 8 × 1.04^2 × 1.02 = 1.3m	197,624 × 8 × 1.04^2 × 1.02^2 = 1.8m

Comment

The decision whether to accept or reject the project critically depends on the discount rate, switching from a negative net present value of €3.3m when the discount rate includes a country risk premium to a positive net present value of €2.8m when there is no premium. Given that there appears to be greater justification for the 13% discount rate it is recommended that the project should be accepted. However, the adjustment to the weighted average cost of capital requires further investigation because it is possible Colvin Co could accept a project that reduces shareholder wealth.

The outcome assumes the contribution and other cash flows are reliably estimated. Other critical inputs include the assumption that land and buildings will increase in value at an annual rate of 30% and that any disposal is tax exempt.

(b) Colvin Co's investment in Canvia does not involve a change in business risk or capital structure. The company's weighted average cost of capital would normally be expected to provide a reasonable measure of risk for the new project. The chief executive's justification for a risk premium is based on the increased risk the company is exposed to in Canvia, a developing economy, compared to the company's existing business in the Eurozone. This perception of increased risk is based on a country risk index, which compares the standard deviation of market indices around the world. The chief executive has incorporated other factors, such as political risk and foreign exchange risk in determining this premium.

However, standard deviation is not the appropriate measure of risk for Colvin Co's investment since any portion of total risk that is uncorrelated across different markets can be diversified away at no cost to investors. For example, adverse political events in Canvia may be partially offset by more favourable events in other parts of the world. No rational investor would pay a premium for risk that can be avoided. In this sense, although Colvin Co's investment in Canvia is exposed to foreign exchange risk, this too can be mitigated by an appropriate hedging policy.

Furthermore, Colvin Co's institutional shareholders are likely to be well diversified across global markets and asset classes. The potential for further risk reduction by Colvin Co from diversifying operations globally is therefore limited when the shareholders can achieve this more efficiently on their own.

The only component of total risk that could justify a premium to Colvin Co's cost of capital is market risk or undiversifiable risk. This assumes returns across countries are significantly positively correlated. For example, there is a strong possibility that a recession in the Eurozone may lead to a downturn in Canvia too rather than offset it, transmitted through trade links and closer integration between markets. This tendency for markets across the world to move together means reduced risk reduction benefits from diversification, hence a higher cost of capital. The key issue therefore is whether the risk of the new investment is diversifiable or not. If returns across markets are significantly positively correlated and the risk undiversifiable, the new project in Canvia may therefore command a risk premium although no justification is provided for the chief executive's premium of 3% which would require further investigation and analysis.

Marking guide			Marks
(a)	Exchange rates		2
	Tax		2
	Working capital		1
	Land and buildings residual value		1
	Remittable cash flows in euros		1
	Contribution from component		2
	Tax on contribution		1
	Net present values		2
	Comment		2 – 3
		Maximum	14
(b)	Up to 2 marks per point (e.g. argument for WACC, total risk vs market risk, correlation across countries)		
		Maximum	6
	Professional skills marks (see below)		5
Total			25

Professional skills marks

Analysis and Evaluation

Appropriate use of the data to determine suitable calculations

Appropriate use of the data to support discussion and draw appropriate conclusions

Appraisal of information objectively to make a recommendation

Scepticism

Effective challenge of information, evidence and assumptions supplied and, techniques carried out to support key facts and/or decisions

Demonstration of ability to consider all relevant factors applicable to a given course of action

Commercial acumen

Recommendations are practical and plausible in the context of Colvin Co's situation

Effective use of examples and/or calculations from the scenario information and other practical considerations related to the context to illustrate points being made

Maximum 5 marks

3 BOULLAIN CO (SPECIMEN EXAM 2022)

Key answer tips

Part (b) of this question covered margins that are payable on futures hedges.

Often the examiner tells you to ignore margins in exam questions, but he did write a technical article about margins, so clearly he expects you to understand how they work.

This shows how important it is to keep an eye on the ACCA website and to fully understand any technical articles presented there.

(a) Rationale for hedging policy

Within the framework of Modigliani and Miller, Boullain Co's CEO is correct in stating that a company's hedging policy is irrelevant. In a world without transaction or agency costs, and where markets are efficient and information symmetrical, hedging creates no value if shareholders are well diversified. Shareholder value may even be destroyed if the costs associated with hedging exceed the benefits.

However, in the real world where market imperfections exist, including the transaction costs of bankruptcy and other types of financial distress, hedging protects shareholder value by avoiding the distress costs associated with potentially devastating foreign exchange fluctuations.

Active hedging may also benefit debt-holders by reducing the agency costs of debt. A clearly defined hedging policy acts as a signalling tool between shareholders and debt-holders. In this sense, hedging allows for higher leverage and a lower cost of debt and reduces the need for restrictive covenants.

Communication of policy with stakeholders

Even when foreign exchange risks are hedged, the funding of variation margin payments on exchange traded futures can create financial distress. A well communicated hedging strategy allows debt providers to make informed decisions about Boullain Co's ability to service its debt.

Agency costs and the risk of financial distress also impact the expected wealth of employees who, unlike shareholders, may not enjoy the risk reduction benefits of a diversified portfolio. A consistent hedging policy reduces the risks faced by employees which may serve to benefit Boullain Co in the form of motivational and productivity improvements.

Customers and suppliers have claims on a company which create shareholder value but are conditional upon Boullain Co's survival. Suppliers may invest in production systems which create value in the form of lower costs. For customers, these claims reflect promises of quality and after-sales service levels which enable Boullain Co to charge higher prices. In both cases, shareholder value is created as long as the customers and suppliers believe these claims will be honoured. One way of achieving this is by implementing a hedging strategy and communicating it to stakeholders.

In conclusion, management should attempt to communicate the principles underlying its hedging strategy and the benefits to shareholder value in the form of reduced agency and distress costs. In this way, stakeholders can make informed decisions about the potential risks and impact on their expected wealth.

(b) **Forward contract**

$18,600,000 × 0.8729 = €16,235,940

Futures

Buy September € futures

Calculation of futures price

Spot rate (US$/€1) = 1/0.8707 = 1.1485

Predicted futures using spot rate = 1.1422 + ((1.1485 − 1.1422) × 1/7) = 1.1431

Or using futures: 1.1422 + ((1.1449 −— 1.1422) × 1/3)) = 1.1431

Number of contracts

Expected receipt = $18,600,000/1.1431 = €16,271,542

Number of contracts = €16,271,542/€200,000 = 81.4, say 81 contracts

Amount underhedged = $18,600,000 − (81 × €200,000 × 1.1431$/€) = $81,780

Receipt at forward rate = $81,780 × 0.8729€/$ = €71,386

Outcome

	€
Futures (81 × 200,000)	16,200,000
Forward market	71,386
	16,271,386

Options

September € call options

Number of contracts

Payment = $18,600,000/1.1420$/€ = €16,287,215

Number of contracts = €16,287,215/€200,000 = 81.4, say 81 contracts

Premium

Premium = 81 × €200,000 × 0.0077$/€ = $124,740

Translate at spot = $124,740 × 0.8711€/$ = €108,661

Amount underhedged = $18,600,000 − (81 × €200,000 × 1.1420$/€) = $99,600

Receipt at forward rate = $99,600 × 0.8729€/$ = €86,941

Outcome

	€
Options (81 × €200,000)	16,200,000
Premium	(108,661)
Forward market	86,941
	16,178,280

Recommendation

The forward and futures contracts fix the exchange rate with the futures contract generating a slightly higher euro receipt compared to the forward. However, the futures contract is exposed to basis risk.

The futures contract is also marked-to-market daily. This means that Boullain Co deposits an initial margin with the clearing house when the futures position is opened. The notional profit or loss at each day's closing settlement price is added to or subtracted from the margin account balance. If the margin account balance falls below the level of the maintenance margin, Boullain Co is required to deposit additional funds to top-up the margin account, known as a variation margin. Boullain Co needs to consider that the initial margin and any variation margins would need to be funded and would impact cash flow in the short term.

The option outcome of €16,178,280 provides a worst-case scenario based on the option being exercised. The option premium is expensive which results in a lower receipt if the option is exercised. Unlike the forward and futures contracts, however, the option allows Boullain Co to retain the upside whilst also protecting against the downside risk. Based on the forward and futures markets, the dollar is expected to strengthen and it is therefore unlikely the option would be exercised.

The final hedging choice depends on the board's attitude to risk. However, assuming there is no default risk associated with the forward contract, this may be the best choice under the circumstances. The board may also wish to consider the possibility of not hedging since the dollar is expected to strengthen.

In order to reduce counter-party risk, Boullain Co deposits an initial margin with the clearing house when the futures position is opened. The notional profit or loss at each day's closing settlement price is added to or subtracted from the margin account balance. If the margin account balance falls below the level of the maintenance margin, Boullain Co is required to deposit additional funds to top-up the margin account, known as a variation margin.

If Boullain Co makes a notional profit on any day, the amount in the margin account will be greater than the specified maintenance margin and no variation margin is required. The profit on each such a day may be withdrawn in cash.

Marking guide		
		Marks
(a)	Rationale for hedging policy	2–3
	Communication of policy with stakeholders (examples of stakeholders may include debt providers, employees, customers and suppliers, policy may include example to reduce agency and distress costs)	3–4
	Maximum	**6**
(b)	Forward	1
	Buy futures and call option	1
	Number of futures contracts	1
	Predicted futures rate	1
	Underhedge futures	1
	Number of option contracts	1
	Option premium	1
	Underhedge options	1
	Outcome	1
	Discussion of outcome	2–3
	Explanation of margin requirements	2–3
	Maximum	**14**
	Professional skills marks (see below)	**5**
Total		**25**

Professional skills marks

Analysis and Evaluation

Appropriate use of the data to determine suitable calculations

Appropriate use of the data to support discussion and draw appropriate conclusions

Appraisal of information objectively to make a recommendation

Scepticism

Effective challenge of information supplied to support key facts and/or decisions

Demonstration of ability to consider relevant factors applicable to hedging options

Commercial acumen

Recommendations are practical and plausible in the context of Boullain Co's situation

Effective use of examples from the scenario information and other practical considerations related to the context to illustrate points being made

Maximum 5 marks